Effective Management
in Therapeutic Recreation Service

Second Edition

Effective Management
in Therapeutic Recreation Service

Second Edition

by
Marcia Jean Carter and Gerald S. O'Morrow

Venture Publishing, Inc.
State College, Pennsylvania

Venture Publishing, Inc.
1999 Cato Avenue
State College, PA 16801
Phone   814-234-4561
Fax   814-234-1651
E-mail   vpublish@venturepublish.com
Web site   http://www.venturepublish.com

Production Manager: Richard Yocum
Manuscript Editing: Valerie Fowler, Michele L. Barbin, Shannon B. Dawson

Library of Congress Catalogue Card Number 2005938309
ISBN-10 1-892132-62-1
ISBN-13 978-1-892132-62-8

As a lasting tribute to Dr. Gerald S. O'Morrow, CTRS

July 18, 1929 – November 9, 2002

His colleagues completed this second edition.

Dr. Gerald S. O'Morrow was an international leader, teacher, and writer in therapeutic recreation who enjoyed helping people with either mental or physical disabilities. For over 40 years, he served as a therapist, administrator and consultant within health care facilities and as an administrator and educator in academic settings. As an early leader, he edited one of the first textbooks, *Administration of Activity Therapy Service* (1966). Dr. O'Morrow's scholarly activity in research and in books and journal article publications had a profound impact on the philosophy, theory, and standards of therapeutic recreation practice. In 1976 he published *Therapeutic Recreation: A Helping Profession*, one of the first texts to identify the role and scope of therapeutic recreation. His professional service included frequent conference presentations and service as President of the National Therapeutic Recreation Society on two occasions. Dr. O'Morrow was a visiting lecturer at colleges and universities in the United States and worldwide in China, Japan, New Zealand, and Spain. He served for many years as a consultant to public and private agencies including the World Health Organization. During his career he received numerous awards and citations for his exemplary service including two of the highest honors given in the profession—the NRPA Distinguished Professional Service Award and the National Literary Award respectively—as well as the NTRS Distinguished Service Award. He was recognized by Palestra for his significant contributions to therapeutic recreation throughout his career. A native of Fort Wayne, Indiana, and fanatic about Notre Dame football, he earned his degree in recreation therapy from Sacramento State

College, his Master's in Hospital Recreation from the University of Minnesota, and his Doctorate in Therapeutic Recreation from Columbia University.

Table of Contents

List of Tables and Figures

Preface

Effective Management in Therapeutic Recreation Service, Second Edition, provides theoretical and practical knowledge about the management of therapeutic recreation service in health and human service organizations. The text was written for therapeutic recreation personnel who will eventually be seeking either a management role or who are new to a management position. This book also speaks to therapeutic recreation managers who have been in a management position for a period of time and are looking for a practical desk reference and major resource to improve their performance.

While therapeutic recreation managers work in a variety of health and human service organizations, this book specifically focuses on the core competencies essential for the therapeutic recreation manager at the first level of managerial responsibility in the organizational chain of command. In other words, the text is being written for a therapeutic recreation specialist who has responsibility for managing direct therapeutic recreation service and the assignment and direction of therapeutic recreation staff who deliver the service.

The challenge and excitement of management stems from the opportunity to see what needs to be done in the interest of the consumer. Therapeutic recreation specialists need to be introduced to the concept of management in these terms; it is a challenge. The manager should know how to spark a group of practitioners into getting the job done while understanding the theory underlying the action taken. Effective managers need to have the skills necessary to function in a health and human service delivery system with assurance, knowing they are well-equipped for their role. In addition, they need to be able to speak the language used by other health and human service managers as well as to articulate therapeutic recreation needs to other managers and administrators who have no specific knowledge of therapeutic recreation.

While we realize all the knowledge that might be useful to a potential manager or practicing manager is not in this one volume, the intent is to present the most important portions of management knowledge relevant to therapeutic recreation service in an organized and useful way. In doing so, we emphasize the essentials of management pertinent to being an effective practicing therapeutic recreation manager in a health and human service setting. This means that to achieve the best kind of practice managers must apply and implement management concepts, functions, techniques, and skills to the realities of any situation. As every practicing manager knows, there is no universal "one best way" of doing things in all instances, and the practical application of management theory and science has always recognized the importance of the realities in a given situation.

While this text is designed for upper-level undergraduate and graduate students as well as practitioners, it is well to note that some chapters are a brief overview and enhancement of what students undoubtedly would consider in an introductory administration course. Where this does occur, the content is associated with the implementation of therapeutic recreation service. Further, the sequence of chapters reflects a management perspective as opposed to a program perspective. Likewise, the chapters are arranged from a practical perspective or functional process organization. As a result, service matters associated specifically with the consumer are considered in later chapters, because consumer service depends on effective accomplishment of earlier managerial functions. Last, because most therapeutic recreation managers appear to work within some type of a health care facility, many of the examples and figures used are from health care facilities. At the same time, however, all of the material herein has direct application in other types of settings, such as community-based leisure service agencies.

One final note: We recognize changes are taking place on a daily basis in health and human service organizations, which in turn affect therapeutic recreation service and its management. Therapeutic recreation service is expanding rapidly even though reengineering and downsizing is occurring in many health and human service organizations. Tomorrow's health and human service delivery, and quite possibly the delivery of therapeutic recreation service regardless of setting, will look totally different from today's. Hence, we foresee that some statements may not be as appropriate as they were at the time the manuscript was prepared.

The second edition is organized into five parts: After introducing the reader to the management discipline and the therapeutic recreation manager's job, including transition from practitioner to manager, Part 1 considers the characteristics of management. Chapter 2 overviews the conceptual foundations of management with particular attention to the human factor of management and contingency theory. Therapeutic recreation managers are able to make clearer sense of complex situations and to formulate the best possible strategies for rational action by using theories. The various functions of managers—planning, organizing, directing or leading, and controlling—are considered. These functions are generally accepted as the universal descriptors of the management process. In Chapter 3 consideration is given to the leader-manager. Clearly, one of the keys to being an effective manager is to become an effective leader. Leadership theories and power are considered. Attention is given to the supervisor as a leader. Introduced in this edition is stress and time management. How a manager handles pressure is a reflection of attitude and influences how employees approach workday demands.

Part 2 examines selective administrative functions that support effective and efficient management. Chapter 4 focuses on the development of vision, mission, philosophy, goals, and objective statements of therapeutic recreation divisions or departments within health and human service organizations. Examples of such statements from various organizations are provided. Chapter 5 provides the therapeutic recreation manager with information on behavior that influences individual and group dynamics in an organization. New to this edition are discussions of organizational change and diversity in the workplace. Managers are ultimately responsible for orchestrating change and addressing diversity among their employees through departmental protocols. Chapter 6 considers ethics as an integral part of therapeutic recreation management. Particular attention is given to the values and rights of consumers, major ethical theories, and ethical decision making as a process. The Health Insurance Portability and Accountability Act (HIPAA) passed in 1996 introduced privacy rules impacting health care delivery. This edition considers practice implications of this law. The last chapter in Part 2, Chapter 7, discusses how to work effectively with management. Successful therapeutic recreation managers establish positive working relationships with supervisors and engage in effective clinical supervision as they mentor staff.

Operational management is the focus of attention in Part 3. The nature and process of financial management and budgets is found in Chapter 8. Attention is given to sources of revenue to support therapeutic recreation services as well as the budget process, types of budgets, budget review, and the role of the first-line manager in the fiscal management process, including budget cutbacks. Chapter 9 provides rudimentary information and knowledge on technology and technology information systems

to assist in therapeutic recreation practice, management, and research to improve health and safety of consumers in therapeutic recreation services. Chapter 10 concentrates on decision making, problem solving, and conflict management. By considering the components of decision-making and problem-solving processes, the manager will become adept at implementing the most appropriate and effective solution to a given problem. Tools and techniques used in decision making and ethical elements of decision making are expanded in this edition. Managing conflict is an important skill to develop, because using appropriate solutions to resolve conflict will prevent its potential destructiveness. Marketing of therapeutic recreation services is discussed in Chapter 11. The nature of marketing in health and human services, marketing the benefits of therapeutic recreation, and the development of a strategic marketing plan for therapeutic recreation are considered in this chapter. New to this edition are suggestions like use of a tag line, logo, and bundling services to market the benefits of therapeutic recreation. Chapter 12 focuses on therapeutic recreation staffing to deliver quality service. Consideration is given to legal and professional regulations and standards, human resource planning, recruiting process, selection process, and issues affecting staffing.

Part 4 considers elements associated with human service management. The hallmark of an effective manager is effective communication. Chapter 13 reviews the strategies and techniques that foster effective interpersonal communication and the nature of supervisory communication to achieve goals. Consideration is also given to organizational and professional communication respectively. Expanded consideration is given to the impact of technology on communication. The manager's use of e-mail is considered. Also addressed is appropriate communication in the multicultural workplace and effective management of meetings. Why do people act as they do? Answers to this question are given in Chapter 14, which covers the subject of motivation. This chapter initially considers individual need fulfillment by examining various motivation theories, and then concludes with a discussion of the therapeutic recreation manager's interaction with the diverse work culture and motivation. Guidelines to follow regarding developing a positive motivational atmosphere are also given. The important managerial function and challenge of performance appraisal is explored in Chapter 15. This function contributes to quality outcomes and ongoing service improvements. Today's managers use action plans as ongoing performance tools with staff. Coaching and positive and progressive discipline techniques are day-to-day processes that promote adherence to desired performance criteria while encouraging service quality. For the first-line manager, Chapter 16 develops the logic for and composition of staff training and development programs, including program implementation and evaluations respectively. Chapter 17 and Chapter 18 focus on two significant topics: volunteer management and intern management. Knowledge needed for the successful management, development, implementation, and evaluation of volunteer and internship programs is provided. These updated chapters contain management checklists and evaluative tools to critique the volunteer/intern/agency interactions and services.

Last, Part 5 considers those matters associated with the consumer. Chapter 19 concentrates on a number of factors concerned with therapeutic recreation service delivery management—scheduling of services, therapeutic recreation processes, protocols, documentation, and monitoring and consulting practitioner performance. The management of risk is discussed in Chapter 20. New to Chapter 20 is a consideration of safety and security. The focus of risk has shifted to safety of all health and human service stakeholders resulting in an interest in evidence-based practices. The final chapter, Chapter 21, examines the management of quality service, which incorporates a historical overview of quality management in health and human service organizations and the implications of total quality management and quality assurance and continuous quality improvement in therapeutic recreation services. New to this chapter is a concluding section on outcome measurement and evidence-based practices. The transition to performance improvement, like its predecessors, intends to ensure accountability and quality in service provision.

Acknowledgments

The author and contributors of chapter revisions in this edition were Dr. Gerald O'Morrow's students and colleagues. We are honored to have the opportunity to show our appreciation and respect for his dedication to the profession through this second edition. Authors of revised chapters in this edition include:

Jane K. Broida, CTRS
Metropolitan State College of Denver
Denver, Colorado

Jean E. Folkerth, CTRS
University of Toledo
Toledo, Ohio

Claire M. Foret, CTRS
University of Louisiana—Lafayette
Lafayette, Louisiana

Kathy Jack, CTRS
Lafayette General Medical Center
Lafayette, Louisiana

M. Jean Keller, CTRS
University of North Texas
Denton, Texas

S. Harold Smith, MTRS
California State University—Northridge
Northridge, California

Glenda Taylor, CTRS
Longwood University
Farmville, Virginia

Karen C. Wenzel, CTRS
Rocky Mountain Multiple Sclerosis Center
Denver, Colorado

As might be expected with a text of this kind, the authors are indebted to many people who helped create this publication, some of whom provided manuals, job descriptions, budgeting reports, vision and mission statements, and similar documents from their health and human service organizations. We would like to acknowledge the following for their contributions:

Angie L. Anderson
Iowa Health Des Moines, Methodist, Lutheran, Blank Hospitals
Des Moines, Iowa

Patricia Ardovino, CTRS
University of Wisconsin LaCrosse
LaCrosse, Wisconsin

Missy Armstrong, CTRS
Harborview Medical Center
Seattle, Washington

joan burlingame, CTRS
Ravensdale, Washington

Sharon K. Entsminger, CTRS, and Erika S. DeWitt, CTRS
Chesterfield County Parks and Recreation Department
Chester, Virginia

Julie Forker, CPRP, CTRS
Maryland National Capital Park and Planning Commission
Riverdale, Maryland

Lynn Griffiths, CTRS
Southwestern Virginia Mental Health Institute
Marion, Virginia

Mead B. Jackson, RTR, CTRS
Los Angeles County/University of Southern California Medical Center
Los Angeles, California

Martha Johnson
INOVA/Mount Vernon Hospital
Alexandria, Virginia

Steven P. LeConey, CTRS
Cincinnati Recreation Commission
Cincinnati, Ohio

Jerri K. Lerch, CTRS
Lindenview Regional Behavioral Center
Fort Wayne, Indiana

Carolyn M. Nagle, CPRP, CTRS
Fox Valley Special Recreation Association
Aurora, Illinois

Bill Parker, CTRS
Virginia Beach Department of Parks and Recreation
Virginia Beach, Virginia

Rhonda Riggleman, CTRS
Sheltering Arms (Midtown) Physical Rehabilitation Center
Richmond, Virginia

Paulette Schuster, RTR, CPRP, CTRS
Department of Recreation and Parks
Los Angeles, California

Lisa Silverman, CTRS
Department of Recreation, Parks and Cultural Activities
Alexandria, Virginia

Jody L. Stock, CTRS
The Virginia Home
Richmond, Virginia

Lisa Turpel, CPRP, CTRS
Portland Parks and Recreation Department
Portland, Oregon

Jeffrey Witman, CTRS
Philhaven Behavioral Healthcare Services
Mt. Gretna, Pennsylvania

—*G.S.O'M* and *M.J.C.*

Chapter 1
Overview

"Today's health care system is continuing to undergo significant changes" (Sullivan & Decker, 2005, p. 3). A number of changes are challenging health and human service organizations. "Health care exists because society deems it worthy of support… yet government agencies and private citizens alike share concern about the future ability to pay for care" (Sullivan & Decker, 2005, p. 6). Informed citizens are participating in health care decisions. An aging population, increasing incidence of life-threatening diseases, bioterrorism, and violence add demands to an overburdened system. Advancing technology promises innovative treatments. As health care continues to move beyond hospital walls to community-based settings, a broader array of health care professionals are providing more holistic care. Information technology contributes to integrative care systems. Evidence-based practice, point-of-care technology, and distance interventions continue to shape care. The health care system continues to change to adapt to market forces, political pressures, and consumer demands (Aiken, 2003; Needleman, 1999; Nosek, 2004; Sullivan & Decker, 2005).

Commencing in the 1950s there was unparalleled growth in the size and scope of health and human service organizations. It was during this same period that therapeutic recreation began to emerge as a professional field of service. As the years passed, therapeutic recreation practitioners carried out their responsibility of direct service ably and often imaginatively. In addition, as therapeutic recreation programs and services developed in varied health and human service organizations, therapeutic recreation practitioners moved into positions of management without any formal organized body of practice knowledge and techniques directly applicable to therapeutic recreation management.

Today all practitioners are managers. To be successful in the evolving health care system, professionals must collaborate with others, both as leaders and team members, and use decreasing resources effectively and efficiently. This chapter addresses the changing nature of health and human services and the emergence of therapeutic recreation as a specific field of service. Also considered is the role of the therapeutic recreation manager as a first-line manager. A first-line manager requires leadership and management skills. Effective professionals strive for the integration of leadership characteristics throughout each management process. Thus, this chapter introduces the integration of management and leadership skills as well as the factors associated with making the transition from practitioner to manager. Initially, however, societal changes that have taken place since the 1950s, the emergence of therapeutic recreation as a profession, the implications of that history for therapeutic recreation service management, and the challenges to therapeutic recreation management today will be examined briefly.

Decades of Change

Few things in life remain unchanged over time. Individuals, families, communities, and organizations grow and adapt according to events and conditions within their environment. During the past several decades societal, political, economic, technological, and legal forces have influenced the content and context of health and human services and the delivery of these services. In addition, these services and their delivery have been under siege from many individuals and organizations.

In the 1950s legislation was passed for the planning and financing of health care. Debate flourished about the notion of health care as a basic right, as something more than a privilege for people with economic means. The debate continues today, with the consumer believing strongly that adequate health care is a right and at the same time a prerequisite for the good life. In the more generic human services arena, those who worked in and received services from human service agencies began to have a voice in determining the destiny of the agencies and the services being provided. Also during this decade, third-party health insurance companies such as Blue Cross and Blue Shield offered an insurance premium plan to pay for health care. In addition, systems theory as a management concept emerged at the same time that social scientists recognized that interdependence of individuals, governments, and societies was a basic fact.

The 1960s witnessed federal policy and legislation (e.g., Civil Rights Act of 1964, P.L. 88-352) that increased citizen access to health and human services. Health care expenditures in 1960 were 5.3% of the gross national product (GNP; Bush, 1994). Lyndon Johnson's call for a war on poverty led to the passage of a vast array of social welfare programs. While some social agencies expanded to address unmet social needs, others were widely criticized for being unresponsive to changing needs and conditions. Government programs such as Medicare and Medicaid were started in 1965. At the same time, a technological explosion occurred based on heavy public investment in medical research. Elaborate technology became available for diagnosis and treatment and for life support and life extension. During this decade social roles were also changing, and there was much experimentation with new lifestyles.

The 1970s ushered in increased government regulation and mandated community-based planning to limit hospital expansion. The goal was to contain rapidly increasing health care costs. Wellness programs designed to promote health and to prevent disease gained momentum, partly in response to the business community's recognition of rising health care costs and insurance premiums. Also, during this period there was a marked increase in legislation that expanded recreation and leisure service opportunities for individuals with disabilities and provided funds for research and demonstration projects.

The 1980s marked the birth of large for-profit hospital chains, the introduction of legislation associated with deregulation and competition, and the inception of marketing to consumers. Also, patients in hospitals came to be redefined as customers. Alternative delivery systems (e.g., substance abuse centers, home health service, outpatient service) proliferated during this period as did new reimbursement arrangements, such as prospective payment systems through diagnostic-related groups (DRGs). Preferred provider organizations (PPOs) in their various guises also became common. This movement led to "managed care" as a major feature of the system, although the forerunner of managed care began with Kaiser Permanente (Kaiser Foundation Health Plan) in the 1930s (Northern, 1995). At the same time consumers demanded a healthy environment in which to live and work. In fact, the direction of the health care industry shifted away from "medical care" and toward "health care." This shift incorporated an emphasis on acute illness rather than chronic illness and the importance played by the environment, lifestyle, and social stress in the onset and progression of disease.

Legislation during this time focused on many aspects of consumer care. Providing access for persons with disabilities so they could participate more fully in society was a major milestone. Congress enacted a hospice option within Medicare benefits in the early 1980s to foster community-based care for the terminally ill. Later in the decade the Omnibus Budget Reconciliation Act (OBRA; P.L. 100-203) was passed with reference to Medicaid

and Medicare standards and emphasis on the inclusion of therapeutic recreation as part of the rehabilitation process. Last, the U.S. Department of Health, Education, and Welfare was restructured to become the Department of Health and Human Services, while Education became a separate department. Such development during the 1980s permanently changed the nature of health and human services and set the stage for the trends of the 1990s.

The dramatic changes in health and human services in the 1980s did not magically end in 1990. By 1990 health care expenditures had risen to 12.2% of the GNP, to 14% by 1992, and it was estimated that by 1994 it would represent 16% of the economy (Bush, 1994). In the early 1990s many health and human service organizations adopted the principles of total quality management (TQM) to improve the quality of their services to consumers. At the same time, the goals and values of health and human services were being rethought.

In the health care arena it became apparent that society was no longer willing to pay for escalating health care costs but wanted changes in all components of the health care delivery system to deal with the emerging health care crises. Further, health care planners agreed they needed to know more about the cost-effectiveness, quality, and safety of the methods health practitioners used for the prevention, diagnosis, and treatment of disease. This was the result, in part, of the continued decline in community hospitals since 1977, which provided inpatient acute care services (Hull, 1994). By the mid-1990s many hospitals were being referred to as "health centers" to distinguish them from the older generation of hospitals which focused on inpatient care. New hospitals or health centers were putting greater emphasis on outpatient care and prevention. In addition, the U.S. Department of Labor reported that the health care industry was the largest single employer of all the industries monitored by the department, outpacing overall employment in the economy and total population growth (Kronenfeld, 1993). Not only had the numbers of people employed in health care increased but also the types of people had changed and the number of different categories of health care workers had increased (e.g., allied health and assistant personnel). Kronenfeld (1993) reported more than 700 different job categories in the health industries.

The mid-1990s brought the health care dilemma to the political forefront. The demand for affordable yet available care was addressed through a number of federally proposed yet failed health care reform measures. As a consequence, the enactment of the Balanced Budget Act of 1997 (P.L. 105-33) reflected a political consensus that may set the direction of health care in the 21st century like the 1965 Social Security Amendment that established Medicare and Medicaid and the then dominant fee-for-service system (Barr, Lee & Benjamin, 2003). The primary objective of the bill was to reduce the spending of federal health care dollars—cost containment. Payment rates are calculated prior to service delivery and are based on price or historical costs (Thompson, 2001). The bill assured Medicare beneficiaries of access to necessary treatment and provided safeguards to assure treatment quality. Legislation in 1999 (i.e., Balanced Budget Reform Act) and 2000 (i.e., Budget Improvement and Protection Act) restored cuts introduced by the 1997 act.

The defeat of comprehensive health care reform shifted concern for cost controls and quality to the private sector and the states. Managed care options emerged as one solution to health care spending and access. The impact on both control and quality was mixed. Many states introduced consumer protection laws that set limits on private sector plans. Consumer trust in governmental resources was further eroded in 1999 when the Institute of Medicine (IOM) reported a high level of deaths from preventable medical mistakes (Sullivan & Decker, 2005). Integrated health care systems evolved as alternatives to reduce hospital expenses and costs incurred by consumers. This focus on primary care is expected to continue throughout the 21st century. Many of these health care systems are relying on continuous improvement systems to evaluate and improve quality. At the close of the 20th century, the health care system had transitioned from a service-oriented to a business-oriented industry.

Another perspective of the 1990s reveals that the number of people with disabilities was rising to a higher level of social visibility and responsiveness than in the past. Acknowledgment of their right to equal opportunity and quality of life was noted with the enactment of the Individuals with Disabilities Education Act (P.L. 101-476, 1990) and the Americans with Disabilities Act (P.L. 101-336, 1990). The latter was considered to be the most significant piece of legislation of the past decade for persons with disabilities. This legislation was designed to provide a clear and comprehensive mandate that would end discrimination against individuals with disabilities relative to housing, employment, public transportation, and communication services. Definitions of places of public accommodation include several categories with direct references to recreation facilities and their programs (Stein, 1993). A year later, in 1991, the U.S. Department of Labor (U.S. Department of Labor, Bureau of Labor Statistics, 1991) reported that recreation therapy was the 12th fastest growing profession requiring a baccalaureate degree in the United States. In the same year, the U.S. Department of Health and Human Services documented the importance of active recreation and accessible programs and facilities in its national health strategy report, *Healthy People 2000: National Health Promotion and Disease Prevention Objectives*; these were restated in the 1995 revision (U.S. Department of Health and Human Services, Public Health Service, 1991, 1995).

The Healthy People Consortium, an alliance of 350 national organizations and 250 state agencies, conducted a series of regional and national meetings in the late 1990s on the development of *Healthy People 2010—Understanding and Improving Health*, an agenda designed to continue the momentum of *Healthy People 2000* initiatives (Howard, Russoniello & Rogers, 2004; U.S. Department of Health and Human Services, 2003). This roadmap for the first decade of the 21st century is designed to achieve two goals: to increase quality and years of healthy life and to eliminate health disparities. The report acknowledged that individual and community health status may be dramatically improved in a relatively short time, yet recognized issues such as (a) the increase in adult obesity by 50% over the two previous decades, (b) the lack of leisure time physical activity by nearly 40% of the adult population, and (c) the minimal attention given to persons with disabilities and secondary conditions (Howard, Russoniello & Rogers, 2004; U.S. Department of Health and Human Services, 2003). The underlying premise of *Healthy People 2010* is that the health of each individual is intertwined with that of the larger community. Thus, this integrated systematic approach called on collaboration among government and private sector agencies as well as professional groups like ATRA and NTRS to address health and quality of life issues.

The aftermath of the September 11, 2001, terrorist attacks renewed an interest in effective partnerships of local, state, and federal agencies to respond to communal health needs and threats. These attacks and the subsequent anthrax attacks demonstrated the need to revisit protocols and to provide better planning, coordination, and communication among agencies. Consequently at the federal level, a new cabinet level department, Homeland Security, was created, while the Model State Emergency Health Powers Act outlined several measures to better prepare communities to address public health emergencies (Annas, 2003). This renewed support for health care from the federal level may breath new life into national issues like public insurance programs, care for an aging population, and disparities in health care access.

Throughout the first decade of the 21st century, a number of health care records were set (Curran, 2004). Health care cost inflation reached double digits in 2000 and remained there (Ferman, 2003). The number of uninsured escalated to its highest level in 2003, and Medicaid spending (a state responsibility) also continued to increase at a double-digit rate. While the Balanced Budget Act of 1997 has tended to reduce public Medicare spending, private expenditures have increased, employee out-of-pocket is increasing, and more employees and employers are dropping health care coverage. Ironically, a number of factors like availability of new drugs, access to specialists without authorization, and more treatment to improve care are continuing to trigger modest increases in medical costs (Coy, 2003).

Health care spending is projected to continue to consume larger portions of the gross national product (GNP) through the first decade of the 21st century. Likewise, the supply of nonphysician clinicians is anticipated to continue on an upward spiral (Aiken, 2003). Integrated health care systems are expected to address increasing consumer demands for an array of health and social concerns. In the midst of these health care dynamics, the first-line manager is living with change—change being experienced as it is predicted (Porter-O'Grady, 2003). New technology is altering professionals' responses to those needing health care as globalization yields common threats and solutions (Nosek, 2004).

Concurrent with those factors that influenced health and human services and recreation and leisure services for individuals with disabilities, therapeutic recreation began to emerge as a specific field of service with a distinctive theory and method of practice between 1950 and 1960. Therapeutic recreation shifted its philosophical basis to include treatment service in addition to participative leisure experiences in both health care facilities and community-based leisure service organizations. This practice theory remains a major influence on much of the practice to this day. The emergence of therapeutic recreation was the result of an expansion of health care services wherein recreation services became common in settings such as psychiatric institutions and hospitals; residential facilities for the mentally retarded and other specific disabilities; local mental health, mental retardation, and developmental disability centers; skilled and long-term care facilities; rehabilitation units in general medical hospitals, comprehensive freestanding rehabilitation centers, and substance abuse rehabilitation facilities; and other health care facilities. At the same time, recreation services for persons with disabilities of all ages were offered more and more through community-based leisure service agencies, primarily parks and recreation departments. Unfortunately, the expansion of therapeutic recreation service with its theory of practice was not accompanied by the development of therapeutic recreation management skills. Managers of therapeutic recreation departments developed their skills on-the-job.

In the decades since therapeutic recreation's emergence as a profession, attention was given to issues critical to its professionalization, including credentialing, accreditation, practice standards, models of service, ethics, advocacy, legislation, definitions, and philosophy of therapeutic

recreation. Further, in the health care arena therapeutic recreation was included in the standards associated with inpatient and outpatient physical rehabilitation issued by the Joint Commission on Accreditation of Healthcare Organizations (JCAHO). Likewise, therapeutic recreation was included within the medical rehabilitation and behavioral health standards (e.g., alcohol and other drug programs, mental health programs) of the Commission on Accreditation of Rehabilitation Facilities (CARF). The Health Care Financing Administration (HCFA; now the CMS—Centers for Medicare and Medicaid Services) also included therapeutic recreation services within federal government standards in skilled nursing and long-term care facilities. Last, during the health care reform debate in 1994, the American Therapeutic Recreation Society (ATRA) and the National Therapeutic Recreation Society (NTRS) issued a joint statement supporting the commitment of President Bill Clinton and the U.S. Congress to making health care a right of all Americans (ATRA & NTRS, 1994).

Today the scope of therapeutic recreation reveals a wide range of services to individuals with an equally diverse set of problems, disorders, and limitations. Services are provided to individuals in institutional and residential facilities, in community-based health and human service agencies as noted previously plus outpatient services, home health agencies, hospices, and various other day treatment and social programs (e.g., summer day camp, adult social clubs, inclusion buddy aquatic programs). According to the National Council for Therapeutic Recreation Certification (NCTRC), there are nearly 30,000 therapeutic recreation professionals in the United States with nearly 70% of the 16,000 CTRSs employed full-time with the title of therapist or therapist supervisor: The majority of the CTRSs practice in hospitals and skilled nursing facilities while others are found in community, residential, school, and day-care settings (NCTRC, 2004).

A changing and somewhat challenging environment will probably continue to confront health and human service managers and providers. At no time in the history of the United States have so many powerful forces been exerting their influence. Forces, trends, and changes in organizational structures, delivery systems, cost containment, quality management and accountability, consumerism, health problems, and health care policy will continue to affect the health and human service professions and the roles, functions, and skill requirements of these professionals. Therapeutic recreation managers and practitioners at all levels of responsibility and in all types of settings will have to respond to ever-changing demands in society and in the field. Perhaps the most significant issue that will challenge the therapeutic recreation profession as a result of economic, social, and political changes will be the implementation, delivery, and monitoring of quality therapeutic recreation services regardless of setting. If therapeutic recreation service quality is to improve and meet the demands of the public, the federal government (e.g., CMS), and regulatory agencies (e.g., JCAHO, CARF), it must come through the development of effective procedures directed by personnel with management and leadership knowledge, understanding, and skills.

Management and Leadership Defined

Many definitions of management exist. Perhaps the most widely quoted one, attributed to management theorist Mary Parker Follett, is that "management is the act of getting things done through other people" (Wren, 1979, p. 3). Since management is an authorized activity inherent in all formal organizations, it will be defined here as a process of working with others to achieve organizational goals in a changing environment (Kreitner, 1992). The manager is responsible and accountable for coordinating and integrating resources to effectively and efficiently accomplish the goals of an organization through delivery of quality safe services that satisfy consumer needs.

The manager's job in many respects is analogous to that of an orchestra leader. If the individual musicians played without a common score and without a conductor, what would be the result? Just noise. The purpose of the score and the conductor is to weld the individual instruments into pleasing music. And so it is with the manager.

A leader is anyone who influences others to accomplish specific goals (Sullivan & Decker, 2005). A leader is important in an organization to create connections that result in high levels of performance and quality outcomes. The leader functions (a) to achieve group consensus and set direction; (b) to maintain a structure to accomplish the group goals; (c) to provide information to clarify, innovate, and change; and (d) to engage others while maintaining cohesion and satisfaction to pursue shared goals (Sullivan & Decker, 2005; Tappen, Weiss & Whitehead, 2004).

Leadership is an informal role determined by a person's behavior (Marquis & Huston, 2003). Through interpersonal skills a person influences and guides direction. "Leadership increases productivity by maximizing work force effectiveness" (Marquis & Huston, 2003, p. 4). The skills of an "effective leader are dynamic and change constantly in response to the rapidly changing world in which we live" (Marquis & Huston, 2003, p. 20). Thus, leadership skills are important to therapeutic recreation managers who find themselves in constantly changing organizational complexity and structure created by increasing availability of information, technology, and competition for scarce resources.

Integrating Leadership and Management Skills

"For managers and leaders to function at their greatest potential… the integration of leadership characteristics throughout every phase of the management process" must occur (Marquis & Huston, 2003, p. 21). Since managers have formal authority and responsibility for the quality of work performed by their employees, they need to be good leaders to be effective managers (Tappen, Weiss & Whitehead, 2004). Good managers are good leaders—both roles can be learned and the skills gained enhance either role (Sullivan & Decker, 2005). To be successful in the 21st century, the leader-manager will not only manage resources well but also lead initiatives to build new structures responsive to the ever-changing health and human service environment.

Integrated leader-managers are identified by several characteristics (Marquis & Huston, 2003): (a) visionary thinking, (b) an understanding of the role of their department in relationship to the bigger organizational picture, (c) political astuteness and sensitivity to the expectations and needs of others, and (d) the ability to rise above bureaucratic boundaries and examine the ever-changing nature of the health and human service environment. Thus, "contemporary management requires communication, leadership, and action" (Sullivan & Decker, 2005, p. 65). The first-line therapeutic recreation manager uses a scientific approach as resources are managed and staff empowered to deliver quality safe consumer-oriented services.

Therapeutic Recreation Manager

While there are various levels of management (e.g., top, middle, first-line), therapeutic recreation managers in health and human service organizations are considered first-line managers because they are responsible for delivery of therapeutic recreation service, assignment and direction of professional practitioners and volunteers, and interaction with other managers in the same organization or with others in the community who deliver therapeutic recreation services. There may be times however, that the manager may be responsible for providing direct service (e.g., vacation, sick leave, special programs). This management responsibility would be true whether one is managing in a health care facility or in a community-based leisure service organization. However, there are exceptions. In some large health and human service organizations (e.g., hospitals, public or private freestanding community-based leisure service centers for persons with disabilities) and depending on the organizational structure, therapeutic recreation managers may occupy a middle management position wherein they would be responsible for implementing basic policies and plans developed by top management and for supervising and coordinating the activities of lower level managers. The coordinator or director of an activity therapy department responsible for varied disciplines (e.g., occupational therapy, music therapy) would be an example of middle management.

First-line manager is often the first position held by a practitioner who enters management from the worker or subordinate personnel rank; however, there are some settings in which the first-line manager is also the sole practitioner (e.g., long-term care settings, small community-based leisure service organizations). It seems reasonable to assume, as has been noted earlier, that most first-line managers have had little or no formal academic preparation in therapeutic recreation management. Their advancement is the result of competency in direct service, program knowledge, and job experience. This is not to say that direct practice experience and program knowledge are not important psrerequisites for first-line managers. A therapeutic recreation practitioner survey noted that of 490 respondents, nearly one half indicated they occupy an administrative or supervisor position (O'Morrow, 2000).

Even though the first-line manager holds a bottom-rung managerial position in the organization, it is one of the most critical and valuable roles within the administration of the organization. The manager's responsibility is to turn a management plan into operational reality. Within the context of a program, the first-line manager is primarily involved with developing and facilitating technical and professional processes, as well as identifying areas of knowledge and skill deficiencies, providing opportunities for upgrading them, and evaluating practitioner performance. The first-line manager also serves as a linking agent by advocating and representing the interests of subordinates to the next managerial level and communicating, clarifying, and enforcing the directives of his or her supervisor.

Effective managers have a common affinity for understanding the nature of the larger organization within which they work. In other words, a special effort is made to understand the inner workings of the larger organization of which their department is a part. Realizing that the needed information cannot be uncovered simply from printed documents, managers are relentless in their probing. They observe, inquire, and integrate until they are satisfied that they have a valid conceptual model of the organization.

The majority of objectives for any therapeutic recreation service, regardless of setting, relates to the consumer, and the first-line therapeutic recreation manager is the administrative channel through which these objectives ultimately succeed or fail. This professional person must ensure that quality services for consumers are delivered efficiently in an ever-changing environment of standards and regulations, consumer activism, and budget limitations. Planning for the department, for example, is in vain if the therapeutic recreation manager cannot translate the objectives into concrete action. To perform effectively as a first-line manager one must have clear ideas of that role and how it relates to the health and human service organization.

Other characteristics of a successful first-line therapeutic recreation manager would include the following: the ability to conceptualize ways to resolve problems by using creative solutions, being able to rebound from the frustrations of today and recognize that tomorrow is another day with its own challenges and rewards, and a sense of humor is vital—without it the environment can rapidly create management burnout.

Therapeutic recreation managers are also considered functional managers, as opposed to general managers, because they are responsible for a specialized service important to the organization. Recently, more therapeutic recreation managers in community-based settings are assuming general managerial responsibilities because of their knowledge of the Americans with Disabilities Act (ADA). While manager is the term most frequently used for the role and function examined in this text, other titles may be used, such as administrator, chief, director, head, or supervisor.

In summary, a manager is both an investor in the organization and its goals, and an integrator and interpreter of its functions. The manager has a professional role, an interpersonal role, a business role, and an informational role. A manager's responsibility, as will be explored further, is to ensure that functions are carried out and tasks are performed to meet the organizational goals, objectives, and plans. If practiced effectively, the result is quality service to the consumer. These responsibilities are achieved through appropriate behavior and competent use of administrative skills, human resource skills, and technical skills.

First-Line Manager Responsibilities and Challenges

While some of these responsibilities were mentioned previously and many will be considered in more detail in subsequent chapters, the concern here is highlighting and briefly describing the many and varied responsibilities and challenging aspects of being a first-line manager.

Setting Objectives

All planning rests on the assumption that the first-line manager has a clear idea of the objectives to be achieved in providing services. These objectives direct activities of the department, although they may vary or be supplemented by interim and ad hoc objectives formulated on the basis of the day-to-day situation.

Planning and Organizing

Reaching objectives entails making a plan concerning what has to be done. This means that the first-line manager analyzes what activities need to be done, sets priorities, and plans the best means to achieve the desired ends. In addition, the plan must assign responsibility, and it must be communicated to staff. The challenge of the first-line manager is to convert planning into action by way of organizing. Planning must deal with the realities of therapeutic recreation service. There is no way the first-line manager can be unrealistic because plans are tied to everyday results, and these results provide loud and clear feedback.

Communicating and Motivating

It seems simple to note that the first-line manager tells the staff what is expected of them. It is an often neglected step, however. The manager may assume that the staff will envision the same objectives as he or she does. This assumption, unfortunately, is often faulty. Even if all staff members are highly motivated to give "good service," there is no reason to assume that all of them mean the same thing by this phrase. Therefore, the manager has a critical obligation to make clear to staff the kind of performance wanted.

As the acknowledged head of the department, the manager lays the groundwork for the exchange of information related to consumer service, organizational matters, and trends. The way information is articulated to staff has a direct bearing on the way it is used and processed.

Effective managers keep communication flowing. Because of the manager's vital role in the organization, the manager's ability to listen to staff is as important as his or her ability to be a good spokesperson. Moreover, managers create an environment conducive to professional behavior when they solicit staff suggestions and act on them.

Measuring and Evaluating

The manager makes expectations explicit and does not assume that staff will always share his or her standards of performance. While staff need to set personal goals that correspond to the department objectives, the manager provides the yardstick against which the individual measures his or her performance. Periodic written evaluations are an essential management tool that should be supplemented by routine feedback on what staff is doing right and what areas need improvement.

The danger in not setting standards is that minimal standards, if any, will prevail. The delivery of quality consumer service depends on each practitioner's striving for excellence. The manager understands that everyone will not perform equally well, but he or she establishes standards to aim for and establishes what is required. Quality assurance (QA) and continuous quality improvement (CQI) form a basis for judging how well a group is performing.

Ensuring Consumers' Welfare

One step the manager can take to ensure quality delivery of service to the consumer is to scrutinize the policies and procedures manual. There are policies and procedures for reporting on and off duty, for transmission of information regarding consumers, for interacting with higher management staff, and for working with interns or fieldwork students and volunteers. All of these practices plus many others impact consumer service. It is important, therefore, that the manager identify the policies and procedures associated with the department and subject them to scrutiny.

The first-line manager is ultimately responsible for and responsible to the consumer. This means that the manager, depending on the setting, must have knowledge about the consumer on an ongoing basis, including achievements and goals the consumer wants to reach. Likewise, the manager also should know the challenges and problems consumers present to staff. The manager acquires such knowledge through QA and CQI measures primarily.

Other Responsibilities and Challenges

Other first-line managerial responsibilities and challenges organized as personnel, administrative, and educational are as follows (Whetten & Cameron, 1984):

Personnel Challenges

1. Organizing and managing time despite so many demands and changes.

2. Managing the frustrations associated with being creative in a bureaucratic agency environment.

3. Managing the guilt feelings regarding the use of supervisory privileges (e.g., conference attendance, travel, larger office).

4. Managing personal job frustrations and insecurities about giving priority to working or to experiencing a lack of knowledge, which often requires a commitment to update oneself.

Administrative Challenges

1. Managing the heavy paperwork demands for accountability.

2. Managing increased workload without increases, or even with reductions, in staff.

3. Translating poorly conceived, untimely administrative directives into a form staff can understand and implement.

4. Managing interagency conflicts based on jealousy, competition, and poor communication regarding differing service standards.

5. Confronting staff with disciplinary action over inadequate performance after years of inattention by previous supervisors.

6. Managing well-organized unit or staff meetings (e.g., maintaining clear focus; avoiding long, boring meetings).

7. Managing staff's concerns for the quality of work with the manager's concern for the quantity of work.

8. Managing top and middle management who violate the chain of command and subordinates who make "end runs" on the manager to higher authorities.

9. Managing work unit issues, such as staff abuse of privileges (e.g., overuse of compensation time), a dominant worker who undermines morale, jealousies among workers, and translation of agency goals and objectives into viable worker activities.

Educational Challenges

1. Motivating staff to plan for their own professional growth.

2. Managing to secure the time and money for staff in-service training and professional development.

In addition to these responsibilities and challenges, the manager should have knowledge and awareness of other health and human service resources, especially those that relate to providing leisure service and ways to make referrals to them. The manager will also possess adequate knowledge and understanding of the therapeutic recreation continuum and therapeutic recreation process and their application regardless of setting. Last, the manager is knowledgeable about the purposes and activities of the national professional membership organizations (e.g., ATRA, NTRS), including state affiliation organizations and the professional certification organization (e.g., NCTRC). The manager is active in these professional organizations, is certified by them and, at the same time, recognizes the importance of certification for his or her staff. The manager is also knowledgeable about other allied health professions and their goals, standards, and

services. Figure 1.1 offers a reflection of the variables that affect the therapeutic recreation manager.

Therapeutic Recreation Department Dimensions

The therapeutic recreation division or department usually operates within the broader context of the health and human service organization. While the therapeutic recreation department must support the overall mission of any organization as a major dimension, its approach must be grounded in therapeutic recreation's values and beliefs as to what constitutes professional quality. The philosophy and goals of therapeutic recreation, regardless of setting, provide a basis for organization and intradepartmental decision making. They also outline the relationship of therapeutic recreation to the overall organization, define what therapeutic recreation is, and point out its unique contribution to the organization. By using recreation and leisure experience in helping individuals with problems, limitations, and disabilities to achieve their optimal intellectual, physical, emotional, and social well-being, the philosophy and goals of therapeutic recreation are affirmed. The promotion of leisure opportunities and wellness, the prevention of disease, and the treatment of illness have been and will continue to be therapeutic recreation foci.

Within this context, programs are the instruments through which the department accomplishes its goals and objectives. The manager's task is to oversee the therapeutic recreation process, which is a model for action that includes establishing outcomes, the nature of the services provided, the consumers served, and the resources required.

In addition to these major dimensions, therapeutic recreation operating practices need to be in congruence with the organization's overall environment. These practices structure the work of the department and its operations. Department dimensions, while not comprehensive, include the following:

- vision and mission

- marketing

- philosophy

- programming, scheduling, staffing

- service scope

- managerial reporting

- objectives

- department policies

- organizational structure

- personnel policies

- standards of practice and ethics code

- job description

- budget

- performance review and evaluation

- information processing

- continuous quality management and research

- advocating, negotiating, and networking

- risk, safety, and security management

Making the Transition: Practitioner to Manager

It is widely recognized that a sizeable proportion of therapeutic recreation practitioners whose professional training is in direct service move into positions of managerial responsibility at some point in their careers. A major reason for this is that a management position continues to be one of the few options open to a practitioner that increases status and salary. Other reasons for taking a management position might include a desire to achieve, to change and improve policies and services, to reach for power, to offer

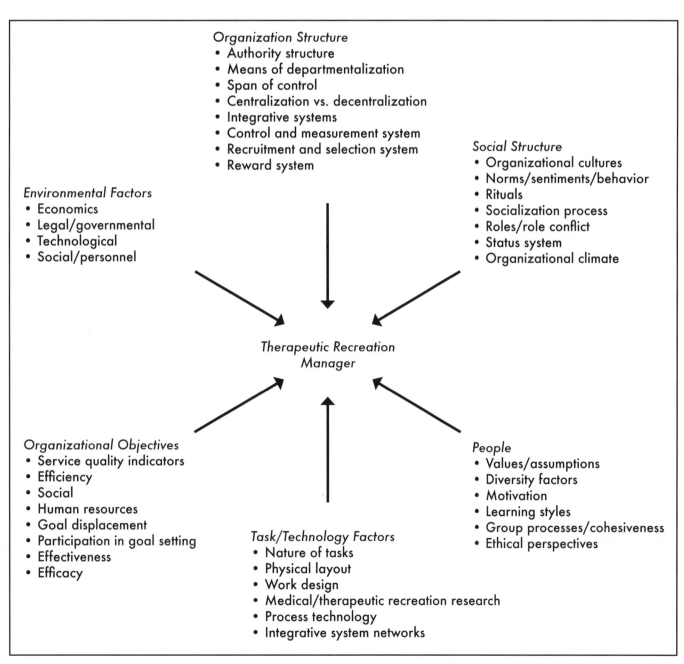

Organization Structure
- Authority structure
- Means of departmentalization
- Span of control
- Centralization vs. decentralization
- Integrative systems
- Control and measurement system
- Recruitment and selection system
- Reward system

Social Structure
- Organizational cultures
- Norms/sentiments/behavior
- Rituals
- Socialization process
- Roles/role conflict
- Status system
- Organizational climate

Environmental Factors
- Economics
- Legal/governmental
- Technological
- Social/personnel

Therapeutic Recreation Manager

Organizational Objectives
- Service quality indicators
- Efficiency
- Social
- Human resources
- Goal displacement
- Participation in goal setting
- Effectiveness
- Efficacy

Task/Technology Factors
- Nature of tasks
- Physical layout
- Work design
- Medical/therapeutic recreation research
- Process technology
- Integrative system networks

People
- Values/assumptions
- Diversity factors
- Motivation
- Learning styles
- Group processes/cohesiveness
- Ethical perspectives

Figure 1.1
Variables Affecting the Therapeutic Recreation Manager

service, and to give of one's self (French & Raven, 1968). Regardless, a practitioner frequently experiences a high degree of difficulty in making the transition to manager and focusing on getting the job done through other people. To some extent this problem is associated with any new job or practice role. An interesting observation the authors have made is that after a period of three to five years as a manager, "a point of no return" is reached—that is, it would not be feasible to return to the position of individual practitioner; a commitment has been made to a career in professional management.

In what follows, several areas in which problems appear to exist when there is a transition from practitioner to management role are discussed briefly.

The move into a manager's position often affects the nature of relationships with colleagues. While still a practitioner, the new manager is likely to have participated in a normative system that valued mutuality and cooperation. He or she probably enjoyed opportunities to vent frustration, to gain support, and to exchange ideas and information. New relationships are likely to be more functionally specific and instrumental. The manager's new status makes it increasingly difficult for him or her to maintain primary group relationships with colleagues who have now become subordinates. The change in structural arrangements usually pushes the manager and practitioners toward an impersonal and neutral level of interaction.

One of the most troublesome areas managers encounter in their first management position is exercising authority over subordinates, especially former colleagues. The problem centers on eliciting support and cooperation in moving toward the goals of the organization, motivating people to change behavior or to improve performance, and gaining cooperation with changes proposed by managers. The manager's direct practice knowledge and skill gained as a practitioner usually help in resolving these kinds of problems. However, if various efforts fail, the manager is often faced with the necessity of using the authority of the office to elicit the desired behavior. The manager who consistently shrinks from using the authority of the position when there are problems will eventually lose the ability to coordinate activities toward the organization's objectives.

The new manager needs to have an appreciation of the organization as a functioning system. While the manager will certainly understand the dynamics of the department as a practitioner, he or she now must develop an understanding of the interdependency of the process and events occurring in the organization, such as the exchange relationships that must occur between the organization and its task environments; the effects of organization, structure, and climate on communication, practitioner satisfaction, and performance; the importance of ideological and occupational commitments and professional vested interests as determinants of individual and group behavior; and the dynamics underlying various problems like goal displacement, ritualism, and intergroup conflict.

Finally, the manager must understand the differences between direct service and management and recognize the unique skills and perspectives needed in each of these roles. While the new manager probably has those skills related to direct service, he or she should be particularly aware that management, as noted earlier, is itself a professional activity that requires the same level of expertise and dedication required of the practitioner in direct practice. Attempting to make the transition to management by remaining a de facto practitioner, who happens incidentally to manage, is to avoid coming to terms with this reality.

Summary

Initial consideration was given to those factors that have changed the delivery of health and human services since the 1950s. Coupled with these factors was a brief review of the emerging professionalization of therapeutic recreation. If professionalization is to continue, attention must be given to the implementation and delivery of quality service regardless of setting. However, for this to be accomplished, it must come through the development of effective procedures directed by personnel with leader/manager skills.

Management was defined as the process of working with others toward goal accomplishment in a changing environment. Leadership was defined as a role that uses interpersonal skills to influence and guide. In the 21st century, the integration of leadership into the management process is essential to manage change and resources while empowering employees to effectively deliver quality, safe consumer-oriented services. While there are several levels of management, the therapeutic recreation manager in a health and human service organization is considered a first-line manager. In most settings, this manager is usually classified as a functional manager because he or she provides a specialized service.

Therapeutic recreation manager responsibilities and challenges were noted as well as the dimensions of a therapeutic recreation department with special attention given to incorporating the philosophy, values, and beliefs of therapeutic recreation. Final consideration was given to factors associated with making the transition from practitioner to manager.

Review Questions

1. Interview a therapeutic recreation manager about the responsibilities of a first-line manager. Compare responsibilities across settings (e.g. hospital, residential, community). Identify common responsibilities and challenges.

2. Conduct an Internet search to discover the types of settings in which therapeutic recreation is practiced.

3. Identify the titles of units and unit managers, their credentials, organization of the departments within the organization, and nature of the agency services.

4. Conduct an Internet search of professional organization Web sites (http://www.nrpa.org and http://www.atra-tr.org) and the certification organization Web site (http://www.nctrc.org). What resources are available to assist the manager?

5. Review the historical development of health care and of therapeutic recreation. Identify the events and regulatory agents impacting the direction and priorities in health and human services and the profession.

References

Aiken, L. H. (2003). Achieving an interdisciplinary workforce in health care. *New England Journal of Medicine, 348*(2), 164–166.

American Therapeutic Recreation Association (ATRA) and National Therapeutic Recreation Society (NTRS). (1994). *Therapeutic recreation: Responding to the challenges of healthcare reform* [Brochure]. Hattiesburg, MS and Arlington, VA: Authors.

Annas, G. J. (2003). Bioterrorism, public health, and civil liberties. In P. R. Lee, C. L. Estes, and F. M. Rodriquez (Eds.), *The nation's health* (7th ed., pp. 324–333). Boston, MA: Jones and Bartlett.

Barr, D. A., Lee, P. R., and Benjamin, A. E. (2003). Health care and health care policy in a changing world. In P. R. Lee, C. L. Estes and F. M. Rodriquez (Eds.), *The nation's health* (7th ed., pp. 199–212). Boston, MA: Jones and Bartlett.

Bush, D. D. (1994, Spring). The insurer's point of view. *Hanover Quarterly*, 10–13.

Coy, P. (2003). Why your premiums are still on the rise. *Business Week, i3856*, 31. Retrieved November 9, 2003, from Infotrac One File database.

Curran, C. R. (2004). The simplified six: A leadership challenge. *Nursing Economics, 22*(1), 52. Retrieved December 15, 2004, from Academic Search Premier (EBSCO host) database.

Ferman, J. H. (2003). The rising cost of healthcare. Cost increases drive healthcare to the top of the domestic policy agenda. *Healthcare Executive, 18*(2), 70–71. Retrieved November 9, 2003, from Medline (Ovid) database.

French, J. R. P., Jr., and Raven, B. (1968). The base of social power. In D. Cartwright and A. Zander (Eds.), *Group dynamics* (3rd ed., pp. 262–268). New York, NY: Harper & Row.

Howard, D., Russoniello, C., and Rogers, D. (2004). Healthy people 2010 and therapeutic recreation: Professional opportunities to promote public health. *Therapeutic Recreation Journal, 38*(2), 116–132.

Hull, K. (1994). Hospital trends. In C. Harrington and C. L. Estes (Eds.), *Health policy and nursing* (pp. 150–168). Boston, MA: Jones and Bartlett.

Kreitner, R. (1992). *Management* (5th ed.). Boston, MA: Houghton Mifflin.

Kronenfeld, J. J. (1993). *Controversial issues in healthcare policy*. Newbury Park, CA: Sage Publications.

Marquis, B. L. and Huston, C. J. (2003). *Leadership roles and management functions in nursing: Theory & application* (4th ed.). Philadelphia, PA: Lippincott Williams & Wilkins.

National Council for Therapeutic Recreation Certification (NCTRC). (2004). *Why hire a CTRS? Certified therapeutic recreation specialists enhance quality care.* [Brochure]. New City, NY: Author.

Needleman, J. (1999). Nonprofit to for-profit conversions by hospitals, health insurers, and health plans. *Public Health Reports, 114*(2), 108–119.

Northern, L. (1995, June 7). Stirring alphabet soup? *Rehab Rap*, 1–2.

Nosek, L. J. (2004). Globalization's costs to healthcare. How can we pay the bill? *Nursing Administration Quarterly, 28*(2), 116. Retrieved from Academic Search Premier (EBSCO host) database.

O'Morrow, G. S. (2000). *Therapeutic recreation practitioner analysis*. Ashburn, VA: National Therapeutic Recreation Society.

Porter-O'Grady, T. (2003). Of hubris and hope: Transforming nursing for a new age. *Nursing Economics, 21*(2), 59–64.

Stein, J. O. (1993). The Americans with Disabilities Act. In *Leisure opportunities for individuals with disabilities: Legal issues* (pp. 1–11). Reston, VA: American Alliance for Health, Physical Education, Recreation and Dance.

Sullivan, E. J. and Decker, P. J. (2005). *Effective leadership & management in nursing* (6th ed.). Upper Saddle River, NJ: Pearson/Prentice Hall.

Tappen, R. M., Weiss, S. A., and Whitehead, D. K. (2004). *Essentials of nursing leadership and management* (3rd ed.). Philadelphia, PA: F. A. Davis.

Thompson, G. T. (2001). Reimbursement: Surviving prospective payment as a recreational therapy practitioner. In N. J. Stumbo (Ed.), *Professional issues in therapeutic recreation:*

On competence and outcomes (pp. 249–264). Champaign, IL: Sagamore Publishing.

U.S. Department of Health and Human Services. (2003). Healthy People 2010: Understanding and improving health. In P. R. Lee, C. L. Estes, and F. M. Rodriquez (Eds.), *The nation's health* (7th ed., pp. 53–61). Boston, MA: Jones and Bartlett.

U.S. Department of Health and Human Services, Public Health Service. (1991). *Healthy People 2000: National health promotion and disease prevention objectives.* Washington, DC: Government Printing Office.

U.S. Department of Health and Human Services, Public Health Service. (1995). *Healthy People 2000: Midcourse review and 1995 revisions.* Sudbury, MA: Jones and Bartlett Publishers.

U.S. Department of Labor, Bureau of Labor Statistics. (1991). *Occupational handbook.* Washington, DC: Government Printing Office.

Whetten, D. A. and Cameron, K. S. (1984). *Developing management skills.* Glenview, IL: Scott, Foresman and Company.

Wren, D. A. (1979). *The evolution of management thought* (2nd ed.). New York, NY: John Wiley & Sons.

Section I
Characteristics of Management

Chapter 2
Conceptual Foundations of Management

chapter revisions by S. Harold Smith and Marcia Jean Carter

Today first-line therapeutic recreation managers operate in an environment in a state of flux. As a result, managers must be thoroughly familiar with a plurality of factors that influence the conditions under which service-giving resources are managed. The roots of present-day management lie with practitioners and writers who sought to develop principles that would make organizations more efficient (Robbins & Decenzo, 2001). Yet "because organizations are complex and varied, theorists' views of what successful management is and what it should be have changed" (Marquis & Huston, 2003, p. 5). Consequently a professional manager draws on a number of theories to guide decision making and problem resolution and to provide a framework for effective practice. The first section of this chapter presents a historical review of six management theories. These theories assist the manager in the following ways:

1. **Organization.** A theory provides a framework in which one can organize ideas and experiences. It detects similarities, differences, and other patterns in data and provides explanation for these patterns. When theory is used, our practices become well thought out, carefully considered, and reflective (Woodward, 2003). The art of therapeutic recreation, helping relationships, and the science of our profession, the APIE (i.e., assessment, planning, implementation, evaluation) process come together as one to address the clients' needs through effective management practices.

2. **Perspective.** A theory also provides a perspective, a certain way of looking at things. Using a particular theory influences how one interprets what one sees. One describes their practice using a particular paradigm rather than using the language of other constructs like the medical model (Woodward, 2003).

3. **Explanation.** Theories not only organize information but also provide explanations of events. Theories are general statements that help one understand why certain things do or do not happen. Why, for example, does therapeutic recreation specialist A work harder than therapeutic recreation specialist

B? One management theory will say that it is because A receives a larger salary than B. Another theory will say that it is because B is not interested in working with that group of consumers on that unit. A third will say that both factors are operating: A has interesting, stimulating work and is paid more than B, who is dissatisfied with her work in several ways. Theories make incidents and situations like this one understandable.

4. **Prediction.** A theory should also help one predict what is likely to happen in a given situation. Developmental theory predicts that certain crises will occur during adolescence, including conflicts between parents and teenagers. Familiarity with this theory enables a specialist to provide leisure guidance to a family with an at-risk youth in a leisure counseling program.

5. **Application.** A theory that predicts what is likely to happen in a given situation can provide some direction regarding what action is to be taken. Management theories serve as guides for selecting the most effective action. Theory also lends itself to research that can define measurable outcomes in one's work and professional environments (Woodward, 2003). Although it takes time to view a situation through a theoretical lens, "the more theory is used, the more it seeds its own value" (Woodward, 2003, p. 222).

The second section of the chapter considers how the presented theories are useful in the decision-making process.

The third section of the chapter introduces the management processes of planning, organizing, directing or leading, and controlling. This management process is universal and describes what managers do. This process accomplishes department and organizational goals effectively and efficiently through and with employees. Planning defines the goals; organizing determines the tasks and structure to achieve the goals; leading occurs through motivating, directing and communicating with others to accomplish the goals; and controlling is the monitoring function to assure goals are accomplished.

A review of the management theories and functions provides a conceptual foundation to consider the integration of leadership and management. Chapter 3 outlines leadership theories and the importance of including leader behaviors in the repertoire of a first-line therapeutic recreation manager.

Theories

As one begins to consider the various theories of management one should recognize that the actual practice of management has been in existence for thousands of years and can be traced back to the Egyptians. The mere physical presence of the pyramids forces one to accept that there had to exist formal plans, organizations, leadership, and control systems. The study of management from a scientific perspective did not begin until the late 19th century, however.

No single theory of management that explains all human behavior is universally accepted. Further, it is not unusual to become frustrated in the study and review of management theories. To help put different theories in perspective, this section shall discuss the following six conventional approaches, keeping in mind there is overlap or refinement from one theory to the next:

1. classical management theory

2. behavioral school

3. quantitative management theory

4. general systems theory

5. contingency theory

6. chaos theory

Classical Management Theory

Classical theory is built around four elements: division and specialization of labor, chain of command, structure of the organization, and span of control (Sullivan & Decker, 2001). Classical theory has had a number of labels since the turn of the century, including scientific management, management science, and operations management.

While several theorists have contributed to classical management theory, Frederick W. Taylor, who played a dominant role in its early development, is considered "the father of scientific management" (Wren, 1987). His innovations in the workplace resulted in higher quality products and improved employee morale. In his book, *The Principles of Scientific Management* (1911), Taylor offered the following four principles of scientific management to maximize individual productivity:

1. Develop a "science" for every job by studying motion, standardizing the work, and improving working conditions.

2. Carefully select workers with the correct abilities for the job.

3. Carefully train these workers to do the job and offer them incentives to produce.

4. Support the workers by planning their work and by removing obstacles. (Wren, 1987)

Henry Gantt, Frank and Lillian Gilbreth, and Morris Cooke added to scientific management. Gantt humanized Taylor's differential piece-rate system by combining a guaranteed day rate (i.e., minimum wage) with an above-standard bonus (Kreitner, 1992; Robbins & Decenzo, 2001; Roth, 2000). Gantt is best known for creating a graphic bar chart managers use to monitor production costs (Roth, 2000). The Gilbreth's devoted their efforts to motion analysis, or "least-waste" method, of labor. Their approach focused not on how long it took to do a piece of work but rather on the best way to do it (Roth, 2000). The "one best way" was the one that required the fewest motions to accomplish (Wren, 1987). Cooke broadened the ideas of scientific management to include their application in universities and municipal organizations. He recognized that the concepts of efficiency, so valuable to the profit sector, could be equally valuable in nonprofit and service organizations (Robbins, 1980).

Although Taylor, Gantt, the Gilbreths, and Cooke focused on the techniques that management might use in the production of goods through the use of individual employees and improving organization efficiency, none addressed management as a function distinct and separate from techniques and individuals.

It was Henri Fayol who attempted to develop a broad and more functional universal approach to management—managing the total organization. Fayol published a study concerned with the principles of general management entitled *General and Industrial Management* (1949). Fayol primarily studied the upper echelon of organizations and felt that the need for managerial ability increased in relative importance as an individual advanced in the chain of command (Fayol, 1949). Fayol's work provided definitions regarding the basic functions for management: planning, organizing, commanding, coordinating, and controlling (Robbins & Decenzo, 2001). If goals are to be accomplished, these functions must be carried out (Fayol, 1949). He defined management in these words:

> To manage is to forecast and plan, to organize, to command, to coordinate, and to control. To

foresee and provide means examining the future and drawing up the plan of action. To organize means building up the dual structure, material and human, of the undertaking. To command means binding together, unifying and harmonizing all activity and effort. To control means seeing that everything occurs in conformity with established rule and expressed demand. (Fayol, 1949, pp. 5–6)

Fayol came to the conclusion that there was a set of management principles that could be used in all types of management situations regardless of organization. Further, these principles should be used to implement the five functions (i.e., planning, organizing, commanding, coordinating, and controlling). Fayol (1949, pp. 19–20) listed the principles of management as follows:

1. division of work
2. authority
3. discipline
4. unit of command
5. unit of direction
6. subordination of individual interest to the general interest
7. remuneration
8. centralization
9. scalar chain (line of authority)
10. order
11. equity
12. stability or tenure of personnel
13. initiative
14. esprit de corps

While not specifically associated with classical theory or scientific management, the work of Luther Gulick and Lyndall Urwick expanded on the contribution of Fayol's management functions. Gulick (1947) expanded on Fayol's contribution, using the acronym POSDCoRB to represent the functions of management. The acronym stands for planning, organizing, staffing, directing, coordinating (or communicating), reporting, and budgeting. Variations of this management scheme are still used by many managers today as well as the authors of this book. Urwick (1944) indicated that administrative skill within management functions is a practical art that improves with practice and requires hard study and thinking. From

his work Urwick concluded that there are three principles of administration. He described the first principle as that of *investigation* and stated that all scientific procedure is based on investigation of the facts. Investigation takes effect in planning. The second principle is *appropriateness*, which underlines forecasting, entering into process with organization and taking effect in coordination. Exercising the third principle the administrator looks ahead and organizes *resources* to meet future needs. Planning enters into the process with command and is effected in control.

Oliver Sheldon departed from earlier writings in scientific study of management by noting the importance of ethics in management and that managers have a social responsibility to their community. To Sheldon, workers as part of a community were more important than machines (Roth, 2000). His philosophy gave management a distinct identity with a major responsibility to serve the community. Lending itself also to the field of scientific study was the work of Leonard White. He argued that management should be separate from politics and that the mission of management is economy and efficiency (Robbins, 1980).

Although Max Weber is identified more with organizational theory, it is important to note his relationship to scientific management. Weber (1947) is credited with attempting to create the ultimate efficient organization by proposing a rational bureaucracy of integrated activities and positions with inherent activities (Sullivan & Decker, 2001). He is credited with using the term *bureaucracy* to describe the concepts implied in the depersonalization of the management function (Roth, 2000; Sullivan & Decker, 2001). Employees occupied roles assigned on the basis of technical qualifications that in turn were determined by formalized impersonal procedures. Rules and regulations were developed for each position regardless of the person who occupied it. The concept of role became paramount in Weber's system, with employees conceived almost as preprogrammed interchangeable robots. Weber's impersonal bureaucracy seemed to outlaw the development of personal relationships in legitimate organizational activities. However, this impersonal bureaucracy contributes to the stability of any organization and the predictability of its performance (Shortell, Kaluzny & Associates, 1988).

The overall approach of Taylor, Gantt, the Gilbreths, Fayol, and others was to provide a rational basis for management and to place it on a more objective and scientific foundation. As the classical management theory developed, it examined in more detail the functions of managers. According to Hax and Majluf (1984), Weber, Taylor, and Fayol have had a lasting impact on management and organizational design, as their views are a frame of reference for many current concepts.

Behavioral School

As more managers began operating under the principles of classical management thought, it became apparent that results were not totally compatible with expectations. Many managers felt the classical approach did not take into account human relations in that people desire social relations, respond to group pressures, and search for personal fulfillment (Sullivan & Decker, 2001). As a result the management field moved gradually from a mechanical approach of following a series of rules to an attempt to understand the worker. Studies focused on democratic structure, multidirectional communications, and promotion of general worker satisfaction. These studies are considered to be the beginning of the human relations approach to management (Edginton, Hudson & Lankford, 2001). Self-development, individualization, initiative, and creativity were identified as attributes to be promoted and encouraged. Since the therapeutic recreation manager may not have too much to say about the way in which the organization is structured, behavioral theory may have special significance for the manager.

Behavioral management theory was stimulated by a number of writers, but the primary catalyst for this movement was Elton Mayo (1933) and his studies at Western Electric Company's Hawthorne Plant concerned with the physical environment and productivity. Mayo initiated a series of studies intended to contribute to the concepts of scientific management but which ultimately demonstrated the impact of small group dynamics on production. Small groups of women and men were selected for an intensive study focusing on the impact of physical working conditions, the psychological capacity of the worker on productivity, and how monetary incentives played a role in work behavior. Mayo found that physical comfort and pay had less impact on productivity than the way workers related to each other socially and economically (i.e., being paid for the group's output rather than individual output). After several years of the Hawthorne experiments concerned with increasing productivity, the researchers concluded that "other factors," or group dynamics, the relationship between workers and supervisors, and the "quantity and quality of job supervision affected employee job satisfaction and production" (Edginton, Hudson & Lankford, 2001, p. 42). These factors were more important than wages and physical working conditions in terms of performance (Roth, 2000).

Mayo (1933) pointed out in *The Human Problems of an Industrial Civilization* that emotional factors are important in productivity. He also urged managers to provide work that stimulated personal satisfaction. He did not argue against the bureaucratic structure approach to management as outlined by Weber, but he proposed that improvements be made by making the structure less for-

mal and by permitting more employee participation in decision making. The implication of Mayo's studies relative to the therapeutic recreation manager is quite clear. Sometimes the only thing required to meet people's needs is to pay attention to them. This applies to consumers, peers, and other health and human service staff.

Mary Parker Follett is another behavioral scientist who suggested to managers that employees are a "complex conviction of emotions, beliefs, attitudes, and habits" (Kreitner, 1992, p. 52). Because she believed that managers had to recognize the individual's motivating desires to get employees to produce more, she suggested that managers motivate performance rather than demand it. By relying on expertise and knowledge to lead staff, rather than the formal authority of their positions, Follett suggested the workplace, like life, is developmental and the lines between one's workplace and life and between workers and managers should be erased (Roth, 2000).

In the development of the behavioral school, Chester Barnard (1938) is recognized as one of the outstanding contributors. Associated with the systems approach to management, Barnard's work was primarily drawn from sociological approaches to management in which he attempted to find answers underlying the process of management. Barnard established a theory for a system of cooperation: willingness to serve, common purpose, and communication are the principle elements in an organization. This theory emphasized the need of individuals to solve the limitation of themselves and their environment through cooperation with others. The success of an organization depended on cooperation of its employees and maintaining good relations with people and institutions outside the organization. Barnard's work brought forth the recognition of the organization as a social organism that must interact with environmental pressures and conflict. The current interest in developing cooperative work groups and teams, making health care more socially responsive, and matching organizational strategies to opportunities (SWOT analysis—strengths, weaknesses, opportunities, threats) in the community is traced to Barnard's original ideas (Robbins & Decenzo, 2001).

Later theorists, such as Kurt Lewin (1951), Abraham Maslow (1954), Douglas McGregor (1960), and others influenced a humanistic approach to management. Maslow is well-known for his theory based on a hierarchy of needs—physiologic, safety, love, belonging, self-esteem, and self-actualization. Organizations and management theories, according to Maslow, ignore the human being's intrinsic nature and are detrimental to the psychic and physical health and well-being of employees. Although these needs, especially higher level ones, may be suppressed, ignoring basic human needs would contribute to lower productivity, high absenteeism, high turnover, low morale, and job dissatisfaction. Maslow's theory of hierarchy of needs led to theories on motivation (Maslow, 1968; refer to Chapter 14).

McGregor furthered the human relations movement. His theme was people are basically good and to stimulate their performance one should humanize work with this philosophy: Let people participate and take an active role in those decisions that affect them, have trust and confidence in people, and reduce external control devices. He developed a set of assumptions called Theory X and Theory Y about human behavior, reflected in Table 2.1. In McGregor's view, Theory X focused on the tasks to be done. In contrast, Theory Y was a more appropriate view for managers to take in regard to viewing employees since its focus was on the employees and their job satisfaction (McGregor, 1960). According to Robbins and Decenzo (2001), there is no evidence to confirm that either set of assumptions is valid.

More recently a Theory Z (Ouchi, 1981) has been proposed that suggests a middle ground between Theories X and Y. The Theory Z model (Ouchi, 1981) attempts to integrate common business practices from the United States and Japan into one middle-ground framework. Theory Z takes a humanistic viewpoint and focuses on developing better ways to motivate people. In addition, Theory Z emphasizes collective or participative decision making, collective responsibility as opposed to personal responsibility, and a recognition of mutual dependence (Ouchi, 1981).

In summary, the behavioral school brought together newly developed theories, methods, and techniques of the relevant social sciences on the study of interpersonal and intrapersonal phenomena, ranging from the personality dynamics of individuals at one end to the relation of cultures at the other end. According to the advocates of the behavioral approach to management today technology, work rules, and standards do not guarantee good job performance. Success depends on motivated and skilled individuals who are committed to organizational objectives. The function of the manager is to obtain employee cooperation so they work toward organizational goals (Tappen, 2001). Our current understanding of employee motivation, organizational cultures, high-performance teams, performance appraisals, conflict management, and negotiation techniques are due in large part to the contributions of behavioral scientists (Robbins & Decenzo, 2001).

Quantitative Management Theory

Quantitative management theory never really claimed to be the overall conceptual base for management theory advocates have implied it to be. However, the approach does use tools that provide management with a greater power for the analysis of problems. Quantitative management theory incorporates two interrelated branches: management science (not related to scientific management) and operations management. Together they focus on decision making, economic effectiveness, formal mathematical models, and the use of computers to stimulate and solve problems. Management science and operations research provide quantitative information used in decision making, particularly planning and control decisions like scheduling and resource allocations (Robbins & Decenzo, 2001).

Table 2.1
Theory X and Theory Y Assumptions

Theory X Assumptions	*Theory Y Assumptions*
1. People do not like work and try to avoid it.	1. People do not naturally dislike work; work is a natural part of their lives.
2. People do not like work, so managers have to control, direct, coerce, and threaten employees to get them to work toward organizational goals.	2. People are internally motivated to reach objectives to which they are committed.
3. People prefer to be directed, to avoid responsibility, to want security; they have little ambition.	3. People are committed to goals to the degree that they receive personal rewards when they reach their objectives.
	4. People will both seek and accept responsibility under favorable conditions.
	5. People have the capacity to be innovative in solving organizational problems.
	6. People are bright, but under most organizational conditions, their potentials are under utilized.

Source: McGregor, D. (1960). *The human side of enterprise* (pp. 33–34, 47–48). New York, NY: McGraw-Hill. Reprinted with permission of the McGraw-Hill Companies.

Techniques like Program Evaluation Review Technique–Critical Path Method (PERT–CPM) and Planning-Programming-Budgeting System (PPBS) are used to design and evaluate project efficiency. These techniques use modeling to help the manager review alternatives and make objective decisions.

General Systems Theory

An organization is a complex sociotechnical system (DeGreen, 1973). In the 1950s von Bertalanffy described a general systems theory that provided a consistent operational model for studying systems at all levels of science from a single cell to complex social systems such as business firms, health care facilities, and political states (Kast & Rosenzweig, 1985). According to von Bertalanffy (1972, p. 411), "In order to understand an organized whole we must know both the parts and the relations between them." General systems theory is interdisciplinary in its study approach; it is based on the assumption that everything is part of a larger, independent arrangement.

A system can be defined as a unitary whole composed of two or more elements in interaction and differentiated by an identifiable boundary from its environment. It is characterized by input (e.g., materials, employees, money, consumers), the transformation process (e.g., technology, interventions, management systems), output (e.g., services, well consumers, employees' behaviors), and feedback (e.g., consumer, factors in the environment) to the system. Feedback enables a system to regulate itself. For example, in the community, laws, rules, and regulations regulate the behavior of citizens. In the family system, parents provide feedback to children to regulate behavior (Kast & Rosenzweig, 1985).

Stumbo and Peterson's (2004) *Therapeutic Recreation Program Design: Principles and Procedures* takes a systems approach to programming. The therapeutic recreation process has characteristics of an open system: it is open, flexible, and dynamic; it is planned and goal directed; it interacts with the environment; and it emphasizes feedback. Input (i.e., data) from the consumer and practitioner is transformed by the process of analyzing, planning, and implementing, all of which occur throughout the therapeutic recreation process. The output (i.e., consumer response) is then evaluated. The Input Process Output (IPO) model of Carter, Van Andel, and Robb (2003) is another example of a systems approach to program design. Moreover, the IPO model is associated with Riley's (1991) outcome evaluation model and quality-of-care indicators.

There are any number of characteristics associated with systems. For example, systems are either open or closed. Closed systems are usually self-contained. However, there is disagreement on whether or not a truly closed system exists. The assumption is that the most important feature of organizations has to do with their internal structure and processes which are relatively isolated from the external environment. Open systems, on the other hand, interact with the surrounding environment for survival (see Figure 2.1). Environmental factors include political, social, and economic variables that influence system performance. By taking into account its environment, the organization's structure, process, and performance are centrally influenced by the nature of the inputs taken in from the environment and the outputs produced. Organizations, such as hospitals and departments of parks and recreation, are open systems because their survival depends on interaction with the surrounding environments.

Another important assumption made by systems theory is that systems are made up of subsystems—a system within a system. According to Kreitner (1992), hierarchies of systems range from very specific systems (e.g., communication, decision making) to general ones. While subsystems have some degree of autonomy, they also depend on the next subsystem. A therapeutic recreation department within physical medicine and rehabilitation (PM and R) can function somewhat independently, but it is eventually dependent on PM and R, which in turn depends on the hospital. A therapeutic recreation division within a community-based parks and recreation department depends on the community-based department, and the department depends on the community. Thus, there is a constant interdependence among various departments.

Sentience—the capacity for thought, abstraction, and feeling—is another characteristic of systems. It brings

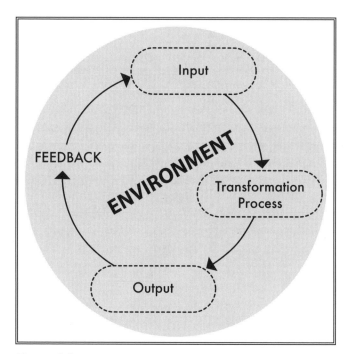

Figure 2.1
Open System

into play the uniquely human importance of emotions, values, and personal and culture-bound meanings. People are not simply aware of the world around them—they are actively involved in trying to make sense of it by attempting to organize or influence their environment (Boulding, 1968). In an open system the therapeutic recreation manager integrates information and resources from the environment, such as legislation and reimbursement factors, so the organization's goals are achieved (Sullivan & Decker, 2001). As the link to the community, the manager assumes an integral role in community relations (refer to Chapter 11).

Contingency Theory

Today virtually any health and human service organization must cope with an environment more complex, more changeable, and therefore more uncertain than the environments health care organizations faced in the past. Likewise, departments of parks and recreation will increasingly be forced to cope with changes in service delivery as a result of the Americans with Disabilities Act. To meet the challenge of change, a new approach to theory and practice of management has emerged.

Most books about management today recognize that it is largely contingency-based. Contingency theory suggests that appropriate managerial behavior is contingent on a variety of elements (Kast & Rosenzweig, 1985). These elements may be the environment (e.g., consumers, third-party payers), personnel (e.g., training, shortage of staff), technology, department or organization size and goals, administrator's power and influence, and clarity and equity of reward systems. According to Shetty (1974, p. 27), "The effectiveness of a given management pattern is contingent upon multitudinous factors and their interrelationship in a particular situation." Taking a universal approach to this theory, Koontz, O'Donnell, and Weihrich (1980, p. 17) noted:

> that there is no one best way to plan; there is no one best way to lead; there is no one best way to organize a group; and there is no one best way to control the activities of an organization. The best concepts and techniques can be selected only after one is aware of the particular circumstances he is facing…

Consequently, what has worked in the past, such as a concept or technique to solve a problem, may not be appropriate in a different situation or under different circumstances. The approach to the delivery of services in a hospital setting is going to be much different from a community parks and recreation department.

Although still not fully developed, the contingency approach is helpful to management because it emphasizes

situational appropriateness. As noted by Kreitner (1992, p. 60), "People, organizations, and problems are too complex to justify rigid adherence to universal principles of organizations." A contingency theorist believes managers enhance agency performance by matching organizational structure to its environment. Therefore, the nature of therapeutic recreation services will vary with the unique features of the setting and each consumer's particular situation.

Chaos Theory

Chaos theory suggests the universe is uncertain, and the life cycle of an organization depends on its responsiveness to changes in the environment (Sullivan & Decker, 2001). Managers build resiliency in the midst of change and create learning organizations where trial-and-error modes to service delivery prevail. This theory incorporates aspects from several earlier theories. Also recognized is the importance of quality and excellence that result from organizational change, and a culture that realizes employees' creative energies to design a preferred future.

Theory Application to Therapeutic Recreation

Although the theories just presented and their application to effective therapeutic recreation management will be considered throughout this text, it should be noted that no single theory is universally accepted. The poem "The Blind Men and the Elephant" (p. 22) humorously illustrates the dilemma in management theory: Where one is and what perspective one takes determines what one sees. Each has its limitations because organizations today are unique, changing, and complex. Consequently, therapeutic recreation managers should use management theory in an elective way.

To assist in determining the usefulness of the presented theories in the decision-making process, as a therapeutic recreation manager one may want to ask the following questions (Tappen, 2001):

1. **Is the theory internally consistent?** Are the different parts of the theory congruent with each other, or is there some inconsistency in the way human behavior is explained or predicted?

2. **Does the theory provide useful guidelines for practice?** The purpose of considering theories that explain human behavior is to apply them to specific situations. However, some theories are so broad or narrow that it is difficult to apply them to specific situations. The general systems theory is so broad that it does not give us answers to a

The Blind Men and the Elephant
by John G. Saxe

It was six men of Indostan,
To learning much inclined,
Who went to see the elephant
(Though each of them was blind,)
That each by observation
Might satisfy his mind.

The first approached the elephant,
And happening to fall
Against his broad and sturdy side,
At once began to bawl:
"God bless me! but the elephant
Is very much like a wall!"

The second, feeling of the tusk,
Cried: "Ho! what have we here
So round, and smooth, and sharp?
To me 'tis very clear
This wonder of an elephant
Is very like a spear!"

The third approached the animal,
And happening to take
The squirming trunk within his hands,
Thus boldly up he spake:
"I see," quoth he, "the elephant
Is very much like a snake!"

The fourth reached out his eager hand,
And fell upon the knee:
"What most this wondrous beast is like,
Is very plain," quoth he;
"Tis clear enough the elephant
Is very like a tree!"

The fifth who chanced to touch the ear
Said: "E'en the blindest man
Can tell what this resembles most:
Deny the fact who can,
This marvel of an elephant
Is very like a fan!"

The sixth no sooner had begun
About the beast to grope,
Then, seizing on the swinging tail
That fell within his scope,
"I see," quoth he, "the elephant,
Is very like a rope!"

And so these men of Indostan
Disputed loud and long,
Each in his own opinion
Exceeding stiff and strong,
Though each was partly in the right,
And all were in the wrong!

Source: Saxe, J. G. (1936). The blind men and the elephant. In H. Felleman (Ed.), *The best-loved poems of the American people* (pp. 521–522). New York, NY: Doubleday.

particular problem yet does suggest the complexity of health care environments.

3. **Has empirical testing yielded evidence in support of the theory?** Some theories have a natural appeal that tempts one to accept them without sufficient evaluation. The evolution of the Z theory suggests popularity of the X and Y theories was not assurance of their utility.

4. **Is the theory congruent with one's values and one's philosophy of therapeutic recreation as well as with the organization's?** A management theory that supports the growth and development of the individual employee implies a very different set of values from one that supports immediate termination when the skills of the specialist are no longer needed. In addition, the theory must be in agreement with the health and human service organization.

In the development of classical management theory, the work of Fayol and his basic functions of management stand out. Although these functions have been modified and expanded, they will provide the nucleus for the discussion of what management is and what managers do. In addition, his guidelines or principles of management, and those of Gulick and Urwick, are intertwined throughout the discussion of the management process.

It can be noted from the review of these theories that goal achievement (e.g., quality service) within any setting is getting things done through people. Further, these people have human needs, perceptions, and aspirations. Material surroundings, wages and hours, or work cannot be considered in isolation from their value in relating a person to a setting. No therapeutic recreation practitioner should be viewed as motivated strictly by economic or rational considerations. Values, beliefs, and emotions are inextricably involved in each practitioner's behavior. Successful goal achievement depends on good human relations, job satisfaction, and an understanding of what motivates people. A sensitive manager is aware of individual differences. A humanistic management atmosphere, with an emphasis on management theories to improve service, is essential for effective organizational goal achievement.

A last point is the approach to management. Today's environment demands diverse approaches to management to cope with more complexity and more uncertainty. It is naive to think that the form of management best for the delivery of therapeutic recreation service in one setting would be appropriate for all settings. While there are similarities, there are also differences, and these differences represent a wide range of factors. The optimal form of management suggested is contingent on the factors faced by the therapeutic recreation manager in any setting—providing the highest possible level of consumer care and service while at the same time meeting other conflicting goals, such as staying within budget and keeping staff practitioners satisfied. The contingency theory of management complemented by the systems approach (e.g., open systems, subsystems) offers a viable management approach. Being aware of a variety of theoretical frameworks helps therapeutic recreation managers know that, as they seek to organize and develop their programs and services, they do have choices. These choices are made even more complex, however, by the very nature of health and human service organizations.

Functions

The management process is universal. It is used in one's personal and professional life. It applies to management of oneself, a consumer, a group of consumers, or a group of practitioners.

The management process is composed of four major functions: (a) planning, (b) organizing, (c) directing or leading, and (d) controlling. They represent the breaking down of the managerial job into its principal parts. However, one should recognize that managers' jobs are shaped by the organizations in which they work. As the organization and its environment change, so does the managerial role (Shortell, Kaluzny & Associates, 1988).

Planning is an organized managerial function of establishing the basic direction and objectives and of laying out a design for reaching the objectives. It is deciding what to do, how to do it, and who is to do it. Further, it is a disciplined way of implementing the sequence of major tasks to meet goals. Because planning bridges the gap from where one is to where one wants to be, it is the most basic of the four functions. Organizing involves determining the activities necessary to accomplish the plans, grouping them, assigning them to specific positions and individuals, and delegating the requisite authority. Directing is principally the managerial function of leading or supervising subordinates toward the achievement of objectives. Finally, the controlling function compares performance with established objectives and, if necessary, initiates corrective action. Every professional manager at every management level performs each of these functions and the activities associated with these functions. The differences are in magnitude and frequency.

Planning

The first element of management defined by Fayol (1949) is planning. Planning is the foundation and framework for all of the other management functions. It is a comprehensive process that includes determining philosophy, goals, objectives, policies, procedures, and rules; carrying out long-range and short-range plans; formulating a fiscal plan; and managing planned change (Marquis & Huston, 2003). Every manager has a planning function to perform. Although it is true that top managers may devote more of their time to planning and work with more vital issues than do managers at the middle or lower levels, the fact remains that every manager has planning to perform within his or her particular area of responsibility.

Planning takes the risk out of decision making and problem solving. Moreover, planning improves with yearly experiences, gives sequence in activities, and protects against undesirable organizational changes. Last, it helps to ensure that probable outcomes will be desirable ones in terms of the use of human resources, budget, and service. As an example, Table 2.2 (p. 24) depicts those management tasks required of a therapeutic recreation manager in association with program planning within a community-based leisure service agency as suggested by Carter, Browne, LeConey, and Nagle (1991). One will note that the therapeutic recreation process format is used in the management plan.

The statement of the vision, mission, purpose, philosophy, goals, objectives, standards, policies, and procedures are all consequences of planning. Conceptual thinking and problem solving are also crucial functions in the planning process. Data are gathered and analyzed so that alternatives can be identified and evaluated in the decision-making process. The manager must forecast what is needed for the future, set goals and objectives for the desired results, and develop strategies for how to achieve the goals. Priorities must be set and strategies need to be sequenced in a time frame to accomplish these goals and objectives. Policies and procedures are also developed in the planning phase. Policies are standing decisions concerning recurring matters and procedures are standardized methods. Budgets are used as planning and controlling tools in the allocation of resources. Planning is the basis for time management which will in turn facilitate the implementation of the plans.

Planning is the essential link between good intentions and action. Without it good ideas rarely become reality. Good planning requires that a manager have a broad knowledge of the organization's operations and goals, a detailed knowledge of the division or department, technical knowledge, and intuition. A keen awareness of the changes and current internal and external trends affecting the area of service delivery is also needed.

Planning is the assessment of the therapeutic recreation department's strengths and weaknesses, covering factors that affect performance and facilitate or inhibit

Table 2.2
Management Planning Tasks

Assessment
- Identify assessment techniques and resources
- Prepare assessment instruments
- Organize advisory committee
- Collect data from participants
- Collect data from agency
- Collect data from community
- Analyze collected data

Planning
- Develop philosophy and program structure
- Select program content
- Identify leadership needs
- Prepare management plan
- Prepare participant and staff schedules
- Prepare program resources
- Develop operating policies and procedures
- Develop risk management plan
- Oversee budget functions
- Prepare documentation and recordkeeping procedures
- Develop staff training
- Prepare marketing program
- Develop evaluation plan

Implementation
- Conduct program registration
- Complete individual participant assessments
- Write individual participant plans
- Conduct activities
- Complete formative participant/program evaluations
- Monitor budget functions and staffing
- Conduct staff supervision and development
- Inspect and document health/safety and participant involvement
- Monitor and communicate with market audiences
- Adjust programs and services

Evaluation
- Conduct summative evaluations on participants and programs
- Analyze collected data
- Update participant files
- Update documentation and recordkeeping procedures
- Adjust budget, staff, programs, and services
- Revise risk management, marketing, and staff training programs
- Prepare transition information
- Prepare final program report
- Present report to Advisory Committee

Source: Carter, M.J., Browne, B., LeConey, S.P., and Nagle, C.J. (1991). *Designing therapeutic recreation programs in the community.* Reston, VA: American Alliance for Health, Physical Education, Recreation and Dance. Reproduced with permission from the American Alliance for Health, Physical Education, Recreation and Dance, Reston, VA 22091.

the achievement of objectives. Planning implies writing specific, useful, realistic objectives (the *why*) that will reflect both strategic and operational goals for the department of therapeutic recreation and its personnel. Objectives become the reasons behind an operational therapeutic recreation management plan that will detail activities to be performed (the *what*), the target dates or time frames for their accomplishment (the *when*), the persons responsible for accomplishing them (the *who*), and strategies for dealing with the technical, economic, social, and political aspects. These operational plans will have control systems for monitoring performance and providing feedback. The summary of planning describes the work of the department; it gives outsiders a bird's-eye view of its totality.

Flexibility is essential in the planning process and the plan is both normative and summative in nature. Therefore, planning is an ongoing process that does not have a final conclusion or finite end point. This dynamic nature of planning is essential to ensure the relevancy of the plan and its resultant decisions to reality. If plans are not revised and reevaluated on an ongoing basis, they soon develop a greater divergence with reality and this divergence increases with the passage of time. Competent managers advocate changing plans at any moment along the way if the change will bring in facilitative resources and alterations. Planning is a continuous process of assessing and establishing goals and objectives, and implementing and evaluating them. The process is subject to change as new facts become known so as to ensure or achieve organization goals for the present and the future. See Figure 2.2.

Reasons for Planning

Why should managers plan? There are a number of valid reasons for planning. Collectively, the reasons for planning include efficiency, effectiveness, accountability, and morale. Efficiency is always desirable. The aim is to achieve goals with a minimum of cost and effort. This oc-

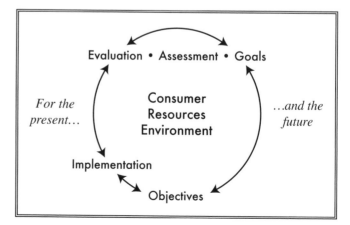

Figure 2.2
Continuous Planning Process

curs only through careful planning, which is an anticipatory process. In therapeutic recreation, regardless of setting, practitioners and resources are limited, so it is particularly important to provide services as efficiently as possible.

Effectiveness is extremely important. If activities are not planned, the desired results may not be achieved. In therapeutic recreation service, the main goal is, of course, to help people. If practitioner efforts and organization and department resources are diffused, and planning involving unity of purpose and integration of effort does not occur, the level of achievement will be low. Thus, the therapeutic recreation manager must do effective planning to create an environment in which therapeutic recreation practitioners will give the service desired and needed by consumers.

Planning is needed for evaluation and accountability. Today, public-spirited citizens, legislators, community leaders, and top managers are asking valid questions. What are the results of therapeutic recreation services? Can one afford them? Can one improve them? These and other questions can be answered only as therapeutic recreation manager's plan carefully in relation to specific objectives and evaluation procedures for measuring their programs and services. Proper planning makes it possible to carry out an objective evaluation of services.

Careful planning is essential for the morale of the therapeutic recreation department. Practitioners need feelings of achievement and satisfaction to perform their best. Such feelings are engendered when the manager and practitioners work together in the planning process making it possible for each practitioner to feel needed and effective. A department that makes it possible for each practitioner to understand exactly what to do and how to do it provides an emotional and administrative climate conducive to high morale. How the staff feels will make a difference in the delivery of therapeutic recreation services.

Strategic, Operational, and Contingency Planning

Strategic planning refers to determining and prioritizing the long-term objectives within the organization and the strategies for implementing these objectives (Sullivan & Decker, 2001). It means looking at where one is, where one wants to go, and how to reach the desired future. This type of planning is usually carried out by the chief administrator of the hospital or the superintendent or director of the department of parks and recreation. Although lower level managers (e.g., middle and first-line managers) are not directly involved in strategic planning, they are affected by the strategic plan, because it will determine both the objectives they must achieve and the means by which they can do so.

Strategic planning provides a forecast for two to five years into the future (Sullivan & Decker, 2001; Tomey,

2000). Strategic planning establishes direction or a mission, collects and analyzes data, assesses strengths and weaknesses, sets goals and objectives, determines a timetable, evaluates, and gives guidance to the therapeutic recreation managers. It is important that therapeutic recreation managers have input into strategic planning; however, it is realized that such an opportunity will vary within each organization. Turpel (1992, p. 72) sees the benefits of the strategic planning process as follows:

1. Identifies unique strengths and builds strategies for the future on the basis of those strengths.

2. Provides a workable mechanism for cooperation among all "players."

3. Separates fact from fiction and tests conventional "wisdom."

4. Places critical issues and problems in the perspective of larger trends.

5. Focuses available energy and resources on the top priorities.

6. Shapes a vision of the future that provides a touchstone for all involved parties.

7. Recruits and develops the leaders of tomorrow.

8. Fosters effective action (gets things done).

Operational planning is performed at the department or service level. Operational planning is usually associated with a specific service within the therapeutic recreation department. For example, a therapeutic recreation manager would assist or have input into developing the overall strategic plan but would only develop departmental goals, objectives, and operational plans related specifically to the department.

Operational plans consist of everyday working management plans. They are developed from both short-range and long-range goals and objectives based on the strategic planning process. In development of operational plans new strategic objectives can emerge or old ones can be modified. Strategic plans and objectives are made into operational plans and carried out at all levels of management, not just at the first-line management level.

First-line managers develop strategies, goals, objectives, and time frames to accomplish the overall strategic plan. They match each department goal or objective to a strategic goal or objective. Departmental goals and objectives may be more detailed and specific than the overall strategic goals and objectives. There can also be numerous departmental objectives that support one strategic objective.

Goals are critical not only to the organization but also to the department. Goals serve four important purposes as noted by Richards (1986). First, they provide guidance and a unified direction for the practitioners in the department. Goals can help practitioners to understand where the department is going and why getting there is important. Second, as an outgrowth of guidance, planning is facilitated. Goals and planning are interrelated. Third, goals can serve as a source of motivation and inspiration for staff. Specific and moderately difficult goals can motivate people to work harder, especially if attaining the goal is likely to result in rewards. Last, goals provide an effective mechanism for evaluation and control.

Operational planning at the department level is related to the delivery of direct program services. It involves matching practitioners to responsibilities, developing policies and procedures specific to the delivery of services, identifying training needs, preparing and conducting training programs, supervising personnel, and evaluating. Evaluation takes place on a continuing basis. Depending on the results, modifications are made in the implementation of the plan as deemed appropriate.

Contingency planning refers to identifying and dealing with the many problems that interfere with getting work done (Sullivan & Decker, 2001). Planning may be reactive in response to a problem or proactive in anticipation of an opportunity. Some examples of potential problems are new, inexperienced staff who do not know the policies and procedures of the organization well; volunteer tardiness or staff absenteeism which leaves the department short of personnel (e.g., sick days, holidays, weekends, vacations); physician request for a special service or program and unavailability of supplies or equipment at that time; and staff quitting without giving notice. Once aware of possible contingencies (i.e., reactive), the therapeutic recreation manager is alert to detect their occurrence and plans accordingly (i.e., proactive). Finally, therapeutic recreation managers should ask themselves what activities are necessary to prevent problems from happening and what the plans are for dealing with problems once they have occurred. For example, does the department have plans for dealing with certain kinds of disasters—external disasters, like the hurricanes in Florida and the earthquakes in California, which prevented therapeutic recreation practitioners from getting to work, or internal disasters, such as loss of power?

Organizing

Organizing is the second managerial function. It refers to the grouping of activities and resources into organizational units, such as departments or sections, and staffing these departments to accomplish the work of the organization (Sullivan & Decker, 2001). In addition, organizing includes the assignment of such groupings to a manager who has authority for supervising each group and the defined means for coordinating appropriate activities with other departments, horizontally and vertically, to achieve organizational objectives. Last, organizing involves establishing an organizational structure to develop and to attain the organization's mission, including goals and objectives.

The grouping of activities and resources into a department may be based on function according to similarity of skills or tasks necessary to accomplish a goal. This arrangement by function, according to Gray and Smeltzer (1989), is a prevalent method of grouping activities. This arrangement facilitates specialization and contributes to economical operations. Functions performed by the same specialists with similar equipment and facility needs are grouped and report to the same manager (Tomey, 2000). Functional structures are usually stable and foster good communication, and managing the coordination of tasks is easily achieved. The formal hierarchic nature of functional structures offers a model for placing large numbers of people into a structure that can be easily identified and programmed. It also provides for easy performance evaluation, promotion based on seniority and achievement, and more fair distribution of awards. In addition, recruitment is enhanced because a cadre of professional colleagues can attract other professionals.

Functional structures also have their disadvantages. Functional structures are rigid and frequently neither prepare practitioners for the future nor train or test them. Functional managers are confronted with situations involving only their narrow field of specialty. In addition, professional skills are emphasized over organizational goals. Consequently, coordination across services is limited and responses to external factors that require coordination across functions is slow (Sullivan & Decker, 2001). Its inherent focus on specialization has a tendency to push the decision-making process upward because only at the top does one find the confluence of all input required for a final decision. Consequently, communication may require additional time.

Organizational structures are changing from hierarchical structures to flat organizations with cross-functional teams empowered to work through multiple tasks (Tomey, 2000). One structure—the service-integrated, product-line, or self-contained unit—combines all the functions necessary to produce a service into self-contained units (Sullivan & Decker, 2001). This structure is decentralized; units are based on geographic areas like regions of a city or type of consumer like individuals with cancer (oncology unit). In large organizations, self-contained units can respond rapidly to meet client needs and service goals receive priority since staff view outcomes as the primary purpose of their organization (Sullivan & Decker, 2001). Disadvantages of this organization format include possible duplication of resources, lack of specialization, the difficulty of coordination across units, and the potential for competition among units for resources.

The matrix structure integrates both service and functional structures (Marquis & Huston, 2003; Sullivan & Decker, 2001). "Function is described as all the tasks required to produce the product, and the product is the end result of the function" (Marquis & Huston, 2003, p. 171). Satisfactory outcome of a client need is the product or service, whereas the actions required to produce the outcome is the function. Different managers are responsible for product and function. To illustrate, a therapist might report to the therapeutic recreation unit manager (function) while also reporting to an inclusion specialist or outpatient services manager (product). Although there are less formal rules and fewer levels of the hierarchy, a matrix structure does require staff to report to more than one manager. Consequently, decision making may be slow because of the frequency of meetings and necessity to share information, and employees may experience confusion as they report to more than one supervisor.

One of the more innovative organizational structures developed in the mid-1980s is shared governance (Marquis & Huston, 2003). Although there is no one model, the common thread among all the models is empowerment of staff to make decisions over their own practice (Marquis & Huston, 2003; Sullivan & Decker, 2001). Integrative care models, multidisciplinary teams, and partnerships characterize shared governance models. In some instances these models incorporate the election of advisory boards and councils of practitioners to decide policies. Departmental structures are disappearing as service configurations address the client care continuum with service efficiency and accountability. Shared governance models result in fiscally responsive services, job retention and satisfaction, positive consumer outcomes, and positive organizational cultures (Marquis & Huston, 2003; Sullivan & Decker, 2001).

Various organizational structures are depicted through organizational charts. An organizational chart is a drawing that shows how the parts of an organization are linked. It depicts the formal organizational relationships, areas of responsibility, persons accountable, and channels of communication. Figure 2.3 (p. 29) shows a conventional mid-size hospital hierarchical organization organized by function while Figure 2.4 (p. 30) illustrates a matrix organization design with dual reporting relationships wherein the practitioner reports to the department manager as well as the unit manager (e.g., rehabilitation unit). An organizational chart is meaningful only to the extent that the system represented on paper is a reality. The organizational chart, like milk, may be dated but not fresh. Its precision sometimes masks what is actually taking place in the organization. In addition, organizational charts alone do not explain functions in great detail, but must be joined by written job descriptions that can provide additional information.

Thus, a final organizational responsibility of the manager is to consider personnel to implement the mission of the department with efficiency and effectiveness. Relationships are delineated relative to the department structure and described in position descriptions that define the scope of responsibilities, relationships, and authority. Job analysis, evaluation, and design help to define qualifications for practitioners in each position within the structure (refer to Chapter 12).

A factor that needs to be remembered in the organizational structure of a health care facility (e.g., hospital) is the unique relationship between the authority of the health care organization and the authority of its medical staff. Consequently, a health care facility frequently has parallel structures rather than one organizational structure. The medical staff usually is separate and autonomous from the organization; it has its own admission requirements, hierarchy, rewards, and sanctions. In recent years however, physicians have taken on greater management and administrative responsibilities (e.g., medical director, vice president of medical services) within general medical hospitals as the result of hospital mergers, rapidly changing concepts of delivery of health care, health care costs, and the expertise and judgment of physicians to assist the administrative staff in decision making.

It must be understood that the health care industry continues to be in a state of change. Because of this, the face and function of therapeutic recreation will need to evolve to fit within these newly structured entities.

Governance Structure

Regardless of setting or type of ownership, the function of the governance structure is best understood as an interface between the demands of the external world and the operations of the internal organization.

Traditional government, community-based leisure service agencies have a recreation board or commission type governance structure, which reflects both policy and advisory responsibilities. The members are either appointed or selected to the governance body as part of the political process. In addition, the commission is responsible for selecting (and firing) the director of the department. In summary, the director selects and supervises all other employees of the department, coordinates the design and operation of the organizational structure, and represents the commission internally and externally. The director is an agent for the commission and in essence is the servant of the commission.

Private, community-based leisure service agencies, nonprofit voluntary organizations, community agencies serving specific disabilities, and various other types of

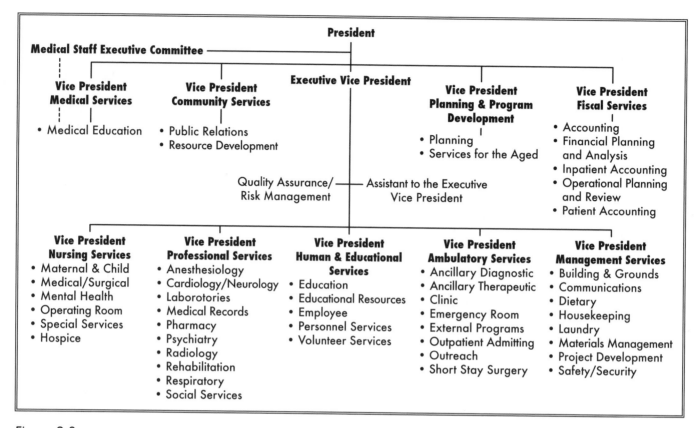

Figure 2.3
Conventional General Medical Hospital Organizational Chart

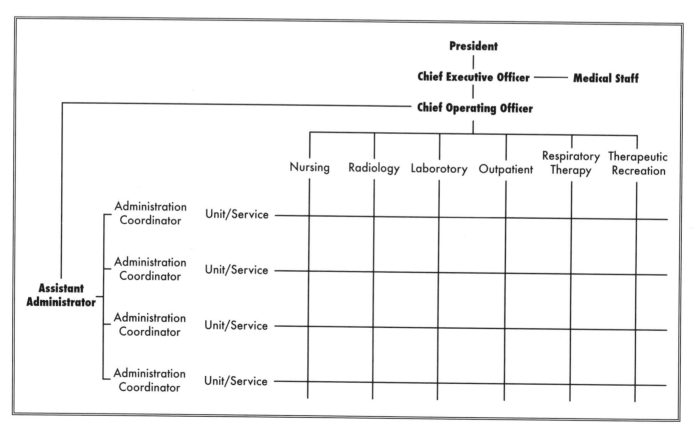

Figure 2.4
Matrix Organization Design

community social service agencies that coordinate or provide recreation and leisure services and resources have a governance structure similar in nature to the public sector, although each may have a unique variation in its organization and function.

Similar in nature to a governing board is the advisory committee. There are many public community-based leisure service agencies that have an advisory committee associated with their therapeutic recreation department. This committee usually has a liaison relationship with the recreation board and commission. Its membership reflects individuals who assist in identifying the recreational needs of individuals with disabilities and may also represent special interest groups (e.g., Special Olympics, United Cerebral Palsy, The Arc). The committee's major input is associated with the planning function, although it may be involved with budgetary matters. Its legal status varies from state to state, and it may or may not operate within a constitution or bylaws.

Administration of hospitals and similar health care facilities has become increasingly complex because of the significant changes that have taken place in service delivery. The basic purpose of a hospital governing board is similar in nature to that of community-based, leisure service agencies—to set policy, to review the budget, and to represent views of the community or shareholders to the organization.

In the for-profit hospital, the focus is on maximizing profit. Subject to legal restrictions designed to protect the owners, board members (usually called *directors*) may choose to maximize profit in either the long or the short run. They may sell all or part of the assets whenever they choose, and they may discontinue all parts of the business and liquidate assets if investment is not profitable. In addition, they are compensated for their service by salary and/or investment opportunities (Griffith, 1992).

In not-for-profit hospitals the governing board consists of trustees who are nominated and selected to serve on the board. Their purpose is accepting the assets of the hospital in trust for the community. Profits derived from the operation of the hospital are put back into the hospital and used for the health care needs of the community. Trustees may or may not be compensated for service. If compensated, it is usually out-of-pocket expenses associated with board meetings (Griffith, 1992).

Some hospitals owned by large units (e.g., churches, government agencies, multihospital systems) may have no governing board. A director, committee, or group performs the essential functions of a board (Griffith, 1992).

At the corporate level (e.g., Columbia/HCA Healthcare Corporation [for-profit], Carilion Health System [not-for-profit]), the function of the directors or trustees is to elect officers, to establish corporate policies, to super-

vise the affairs of the corporation, and to carry out the expressed purposes of the bylaws. As related to the hospitals within the corporation, each hospital may only have a director or manager who reports back to the corporation as noted previously.

While the governing board in either a for-profit or not-for-profit hospital is legally responsible for everything that goes on in the hospital, it delegates this authority and overall responsibility for making decisions for the organization and placing the hospital in a place of effectiveness and efficiency to the chief executive officer (CEO) or president of the hospital. In addition to this specific responsibility, the board does carry out a number of other essential functions as noted by Griffith (1992, p. 145):

1. Establish the vision, mission, and long-range plan.

2. Approve the annual budget.

3. Appoint members of the medical staff.

4. Monitor performance against plans and budgets.

In most community-based leisure service agencies, the agency director and hospital CEO are empowered to implement the decisions of the commission or board as well as to assist these bodies in making decisions. To manage the day-to-day operations, the agency director and CEO rely on an administrative staff with specialized knowledge in financial management, personnel management, public affairs, strategic planning and development, and professional services. In health care facilities there is usually a chief operating officer (COO) or senior vice president responsible for most of the operating expectations (e.g., resource and revenue expectations, quality of care, quality of work life). In meeting these expectations he or she works through subordinates with titles such as vice president, associate administrator, or assistant administrator depending on the scope of the responsibilities involved. The number of executive or specialized senior administrative staff will depend on the size of the setting and the services provided. In addition, these senior administrators make up an "administrative council" type of structure to promote participative management. They usually meet one or more times a week. All major problems, plans, and budgets are brought by the administrators to these meetings for discussion and resolution (Griffith, 1992).

Departmentalization

Departmentalization is the allocation of function and responsibilities designed to achieve goals through a formalized arrangement of human and material resources in organizational units. It is the result of the grouping in organizing, as noted earlier, including both advantages and disadvantages. Departmentalization is most appropriate where there is a need for highly specialized expertise to be consolidated. Thus, the therapeutic recreation department in a health care facility is considered a functional structure, because it provides a specialized service and practitioners perform similar tasks. Special recreation or therapeutic recreation divisions in community-based leisure service organizations would also be considered a functional structure.

The place of the therapeutic recreation department within a health care facility and on the organizational chart will vary from facility to facility and influence its scope of service. It may be a separate department reporting to a middle-management administrator, or it may be a unit within a physical medicine and rehabilitation (aka, "PM and R") department. It may even be considered a service wherein therapeutic recreation practitioners are assigned to various treatment teams but have no specific department identification. More and more it appears therapeutic recreation practitioners are being assigned to interdisciplinary teams but remain identified with a therapeutic recreation department.

A PM and R department is a form of departmentalization, because it is considered a functional structure providing specialized services. In this department it is the grouping of activities (e.g., physical therapy, occupational therapy, speech therapy, therapeutic recreation) that might be carried on in other departments or independently but are brought together in a specialized department for purposes of better service, efficiency, control, or all three.

In community-based leisure service organizations, therapeutic recreation may be an independent division within a department or a special service unit or program section of a department. Therapeutic recreation services may also be found in a freestanding voluntary agency that focuses specifically on individuals with disabilities (e.g., The Ability Center, Toledo, Ohio). A study of therapeutic recreation practitioner ($N = 480$) employment characteristics conducted in 1999 by O'Morrow (2000, p. 9), noted the following location of practitioners within the organizational structure:

- 21.5% independent therapeutic recreation division or section within a health care facility.

- 17.1% independent therapeutic recreation division, department or section within a community park and recreation department, and special recreation districts or associations.

- 13.8% within a rehabilitation division or department with discipline designations (e.g., OT, PT, TR).

- 13.5% within an activity therapy service with no discipline designations (e.g., nursing home).

- 34.2% other structures.

Directing (Leading)

After the manager has planned and organized, consideration is given to directing personnel and activities to accomplish the goals of the organization. A majority of first-line managers give 50% or more of their time to directing (Kraut, 1989; Robbins, 1995). Directing is the connecting link between organizing for work and getting the job done. Directing assures some uniformity of quality and quantity in the work of the staff. Knowledge of one's leadership style, managerial philosophy, sources of power and authority, and political strategies are important. To get work done by others, the manager must resolve conflicts, motivate staff, and discipline staff. These tasks require good communication skills and assertive behavior.

There are many definitions and concepts of directing. Robbins (1995) noted that directing is within the management process of leading. According to Robbins (1995, p. 8): "When managers motivate employees, direct the activities of others, select the most effective communication channel, or resolve conflicts among team members, they are leading." Directing entails motivating, managing conflict, delegating, communicating, and facilitating collaboration (Marquis & Huston, 2003). In today's health and human service organizations, the manager "coaches and counsels to achieve the organization's objectives" (Sullivan & Decker, 2001, p. 60). Professional staff are autonomous and require guidance rather than direction. The first-line manager "is responsible for supervising the work of nonmanagerial personnel and the day-to-day activities of a specific work unit or units" (Sullivan & Decker, 2001, p. 63). One may conclude from these statements that directing/leading is a physical act of therapeutic recreation management—the interpersonal process by which therapeutic recreation personnel accomplish the objectives of the therapeutic recreation department.

To understand fully what directing/leading entails, the therapeutic recreation manager examines the conceptual functions of therapeutic recreation management (i.e., planning and organizing). The therapeutic recreation manager develops management plans for the organization from the statements of vision, mission, philosophy, and written goals and objectives. Developing such plans involves the process by which methods and techniques are selected and used to accomplish the work of the therapeutic recreation department. Directing or leading is the process of applying the management plans to accomplish therapeutic recreation goals and objectives. It is the process by which therapeutic recreation practitioners are inspired or motivated to accomplish work.

The amount of guidance needed varies with the knowledge, experience, and initiative of individual practitioners and the staff as a whole. It may take a strict form (e.g., emphasis on clear-cut delegation of responsibility and formal communication), or it may be loose, low-awareness direction (e.g., flexibility, fluid lines of responsibility and communication). However, everyone needs some direction no matter how small the department. Staff practitioners need to know (a) what is expected of them and (b) how to do it. A knowledgeable staff practitioner will either know how to do the assigned responsibility or how to obtain information to complete the task. Nevertheless, he or she will still need some direction as to how the responsibilities have been divided among staff. The less experienced, less knowledgeable staff member will also need assistance with the "how to do it" part. This assistance does not necessarily have to come from the therapeutic recreation manager; it may be delegated to an experienced staff practitioner or mentor.

The therapeutic recreation manager is responsible for motivating personnel. No matter how fine the plans, nothing usually happens until the people who make up the department are stimulated to perform. Although money is a motivating power, personnel seek in their work the intrinsic qualities of recognition, achievement, growth, and advancement. Frederick Herzberg (1976), called the father of job enrichment, came to the conclusion from his many studies of workers that salaries and salary increases were important factors in fulfilling basic needs but not major motivating factors in work production. Motivation is considered in depth in Chapter 14.

The manager must also be able to communicate effectively, to bring about necessary changes, and to manage conflict within and between his or her department and other departments. Change, conflict, and communication are three highly interwoven concepts. Some practitioners resist change, yet it is necessary if the therapeutic recreation department is to be adaptable. Resistance to change can create conflict; at the same time, conflict can bring about change. Effective communication can facilitate the acceptance of change and minimize destructive conflict. See Chapter 13 for further discussion of effective communication.

Effective guidance/leadership increases the contribution of practitioners to the achievement of therapeutic recreation management goals. Effective directing creates harmony between therapeutic recreation management goals and the goals of the therapeutic recreation practitioner. An effective manager seeks to understand change, conflict, and communication to lead his or her practitioners more effectively.

Controlling

Controlling is the last step in the management process. Fayol (1949, p. 107) defined control as verifying whether everything occurs in conformity with the plan adopted, the instructions issued, and principles established.

Controlling is closely related to planning for therapeutic recreation managers. The planning function provides the basis on which the control function is predicated. Feedback from the planning function provides input for the modification and adjustment of the organizational plan. Therefore, one should view planning and control as being closely linked, each influencing the other.

Control includes coordinating numerous activities, making decisions related to planning and organizing activities, and gaining information from directing and evaluating each practitioner's performance. The control function is also concerned with records, reports, organizational progress, and effective use of resources. Finally, control uses standards, regulation, and evaluation to attain organizational goals and objectives. "The efficient manager constantly attempts to improve productivity by incorporating techniques of quality management, evaluating outcomes and performance, and instituting change as necessary" (Sullivan & Decker, 2001, p. 60).

A systems theory is used in controlling. Feedback and adjustment comprise the control element of therapeutic recreation management. Output is described in terms of the consumer in the program and is measured by quality indicators. When the outcomes or indicators fall short, the information is fed back to the therapeutic recreation practitioner, who makes adjustments in the program. Both the consumer and the practitioner are systems input, whereas the process consists of therapeutic recreation interventions related to consumer outcomes and managerial actions related to setting goals for practitioners' behavior. Continuous quality improvement (CQI) measures the therapeutic recreation process and action is taken to improve services.

Similarly, systems theory can be applied to performance evaluation. For example, input is still the consumer and the practitioner, with process being the managerial actions related to goals of the therapeutic recreation practitioner. A performance review and improvement plan between the therapeutic recreation manager and staff practitioner spell out agreed-on performance goals. The output is corrected actions.

A prime element of the management of therapeutic recreation service is a system for evaluation of the total effort. This includes a system for evaluation of the management process as well as the practice of therapeutic recreation and the delivery of quality service. Evaluation requires standards that can be used as yardsticks for gauging the quality and quantity of services. The key sources for these standards, available for both management and practice, are the American Therapeutic Recreation Association (ATRA) *Standards for the Practice of Therapeutic Recreation and Self-Assessment Guide* (2000) and the National Therapeutic Recreation Society (NTRS) *Standards of Practice for a Continuum of Care in Therapeutic*

Recreation (2004), supplemented by the Joint Commission on Accreditation of Healthcare Organizations (JCAHO) and Commission on Accreditation of Rehabilitation Facilities (CARF) standards associated with therapeutic recreation in hospitals and rehabilitation facilities.

Several yardsticks can be developed using these source documents, which can be of assistance in developing department objectives. Performance standards can be used for individual performance and criteria can be developed for evaluation of delivery service. Koontz and Weihrick (1988) noted that standards are an established criteria of performance based on elements such as planning goals, strategic plans, physical or quantitative measurement of service, cost, programs, and others not specifically related to therapeutic recreation.

A financial control system is implemented by a budget, defined as a tool for planning, monitoring, and controlling cost, or a systematic plan for meeting expenses (Hellriegel & Slocum, 1986). Budgets form the last link in the management process that began with goals and strategies; they are the most detailed management practice used to ensure that organization and department goals are achieved. Budgets are powerful instruments because they serve as a guide for therapeutic recreation performance and allocation of personnel, supplies, support services, and facilities.

Control is necessary because internal and external forces affect the intent of departmental goals. Establishing standards is perhaps the first step in the control process. Standards are the gauge against which performance is measured, and different types of standards must be established to measure the various functions within the department. Today's managers share the control function with staff through such processes as continuous quality improvement activities and the peer reviews that occur with performance reviews.

Summary

Therapeutic recreation managers operate in a dynamic environment that places heavy demands on them to cope with a range of factors influencing the delivery of therapeutic recreation service. It was noted that social forces, economic forces, and political forces influence management. The various theories of management were reviewed as follows: classical theory, behavioral theory with its human relations approach, quantitative management theory, general systems theory, contingency theory, and chaos theory. Within these theories the contributions of various individuals, such as Taylor, Fayol, Mayo, Maslow, and McGregor, were highlighted. Systems theory and

contingency theory were discussed as potential approaches to management.

Consideration was given to the application of these theories to therapeutic recreation management. Initial consideration was given to questions the manager might want to ask regarding what theory is best to use in a particular situation. Thereafter it was indicated that the management functions outlined by Fayol and expanded on throughout the years will be used as a guide in this text. Further, goal achievement cannot be obtained without consideration of individual needs, perceptions, and aspirations. Perhaps the most logical theoretical approach to management discussed was the use of the contingency theory, which stresses situational appropriateness in solving complex problems of today. Yet, because the rate of change is so fast and agencies are so complex, no one theory adequately explains today's health care and human service systems.

Another section of the chapter highlighted the traditional four functions of management: planning, organizing, directing, and controlling. It was noted that planning, a principal duty of all managers, is a dynamic, intellectual, future-oriented process directed toward meeting objectives once objectives have been defined. Reasons were given for planning and the importance of strategic, operational, and contingency planning. Organizing is the grouping of activities into organized units to achieve goals. While various organizational structures exist, the therapeutic recreation department is a functional structure because it provides a specialized service and practitioners perform similar tasks. Directing (i.e., leading) initiates and maintains action toward objectives, although the amount of leadership needed varies with the knowledge, experience, and initiative of the practitioner and the staff as a whole. The integration of leadership with management is noted as the manager coaches and guides employees to attain organizational goals. Controlling, the final element of the management process, is the process of seeing that actual expenditures and activities conform to plan. A systems approach is used frequently in controlling. Through this process, standards are established and then applied, followed by feedback that leads to improvement. The process is kept continuous.

Review Questions

1. Why should a student in therapeutic recreation who is considering therapeutic recreation management as a career goal know management theory?

2. Why is a historical review of management theories helpful to understanding the functions of today's first-line therapeutic recreation manager?

3. What is the relationship between planning and each of the other management functions?

4. Visit a health care facility and/or local park and recreation department and note where therapeutic recreation is on the organization chart. Discuss its relationship to middle management and top-level management.

5. Of the principle management theories or approaches discussed, which one do you find most appealing to you as a therapeutic recreation manager of a therapeutic recreation department in a general medical hospital and in a community-based parks and recreation department?

References

American Therapeutic Recreation Association (ATRA). (2000). *Standards for the practice of therapeutic recreation and self-assessment guide.* Alexandria, VA: Author.

Barnard, C. I. (1938). *The functions of the executive.* Cambridge, MA: Harvard University Press.

Boulding, K. E. (1968). General systems theory—The skeleton of science. In W. Buckley, *Modern systems research for the behavioral scientist.* Chicago, IL: Aldine Publishing.

Carter, M. J., Browne, B., LeConey, S. P., and Nagle, C. J. (1991). *Designing therapeutic recreation programs in the community.* Reston, VA: American Alliance for Health, Physical Education, Recreation and Dance.

Carter, M. J., Van Andel, G. E., and Robb, G. M. (2003). *Therapeutic recreation: A practical approach* (3rd ed.). Prospect Heights, IL: Waveland Press.

DeGreen, K. B. (1973). *Sociotechnical systems.* Englewood Cliffs, NJ: Prentice Hall.

Edginton, C. R., Hudson, S. D., and Lankford, S. V. (2001). *Managing recreation, parks, and leisure services: An introduction.* Champaign, IL: Sagamore Publishing.

Fayol, H. (1949). *General and industrial management* (C. Starrs, Trans.). London, England: Isacc Pitman and Sons.

Gray, E. R. and Smeltzer, L. R. (1989). *Management: The competitive edge.* New York, NY: Macmillan Publishing.

Griffith, J. R. (1992). *The well-managed community hospital* (2nd ed.). Ann Arbor, MI: Health Administration Press.

Gulick, L. (1947). Notes on the theory of organizations. In L. Gulick and L. F. Urwick (Eds.), *Papers on the science of administration* (pp. 15–30). New York, NY: Columbia Press.

Hax, A. C. and Majluf, N. S. (1984). *Strategic management: An integrative perspective.* Englewood Cliffs, NJ: Prentice Hall.

Hellriegel, D. and Slocum, J. (1986). *Management* (4th ed.). Reading, MA: Addison-Wesley Publishing.

Herzberg, F. (1976). *The managerial choice: To be efficient and to be human.* Homewood, IL: Don Jones-Irwin.

Kast, F. E. and Rosenzweig, J. E. (1985). *Organizations and management: A systems and contingency approach* (4th ed.). New York, NY: McGraw-Hill.

Koontz, H., O'Donnell, C., and Weihrich, H. (1980). *Management* (7th ed.). New York, NY: McGraw-Hill.

Koontz, H. and Weihrick, H. (1988). *Management.* New York, NY: McGraw-Hill.

Kraut, A. I. (1989). The role of the manager: What's really important in different management jobs. *Academy of Management Executive, 3*(4), 286–293.

Kreitner, R. (1992). *Management* (5th ed.). Boston, MA: Houghton Mifflin.

Lewin, K. (1951). *Field theory in social science.* New York, NY: Harper.

Marquis, B. L. and Huston, C. J. (2003). *Leadership roles and management functions in nursing: Theory and application* (4th ed.). Philadelphia, PA: Lippincott Williams & Wilkins.

Maslow, A. (1954). *Motivation and personality.* New York, NY: Harper.

Maslow, A. (1968). *Toward a psychology of being* (2nd ed.). New York, NY: Van Nostrand.

Mayo, E. (1933). *The human problems of an industrial civilization.* New York, NY: Macmillian.

McGregor, D. (1960). *The human side of enterprise.* New York: McGraw-Hill.

National Therapeutic Recreation Society (NTRS). (2004). *Standards of practice for a continuum of care in therapeutic recreation.* Retrieved September 12, 2004 from http://www.nrpa.org/content/default.aspx?documentID=530

O'Morrow, G. S. (2000). *Therapeutic recreation practitioner analysis.* Ashburn, VA: National Therapeutic Recreation Society.

Ouchi, W. G. (1981). *Theory Z: How American business can meet the Japanese challenge.* Reading, MA: Addison-Wesley Publishing.

Richards, M. D. (1986). *Setting strategic goals and objectives* (2nd ed.). St. Paul, MN: West Publishing.

Riley, B. (1991). Quality assessment: The use of outcome indicators. In B. Riley (Ed.), *Quality management: Applications for therapeutic recreation* (pp. 53–67). State College, PA: Venture Publishing, Inc.

Robbins, S. P. (1980). *The administrative process.* Englewood, NJ: Prentice Hall.

Robbins, S. P. (1995). *Supervision today.* Englewood Cliffs, NJ: Prentice Hall.

Robbins, S. P. and Decenzo, D. A. (2001). *Fundamentals of management* (3rd ed.). Upper Saddle River, NJ: Prentice Hall.

Roth, W. F. (2000). *The roots and future of management theory: A systems perspective*. Boco Raton, FL: St. Lucie Press.

Saxe, J. G. (1936). The blind men and the elephant. In H. Felleman (Ed.), The *best-loved poems of the American people* (pp. 521–522). New York, NY: Doubleday and Company.

Shetty, Y. K. (1974). Contingency management: Current perspective for managing organizations. *Management International Review, 14*(6), 114–123.

Shortell, S. M., Kaluzny, A. D., and Associates. (1988). *Healthcare management: A text in organization theory and behavior* (2nd ed.). New York, NY: John Wiley & Sons.

Stumbo, N. J. and Peterson, C. A. (2004). *Therapeutic recreation program design: Principles and procedures* (4th ed.). San Francisco, CA: Pearson Benjamin Cummings.

Sullivan, E. J. and Decker, P. J. (2001). *Effective leadership and management in nursing* (5th ed.). Upper Saddle River, NJ: Prentice Hall.

Tappen, R. M. (2001). *Nursing leadership and management: Concepts and practice* (4th ed.). Philadelphia, PA: F. A. Davis Company.

Taylor, F. W. (1911). *The principles of scientific management.* New York, NY: Harper & Bros.

Tomey, A. M. (2000). *Guide to nursing management and leadership* (6th ed.). St. Louis, MO: Mosby.

Turpel, L. T. (1992). Strategic management. In R. M. Winslow and K. J. Halberg (Eds.), *The management of therapeutic recreation services* (pp. 71–83). Arlington, VA: National Recreation and Park Association.

Urwick, L. F. (1944). *The elements of administration.* New York, NY: Harper & Row.

von Bertalanffy, L. (1972, December). The history and status of general systems theory. *Academy of Management Journal, 15,* 447–465.

Weber M. (1947). *The theory of social and economic organizations* (A. Henderson and T. Parsons, Trans.). New York, NY: Free Press.

Woodward, W. (2003). Preparing a new workforce. *Nursing Administration Quarterly, 27*(3), 215–222.

Wren, D. (1987). *The evolution of management theory* (3rd ed.). New York, NY: John Wiley & Sons.

Chapter 3
The Leader-Manager

The terms *manager* and *leader* are often used interchangeably, yet there are differences in the two. A manager (a) has an assigned position with formal authority to direct the work of employees, (b) is formally responsible and accountable for the quality of that work and what it costs to do it, and (c) has a legitimate source of power due to delegated authority that accompanies the position with expected functions, duties, and responsibilities (Marquis & Huston, 2003; Tappen, Weiss & Whitehead, 2004). A leader is "anyone who uses interpersonal skills to influence others to accomplish a specific goal" (Sullivan & Decker, 2005, p. 44). A job title does not make one a leader; rather, the person's behavior determines whether a leadership position is occupied (Marquis & Huston, 2003). A leader uses a repertoire of personal behaviors to guide and link others so a sense of direction is created to accomplish high levels of performance and quality outcomes.

To become an effective leader-manager, the integration of "leadership skills with the ability to carry out management functions is necessary" (Marquis & Huston, 2003, p. 23). Good managers are good leaders. One may be a good manager of resources yet not be a leader of people while a good leader of people may not manage well (Sullivan & Decker, 2005). Yet, professional managerial judgment and successful leadership decision making can be learned, and skills gained can enhance either role. Effective therapeutic recreation managers are those who blend the qualities of leadership and apply the principles of management to practice.

Managers, regardless of level, are usually appointed. They have a legitimate power base and can reward and punish. Their ability to influence is founded on the formal authority inherent in their positions. The manager as has been noted frequently, is concerned with coordination and integration of resources through planning, organizing, directing (i.e., leading), and controlling to accomplish specific organization or department goals and objectives. In contrast, leaders may either be appointed or emerge from within a group. Leadership is an interpersonal relationship in which the leader employs specific behaviors and strategies to influence individuals and groups toward goal setting and attainment in specific situations. One must keep in mind, however, the fact that a person can influence others does not indicate whether that person can also plan, organize, or control. One of the few common threads between both management and leadership literature is that effective leaders are important to a successful organization (Robbins, 1980). In other words, effective managers must be effective leaders. Thus, ideally all managers should be leaders. But one is cautioned that not all leaders necessarily have capabilities in other management functions.

A body of knowledge and theory germane to therapeutic recreation leadership is in its embryonic stage. It is important to provide a brief overview of the better known leadership theories because the wise and systematic use of self influences the achievement of organization and department objectives. The authors have cited a perspective that leadership theory has evolved in response to changes in society and culture. Because society and culture are ever evolving, even the most recent leadership theories will probably be insufficient to describe, explain, or predict leadership behavior in the near future. However, these theories do provide a springboard for action to be taken by therapeutic recreation managers.

Following the presentation of leadership theories, other key concepts inherently associated with leadership will be considered. An effective leader-manager understands the nature of power and how to use it to accomplish organizational goals through employees. Through the process of supervision the leader-manager helps practitioners to increase their effectiveness in service delivery. The dynamics of a constantly changing work environment can result in a stressful position as a leader-manager. The first-line manager seldom has the luxury of working on one project at a time. The closing portion of the chapter briefly considers the importance of stress and time management to the first-line manager. The successful integration of leadership and management skills contributes to the first-line manager's effectiveness. A concluding note summarizes leadership considerations of the first-line manager.

Theoretical Explanations of Leadership

The successful organization sets itself apart from the unsuccessful through effective leadership (Russell, 2005). Several theories have attempted to explain how a person becomes an effective leader. To understand today's beliefs about leadership, it is necessary to review how leadership theory has evolved (Marquis & Huston, 2003). One approach has been to identify the characteristics that contribute to leadership. Another approach has been to consider the leader's actions or behaviors. A third approach has been to explore the situation or contingencies that explain leadership. Lastly, contemporary theories have evolved as the result of "the need to humanize working environments and improve organizational performance" (Sullivan & Decker, 2005, p. 561).

Trait Theories

Until the mid-1940s trait theory was the basis for most leadership research. By 1950 the list had grown to over 100 characteristics identified as essential to successful leadership (Adorno, Frenkel-Brunswik, Levinson & Sanford, 1950). It postulated that individuals possessing a certain combination of physical, personal, and social traits would be effective leaders. Bass (1981) listed 16 personality traits that have been positively correlated with leadership. Dominance and self-confidence are most frequently related to leadership; emotional control, independence, and creativity are the next most frequent. Social skills, such as sociability and administrative ability, have also been associated with leadership. The following list by Hein and Nicholson (1990) is an example of other common leadership traits associated with this theory:

1. Leaders need to be more intelligent than the group they lead.

2. Leaders mostly possess initiative or the ability to perceive and start courses of action not considered by others.

3. Creativity is an asset.

4. Leaders also possess emotional maturity, integrity, a sense of purpose and direction, persistence, dependability, and objectivity.

5. Communication skills are important.

6. Persuasion often is used by leaders to gain the consent of followers.

7. Leaders need to be perceptive enough to distinguish their allies from their opponents and to place subordinates in suitable positions.

8. Leaders participate in social activities. They can socialize with all kinds of people and adapt to various groups.

While research studies have shown the importance of some traits, they have not consistently identified traits common to all leaders. Trait theory does not view personality as an integrated whole, does not deal with subordinates, and avoids environmental influences and situational factors (Stogdill, 1974). On the other hand, Gibb (1969) concluded that the traits associated with leadership are contingent on the nature of the task, the goal pursued, and the characteristics of group members. This view is supported by McGregor (1966, p. 73) who stated, "research findings to date suggest that it is more fruitful to consider leadership as a relationship between the leader and the situation than as a universal pattern of characteristics possessed by certain people." Megginson, Mosley, and Pietri (1991) concluded after a review of the leadership literature associated with the traitist approach that leaders have vision, communicate well, are highly motivated, and motivate their followers. As the traitist approach did not prove completely valid, theorists moved toward examining leadership in relation to the groups being led. It is interesting to note, however, that despite their limitations and contradictions, aspects of trait theory are often used as the basis for management decisions and to identify successful leaders today (Marquis & Huston, 2003; Sullivan & Decker, 2005). The most physically imposing or most highly skilled therapeutic recreation practitioner in a group may be chosen as a manager on the basis of this particular leadership trait.

Behavioral Theories

The behavioral theorists, sometimes called functional theorists, concentrated on the leader's action rather than the traits of the leader. Among the most influential and comprehensive of the behavioral research and theories are those of Lewin and Lippit (1938) at the University of Iowa, Rensis Likert's (1967) Michigan Studies, the Ohio State University group (Stogdill, 1974), Blake and Mouton's (1964) managerial grid, and Douglas McGregor's (1966) Theory X and Theory Y.

The behaviorists viewed leadership as including not only the qualities of the leader but also the task, expectations, and capabilities of the group. Groups have two major functions. The first function is the performance of a task or achievement of a goal. In therapeutic recreation service the goal is the delivery of quality service. The second function of a group is to strengthen the group itself. In therapeutic recreation service this would include professional development and actions taken to maintain high staff morale.

In relation to these functions, leadership functions have been described primarily by the Ohio State University group (Stogdill, 1974) as "initiating structure" or task-oriented and "consideration" or human-oriented. Other terms for task-oriented leadership are job-centered, production-oriented (Likert, 1967), and autocratic. According to Robbins (1980), structure or task refers to the extent to which the leader is likely to define his or her role and those of subordinates in the search for goal attainment. Behaviors that attempt to organize work, work relationships, and goals are also included in this definition. This task-oriented behavior reflects McGregor's (1966) Theory X authoritarian (or autocratic) management style (Megginson, Mosley & Pietri, 1986). Terms for human-oriented leadership are employee-centered, people-oriented (Likert, 1967), and democratic. Human-oriented is described as the extent to which a person is likely to have job relationships characterized by mutual trust, respect for subordinates' ideas, and regard for their feelings. A leader high in human factors could be described as one who helps subordinates with personal problems, is friendly and approachable, and treats all subordinates as equals (Robbins, 1980). Theory Y is employee-centered (McGregor, 1966).

Taking the dimensions developed by the Ohio State University and Michigan groups respectively, Blake and Mouton (1964) proposed a managerial grid. The grid was based on the styles of "concern for people" and "concern for production" using a high-low axis. Results showed that administrators perform best where they facilitate task efficiency and high morale by coordinating and integrating work-related activities.

Lewin identified three popular behavior styles of leadership: autocratic, democratic, and laissez faire (Marquis & Huston, 2003; Russell, 2005; Sullivan & Decker, 2005). The autocratic style is authoritarian, leader-centered, with close supervision. The style is evident in large bureaucracies and useful in crisis situations. Democratic or participatory leadership shares decision making and responsibility for outcomes with the group. This style promotes individual employee growth and autonomy, and is effective in collaborative efforts. Lastly, a laissez-faire or permissive style assumes employees are mature, internally motivated, and self-directed. This style promotes creativity and brainstorming. A fourth behavioral style, referred to as bureaucratic leadership, assumes employees are motivated by external forces (Sullivan & Decker, 2005). As a consequence the leader-manager relies on organizational policies to make decisions. Theorists have come to realize leadership tends to fall on a continuum and varies with the situation rather than fitting one behavioral style regardless of the nature of the experience.

Further, the behaviorists found very little success in identifying consistent relationships between patterns of leadership behavior and successful performance. The ideal leadership behavior according to the behaviorists is one that combines structure (i.e., task) with consideration (i.e., human). As an example, the therapeutic recreation manager using the ideal approach would focus on accomplishing the goals, while at the same time maintaining open communication and an environment of mutual trust and respect among staff members.

Situational Theories

Situation theories became popular during the 1950s and developed from the failure of the other types of theories to address the significance of the environment, organization, goal, or situation on leadership. In addition, reference to these models is sometimes found under the heading of leadership styles. A number of situation or contingency theories exist and are explained next.

Fiedler's Contingency Model

One of the earliest situational theories was Fiedler's Contingency Model of Leadership Effectiveness (Fiedler, 1967). The focus of attention in this model was on the performance of the group. There must be a group before there can be a leader. Fiedler argued that effective group performance depends on the proper match between the leader's style of interacting with subordinates and the degree to which the situation gives control and influence to the leader. He identified three aspects of a situation that structure the leader's role: (a) leader-member relations, (b) task structure, and (c) leader position power.

Leader-member relations involve the amount of confidence and loyalty the subordinates have in their leader. Task structure refers to the degree to which a task can be defined and measured in terms of progress toward completion. Structure is generally high if easy to define and measure and low if difficult to define and measure. Position power relates to the leader's authority in the organization (e.g., hiring, firing, reward, punishment).

Fiedler stated that the more positive the leader-member relationship, the more highly structured the task, and the greater the position power, the greater the influence. In addition, of the three situational dimensions, the most important is leader-member followed by task structure. The least important is position power. In summary, Fiedler (1967, p. 32) said, "successful leadership was an interaction of leadership styles and the situation." The most effective leadership style "is the one that best complements the organizational environment, the tasks to be accomplished, and the personal characteristics of the people involved in each situation" (Sullivan & Decker, 2005, p. 47).

Life-Cycle Model

The life-cycle theory of Hersey and Blanchard (1982) states that the leader's behavior will vary based on the maturity of the subordinates and the situation. Job maturity is defined by the individual's technical knowledge and skill in performing a task. This is combined with the individual's feeling of self-esteem and confidence. An individual can be extremely mature, both personally and in relation to the task, in one particular situation. If the situation changes, the person will experience a decrease in maturity in relation to either the task itself or feelings of self-confidence. For example, an experienced psychiatric therapeutic recreation practitioner understands his or her role, has the knowledge and skills necessary to provide quality service to the patient, and is confident in the relationship with both peers and other professionals. The therapeutic recreation manager gives this practitioner a great deal of program freedom and finds ways of intellectually challenging the staff member. If this practitioner transfers to the physical rehabilitation unit within the hospital, the practitioner will have to learn new skills and develop a new set of relationships. Temporarily, the practitioner will experience feelings of insecurity. Both personal and job maturity will decrease and the practitioner will require direction from the manager in this unit. As the practitioner gains knowledge and confidence, the manager allows more freedom and supports the practitioner in making decisions and implementing service. The life-cycle model therefore emphasizes the importance of the maturity level of the staff. As employees mature, "leadership style becomes less task-focused and more relationship-oriented" (Marquis & Huston, 2003, p. 15).

Path-Goal Model

According to House and Mitchell (1974), the leader will look at the situation and the characteristics of the individual involved and determine what leadership style (e.g., directive, supportive, participative, achievement-oriented) will increase the subordinate's motivation to perform the task or reach the goal. The theory "proposes removing obstacles to goal attainment, coaching, and providing personal rewards for achievement will result in high levels of performance and productivity" (Sullivan & Decker, 2005, p. 51). The leader rewards personnel for task achievement and provides additional opportunities for satisfying goal accomplishment. In brief, the leader shows the way down the "path" to reach the goal and provides rewards for the individual as an incentive.

The application of situational theories to practice requires continuous monitoring of employees' abilities, motivations, understanding of the task, and options for completing it (Sullivan & Decker, 2005). The manager observes the cause-and-effect relationship between their behavior and the employees' responses and considers the environmental factors that influence these interactions.

Contemporary Theories

Managers in today's health and human service environment place increasing value on collaboration and teamwork. The complexity of the work environment requires coordination among managers and staff. To create collegial work environments leaders use group and political leadership skills (Sullivan & Decker, 2005). The newer theories emphasize mutual goals of leaders and followers focusing on the relational nature of leader-participant interactions (Russell, 2005).

Interactional/Relational Leadership

The basic premise of interactional leadership is that "leadership behavior is generally determined by the relationship between the leader's personality and the specific situation" (Marquis & Huston, 2003, p. 15). These theories can be viewed as the compilation of everything that has been theorized before in an attempt to pull together the three elements of leader, follower, and environment. Schein (1970) proposed a complex man and open systems framework in an attempt to synthesize trait, behavior, motivation, and situation theories. Schreisheim, Mowday, and Stogdill (1979) emphasized the interdependence between the leader and group in any given complex situation as determining the leadership process.

In today's health and human service environment, the purpose of relational leadership is to better coordinate client services in a caring, noncompetitive manner (Sullivan & Decker, 2005). "Hierarchical relationships break down and leadership develops at all levels in the organization" (Sullivan & Decker, 2005, p. 55). Thus "no single leadership strategy is effective in every situation" (Marquis & Huston, 2003, p. 16). This theory, therefore, recognizes the need for flexible open systems to empower all of the stakeholders interacting with clients.

Tannenbaum and Schmidt (1983, p. 163) summarized the synthesis of personality and interpersonal relationships in leaders that result in success as follows: "The successful leader is one who is keenly aware of those forces which are most relevant to behavior at any given time [and] who is able to behave appropriately in the light of these perceptions."

Transactional Leadership

Leadership is viewed as a series of transactions or exchanges. A leader is successful to the extent to which staff needs are met and incentives are used to enhance employee loyalty and performance (Sullivan & Decker, 2005). Transactional leaders help staff to recognize task responsibilities, identify goals, and meet desired performance levels. Transactional leadership is aimed at maintaining the status quo by performing work according to desired standards of practice emphasizing interpersonal dependence and reward for achieving the standard.

Transformational Leadership

Transformational leadership motivates individuals to perform beyond the status quo. The manager who has a vision and empowers staff to effect change as a result of their commitment to this ideal is transformational. This manager has a strong commitment to the profession and organization and is able to create synergistic environments that enhance change (Marquis & Huston, 2003). "The effectiveness of this style depends on the leader's ability to stimulate growth and development of others" (Sullivan & Decker, 2005, p. 54).

Charismatic Leadership

One of the important features of a transformational leader is charisma (Russell, 2005). The ability to convey a vision that inspires followers is based on the leader's personality. This charismatic leadership engenders a commitment to the leader as well as to the beliefs espoused by the leader. Consequently, this form of leadership promotes high expectations and self-confidence among staff.

Servant Leadership

Servant leadership purports that leadership "originates from a desire to serve and that in the course of serving, one may be called to lead" (Sullivan & Decker, 2005, p. 55). A manager who puts serving others, including employees, clients, and the community, as the first priority is termed a servant leader. The servant leader sees the whole and senses the relationships and connections (Marquis & Huston, 2003). Servant leaders are helpers and teachers first, then leaders—as a consequence, application to therapeutic recreation practice is appealing because our intent is to serve others so they grow in their health and well-being.

The new generation of leadership has emerged in response to a need to create a synergistic work environment that improves organizational performance. The integration of a number of variables, including the culture, the values of the manager and staff, and the complexities of the situation, are apparent in contemporary leadership theories. The effective leader needs skills that are dynamic and change in response to a rapidly changing health and human service environment. As noted by a review of all the theories of leadership, what is considered to be essential as an effective leader has changed since the formal study of leadership began and is likely to continue to evolve as challenges are addressed in the not too distant future.

Leadership and Power

Regardless of the explanation chosen to describe effective leadership, an underlying factor is the ability of the leader-manager to make things happen or to influence others (Russell, 2005). Power is an important source of an individual's influence. A leader leads by influencing. The therapeutic recreation manager brings about change by influencing others through the use of power and motivation (refer to Chapter 14).

Effective leaders understand the nature of power and how to use it. For one thing, they know that power is found in relationships—in connections and associations between and among people. They also know that power is based on formal relationships and informal relationships; that is, on what is given them by their formal position in the organization as well as on what they are blessed with in terms of charisma and persuasiveness. Further, they know that power may be good or evil—good if used for positive purposes or evil if sought as an end in itself. A consensus of most authors shows that the essence of power is the ability to affect something or to be affected by something (i.e., the ability to cause or prevent change).

Base of Power

Generally speaking, organizations are made up of people consistently vying with one another for power, status, and prestige. Power is the ability to impose the will or desire of one person or group of persons on another individual or group of individuals to influence and alter behavior. However, one must keep in mind that power itself is neither good nor bad. It is how an individual or group uses or abuses power that ultimately colors its perception. Power is inherent in the ability to lead. How that power is used ultimately determines the effectiveness of the leader (Hersey & Blanchard, 1982).

French and Raven (1968) are credited with identifying five types of power. They explained the sources or bases from which power emanates and called these bases legitimate, coercive, reward, expert, and referent. The therapeutic recreation manager has legitimate power and authority based on his or her position. Reward and coercive powers are present based on the right to hire, evaluate, promote, or discharge individuals. Expert power is derived from professional knowledge and demonstrated management skills. Referent power may also be present based on attractiveness and a pleasant, motivating personality. Hersey and Blanchard (1982) added information power and connection power to these five powers. Besides the sources of their own power, the therapeutic recreation manager needs to be aware of and concerned with the power of others since the source of others' power can dilute his or her power. These seven types of power will be considered in a bit more detail next.

1. *Reward power* comes from the ability of the manager to give awards. The use of positive sanctions is the hallmark of a good manager. This is demonstrated through compensation, verbal praise, taking staff to lunch, and so forth. When monetary rewards are insufficient or nonexistent, then subtle forms of reward and acknowledgment assume special importance. One who can distribute rewards that others view as valuable will have power over them.

2. *Coercive power* is the opposite of reward power—a manager deliberately withholds rewards or punishes to promote compliance. Staff react to this power out of fear of the negative ramifications resulting from failing to comply. Withholding sanctions is clearly part of the system. For example, an employee whose performance is unsatisfactory does not deserve a merit increase. A caution here is that this type of power can be somewhat subjective.

3. *Legitimate power* relates to official position in the organizational hierarchy. Most people recognize this, but there is something peculiar that has to be faced in providing health care services that other businesses do not have to confront—the impact of physicians.

4. *Referent power*, sometimes called *charismatic power*, is the therapeutic recreation manager's ability to use influence because the staff identifies with the manager as a leader. Employees generally identify with a person who has the resources or personal traits they believe are desirable. If a manager's leadership style is working, staff practitioners will choose to emulate some of the manager's more attractive qualities. Thus, the greater the attraction, the greater the identification, and subsequently the greater the referent power.

5. *Expert power* is the influence a manager wields as a result of his or her expertise, special skill, or knowledge. Therapeutic recreation managers gain power through knowledge because respect and compliance from the people they interact with will follow. Managerial knowledge and knowledge of the organization, including its mission, goals, objectives, and operations, will help a manager to acquire power.

6. *Informational power* is the power that proceeds from the ability of an individual to gain and share valuable information.

7. *Connection power* becomes a reality when the manager is perceived as having close contact with other influential people.

The wise therapeutic recreation manager will use all sources of power while moving between the various sources as circumstances warrant. However, many authors (Fiedler, 1967; Moore & Wood, 1979; Stoner, 1982) contended that no other power source is as valuable as expert power. Having the knowledge and the ability to apply it will go a long way toward establishing the therapeutic recreation manager's credibility with superiors, peers, and subordinates. However, the manager is cautioned that having access to one or even all of these powers does not guarantee the ability to influence particular individuals or groups in a specific way. A manager may be widely accepted and admired as an expert but still unable to influence his or her staff to be more creative and productive in their jobs or even get to work on time.

Power Strategies

Assuming one has the desire, ability, and will to be powerful and occupies a management position, what are some of the other strategies used to assist in acquiring power? Benziger (1982) noted several strategies designed to increase an individual's power. Although these strategies were formulated with women in mind, they are certainly applicable to this discussion. Benziger cited the following 12 organizational power strategies:

1. Learn to speak the organization's language and don't expect it to use the manager's.

2. Learn the organization's priorities and explain one's needs in terms of how it will aid in meeting the organization's needs.

3. Learn the power lines and who has the power. Time and energy can be wasted when the wrong people are contacted.

4. Become acquainted with those who are powerful. One may find one shares an interest and discussion of that interest will enhance the relationship. This is a form of networking, which at times takes some meticulous attention to details and patience.

5. Develop professional knowledge. Develop knowledge based on the needs of the organization.

6. Develop power skills. Develop one's bases of power remembering that they are additive in their effect.

7. Be proactive rather than passive or reactive. Not only does the person get the work done faster and

better but also the person generates alternative solutions if something does not meet expectations. In addition, the person plans for the future.

8. Assume authority in one's dealings. Once power is activated, it either results in authority or force. Only when authority is disregarded does an individual choose to use force over authority. An individual will not be seen as displaying authority if his or her power bases have not already been established.

9. Take risks. Men are introduced early to taking risks while women do not generally have the opportunity to practice this.

10. Be verbal with achievements. One may not like this approach and may feel uncomfortable, but it will move one into a more visible and powerful situation.

11. Meet one's supervisor's needs. Become knowledgeable about his or her goals because one's performance can give the supervisor credit.

12. Take care of oneself. In the process of becoming powerful, remember to take care of oneself physically, emotionally, and socially.

A word of caution to the manager: According to Lewis and Lewis (1983), in health and human service settings, issues of power are often especially difficult because managers as supervisors tend to be wary of overcontrolling others' efforts. Professionals want to be mentors but might feel uncomfortable about evaluating and influencing other practitioners' progress toward effectiveness. The manager-supervisory relationship must recognize the existence of power while taking into account the unique aspects of the human service environment.

Leadership and Supervision

If leadership is defined as the process of influencing human behaviors in the interest of achieving particular goals, it is a key factor in supervision. The supervisor is clearly interested in influencing the practitioner's behavior; therefore, some kind of "leadership event" must take place. The process of supervision involves helping practitioners increase their effectiveness in service delivery. The supervisor provides support and encouragement, builds skills and competencies, and oversees the practitioner's work. The nature of the relationship depends to a large degree on the supervisor's leadership style, the practitioner's motivation, and the department's needs.

Much of what has already been discussed can be related to the manager as a supervisor. However, it is important to highlight those factors that make the first-line manager, as a supervisor, a special case of leadership because the activity is associated with directing subordinates. The first-line manager functions in a situation that requires management of professionally knowledgeable practitioners—people who base their work activities on a compendium of knowledge, skills, and abilities too extensive to be translated into a routine, standardized pattern of behavior.

Knowledgeable workers, it is well-known, are a difficult group in some respects. They expect more than mere wages from their work—they expect to derive a sense of satisfaction and self-esteem from work well done. They do not require a great deal of externally based motivation. They are, in effect, practitioners who can be defined both as achievement motivated and as possessing high task maturity. They also may be quite determined about holding to internalized goals and values that dictate how they will proceed in work.

As first-line managers, supervisors must, by definition, occupy the only level of management charged with the responsibility of directing the work of nonmanagement personnel. As supervisors, managers are directly responsible for the daily, face-to-face, immediate, and operative activities of a group of personnel. Getting the most out of knowledgeable workers requires special managerial skills. Those who are enthusiastic and perform exceptionally well in their jobs usually feel challenged by their work itself and take responsibility for their own jobs. Managing professionals requires more than overseeing; managers serve as guides and teachers who provide information and set standards. The uniqueness of being a manager or supervisor calls for, but is not limited to, the following abilities:

1. *Heavy reliance on technical expertise.* Supervisors are required to know the job they supervise. They spend a large portion of their time directing and overseeing the activities of their subordinates. Because of the problems they face at this level—experienced and inexperienced personnel—they must have expert knowledge of jobs that their subordinates perform.

2. *Skills assessment.* After learning the skills required of each position, the manager must assess each practitioner's suitability for the varied positions in the department. It is up to the manager to identify areas of excellence, competence, and deficiency for every practitioner under supervision. It is important to differentiate between performance and ability.

3. *Facilitation of work.* The work environment needs to be monitored to identify barriers to accomplishments. Thus, the therapeutic recreation manager

must look for barriers within the practitioner, the staff as a group, and the organization with its various support systems. One of the manager's most important tasks is the challenge of developing positive feelings of capability and potential achievement in each practitioner. In addition, the manager attempts to manage and to facilitate change rather than regarding change as a threat to the status quo. As has been noted previously, the external environment for any organization today is changing rapidly. The manager, therefore, should attempt to lead practitioners to embrace change as a permanent way of life.

4. *Communication in two languages.* Communication is a problem at all levels of management. First-line managers are required to communicate in two distinct languages—that of management and that of workers. Differing educational backgrounds, value systems, and points of reference are just several of the major disparities between the two groups.

5. *Coping with role conflict.* Managers are neither fish nor fowl. They are not practitioners, and although they are officially classified as managers, they are not often accepted by other middle-level or top-level managers. A first-line manager may be assumed to be like other managers, but the individual's activities, status, and security are at times quite different. The activities are associated with nonmanagement personnel, the status is "low person on the totem pole" when it comes to management, and security is not always solid if performance is not tops. Finally, managers promoted from within face the task of learning new behaviors when being subtly or not so subtly coerced to retain the behaviors of the past role as a practitioner.

6. *Coping with constrained authority.* Today managers must adapt to a less autocratic style than their predecessors. Managers must also adapt to the constraints imposed by internal and external factors, such as the intricate appeals systems that most organizations provide for their workers. In addition, managers are required to interact in an authority relationship with two groups: subordinates and supervisors who are their superiors.

7. *Reinforcing employees' good performance.* On a day-to-day basis this reinforcement mainly takes place verbally or via e-mail with compliments and praise when a job has been done well. For the longer term, a variety of rewards may be used to recognize good performance (e.g., material rewards).

8. *The management's representative.* Rules, policies, procedures, and other dictates are implemented at the first-line manager level, so when practitioners think of management, their usual point of reference is their manager. This obviously places high responsibility on the managers to reflect accurately the vision, philosophy, and attitudes of the management, a task made even more difficult because they rarely have the opportunity to participate in major policy decisions that may affect the people they directly supervise.

Stress and Time Management

The leader-manager is a resource and a role model to subordinates in how to cope with stress and manage time (Marquis & Huston, 2003). "The attitude and energy level of managers directly affects" staff productivity and satisfaction (Marquis & Huston, 2003, p. 325). The leadership skill of self-awareness is necessary in stress and time management. How managers handle the pressure of the workday and use time is a reflection of their own attitude and influences how they expect employees to approach workday demands and use time. Successful managers are able to control constraints and pressures in their personal lives and to guide employees as they balance personal and professional demands. This translates into a more effective work unit and reduces negative organizational outcomes, like illness and turnover, which decrease productivity and impede service quality.

Managing Stress

Today's health and human service system has adopted the "corporate mindset" (Tappen, Weiss & Whitehead, 2004). Redesigning, changing staffing patterns, documentation requirements, and the expectation that work does not end when one goes home are ever present. In addition, challenges like increased expectations from clients, new technology, decreased length of patient stay, and maintaining proper staffing ratios precipitate tension and lead to constraints on the ability to manage time effectively. Like anyone else, the first-line manager cannot always control the demands from middle and upper management, employees, colleagues, or caregivers; yet reactions can be managed and choices can be made that better prepare the manager to address workplace expectations. Additionally, the manager who is aware of the subjective and individual nature of experiences resulting in stress is astute to workplace factors causing stress among employees and others in the organization (e.g., participatory rather than autocratic leadership style can reduce job stress). Lastly, the first-line manager who has recently moved from direct service is aware that such a transition may create disequilibrium and raise questions about effectiveness in the new role causing a degree of perceived stress.

Personal Management Methods

Awareness of stressors in the environment is one of the first steps in managing stress. Identifying sources of stress and signs of impending burnout are prerequisites to controlling stress. What are the consequences of too much stress? A second step is believing that behavior can be changed and that one controls one's destiny in life and at the work setting. Finally, a commitment to recognize and to reduce stress requires the adoption of an action plan to prevent engagements that cause stress and to develop coping strategies (Tappen, Weiss & Whitehead, 2004).

Caring for one's self physically is an essential health promotion and stress reduction strategy. Eating a well-balanced diet, exercising regularly, getting adequate rest, taking "time-outs" during the day, proper posture, and deep breathing are behaviors that promote a healthy lifestyle and coping with stressful situations. Developing effective mental habits is also important. Each person is a product of his or her own attitude. Therefore, a question one may ask is "How realistic are one's expectations or is the perception of the situation causing frustration?" Role redefinition lessens ambiguity, reduces overload, and integrates responsibilities (Sullivan & Decker, 2005). The first-line manager may rely on a supervisor or mentor to clarify new responsibilities during the transition from direct practice to entry-level management. The social-emotional support gained in this relationship alleviates perceptions of ineffectiveness by creating a sense of belonging or community that reduces fear of failure and negative self-talk. The humor that occurs during the workday and with friends also relieves tension. The new first-line manager also recognizes the importance of learning to say "no" and that employees as well as managers can be taught how to treat each other.

Organization Management Methods

The first-line manager is in a position to help staff identify sources of stress and to decide how these can be reduced or eliminated (Sullivan & Decker, 2005). Awareness of workplace stressors begins with questions such as the following:

- Does the manager need to clarify staff goals and roles?

- Are there barriers interfering with employee goal attainment or recognition?

- Would additional training or development help to reduce stress?

- Is the work culture conducive to effective communication and sensitive to employees building a supportive network?

- Is the staff empowered to make decisions and are resources available to resolve problems?

When stress is job-related, managers introduce strategies that enable relaxation and an opportunity to set priorities. These may include skills training, team building, time management, participatory opportunities, and policies that give permission to take "personal time-outs." A relaxed attitude by the manager sets a tone that permeates the work environment and encourages staff to calmly approach their goals and achieve organizational expectations.

Managing Time

"Time is the essence of living, and it is the scarcest resource" (Sullivan & Decker, 2005, p. 207). "Time can not be saved and used later, so it must be used wisely" (Tappen, Weiss & Whitehead, 2004, p. 138). Learning to take charge of time is critical to the manager's success and a key to time management. A successful leader-manager accomplishes the unit goals "in a timely and efficient manner in a concerted effort with subordinates" (Marquis & Huston, 2003, p. 112). Time is a valuable unit resource and responsibility for use of the resource is shared with employees. Time management commences with setting aside time to plan and establish priorities. Hourly and daily goals are identified and prioritized. Tasks are identified that can be realistically accomplished by staff. Schedules enable staff performance. After each major task is accomplished, time is taken to reprioritize, reorganize, communicate, and delegate the new plan. At day's end, when goals are clearly delineated, there is a sense of achievement. Staff and management feel productive and satisfied. The leadership skills to manage time resources draw on interpersonal communication skills, whereas the management functions inherent in wise use of time resources are concerned with productivity (Marquis & Huston, 2003).

While one likes to think that the various management functions can be divided into distinct equal time elements, in reality this is not true. Few managers have the luxury of working on only one project at a time. The skill of time management enables the first-line manager to separate the important from the unimportant. Time management is a habit pattern characterized by but not limited to the following points:

- *Make a written list of "things to do" today.* It is a common sense rule that implies the need to do some advance planning each day in response to upcoming problems and demands and not rely solely on memory.

- *Set goals. Establish a time frame.* Goals provide direction and vision for actions. With goals and time frames, when confronted with multiple tasks, managers are less likely to panic (Sullivan & Decker, 2005).

- *Prioritize tasks.* Arrange the things to do in order of priority as determined by the expected payoff of each item. Keep in mind that these priorities usually take in both short-term and long-term tasks. Don't spend the whole day on one task.

- *Learn to delegate.* There are many positive reasons for effective delegation. One such reason is that delegation demonstrates a manager's trust and confidence in subordinates, which leads to more effective performance and better interpersonal relationships for all.

- *Control interruptions.* Meeting visitors in the doorway helps managers to maintain control of their time by controlling the use of office space. Other factors include having someone else answer calls, having a place to work uninterrupted, and going to practitioners' offices if matters warrant it.

- *Plan meetings.* Prepare and distribute agendas in advance (Marquis & Huston, 2003). State goals of the meetings in terms of actions. Set start and stop times. Adhere to the agenda and scheduled time. Come on time and prepared. Delegate responsibility when the agenda is distributed (Russell, 2005).

- *Minimize routine work.* List a few 5- or 10-minute tasks. This helps use the small bits of time almost everyone has during his or her day. One can accomplish a lot by doing more than one thing at a time when tasks are routine, trivial, or require little thought.

- *Know one's own productivity period.* Most individuals know their productivity period. Some are morning people, while others are afternoon people. Managers should handle their most demanding problems during their peak period. Also know one's preferred time management style. Some prefer to work on one task at a time while others tend to multitask (Marquis & Huston, 2003). The manager aware of his or her own style is sensitive to how staff will accomplish assigned work.

- *Respect time.* Managers who respect their time are likely to find others respecting it as well. Managers must reciprocate by respecting the time needs of their staff. One should continually ask: "What is the best use of my time for myself and my goals,

staff and their goals, and the organization and its goals?" (Sullivan & Decker, 2005, pp. 213–214).

The Leader-Manager

The department goal is for its manager to adopt a management style that promotes a high level of work performance in a wide variety of circumstances as efficiently as possible and with little disruption. A successful leader accurately assesses the forces that determine what the most appropriate behavior at any given time should be and actually is able to behave accordingly while motivating staff to contribute. The leader-manager is "a change agent—challenging, questioning the status quo, and creating an atmosphere where self-directing activities, workplace partnerships and shared critical outcomes become the norm" (Porter-O'Grady, 1993, p. 52). Due to the rapid and dramatic rate of change in health and human services, the first-line therapeutic recreation manager "must strive for the integration of leadership characteristics throughout every phase of the management process" (Marquis & Huston, 2003, p. 21). A number of behaviors and characteristics drawn from the theories presented in this chapter offer general guidelines regarding leadership and the first-line manger, including the following:

- Assess how one's behavior affects others and vice versa.

- Be sensitive to forces acting for and against change.

- Express an optimistic view about human nature.

- Be energetic.

- Be open and encourage openness so that real issues are confronted.

- Facilitate personal relationships.

- Plan and organize activities of the group.

- Be consistent in behavior toward group practitioners.

- Delegate tasks and responsibilities to develop practitioners' abilities, not merely to get tasks performed.

- Involve practitioners in all decisions appropriate for them.

- Value and use group practitioners' contributions.

- Encourage creativity.

- Encourage feedback about management's leadership style.

After reviewing various theories and definitions of leadership as well as the types of power and their uses in addition to the aforementioned guidelines, Frank (1993) noted, "…interacting with others is the foremost ability one needs to successfully lead" (p. 387). Other major characteristics of effective leadership suggested included assertiveness (not aggressiveness), personal and professional goal setting, time management coupled with the ability to delegate work, effective communication skills, negotiating abilities so that both sides feel they are a winner, knowing when and how to use power, and the ability to recognize and to understand the stress that may be associated with leadership obligations.

To address expanding responsibilities and demands, the first-line manager must assume new roles that facilitate quality outcomes and meet organizational goals. Managers are now more than ever involved in financial and marketing aspects of their programs. Additionally, leadership skills are necessary to build teams at the organizational level (Marquis & Huston, 2003). Successful team building ensures hiring and retention of competent personnel critical to maintaining high-quality programs and services. The manager's leadership ability increases productivity by maximizing workforce effectiveness. The manager who leads is building new service delivery models that enable both the individual and the organization to grow (Marquis & Huston, 2003).

Summary

While leadership is a complex, multidimensional concept, it is at the same time a process of influencing a group to set and to achieve goals. There are several major theories of leadership. One of the earliest theories of leadership is trait theory. This theory has been succeeded by other leadership theories, including behavioral, situational, and contemporary; however, none of these approaches has adequately defined successful leadership.

Power is the capacity to influence others. Effective leaders understand the sources of power and how to use it. As supervisors, managers influence the work of subordinates. Consideration was given to the nature of power, its sources, and its use as first-line managers engage in supervision.

Managers and staff experience a variety of daily pressures and challenges to the use of their time. As a role model, the manager's perceptions and management of stress and time influence staff responses and interactions. Effective managers are intimately aware of their coping strategies and create a supportive environment so staff maintain their productivity and satisfaction with their positions.

The chapter concluded with a brief discussion of the leadership characteristics found with effective first-line managers. When the manager affects the universal functions (e.g., planning, organizing, directing or leading, controlling) to operate a department, status quo is evident. Today's ever-changing, unstable, resource conscious environment requires integration of traditional management functions with leadership skills. As noted in the preceding chapter and with the concluding section of this chapter, an effective leader-manager uses interpersonal skills to coach and to counsel enabling subordinates to achieve the organization's objectives while creating new service delivery options.

Review Questions

1. What do you see as the essence of leadership?

2. "All managers should be leaders, but not all leaders should be managers." Do you agree or disagree with this statement? Support your position.

3. Which of the various leadership theories discussed in this chapter do you think is the most applicable in a therapeutic recreation setting? Support your position.

4. Do an Internet search on time and stress management. What strategies will work best for you?

5. Visit with a manager. What strategies does the manager incorporate to assist as staff cope with work pressures and demands on their time?

References

Adorno, T. W., Frenkel-Brunswik, E., Levinson, D.J., and Sanford, R. N. (1950). *The authoritarian personality.* New York, NY: Harper & Row.

Bass, B. M. (1981). *Stogdill's handbook of leadership* (Rev. ed.). New York, NY: Free Press.

Blake, R. R. and Mouton, J. S. (1964). *The managerial grid.* Houston, TX: Gulf Publishing.

Benziger, K. (1982). The powerful woman. *Hospital Forum,* 25(3), 15–20.

Fiedler, F. E. (1967). *A theory of leadership effectiveness.* New York, NY: McGraw-Hill.

Frank, M. S. (1993, Fall). The essence of leadership. *Public Personnel Management, 22*(3), 381–389.

French, J. R. P., Jr. and Raven, B. (1968). The base of social power. In D. Cartwright and A. Zander (Eds.), *Group dynamics* (3rd ed., pp. 262–268). New York, NY: Harper & Row.

Gibb, C. A. (1969). Leadership. In G. Lindsy and E. Aronson (Eds.), *The handbook of social psychology* (2nd ed., pp. 216–228). Reading, MA: Addison-Wesley Publishing.

Hein, E. C. and Nicholson, M. J. (1990). *Contemporary leadership behavior* (3rd ed.). Glenview, IL: Scott, Foresman and Company.

Hersey, P. and Blanchard, K. H. (1982). *Management of organizational behavior: Utilizing human resources* (4th ed.). Englewood Cliffs, NJ: Prentice Hall.

House, R. J. and Mitchell, T. R. (1974, Autumn). Path-goal theory of leadership. *Journal of Contemporary Business*, 81–97.

Lewin, K. and Lippit, R. (1938). An experimental approach to the study of autocracy and democracy: A preliminary note. *Sociometry, 1*, 292–300.

Lewis, J. A. and Lewis, M. D. (1983). *Management of human service programs*. Belmont, CA: Brooks/Cole Publishing.

Likert, R. (1967). *The human organization*. New York, NY: McGraw-Hill.

Marquis, B. L. and Huston, C. J. (2003). *Leadership roles and management functions in nursing theory & application* (4th ed.). Philadelphia, PA: Lippincott Williams & Wilkins.

McGregor, D. (1966). *Leadership and motivation*. Cambridge, MA: MIT Press.

Megginson, L. C., Mosley, D. D., and Pietri, P. H., Jr. (1991). *Management: Concepts and applications* (4th ed.). New York, NY: HarperCollins.

Megginson, L. C., Mosley, D. C., and Pietri, P. H., Jr. (1986). *Management: Concepts and applications* (3rd ed.). New York, NY: Harper & Row.

Moore T. and Wood, D. (1979). Power and the hospital executive. *Hospital and Health Services Administration, 24*, 30–41.

Porter-O'Grady, T. (1993, April). Of mythspinners and mapmakers: 21st century managers. *Nursing Management, 24*(4), 52–56.

Robbins, S. P. (1980). *The administrative process* (2nd ed.). Englewood Cliffs, NJ: Prentice Hall.

Russell, R. V. (2005). *Leadership in recreation* (3rd ed.). Boston, MA: McGraw-Hill.

Schein, E. H. (1970). *Organizational psychology* (2nd ed.). Englewood Cliffs, NJ: Prentice Hall.

Schreisheim, C. A., Mowday, R. T., and Stogdill, R. M. (1979). Critical dimensions of leader-group interactions. In J. G. Hunt and L. L. Larson (Eds.), *Cross-currents in leadership* (pp. 113–121). Carbondale, IL: Southern Illinois University Press.

Stogdill, R. M. (1974). *Handbook of leadership: A survey of the literature*. New York, NY: Free Press.

Stoner, J. A. F. (1982). *Management* (2nd ed.). Englewood Cliffs, NJ: Prentice Hall.

Sullivan, E. J. and Decker, P. J. (2005). *Effective leadership & management in nursing* (6th ed.). Upper Saddle River, NJ: Pearson/Prentice Hall.

Tannenbaum, R. and Schmidt, W. H. (1983). Effective Leadership. In E. G. C. Collins (Ed.), *Executive success: Making it in management* (pp. 151–168). New York, NY: John Wiley & Sons.

Tappen, R. M., Weiss, S. A., and Whitehead, D. K. (2004). *Essentials of nursing leadership and management* (3rd ed.). Philadelphia, PA: F. A. Davis.

Section II
Administrative Management

Chapter 4
Vision, Mission, Philosophy, and Objectives

chapter revisions by Glenda Taylor

The challenges of the 21st century have created the need to reengineer our organizations, management, and leadership (Heifetz & Halle, 1996). The organization needs to adapt to changes brought about by forces such as shifts in political power, global trade, and technological advancement (Birkner & Birkner, 1998). The organization must have a strategy and a structured process to keep at the "cutting edge" of the competitive environment—a sound strategy is no longer a luxury, but a necessity (Montgomery & Porter, 1991). Reading (2002) suggested all organizations need a robust strategy to achieve identified targets… ownership of the strategy by all members of the leadership team, is critical to advancing the mission of the agency.

A statement heard most frequently in the workplace is: "Today we have to get organized." Individuals who express this view are in many instances venting frustration about the fact that the workplace is not functioning in a smooth and systematic manner. A major reason for this is the lack of statements associated with the workplace vision, mission, philosophy, goals, and objectives. Strategic business planning requires the agency to have a focus. A focus provides a forum and structured process to resolve internal confusion and to channel energy and effort in a commonly agreed direction (Reading, 2002). Ensuring successful organizational change may require a process that addresses, according to Birkner and Birkner (1998), the establishment of a sense of urgency, creation of a guiding coalition, development of a vision, communication, and the empowerment of employees.

Statements regarding the vision, mission, or purpose of the therapeutic recreation department in a health care facility or a division of a public park and recreation department that espouse the philosophy, beliefs, goals, and objectives are part of the planning function or process. These statements provide the framework for all plans and activities within the department. These statements evolve from and support those that have been developed by the top management of the organization. These statements are the blueprints for effective management, and they set the stage for smooth operations. They are also the reasons for being. They are the basic tools of management planning (Swansburg, 1996), as they articulate the major tasks to be carried out and the kinds of technologies and human resources to be employed.

This chapter focuses on the written statements that reflect the agency's vision, and incorporates the mission/purpose, values, philosophy, and objectives. Written operational plans are the blueprints for effective management of any enterprise, including health and human service agencies (Swansburg, 1996). A *vision statement* is like a cascade, a series or succession of statements that act on the preceding statement, flowing from one component or statement to the next, or as a descriptive story of the desired future in action (Levin, 2000). Not all organizations, agencies, or therapeutic recreation departments have implemented a total vision statement into their management operation or planning process. Some organizations tend to have independent components, such as a mission or philosophy, while others tend to be a mixture of values, purpose, philosophy, beliefs, goals, and operations. The concern here is to clarify those components of a vision statement using examples from various types of organizations and their respective departments of therapeutic recreation. Likewise, to give some consistency to the various components or statements, illustrations of various statements of vision, mission, philosophy, goals, and objectives have been used from the same organization and its department of therapeutic recreation where possible. One is cautioned there is some variance in the content from one component or statement to another.

Vision

Vision was the buzzword of the 1990s. Vision is an intriguing phenomenon that touches on issues of leadership, motivation, empowerment, cognitive complexity, and self-transforming organizations (Nathan, 1996). In recent years many health and human service organizations such as hospitals and community-based leisure service agencies, like business and industry before them, have developed vision statements. Further, some therapeutic recreation departments have developed vision statements in consonance with their organization or agency.

The term *vision* implies the ability to see… In planning, vision always deals with the future. A vision also encompasses "values" that are worthwhile and important to people. The premise of a vision is that if you can dream it, you can do it. For a vision to serve more than one person, it must be shared. (Kolzow, 1999)

A limited random sampling of therapeutic recreation departments regarding vision, mission, and philosophy statements taken by the authors produced few vision statements, but a large percentage of mission and philosophy statements were evident. However, a vision and a mission can be one and the same: "Vision refers to a future state (i.e., a condition that is better than what now exists), whereas mission more normally refers to the present" (Campbell, Nash, Devine & Young, 1992, p. 32). Strategic management wisdom has it that "vision" is all-important. It sets the heights to which an organization can climb, and yet is the sensible foundation of a solid operation (Nathan, 1996).

A vision is a dream of greatness (Block, 1987). It is a word picture—a description of the future that provides a focus for coordinating the efforts in an organization or agency. Its expression is to provide a unifying theme and a challenge to all-organizational departments or units. The vision communicates a sense of achievable ideals, serves as a source of inspiration for confronting the daily activities, and becomes a contagious, motivating, and guiding force congruent with the organization's ethics and values (Hax & Majluf, 1984). "A vision is a target that beckons" (Campbell, Nash, Devine & Young, 1992, p. 38). From another perspective, the vision must relate to the wants of the customers while being grand enough and imaginative enough to fuel the employees' spirit (Block, 1987). From still another perspective a vision statement indicates quality and "a benchmark for value measurement" (Russoniello, 1991, p. 26).

Russoniello (1991, p. 22) defined a vision statement as "a description of a desired state that an organization or therapeutic recreation department commits to." According to Silvers (1994/95, p. 11) a vision is a "statement of what an organization stands for, what it believes in, why it exists, and what it intends to accomplish." A vision focuses on end results but not necessarily on how to get there. Goals focus on the direction, while objectives focus on how to get there. "A powerful vision provides the sense of where one is going. It empowers people. It provides the force, or guiding principle, behind why we do what we do" (Turpel, 1992, p. 4). As noted by Schroll (1995a, p. 25), "When the organization has a clear, widely shared vision of its purpose and direction, it empowers individuals and confers status on them. They see themselves as part of a worthwhile enterprise in pursuit of a shared mission."

Although the vision is initiated and developed by top management, the practitioner working for the organization has to become an active collaborator in the pursuit of the organization mission or purpose; he or she must share the vision of the organization and feel comfortable with the way in which it is translated or expressed in values. This framework conditions the behavior of practitioners, and they must intimately sense that by following the vision, they are fulfilling a personal need for achievement. The vision of the organization becomes a personal drive for their own lives. Russoniello (1991) noted that a vision statement provides motivation while Turpel (1992, p. 74) commented, "…that the vision must be fertile. The vision must excite people… Focused vision inspires, empowers, and generates the commitment needed for innovation and effective action." Employees may live the vision (Swansburg, 1996), particularly those who participate in developing the vision. Employees who participate in the design of a vision are more committed to the organization than those who do not participate in this process.

While a vision statement in its development is usually confined to senior management, there is no reason that a therapeutic recreation department cannot form a vision that is relevant to its own department by building on the organization's vision, mission, and objectives. The development of a vision may improve department planning and performance. If the organization does not have a vision, the initiation of one by the therapeutic recreation department may stimulate the organization as a whole to think about a vision.

Creating a Vision

In developing a vision statement for the therapeutic recreation department, intense focus must be on the consumer, and it must describe something markedly better than the current state. The vision is based on the values and beliefs of the department and its practitioners; on knowledge of the department's capabilities; on technical, regulatory, and environmental conditions; and on consumer requirements. "A vision statement is the collective identification of those aspects of care that recreational therapists feel are critical in the quest for quality" (Russoniello, 1991, p. 23). Effective visions should describe a future world where the mission is advanced and where goals and strategy are being successfully achieved in lockstep with the organization's guiding philosophy and values (Levin, 2000).

How does one create a vision statement? Silvers (1994/95) suggested incorporating four basic components into the vision statement, including values and beliefs, purpose, mission, and goals. The foundation of the statement consists of core values and beliefs. Achievement may be one of the core values of the department. Consumer satisfaction may be the measure of that value. Purpose is the second aspect of the vision and is an outgrowth of the department's values and beliefs. "A statement of purpose should clearly convey the basic human needs which are fulfilled by the department" (Silvers, 1994/95, p. 12). Mission comes next and states what the department does. The last aspects of the vision are goals. Goals are built on the previous three statements. Goals focus on the future and guide the efforts of the department. "The goals should have a long-range outlook and reflect lofty ideals" (Silvers, 1994/95, p. 12).

Once the statement is completed and approved, the manager needs to communicate it to staff and motivate them to embrace it. By enthusiastically communicating the vision to practitioners, the manager begins the process of motivating them toward achievement of the vision (Silvers, 1994/95). Facilitating shared vision in the organization requires the administrators to convey an understanding of needs, building futures scenarios, pointing out hurdles, and deciding on action items (Eigeles, 2003). Figure 4.1 illustrates the vision statement of Sheltering Arms (Midtown) Physical Rehabilitation Center, a branch of the freestanding rehabilitation hospitals, Richmond, Virginia.

Mission or Purpose

Every organization, whether it is a company in business to make a profit or a charitable organization with nonprofit status, needs a mission statement (Abrahams, 1995). The mission defined by an organization identifies its basic thrust—its business. Shaping the identity of an agency really begins with determining its mission, its reason for being, its purpose, focus, and goal (Abrahams, 1995). For example, Southern Health (1995, p. 67), a managed care organization, states its mission as follows: "Southern Health's mission is to be the preferred manager of high-quality, cost-effective health benefit services." In many instances this statement is drawn from the vision statement but is more concise or focused on the type of services provided. Hospitals exist to provide health care services to the community. Local public park and recreation departments exist to provide recreation and leisure facilities and experiences to meet individual needs within the community. Each department or unit within an organization has

a mission that contributes to the overall purpose of the organization. In a broad sense, the therapeutic recreation department in a general medical hospital exists to provide quality therapeutic recreation to patients. In the therapeutic recreation division of a community-based park and recreation department, the same purpose is intended but directed toward individuals with disabilities who live in the community.

The mission states the reason this particular therapeutic recreation department exists and the intent it serves. A mission influences the philosophy, scope of service, goals, and objectives as well as the policies and procedures of an organization. For example, if a therapeutic recreation department in a general medical hospital is responsible for providing services in a psychiatric unit and that unit prepares patients for community adjustment, it should be staffed with a therapeutic recreation specialist particularly skilled in leisure education. How broad or narrow a mission statement should be is a controversial question. There are advantages and disadvantages to both narrow and broad mission statements. A narrow statement carefully specifies the area within which the department will consider its service, whereas a broad mission statement widens the areas of service. Too narrow a statement can blind the department to significant threats and opportunities from other departments or service units. Too broad a statement, on the other hand, encourages the department to expand into services where it has limited expertise.

The mission of the department should be known and understood by other facility staff, consumers and their families, and the community. "An individual feels a sense of purpose when the organization has a strong mission and its values are attractive to the individual" (Campbell, Nash, Devine & Young, 1992, p. 65). A mission statement must be dynamic, giving action and strength to evolving statements of philosophy, objectives, and management plans. Statements of mission can be made dynamic by indicating the relationship between the therapeutic recreation department and consumers, personnel, and community. Above all, it must be realistic. As Schroll (1995b, p. 22) commented, "If wrongly formulated, mission can become a straitjacket that prevents a company from moving forward."

The worded mission statement may be given from several different perspectives. First, it may state the purpose of the therapeutic recreation department *qua* organization; that is, the desired *structure* that provides for and controls therapeutic recreation service. A second option is to word the mission so as to describe the *process* of therapeutic recreation service desired. Other mission statements are worded in terms of desired consumer *outcomes*. In this regard, Russoniello (1991) commented that the mission statement "should reflect…what the consumer can expect as a result of the [therapeutic recreation] service" (p. 25).

Sheltering Arms (Midtown) Physical Rehabilitation Center, Community Recreation Services

Vision Statement
The Department of Community Recreation Services will offer a variety of comprehensive, quality programs and services that will enhance the promotion of healthy lifestyles.

Figure 4.1
Sample Vision Statement

Some statements of mission choose to include all of these perspectives: structure, process, and outcome.

According to the management style of the organization, its size, and its structure, the therapeutic recreation manager may have more or less leeway in developing the department's mission and in defining the boundaries of therapeutic recreation's role.

Sheltering Arms (Midtown) Physical Rehabilitation Center, Community Recreation Services
The mission of Community Recreation Services is empowering people of all abilities to embrace a lifetime of recreation and wellness. Our staff will project a creative and caring attitude, which is sensitive to the needs of the community. Through recreation, special events, and fitness and wellness programs, the Department of Community Recreation Services will provide a safe environment while enhancing the quality of life for our participants.

Rocky Mountain Multiple Sclerosis Center
The mission of The Rocky Mountain Multiple Sclerosis Center is to improve the quality of life of individuals with MS and their families through patient care services, education and research.

King Adult Day Enrichment Program
The mission of the King Adult Day Enrichment Program is to provide a client centered, community-based program designed to enhance participant's quality of life by improving their physical, emotional, social, cognitive and spiritual well-being.

Chesterfield County Parks and Recreation Department
The mission of the Chesterfield County Parks and Recreation Department is to provide a comprehensive system of leisure programs, educational opportunities and recreational facilities for all its citizens while conserving and protecting environmental, historical, and cultural resources. We will promote community involvement in developing and providing leisure services. The department will ensure customer service excellence, affordability, equal opportunity, a safe environment, and access for all citizens.

The Virginia Home
The Virginia Home is a private nonprofit 130-bed facility providing nursing, therapeutic and residential care to adult Virginians with irreversible physical disabilities. The home exists to provide compassionate, professional care and to ensure that the lifelong comfort and security of these individuals will never be compromised regardless of ability to pay. The staff develops and seeks to improve the physical, social and emotional lives of those living with a severe disabling condition, helping them to live active meaningful lives.

Figure 4.2
Sample Mission Statements

Like the organization's mission, the therapeutic recreation department's mission is elaborated into a number of specific objectives. Otherwise, they remain good intentions that are not operationalized. Figure 4.2 shows a variety of mission statements.

Philosophy

Philosophy is a statement of beliefs and values that direct one's practice. A written statement of philosophy sets out values, concepts, and beliefs that pertain to therapeutic recreation administration and practice within the organization (Swansburg, 1996). It states their beliefs as to how the mission or purpose will be achieved, giving direction toward this end. It creates a climate for achieving professional excellence by stressing high standards. If a philosophy is stated in vague, abstract terms that are not easily understood, it is useless. Practitioners are most likely to interpret a philosophy from the pronouncements and actions of others in the organization. Therefore, conformity of action to belief is important. In addition, William G. Ouchi (1981) argued in Theory Z that a philosophy is critical because it enables individuals to coordinate their activities to achieve a purpose even in the absence of direction from managers.

The advantages of a philosophy statement are twofold. The first is that it can be used to guide behavior and decisions. Values, which a philosophy statement expresses, by their very nature define what course of action and outcomes "should be." Thus the statement can help direct practitioners' attention in some ways and not others. A second potential advantage is that it may contribute to organization and department performance by motivating practitioners or inspiring feelings of commitment.

One does not need to be a philosopher to express ideas underlying therapeutic recreation practice. A philosophy simply represents the central beliefs and values of the department relative to therapeutic recreation and therapeutic recreation practice. Philosophies are not right or wrong, and their content varies from organization to organization depending on what values are perceived as central to therapeutic recreation. In some settings a value statement is expressed in lieu of a philosophy statement.

A philosophical statement that is clear, succinct, powerful, and advocates for the rights of the individual is exemplified in the statement by The Virginia Home, Richmond, refer to Figure 4.3.

Before proceeding it is important to note that a therapeutic recreation department's vision, mission, and philosophy statements usually complement those of the organization or larger divisions or departments within the organization. In such situations, the therapeutic recreation statements would need to be consistent with the organization or division statement. It is not unusual to begin the various statements with, "We concur," "We believe," or "We are committed." The various statements do not repeat generalities that might be found in the organization or larger division statements. Instead, it focuses on the uniqueness within the context of the therapeutic recreation department.

Goals and Objectives

The two terms *goals* and *objectives* are in many instances used interchangeably and should be considered as ends toward which all activity is directed. These terms suggest aspirations or the desired end that any organization or department of therapeutic recreation attempts to realize. This discussion will consider them separately. A *goal* is a state or condition that the organization and department want to achieve; it offers direction. An *objective*, on the other hand, is the result to be achieved to reach the goal; it is the action taken to achieve the goal.

The reader is also reminded that within some therapeutic recreation departments there may be a scope of care or service section before the goals and objectives section or as a part of the section. Such a section may address the services provided and if within the goals and objectives section notes the goal of a specific service and how it will be met through various objectives. Figure 4.4 provides an example of a scope of service statement relative to therapeutic recreation services within a physical rehabilitation department of a general medical hospital. The service activities in the example could be expanded to include the types of activities or specific focus of the activities found in each service area depending on the department's or hospital's policies and procedures addressing rehabilitation care planning.

Goals and objectives state actions for achieving the mission and philosophy. They are specific statements that therapeutic recreation managers seek to accomplish. Performance standards, deadlines, budgets, to-do lists, and work objectives are all examples of work goals. The best way to manage one's workload efficiently is the use of the management-by-objective model. This model helps push workers to establish priorities and provides an order to getting the job done (Brill, 1990).

If the mission and philosophy are to be more than good intentions, they must be translated into explicit goals. A major characteristic of effective goal setting is the avoidance of ambiguity in determining the exact goal. Goals are central to the whole management process—planning, organizing, directing, and controlling. Planning defines goals. The organization is organized and staffed to accomplish goals. Directions stimulate personnel to accomplish objectives, and control compares the results with objectives to evaluate accomplishments. An example of the operationalizing of the mission statement with clear and succinct goals is viewed in Figure 4.5 (p. 54).

Goals

According to Richards (1986), goals serve four important purposes. First, they provide guidance and a unified direction for all people in the organization. Goals help everyone to understand where the organization is going and why getting there is important. Second, planning, as noted earlier, is facilitated. Goals and planning are highly interrelated. Third, goals can serve as a source of motivation and at times inspiration to the employees of the organization. Specific and moderately difficult goals can motivate people to work harder, especially if attaining the goal results in a reward. Last, goals provide an effective mechanism for evaluation.

Who sets goals? The answer is actually quite simple. All managers at all levels within the organization should be involved in the goal-setting process. Moreover, goal setting incorporates short-term, intermediate, and long-term

---

The Virginia Home Philosophy

All residents should be as independent as they can possibly be. Therefore, The Home effectively removes the day-to-day barriers faced by people with disabilities, freeing its residents to pursue constructive endeavors.

Figure 4.3
Sample Philosophy Statement

Therapeutic Recreation Services of Community Memorial Hospital serves all patients, both inpatients and outpatients, with services provided by certified therapeutic recreation specialists in a professional, effective, and efficient manner. Services are delivered, only when medically indicated, under the direction of physicians and in collaboration with the rehabilitation interdisciplinary team. The hours of service are between 8:30 a.m. and 4:30 p.m., Monday through Friday. Some services are scheduled in the evenings and on weekends when appropriate.

The scope of services includes an initial assessment to determine patient needs. Based on this assessment, services are provided to achieve maximal rehabilitation or functional ability through the use of activities which focus on treatment, leisure education, community integration, and general recreative participation.

Figure 4.4
Sample Scope of Service Statement

goals. There tends to be more organizational long-term goals than short-term goals associated with top management, whereas first-line managers are usually responsible for short-term goals, and there tends to be a balance or mix of management regarding intermediate goals (Griffin, 1990). As a final note, all organizations and departments have a multiple set of objectives, all of which should be compatible.

Making Goal Setting Effective

Goal setting is an important task. There are several guidelines reflected in the literature for making goal setting effective. The following five guidelines noted by Griffin (1990) are the ones most frequently mentioned:

1. *Understanding the purposes of goals.* The best way to facilitate the goal-setting process is to make sure all managers and practitioners understand the four main purposes of goals as noted earlier: (a) source of guidance and direction, (b) catalyst for planning, (c) stimulus for motivation and inspiration, and (d) mechanism for evaluation and control (Richards, 1986). Goal setting and implementation should be undertaken with those purposes in mind.

2. *Stating goals properly.* Making sure that goals are properly stated is another way to improve the goal-

setting process. To the extent possible, goals should be specific, concise, and where necessary, time related.

3. *Goal consistency.* A third way to improve the goal-setting process is to be sure that goals are consistent throughout the organization. All goals must agree with one another (i.e., be compatible).

4. *Goal acceptance and commitment.* People, regardless of their place in the organization, need to have a high level of acceptance and commitment to work toward organization and department goals. Managers need to demonstrate their vision for the organization in everything they do to encourage goal acceptance and commitment by those who work for them. Moreover, managers should also allow for broad-based participation in the goal-setting process whenever appropriate, and they should make sure that goals are properly communicated. People are much more likely to accept and to become committed to goals if they help set them or at least know how and why the goals were established.

5. *Effective reward systems.* Goal setting can also be improved if it is integrated with the reward system of the organization or department. People should be rewarded first for effective goal setting and then for successful goal attainment. However, since failure sometimes results from factors outside the manager's control, people should also be assured that failure to reach individual goals would not necessarily bring punitive consequences.

It is important also to recognize that while these guidelines are positive in nature, the reverse of these guidelines can disrupt things. An inappropriate goal would be one that is not consistent with the organization or department mission. Another obstacle would be goals so extreme that accomplishing them is virtually impossible. Over-emphasis on quantitative or qualitative goals is another problem. And finally, improper reward systems act as a barrier to the goal-setting process.

Objectives

Objectives are concrete statements that become the standards against which performance can be measured (Swansburg, 1996). Good objectives have two principal characteristics. They should be (a) specific and verifiable and (b) attainable. Specific and verifiable means, that where possible objectives should be stated in quantitative terms like goals. The more quantitative the objective, the more likely it is to receive attention toward its accomplishment and the less likely it is to be distorted. Unfortunately,

---

> *King Adult Day Enrichment Program*
>
> *Mission Statement and Goals*
>
> The mission of the King Adult Day enrichment Program is to provide a client centered, community-based program designed to enhance participants' quality of life by improving their physical, emotional, social, cognitive, and spiritual well-being.
>
> The goals of the King Adult Day Enrichment Program are as follows:
>
> 1. To maximize independent functioning
> 2. To facilitate adjustment to disability and decrease depression and isolation
> 3. To provide opportunities for socialization and community integration
> 4. To provide wellness monitoring and preventative health care
> 5. To provide respite
> 6. To provide a cost-effective alternative to institutionalization
> 7. To enhance life satisfaction

Figure 4.5
Sample Mission Statement and Goals

it is not possible to quantify all objectives. Some objectives, because of the nature of the plan, will have to be qualitative. Nevertheless, even qualitative objectives should be made as specific and verifiable as possible.

Sometimes it is said that qualitative objectives are gauged by the standard of "how well," and quantitative objectives by "how much." To some extent this is true, but in the author's experience, a qualitative objective can be made highly verifiable by spelling out the characteristics of the programs or other objectives sought and a date of accomplishment.

The second important characteristic of a good objective is that it is attainable. Optimally, an objective should be fairly difficult but not impossible to reach. Objectives that are too high tend to discourage managers and practitioners. Those that are too low have little motivational impact and may result in under accomplishment.

Writing Objectives

Developing and writing objectives should not be a difficult undertaking providing there has been a thorough collection of data and a definition of the needs of the situation have been established. The essentials of developing and writing objectives are quite simple: set meaningful goals written in the form of objectives and evaluate how well the objectives have been met. In general, the objectives should begin with an action verb and describe an activity that can be measured or at least observed. Whenever possible, the objective should be specific, time bound if feasible, and state a measurable or observable end result to increase the objectivity of the evaluation done at the endpoint.

The objective should also be meaningful and either congruent with the goals of the organization or department or deliberately aimed at changing the goal. The time set for completing the objective depends on the nature of the work being planned and other factors that will affect the speed with which the work can be completed. Time lines are particularly helpful in working out the specific objectives leading to a long-term goal. When the objective is complex, it may also be necessary to break it down even further into separate steps or components to have an adequate guide to work by and to evaluate the progress toward meeting the goal. Objectives and time estimates should be considered as flexible guides, not unbendable demands.

Objective Areas

Because organizations or departments have more than a singular objective, it is valuable to consider areas from which goals can emanate. Goals may be internal or external. They either relate to the direct needs of the organization or to the consumer and society it serves. *Internal goals* are primarily concerned with human, physical, and financial inputs and their transformation into desirable outputs. *External goals* focus on consumer satisfaction, social awareness, and social responsibility. Every organization or department must satisfy the needs of consumers who have the power to curtail its livelihood.

The therapeutic recreation staff, specifically the therapeutic recreation manager, must decide where efforts will be concentrated to achieve results. A major objective area is evaluation of consumer service, or developing methods of measuring the quality of patient care. Certainly, the American Therapeutic Recreation Association's (ATRA) *Standards for the Practice of Therapeutic Recreation and Self-Assessment Guide* (2000) and the National Therapeutic Recreation Society's (NTRS) *Standards of Practice for a Continuum of Care in Therapeutic Recreation* (2004) should be used as guidelines in the development and evaluation of consumer service and patient care. In addition, the concepts of appropriateness and continuous quality improvement should be incorporated.

Other internal objectives would include evaluation of personnel performance and staffing in accordance with practitioner's skill levels, educational program planning, requisition of supplies and equipment to facilitate consumer service, innovation to introduce new methods, and particularly, the application of new knowledge.

No organization can survive very long if it does not meet the needs of some constituency. When an organization no longer satisfies its consumers, it finds its charter rescinded, its revenues shrinking, and a lack of public support for its objectives. Therefore, all organizations must serve a constituency and satisfy the needs of consumers. The same is so for the therapeutic recreation department. As part of the health and human service delivery system, it must provide quality service.

Implications for Therapeutic Recreation

Objectives are the fundamental strategy of therapeutic recreation, because they are the end product of all therapeutic recreation activities. Objectives must be capable of being converted into specific targets and specific assignments so that therapeutic recreation personnel will know what they have to do to accomplish them. Further, objectives become the basis and motivation for therapeutic recreation work and for measuring therapeutic recreation achievement regardless of setting.

In therapeutic recreation, all objectives should be performance objectives. They should provide for existing therapeutic recreation services and for existing consumer groups. They should provide for abandonment of unneeded and outmoded therapeutic recreation services. They should provide for new services, for new consumers, and for standards of therapeutic recreation service and performance.

Objectives are the basis for work and assignments. They determine the department structure, key activities, and allocation of staff to tasks. Objectives make the work of therapeutic recreation clean and unambiguous—the results are measurable, there are deadlines to be met, and there is a specific assignment of accountability. Objectives also give direction and make commitments that mobilize the resources and energies of therapeutic recreation for the future. Finally, objectives should be changed as necessary, particularly when there is a change in mission or purpose or when they are no longer functional.

Critical to the operation of any therapeutic recreation department is the provision of an education function—to transmit knowledge and skills to the student learner. A comprehensive set of objectives is developed to operationalize the goal of the internship program. These objectives guide clinical education practices as the student learner transitions from novice to apprentice to expert (Muscari, 2000). An example of a goal and objectives of an intern program are illustrated in Figure 4.6.

Goal

To provide a well-rounded intern program that enhances professional growth and development.

Objectives

- To orient the intern to the practical aspects of the leisure services profession and further his or her knowledge of the profession.

- To introduce the intern to the goals and objectives of the Chesterfield County Parks and Recreation Department.

- To provide through practical experience within the department as many opportunities as possible for the intern to mature, practice, improve and evaluate the skills, techniques, principles, and theories to which the intern has been exposed in the academic setting.

- To help the intern understand and appreciate the duties and responsibilities of all persons employed in the field of leisure services.

- To provide feedback to the university or college regarding student participation, intern program, and curriculum.

- To evaluate the intern on his/her performance and provide professional recommendations.

- To prove mutually beneficial to the intern and the agency by providing both challenge and growth.

Figure 4.6
Sample Goal and Objectives of an Intern Program

Summary

It was noted that the development of a statement of the vision, mission or purpose, philosophy, goals, and objectives of an organization at the division or department level sets the stage for smooth operations. Moreover, all managers use such statements in their management operation and planning process to accomplish the work of therapeutic recreation.

The vision statement articulates what an organization and department considers important and what it hopes to achieve. The mission or purpose articulates the reason for the department's existence within the organization while the philosophy reflects the values and beliefs of the organization and the department. Goals and objectives state actions for achieving the purpose and philosophy and serve as a guide in planning work, setting priorities, and evaluating effectiveness. Objectives should be verifiable and attainable can be short-term, intermediate-term, or long-term. Guidelines for setting effective goals and the areas from which goals can emanate were given. This chapter concluded with the implications of objectives for therapeutic recreation.

Review Questions

1. Make a list of goals you wish to achieve in the next five years. Are they verifiable? Are they attainable?

2. Write a concise vision statement (including mission, philosophy, values, goals, and objectives) for a department of therapeutic recreation with which you are familiar.

3. Interview the head of the parks and recreation department in your community or the director of therapeutic recreation at the local hospital to ascertain what the mission, philosophy, and objectives of his or her department are.

4. Collect and critique vision, mission, purpose, philosophy statements and write statements according to guidelines presented in this chapter from a therapeutic recreation department in a clinical setting, a community park and recreation setting, and a private agency.

5. Develop a mission statement reflective of structure, process, and outcome per descriptions in this chapter.

6. Write objectives for the goal statements presented in Figure 4.5 (p. 54).

References

Abrahams, J. (1995). *The mission statement book.* Berkeley, CA: Ten Speed Press.

American Therapeutic Recreation Association (ATRA). (2000). *Standards for the practice of therapeutic recreation and self-assessment guide.* Alexandria, VA: Author.

Birkner, L. R. and Birkner, R. K. (1998). Making successful change. *Occupational Hazards, 60*(6), 13–14.

Block, P. (1987). *The empowered manager.* San Francisco, CA: Jossey-Bass.

Brill, N. L. (1990). *Working with people: The helping process.* New York, NY: Longman.

Campbell, A., Nash, L. L., Devine, M., and Young, D. (1992). *A sense of mission—Defining direction for the large corporation.* Reading, MA: Addison-Wesley Publishing.

Eigeles, D. (2003). Facilitating shared vision in the organization. *Journal of European Industrial Training, 27*(5), 208–219.

Griffin, R. W. (1990). *Management* (3rd ed.). Boston, MA: Houghton Mifflin.

Hax, A. C. and Majluf, N. S. (1984). *Strategic management: An integrative perspective.* Englewood Cliffs, NJ: Prentice Hall.

Heifetz, M. and Halle, S. (1996). Leading change, overcoming chaos—Making change succeed in your organization. *Hospital Materials Management Quarterly, 18*(1), 17–28.

Kolzow, D. (1999). A perspective on strategic planning: What is your vision? *Economic Development Review, 16*(2), 5–15.

Levin, I.M. (2000). Vision revisited: Telling the story of the future. *Journal of Applied Behavioral Science, 36*(1), 91–107.

Montgomery, C. A. and Porter, M. E. (Eds.). (1991). *Harvard business review on strategy: Seeking and securing competitive advantage.* Boston, MA: Harvard Business School Press.

Muscari, M. E. (2000). Developmental Framework. In J. Kasar and E. N. Clark (Eds.), *Developing professional behaviors* (pp. 19–26). Thorofare, NJ: Slack.

Nathan, M.L. (1996). What is an organizational vision? *The Academy of Management Executive, 10*(1), 82–83.

National Therapeutic Recreation Society (NTRS). (2004). *Standards of practice for a continuum of care in therapeutic recreation.* Retrieved September 12, 2004, from http://www.nrpa.org/content/default.aspx?documentID=530

Ouchi, W. G. (1981). *Theory Z: How American business can meet the Japanese challenge.* Reading, MA: Addison-Wesley Publishing.

Reading, C. (2002). *Strategic business planning* (2nd ed.). London, England: Kogan Page.

Richards, M. D. (1986). *Setting strategic goals & objectives* (2nd ed.). St. Paul, MN: West Publishing.

Russoniello, C. V. (1991). "Vision statements" and "mission statements:" Macro indicators of quality performance. In B. Riley (Ed.) *Quality management: Applications for therapeutic recreation* (pp. 21–28). State College, PA: Venture Publishing, Inc.

Schroll, C. (1995a, Spring). Strategic planning to strategic management: Incorporating vision and mission. *Virginia Parks and Recreation, 22*(1), 25–26.

Schroll, C. (1995b, Summer/Fall). Part two: Strategic planning to strategic management: Incorporating vision and mission. *Virginia Parks and Recreation, 22*(2), 22–23, 28.

Silvers, D. I. (1994-95, Winter). Vision—Not just for CEOs. *Management Quarterly, 35*(4), 10–14.

Southern Health. (1995, August 13). *Who is Southern Health? Discover by the Seasons* (Supplement to the *Roanoke Times*).

Swansburg, R. (1996). *Management and leadership for nurse managers* (2nd ed.). Boston, MA: Jones and Bartlett.

Turpel, L. T. (1992). Strategic management. In R. M. Winslow and K. J. Halberg (Eds.), *The management of therapeutic recreation service* (pp. 71–83). Arlington, VA: National Recreation and Park Association.

Chapter 5
Organizational Behavior

Therapeutic recreation managers can benefit from the study of organizational behavior because it helps them to understand and predict human behavior within individual groups and teams in an organization—and at the department level—even though therapeutic recreation departments in health care facilities and community-based leisure service agencies are relatively small in comparison to other organizational departments. Before considering the behavior of individuals, groups, and teams in an organization it is important to realize that organizations, regardless of size, have a culture and a climate that affect individual and group behavior throughout the organization. The diversity that exists in the workplace requires that managers be sensitive to differences as they motivate individual employees and create an organizational climate in which diverse work groups mature.

"The health care system is in the midst of unprecedented change in a climate of uncertainty" (Sullivan & Decker, 2001, p. 249). Many of the changes are external to the organization, especially those resulting from economic forces. Therapeutic recreation managers are change agents. They may alter the work environment, technology, or people (Robbins & Decenzo, 2001; Sullivan & Decker, 2001). The organizational culture and climate influence adjustments in any or all of these.

Organizational Culture and Climate

Organizational culture is similar to societal culture in that both are pervasive and powerful forces that shape behavior. Every organization has a culture of values and behaviors. A culture consists of both the implicit and explicit contracts among individuals, including what is expected of them and the rewards or sanctions associated with compliance or noncompliance of these contracts. Further, a culture is based on a pattern of basic assumptions or behaviors that have worked in the past and are taught to new individuals as the correct way to perceive, to think, to feel, and to act. When someone speaks of "the way we do things here," they are referring to the corporate culture of the agency.

One often assumes that everyone, particularly managers, are savvy about organizational culture just as one

assumes everyone is politically savvy or "street smart." Indeed, culture smart is part of street smart or political savvy. Unfortunately, many managers and employees, regardless of setting, are naive about the concepts, application, or importance of organizational culture. Thus, a brief discussion about this matter is in order.

Organizational culture is the sum total of symbols, language, philosophies, traditions, rights and rituals, and unspoken gestures that overtly reflect the organization's norms and values. An organization's culture "is the customary way of thinking and behaving that is shared by all members of the organization and must be learned and adopted by newcomers before they can be accepted into the agency" (Tomey, 2000, p. 269). For the most part, these shared, and unquestioned assumptions and behaviors have a profound effect on both the organization's decision making and the staff's performance (Wilkins, 1984).

Cultural norms and values are reflected in policies and practices, social decorum, physical environment, communication networks (i.e., formal and informal), status symbols, and virtually every other aspect of the organization work life. Management style, whether authoritarian or participatory, is also part of organizational culture.

The basic assumptions that form the foundation of the culture are illuminated and understood through organizational tropes, metaphors, stories, myths, rituals, and ceremonies. A culture characterized by militaristic metaphorical expressions such as "we run a tight ship here" is quite different from one with family metaphors like "people care about each other here." Other metaphors identified by del Bueno and Vincent (1986) to characterize personalities and work styles include sports, anthropology, television, mechanics, and animals. The underlying culture of an organization can be determined by listening carefully to the tropes, metaphors, and other cultural indicators.

A successful therapeutic recreation manager identifies quickly and accepts the prevailing culture before attempting to bring about change. Organizational culture is difficult to change because it operates at the level of basic beliefs, values, and perspectives. Yet to accomplish change, the manager must understand and appreciate the prevailing culture, because it is the primary informal means of communication in the organization (Tomey, 2000).

Organizational climate, as opposed to the values and behaviors of organizational culture, is the emotional state shared by members of the organization. More specifically, it is a "measure of whether people's expectations about what it should be like to work in an organization are being met" (Schwartz & Davis, 1981, p. 31). The climate can be formal, relaxed, defensive, cautious, accepting, trusting, and so on. A work climate set at the top management level impacts the first-line manager, and in turn this determines the behavior of the staff in the department.

Staff members want a climate that will give them job satisfaction, high salaries, good working conditions, and opportunities for professional growth that increase self-esteem through self-actualization. Therapeutic recreation managers can establish this type of climate by emphasizing tasks that stimulate motivation and by using discipline fairly and uniformly to provide opportunity for committee assignments, to promote participation in decision making, and to reduce boredom and frustration (Conway-Rutkowski, 1984). In addition, a successful manager will be not only professionally competent but also organizationally acculturated.

The organizational climate and culture is also supported directly and indirectly by work rules. In addition, these rules provide assistance in motivating the employee. Liebler, Levine, and Rothman (1992, p. 222) suggested work rules serve the following functions:

- Create order and discipline so that the behavior of workers is goal oriented.

- Unify the organization by channeling and limiting behaviors.

- Give members confidence that the behavior of other members will be predictable and uniform.

- Make behavior routine so managers are free to give attention to nonroutine problems.

- Prevent harm, discomfort, and annoyance to clients.

- Ensure compliance with legislation that affects the institution as a whole.

Organizational Change

"Health care organizations are undergoing major changes because of social, consumer-related, governance, technology, and economic pressures" (Cox, 2003, p. 153). To survive, they must be focused yet flexible. Care systems must maximize efficiency and quality while controlling cost (Sullivan & Decker, 2001). Changes require modifications in technology, employees, and the work environment. Managers anticipate these modifications and become change agents who plan change within the prevailing organizational culture. As change occurs, managers realize they actually may be changing an organization's culture. As a consequence, the organizational climate is impacted.

Organizational development is long term: The focus is on constructive change in employee attitudes and values so they adopt effective behaviors to move the organization in new directions (Robbins & Decenzo, 2001). Employees may experience adjustments in their expectations, perceptions, attitudes, and motivation when their work environment is altered. Adjustments in the work environment may include job redesign, increases or decreases in the span of control, and reconfigured authority relationships. The marketplace, economic variables, and technology create the need for change and are factors within the workplace that change. Technology changes work methods, processes, and equipment. Reimbursement and fee processes change as a consequence of economic swings. Marketing addresses altered target markets to compensate for prevailing financial protocols.

Managers assume entrepreneurial roles as they orchestrate change within their units. Sullivan and Decker (2001, p. 258) believe successful change agents demonstrate the ability to

- Combine ideas and think realistically.

- Energize others and handle resistance.

- Articulate a vision and remain confident in the outcomes.

- Project the big picture yet see the details.

- Have sufficient flexibility, yet persistence enough to resist nonproductivity.

- Maintain a track record of integrity and successes with change experiences.

Organizational development, or planned change, assumes a problem-solving approach like APIE (assessment, planning, implementation, evaluation; Sullivan & Decker, 2001)—a process familiar to first-line managers. During assessment, the manager conducts an organizational audit. This includes identifying what kind of change is required, the costs and benefits of the proposed changes, and the information or data needed to address the problem or opportunity. In the planning phase, the who, how, and when of change are identified. Resources are identified to make the changes, and people are contacted who will provide feedback and evaluate progress. During implementation, the manager creates a supportive climate, provides feedback, and manages resistance to change. In the final stage, evaluation, the manager weighs the costs and benefits of each change from gathered financial and qualitative information. Although change will continue at a rapid pace, managers using the APIE process create an organizational climate in which change is stabilized.

Response to change varies from acceptance to resistance. "People tend to consider the effects of the change on their personal lives… more than on the welfare of the agency" (Tomey, 2000, p. 281). People go through the grieving process when they experience change. When people do not work through acceptance, they may disengage or withdraw, disidentify or worry and continue to do the old job, become disoriented or confused and do the wrong things, and/or become disenchanted or angry and negative and sabotage change efforts (Tomey, 2000). Causes of resistance to change may include inaccurate perceptions, low tolerance to change, insecurity, embarrassment, fear of the unknown, belief that change is not good for the organization, fear of losing something of value, and perceived loss of rewards or relationships (Robbins & Decenzo, 2001; Tomey, 2000). Resistance is both good and bad. The positive side of resistance requires the manager to clearly articulate why the change is needed. Resistance itself may motivate the group to do better what it is currently doing so it won't have to change. On the negative side, resistance can wear down the change agent and morale suffers (Sullivan & Decker, 2001). Gradual or planned change made in progressive stages is usually less disruptive than unpredicted change.

The following strategies can be used during the APIE approach to planned change or organizational development to build consensus and minimize resistance (Robbins & Decenzo, 2001; Sullivan & Decker, 2001):

- Educate and communicate with those who oppose change so they see the logic behind the change effort.

- Encourage participation of resisters and those affected by the changes, presenting both the negative and positive consequences of the change.

- Maintain a climate of trust and support by helping employees deal with their fear and anxiety associated with the change effort.

- Negotiate and remain open to revisions yet clear as to the desired outcome.

- Pace the change process according to the political climate (i.e., Don't change too much too fast).

- Build a coalition for support before commencing the change process by becoming familiar with the roles and functions of key staff in the department or organization.

Like people, departments and organizations grow and advance when there is planned change. Progress leads to evaluated outcomes. This leads to new actions or continuous quality improvement. Managers as change agents guide this process. Managers make decisions that guide the unit toward its vision. Resistance to change is reduced with appropriately timed communication and adequate feedback that builds employee confidence (Tomey, 2000).

Principles of Organizational Behavior

It is well-known that people differ in their work performance. Numerous factors have been identified as affecting individual performance in an organization, including attitude, personality, motivation, perception, learning styles, group size, and organizational support (Baron, 1983; Robbins & Decenzo, 2001; Tomey, 2000). Each of these is discussed next.

Attitude

Attitudes are mental states of readiness that exert influence on peoples' responses to others, situations, and objects (Tomey, 2000). They are value statements that reflect how people feel about something, their likes and dislikes. Managers are interested in job-related attitudes, in particular job satisfaction, job involvement, and organizational commitment (Robbins & Decenzo, 2001). People tend to seek consistency between their attitudes and behavior. This is evident when people change what they say so their behavior is not contradictory. The cognitive dissonance theory suggests that the inconsistency created by differences between attitudes and behaviors is uncomfortable so people work to reduce this dissonance. When people perceive dissonance is uncontrollable they are less likely to feel a need to change their attitude to reduce the dissonance. Likewise, when rewards like one's paycheck offset the tension created by the dissonance, individuals are less likely to feel the need to align their behavior with their responses. Positive job attitudes are generated when rewards lessen the tension created by dissonance. When employees engage in activities that appear inconsistent, like completing comprehensive assessments when clients are anticipating abbreviated intervention periods, the manager may reduce employee discomfort by reaffirming that length of stay (LOS) is controlled by reimbursers over which neither the staff member or manager has control. Attitudes, therefore, influence behavior and are close to the core of one's personality.

Personality

Each person exhibits a unique combination of relatively stable behaviors and characteristics. All personalities exhibit demographic, competency, and psychological characteristics. A manager seeks to have a blend of personalities on staff, including volunteers where possible, who will be able to interact not only with one another but also with a diverse consumer population. Persons of varied demographic characteristics (e.g., a 24-year-old single male graduate practitioner and a 55-year-old female practitioner aide and grandmother) present different developmental concerns, societal role expectations, and past experiences. These differences may enrich the lives of both staff members, or they may present obstacles to their working together. Encouraging acceptance and respect for the uniqueness of each person and emphasizing what each person can contribute to the organization and department is an essential role of the therapeutic recreation manager.

Just as people vary in demographic characteristics, they also have individual competency differences. The abilities, aptitudes, and skills of each staff member must match the tasks they are expected to perform. Frustration grows quickly if one's capabilities are overused or underused. Continuing education or training activities can be practiced and/or adopted to develop or enhance job skills, but they cannot correct for the lack of a person's ability to perform the job.

Psychological characteristics also contribute to one's personality. Values, interests, and traits provide other sources of differences among individuals. Values are belief systems about what is important. Values provide the foundation for attitudes, perceptions, and personality. They are rather stable and influence decisions and behaviors. Interests are based on likes and dislikes of different activities. Determining which activities are most relevant to the department's purpose helps the therapeutic recreation manager accurately describe the department tasks to prospective staff members. When the interests and the needs of the department's practitioners and the department's needs are congruent, work performance is enhanced. Traits are particular ways that people vary from one another; they are descriptors of the way people act or are perceived (e.g., sensitive, aggressive, self-starter).

For therapeutic recreation managers, an understanding of personality characteristics can be useful in employee selection and when trying to improve individual performance and group behavior. "Personality has been established as an important determinant in vocational interests and choices" (Jin & Austin, 2000, p. 34). The Myers-Briggs Type Indicator (MBTI) is one of the more commonly used methods to identify personalities. The MBTI is a forced-choice instrument that measures four dimensions of personality to identify 16 different personality types. The dimensions include extroversion versus introversion (EI), sensing versus intuitive (SN), thinking versus feeling (TF), and judging versus perceiving (JP). These dimensions influence the way people interact and solve problems (Robbins & Decenzo, 2001). Although results have varied, one study (Jin & Austin, 2000) identified the dominant personality types of undergraduate therapeutic recreation majors as ESFJ and ENFP. Employees must continually learn on the job. The results of evaluations like the MBTI are also useful in explaining learning styles. With this information managers design professional development programs to match employee personality characteristics.

Motivation

People employ certain behaviors to attain certain goals. Motivation derives from the needs and drives of a person. Needs are related to goals toward which behavior is directed. Staff practitioners with a high need for recognition will be most productive if their participation in department activities is recognized by the manager. If a staff practitioner is asked to coordinate a staff meeting for the purpose of clarifying patient goals and objectives because the manager is off that particular day, early recognition by the therapeutic recreation manager of this meeting and its contribution to the delivery of service will reinforce the staff practitioner's action.

Drives are directed energy. Some therapeutic recreation practitioners continually strive to be the most knowledgeable person in the department concerning the delivery of services to a particular group of consumers. If this drive is identified and responded to positively by the manager, the department can benefit from the expanded knowledge base of this practitioner. By supporting the practitioner's quest for continued education through attendance at conferences or additional course work, the therapeutic recreation manager can request that the practitioner share information with the rest of the staff through an in-service training program.

Motives cannot be directly observed; they can only be inferred. Motives may raise from curiosity, activity, or exploration. Because motives are often difficult to ascertain, therapeutic recreation managers need not focus on the reason for the behavior, but rather on the behavior itself and its results.

Therapeutic recreation managers can motivate staff by setting specific expectations, providing prompt feedback, and giving plenty of encouragement. More about motivation is found in Chapter 14.

Perception

People tend to organize the sensory input from their environment selectively into meaningful patterns. Past experience is related to the present situation. A certain amount of selective attention allows a person to fill in missing data or to simplify his or her response to a wide range of situations. Varied individual perceptions of a situation are evident when people are asked to describe an incident they witnessed. No two accounts of it will be exactly the same. There is also a certain amount of self-preservation in one's perception. The uniqueness with which each person perceives helps that person to create and to maintain a sense of order and constancy in a complex and changing world by filtering some of the sensory stimuli.

The therapeutic recreation manager must remain aware of the fact that perceptions vary from person to person. To keep perceptions fairly uniform, the manager must

- Update information
- Use written rather than verbal methods of information giving
- Repeat information periodically
- Report information in group meetings
- Encourage asking questions for clarification
- Keep minutes of meetings
- Check the minutes for accuracy

Employees react to perceptions, not to reality (Robbins & Decenzo, 2001). Employees organize and interpret what they see, consequently selecting cues that may cause them to misperceive another person, group, or object (Tomey, 2000). This selectivity leads to shortcuts in judgment. For example, we may assume others are like us because they possess one of our traits or we may judge one person on the basis of our perception of a group (i.e., stereotyping). In either situation, judgment is distorted and accuracy is compromised. Therapeutic recreation investigators have considered the influence of perceptions on workplace equity (Anderson & Bedini, 2002). Results suggest managers may reduce inequities by considering differences in perceptions between males and females on promotions and job satisfaction. When employees perceive inequities, they behave as if the condition actually exists. As a consequence, whether the manager's behavior is objective is less relevant than what the employee perceives (Robbins & Decenzo, 2001).

The more an individual disagrees with the sensory stimuli, the greater the chance for distortion of it. When a department policy is changed and announced at a staff meeting, the actual change is frequently lost. Some staff members, usually in favor of the change, may be able to articulate clearly the difference from the old and new policy requirements. However, other members, often those not in agreement with the change, may leave the meeting unable to describe the policy change and quickly forget that they are expected to change their behavior in accordance with the change in policy. To prevent this kind of discordance in perception, therapeutic recreation managers need to seek out ways to make staff perception uniform (e.g., policy changes may be presented in writing).

Learning Styles

Almost all complex behavior is learned, so a manager needs to understand how people learn to predict and explain practitioner responses (e.g., to policy changes). Likewise, to remain successful on the job, practitioners continue to learn. Therefore, a knowledge of learning styles enables therapeutic recreation managers to design training processes so practitioners gather and process information with their dominant personality characteristics.

The MBTI indicates that professionals "gather information through sensing and intuiting and process or evaluate the information through thinking and feeling" (Tomey, 2000, p. 264). Consequently, the personality type suggests how learning occurs. To illustrate, the dominant personality types of undergraduate therapeutic recreation majors, ESFJ and ENFP (Jin & Austin, 2000) are best accommodated with structured courses with clearly stated objectives and deadlines and opportunities to discuss the gathered information.

Managers desire employees to display behavior that benefits the organization. To accomplish this the manager "shapes" staff by guiding their learning using behavior strategies like reinforcement, reward, modeling, and if necessary, punishment (Robbins & Decenzo, 2001). Therapeutic recreation managers sensitive to these techniques are aware of the significance of, for example, pay increases or promotions to reward exemplary behavior. Managers should expect practitioners "to read the message they are sending and model their behavior accordingly" (Robbins & Denenzo, 2001, p. 276).

Group Size

Group size influences the possible relationships, communication patterns, and responsibility for participation in a group. Researchers have found that as the number of group members increases, so does the number of possible relationships among the members. Thus, more group members means more avenues of communication and consequently the possibility that multiple communication difficulties will arise. Large groups may inhibit member participation and may result in domination by a few and the split into subgroups. These factors can have a negative effect on the attractiveness of the group and can contribute to greater turnover and absenteeism of its members. The larger the group, the more effort needed by the manager to coordinate and organize the collective potential of membership.

There are times, however, when a large group is advantageous. Increasing group size offers more human resources and helps accomplish the group task especially when the task is complex. Small groups tend to foster more personal discussion and more active participation, but fewer people exist to share in the work responsibilities. Problem solving is handled more efficiently in groups of five to seven members because there is less chance for differences between the leader and members, less chance of domination by a few members, and less time required for reaching decisions (Megginson, Mosley & Pietri, 1992; Robbins & Decenzo, 2001). Any size group can be well-managed and can achieve a high task level performance through attention to the group process and group dynamic, and with good decision-making strategies.

Organizational Support

Work group dynamics significantly affect individual performance. Individuals may perceive their role is diminished as the responsibility to complete tasks is dispersed among group members. When individual members rely on group efforts, assuming their contributions are not being measured, the reduction in efficiency becomes a management concern. Individual performance is integral to the success of work groups and teams; yet, the development of work groups and teams is a dynamic process that impinges on the effectiveness of each of its members. The following sections discuss factors relevant to individual performance and work group dynamics.

Diversity in the Workplace

The workplace is becoming more culturally diverse each day. This diversity requires the manager to become more sensitive to the differences each individual and group brings to the work setting. Managers help staff with cultural diversity through awareness building. The manager is also ultimately responsible for organizational mission and goal statements that address diversity (Tomey, 2000). Likewise managers are responsible for clearly written policies and the provision of career development resources that support diversity and embrace sensitivity. Finally, managers are responsible for training programs that will "increase their staff members' perception of themselves as multiculturally competent and subsequently will increase the likelihood of their ability to deliver effective services to minorities" (Stone, 2003, p. 171).

Diversity is a state of difference or variety (Getz, 2002; Tomey, 2000). Culture includes all the values, inter-

ests, traits, beliefs, and attributes common to a particular group of people (Getz, 2002; Tappen, 2001). Cultural diversity refers to differences in patterns shared by the group. These shared patterns are learned and may lead to misunderstandings between people of different cultures—another reason managers address workplace diversity.

One's personality is at the center of diversity (Tomey, 2000). Other personal factors are age, gender, race, education, work experience, religion, personal habits, recreational habits, and appearance. Respect for diversity comes from acknowledging the strength that comes from these differences. A number of other differences across cultures are important to managers because they impact individual and group performance, including differences in the following (Tappen, 2001; Tomey, 2000):

- relationship to people in authority
- sense of self and space
- use of eye contact
- expressiveness
- communication and language
- mental processes and learning styles
- preferred leadership and management styles
- time and time consciousness
- work habits and practices

Managers who recognize individual differences that result from these factors are likely to respond in a way that promotes employee productivity and retention.

Cultural competence is defined as the pursuit of increasing awareness of cultures other than one's own over the life course (Getz, 2002). The health care field attracts and interacts with people from many different cultures; multiculturalism prevails at most workplaces. Gaining multicultural competence commences with preservice therapeutic recreation training programs (Getz & Austin, 2001; Stone, 2003). One study (Stone, 2003) reported "even though CTRSs self-reported moderate levels of multicultural competence, they may be in the unconsciously incompetent level, especially in the area of multicultural awareness" (p. 170). Competencies critical to multicultural education have been organized into two lists: Those that deal with the students' awareness of their own culture and their impact on others and those related to understanding of how clinical practice and communications are impacted by culture (Getz & Austin, 2001). If entry-level CTRSs are unaware of their reactions toward culturally different groups and clients (i.e., unconsciously incompetent), one approach is to commence awareness and sensitivity through embracing recommended cultural competencies in preprofessional education programs.

The challenge to managers is to recognize and celebrate differences in the workplace by addressing individual and group variances in a number of factors, such as age, religion, work experience, group size, and organizational support. Differences are descriptors of group tendencies and not predictors of individual behavior. Yet, people are born into groups each with a unique culture that affects individual and group performance.

Groups and Organizations

People are born into a group (i.e., family) and interact with others at all stages of their lives in various groups, including peer groups, work groups, focus groups, recreational groups, and religious groups. A group is a collection of two or more people interacting with and influencing one another over a period of time. People join groups for many reasons, including security, proximity, goals that would be unattainable by individual effort alone, economics, social needs, and self-esteem needs. Much of a therapeutic recreation manager's or practitioner's professional life is spent in a wide variety of groups, ranging from dyads to large professional organizations.

Groups and their performance are assuming today greater importance in modern organizations. The complexity and interactions of both technology and social systems are increasing. In various forms (e.g., matrix organizations, cross-functional teams), team effort and performance have taken on greater importance in integrated health care systems. Indeed, many organizations are consciously and deliberately moving toward organizational structures based on group concepts as a means of improving responses to an increasingly complex environment. The emphasis on quality circles and self-managed work teams in various organizations provides excellent examples (Robbins & Decenzo, 2001).

Groups usually form by the same process regardless of the type of group. Members develop a mutual acceptance of each other, discuss and experiment with decision, select a leader, develop motivation, and establish norms of operation. Each member influences, and is influenced by, the others with some degree of dependence on each other in respect to the attainment of one or more common goals.

Groups and teams appear in various forms in the work setting of an organization. Examples include ad hoc task groups, quality improvement teams, quality circles, self-directed work teams, councils, virtual teams, committees, and focus groups (Sullivan & Decker, 2001). Health and human service professionals work in close proximity and depend on each other to perform their work; therefore the quality of the interaction is vital. Consequently, understanding the nature of groups and how groups are transformed into teams is essential to the first-line therapeutic recreation manager's effectiveness.

Teams tend to outperform individuals when tasks like designing client intervention plans require judgment, experience, and multiple skills (Robbins & Decenzo, 2001). Teams are more flexible and tend to respond to changing environments better than departments. Yet managers are challenged to work with group members to identify goals, to manage conflict, and to achieve balanced relationships (Sullivan & Decker, 2001). Maintaining a positive work group climate and building a team is a complex leadership task. Understanding group behavior and dynamics promotes a positive work climate. Three major groups can be found in organizations: formal, work or task, and informal.

Formal Group

A formal group is created by the formal authority of the organization to accomplish specific goals. It is part of the formal structure of the organization and usually appears on formal organizational charts. The formal group has goals specifically created to achieve the goals of the organization and typically has clear-cut superior-subordinate relationships as opposed to meeting needs of group members. Committees and task forces are additional examples of a formal group. Traditional features of formal groups include the following (Kaluzny, Warner, Warren & Zelman, 1982):

1. Authority is imposed from above.

2. Leadership selection is assigned from above and made by an authoritative and often arbitrary order or decree.

3. Managers are symbols of power and authority.

4. The goals of the formal group are normally imposed at a much higher level than the direct leadership of the group.

5. Fiscal goals have little meaning to the members of the group.

6. Management is endangered by its aloofness from the members of the work group.

7. Behavioral norms (i.e., expected standards of behavior), regulations, and rules are usually superimposed. The larger the turnover rate of members, the greater the structuring of rules.

8. Membership in the group is only partly voluntary.

9. Rigidity of purpose is often a necessity for protection of the formal group in the pursuit of its objectives.

10. Interactions within the group as a whole are limited, but informal subgroups are generally formed.

Work or Task Group

The work or task group is created by the formal authority of an organization for a clearly defined purpose (Sullivan & Decker, 2001). Specifically, a work group is any number of people who (a) interact with one another, (b) are psychologically aware of one another, (c) perceive themselves to be a group, and (d) are motivated to participate in the group (Kaluzny, Warner, Warren & Zelman, 1982; Shortell, Kaluzny, and Associates, 1988). The work done by this group is goal-oriented and time-limited. There are usually clear specifications of the procedures or methods needed to achieve the task. In community-based leisure service agencies and health care facilities this means providing quality service according to clearly defined therapeutic recreation standards. In addition to providing quality service, therapeutic recreation work groups have other reasons for forming: to hear reports, to impart assignments, to solve consumer problems, or to engage in committee activities.

The work group enables organizations and their members to accomplish things that individuals cannot do alone. A group can pool resources, divide responsibility, represent more interest in a decision, and may provide better communication. Schermerhorn, Hunt, and Osborn (1982) described the work group as created by a formal authority to transform inputs (e.g., ideas, materials, objects) into outputs (e.g., report, decision, service). Some of these groups are permanent (e.g., therapeutic recreation department, standing committees), while others are temporary (e.g., ad hoc or task forces) and usually dissolve after the group has accomplished its task. Permanent or standing committees are usually advisory in authority, but some may have collective authority to make and implement decisions.

According to Schermerhorn, Hunt, and Osborn (1982), an effective work group is one that achieves high levels of both task performance and human resource maintenance overtime. A number of forces or dynamics facilitate the effectiveness of the work group (e.g., purpose, norms, status, role). And group dynamics affect task performance and membership satisfaction as well.

While work groups have advantages, they also have disadvantages. The division of responsibility may be considered a disadvantage in many situations because there is no place to assign blame. Groups may successfully avoid action. Most group decisions are compromises; therefore, they are neither the best nor the worst decision that could be obtained. Often a group assumes no responsibility for decisions or actions. A group may engender a false sense of democracy in the organization, especially when it is dominated by a powerful chairperson. Last, groups within an organization may be in conflict. The limit to available resources, a difference in goals, a failure to clearly define tasks, and a false perception of the role of the group may lead directly to conflict within the group and between groups.

Informal Group

The informal group is a group formed by coworkers to satisfy their own personal needs. Its major difference from the formal group is that the informal group is not created by the formal authority. In a strict sense, informal group activity constitutes those activities not officially sanctioned in any organization policy or manual. The informal group affords its members a sense of affiliation, emotional support, identification, belonging, and security. Moreover, the informal group develops its own communication network known as the "grapevine," which is outside the formal communication channel designed by management. As noted by Mayo (1933), research showed that the lack of opportunity for social contact resulted in employees experiencing a loss of self-esteem and perceiving their jobs as unsatisfying.

The informal group can serve to complement the formal organization by generating optimal task performance and productivity and by giving social values and stability to the workplace. The informal group can also have negative and more destructive effects on the organization when it works directly in opposition to the organization's goals and objectives and creates only negative conflict that affects group task performance and productivity.

The astute therapeutic recreation manager needs to become familiar with these effects to gain a better understanding of how the informal group operates in relation to the formal organization and to one's own department. In all cases, the formal structure must prevail; the informal group should always complement and assist the effort of the formal group.

Group Development

Groups, whether formal or informal typically go through stages of development. "They typically form, organize, solve problems, implement solutions, and disband" (Tomey, 2000, p. 318). Like individuals, not every group achieves maturity nor does it complete the tasks of one stage prior to moving to the next stage. Some groups terminate before they have progressed through all the stages (Tappen, 2001). The model of small group development (Tuckman, 1965; Tuckman & Jensen, 1977) identifies the stages of growth as forming, storming, norming, performing, and re-forming/adjourning.

Forming

In this stage individuals first come together and form initial impressions. They begin by determining the task of the group, although some purposes, objectives, and goals may already have been set by management. In addition, individuals try to determine role expectations of one another. Because group members are unsure of their roles, considerable attention is given to the leader in establishing the agenda (Sullivan & Decker, 2001). The stage is complete when individuals begin to perceive themselves as group members.

Storming

In the second stage individuals begin to express themselves about goal setting, who is responsible for what, and a standard of behavior. It is not unusual for conflict among group members to arise. Members accept the existence of the group yet resist the control the group imposes on individuality. Informed leadership emerges as members compete for power and status. The manager helps the group acknowledge the conflict and resolve it in a win-win situation (Sullivan & Decker, 2001). This stage is complete when relatively clear leadership emerges.

Norming

This stage is viewed as sharing group norms. In other words, teamwork begins to develop; there is a sense of group cohesiveness and openness of communications with information sharing. Trust and cooperation develop and goals and standards by which the group will operate are finalized. The manager interprets standards of performance and encourages consensus building. Decisions are made about what has to be done and who will do it. If problems continue to exist or are carried over from any of the earlier stages, progress to the next stage will be slow, if at all. If the group is maturing, by the end of this stage group members feel a sense of progress and have assimilated a common set of expectations of appropriate work behavior (Robbins & Decenzo, 2001).

Performing

This is the most productive stage in group development. There is a stable pattern of personal interaction, joint problem solving and shared leadership including achievement of goals and objectives. The group's energy becomes task-oriented. The group has reached maturity. The manager gives feedback on work effort, and, if necessary, critiques poor work and takes steps to improve performance.

Re-forming/Adjourning

Some work groups continue indefinitely while others have a specific time-limited purpose and are dissolved after this purpose is achieved. Those that are indefinite may be re-formed to accomplish new goals or to accommodate changes in the work environment; as a consequence, the group refocuses its activities and recycles through the previous four stages. When a group adjourns, the manager helps the group to summarize the activities that occurred over the life of the group, and assists in the evaluation of the group process and the degree to which the group achieved its purpose. When a group reforms, the manager explains the new direction and provides guidance as the group redevelops to accomplish new tasks.

A mature group develops over time with the careful interventions of the manager. Regardless of the stage of group development, affirmative action on the part of the therapeutic recreation manager helps to develop the kind of member participation that ensures a high level of group productivity and member satisfaction.

Group Dynamics

How the group functions, communicates, and interacts to achieve its goals relate to group dynamics. Effectiveness of the group is influenced by group rank, group status, group role, group norms, and group cohesiveness (Shaw, 1971).

Group Rank

When an individual joins a group, he or she will be implicitly evaluated by the other group members. This is called *group rank*, or the position of a group member relative to the evaluation of other members of the group. The rank order can influence an individual's behavior in a group by affecting (a) the member's interactions with other group members, (b) the individual's level of aspiration, and (c) the individual's self-evaluation. All of these can combine to affect the group member's ability to perform the task assigned to him or her in the group.

Group members rank each other on a variety of characteristics, including intelligence, verbal performance, and popularity. The first-line therapeutic recreation manager as a group leader should be aware that all group members, including the group leader, will be evaluating each other throughout the life of the group and that this evaluation can affect the group member's and the group's work. It is important to note that the manager as group leader may rank a member high on a particular characteristic, but this member may not rank high on this same characteristic according to other group members. Being aware of the group rank dynamic can help the manager to avoid communication problems that affect the group's work.

Group Status

Group status is the prestige attributed to particular positions in the group. Cohen, Fink, Gadon, and Willitis (1988) described status as a collection of rights and duties. A group member can bring status into the group from outside or can be assigned status as a result of behavior within the group. Status can be based on a number of characteristics, such as age, work seniority, past positions held within the organization, performance in the group, and education. Status congruence occurs when a group member's standing in each factor is consistent with the standing in other factors. When standings vary among factors, status incongruity occurs. Status incongruity can affect individual and group performance because members that experience a range of status incongruities are not sure how to react to it. Because status is a significant motivator and has behavioral consequences, status incongruities can pose challenges to department managers who want to assure group effectiveness. The following is an example of status incongruity.

An assistant therapeutic recreation manager position is available in a large staff therapeutic recreation department in a general medical hospital. One applicant has been working in the department for only a short time in the psychiatric unit. However, the applicant had leadership positions in two previous jobs in other hospitals. In addition, the applicant has advanced education. The incongruities among these factors can pose questions in the minds of the staff as to how best to react to these inconsistencies if a new (or different) applicant is appointed to this position. Some staff may find it is difficult to work with this. It might be helpful for the manager and/or the committee choosing the assistant to arrange an interview with some staff representatives and this applicant so that the staff can discuss with the applicant some of the questions or concerns.

Group Role

A group role is the function a person assumes as a member of a group. It is often referred to as the part a person plays in a group. Role and status can be viewed as inseparable; role is the dynamic aspect of status that operationalizes the rights and duties granted by other group members. Role is often referred to as the set of expectations that group members share concerning the behavior of a person who occupies a given position in a group (Sullivan & Decker, 2001). A role acted out by a group member may or may not be useful for the task. Further, an individual in a group receives multiple role expectations and occupies multiple roles. It is important for all group members to develop role flexibility, skill, and security in a wide range of roles as well as an awareness of those roles that negatively affect the work of the group.

A broad range of group task roles are assumed by members who attempt to coordinate the group's efforts to remain focused and implement strategies to resolve problems. A number of authors have categorized the following positive task roles that promote group functioning (Benne & Sheats, 1984, p. 47; Sullivan & Decker, 2001, p. 240; Tappen, 2001, p. 126; Tomey, 2000, p. 317):

- *Initiator-Contributor:* suggests new ideas
- *Information Seeker:* clarifies suggestions
- *Opinion Seeker:* clarifies values
- *Information Giver:* offers facts or generalizations
- *Opinion Giver:* states beliefs or opinions
- *Elaborator:* spells out suggestions
- *Coordinator:* clarifies relationships
- *Orienter:* summarizes what has occurred
- *Evaluator-Critic:* evaluates the logic of group discussion
- *Energizer:* prods group interaction
- *Procedural Technician:* does things for group
- *Recorder:* writes down suggestions

Group maintenance roles nurture and facilitate group functioning and interpersonal needs. These positive roles focus on how group members treat each other as the task is accomplished and include the following (Benne & Sheats, 1984, p. 47; Sullivan & Decker, 2001, p. 240; Tappen, 2001, p. 126; Tomey, 2000, p. 317):

- *Encourager:* praises contributions of others
- *Harmonizer:* mediates differences between members
- *Compromiser:* offers compromise by coming "halfway"
- *Gatekeeper:* tries to keep communication channels open
- *Standard Setter:* applies standards to group
- *Group Observer:* keeps records of group process
- *Follower:* goes along with group movement

Any positive role taken too far can have a negative impact on the group. Individuals may attempt to satisfy their own needs irrespective of the group task and maintenance roles. Roles that have an inhibiting effect on groups include the following (Benne & Sheats, 1984, p. 49; Jordan, 2001, pp. 92–93; Tappen, 2001, p. 126; Tomey, 2000, p. 318):

- *Aggressor:* disapproves, deflates status of others
- *Blocker:* is resistant and negative

- *Recognition Seeker:* calls attention to self

- *Self-Confessor:* uses group as an audience to express personal feelings

- *Playboy:* exhibits general lack of involvement

- *Dominator:* tries to control groups

- *Help Seeker:* tries to provoke sympathy response from group members

- *Special Interest Pleader:* states biases in his or her own stereotypic fashion

Because the group leader can assume any or all of these roles, the therapeutic recreation manager should become familiar with those roles that have a more facilitating or vitalizing effect on the group's task or functioning and should strive to assume more of those positive roles. If a therapeutic recreation manager has an awareness of the roles that inhibit a group's work and are irrelevant to the group task and functioning, the manager can begin to create some sort of harmony within the group.

Group Norms

Group norms are the organized and largely shared unwritten rules or ideas that evolve in every group and determine the behavior of the group. They also function to regulate the performance of a group as an organized department. The collective will of a group determines its group norms. Norms dictate output levels, amount of socializing allowed on the job, dress, loyalty, and levels of effort and performance (Robbins & Decenzo, 2001). The norms adopted by the group are many and can be both positive and negative. A manager wants the group to acquire norms supportive of organizational goals.

The performance norm is especially important for the work group. Members of a group with a positive performance norm give the best they can to a task or project, always striving for success. Group members with a negative performance norm may do just enough work to get by and may have an attitude of "not really caring" if they fail or if a project does not turn out well. Other group norms especially important for the work group include the adaptation or change norm, the interaction-communication norm, and the leadership-support norm. Researchers report that work groups with more positive norms tend to be more successful in accomplishing organizational objectives than groups with more negative norms (Heidman & Hornstein, 1982; Homans, 1961).

Conformity to norms is strongly influenced by group cohesiveness. In a highly cohesive group there is strong conformity to group norms. Therapeutic recreation managers as group leaders can help groups build positive norms. The following are ways to influence positive norm

building (Heidman & Hornstein, 1982; Homans, 1961; Napier & Gershenfeld, 1973):

- Emphasize positive role modeling.

- Reward desired behavior.

- Give regular feedback and performance reviews.

- Work with new group members to adopt desired behavior.

- Include desired behaviors in group member selection criteria.

- Hold regular meetings to look specifically at task performance and member satisfaction.

- Utilize group decision making to agree on desired behaviors.

Group Cohesiveness

Group cohesiveness is the end result of all the forces operating in a group that motivate members to remain or to leave the group. It is often referred to as group "we-ness" or the amount of "group-ness." "The more the members are attracted to one another and the more the group's goals align with their individual goals, the greater the group's cohesiveness" (Robbins & Decenzo, 2001, p. 280). Group cohesion can be viewed as an "organizing" force that contributes to overall group potency and vitality. This cohesive force increases the significance of membership for those who belong. When a person is attracted to a group, he or she is motivated to behave in accordance with the wishes of other group members. Important characteristics of high cohesive groups include the following: trust among members, high group productivity, group satisfaction with work, tasks accepted readily, more group energy for projects, commitment to group goals, high member interaction, low turnover, and promptness (Homans, 1950, 1961; Sullivan & Decker, 2001).

According to Homans (1950, 1961) the therapeutic recreation manager can employ the following methods to build a cohesive group:

- Induce agreement on group goals.

- Increase member homogeneity.

- Support member interactions.

- Introduce competition with other groups.

- Provide groups with individual rewards and praise.

- Decrease group size.

On the other hand, examples of how the therapeutic recreation manager could help decrease group cohesion include the following:

- Induce disagreement on group goals.

- Increase member heterogeneity.

- Inhibit interaction among staff.

- Provide individual awards and praise.

- Remove physical isolation.

- Enlarge group size.

- Introduce a dominating staff member.

- Disband the group.

When a group is highly cohesive, there is greater conformity to group norms. Also, when the performance norm of a highly cohesive group is high, there is a positive effect on task performance and productivity. In this case increased conformity to the group norm serves the organization well (Cartwright & Zander, 1968). Sometimes a group will be congenial, agree on goals, and feel like a team yet fail in its mission. In such instances, what may have caused the failure is a phenomenon called *groupthink*. This factor is examined in the next section.

Groupthink

The groupthink phenomenon occurs when highly cohesive groups lose criteria evaluative capabilities for one another's ideas and suggestions (Janis, 1982). The group no longer becomes willing to disagree or appraise alternative courses of action when problem solving. "Members either abandon or suppress their own views, and uncritically accept the prevailing attitude or overidentify with either the leader or the group" (Tappen, 2001, p. 108). Loyalty and unity norms are weak when members become unable to challenge each other. Groupthink is often referred to in the literature as negative cohesion, and it has a negative influence on decision making in the group. Highly cohesive groups can be conducive to groupthink except when certain conditions are present, or special precautions are taken to counteract the group's push for unanimous agreement.

Irving Janis (1968) is known for describing the following eight main symptoms of the groupthink phenomenon:

1. The group experiences an illusion of invulnerability that promotes excessive risk taking, optimism, and confidence in the group's work.

2. The group makes collective efforts to rationalize its decisions stopping any warnings that might promote reconsideration of other assumptions.

3. The group unquestionably believes its morality and does not address ethical and moral consequences of the decision.

4. All group members look at any possible opposing factions in a stereotypical way, as being too weak or stupid to challenge the group's decision.

5. Group members put strong, direct pressure on any dissenters in the group, forcing a hard (or solid) loyalty norm.

6. Each group member self-censors any of his or her own doubts or objections.

7. The group members share the illusion that all decisions and judgments are unanimous; the group relies on consensual validation versus individual thinking or reality testing.

8. "Mindguards" emerge from the group who serve to protect everyone from thoughts that might present opposing views and that question the group's morality or effectiveness.

Therapeutic recreation managers as leaders of a variety of groups are in a key position to identify a group's movement toward the groupthink phenomenon. A manager can ask the following questions when suspecting groupthink according to Janis (1968):

1. Do I, as the group leader, cause members to "fall into line" with my way of thinking thereby strongly influencing their decision making?

2. Are there discussions of any opposing views or possibilities?

3. Is the group able to look at the advantages and disadvantages of any decision?

4. Are objectors or opposing views tolerated by the group?

5. Is decision making rushed or do group members take time to reach a decision?

6. Does the group feel overly confident with its decision making?

7. Are various ideas criticized or pulled apart?

8. Does the group look at the possible consequences of its decisions?

9. Does the group reach a decision too easily with a general consensus?

Several means to decrease groupthink by the therapeutic recreation manager have also been described in the literature (Janis, 1982; Tappen, 2001), including the following:

1. Give priority to verbalizing objections while assigning each group member the role of critical evaluator.

2. Remain impartial about own preferences and expectations, especially at onset.

3. Encourage group members to discuss periodically the group's deliberations with two trusted associates and report back.

4. Invite outside qualified experts into the group periodically.

5. Promote a collegial environment, support people who dare to disagree, and encourage critically reflective thinking.

A final note about groupthink. It is important for the therapeutic recreation manager to understand that conflict is not always dysfunctional and dissent must be allowed if good decisions are to be made.

The next section addresses specific behaviors within groups and suggests both a philosophy and first-line manager activities to promote effective behavior within groups.

Affirmative Action in Groups

Activities most beneficial in groups can be categorized as (a) information gathering, (b) discussion, (c) problem solving, (d) making and implementing decisions, and (e) evaluating the outcome of the group's work (Cartwright & Zander, 1968).

The therapeutic recreation manager needs to monitor the information flow within the group—who introduces new information, how it is received by the staff, and what action follows it can be indicative of the maturity of the group. The manager can check the facts with the staff and supply missing or misconstrued data.

Closely related to information gathering is the kind and amount of discussion that takes place within the group. For example, are staff freely exchanging their ideas, or are they exchanging glances? Does discussion of a topic cease after one staff member speaks, or is a topic fully explored by those present? The manager can help the group become conscious of topic hopping if it continues for a few minutes.

Modeling behavior helps the group to become aware of its own behavior and to move on to address less obvious issues that are blocking the group.

Problem solving is a significant task of most work groups. The manager must be sure the group is given problems it has the capability, capacity, and authority to solve. Groups will soon learn if their solutions are taken seriously. If they are not, the group will either stop participating in the process or offer hastily considered solutions just to be done with the process. Decision making requires much forethought on the part of the manager before the group is asked to participate in the decision-making process. Managers must be willing to abide by the group's decision even if it is different from their own. Groups become frustrated when asked to participate in a decision only to find themselves trying to guess what their manager wants. This behavior promotes distrust and apathy in the group. Staff can learn to live with an autocratic therapeutic recreation manager more easily than a so-called participative manager who changes the decision after the staff is dismissed (Maier, 1967).

While a manager may not agree with the group's decision, if the manager has delegated decision-making responsibility to the staff, he or she must abide by the decision. Abrupt changes by the manager who favors a different approach will negate effective functioning of the group. If the decision presents a serious problem, the manager is bound by the group process to take the issue back to the group for further discussion. However, a wise therapeutic recreation manager will not use this mode of action too often, or the group will refrain from decision making.

Once a decision has been made, all staff should be aware of when and how the decision will be implemented and by whom. When these details are left vague, confusion and a delayed implementation of the decision occurs at best. Poorly implemented decisions often lead group members to grumble that "nothing ever changes," or "I'm not going to waste my time trying to make changes." Routine evaluations of the outcomes of the group's work helps everyone to see how the organization or department is developing and how they can learn from mistakes, and it allows them to feel appreciated for fruitful efforts. Further discussion of decision making and group process will address some of the guidelines and factors facilitating group decision making (see Chapter 10).

Effective groups do not just happen—they emerge as the therapeutic recreation manager and members share common goals, communicate openly, make mutual decisions, engage in ongoing feedback, and share leadership roles congruent with situational and group needs. In effective, mature groups, each employee's talents are used and the diversity among group members is appreciated. The effective manager thinks in terms of the group as a whole while recognizing each member's performance is unique yet influenced by group participation. The astute manager is aware of the qualities of effective and ineffective groups (see Table 5.1). Productivity and worker satisfaction are increased with group cohesiveness and alignment between the group's and organization's goals.

Group Meetings

The therapeutic recreation manager will participate in a variety of conferences, committee meetings, and department meetings. Conferences are usually one-time affairs, held for a limited time and dealing with a specific topic or problem. Committees are relatively permanent groups with organizational sanction. They are usually directed toward a specific purpose or task, have some mechanism for selecting members, and have authority to make recommendations or decisions. Both types of groups involve persons representing several units or departments.

A number of characteristics influence the nature and effectiveness of small group communication. For instance, the status and authority of each member in relation to the other, his or her past experiences together and current relationships both individual and as a group, and the expectations and preconceptions he or she has of each other will influence the communication patterns they use. Second, the structure of the group imposes certain patterns of interaction. Time and place characteristics are additional determinants of communication (see Chapter 13). A final characteristic is the expertise of each member in relation to the assigned task. Department meetings are similar to committee meetings. Most organizations expect their various departments to have staff meetings. These meetings are broader in scope than committee meetings and have authority to make recommendations and decisions concerning the function of the department.

Agendas are essential for conducting efficient meetings. They allow group members to prepare for meetings and ensure that all necessary items are addressed. Whether conducting a committee meeting or a department meeting the following steps are important (Davis, Skube, Hellervik, Gebelein & Sheard, 1992):

- Prepare an agenda in advance and distribute it to those who will be attending. This enables participants to gather materials, if needed, and to be prepared for any discussion.

- State the purpose of the meeting at the top of the agenda.

- State a definite start and stop time for the meeting and stick with it.

- Structure a content and process agenda and determine the type of process and action desired on each agenda item. One is likely to have "information only," "decision only," and "decision required" items.

- Set priorities for each agenda item so that group members focus on addressing the most important items.

- Determine the order of the agenda items. Place important items toward the beginning of the agenda.

- Establish time limits on items by deciding on an approximate amount of time to be spent on each agenda item. On "decision required" items acknowledge when the time limit has been reached; then ask the group to decide whether and how to continue with these items.

- Appoint a recorder who will take minutes and monitor time.

- Express concern if the group is straying from the agenda.

- Take a few minutes at end of meeting to "process" the meeting and discuss what went well, what problems came up, and what can be done about the ways in which the group works together.

- Follow up by distributing copies of meeting minutes including reminders about assignments and deadlines to all persons who attended.

One key to successful meetings is preparation of the agenda and structure of the meeting. A second is management of meeting stakeholders. The attendees should include the fewest number of participants who have the skills and knowledge to represent those affected by the decisions. The manager helps attendees to understand they share responsibility for successful meetings by arriving on time, stating disagreement openly or revealing hidden agendas, and implementing decisions following the meeting. Meeting effectiveness is increased when the manager periodically summarizes the group's progress, facilitates reconciliation of openly discussed disagreements, and ensures that hidden agendas either contribute positively to group performance or are neutralized (Sullivan & Decker, 2001).

Teams

Considerable emphasis in recent years has been placed on self-managed teams in the workplace. McHenry (1994) suggested that self-managed teams are a "tool for the 21st century workplace" (p. 801). It is argued that individuals

Table 5.1
Comparative Features of Effective and Ineffective Groups

Factors	Effective Groups	Ineffective Groups
Atmosphere	Informal, comfortable, and relaxed. It is a working atmosphere in which people demonstrate their interest and involvement.	Obviously tense. Signs of boredom may appear.
Goal setting	Goals, tasks, and objectives are clarified, understood, and modified so that members of the group can commit themselves to cooperatively structured goals.	Unclear, misunderstood, or imposed goals may be accepted by members. The goals are competitively structured.
Leadership and member participation	Shift from time to time, depending on the circumstances. Different members assume leadership at various times, because of their knowledge or experience.	Delegated and based on authority. The chairperson may dominate the group, or the members may defer unduly. Members' participation is unequal, with high-authority members dominating.
Goal emphasis	All three functions of groups are emphasized: goal accomplishment, internal maintenance, and developmental change.	One or more functions may not be emphasized.
Communication	Open and two-way. Ideas and feelings are encouraged, both about the problem and about the group's operation.	Closed or one-way. Only the production of ideas is encouraged. Feelings are ignored or taboo. Members may be tentative or reluctant to be open and may have "hidden agendas" (personal goals at cross-purposes with group goals.)
Decision making	By consensus, although various decision-making procedures appropriate to the situation may be instituted.	By the highest authority in the group, with minimal involvement by members; or an inflexible style is imposed.
Cohesion	Facilitated through high levels of inclusion, trust, liking, and support.	Either ignored or used as a means of controlling members, thus promoting rigid conformity.
Conflict tolerance	High. The reasons for disagreements or conflicts are carefully examined, and the group seeks to resolve them. The group accepts unresolvable basic disagreements and lives with them.	Low. Attempts may be made to ignore, deny, avoid, suppress, or override controversy by premature group action.
Power	Determined by the members' abilities and the information they possess. Power is shared. The issue is how to get the job done.	Determined by position in the group. Obedience to authority is strong. The issue is who controls.
Problem solving	High. Constructive criticism is frequent, frank, relatively comfortable, and oriented toward removing an obstacle to problem solving.	Low. Criticism may be destructive, taking the form of either overt or covert personal attacks. It prevents the group from getting the job done.
Self-evaluation as a group	Frequent. All members participate in evaluation and decisions about how to improve the group's functioning.	Minimal. What little evaluation there is may be done by the highest authority in the group rather than by the membership as a whole.
Creativity	Encouraged. There is room within the group for members to become self-actualized and interpersonally effective.	Discouraged. People are afraid of appearing foolish if they put forth a creative thought.

working as a team can bring results that surpass in quantity and quality the contributions of individuals working independently. According to Katzenbach and Smith (1993) teams are the key to improving performance. They further commented that organizations cannot meet the challenges from total quality to customer service without teams. To remain competitive in today's marketplace, the survival of health care systems depends on their ability to respond quickly to client needs with high-quality care and reduced length of stay (Rudan, 2003). The primary building block of reengineered organizations is the establishment of teams to supplant individuals as the fundamental work unit. "Through teamwork, organizations are able to focus on integrative work processes rather than on fragmentation of work through tasks" (Rudan, 2003, p. 179). Diversity in work teams is a relatively new concept, as the arrival of the 21st century saw pieces of the workplace pie shared by men, women, and persons with varying worldviews. "Managing diversity on teams is a balancing act" (Robbins & Decenzo, 2001, p. 303). New perspectives are brought to the team yet the manager is challenged to facilitate team efforts to reach agreement.

The implementation of self-managed teams within health and human service organizations has been primarily associated with total quality management (TQM) and other employee involvement practices wherein the work relationships are interdependent (e.g., nursing service, psychiatric unit, physical rehabilitation unit). Therapeutic recreation managers and practitioners are involved as members of TQM or continuous quality improvement (CQI) teams, which focus on improving quality and consumer satisfaction as well as being members of various unit treatment teams (Shank & Coyle, 2002). Accreditation standards require comprehensive intervention plans that incorporate the work of all clinical professionals into one integrated care document. This usually occurs through team effort.

Although there is similarity in the development process of groups and teams (Smith & Hukill, 1994; Tuckman, 1965; Tuckman & Jensen, 1977), there are differences in the goals and functions of work groups and work teams (Robbins & Decenzo, 2001; Tomey, 2000; refer to Tables 5.2 and 5.3). Work groups interact to share information and to make decisions that will help each staff member independently perform their duties. Teams, on the other hand, generate positive synergy through coordinating their efforts. This results in performance levels greater than the sum of each individual's efforts. Thus, through teams

Table 5.2
Summary of Stages of Team Development

Stage	Team Behaviors	Leadership Behaviors
Orientation	• Uncertainty • Unfamiliarity • Mistrust • Nonparticipator	• Directive style • Outline purpose • Negotiate schedules • Define the team's mission
Forming	• Acceptance of each other • Learning communication skills • High energy, motivated	• Plan/focus on the problem • Positive role modeling • Actively encourage participation
Storming	• Team spirit developed • Trust developed • Conflict may arise • Impatience, frustration	• Evaluate group dynamics • Focus on goals • Conflict resolution • Establish goals and objectives
Norming	• Increased comfort • Identify responsibilities • Effective team interaction • Resolution of conflicts	• Focus on goals • Attend to process and content • Supportive style
Performing	• Clear on purpose • Unity/cohesion • Problem solve and accept actions	• Act as a team member • Encourage increased responsibility • Follow up on action plans • Measure results
Terminating	• Members separate • Team gains closure on objectives	• Reinforce successes • Celebrate and reward

Source: Smith, G. B, and Hukill, E. H. (1994). Quality work improvement groups: From paper to reality. *Nursing Care Quality, 8*(4), 1–12. Reproduced with permission of *Journal of Nursing Care and Quality,* Lippincott, Williams & Wilkins/WoltersKluwer Health.

integrative work processes result in more efficient and responsive client care.

People-oriented and goal-directed organizational cultures are conducive to team development (Tomey, 2000). Effective teams possess a number of qualities, including the following (Robbins & Decenzo, 2001; Sullivan & Decker, 2001; Tomey, 2000):

- a clear sense of direction and understanding of their team goals

- relevant technical and interpersonal skills

- high mutual trust and collegiality among members

- unified commitment to the team

- open and effective communication skills and negotiation skills

- supportive internal and external environment and relationships

- effective leadership and efficient operating procedures

Effective managers can motivate teams to undertake even the most difficult quality improvement responsibilities. The manager assumes the role of a coach or facilitator, guiding and supporting efforts. Additionally, the manager encourages development of self-managing teams by training and educating team members, acquiring resources, allowing processing time, protecting the team from political obstacles, and recognizing member contributions (Tomey, 2000).

The manager faces a number of challenges as teams are created and used in health care settings. The challenge of creating team players in a highly individualistic culture or an established organization that rewards individual per-

formance may be evident. To perform well as team members, individuals must "place lower priority on personal goals for the good of the team" (Robbins & Decenzo, 2001, p. 297). This emphasis may counter their views of work and life (e.g., individual rather than collective values of teamwork). Another concern when teams operate within departments is that department managers' responsibilities are absorbed within the team. Diversity in the workplace leads to another challenge. Diversity provides fresh perspectives yet may result in the team taking more time to reach agreement (Robbins & Decenzo, 2001; Tappen, 2001). A diverse team may spend more time discussing issues yet the chance decreases that a weak alternative is chosen.

In general, employees that have moved into self-managed teams are better satisfied and quality is improved. It is incumbent on the manager to articulate the challenges as well as the benefits of using self-managed teams to promote continuous improvements and more efficiently manage client intervention plans. Teams are a natural way "for employees to share ideas and implement improvements" (Robbins & Decenzo, 2001, p. 302). When team members' skills complement each others' expertise complex situations are addressed through more comprehensive care. Efforts of one team member reinforce others resulting in a synergy that contributes to a highly motivated and committed group of people producing high-quality work (Tappen, 2001; Tomey, 2000). In the end, a positive work climate is created.

Summary

Organizational culture is the customary way of behaving in an organization, whereas organizational climate is the emotional state shared by members of the organization. Managers guide planned change or organizational development as they respond to economic exigencies. Changes in the work environment, technology, and employees impact organizational culture and climate. People differ in their work performance and a number of factors affect individual performances. They include attitude, personality, motivation, perception, learning styles, group size, and organizational support. The workplace is becoming more culturally diverse. Managers assume a variety of responsibilities as they create an environment and uphold policies that embrace awareness and sensitivity of differences that affect individual and group performance.

Groups appear in various forms in the work setting of an organization. Three major groups are usually found in the organization: formal, informal, and work groups. The formal group is created by the formal authority of the organization, whereas the informal group is formed

Table 5.3
Differences Between Groups and Teams

Groups	Teams
Sharing of information goals	Collective performance
Varied and random skills	Complementary skills
Individual accountability	Individual and mutual accountability
Neutral energy	Synergy
Appointed or elected leadership	Shared leadership
Delegation of responsibility	Shared responsibility

Sources: Robbins and Decenzo, 2001; Tomey, 2000

by people who work together mainly to meet the social needs of its members. The work group is created by a formal authority for a clearly defined purpose. It is goal-directed and reality-oriented. Work groups can be permanent or temporary.

Group development occurs in stages (i.e., forming, storming, norming, performing, and re-forming/adjourning); the nature of group functioning varies with the stage of maturity reached.

Several dynamics affect work group effectiveness, including group rank, group status, group roles, group cohesiveness, and group norms. Characteristics associated with each group were identified by listing the roles that function to enhance the group task and promote group functioning as well as those roles that inhibit effective group task.

Consideration was also given to groupthink, a phenomenon that occurs when highly cohesive groups lose their ability to evaluate critically one another's ideas and suggestions. Symptoms of the groupthink phenomenon were identified.

The mature work group is characterized by a shared sense of ownership of the group. The therapeutic recreation manager can encourage a high level of group productivity and staff satisfaction by engaging in affirmative actions, which include information gathering, discussion, problem solving, decision making, and evaluation of outcomes.

Last, consideration was given to self-managed teams, which in the opinion of some authors surpass the contribution of individuals working independently. Qualities associated with teams as well as the role and responsibilities of the manager were identified. In addition, challenges associated with teams were noted.

It may be concluded from this chapter that an awareness of behavior and its effect on an individual or a group within an organization or department helps the therapeutic recreation manager to anticipate and predict reactions to particular activities and situations.

Review Questions

1. Consider a setting wherein a therapeutic recreation department exists. What cultural factors lead to managerial effectiveness?

2. Compare and contrast formal groups with informal groups. Is leadership important in both types? Why or why not?

3. If groups have so many limitations (i.e., ineffective), why are they so popular?

4. As a therapeutic recreation manager for a division or department, regardless of setting, how would you deal with an informal leader in a work or task group who seems to be totally opposed to the objectives of the task group?

5. Identify conditions within a health care facility where self-managed work teams would not be the way to organize, and vice versa.

6. Identify some typical tendencies in perception. Does any one apply to you? What are the implications for your everyday life? How can you guard against perceptual fallacies?

7. Consider the impact of diversity and change on the organization culture and climate. What steps can managers take to enhance the work environment and benefit from each employee's perspective?

References

Anderson, D. M. and Bedini, L. A. (2002). Perceptions of workplace equity of therapeutic recreation professionals. *Therapeutic Recreation Journal, 36*(3), 260–281.

Baron, R. A. (1983). *Behavior in organizations: Understanding and managing the human side of work.* Boston, MA: Allyn & Bacon.

Benne, K. and Sheats, P. (1984, Spring). Functional roles of group members. *Journal of Social Issues*, 42–49.

Cartwright, D. and Zander, A. (1968). *Group dynamics* (3rd ed.). New York, NY: Harper & Row.

Cohen, A. R., Fink, S. L., Gadon, H., and Willitis, R. D. (1988). *Effective behavior in organizations.* Homewood, IL: Irwin.

Conway-Rutkowski, B. (1984, February). Labor relations: How do you rate? *Nursing Management*, 13–16.

Cox, K. B. (2003). The effects of intrapersonal, intragroup, and intergroup conflict on team performance effectiveness and work satisfaction. *Nursing Administration Quarterly, 27*(2), 153–163.

Davis, B. L., Skube, C. J., Hellervik, L. W., Gebelein, S. H., and Sheard, J. L. (1992). *Successful manager's handbook.* Minneapolis, MN: Personnel Decisions.

del Bueno, D. J. and Vincent, P. M. (1986, May/June). Organizational culture: How important is it? *Journal of Nursing Administration*, 7–21.

Getz, D. (2002). Increasing cultural competence in therapeutic recreation. In D. R. Austin, J. Dattilo, and B. P. McCormick (Eds.), *Conceptual foundations for therapeutic recreation* (pp. 151–164). State College, PA: Venture Publishing.

Getz, D. A. and Austin, D. R. (2001). Key competencies in multicultural education for entry-level therapeutic recreation professionals. In B. Riley (Ed.), *Annual in therapeutic recreation* (Vol. 10, pp. 23–31). Alexandria, VA: American Therapeutic Recreation Association.

Heidman, M. E. and Hornstein, H. A. (1982). *Managing human forces in organizations.* Homewood, IL: Irwin.

Homans, G. C. (1950). *The human group.* New York, NY: Harcourt Brace Jovanovich.

Homans, G. C. (1961). *Social behavior: Its elementary forms.* New York, NY: Harcourt Brace Jovanovich.

Janis, I. L. (1968). *Victims of groupthink.* Boston, MA: Houghton Mifflin.

Janis, I. L. (1982). *Groupthink: Psychological studies of policy decisions and fiascos* (2nd ed.). Boston, MA: Houghton Mifflin.

Jin, B. and Austin, D. R. (2000). Personality types of therapeutic recreation students based on the MBTI. *Therapeutic Recreation Journal, 34*(1), 33–41.

Jordan, D. J. (2001). *Leadership in leisure services: Making a difference* (2nd ed.). State College, PA: Venture Publishing, Inc.

Kaluzny, A. D., Warner, D. M., Warren, D. G., and Zelman, W. N. (1982). *Management of health services.* Englewood Cliffs, NJ: Prentice Hall.

Katzenbach, A. E. and Smith, L. R. (1993). *Wisdom of teams: Creating the high performance organization.* Boston, MA: Harvard Business School Press.

Liebler, J. G., Levine, R. E., and Rothman, J. R. (1992). *Management principles for health professionals.* Gaithersburg, MD: Aspen Publishers.

Maier, N. R. F. (1967). Assets and liabilities in group problem solving. *Psychological Review, 74*(4), 239–249.

Mayo, E. (1933). *The human problems of an industrial civilization.* Cambridge, MA: Harvard University Press.

McHenry, L. (1994). Implementing self-directed teams. *Nursing Management (Critical Care Management Edition), 25*(3), 80I–80L.

Megginson, L. C., Mosley, D. C., and Pietri, P. H., Jr. (1992). *Management: Concepts and applications* (4th ed.). New York, NY: HarperCollins.

Napier, R. and Gershenfeld, M. (1973). *Groups: Theory and experience.* Boston, MA: Houghton Mifflin.

Robbins, S. P. and Decenzo, D. A. (2001). *Fundamentals of management essential concepts and applications* (3rd ed.). Upper Saddle River, NJ: Prentice Hall.

Rudan, V. T. (2003). The best of both worlds: A consideration of gender in team building. *Journal of Nursing Administration, 33*(3), 179–186.

Schermerhorn, J. R., Hunt, J. G., and Osborn, R. N. (1982). *Managing organizational behavior.* New York, NY: John Wiley & Sons.

Schwartz, H. and Davis, S. (1981, Summer). Matching corporate cultures and business strategy. *Organizational Dynamics,* 30–48.

Shank, J. and Coyle, C. (2002). *Therapeutic recreation in health promotion and rehabilitation.* State College, PA: Venture Publishing, Inc.

Shaw, M. E. (1971). *Group dynamics: The psychology of small group behavior.* New York, NY: McGraw-Hill.

Shortell, S. M., Kaluzny, A. D., and Associates. (1988). *Healthcare management: A text in organization theory and behavior* (2nd ed.). New York, NY: John Wiley & Sons.

Smith, G. B. and Hukill, E. (1994). Quality work improvement groups: From paper to reality. *Journal of Nursing Care Quality, 8*(4), 1–12.

Stone, C. F. (2003). Exploring cultural competencies of Certified Therapeutic Recreation Specialists: Implications for education and training. *Therapeutic Recreation Journal, 37*(2), 156–174.

Sullivan, E. J. and Decker, P. J. (2001). *Effective leadership and management in nursing* (5th ed.). Upper Saddle River, NJ: Prentice Hall.

Tappen, R. M. (2001). *Nursing leadership and management: Concepts and practice* (4th ed.). Philadelphia, PA: F. A. Davis Company.

Tomey, A. M. (2000). *Guide to nursing management and leadership* (6th ed.). St Louis, MO: Mosby.

Tuckman, B. W. (1965, May). Developmental sequence in small groups. *Psychological Bulletin,* 384–399.

Tuckman, B. W. and Jensen, M. A. (1977). Stages of small group development revisited. *Group and Organizational Studies, 2,* 419–427.

Wilkins., A. L. (1984). The creation of company culture: The soul of stories and human resource systems. *Human Resource Management, 23*(1), 41–60.

Wilson, H. S. and Kneisl, C. R. (1983). *Psychiatric nursing* (2nd ed.). Menlo Park, CA: Addison-Wesley Publishing.

Chapter 6
Ethical Perspectives

chapter revisions by S. Harold Smith and Marcia Jean Carter

All persons, whether in business, government, health care, or any other enterprise are concerned with ethics. Ethics is "the study of what is morally good and bad, right and wrong regarding human behavior and human characteristics" (Sylvester, Voelkl & Ellis, 2001, p. 52). In *The Social Work Dictionary* (Baker, 1995, p. 124), ethics is defined as "a system of moral principles and perceptions about right versus wrong and the resulting philosophy of conduct that is practiced by an individual, group, profession, or culture." As noted in this definition, professional organizations often choose to establish rules or standards governing the conduct of members of its profession. One attribute of a profession is its ethical code (Greenwood, 1957). By articulating standards in a code of ethics, professions establish expectations for every member of the profession and provide a basis for the evaluation of professional behavior. According to Levy (1982), social organizations and institutions also have ethical obligations. Organizational ethics are based on the selection and pursuit of organizational purposes and functions in consideration of the many people and groups the organization affects. Organizational ethics are put into practice by employees who are bound by those moral and ethical obligations in their role as employees. In addition, "once managers take action, they are deeply involved in ethics all the time, whether they are conscious of it or not" (Williams, 1991, p. 245).

Health care facilities, for instance, are ethically obligated to maximize patient health. They also have obligations to their employees and communities. These ethical obligations are separate from, but may be reinforced by, legal, political, business, and other considerations.

Often ethical standards are enacted into laws, but ethical behavior is just and fair conduct that goes beyond observing laws and government regulations. Ethical behavior is behavior that adheres to moral principles and is guided by particular values.

While definitions capture the spirit of the ethics concept, ethics has three specific implications that warrant a brief comment. Ethics are individually defined. How the individual operates in a management role is influenced by his or her beliefs and values. Second, what constitutes ethical behavior can vary from one person to another. The manager is influenced by the experiences that form him

or her as an individual and as a leader. Third, ethics are relative, not absolute. Thus, ethical behavior is in the eye of the beholder, but it is usually behavior that conforms to generally accepted social norms, whereas unethical behavior does not.

In an era of limited resources, decision making by managers involves ethics (Marquis & Huston, 2003). A number of environmental factors ensure that ethics will become an even greater element in management decision making in the future, including increasing technology, regulatory pressures, and competitiveness among health care providers; reduced fiscal resources; spiraling health care costs; and the public's increasing distrust of the health care system (Marquis & Huston, 2003).

Only in the last few years has there been serious discussion in journal articles and at professional conferences regarding the ethical aspects of therapeutic recreation practice (Nisbett, Brown-Welty & O'Keefe, 2002; Sylvester, 2002). A first-line therapeutic recreation manager often receives the first level of inquiry from staff, volunteers, and interns as to what is ethical and legal. As a leader the first-line manager is aware of his or her values and beliefs about the rights and duties of others. As an ethical person, therefore, the leader-manager is a role model for their subordinates in their decision making. Likewise, the therapeutic recreation manager is responsible for directing the ongoing professional growth and development of staff and interns. This task involves knowing how to recognize the ethical dimensions of therapeutic recreation and how to make ethical decisions in practice. Because ethical decisions are complex and the cost of poor decision making is high, the manager attempts to make decisions that increase "the chances that the best possible decision will be made at the least possible cost in terms of fiscal and human resources" (Marquis & Huston, 2003, p. 564).

Initially this chapter considers an overview of several schools of ethical thought followed by a discussion of the role values and rights play in ethical dilemmas and moral reasoning. Next consideration is given to ethics as related to cultural and individual conflicts followed by a discussion of ethics as an integral part of therapeutic recreation management. A model for ethical decision making is presented. A concluding section considers practice and professional dilemmas with special attention given to HIPAA. Please note, while the focus of the discussion will be health care related its application is appropriate in all health and human service settings.

Ethical Theories

Examination of societal values and moral issues has led to the study of ethics. Ethics is a branch of philosophy that deals with questions of human conduct, the values and beliefs that determine human conduct, and how these elements change over time. Metaethics focuses on the study of moral judgments to determine if they are reasonable or in some way justifiable. As the study of ethics has developed, ethical theories have been proposed to identify, organize, and examine as well as to justify human behavior through the application of the concepts and principles of human rights and values. The ultimate goal of ethics is to be able to determine what is right or good to do in a given situation.

Teleology

The outstanding example of a teleological approach to ethical decision making is utilitarianism. The manager makes decisions "based on what provides the greatest good for the greatest number of people" (Marquis & Huston, 2003, p. 53). Teleology gauges the rightness or wrongness of actions by their ends or consequences. The Greek *telos* means end, so it may not be surprising that one way of summarizing the utilitarian approach is that the end justifies the means. "Human action is ethical to the extent that it produces the greatest good or best overall consequences" (Shank & Coyle, 2002, p. 256). In health care, for example, a shot may hurt but it prevents a crippling disease; the pain is for a good cause. This perspective has its critics.

The founders of modern utilitarianism, Jeremy Bentham and John S. Mill, were concerned with the greatest good, or maximizing the good. The good is sometimes identified with happiness or pleasure and the absence of pain (Bentham, 1969). Pleasure may be reading a good book or eating a good meal. Mill defined happiness on a broader level to mean social utility. Human actions contain a moral aspect, an aesthetic aspect, and a sympathetic aspect. All of these aspects contribute to the rightness or wrongness of an action and its ultimate worth to society (Mill, 1950).

The greatest number may be simply those in power or those with the ability to pay, which is not an unusual situation in health care. This concept of the greatest good for the greatest number appears to be the ethical basis of the various national health care initiatives. On a large scale it is difficult to consider the individual. For this very reason, some would say utilitarianism is an inadequate ethic for health care because of its lack of concern for the individual patient.

Deontology

The Greek *deon* means rule or principle. Deontology focuses on universal duties and obligations regardless of consequences and holds that the features of actions themselves determine whether they are right or wrong. However, there is an overlap here with moral rules, which is why some do not make the distinction between morals and ethics. The Ten Commandments of the Judeo-Christian tradition are a familiar example of moral rules.

Theoretically, there is no limit to the number of ethical principles. The Golden Rule, "Do unto others as you would have others do unto you" or "Do not do unto others that which is hurtful to thyself," is common to many of the religions of the world. Deception is commonly seen as immoral or unethical; it violates the principles of truth telling. The relief of pain or suffering is a major principle in health care. The law of double or secondary effect says that if the primary aim is good, a negative side effect may be acceptable. The hair falls out, but the cancer is cured (Beauchamp, 1982).

Beauchamp and Childress (1989) suggested many ethical principles can be organized under larger umbrella units: autonomy, do no harm (i.e., nonmaleficence), do good (i.e., beneficence), and justice. These principles, according to the authors reflect strong values, are universal, and are framed in terms of the welfare of others. To a large degree these four principles provide the foundation for the principles of biomedical ethics.

Under the first is personal autonomy, "being one's own person, without constraints either by another's action or by psychological or physical limitations" (Beauchamp & Childress, 1989). Autonomous people are self-governing or self-regulating; they exercise control over their actions and circumstances. As an ethical principle, autonomy guides one to respect others as autonomous and to enhance, support, or restore autonomy insofar as possible (Beauchamp & Childress, 1989). Other writers would include informed consent, privacy, and free choices and actions as part of personal autonomy (Sylvester, Voelkl & Ellis, 2001). Regarding this principle, the therapeutic recreation manager or practitioner, in attitudes and actions, shows respect for the self-governing of consumers by recognizing their diverse abilities and viewpoints while respecting their prerogatives to make independent decisions and take actions accordingly.

Primum non nocere comes from the famous Hippocratic oath which says do good, or at least no harm. This ethical principle is so obvious that it is often overlooked or taken for granted. This principle is reflected by a therapeutic recreation practitioner who discourages a consumer from seeking involvement in a specific activity that involves risk of harm.

The third category includes beneficence, the doing of good. In many respects, it is not unlike the principle of nonmaleficence. The distinction between the two comes in the degree of activity required to act. Beneficence requires action that contributes to the welfare of others. It is a principle that underlies the goals of many social and health care organizations. The manager who uses this principle to plan performance reviews is more likely to view them as a means of employee growth (Marquis & Huston, 2003). Beauchamp and Childress (1989) pointed out that in health care facilities this principle is often expressed in the form of paternalism. Paternalism is doing what one believes is for someone else's good without necessarily having obtained the other person's knowledge or consent.

Justice is usually considered an umbrella term and has to do with how people are treated when their interests compete and are compared with the interests of others. Most often, justice is equated with fairness or merit. In addition, justice incorporates just allocations of scarce resources (Beauchamp & Childress, 1989). Three types of justice are of concern to managers: distributive justice, procedural justice, and compensatory justice. *Distributive justice* requires that differentiated treatment of individuals not be based on arbitrary characteristics (e.g., men and women doing the same job should be paid equally). *Procedural justice* requires that rules be fair to all concerned and be administered consistently and impartially (although mitigating circumstances should be considered). *Compensatory justice* is concerned with compensating people for past harm or injustice (Gray & Smeltzer, 1989).

Teleology (i.e., utilitarianism) and deontology are the two predominant approaches of analysis for thinking through ethical problems. Both have developed a number of moral principles used to explore what beliefs and values form the basis for decision making. In time, other approaches to ethical decision making have evolved some combining concepts from these two.

Bioethics

While ethics is concerned with the rightness or wrongness of human behavior, bioethics is concerned with the application of ethics to issues pertaining to life and death (Tappen, Weiss & Whitehead, 2004). Moral judgments about the rightness and goodness of health care practices are the purview of bioethics. While ethics tends to refer to a standardized code as a guide to behavior, morals refers to an individual's own code of acceptable behavior. Bioethics incorporates moral reasoning into dilemmas and

obligations of health care professionals. Thus, the perspective of the health care provider is considered during intervention and management decisions.

Contextual Ethics

This approach considers the consequences of each alternative in the context of the situation (Shank & Coyle, 2002). The client is the center of the process, yet the relationship of the therapist with the client is factored into decisions (Husted & Husted, 1998). The feelings of the therapist are considered, as are the factors that describe the problem. A manager analyzes moral situations reflecting on his or her personal awareness of what is right and wrong and the merits of various courses of action.

Caring Ethics

This perspective suggests that each situation is unique and requires sensitivity to the other's needs and the dynamics of the helping relationship (Husted & Husted, 1998). The manager acts with empathy through thinking about what it is to be a manager, a client, and a human being. Caring is essential to growth and development (Sylvester, 2002). Moral conflict is resolved through communication to understand the needs of those involved.

Virtue Ethics

The essence of virtue ethics is that the professional consistently displays honesty, integrity, and respect because these behaviors are inherent in their character (Sylvester, 2002). A professional's ethical obligation to act in the interest of the client outweighs one's self-interest (Shank & Coyle, 2002). Moral conduct is a reflection of one's character. "Virtuous individuals are more likely not only to follow ethical rules but also to aspire to the highest ideals" (Sylvester, Voelkl & Ellis, 2001, p. 68). A virtuous manager possesses the kind of character "that disposes them toward morally good action and the highest ethical ideals" (p. 69).

Ethical Dilemmas and Moral Reasoning

How do managers decide what is right and wrong? Dealing with moral situations is difficult and there may be no clear alternative. The manager must use a professional approach that eliminates trial and error. "Moral reasoning entails identification of relevant theory principles, and rules, as well as pertinent facts and circumstances" (Sylvester, Voelkl & Ellis, 2001, p. 64). Moral reasoning tends to take place at the level of rules and principles, which become the guidelines for moral behavior.

Dilemmas occur when there are good reasons to support a number of alternatives. No theories or rules exist to cover all aspects of ethical dilemmas. An individual's values and beliefs play a major role in the manager's daily decision making (Marquis & Huston, 2003). The way the manager solves ethical dilemmas is a reflection of values and beliefs about the rights of human beings. Self-awareness is a leadership role in ethical decision making. The manager is prepared to live with a degree of uncertainty in practice situations.

Values and Rights

Values are a set of beliefs and attitudes about the truth, beauty, or worth of any thought, objective, or behavior. Values are qualities intrinsically desirable to everyone. Every decision made, or course of action taken, is based consciously or unconsciously on such beliefs and values. In other words, what is really important, and what are the priorities in life, what is one willing to sacrifice or suffer in order to achieve, obtain, protect, or maintain are basic value issues for everyone. Values become a part of a person's worldview that guide behavior and assist in making choices (Tappen, Weiss & Whitehead, 2004). The majority of people in today's society have not had to answer these kinds of tough questions consciously. As a result, there is a lot of unnecessary confusion, inconsistency, and ambivalence exhibited in people's behavior. A person is frequently confronted with this confusion and ambivalence concerning his or her own values and rights during a difficult decision-making time.

Values

Values provide individuals with the ideological justification for roles and norms within society (Vustal, 1977). Without values, there are no standards and hence no moral code, no right nor wrong, and ultimately chaos results. When a person has at least a tentative idea of what is considered to be truth, beauty, and right or wrong, he or she is able to act in a manner consistent with those values. This behavior is more organized and predictable not only for the individual but for society as well. Jourard (1964, p. 27) wrote: "That until an individual knows his values he cannot know himself. Until one knows what he values or what lines in life he is going to cross, an individual doesn't know himself very well."

Values are both simple and complex and vary in the degree to which they are believed to be important to the person. Raths, Harmin and Simon (1966) identified three processes that individuals go through as they attempt to clarify their values. The first process is the *choosing process*. Values are considered completely unique to each individual. Although two people may share the same value, they each arrived at that value individually. Theoretically, the choice of these values is made freely without indoctrination or coercion. Since values involve choosing, it is explicitly assumed that alternative values exist simul-

taneously. Because alternatives exist and because all decisions have consequences, the individual considers the consequences of all choices in making the ultimate decision.

The second process in the value clarification process is labeled *prizing*. This occurs when the individual acknowledges first to himself or herself and then publicly what choice has been made and how he or she feels about it. Generally, the individual is proud of his choice. In addition to publicizing his values, the individual will also actively support his values (Raths, Harmin & Simon, 1966).

The third process in value clarification according to Raths and colleagues (1966) is called *acting*. It is at this point that the individual has truly internalized the value. In this aspect, the individual's behaviors are a direct reflection of that value. Likewise, as an integral part of the individual's behavior, the value is then expressed not just episodically, but repeatedly.

As an individual grows, develops, and matures, values are defined and clarified, tested and revised, and gradually become all-pervasive to the individual's existence. As such, the individual becomes an agent of value or, more commonly, a moral agent. The terms value and moral frequently are used interchangeably because they both deal with human behavior and values (Vustal, 1977).

When individuals have developed values, generally their decisions are made in terms of those values. Thus, it is easy to understand the magnitude and extent of the effect that values have on lives. Values have significance for people as individuals and collectively as societies. Values are useful because they provide order and predictability. Values can be considered as a means to a good end. Inherently, values can make an individual feel good inside. Finally, values contribute to social order and societal maturation. Professional values are established as being important to practice like caring and ethical behavior (Tappen, Weiss & Whitehead, 2004).

Values Clarification

Because every person holds individual and shared values, both consumer and therapeutic recreation managers and practitioners hold wide ranges of values. Given this reality, it is apparent that often therapeutic recreation managers and practitioners and their consumers will hold dissimilar values. Dissimilar values can contribute to misunderstandings or even to serious conflict. If therapeutic recreation specialists are going to give service, they will need to find ways to accommodate these differences. This accommodation must be achieved both for the sake of the consumer and for the sake of therapeutic recreation specialists' own personal and professional well-being. Understanding one's own values can be a first step that helps a therapeutic recreation manager or practitioner to identify, understand, and learn strategies that accommodate these differences.

Values clarification is, as the name suggests, clarifying what values are important to a person. It is a self-awareness process that not only identifies what values are "me" but also asks the individual to prioritize or rate different values to determine which are most important. The following values clarification exercise is associated with professional values:

- How much do I value therapeutic recreation as a commitment to a lifelong career of learning and competence?

- Do I like to provide service for some kinds of consumers and not others?

- Do I prefer working with healthy consumers to working with ill ones? young to old? physical to psychological disabilities?

A first step in accomplishing the preceding exercise is to reflect on such questions privately. A second and more enlightening step is to participate in values clarification with one's classmates. More specific reasons exist for potential therapeutic recreation managers to examine their value systems include the following:

- Some inconsistencies in personal values are not apparent until consciously examined.

- Some inconsistencies may cause problems if conflicting values are caught in the decision-making process.

- Personal value may conflict with certain professional practice responsibilities.

- Examining values can guide ethical choices in professional practice.

- Values clarification contributes toward functioning at a higher level of moral reasoning.

Rights

Individuals struggling to clarify their values do not always identify rights as values. However, as values are peeled away to their basic layer, the rights of humans usually become clear. Individuals have the human right to existence and therefore have the right to choose or to make decisions concerning themselves as long as they are willing to accept the consequences. The concept of self in this respect refers to an individual's body, life, property, and privacy. Nevertheless, because individuals exist within societies, the actions associated with these choices cannot infringe on another person's rights. Within the concept of human rights is the associated concept of duties and re-

sponsibilities. Rights equate with responsibilities. If one has a right to his or her existence, other persons and society have a duty or obligation not to kill him. Moreover, in the opinion of the authors, health professionals, because of the roles they assume within society, assume additional responsibilities toward others that other individuals do not assume.

Scholars suggest the existence of six conditions associated with the fundamental rights of individuals. In some respects Thomas Hobbes and John Locke developed early rights theories in the 1600s. First, there is an accompanying condition of the freedom to exercise the right or not to exercise the right if the individual so chooses. Second, rights are associated with duties for others to facilitate, or at least not to interfere with, the exercise of those rights. Third, rights are usually defined or defended in basic terms that equate with the principles of fairness, impartiality, or equality. Fourth, a basic fundamental or significant right is considered enforceable by society. Fifth, is the right to express oneself without fear of punishment. The final condition is also the result of societal maturation because this condition concerns compensation due an individual whose rights have been violated (Cavanaugh, Moberg & Velasquez, 1981).

In decision making the rights of the individual need to be respected. The decision maker need only avoid violating the rights of the individual affected by the decision. As an example, firing an employee for wrongdoing on the basis of hearsay evidence would violate that person's right to due process. Of course, there are many situations where the issue is clouded. For instance, to what degree does a therapeutic recreation manager have the right to interfere with a staff member's right to privacy if that member's use of drugs or alcohol is affecting his or her job performance?

One must remember that human beings have rights because they are unique creatures that possess the ability to know and think. What a person knows about himself or herself and what he or she defines as unique becomes the source of human right. As a unique, self-contained human, an individual possesses certain needs in order for that existence to continue. Humans have a common origin which results in having common needs and a subsequent interdependence on one another. Because of these principles human needs exist whether they are recognized or not.

Specifically, defined sets of rights have developed in society as a result of the increased attention being devoted to the field of moral and ethical issues. For instance, the American Hospital Association (1985) has a Patient's Bill of Rights. Nursing homes are another example. For nursing homes to participate in Medicare and Medicaid programs, they have been required by the federal government to establish resident's rights policies. The Universal

Declaration of Human Rights of the United Nations claims "everyone has a right to a standard of living adequate for the health and well-being of himself or his family, including… medical care…" (as quoted in Beauchamp, 1982, p. 38). These policies focus on the right to respectful and considerate care and treatment, right to information about treatment and cost, informed consent about procedures and outcomes, patient autonomy, right to refuse treatment, and right to privacy and confidentiality. Other health-related organizations and even particular facilities have developed "sets of rights," which contain many of the same basic elements noted previously. As a result, today's consumers are appropriately aware of what is being done to and for them.

Cultural and Individual Conflicts

The practice of therapeutic recreation occurs in a multicultural context. The workplace is becoming more culturally diverse each day. Managers are ultimately responsible for the policies that address diversity and the processes that support awareness and sensitivity in the workplace. Multiculturalism, while respecting differences among people, recognizes common values, beliefs, and rights like justice and well-being that enable a sense of unity among people of different cultures (Sylvester, Voelkl & Ellis, 2001).

The population of the United States and Canada is a mixture of many ethnic groups and cultures. While there are differences in the ethics between cultures, there are also universal elements. Many, if not all, cultures have some form of the Golden Rule ingrained into their system. While different cultures have different perspectives on health and illness care service, the common ethic calls for respect of their differences. Native Americans, for example, tend to value harmonious relations with the world around them. Each rock, tree, animal, flower, and person is equally respected, and all are seen to coexist in harmony. A state of health exists when a person is in total harmony with nature. Illness, on the other hand, is seen as an imbalance between the person who is ill and the natural or supernatural forces around the person rather than an altered physiologic state (Spector, 1985).

Understanding other cultures takes time and communication. It also takes knowledge and requires a personal investment and commitment to learning. It is not always easy to know or to understand how another will respond to health or illness. However, such knowledge is important for ethical decision making.

Another source of conflict is the differences in values. Value clarification helps individuals to explore what it is they believe in and how to put those beliefs into daily practice. Such clarification may be vital to the provision of ethical service not only in the health care setting but also in the community-based leisure service arena. Therapeutic recreation practitioners need to be aware of value differences so that they can avoid the unconscious imposition of either their personal or professional values on consumers. Likewise, if practitioners know what consumers value, these values can be respected in daily service whenever possible.

Providers of service to persons with disabilities work in an environment oriented toward ethical situations. To ignore this is to ignore reality. Williams (1991) noted that the three most important factors in personal and organization ethics are "integrity, purpose, and responsibility" (p. 245). The two main group providers of therapeutic recreation have recognized the ethical essence of their work and have developed professional codes of ethics. Both the American Therapeutic Recreation Association (ATRA) and National Therapeutic Recreation Society (NTRS) Codes of Ethics contain principles or statements that recognize human rights. The responsibility of providing quality service and concern for the dignity of the consumer are noted. Confidentiality and privacy are also recognized as ethical issues. Besides the positive actions of these provisions, the manager or practitioner prevents harm from occurring by safeguarding of the consumer from incompetent providers. Honesty is another ethical principle embraced by the code for therapeutic recreation specialists. Other professional associations, especially health-related associations and individual facilities, have developed similar ethical guidelines or principles. These statements intend to serve daily practice as well as to provide a basis for dealing with more complex ethical dilemmas.

A professional challenge is to assure that professional codes of ethics reflect cultural diversity (Sylvester, Voelkl & Ellis, 2001). To illustrate, ethical principles like privacy must be viewed from the multicultural context in which service occurs. A manager sensitive to various cultural interpretations of privacy accommodates employee needs during supervisory interactions.

One of the most difficult aspects of professional therapeutic recreation practice is the daily source of conflict. For the therapeutic recreation specialist these conflicts usually are associated with allocation of resources and practice respectively. Resource allocation, including staff, supplies, and equipment, is given considerable attention because of the commonalities between economics and ethics. The need for more staff or supplies and equipment to provide better service is not an infrequent dilemma. The clinical area in health care facilities provides ground for ethical dilemmas. Some of this conflict is territorialism, a power struggle for influence and space. Some conflict may also reflect differences in value systems. When professionals disagree, ethical practice requires time, listening, respecting, and sharing the sources of conflict to seek jointly an acceptable solution.

The therapeutic recreation manager as a first-line manager may be the first source of help when therapeutic recreation staff find themselves in conflict with other professionals. The manager then needs to be able to sort out the reasons for the conflict and determine which values are involved. Conflicts over power and territorialism will be handled with different approaches. The therapeutic recreation professional remains mindful that the primary goal of any professional practice is an ethical concern for the best service possible.

Individual conflicts involving unethical or illegal practice of a peer or other professional staff are probably the most difficult for the therapeutic recreation manager. Clarity of thought, responsiveness, listening, and data collection are needed. Support networks for substance abusers, consultation for legal concerns, and confidentiality in handling these difficult situations are vital. Likewise, knowing when to take what action is crucial. All are learned through experience and support from other colleagues.

Ethics and Therapeutic Recreation Management

How the therapeutic recreation manager operates in a management role is influenced by the beliefs, values, and experiences (e.g., family, peers, situations) that inform him or her as an individual and leader. In the language of Mark Pastin (1986), the individual's values are the set of "ground rules" for making what the individual considers to be a "right" decision. In addition to personal value, the therapeutic recreation manager is guided by values of the profession (e.g., responsibilities to consumers and to society). ATRA and NTRS have each published a Code of Ethics in addition to several position statements and guidelines that seek to assist therapeutic recreation managers and practitioners in making ethical decisions in practice (e.g., see McFarlane, Keogh-Hoss, Jacobson & James, 1998). Not only should ethics be ingrained in staff to create a strong sense of professionalism but also the codes should be the basis of a planned approach to all management functions of planning, organizing, directing, and controlling.

These codes articulate the core values and ethical principles of the profession and provide guidelines for ethical conduct among all professionals (Shank & Coyle, 2002). These codes are dynamic—"Changes occur as society and technology evolve" (Tappen, Weiss & Whitehead, 2004, p. 231). Technology has increased our knowledge and skills, yet our ability to make decisions and resolve moral dilemmas about ourselves and our consumers is guided by the principles found in these codes: autonomy, beneficence, nonmaleficence, justice, fidelity (i.e., loyal to client), veracity (i.e., honesty), privacy, and confidentiality.

Last, the manager, because of his or her role in the organization, is expected to further the organization's ethics and to assist staff and other practitioners in doing the same. The manager has a responsibility to create a climate in which ethical behavior is the norm (Marquis & Huston, 2003). Managers have special obligations to exercise their power—derived from their position, responsibility, and relationships—responsibly and ethically (Levy, 1982).

Spurred in part by scandals in both industry and health care, many organizations have increased their emphasis on ethical behavior (Carroll, 1987). Leaders of some organizations have initiated internal conferences on ethics (Lee, 1986). Others offer their employees training in how to cope with ethical dilemmas (Businesses Are Signing Up for Ethics 101, 1988). Organizations have also prepared detailed guidelines describing how employees are to deal with suppliers, competitors, and other constituents. Last, some organizations have developed a policy on ethics.

Of course, no code, guideline, or training program can truly replace an individual's personal judgment about what is right or wrong in any particular situation. Such devices may explain what people should do, but they often fail to help people deal with the consequences of their choice. To make ethical choices may lead to unpleasant outcomes—firing, rejection by ones colleagues, and so on. Thus, the manager must be prepared to confront his or her own conscience and weigh it against the various options available when making the difficult decisions that every manager must make (Cadbury, 1987). No guidelines or theories exist to cover all the dilemmas a manager faces. The manager accepts uncertainty knowing that to postpone action leads to paralysis (Marquis & Huston, 2003).

However, the stress associated with ethical behavior in management can be reduced if therapeutic recreation managers attempt to practice management that realizes the highest good. The highest good may be found in the comments of Kenneth Blanchard (as cited in Fernicola, 1988). When translated into therapeutic recreation theory, Blanchard's comments can be summed up as follows:

1. Therapeutic recreation managers can influence the ethical behavior of therapeutic recreation personnel by treating them ethically.

2. Therapeutic recreation managers have a code of ethics that peers have agreed upon. They enter into ethical dilemmas when they go against that code.

3. Therapeutic recreation managers fall into moral dilemmas when they go against their internal values.

4. While ethical and moral dilemmas differ, an ethical therapeutic recreation manager is a moral manager.

5. Ethical functions can be confronted by three questions:

   (5.1) Is it legal?

   (5.2) Is it balanced?

   (5.3) How will it make me feel about myself?

6. Therapeutic recreation managers with high self-esteem usually have the internal strength to make the ethical decision.

7. An ethical leader is an effective leader.

8. Therapeutic recreation managers should apply six principles of ethical power:

   (8.1) The manager promotes and ensures pursuit of the stated mission or purpose of the department, division, or unit since this statement reflects the vision of its practitioners. While the mission should be reviewed periodically, goals or objectives are set for yearly achievement.

   (8.2) Therapeutic recreation managers should build a division or department to be outstanding, thereby building self-esteem of staff through pride in the workplace.

   (8.3) Therapeutic recreation managers should work to sustain patience and continuity through long-term effect on the agency or organization.

   (8.4) Therapeutic recreation managers should plan for persistence by spending more time following up on education and activities that build commitment of personnel.

   (8.5) Therapeutic recreation managers should promote perspective by giving staff time to think. They should practice good management for the long term.

   (8.6) Therapeutic recreation managers should consider developing a department code of ethics expressed in observable and measurable behaviors.

Ethical Decision Making and Moral Reasoning

To make appropriate decisions "the manager must use a professional approach that eliminates trial and error and focuses on proven decision-making models or problem-solving processes" (Marquis & Huston, 2003, p. 544). The quality of ethical problem solving is evaluated in terms of the process used to make a decision. With a structured approach similar to APIE (assessment, planning, implementation, evaluation), data gathering is adequate and multiple alternatives are analyzed: "The manager should accept that the best possible decision was made at that time with the information and resources available" (Marquis & Huston, 2003, p. 546).

Ethical decision making is theoretically based on moral reasoning, decision theory, moral development, values and valuing, and evaluation. It differs from traditional decision making in that the step-by-step process focuses on the moral or ethical dimensions of therapeutic recreation service. The reasoning process concludes when a decision of a morally acceptable action to be taken in a given situation is reached. Knowledge of ethical theories and principles helps a manager to identify the ethical issues or dimensions of the situation while providing the moral justification for the final selection of action to take.

The authors have developed a ten-step model for ethical decision making based on moral reasoning:

1. Identify the problem including decisions needed, ethical components, and key individuals.

2. Gather additional information to clarify the situation.

3. Identify the ethical issues of the situation.

4. Define personal and professional moral positions of the problem.

5. Identify moral positions of key individuals involved in the situation.

6. Identify value conflicts.

7. Determine who should make the decision.

8. Identify the range of actions with anticipated outcomes.

9. Decide on a course of action and carry it out.

10. Evaluate and review the results of the decision or action, including monitoring the situation over time.

Like the APIE process, the nature of this model allows for feedback at each step. Additionally, this approach clarifies the values and beliefs of the people involved.

Therapeutic recreation managers are in key positions regarding ethical decision making. One of the major responsibilities of the therapeutic recreation manager is to encourage and to guide ethical decision-making efforts. Such decisions take time and effort, and both should be encouraged among staff members. Ethical dilemmas arise as a result of conflict in values. Difficult ethical dilemmas (e.g, consumer abuse, practitioner substance abuse) that go unnoticed and/or unresolved may lead to unethical (i.e., unprofessional) service as well as job dissatisfaction and apathy on the part of staff. If therapeutic recreation practitioners wish to be accorded professional status, they must also accept responsibility for decision making. All daily decisions have an ethical dimension that requires ethical decision making. Many of these are relatively minor; some are major. One of the greatest challenges of management is making right, good decisions.

Practice and Professional Dilemmas

Today's health and human service delivery systems present a number of ethical dilemmas. "Advanced technology, escalating health care costs, a growing elderly population, and social and economic pressures are just a few of the factors posing ethical dilemmas" (Sullivan & Decker, 2005, p. 68). Questions are being raised about who should receive the benefits of technology. Competition for resources, managed care, regulatory pressures, costs attributed to poor health care practices or the uninsured, and information management are areas that trigger ethical and moral dilemmas. The manager is also faced with supervisory issues, such as incompetent personnel and impaired workers. The manager is ultimately held responsible for decisions concerning adherence to consumer rights issues and professional standards of practice and ethical codes of conduct.

Congress passed the Health Insurance Portability and Accountability Act (HIPAA) in August of 1996 (P.L. 104-91), with implementation in the spring of 2003. Its objectives are to improve the portability (i.e., ability to move or be carried) and continuity of health benefits, to minimize health care fraud, and to simplify administration of health insurance (Denker, 2002). Privacy and confidentiality rules are included in the act and are issues to be considered in ethical health care delivery. Because of therapeutic recreation's direct role in the provision of services in health and human service organizations, privacy and confidentiality expectations are relevant to practice and ethical conduct.

This act is the first comprehensive federal regulation for privacy and confidentiality of health information (Denker, 2002). The intended objectives of the act are to:

1. Define the circumstances in which protected health information may be used and disclosed;

2. Establish certain patient rights regarding protected health information; and

3. Require that the organizations adopt administrative safeguards to ensure the privacy of protected health information" (Nowicki, 2001, p. 96).

The privacy rule (a) enables consumers to find out how their identifiable health information is being used, (b) limits release of information to the minimum reasonably needed, and (c) gives consumers the right to review their records (Denker, 2002).

Managers are obligated to formalize their privacy practices and to adopt clear procedures for intervention, payment, and operations. Employee training to ensure compliance is a managerial task. Likewise, protecting disclosure of client names and identifying information in public places falls to the manager. To illustrate, during discharge planning or inclusion experiences the manager must assure that the client has completed a release that permits communication between service providers. Under certain circumstances the manager considers the welfare of the person or group as confidential information is used, for example, when a personal injury or workers' compensation claim is filed (Sullivan & Decker, 2005).

In today's world it is imperative that the therapeutic recreation manager understands and follows both the practical and ethical expectations of HIPAA. Likewise, individual staff members are responsible to understand and comply with HIPAA standards in their day-to-day practice with clients and caregivers. The manager encounters client and employment issues that result in ethical and moral dilemmas. Nearly all decision making by a manager involves some ethical component for which the manager is responsible and liable. Thus, the first-line manager is cognizant of the ethical principles and legal directives that impact service delivery: A systematic decision-making process is used to assure compliance with relevant codes while providing moral justification for actions taken by the manager.

Summary

Ethics involve an individual's personal beliefs about what is right and wrong or good and bad; however, ethical behavior varies from person to person and is relative. In addition to personal beliefs and values, the therapeutic recreation manager is governed by the values of his or her profession.

The major ethical theories of teleology and deontology were presented. Utilitarianism or teleology holds that plans and actions should be judged in terms of their consequences. On the other hand, deontology theories take the perspective that existing rights require certain duties, behaviors, and obligations among individuals. A number of ethical principles, including the emerging concerns in bioethics were also discussed.

As the manager analyzes ethical dilemmas, decisions of what is right and wrong result from moral reasoning about the rights of human beings. How individuals develop values and rights was considered. It was noted that without values, there are no standards and hence no moral code. The concept of rights generally include the existence of six conditions: free consent, privacy, freedom of conscience, free speech, fairness, and due process.

Multiculturalism and individual ethical conflicts found in the workplace were considered. Professional codes of conduct developed by ATRA and NTRS present guidelines yet are limited in their interpretation of diversity needs. Strategies a manager might use to promote and model ethics in the workplace were suggested. A model of ethical decision making suggested ten steps to aid in moral reasoning. Finally, a brief overview of practice issues with a focus on the Health Insurance Portability and Accountability Act (HIPAA) was provided. Practical and ethical implications to therapeutic recreation practice were considered.

Review Questions

1. What ethical dilemmas do you feel most therapeutic recreation managers face? Why? How would you handle one of the ethical dilemmas presented in this chapter?

2. What are some types of behavior that would be unethical for students? What are some that would be ethical? Compare your responses with those of other students. Are these unethical and ethical behaviors carried over into the work environment?

3. Do you think you will be able to solve an ethical dilemma you might face in the future by applying the theories presented? Explain.

4. Conduct an Internet search for the ATRA and NTRS ethics codes. Apply them to situations identified in Questions 1 and 2.

5. Can a therapeutic recreation manager act in a way that is legal but unethical? Illegal but ethical? Why or why not?

6. Do you think a therapeutic recreation manager has a responsibility to disclose illegal or unethical conduct by others within the organization? Why or why not? If the manager may lose his or her job, does the same responsibility exist? Why or why not?

References

American Hospital Association. (1985). *Values in conflict: Resolving ethical issues in hospital care. Report of the Special Committee on Biomedical Ethics.* Chicago, IL: Author.

Baker, D. L. (1995). *The social work dictionary* (3rd ed.). Washington, DC: National Association of Social Workers.

Beauchamp, T. L. (1982). Ethical theory and bioethics. In T. Beauchamp and L. Walters (Eds.), *Contemporary issues in bioethics* (2nd ed.). Belmont, CA: Wadsworth Publishing.

Beauchamp, T. L. and Childress, J. F. (1989). *Principles of biomedical ethics* (3rd ed.). New York, NY: Oxford University Press.

Bentham, J. (1969). An introduction to the principles of morals and legislation (1780). In M. P. Mack (Ed.), *A Bentham reader* (pp. 78–144). New York, NY: Pegasus.

Businesses are signing up for ethics 101. (1988, February 15). *Business Week*, 56–57.

Cadbury, A. (1987, September–October). Ethical managers make their own rules. *Harvard Business Review*, 69–73.

Carroll, A. B. (1987, March–April). Search of the moral manager. *Business Horizons*, 7–15.

Cavanaugh, G. F., Moberg, D. J., and Velasquez, M. (1981, July). The ethics of organizational politics. *Academy of Management Review, 6*(3), 363–374.

Denker, A. L (2002). What HIPAA means for your clinical practice. *Seminars for Nurse Managers, 10*(2), 85–89.

Fernicola, K. C. (1988, May). Take the high road…to ethical management: An interview with Kenneth Blanchard. *Association Management*, 60–66.

Gray, E. R. and Smeltzer, L. R. (1989). *Management: The competitive edge*. New York, NY: Macmillian Publishing.

Greenwood, E. (1957, July). Attributes of a profession. *Social Work, 2*, 45–55.

Husted, J. H. and Husted, G. L. (1998). Ethical decision making and the role of the nurse. In G. Deloughery (Ed.), *Issues and trends in nursing* (3rd ed., pp. 216–242). St. Louis, MO: Mosby.

Jourard, S. (1964). *The transparent self: Self-disclosure and well-being*. New York, NY: Van Nostrand Reinhold.

Lee, C. (1986, March). Ethics training: Facing the tough questions. *Training*, 30–33, 38–41.

Levy, C. S. (1982). *Guide to ethical decisions and actions for social service administration: A handbook for managerial personnel*. New York, NY: Haworth Press.

Marquis, B. L. and Huston, C. J. (2003). *Leadership roles and management functions in nursing: Theory & application* (4th ed.). Philadelphia, PA: Lippincott Williams & Wilkins.

McFarlane, N., Keogh-Hoss, M., Jacobson, J., and James, A. (1998). *Finding the path: Ethics in action*. Hattiesburg, MS: American Therapeutic Recreation Association.

Mill, J. S. (1950). *On Bentham and Coleridge.* New York, NY: Harper & Row.

Nisbett, N., Brown-Welty, S., and O'Keefe, C. (2002). A study of ethics education within therapeutic recreation curriculum. *Therapeutic Recreation Journal, 36*(3), 282–295.

Nowicki, M. (2001). *The financial management of hospitals and healthcare organizations* (2nd ed.). Chicago, IL: Health Administration Press.

Pastin, M. (1986). *The hard problem of management: Gaining the ethics edge.* San Francisco CA: Jossey-Bass.

Raths, L. E., Harmin, M., and Simon, S. B. (1966). *Values and teaching.* Westerville, OH: Charles E. Merrill Books.

Shank, J. and Coyle, C. (2002). *Therapeutic recreation in health promotion and rehabilitation.* State College, PA: Venture Publishing, Inc.

Spector, R. E. (1985). *Cultural diversity in health and illness* (2nd ed.). New York, NY: Appleton-Century-Crofts.

Sylvester, C. (2002). Ethics and the quest for professionalization. *Therapeutic Recreation Journal, 36*(4), 314–334.

Sylvester, C., Voelkl, J. E., and Ellis, G. D. (2001). *Therapeutic recreation programming: Theory and practice.* State College, PA: Venture Publishing, Inc.

Sullivan, E. J. and Decker, P. J. (2005). *Effective leadership & management in nursing* (6th ed.). Upper Saddle River, NJ: Pearson/Prentice Hall.

Tappen, R. M., Weiss, S. A., and Whitehead, D. K. (2004). *Essentials of nursing leadership and management* (3rd ed.). Philadelphia, PA: F. A. Davis Company.

Vustal, D. B. (1977). Searching for values. *Image, 9*(1), 15–17.

Williams, L. R. (1991). Ethics in management. In G. S. Fain (Ed.), *Leisure and ethics* (pp. 244–246). Reston, VA: American Alliance for Health, Physical Education, Recreation and Dance.

Chapter 7
Working Effectively With Management

chapter revisions by Karen C. Wenzel

Organizations are two or more people working together in a structured, formal environment to achieve common goals. In an organization, a manager's job is to provide guidance, implementation, and coordination so that the organization's goals are achieved. The manager coaches employees of the organization to develop teamwork, which effectively fulfills their needs and achieves organizational objectives. A manager's job is also to create and maintain an environment that allows others to work efficiently. The manager is responsible for planning, organizing, directing/ leading, and controlling the resources of the organization. The extent to which managers perform the functions of management varies by the level they serve in the management hierarchy. The term *supervisor* is often applied to those management levels of the organization that direct the work of others. A supervisor is a manager whose major function is to work directly with employees to achieve organizational goals. In common usage, however, the title tends to be used to refer to the first level of the management hierarchy. Supervisors manage the actual work of the organization at the direct service provision level and their primary functions are directing/leading and controlling. In contrast, top management spends most of their time on the functions of planning and organizing. The top manager determines the mission and sets the goals for the organization. His or her primary function is long-range planning. Middle management implements top management goals. Supervisors and first-line managers direct/lead the actual work of the organization at the operating level.

Most therapeutic recreation specialists will readily state that the reason they entered the profession is to work in a meaningful way with people. The therapeutic relationships established provide the incentive for going to work on a daily basis. However, it is often the relationship, or lack thereof, with a supervisor or management and the organization's hierarchy that are most frequently cited reasons for leaving an otherwise satisfying position. Work becomes miserable when an employee and their supervisor or higher management are not in agreement or have a compatible working relationship. Often, it isn't the job that an employee quits; they quit their manager or supervisor. Dissatisfied employees rarely attribute their unhappiness to the nature of the work, long hours, or even less than desirable pay—but rather to a less than desirable relation-ship with a manager. Employees who set an intention of forging a harmonious, productive, and mutually beneficial relationship with their supervisor reap rewards for these efforts. Getting along with a supervisor or manager has more bearing than any other factor on one's ability to do their best work on the job.

Every employee in an organization contributes to the culture of the organization. However, the senior management play a more significant role. A first-line manager's success is often gauged by how well relationships are developed and how well they support the department and organization. In all their actions and interactions, they demonstrate the values they believe are important. It is their responsibility not only to set the example but also to demonstrate commitment to the mission of the organization, its employees, and stakeholders. An effective manager is not just a charismatic leader but is also accountable for the well-being of the larger organization by operating in service, rather than in control, of those around them. Essentially, the manager is responsible for monitoring and improving the work of others. The manager is expected to develop relationships and environments that enable people to work together, respond to change, and achieve organizational goals. Such "joint performance" involves having common goals, common values, the right structures, and continuing training and development (Drucker, 1988).

A manager has administrative, educational, and supportive responsibilities. Administratively they must promote and maintain the standards of the agency, coordinate practice with policies, and assure that the program, department, and agency run smoothly and efficiently. The manager is also responsible for the educational development of each individual employee in a manner designed to maximize the employee's potential. Finally, the manager serves in a support role, maintaining harmonious working relationships and cultivating the esprit de corps (Kadushin, 1992).

To promote these working relationships, an effective manager must be willing to share relevant information. An effective manager is also readily able to share credit and to give credit where credit is due. Collaboration will not happen when one person, especially a "boss" or supervisor takes credit for the work produced by a team. An effective manager rewards and recognizes honesty and openness. First-line managers foster the creation of an environment that promotes and rewards partnerships. As organizations have grown, many have moved away from the heroic personality of executive leadership or the "great individual" model of leadership toward team leadership. This model of executive team leadership is on the rise, as effective leadership today requires cross-disciplinary and cross functional approaches. Organizations function maximally when there are groups of people with shared responsibilities, clear delegation of tasks, and clear accountability for results. It is the responsibility of the first-line manager to create a high-functioning team.

This chapter explores employee-supervisor expectations, including the nature of supervision, working relationships between employees and supervisors, the challenges associated with a difficult manager, the political nature of relationships, and the importance of reflecting the "boss" and the organization. Additionally, the significance of establishing relationships with other healthcare professionals especially physicians is presented. The chapter concludes with a brief discussion of the interaction between organizational control and self-supervision. Characteristics of principle-centered leaders (Covey, 1990) serve as one barometer of organizational success and effective employee self-supervision.

Expectations of a Supervisor

When an employee is hired to fulfill a position within an agency, the agency has the responsibility of providing sufficient orientation to assure successful job performance. Orientation is a program that introduces the new employee to the organization as a whole, their work unit, their co-workers, and their job duties. New employees need to know their job-related expectations and reporting relationships. The employee is informed about benefits, policies, and procedures. The agency will expect that the employee arrives with the basic entry-level skills and competencies to perform the job that he or she was hired to fulfill. Even an entry level professional should not expect that the manager or supervisor will "teach" him or her how to do the job or provide extensive on-the-job training and coaching. A professional is expected to enter the field and start performing. A certain degree of resourcefulness is implied. If there are areas in which the employee feels uncertain, it is up to the individual to remedy the situation, and seek-out additional training and support. Agencies vary in their commitment and resources dedicated to staff development.

A manager is responsible for the development and growth of the employees he or she supervises. First-line managers must capture the processes by which people at work increase their skills and expand their insights. Organizations invest a great deal on training employees, and management support for staff development programs is necessary for training to be effective. This includes promoting training and development efforts through financial support and released time to engage in staff development. An employee shares the responsibility for their own continued professional growth and development. When financial support from the organization is limited, a professional assumes a degree of responsibility to personally invest in professional development opportunities.

In addition to selecting, orienting, training, and supervising an employee, a manager also has the responsibility of evaluating the performance of the employee. The evaluation process is part of the control function in management. Evaluation ties performance feedback to rewards and corrective actions. Employee evaluation is an ongoing process, taking place informally on a daily basis and formally. A performance appraisal is the formal, structured system that compares an employee's performance to established standards. An effective evaluation process is designed to promote the effectiveness of the employee and support their professional development. The value of the evaluation process depends on the skills of the manager, the soundness of the selected evaluation process and tools, and the working relationship established between the employee and supervisor.

Managers are also responsible for providing the resources needed by their employees to effectively fulfill their job responsibilities. They are the gatekeepers for the resources in the organization and need to realize what the resource needs are, and effectively advocate for them. The manager develops and manages the budget so the needed resources are available to effectively deliver quality services.

Successful employees need ongoing feedback, information, and guidance. The most common process for ongoing feedback is supervision. Supervision is a necessary tool to build competence. Kadushin (1992) identified three basic types of supervision, commonly referred to as administrative (or managerial), clinical (or educational) and supportive supervision.

Administrative supervision, also referred to as managerial supervision is concerned with the correct, effective and appropriate implementation of agency policies and procedures. The primary goal is to ensure adherence to policy and procedures (Kadushin, 1992). It also ensures that the mission of the agency is being met. Administrative supervision includes issues such as policy changes, budget and financial performance, and outcome monitoring.

Clinical or educational supervision is designed to upgrade the skills and knowledge of the employee. Clinical supervision is a formal process of professional support and learning which enables individual practitioners to develop knowledge and competence, assume responsibility for their own practice, and ensure consumer safety and well-being. Clinical supervision focuses on the employee's actual work practice and encourages the employee to reflect on their practice with the support of a skilled supervisor. The primary goal of clinical supervision is to maintain and improve standards of care. The ideal is often to receive clinical supervision from a practitioner of the same professional discipline, but this is not always available in the practice of therapeutic recreation.

Supportive supervision focuses on the morale and job satisfaction of an employee. Employees face a variety of job-related stresses, which may seriously affect their work and lead to a less than satisfactory service to clients. For employees, the ultimate problem is "burnout." Supportive supervision should not be confused with counseling, in which the primary goal is the well-being of the individual. Supportive supervision is provided to ensure that the employee is able to provide the best possible services to the client. Supportive supervision also focuses on maintaining harmonious working relationships, cultivating high-performing teams and developing esprit de corps. Refer to the Table 7.1 for a summary of the intent of each form of supervision.

Professional Clinical Supervision

Knowing that clinical supervision enhances professional competence does not alter the fact that many therapeutic recreation practitioners do not have access to it. Many therapeutic recreation practitioners function independently and are supervised by managers from other disciplines. An experienced professional of any discipline may provide clinical supervision, in particular, supervision related to the specific client group served. Thus, a therapist working in mental health may receive clinical supervision from a psychiatrist or psychologist regarding diagnosis and intervention approaches. The ideal is to have clinical supervision from an experienced therapeutic recreation professional within the agency whose focus is on the therapist's growth as a reflective practitioner, which ultimately impacts client

outcomes. Often clinical supervision is sought out in other ways. To have discipline specific supervision, practitioners seek out professional mentors and participate in professional development opportunities available through professional membership organizations. State, regional, and national conferences provide important discipline-specific learning opportunities as well the opportunity to meet and interact with experienced practitioners.

Professional clinical supervision is a developmental process, which is designed to meet the practitioner at their particular developmental level and promote their continued learning and development. Issues addressed in clinical supervision include skills competence, assessment techniques, interpersonal assessment, client conceptualization, individual differences, intervention plans and goals, and professional ethics (Shank & Coyle, 2002). Clinical supervision occurs in individual sessions, in small groups, or in peer-facilitated groups. Techniques used in clinical supervision include face-to-face dialogue, observation, journaling, prescribed learning exercises and case presentations. The ultimate goal of the clinical supervision process is "practice wisdom," which is the accumulation of lessons learned and insights gained from years of experience (Krill, 1990). Clinical supervision is a highly valued resource that promotes competent professional practice.

Establishing Working Relationships With a Supervisor

The key to a healthy working relationship with a supervisor is effective communication. Effective communication in the employee-supervisor relationship leads to a positive work environment. It is the mechanism that over time cultivates trust, respect, and understanding. Every employee needs to find the best ways to cultivate and assume open communication channels. It is important that a supervisor receives accurate appropriate "doses" of information so that he or she knows what is happening within his or her area of responsibility. A supervisor needs to be apprised of current projects as well as the success and the challenges facing employees.

Table 7.1
Forms of Supervision

	Clinical Supervision	**Managerial Supervision**	**Supportive Supervision**
Nature	Performance centered	Agency centered	Employee/team centered
Focus	Skill development	Operations and controls	Morale and relationships
Goal	Practice wisdom	Organizational effectiveness	Job satisfaction and high-functioning teams

Determining the most effective way to communicate with a supervisor promotes the establishment of a positive working relationship. Each individual has his or her preferred communication methods. Some individuals prefer written memos, sticky notes, e-mail, voice messages, or face-to-face communication. Some supervisors are able to integrate messages given "on the fly"—in passing in the hall or a comment made by popping in at their door. Others need to have a focused interaction, during a prescheduled supervision time, and want all concerns and comments held until that scheduled meeting. Drucker (1967) identified two types of managers, the readers and the listeners. The reader is one who studies volumes of background information before making a decision. The listener, on the other hand, prefers information be delivered orally, followed by a brief written summary of what has been discussed. Likewise, some managers prefer to stay close to the front line and are active in the decision-making process while others prefer that the employee closest to the situation retain complete responsibility (Drucker, 1967). Those who prefer to be close to the decision-making process require ongoing, detailed communication. Those who allow one to retain responsibility usually require summary information of what is going on with notes on decisions as they are made.

Some supervisors are willing to listen to emotional content; others want just the facts. Some will tolerate "venting," while others view this as unprofessional conduct. Complaints made with proposed solutions or remedies are usually more palatable than complaints without alternatives. An employee who anticipates problems and lets their supervisor know about those that will affect him or her as soon as possible gains trust and credibility. No one likes to be surprised or embarrassed. It is essential to keep the supervisor informed of activities, progress, obstacles, and when assistance is needed. Assumptions are always dangerous. There is an art to presenting issues to a supervisor, and employees who hone that skill stand a better chance of obtaining positive results. Knowing the preferred communication style of a supervisor ensures that the message is received.

Employees also must share the responsibility for their relationship with a supervisor. Many employees mistakenly assume that in a supervisor-employee relationship, the supervisor is responsible for establishing and maintaining the relationship. The employee shares the responsibility of scheduling meetings, requesting supervision times, and making their needs known. An employee should come to meetings with an agenda versus waiting for the supervisor to initiate and structure the meeting. Additionally, the employee brings information that the supervisor is able to use to make decisions and act upon. There is information at times that one need not know, therefore it is important to respect and use a supervisor's time wisely. Most supervisors prefer that employees work independently and handle the day-to-day problems that arise. Keeping a list of supervision topics helps to organize a supervision meeting so as to make it effective for both the employee and the supervisor.

An employee should also find ways to help their supervisor be successful. A supervisor is responsible for assuring the effectiveness of those he or she supervises. Likewise, the employee is responsible for assuring the success of their supervisor. In a team-oriented environment, the success of one is linked to the success of all. Often a supervisor is hired for their skills in managing people: They may have limited knowledge about the professional practice of therapeutic recreation. The employee may need to take the initiative to educate their supervisor about the work they do. Supervisors also need to receive feedback on their effectiveness, and to direct communication regarding what the employee needs from them, what facilitates their work, and what makes work more enjoyable for the employee. It is important to communicate recognition of work done well. Managers and staff alike need the warmth of positive strokes.

Honesty is the essence of a good working relationship with one's supervisor. A climate of trust and honesty must be built and established over time. Dishonesty in a working relationship is quickly discovered. Often the dishonesty generated in an agency or organization can be attributed to the employee's need, or manager's need, to appear knowledgeable and competent. Regardless of the reason, the impulse to provide a supervisor with potentially incorrect information must be resisted. Personal integrity, honesty, principles, and commitment to the truth will facilitate and enhance all other aspects of the relationship.

In the course of a professional career, employees will work with a variety of supervisors. Some will be more skilled and helpful while others may be more challenging. Recognize that employees may work with or against their supervisor, and it is easier to work with him or her. A therapeutic recreation professional is trained to accommodate in a variety of ways to work effectively with a client. The client has his or her needs and expectations, and based on these needs and expectations a care plan and interaction strategy is developed. It may be helpful to think of a supervisor as a client. Develop a plan and interaction strategy based on an assessment of needs and expectations. Have a goal-oriented plan to establish and maintain a constructive working relationship. One of the cardinal rules of management is that a commitment to a direction or goal must be supported by all. This does not mean that everyone always agrees. It is important that a way to support the decision without compromising one's values is found. In a professional relationship the outcomes positively impact both parties. An effective supervisory relationship impacts both the employee's ability to successfully do their job, and their overall job satisfaction as well as the supervisor's effectiveness as a manager and his or her job satisfaction.

Finally, it is important to give the relationship time to develop and mature. Don't rush things. As with any good relationship, it takes time to build trust and rapport. Often the strongest and most effective working relationships are those that have been tested and have worked through conflict and challenge. Creating a good working relationship with one's supervisor and working toward the organization's goals will give one a reputation for trustworthiness. Once a relationship is established, free and open communication will sustain and nurture that relationship.

Dealing With Difficult Supervisors

This chapter is predicated on establishing a relationship with a competent supervisor, but not all supervisory situations are ideal. In some cases, an employee may find him or herself in a situation of having a very difficult supervisor. In this situation, Kiechel (1984) advised that one perform to the best of one's ability while continuing to communicate with others in the organization. This allows others to distinguish between one's level of competence and the supervisor's level of incompetence. Potential employee-supervisor scenarios include the following:

The Micromanager

This is a supervisor who is controlling and overly involved. The possible cause for this type of behavior may be a lack of trust and confidence. Providing this type of manager more information than less is an effective strategy. Also, employee consistency in performing job responsibilities may remedy the situation.

The Nonmanager

This is a supervisor who is indecisive, hesitant, vague, and frequently not accessible. The course of action for an employee working with a nonmanaging manager is to avoid asking open-ended questions, but to give the supervisor a few recommendations with one clear recommendation. Counteract vagueness by asking for clarification, and avoid procrastination by communicating timelines and deadlines. Essentially, the employee needs to assume the manager's responsibilities in order to get their work done. It may be important to distinguish between a supervisor who lacks decisiveness and one who lacks accessible information (Kiechel, 1984).

The Unreasonable Manager

This is a manager who is overly demanding and unrealistic with work expectations and assignments. The employee will need to schedule a meeting to discuss priorities and options for what cannot be completed. Suggest solutions when possible, but set realistic expectations.

The Explosive Manager

This is a manager who yells at, insults and bullies his or her employees. In dealing with or managing these individuals, it is helpful to use the principle of disengagement; that is, exiting the situation and letting the individual know that one will return at a time when the matter can be discussed less emotionally. If the outbursts continue, it may be necessary to tell him or her any observations and concerns with the communication difficulty indicating concerns for one's well-being to the appropriate human resource personnel.

At some point, it may become necessary to dissolve or change the existing relationship with a supervisor. Often this means requesting a transfer or leaving an organization. It is always desirable to end relationships positively, but there are instances when this is not possible. Unless the situation is drastic, one in which morals or ethics are being compromised, the employee should make every effort to leave while ensuring a smooth transition and continuation of work in progress including making it as comfortable as possible for those who remain.

The Political Climate

The word *politics* brings a grimace to the face of many therapeutic recreation practitioners. It is cited as a reason for leaving positions and not seeking others. It is often given as a reason for failure or unearned success. It is a word often spoken with skepticism and sometimes as though it were slightly obscene. It is seen as manipulative and not quite respectable. Politics is not a four-letter word. In fact, politics is in the eye of the beholder. What is politics to one is very likely characterized by another as effective management. One cannot escape the fact that it is highly unlikely that an organization is free of politics.

Politics is often defined as the art of influencing others so that the events move toward a desired outcome. In a positive sense, it connotes "campaigning, lobbying, bargaining, negotiating, concurring, collaborating, and winning votes" (Kanter, 1983, p. 213). Politics is associated with leadership and the exercise of power. To be politically successful is to be able to move smoothly through the environment, exerting one's influence in an attempt to accomplish goals. The successful manager understands that this ability is equally important in the management of one's relationship to one's supervisor and employees.

To be sensitive to a political environment implies the understanding of power and its source. This environment is like a body of water on which one must sail a boat. Understanding the wind direction and velocity is critical to plotting a course. One has a choice to try to maneuver against the wind, with the possibility of being stalled, or working with the wind by choosing the appropriate tack, so that progress can be made and the destination is reached.

An employee may be depending on a manager to employ his or her understanding to win a race or achieve a goal, just as a first-line manager depends on his or her "boss" to achieve the department's goals. If one is stalled, has misread the political winds and has capsized due to turbulence, the skipper may be called on for rescue. While that rescue may be forthcoming, one should not grow dependent on it. If one keeps getting thrown overboard because one has not learned the winds, one may expect to stay in the water. No matter how the employee or first-line manager feels about their "boss," the race cannot be won if he or she continually needs to be pulled out of the water. At some point the rescue will interfere with the goal.

The sooner a therapeutic recreation manager becomes aware of the political aspects of a job, the sooner that manager will find that results begin to impact his or her position. A first-line manager like an employee will win some and lose some, but win or lose, he or she must always be ready to return and play the game again. Involvement in the politics of a job is a do-it-yourself endeavor. In reality, waiting around for others to invite one into the arena is a passive posture that signals powerlessness.

To develop and improve political skills Robbins (1995, pp. 423–425) suggests the following:

1. Frame arguments in terms of organizational goals.

2. Develop the right image.

3. Gain access to organizational resources.

4. Make oneself appear indispensable.

5. Be visible.

6. Get a mentor.

7. Develop powerful allies.

8. Avoid "tainted" members.

9. Support the boss.

Reflecting One's Supervisor

Effective managers realize the importance of activating the strengths of their supervisors and employees. Drucker (1967, p. 116) stated, "Contrary to popular legend, subordinates do not, as a rule, rise to the position and prominence over the prostrate bodies of incompetent bosses."

For better or worse, bosses in any organization are perceived and judged not only on their own merits and accomplishments but also on the merits and accomplishments of those who report to them. This means that work, attitudes, and values reflect on the supervisor in the same way that staff's work and attitudes reflect on the manager. Of course, the reverse is also true; a manager is also seen in the light of the supervisor (Drucker, 1967).

In an organization the manager's appearance and attitude communicate the attitude of the supervisor. To the extent that the picture is positive, the employee's work and effort will be enhanced and the employee will feel valued. The wisdom of making others look good, whether they are supervisors or subordinates, is clearly demonstrated in the creation of a positive atmosphere where accomplishments are recognized.

Part of the benefit and expectation of being a manager is participation in activities outside the organization. Whether it is serving on a committee of another organization, serving on citizen committees, or merely appearing at a public hearing, a manager will be perceived as a representative of the organization, even if the service is of purely a personal interest. Behavior and image will be as much a reflection of the boss and the organization as it is of one personally. For the most part, this external visibility does not become an issue of importance unless the values expounded on the community are in conflict with the values of the organization. It might be wise to give thought to what might be said in certain situations rather than having to face the many small decisions about expressing or not expressing a point of view.

Managing Physicians and Other Healthcare Professionals

Therapeutic recreation professionals and most health and human service professionals are taught to be team players and typically work well with others as a prerequisite to the work they pursue. Physicians, on the other hand, are encouraged to develop their individuality and autonomy even though there has been a significant change in attitude in recent years. Medical students are taught to be in control—imperative in critical medical emergencies. Physicians often have not had much exposure to the practice of therapeutic recreation and may not fully understand the value of the services provided. So it is not unusual that therapeutic recreation practitioners experience challenges in their working relationships with physicians.

Often the therapeutic recreation practitioner needs a physician's referral to provide the services indicated from the client assessment. To secure reimbursement of therapeutic recreation services from third-party payers, the therapist incorporates these orders in the client's intervention plan. Thus, cooperation and collaboration among health care professionals on the team, including the referring physician, is fundamental to client intervention.

The following strategies may assist in establishing a positive working relationship with physicians:

- The therapeutic recreation practitioner is an equal member of the healthcare team. Often the therapist may represent themselves with a less than confident presentation.

- Be present at care planning conferences and team meetings with physicians. It is important to have the opportunity to develop a working relationship by establishing an actual face-to-face relationship, being known, and providing direct feedback.

- All the members of the healthcare team should focus on the task to be accomplished or the problem to be solved, rather than personal differences. Discipline-defined boundaries and differences are respected.

- Remain client centered, and remember the reason for working together is the attainment of client goals and high-quality, safe client services.

- Establish clear roles and responsibilities for the physician, other team members, oneself, and one's staff.

- Always be prepared with the facts, assessed needs, and data when talking with physicians. Information on client outcomes is especially relevant.

- Ask clearly and concisely for referrals or other requests of physicians. Make it as easy as possible for them to meet requests.

- Competency in professional practice is the best way to win the respect and confidence of physicians and other healthcare professionals.

- Find opportunities to educate physicians and other healthcare professionals about therapeutic recreation services and outcomes. The celebration of Therapeutic Recreation Week is one avenue to foster knowledge about therapeutic recreation among professionals in health and human services; likewise, participating in the annual professional recognition weeks of other disciplines is both educational and conducive to team development and support.

- Respect the physician as a person, not as "just a doctor."

Therapeutic recreation managers serve as role models for their staff when they are seen working effectively with physicians and practitioners from disciplines like occupational, physical, and speech therapy. An attitude of collaboration and cooperation rather than an adversarial one encourages a similar interaction among staff. The manager may also need to intervene and serve as a mediator in conflicts that may arise between therapeutic recreation practitioners and physicians or professionals from other disciplines. It is important to support staff, while at the same time working in a collegial fashion with other healthcare providers. This is critical for the manager's success with staff and success in the organization.

Organization Control Versus Self-Supervision

In an organization that has a healthy balance of organizational control and self supervision, an employee knows the desired end results, not just methods, and what is to be done and when. Guidelines are provided that specify the parameters (i.e., policies and protocols) within which the results are to be accomplished. Resources are provided, including the human, financial, technical, and organization support to accomplish the results. Standards of performance are predetermined. Individuals are held accountable because they know the standards and methods of measuring progress. Consequences are also defined. Control does not mean that some people control others, it means that the organization is in control—and the parts work together ethically and responsibly to create the desired results.

Supervising oneself means that the employee knows what is expected and is accountable for meeting the expectations. The employee knows their job description, the agency policies and procedures, and accesses the resources needed to fulfill their job. They are self-motivated to pursue their own professional growth and development. These professionals have the foundation they need to work independently to achieve organizational goals, to make informed decisions, and to work effectively as closely as possible to the action front. The empowered organization is one in which individual employees are empowered and have the knowledge, skill, desire and opportunity to personally succeed in a way that leads to collective organizational success.

Stephen Covey (1990) identified eight discernible characteristics of people who are principle-centered leaders. Principle-centered leaders are those who are effectively managing and "self-supervising" their lives. These eight characteristics provide a rubric by which an employee or manager measures their own performance.

1. *They are continually learning.* They read, seek training, take classes, attend conferences, listen to others and are constantly seeking to expand their competence.

2. *They are service oriented.* They see life and their work as a mission and not a career. They have a sense of responsibility, of service and a need to contribute.

3. *They radiate positive energy.* They have an optimistic, positive, enthusiastic, and hopeful outlook on life.

4. *They believe in other people.* They don't overreact to negative behaviors, criticism or human weaknesses. They believe in the unseen potential of all people.

5. *They lead balanced lives.* They aren't workaholics, or unbalanced in any of their life pursuits. They seek variety, know how to play, laugh and enjoy life.

6. *They see life as an adventure.* They savor life, novelty and seek new experiences.

7. *They are synergistic.* Synergy is the state in which the whole is more than the sum of the parts. Synergistic people work well in teams, and readily delegate since they believe in others' strengths and capacities.

8. *They exercise self-renewal.* They regularly take time to exercise physically, mentally, emotionally, and spiritually.

The success of a working relationship depends on the consistent effort applied toward development, the thoroughness of the understanding of the needs, goals, pressures, and work styles of the parties involved, and the willingness to suspend one's personal agenda in favor of the organization's goal. Staff and managers who emulate the characteristics of principle-centered leaders are likely to establish working relationships built on trust, respect, and good communication. Once established a good working relationship enables a uniform approach to meeting goals, completing projects, and allocating resources. This free and open communication nurtures relationships and ensures organizational stability and progress.

Summary

Managing the relationship between employee, manager, and supervisor requires skill, insight, patience, and perseverance. It requires self-knowledge, careful observation, analysis and the ability to take risks. The effort required is great, but the reward for success is equally great. Mutual growth, mutual success, and ultimately an effective work environment that benefits the clients served are the rewards. Whether the therapeutic recreation professional is a department of one, or part of a large organization, and wherever they may be in the organizational hierarchy, the employee-supervisor relationship is critical to effective service provision.

In this chapter, consideration was given to the role of a supervisor or manager, and responsibilities that a manager has within the organization. The three primary types of supervision were reviewed and managerial responsibilities within each supervisory role were discussed. Expectations that an employee has of a supervisor were reviewed as well as strategies for working effectively with a supervisor. Strategies to utilize when working with a "difficult" manager were also presented as were considerations for addressing the political nature of the work environment. The importance of reflecting the manager's and organization's goals through professional and respectful behaviors was addressed. Working with physicians, and other healthcare providers may present challenges; yet the establishment of positive collegial relationships is fundamental to quality client results. Self-supervision was defined and introduced as a job skill that all employees and managers should work to further develop as a means to nurture effective working relationships.

Review Questions

1. Do you support the idea that a supervisor should receive recognition for work you have done? Explain your response.

2. Explain administrative, educational, and supportive responsibilities of a manager. Give an example of each that impacts an employee.

3. Explain two manager communication styles and how each influences interactions between the employee and manager.

4. Interview practicing therapeutic recreation professionals. Collect success stories about their interactions with physicians and other healthcare professionals. Create your own list of effective

strategies to build working relationships among colleagues.

5. Shadow a manager. Identify examples of micromanagement, nonmanagement, unreasonable expectations and emotionally charged employee-manager behavior.

References

Covey, S. (1990). *Principle-centered leadership.* New York, NY: Simon & Schuster.

Drucker, P. F. (1988). Management and the world's work. *Harvard Business Review, 66*(5), 65–76.

Drucker, P. F. (1967). *The effective executive.* New York, NY: Harper & Row.

Kadushin, A. (1992). *Supervision in social work* (3rd ed.). New York, NY: Columbia University Press.

Kanter, R. M. (1983). *The change master.* New York, NY: Simon & Schuster.

Kiechel W., III. (1984). How to manage your boss. *Fortune, 110*(6), 206–210.

Krill, D. (1990). *Practice wisdom: A guide for helping professionals.* Newbury Park, CA: Sage Publications.

Robbins, S. P. (1995). *Supervision today.* Englewood Cliffs, NJ: Prentice Hall.

Shank, J. and Coyle, C. (2002). *Therapeutic recreation in health promotion and rehabilitation.* State College, PA: Venture Publishing, Inc.

Section III
Operational Management

Chapter 8
Financial Management and Budgets

The therapeutic recreation manager today who believes it is not necessary to be aware of the financial side of delivering health and human services is very much like the proverbial ostrich that sticks its head in the sand and hopes that what it cannot see will not hurt it. Given the choice, it is likely the majority of first-line managers would relinquish the budgetary aspects of their jobs. However, as noted by Thompson (2001), the survival of therapeutic recreation service in health care systems may be dependent on therapeutic recreation specialists having "competencies associated with sound financial management" (p. 249) as the "viability of most healthcare organizations today depends on their ability to use their fiscal resources wisely" (Marquis & Huston, 2003, p. 121).

In the past, financial management, to a large degree, was associated with the complex and technical work of accounting. It was viewed as a specialized area delegated to a number of individuals who were separated and apart from general management and operation. This has changed dramatically. Today the role of the therapeutic recreation manager with respect to the costs of providing therapeutic recreation service in health and human services, especially in health care facilities, has changed. In the health care arena budgeting has become increasingly decentralized, with managers taking on a growing role (Tappen, 2001). A focus on cost containment requires that managers fully understand how to make changes to control costs to deliver services effectively and efficiently (McCormick, 2002). Additionally, the scarcity of financial resources, a move toward capitation systems, increased competition among health care providers, and the increased responsibility of consumers to bear the costs of medical care are forces behind fiscal planning and accountability that fall to the manager of a unit (Sullivan & Decker, 2001). In the community-based leisure service agencies and organizations there is a climate of fiscal austerity.

Therapeutic recreation managers need to look at money matters and budgets philosophically as well as pragmatically. They also need to recognize and to maintain a realistic attitude toward obtaining and dispensing funds. Managers, and to a lesser degree staff, can be appreciative or critical toward funds allocated to them, and the position they take does make a difference. Managers are likely to achieve better results in the delivery of ser-

vices if they are realistic about the money available. Managers who overemphasize the value of money in their department may have morale problems with staff and difficulties with supervisors that surpass financial realities. Likewise, managers and practitioners who are constantly critical about budgetary matters will eventually hurt their program delivery of services and lessen the contributions they make. This does not mean financial questions and concerns should not be raised or addressed and budgetary suggestions should not be made. In fact, managers and staff should have input in making suggestions about the budget so the department budget reflects the needs of the unit and is congruent with the goals of the organization.

This chapter makes no pretense of covering the complexities of financial management and budgeting in detail. Initially its purpose is to provide a brief historical overview of sources of revenue to support services coupled with why there is a need for proper fiscal management. This is followed by a discussion of the various revenue sources that organizations presently use. Thereafter, there is a review and consideration of the basic concepts of financial management, including budgeting, budget process, types of budgets, and budget control. The role of the first-line manager in cost containment concludes this chapter.

Historical Overview

Financial management and budgeting were common practices in public community-based leisure service agencies before their use in private sector planning. In the 1950s budgeting began to be seen as a planning tool, and planning was increasingly adopted as a management tool. Subsequent to the enormous investments of the Great Society era, the concern for better leisure resource allocation and program evaluation gave rise to the concept of cost-effectiveness evaluation and cost-benefit analysis (Anthony & Herzlinger, 1980), zero-base budgeting (Cheek, 1977), and social accounting (Melton & Watason, 1977). Other factors that contributed to fiscal stress within the park and recreation field outside of the tax revolt movement included economic recessions, forced reduction in the size of the work force, growing interdependency of the public and private sector, increasing complexity of the law coupled with legislation (e.g., Americans with Disabilities Act [ADA]), erosion of the tax base in metropolitan areas, a growing national debt, and an increase in the gross value and maintenance costs of publicly owned park and recreation resources (Crompton, 1999).

The current crisis in the United States relating to the cost of health care has been brought about by increased use of health care facilities, inflation, population increase, increasing numbers of elderly, focus on illness care, cost reimbursement, fee for service reimbursement, technology, care of the uninsured, malpractice, administrative overhead costs, and the care of chronic and catastrophic diseases (e.g., AIDS). These cost factors have been further complicated by hospital competition, redesigned care delivery service (e.g., freestanding clinics, home care, outpatient surgery, other ambulatory services that focus on preventive or rehabilitative health care and service), and marketing of health care services.

Depending on the source, various approaches can explain the high cost of health care. Hospitals in the early 1900s had a basic mission to care for the sick and poor. In many cases the family was surprised by a patient's discharge, not by a patient's death. Hospitals were financially supported by philanthropy, and there was no hospitalization insurance (Rosenberg, 1987). However, when an individual did pay, it would be on what is now called an *all-inclusive rate*. That is, hospitals charged all patients the same daily rate. This single rate covered all services that the hospital provided.

By the 1920s it was not unusual for patients to be charged a regular daily service and special service charges for specific techniques in surgery, anesthesia, X-ray, laboratory services, drugs, physical therapy, and so forth. The intent of the special service charge system was simply to maintain equity between patients who used particular services and those who did not (Berman, Weeks & Kukla, 1990).

During the late 1920s, an inclusive rate system was applied to certain admissions according to diagnosis, such as tonsillectomies and maternity service. In the 1930s all-inclusive rates were established by many hospitals for all inpatients. These rates varied only as to the length of stay of the patient and the type of accommodations (e.g., ward, semi-private room, private room). Also during the 1930s, the federal government became involved in hospital care reimbursement through the Children's Bureau. As opposed to full hospital costs, the Children's Bureau only paid the cost per day that was applicable to patient care, excluding costs that were not for direct patient care, such as administrative and benefits costs (Berman, Weeks & Kukla, 1990). During this same period Kaiser Permanente in California developed the forerunner of today's

health maintenance organization (HMO); payment and delivery of health care were merged into a single system.

Meanwhile in 1929 Dr. Justin Ford Kimball, the executive vice president of Baylor University, found that the University Hospital in Dallas, Texas, was in serious financial trouble because of the large amount of outstanding accounts receivable. It was noted by Dr. Kimball that a large number of delinquent debtors were teachers. As a result, he initiated a prepayment plan for teachers to aid in hospital care costs. The teachers who joined the plan could pay a fixed sum (e.g., 50¢ per month premium) and be assured of up to 21 days of hospital care in a semi-private room at Baylor University Hospital. The Baylor prepayment idea caught on in other parts of the country where other hospitals faced a problem of collecting unpaid bills. Eventually, these various plans came together under the term Blue Cross (Berman, Weeks & Kukla, 1990; Nowicki, 2001).

Throughout the next four decades, with the exception of the period in the 1930s when Blue Cross plans were getting started and a flat rate system was used, a variety of retrospective, prospective, incentive, and disincentive systems were used to pay hospital bills (Berman, Weeks & Kukla, 1990). These systems shifted the responsibility of health care costs from the individual to private sector (i.e., insurance companies) and government-supported sources.

During World War II, Congress enacted wage controls. As a result employers attracted employees with fringe benefits, such as health insurance, instead of higher wages (McCormick, 2002). Health insurance became a fringe benefit and by 1952 "more than half of the U.S. population was covered by some form of health insurance" (McCormick, 2002, p. 190).

The end of World War II brought a demand for more beds to care for the injured. The passage of the Hill-Burton Act provided funding for construction to expand existing hospitals and build new ones. The Hill-Harris Hospital and Medical Facilities Amendments were enacted in 1964. They dealt with modernization grants, area-wide planning, and long-term care facilities (Tillock, 1981). With the passage of the Social Security Act Amendments of 1965 (PL 89-97), a cost-based retrospective reimbursement system was established (Skalko, 1998). The federal government became the primary insurer of the elderly, the poor, and certain individuals with long-term illnesses through Medicare and Medicaid programs (McCormick, 2002). Federal and state governments became major purchasers of health care services. Additionally, because hospitals were reimbursed retrospectively at a reasonable rate for services provided, they were reinforced financially resulting in the delivery of more services. This resulted in rising health care costs (Marquis & Huston, 2003; Skalko, 1998).

By 1970 medical care costs were escalating at an astonishing rate with no end in sight (Rosenberg, 1987).

"The federal government discovered early that Medicare and Medicaid use and resulting costs had been underprojected, and that retroactive cost-based reimbursement to hospitals...was inflationary" (Nowicki, 2001, p. 88). Initial efforts to control rising health care costs came with the creation of Professional Standards Review Organizations (PSRO) by the 1972 Social Security Amendments. PSROs denied payments for Medicare and Medicaid patients if services were deemed unnecessary (McCormick, 2002). Another alternative to traditional health insurance plans—managed care—came into existence as the result of the Health Maintenance Organization Act (PL 93-222) of 1973 (Marquis & Huston, 2003). The intent of the law was to create HMOs as competitors to drive down costs of traditional care. HMOs are characterized as independent plans that offer comprehensive medical service through a group of medical practitioners, often in one location. The subscriber to an HMO pays a set monthly premium, and physicians and other health professionals employed by the HMO typically are paid on a salaried basis rather than a fee-for-service basis.

The rapid expansion of health care services and the corresponding escalation in health care cost coupled with a significant increase in premiums for malpractice insurance prompted numerous cost-containment efforts during the 1970s and into the 1980s (Rosenberg, 1987). For the first time, the government curtailed unnecessary expansion of the health care delivery system with the passage of the 1974 National Health Planning and Resource Development Act (PL 93-641; McCormick, 2002). This was viewed as a cost-containment effort since it was believed that surplus services tended to create unnecessary use. Utilization review was introduced as a program designed to place limits on consumer stays in hospitals. An attempt to control the expansion of hospital physical facilities and technological equipment was done through a certificate-of-need program. At the urging of the American Hospital Association (AHA), hospitals developed programs to control health expenditures. By the end of the 1970s, third-party payers were paying two thirds of all hospital care costs (American Hospital Association, 1983).

Third-party payers include the federal government Medicare program, state government Medicaid programs, Blue Cross and Blue Shield (BC/BS) plans (separate statewide or substatewide area operations coordinated through the BC/BS Association), commercial insurance companies (e.g., Prudential, Travelers), HMOs, PPOs (i.e., preferred provider organizations), and third-party administrators (i.e., for-profit general business corporations that provide all services of a BC/BS plan or a commercial insurance company with the exception of the insurance underwriting).

Blue Cross and Blue Shield plans are the market leaders. Most operate as not-for-profit health service corporations although there is a trend to convert to for-profit organizations. In addition, people are now making higher copayments for insurance than ever before.

The federal government began exploring alternative cost-containment strategies because the measures enacted during the 1970s were ineffective. Two pieces of legislation—the Tax Equity and Fiscal Responsibility Act (TEFRA; PL 97-248) of 1982 and the Social Security Amendment Act of 1983 (PL 98-21)—changed the way health care was purchased (McCormick, 2002). Health care was to be reimbursed on a prospective payment system (PPS) rather than a cost-per-case basis or retrospective system (Skalko, 1998). This system provided payment to most hospitals at a predetermined specific rate for each Medicare discharge based on the consumer's diagnosis. Under this system, discharges are classified into diagnosis-related groups (DRGs), with 24 major diagnostic categories (MDCs) organized by organ system and disease etiology, and 470 DRGs applicable to Medicare. The PPS system provided hospitals the opportunity to realize a direct savings for the first time in providing services. This system not only provided a savings for hospitals but also assisted greatly in the development of fixed payment plans with employers, HMOs, PPOs, and other health provider organizations. Moreover, the PPS provided a strong incentive for hospital management to organize its operations and to provide services to consumers in the most cost effective and efficient manner (American Hospital Association, 1983). In 1985, the Consolidated Omnibus Budget Reconciliation Act (COBRA; P.L. 99-272) was passed. This act and various amendments to it in succeeding years have modified the reimbursement provisions of PPS.

"Managed care became widespread during the 1980s" (Tomey, 2000, p. 196). The PPS provided the incentive "to third-party carriers to contract with health care systems to receive discounted medical services" (Skalko, 1998, p. 449). Managed care organizations (MCOs), like HMOs, monitor the delivery of care and are gatekeepers to providers of care. Comprehensive health care services are provided to enrolled consumers for a fixed periodic payment. Employers may prepay fixed rates to health care providers per employee or for a defined population per month for specified health care services. With capitation, if the cost of care per month is less, the provider profits.

There are a number of types of MCOs as well as different types of plans within HMOs (Marquis & Huston, 2003). In some instances HMOs have been created by private insurers like Blue Cross/Blue Shield who also maintain their traditional indemnity plans. In independent practice association (IPA) HMOs, "the HMO contracts with a group of physicians through an intermediary to provide services for members of the HMO" (Marquis & Huston, 2003, p. 138). In preferred provider organizations (PPOs), services are rendered on a fee-for-service basis with incentives of lowered rates when the preferred provider is used. The types of plans within HMOs vary according to the degree of provider choice available to enrollees. In point-of-service (POS) plans, at the time of service the patient has the option to select a provider outside the network of HMO contracted providers, but pays a higher premium and a copayment (Nowicki, 2001). With exclusive provider organization (EPO) options, the enrollee who seeks care outside of the designated HMO provider will pay all of the cost out-of-pocket.

The intent of managed care is to integrate efficiency of care, access, and cost of care (Nowicki, 2001). By the late 1980s, with the continuing growth of MCOs, measures like case management, utilization review, clinical (critical or care) pathways with outcome criteria as quality indicators, and continuous quality monitoring and improvement were instituted to manage and evaluate cost-effectiveness and efficiency. The managed care movement remains controversial. Proponents suggest that health care costs have been decreased by between 10% and 40% and the rate of increase of health care costs has been reduced (Marquis & Huston, 2003; Nowicki, 2001). Critics suggest practices may lead to early patient discharge, lower level of care continuity and consumer confusion about the many rules to follow (Marquis & Huston, 2003; Tomey, 2000).

MCOs impact health care delivery and reimbursement strategies and affect how therapeutic recreation managers develop department budgets and market to internal and external audiences. Astute managers are aware that incremental changes in payment systems create windows of opportunity to promote services. Awareness of legislation like the 1997 Balanced Budget Act (PL 105-33) enables the manager to advocate for the most cost-effective mix or bundle-of-services, including therapeutic recreation, to meet individual needs (Thompson, 2001). Revisions in coding and identification have resulted in inclusion of recreation therapy in billing codes and as service options on federally mandated assessments (e.g., Rehab Prospective Payment System Minimum Data Set Post Acute Version 1). This legislation maintained the PPS initiated with TEFRA and introduced the use of RUGS—resource utilization groups—the case mix for reimbursement based on data from resident assessments (Nowicki, 2001).

The challenge to therapeutic recreation managers in an economically constrained and competitive environment, regardless of setting, is to have an understanding of the relationship among agencies and organizations, the environment, and the evolving social, political, and economic initiatives and trends. Legislation like the Health Insurance Portability and Accountability Act (HIPAA) of 1996 designed to improve health insurance availability also effects Medicare and Medicaid reimbursement and the processing of client information. Managers are cognizant of laws and trends like the aging baby boomers that will shape health care financing.

Revenue Sources

Health and human services are funded through a variety of sources: appropriations; contributions; grants and contracts; fees, charges, and reimbursement; or a combination of two or more of these sources. The nature of the organization—public or private, not-for-profit or for-profit—determines the funding sources as well as the implications for the planning and budgeting process to a large degree.

Appropriations

Although declining in recent years, the major source of funds for most public health and human service organizations remains tax-based revenues in the form of appropriations or grants. These tax-based funds may be federal, state, or local allocations. Then, too, a community, freestanding, leisure service center for persons with disabilities, which is part of a local department of parks and recreation, may get a fixed-dollar allocation from the city budget through the department in addition to possible federal or state funds that supplement the allocation by a grant. This may further be supplemented by a grant from a foundation or a large contribution from a private donor.

Public state agencies (e.g., institution for the blind) receive appropriations through the legislative branch of state government, usually on a yearly basis. These funds may also be supplemented by specific organizations or programs with other government and nongovernment grants.

Normally, a public entity can expect support on a long-term basis, with yearly appropriations primarily affecting the level of increment or decrement. This continuity, however, can sometimes limit the flexibility of the organization and its program unit's attempt at innovation. Many functions of public health and human service organizations and the services they offer are prescribed by legislation. As a result, this leaves little room for deviation even when outside funds are available to support growth and change.

Dependency on tax-based revenue and legislative appropriations also means that a public health and human service organization is subjected in a direct way to changes in funding level brought about by broad economic and political changes. Governmental bodies are immediately affected by economic stress and shifting political tides; consequently, the level and allocation of resources becomes a focal point for political processes. Agencies or organizations that do well in times of economic stress tend to have strong, cohesive, and politically active consumer groups. Public agencies cannot lobby, but citizen support groups can.

Funding by appropriation has a strong impact on the budgeting process and on the nature of agency or organization accountability. Ongoing use of public funds tends to allow for continuity and consistency in meeting organizational missions and goals. There still appears to be a strong tendency, however, for accountability to be measured in terms of traditionally understood services, regardless of setting, rather than in terms of community or individual impact. Because public health and human service organizations are held accountable for the means they use rather than the ends they seek in so many situations, they tend to have difficulty reforming budgetary processes or attempting innovations in service delivery unless these innovations have gained political acceptance.

Contributions

Contributions to health and human service agencies (e.g., Easter Seals self-supporting therapeutic recreation service agencies) can run the gamut from $5.00 donations by individuals to multimillion-dollar endowments. The process of fundraising can mean anything from direct mailings, to knocking on doors of corporate offices, to sponsorships, to mounting campaigns, to special events (e.g., walk-a-thons), to arts and crafts sales, to garage sales. Some agencies depend on professional fundraising or development specialists, which also encourages the fundraising efforts of board members.

The implications of contributed funds for the budgeting process depends more on the type of contribution than on its size. Unrestricted donations can be used to carry out any of the normal agency functions; thus, they become part of the operating budget. Sometimes, however, contributions are restricted to use for specific purposes. These funds may be earmarked either for specific current activities or for specified future use. Endowment funds may be restricted or unrestricted in terms of activities supported but involve the use of only the income earned from assets. An agency depending on various types of large contributions that include endowments must either develop or purchase investment expertise. In addition, an agency depending on contributions for a major portion of its revenue must also develop mechanisms for recording pledges or bequests.

For small agencies, participation in consolidated fundraising efforts is the norm. Contributions are received indirectly through participation in such programs as United Fund, United Way, or local community chests. In some respects, receiving funds from such campaigns is more similar to obtaining grants than it is to mounting direct campaigns for donations. Agencies that apply for funding indicate the objectives to be met by the funds, follow specified reporting procedures, and must fit the program's funding priorities.

Grants and Contracts

Grants involve obtaining funds from governmental agencies, particularly the federal government, and from private corporations and individuals. The process of funding can be both enriching and overwhelming. Applications for funds are usually made in accordance with printed guidelines supplied to help applicants define their objectives and describe their framework and methodology. The applications also include a systematized, built-in evaluation procedure to help the applicant. Still, the process can be daunting because of the many details and decisions that must be included and made. This is an area that requires much knowledge, and managers who are interested in obtaining grant money should increase their understanding of it.

The best source for learning about private foundations is the Foundation Center (79 Fifth Avenue, New York, NY 10003; http://fdncenter.org). The Foundation Center's Web site offers general and specialized information on the nonprofit sector. Links to grant makers are categorized by type, including private, corporate, public charities, and community foundations. The Foundation Directory Online Subscription Service provides access to an extensive database of grant makers. To obtain information on smaller foundations one should contact the local office of the Internal Revenue Service (IRS) or nearest Foundation Center Library for the latest Form 990PF. Small foundations must submit this form annually to the IRS on which they list all their grantees, finance details, funding interest and restrictions, and application procedures and deadlines. Additional avenues to locate foundations that have funds available include the following:

1. Conduct online searches through search engines like Yahoo! (e.g., http://dir.yahoo.com/Society_ and_Culture/Issues_and_Causes/Philanthropy/ Organizations/Grant_Making_Foundations).

2. Review publications from organizations like the Grantsmanship Center (http://www.tgci.com/ publications/puborder.htm).

3. Contact foundations known to fund specific causes directly, like the Christopher Reeve Paralysis Foundation (http://www.christopherreeve.org/ qlgrants/qlgrantsmain.cfm).

Tracking government funds may be even more challenging than searching for grants from foundations. Despite a general decline in support, the federal government is still the largest resource of external funding. Information on government funding may be obtained through a number of sources. A primary source is the U.S. Government Printing Office (http://www.gpoaccess.gov); the Catalog of Federal Domestic Assistance (http://www.cfda.gov) and the Commerce Business Daily (http://www.cbd-net.com/index.php/doc/home) which also identify available grants. Relative to federal agency priorities and applications, the program officer who is responsible for the grant in one's regional office or in Washington, DC, can be contacted as can the person whose name and number are listed in the Federal Register (http://www.ed.gov/legislation/fedregister/index.html). The program officer will be able to provide criteria for selection and an application packet for the grant program that includes forms, rules and regulations, and guidelines. Most grants in therapeutic recreation are obtained through the Office of Special Education and Rehabilitation Services (OSERS) and the National Institute on Disability and Rehabilitation Research (http://www.ed.gov/offices/OSERS/NIDRR).

Obtaining grants usually depends on the following: (a) a clear understanding of the guidelines and specific instructions, (b) careful formulation of the application, and (c) effective submission of the application to the funding agency and its representatives. Careful reading of the announcements and guidelines is essential in the grants process. The clearer the understanding of what is suggested and what is possible, the more likely it is that the application will be on target. The better the preparation for the proposed action, the more likely its acceptance.

The application needs both to be well-organized and related to the objectives of the funding agency. Governmental proposals have a highly structured format while proposals for foundations are less structured. Regardless, the more the application touches on specific areas, the more likely it is to be approved. Because many applications are ordinarily reviewed for most grant programs, the more unique and ingenious the application the better. Whenever a new approach can be introduced with anticipated pragmatic results, the more likely it is to be accepted. Creativity and organization are paramount.

The following format is offered as a guide to be modified if the funder requests a different outline:

1. summary statement

2. statement of need

3. goals and objectives

4. components of the program (e.g., activities, tasks)

5. evaluation

6. capability of the organization (i.e., ability to implement project)

7. continuation of the program

8. dissemination plan

9. budget

10. appendices (e.g., letters of support, affirmative action policy)

If the application does meet the funding organization's goal, it will be considered, in most instances, on the basis of the following questions:

- How well does the applicant demonstrate that there is a real need for the proposed project?

- How clear and attainable are the project's objectives?

- Does the proposal spell out a plan of action that suits project goals and objectives?

- Is the applying agency likely to be able to carry out the proposed project and meet the specified goals within the suggested time frame?

- Is the budget clearly thought out and appropriate for the scope of the project?

- Are the plans for evaluation well-documented, feasible, and appropriate?

In addition to routine answering of questions and following of suggestions outlined, if personal contacts can be made, the more likely a grant may be obtained. Contact, especially with private agencies, allows enthusiastic interest and comprehensive knowledge of the program area being considered to be expressed. Person-to-person contact before and during the grant preparation is desirable and may make the difference.

As the result of the ADA, more therapeutic recreation practitioners are developing small corporations to provide services to consumers with disabilities on a contractual basis. In fact, more and more public park and recreation departments are contracting for specific services because of a more conservative economic and political climate (Crompton, 1999).

Contracts are more specific than grants. They usually specify an outcome to be accomplished or a procedure to be followed or performed before the recipient of the funds is selected. When a funding source utilizes a performance contract or subcontract as a funding mechanism, its own personnel might spell out the specific activities to be performed and then select, as the recipient of the allocated funds, the individuals or organization deemed most likely to be successful in carrying out the specified functions.

Fees, Charges, and Reimbursement

Nearly all private community-based leisure service agencies and organizations charge a direct fee for their services. As noted earlier, some public community-based leisure service agencies may receive appropriated funds as well as charge a direct fee for their services. For therapeutic recreation service in these various community-based settings, a regular fee may be charged, or fees may be based on a sliding scale with the consumer paying differing amounts depending on his or her financial status. In freestanding public or private recreation and leisure centers for persons with disabilities there may be a membership fee or a combination membership and special fee or charge for specific courses or activities. Again, these types of fees and charges may be offset by grants, corporations, civic organizations, individual contributions, or gifts.

Sometimes these fund-giving organizations can have the same kind of effect on agency practices as other funding sources might have. "Strings" attached to funding can provide restrictions on an organization's activities. Likewise, fee-based services sometimes have difficulty moving into innovative service areas when their funding depends almost completely on the number of consumers personally served.

Another implication of the use of fees as a funding base is the inherent difficulty in predicting income. The therapeutic recreation manager must be able to estimate very accurately the number of consumers likely to be served in a given time period. Estimations become more complex when sliding scales mean that not all consumers generate the same amount of revenue.

Within health care facilities, and to a lesser degree in school systems and other community cooperatives, organization agreements exist where a majority of consumers are charged direct fees for services rendered. These fees are paid through a third party. For reimbursement, an agency acts on behalf of an organization or consumer to reimburse the provider for all or some portion of the provider's cost or charges of providing services. In such an arrangement the consumer is called the *first party*, the health care organization is the *second party* and the agency acting on behalf of the consumer is the *third party*. Thus, the third party is a highly important factor in the operation of a hospital or any health care agency (e.g., home health care agency). There are two primary third-party payer types for health care in the United States. The largest is public payers—state and federal government through Medicare and Medicaid (McCormick, 2002). Medicare is federally administered while Medicaid is administered by the individual states. Medicare is financed through social security payroll taxes and is available to persons meeting the enrollment criteria. Medicaid is administed on a state-by-state basis for persons unable financially to access health care services with the federal government supplementing state programs as needed. The second third-party type is represented by private companies and organizations like Blue Cross/Blue Shield. Managed care companies and self-insurance by the employer make up the remaining types of private reimbursers.

Third-party reimbursement in health care services is usually associated with active treatment. To satisfy this definition, recreational therapy must be (a) provided under an individualized treatment plan, (b) considered as reasonable and necessary to improve the patient's condition, and (c) supervised and evaluated periodically by a physician (Skalko, 1998; Thompson, 2001). The physician's orders must indicate the need for recreation therapy, including the scope, intensity, and duration of treatment services. Thus, the initial step to third-party reimbursement is administrative and medical support for services provided by qualified professionals (CTRSs) expected to enable the accomplishment of the outcomes found in patient care plans.

Third-party payers, public payers, and private companies and organizations use a variety of reimbursement methods. As a consequence, at any given health care organization because consumers have different health care plans, a number of reimbursement methods may be in evidence (McCormick, 2002). Fee-for-service methods are one of the simplest and oldest forms of health care payment. The health care organization presents the insurer the bill for services rendered. Discounts maybe negotiated between the agency and the insured. Cost-based reimbursement is based on the charges incurred by the agency for the services rendered. A per diem reimbursement provides one daily charge for allowable costs; consequently, specific services need to be identified for inclusion in the coverage. A fourth type of reimbursement is based on case groups (McCormick, 2002). The average costs per case are set by "per diem (i.e., a fixed rate per person per day) per admission (i.e., a fixed rate per person per admission), by patient characteristics (e.g., diagnosis, resource utilization, functional ability), and by capitation (e.g., payment is based on number of plan enrollees)" (McCormick, 2002, p. 201). Reimbursement of therapeutic recreation services varies across the health care continuum and in each setting is influenced by regulatory standards and governing bodies like CMS, JCAHO, and CARF. Knowledge of the reimbursement methods is a precursor to rate setting and financial management.

The rules and regulations involving Medicare and Medicaid reimbursement are voluminous, and any discussion of the respective reimbursement programs is beyond the scope of this chapter or even this book. Likewise, a discussion of the various Blue Cross plans and other health insurance policies is impossible. One thing is clear regarding health insurance policies—policies are no longer simple contracts providing hospital care coverage for subscribers as noted in the Historical Overview section of this chapter. Insurance companies will usually pay up to a certain fixed amount for various procedures. This amount is specified in the contract between the first party and the insurance company. The difference is usually written off or paid directly by the consumer. Changes taking place in reimbursement design make it essential that an organization have accurate data on what costs are actually incurred by individual consumers and separate departments.

Therapeutic recreation within health care facilities or clinical settings, as a reimbursable revenue source, varies nationwide among Blue Cross plans, commercial insurance companies, workers compensation, and Medicare and Medicaid.

A 1999 survey conducted by O'Morrow (2000) for the National Therapeutic Recreation Society (NTRS) reported that only 26 percent of the respondents ($N=486$) indicated that therapeutic recreation received reimbursement within their employment site. The percentage may be even lower because the survey did not consider multiple responses from practitioners working in the same setting. Moreover, the survey did not consider whether the reimbursement was in association with inpatient service, outpatient service, or home care. The major sources of reimbursement in the survey in rank order were Medicare and Medicaid, Blue Cross/Blue Shield, consumer pay, and private insurance.

Charges and Rate Setting

Therapeutic recreation services in health care facilities, primarily acute care hospitals and HMOs are classified as either routine services or ancillary services. Routine services are provided to the consumer as part of basic services or per diem charges. These services are usually incorporated into the operating cost or overhead of the facility and the department is supported as a cost center. Ancillary services are services prescribed or ordered by the physician to meet a specific consumer need (i.e., treatment). The consumer is charged directly for these services, and the hospital or facility is reimbursed for these services in part or whole by a third party. Consequently, recognition as an ancillary service allows therapeutic recreation services to be a revenue rather than cost center.

Charges or rate setting for unit of service vary from one facility to another and are relatively complex. A unit of service is a statistical measure for output of service

consumed. There are various methods or techniques used for determining the rates applicable to the provided services. Environmental service departments use square footage, the dietary department uses meals served, the emergency room uses consumer visits, nursing care units use consumer days. The one most frequently used method in association with therapeutic recreation services is the hourly rate method. The method is based on consumer use in terms of rate per hour. These rates may be broken down into fractions of an hour (e.g., 15-minute units). The rate usually incorporates therapist cost and time and could be further affected by adding material cost. In some settings, depreciation of equipment cost and other overhead costs such as electric, phone, and administrative costs could be added to the rate. Hourly rates or units of service cost are based on past and present trends and changes in the services provided. Unfortunately, the nationally used Medicare reimbursement system does not use a time-dependent unit. The reimbursement is per consumer, which is not a natural measurement. For example, some consumers may participate in a treatment procedure or rehab program for one hour while others may be involved only for 15 minutes.

Annually the American Medical Association (AMA) publishes the CPT (*Current Procedural Terminology*) codes manual that indicates specific codes for treatment procedures performed by physicians and therapists.

A code is assigned to a therapeutic procedure like aquatic therapy or therapeutic activities. The five-digit number and descriptor describe each intervention in 15-minute intervals or service units. Without these codes, interventions are not reimbursable; yet, the use of the codes by recreation therapists does not guarantee coverage. Therapists using the CPT codes accurately depict procedures for billing purposes while supporting the manager's need to document outcomes of services as revenue streams.

A study commissioned by the National Council for Therapeutic Recreation Council (NCTRC; Connolly & Garbarini, 1996) regarding pricing and cost of therapeutic recreation services in health care facilities noted the following:

1. Charges for services vary depending on "type of facility, the area, staff time, staff qualifications, individual versus group rates, and direct and indirect costs."

2. Cost may vary by diagnostic group to include individual or group services to a package of services—recreation therapy, physical therapy, and occupational therapy for a specific amount. This process can be found primarily in managed health care services. On the other hand, the cost may

vary by services provided (e.g., aquatic therapy) wherein the cost to provide is based on the service as opposed to a community outing which takes longer and may include more staff.

3. Cost varies by how often the consumer is seen coupled with whether the treatment is individual or in a group. This cost is compounded by consumer stay and what insurance companies will pay for the treatment.

4. A key element in the cost is having qualified therapeutic recreation personnel (e.g., certified therapeutic recreation specialist [CTRS]).

In the conclusions reached, the study noted, "In harmony with agency practices and client diagnostic needs, the qualified CTRS can provide effective, cost-efficient services in health care today" (p. 3).

In conclusion, charges and rate setting are very complicated procedures that incorporate the philosophy behind third-party payment contracts, economics, political factors, local managed care arrangements, and whether the hospital is for-profit or not-for-profit. Additionally, the therapeutic recreation manager needs to realize that whether the facility is for-profit or not-for-profit, the facility administrators are concerned with the amount of revenue that can be expected from the department so as to balance facility financial needs and income (Needleman, 1999).

The history of therapeutic recreation service being reimbursable through government or commercial insurance carriers has been uneven. It is difficult to determine to what extent therapeutic recreation service is being reimbursed for inpatient or outpatient service due to the limited number of studies conducted (Esneault, Malkin & Sellers, 1992; Malkin & Skalko, 1992; Teaff & Van Hyning, 1988) and the lack of clarity among factors within the studies (e.g., consumers treated, respondents). These investigators concluded from their studies a need for additional research in all factors associated with reimbursement. Additionally, authors suggest managers must become more astute concerning the environments of their practice settings while marketing the unique features of services (McCormick, 2002; Thompson, 2001). Recreation therapists provide services at reasonable costs. Resources required to deliver programs and services are nominal in cost—therapists usually do not rely on expensive technology to facilitate outcomes—and salaries have been lower than other health professions for a number of years.

Financial Management

In commercial enterprises the objective of management is not difficult to identify. It is basically that of maximizing owner's profits. In the case of a hospital, whether for-profit or not-for-profit, the bottom line profitability is not easily definable. Hospitals, like other public health and human service organizations and agencies, are vital community resources. As such they must be managed for the benefit of the community. The objective of hospital management, for example, must be to provide the community with the services it needs at a clinically acceptable level of quality, a publicly responsive level of amenity, and at the least possible cost (Berman, Weeks & Kukla, 1990). The same can be said for a community-based leisure service agency.

The financial management of the organization affects many aspects of work in the organization. It affects program services, salaries, staffing, quality of services, and quality and quantity of equipment and supplies available. The notion that competent financial management is necessary for efficient and effective organization operation is by any standard an accepted truism.

Financial management requires planning and predicting how much money the organization will bring in during the next year and how much it will need to spend to continue operating. The people who prepare the organization's budget must look ahead and consider trends such as economic inflation, recession, community needs, public demands, availability of quality staff, changes in service delivery, and competition from other organizations. Failure to consider these factors and others can result in an inadequate budget and eventual depletion of resources.

Budgeting is a management responsibility. In authoritarian-style organizations, the process is highly centralized, so that only a few people at the higher levels of administration are involved in preparation of the budget. This top-down approach leaves the implementers of the budget without autonomy or the right to appropriate or control expenses. In others, budgeting may be widely decentralized, involving all managers at all levels within the organization, who in turn seek input from their staff. Many organizations are recognizing the value of having budgets prepared by those who must implement them. For the first-line therapeutic recreation manager this bottom-up approach has distinct advantages:

1. The therapeutic recreation manager has a more intimate view of his or her needs than do those at the top.

2. The manager can provide a more realistic breakdown to support requests.

3. There is less likelihood of overlooking vital needs.

4. Morale and satisfaction are usually higher when the manager and staff participate actively in making decisions that affect them.

5. There is room for more flexibility and quicker action.

Whichever way is used, the final authority for the organization-wide budget rests with the governing board and chief executive office (CEO) because they are in a position to study population changes; to consider any changes, such as closing or opening of facilities or services; and to take account of any regulating changes that might result in policy change or legislation.

Prerequisite to Budgeting

Before the actual process of budgeting can occur, several prerequisites need to be met. If the organization desires commitment to its goals and budget, it is essential that the therapeutic recreation manager be involved in budget development. Budget development begins at the top man-

agement level with the vice president of finance or chief financial/fiscal officer (CFO; sometimes called the *comptroller*), who provides the information on past budgets and expenses needed to begin the process of preparing a new budget. In some organizations a budget calendar is prepared to indicate when specific budget activities are to be carried out and completed. A set of guidelines is also prepared to assist managers in completing their portion of the budget. These guidelines include explanations of the budget forms and reporting procedures and, of course, the deadlines for submitting budget requests. Procedures for review, revision, and approval of budgets are usually provided.

An example of a hospital budgeting organization structure is illustrated in Figure 8.1. The structure notes the accountabilities of the various management levels. Therapeutic recreation's place in the structure would obviously differ from one hospital to another, although more than likely it would be at the department or section manager's level.

In some hospitals the creation and use of a staff-level budget committee is an optional component of the budget preparation. Its place in Figure 8.1 represents a logical extension of the principles of participatory management

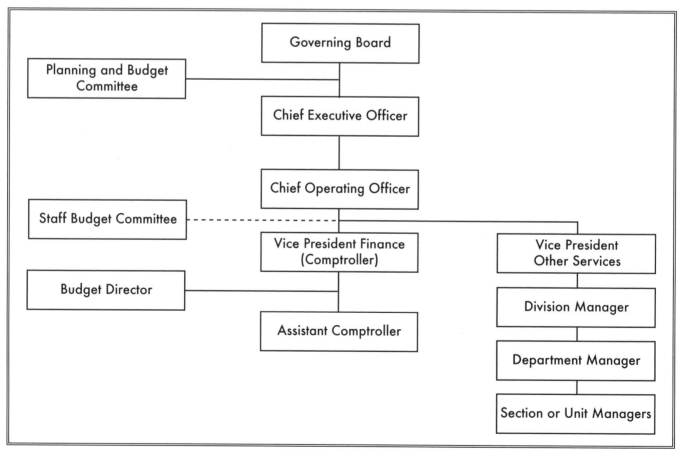

Figure 8.1
Prototype: Hospital Budgeting Organization Structure

and provides a vehicle that can yield operational as well as political dividends. Ideally, the committee would be multidisciplinary in nature.

In the decentralized, participative approach to budgeting, every department head and manager is responsible for preparing his or her section of the budget. Likewise, these same managers are also responsible for defending the budget. Because it may not be possible to implement all goals and projections, the manager must be prepared to discuss the relative priority of budget items and the potential impact of implementing or not implementing them. The therapeutic recreation manager needs to be consciously aware of the department's goals and objectives. It is also important that the needs and goals of the department be congruent with the organization's goals. Although decisions and approvals on budget proposals are the responsibility of top management, these proposals are influenced many times by the information presented through the negotiation process. Compromise invariably has to play a part in working out differences; the manager who is too rigid will ordinarily end up with fewer funds. Finally, if the manager is new, it is essential that the budget process be understood. Even managers who have had previous budget experience will need an orientation to the format or process utilized in a specific organization.

Data must be available to facilitate forecasting or project activity. Revenue and expense data, such as income from services and cost of services, may be provided with the budget information compiled by the CFO. If not, it is the manager's responsibility to gather such information. In addition, nonmonetary statistical information, such as number of services provided and number of consumers participating, is needed for planning the budget.

It is well to recognize at the prerequisite stage that negotiations usually take place regarding each department's budget. Further, one should be aware that power and influence enters into budget negotiations. The therapeutic recreation manager must be willing to devote time and energy to the budgeting process.

Budgets and Budgeting

The process of budgeting has gained importance in recent years. Traditionally, budgeting has been the process of asking for a percentage increase over what was offered the previous year with specific justification for innovative requests. However, this is no longer acceptable because of the rising service costs and the emphasis on cost containment. Today, budgeting should be looked on as a living process with a reasonable degree of flexibility, fluidity, and mobility to meet changing conditions and unforeseen exigencies. If the position is taken that budgeting is a

dynamic rather than a static process, one must be prepared to adjust to changes in demand for services, changes in the cost of services or supplies, and changes in a variety of other conditions that force adjustments in budgeting projections.

Using data from budgets to guide decision making is important for every level of management regardless of setting. It is essential that budgeting be accomplished in such a way that it facilitates goal achievement. Further, it is important that therapeutic recreation managers, even at the first-line management level, participate in the development of the budget.

Consideration of therapeutic recreation budgets and budgeting will be focused primarily within health care facilities. Even here there is much variation in budgets and fiscal management. No attempt is purposely made to ignore therapeutic recreation budgets and budgeting in profit and nonprofit community-based leisure service agencies or organizations. To a large degree there is considerable similarity and overlapping. On the other hand, health care facilities have the following unique characteristics not found in community-based leisure service agencies: cost-based reimbursement programs and private expenditures, shared hospital expenses and other multihospital arrangements, MCO models of service, and large administrative structures.

Regardless of the type of agency, hospital, or community-based leisure service, the budgeting process takes three to six months or more with the process beginning at the first-line manager's level (Sullivan & Decker, 2001). The therapeutic recreation manager may not actually draft the budget, yet may identify needed resources, obtain information from staff, prioritize objectives, review unit productivity, predict future costs and revenues, identify capital equipment needs, and conduct cost comparisons (Tappen, 2001). This initial step in budgeting is followed by drafting the budget document. During this step, managers translate objectives into projected costs and revenues, write justifications for requested expenses, submit capital requests, and present the proposed budget. The proposal is presented to each level within the organization with each administrator evaluating the proposal and making adjustments. After approval by executive management, the proposal is presented to the governing body (e.g., City Council, Board of Directors) for final approval. This process is completed prior to the new fiscal year (e.g., January 1–December 31, October 1–September 30, July 1–June 30, April 1–March 31).

Once approved, the execution phase of fiscal management occurs. During this step, the therapeutic recreation manager monitors monthly and quarterly reports to avoid either surplus or deficit accounts at the conclusion of the fiscal year (Marquis & Huston, 2003). Actual and budgeted expenses are compared to determine variances and the budget is adjusted or performance modified to accomplish targeted objectives (Tappen, 2001). A concluding step in the budgeting process is evaluation. With each successive year, managers more accurately predict their unit's requirements like accounting for seasonal variations or adjustments in FTEs (full-time equivalents; Marquis & Huston, 2003). The four budget steps parallel the APIE process. The outcome is a plan for managing monetary resources similar to the plan resulting from the APIE process that manages client intervention.

Budgets

The word budget is derived from an old French term *bougette*, which means a "little bag," a sack or pouch:

> The British adopted the word to describe the motion engaged in by the chancellor of the exchequer when he presented his annual financial statement to Parliament. He was said to open his "budget" or bag, which contained the various financial documents. (United Way of America, 1985, p. 3)

A budget is an operational management plan for the allocation of resources and a monitor and control for ensuring that results comply with the plans. Results are expressed in quantitative terms. Although budgets are usually associated with financial statements, such as revenues and expenses, they also may be nonfinancial statements covering output, materials, and equipment. Budgets coordinate the efforts of the agency by determining what resources will be used by whom, when, and for what purpose. Budgets are frequently prepared for each organizational unit and for each function within the unit.

Every budget starts with a plan. Planning is done for a specific time, usually a fiscal year but perhaps subdivided into monthly, quarterly, or semiannual periods. The plan and the resultant budget(s) are formulated in the context of the overall objectives of the therapeutic recreation department and the short-range and long-range goals of the organization. In setting objectives for the department, resource requirements need to be built-in. Budgeting translates objectives to be accomplished into financial terms. The budget should help to guide first-line managers in their decision making. The future is unknown, and so any plan has to be flexible enough to allow for changing conditions. For example, an unexpected shortage of therapeutic recreation personnel will adversely affect the staffing budget resulting in more overtime or a reduction in services. Budgets help managers to plan program activities by making staff accountable and responsible to analyze their operations and control resource use. Waste is minimized and resources are allocated to accomplish unit goals. Budgets promote communication and cooperation among

agency personnel as services are planned and resources allotted to accomplish consumer outcomes (Tomey, 2000).

Although one thinks of budgets in a positive way, there are disadvantages to budgeting. One major problem is that budgets convert all aspects of an agency or organizational performance into monetary values for a single comparable unit of measurement. "Consequently, only those aspects that are easy to measure may be considered, and equally important factors such as development and research efforts may be ignored" (Tomey, 2000, p. 204). Another problem may arise when budget goals supersede agency or organization goals, which in turn affect department goals. Budgets may also be applied too rigidly, affecting innovation and change. Last, budget development is time-consuming (Bart, 1988). However, careful planning provides an opportunity for examining options and alternatives in a calm, rational setting. The result is generally a more satisfactory outcome with fewer crisis situations arising.

Types of Budgets

There are numerous types of budgets used to express the plans and to meet the goals and objectives of health and human service agencies and organizations. They are powerful instruments because they serve as a guide to therapeutic recreation performance and allocation of personnel, supplies, support services, and facilities. The format of these budgets is usually line item, a procedure that notes specific expenditures and revenues for specific items. It does not present the organization or department goals, targets, programs, or results. This text will consider only those budgets prepared and used most frequently by first-line managers.

Revenue and Expense Budget (Operating Budget)

By far the most common budgets are the revenue and expense budgets. Combined, they are frequently referred to as the operating budget or the annual budget. This budget spells out the plans for day-to-day operating revenue and expenses in dollar terms for one year. In other words, this budget projects the services to be provided, the revenue that will be generated from these services, and the expenses associated with providing the services (see Table 8.1). In many agencies the operating budget is usually based on the previous year's budget. This practice is sometimes referred to as historical or incremental budgeting. Another practice is program budgeting and zero-base budgeting, which will be discussed shortly.

Some may wonder about for-profit and not-for-profit organizations as related to the operating budget. In general, if the budget shows an excess of revenues over expenses, it means that the organization expects to make a profit from its activities for the year. If the organization is a for-profit company, some of the profits can be paid to the owners of the company in the form of a dividend. Even not-for-profit organizations, such as hospitals and community-based leisure service agencies, need to earn profits. These profits are used to replace worn-out equipment and old buildings or to expand the services available to the community.

Returning to budget development, in some organizations, based on an analysis of the organization's past budget and future plans, dollar figures are assigned to all departments and to all categories on both income and expenditure sides of the budget. In other organizations, individual departments are given some flexibility in requesting or allocating funds for various categories. However, in many other organizations, departments are restricted to using funds only as designated by the CFO unless a justification is offered and approved. In some instances, the manager may be required to balance the budget (i.e., expenses equal income). Considering present cost containment efforts, more demands for balanced budgets may be seen in the future.

Expense factors that the therapeutic recreation manager might consider in the operating budget are personnel salaries, employee benefits, insurance, activity programs, special events, supplies and equipment for both activity programs and office, laundry service (if personnel are required to wear uniforms), repairs and maintenance, depreciation and replacement of supplies and equipment, travel, education, books, periodical subscriptions, dues and membership fees, legal fees, and contractual services. In freestanding recreation centers for persons with disabilities, one would have additional expenses of depreciation on the center, insurance, utilities, mortgage interest or rent, and possibly bad debts. Depending on the budget system of the hospital or agency, some of the aforementioned expenses (e.g., utilities, postage, mortgage rate or rent, maintenance) are considered overhead expenses or indirect costs. These expenses are allocated to all areas

by the accounting department according to a specific formula. On the other hand, direct costs (e.g., supplies and equipment associated with specific client interventions) are expenses charged directly to the unit's budget. Some costs (e.g., insurance) are fixed and remain the same for the budget period while others like supplies are variable as they depend on client volume and activity. Expenses may also be classified as controllable and noncontrollable. The number of personnel needed is controllable while depreciation on the center and bad debts are noncontrollable. The manager includes cushion funds in the unit budget to compensate for noncontrollable expenses and rises in material and labor costs.

In some organizations, salaries, benefits, and insurance are provided by the CFO when budget guidelines and budget forms are forwarded to various departments. In other organizations, a formula is provided to assist the manager in determining benefits and insurance. In addition, many organizations require a written justification for each expense or category of expenses.

The largest budget expenditure is the personnel budget. The manager must be aware of the numbers of staff and the staffing mix to ensure the appropriate number of staff with the proper skills are available to meet client needs. The manager also includes in the personnel budget continuing education costs, professional memberships, health insurance, retirement benefits, social security, merit or cost-of-living increases, overtime, and state and federal unemployment taxes.

Calculating full-time equivalents (FTEs) is fundamental to determining staffing number and mix. A full-time employee is one who is paid 40 hours per week for 52 weeks or 2,080 hours of pay in a calendar year. An FTE of 1.0 represents 40 hours worked/week on the unit payroll and may be either one person who has worked a traditional week or several part-time employees (one working two days or 16 hours or 0.4 FTEs and a second working three

Table 8.1
Components of the Operating Budget

Expenses (Cost)		**Revenue (Income)**	
Payroll	Salary, vacation, holidays, social security, education, other fringe benefits	Consumer services	Fees and charges, Medicaid, Medicare, other insurance
Supplies	Office supplies, program supplies, etc.	Contributions	Philanthropic, grants-in-aid, research and program grants
Equipment	Program and office equipment	Other	Interest, rent, contract
Overhead	Building maintenance, water, electric		
Other	Mortgage, interest, loans, insurance, maintenance service contracts, contractual arrangements, education materials, transportation, marketing, and so forth.		

days or 24 hours or 0.6 FTEs). Any time a full-time employee is paid but not working due to illness, vacation, jury duty, or funeral leave, the hours must be covered by another person. The manager, therefore, must adjust the FTEs upward to cover unproductive or benefit time of full-time employees. This factor can be calculated by determining the average number of allotted benefit days with pay and the average number of sick days per employee experienced by the unit (Sullivan & Decker, 2001; Tappen, 2001). Once calculated, these hours are totaled and divided by 2,080 to determine the FTE requirement to cover benefit time. Seasonal fluctuations, personnel policies like number of days allowed for educational and personal leave, and productivity or staffing requirements affect personnel budgets. Additionally the manager plans for employee turnover, recruitment, and orientation costs (Tomey, 2000).

The next step in developing the operating budget is to determine the revenues associated with the provision of services. As noted earlier, revenue development varies from organization to organization. In some organizations, such as health care facilities, therapeutic recreation is reimbursable through various insurance programs. However, other similar organizations make therapeutic recreation part of consumer cost by incorporating it into the consumer's bill. Other sources of revenues include general donations, donations and grants for specific programs, United Fund, investment revenues, and funding from various tax levies in the form of budget appropriations from governmental units. Revenue projections are based on a number of factors. As noted earlier, third-party reimbursement methods vary, as do the rates of reimbursement (e.g., per diem, capitated). Managers consider the percentage of revenues derived from Medicare, Medicaid, private insurance, MCOs, and private pay. Projections are also based on historical client volume data, program modifications (e.g., inpatient to outpatient) and adjustments in taxing levels or general fund sources.

In an organization where a program budgeting approach is used, projected service revenue is determined by multiplying the projected volume of service by the price charged for the service. The volume estimates are derived in the planning process when the number of consumers using a service or program is projected.

The operating budget presents revenues and expenses as separate components with bottom-line net profit or loss calculated (see Figure 8.2). The personnel budget is a dominant share of the expense budget (see Figure 8.3, p. 118). If an agency has successfully garnered external funds to enhance their revenue budget, separate components within the revenue budget contain notation of these sources; separate budgets are maintained to facilitate reporting account balances to funding authorities. Managers monitor and reconcile monthly and quarterly revenue and expense items in the operating budget using ledgers provided by the comptroller or accounting department.

Capital Expenditure Budget

Capital expenditure budget is usually related to long-range planning that spans a three to five years. The capital budget looks at a capital investment to determine whether the expenditure is economically feasible over the lifetime of the asset. As a result of this time period, more expensive "vision" on the part of the manager is required to identify needs. The capital budget can go beyond simply dollars and cents and look at costs and benefits in a broader sense. The general service provided to the community or to the consumer can be considered. Capital expenditures include physical changes (e.g., replacement or expansion of the facility, property, and equipment) and items that exceed certain dollar amounts (e.g., $50.00 to $500.00; varies from agency to agency).

It is well-established that the health and human service industry operates in an era of limited resources and increased cost. Thus the capital budget process in this industry will become more critical. In most settings, the agency or organization administrator establishes a ceiling for capital expenses. Therefore, it is important that the therapeutic recreation manager recognize and be prepared to identify capital needs on a priority basis and defend those needs when the capital budget is considered.

In brief, the manager should begin development of the capital budget by conducting a thorough review of all capital equipment and fixtures presently in use. Once this process is completed, the manager needs to review goals and objectives of the department for the next several years so as to identify new programs of service that may require new equipment or property. This procedure may also identify programs that will be phased out or equipment that will need replaced.

The manager should now be prepared to construct a capital budget. The budget should include a description of each item needed, a statement of whether it is a new or replacement item, and an estimate of the item cost. The manager will need to justify the item and will likely be required to prioritize the entire budget. Depending on the agency or organization, the names of manufacturers and suppliers, trade-in credits, and estimates of delivery, installation, and maintenance costs may be required.

As a final note, the therapeutic recreation manager should remember that the individuals making the decisions regarding this budget may not be familiar with many of the areas or aspects of therapeutic recreation service. Therefore, it is the manager's responsibility to make the justification, whether verbally or in writing, and to be very clear about what is needed.

Program Budgeting

This budget focuses on specific programs to meet specific goals and objectives. It is a means for providing a systematic method for allocating resources in ways most effective to meeting specific goals. The budget is structured so program outcomes are related directly to specific goals. As a consequence, managers have information on the cost-effectiveness of their programs. The program may be an existing one that the department is considering expanding, contracting, or adding. While most budgets focus on department revenues and cost, program budgets compare revenues and expenses for an entire program over its lifetime. In doing this, the program budgeting method identifies costs and benefits of different programs aimed at the same purpose or of different approaches to one program. By emphasizing goals and programs, program budgeting overcomes the common weakness of many budgets tied to a time frame. Also, it does away with the line-item

FUND 323 STATUS REPORT
Through July 31, 2004

Description — Service Area	1-1-04 Beg Bal Plus Prior Year Cancellations	Prior Year Total Revenue 12-31-03	2003 YTD Revenue	2004 YTD Revenue	Prior Yr Total Expense 12-32-03	2003 YTD Expenses +Fringes	2004 YTD Expenses +Fringes	2004 YTD Encumbrance	2003 Exp/Enc (Over)/Under Resources
	{AB}			{C}			{E}	{F}	{AB+C−E−F}
REGION 1 West Region									
1000 REGON 1 ADMIN	0	79	79		17,911	545	710		−710
2000 PRICE HILL	−44,840	44,957	32,881	34,185	59,210	32,170	35,802	2,191	−48,647
3000 DUNHAM/SAYLOR PARK	126,438	328,087	253,144	236,878	214,281	127,333	143,491	23,269	196,555
4000 Millvale/English Woods	9,191	20,061	11,438	11,363	9,090	793	3,887		16,667
5000 Westwood Town Hall	55,255	91,792	78,471	56,517	91,971	50,293	61,642	18,569	31,561
6000 Hartwell/Winton Hills	40,326	77,270	58,346	61,484	67,253	42,029	43,011	2,188	56,612
3000 THERAPEUTICS	90,843	79,098	49,185	35,598	60,812	33,323	39,564	16,877	70,000
8000 Lincoln/North Fairmount		10,596	2,759	24,291	53,418	14,051	46,403	2,778	−24,890
TOTAL REGION 1	277,214	651,939	486,302	460,316	573,946	300,538	374,511	65,871	297,148
REGION 2 East Region									
1000 REGION 2 Admin					3,068	3,184	603		−603
2000 PL RDG/KEN WD	−6,542	195,397	143,452	123,524	186,413	113,782	112,849	12,175	−8,041
3000 BUSH	24,391	34,223	22,393	23,444	30,336	15,607	35,382	3,318	9,135
4000 EVANSTON	−6,346	52,534	37,354	31,836	51,617	29,416	19,058	1,415	5,016
5000 MT AUB/LEBLND	−16,732	87,753	61,884	74,434	106,714	70,125	57,678	9,125	−9,101
6000 CENTER COMP LABS	−376			165	376	197	134		−346
7000 Madisonville	40,167	64,384	42,350	41,993	19,875	11,939	15,094	903	66,164
8000 Mt Wash/Oakley/Ebersole	28,104	375,395	273,842	291,764	354,301	217,630	200,436	17,552	101,879
9000 Youth/Family Services					711	263	1,427	720	−2,147
TOTAL REGION 2	62,665	809,686	581,276	587,159	753,411	462,145	442,661	45,207	161,956
REGION 3 Central Region									
1000 REGION 3 ADMIN					28,954	376	1,005		−1,005
2000 OVER-THE-RHINE	1,180	12,042	8,621	5,824	7,151	1,698	6,471	428	106
3000 CAMP WASH/Mckie	2,920	59,477	32,430	32,628	63,907	42,322	34,145	4,470	−3,067
4000 CLIFTON/KRUECK	42,972	208,280	138,278	122,404	197,972	122,052	119,212	6,353	39,811
5000 COLLEGE HILL/Mt Airy	49,261	258,154	176,341	198,534	174,822	89,027	154,871	18,665	74,259
6000 CORRYVILLE	24,395	115,633	77,816	68,190	107,042	66,783	62,753	10,703	19,129
7000 Hirsch/North Avondale	115,464	142,190	92,890	88,697	87,499	38,522	41,458	7,917	154,786
2000 SENIORS	47,811	24,727	17,025	17,058	23,787	14,955	18,433	9,932	36,505
8000 Bond Hill/Carthage	16,555	44,570	32,587	29,486	40,685	16,973	34,195	2,318	9,528
TOTAL REGION 3	300,558	865,074	575,988	562,822	731,818	392,708	472,543	60,786	33,0051

Source: Cincinnati Recreation Commission, 2004a

Figure 8.2
Service Area Status Report

050 SUMMARY REPORT West Region for Month Ended July 31, 2004

	2004 Approved Budget	2004 Encumbrances	Estimated YTD Expenditures	2004 Expenditures	(Over)/Under Est. Expenditures	Budget Variance OK/Report Due
1000 Administration						
7100 Payroll	110,504	0	53,075	60,515	−7,440	Report Due
7200 Contractual Services	1,500	0	1,025	3,336	−2,311	Report Due
7300 Materials/Supplies	4,000	373	1,100	1,230	−130	OK
7400 Fixed Costs	500	224	500	225	275	OK
Total	**116,504**	**596**	**55,700**	**65,306**	**−9,606**	**Report Due**
2000 Price Hill						
7100 Payroll	191,764	0	102,555	101,668	887	OK
7200 Contractual Services	8,004	400	4,754	7,970	−3,216	Report Due
7300 Materials/Supplies	8,400	0	5,525	4,729	796	OK
7400 Fixed Costs	600	428	600	599	2	OK
Total	**208,768**	**827**	**113,434**	**114,967**	**−1,532**	**OK**
3000 Dunham/Sayler Park						
7100 Payroll	288,000	0	179,301	181,517	−2,216	OK
7200 Contractual Services	9,000	1,865	5,000	9,569	−4,569	Report Due
7300 Materials/Supplies	7,000	0	3,300	4,644	−1,344	Report Due
7400 Fixed Costs	750	0	700	0	700	OK
Total	**304,750**	**1,865**	**188,301**	**195,730**	**−7,429**	**OK**
4000 Millvale						
7100 Payroll	211,629	0	112,850	116,127	−3,277	OK
7200 Contractual Services	5,500	400	2,800	3,684	−884	OK
7300 Materials/Supplies	6,600	0	3,450	2,393	1,057	Report Due
7400 Fixed Costs	200	0	100	0	100	OK
Total	**223,929**	**400**	**119,200**	**122,204**	**−3,004**	**OK**
5000 Westwood Town Hall/English Woods						
7100 Payroll	128,452	0	70,941	76,761	−5,819	Report Due
7200 Contractual Services	5,196	400	3,031	3,353	−322	OK
7300 Materials/Supplies	3,496	0	2.206	1,754	452	OK
7400 Fixed Costs	450	0	450	0	450	OK
Total	**137,594**	**400**	**76,628**	**81,868**	**−5,240**	**Report Due**
6000 Winton Hills/Hartwell						
7100 Payroll	235,750	0	131,280	130,425	855	OK
7200 Contractual Services	5,000	800	2,600	2,050	550	OK
7300 Materials/Supplies	8,400	0	4,075	2,731	1,344	Report Due
7400 Fixed Costs	1,400	0	840	0	840	OK
Total	**250,550**	**800**	**138,795**	**135,205**	**3,590**	**OK**
196x3 Therapeutics						
7100 Payroll	484,000	0	261,193	270,253	−9,060	OK
7200 Contractual Services	17,500	0	9,500	4,646	4,854	Report Due
7300 Materials/Supplies	6,000	0	5,000	2,122	2,878	Report Due
7400 Fixed Costs	1,400	0	800	0	800	OK
Total	**508,900**	**0**	**276,493**	**277,021**	**−528**	**OK**
8000 Lincoln/North Fairmount						
7100 Payroll	272,000	0	146,890	148,527	−1,637	OK
7200 Contractual Services	6,000	500	3,500	5,014	−1,514	Report Due
7300 Materials/Supplies	6,000	0	3,500	6,134	−2,634	Report Due
7400 Fixed Costs	35,200	9,003	26,300	30,091	−3,791	Report Due
Total	**319,200**	**9,503**	**180,190**	**189,766**	**−9,576**	**Report Due**
9000 Open						
7100 Payroll	0	0	0	0	0	OK
7200 Contractual Services	0	0	0	0	0	OK
7300 Materials/Supplies	0	0	0	0	0	OK
7400 Fixed Costs	0	0	0	0	0	OK
Total	**0**	**0**	**0**	**0**	**0**	**OK**
Summary						
7100 Payroll	1,922,100	0	1,058,086	1,085,793	−27,707	
7200 Contractual Services	57,700	4,364	32,210	39,623	−7,413	
7300 Materials/Supplies	49,896	373	28,156	39,623	2,419	
7400 Fixed Costs	40,500	9,654	30,290	30,914	−624	
Total	**2,070,196**	**14,391**	**1,148,742**	**1,182,067**	**−33,325**	

Source: Cincinnati Recreation Commission, 2004b

Figure 8.3
Regional Budget Summary Report

approach to budgeting. In other words, a program budget is constructed by regrouping all line-item expenditures into their respective program area. For example, the line items of personnel and/or utilities could be regrouped according to some rational formula of direct and indirect cost factors to reflect the various programs that these resources support.

Zero-base Budgeting

Zero-base budgeting (ZBB) is designed to require even more justification than is found in an operating or capital expenditure budget. With ZBB no service or program is taken for granted. This approach is based on the idea that no expense should be assumed to be absolutely necessary. The goal of ZBB is to reorient the manager's thinking and to reevaluate all programs. For example, just because a program received funds in the past does not mean that the program should again be funded or at least funded at the same level in the future. In theory, ZBB begins with a blank slate every year.

The use of the decision package is the core of the ZBB process and is the feature that particularly distinguishes it from the traditional historical budgeting process (Pyhrr, 1973). In brief, a decision package is a description of one or more activities, services, or programs; the cost and justification of the activities; "alternative ways of carrying out these activities and the different costs of each alternative; the advantages of continuing the activity; and the consequences of discontinuing the activity" (Tappen, 2001, p. 303). After decision packages are developed, they are ranked in order of decreasing benefits to the agency or organization. They can be divided into high, medium, and low categories and reviewed in order of rank for funding. Resources are allocated based on the priority of the decision package.

A major advantage to ZBB is that it forces the manager to set priorities and justify resources. The process is complex and time consuming as the manager is required to review and justify the cost efficiency of each program.

Flexible Budgeting

In recent years, flexible budgeting or variable budgeting as a managerial tool has been introduced into health and human service organizations. A flexible budget, as opposed to a fixed budget (one which remains the same regardless of the activity level; e.g., a program budget), is defined "as a statement of expected performance that can be adjusted to reflect the effects of operating at different levels of volume" (e.g., number of participants; Berman, Weeks & Kukla, 1990, p. 499). In other words, flexible budgeting allows department management to adapt to changes in the volume once the fiscal year has started. From another perspective, a flexible budget is a series of fixed budgets

covering a specified range of volume alternatives (Berman, Weeks & Kukla, 1990). To a large degree, flexible budgeting is limited in application to expense budgets such as therapeutic recreation routine services and therapeutic recreation services provided in community-based leisure service organizations.

A flexible budget takes into account costs of personnel, equipment, supplies, and overhead per unit of service and compares that to the actual units of service. Variance results are then compared to a flex standard rather than a budgeted standard. Figure 8.4 and the following discussion concerning supplies used in a large therapeutic recreation department for one month are an example of flexible budgeting.

The supply budget illustration is based on 100 consumers with a disability participating in an arts and crafts program over one month. The budgeted expense is $250. The supply cost per consumer (unit of service) is $2.50 ($250 per 100 consumers). However, during this month, instead of 100 consumers, 75 consumers attended. Thus, the expected supply cost (flex budget) would be $187.50 (75 times $2.50). The actual dollars spent were $260. In this example, actual supply costs were $72.50 (negative variance) over what was expected (flex budget). Any variance, positive or negative, needs to be investigated by the therapeutic recreation manager. In this example the manager spent more than $2.50 per consumer.

Performance Reporting

A good budget can only be effective if it is used as a tool for managing in a person's area of responsibility. This means that the budget must be regularly used to measure the effectiveness of actual performance in comparison to the goals established in the budget process.

The therapeutic recreation manager can expect to receive several types of financial accounting reports of the department's operation on a periodic basis from the budget office or the department responsible for monitoring the cost of programs or services within the organization. These

Supplies	
Actual Expense	$260.00
Budget Expense	$250.00
Flex Budget	$187.50
Variance to Actual	$72.50

Figure 8.4
Flexible Budgeting

reports, generated by a computer system and usually provided monthly, include expenditures, income, and perhaps depreciation costs. If the department receives funds through special funds accounts (e.g., grants), a separate report is provided for each account. These reports include not only the current month's performance but also the year-to-date performance. Some reports may include percentage of budget spent by line item or category.

The monthly report will show the actual bimonthly or monthly annual salary and hourly employee expenditures. In relation to hourly employees, it should include the scheduled hours for each employee and an analysis of the hours actually paid. It should also identify any hours or days for which the employee was paid but did not work, such as vacation, holiday, illness, education, jury duty, or funeral leave. This report will also include expenditures for supplies and equipment in comparison to the budget.

The governing board of an organization reviews the agency budget on an annual basis and managers from the CEO level to the first-line manager are evaluated on budget compliance. Variance analysis is the most common method of evaluating budget performance (Nowicki, 2001). Budgeted revenues and expenses are compared to actual revenues and expenses. Variance is the difference between the actual and budgeted amounts. Organizations usually have established levels at which variance needs to be justified by the unit manager; this may be a dollar amount or a percentage (e.g., 5% over/under budget; Sullivan & Decker, 2001). The therapeutic recreation manager may be called on to ensure favorable variances reoccur while negative variances are reconciled. Variances may be interdependent (e.g., resulting from seasonal expenses). Regardless, the manager needs to be prepared to identify the reason and to provide an explanation to the CEO. Thus the importance of attending to monthly or quarterly accounting reports.

In addition to reviewing reports to ascertain variance levels, managers are also astute to potential errors made by the accounting department. For example, expenditures made by other departments may erroneously be charged to one's department. It is important that these errors are spotted and called to the attention of the accounting department.

The results of these financial analyses frequently can be used to support the manager's arguments in favor of needed improvements, more staff, and increased recognition of the contribution of therapeutic recreation to the overall success of the agency or organization. While financial management is time-consuming, it often provides persuasive data to support any request for changes in the budgets or management of the division, department, or unit. A budget is only as good as the effective use one makes of it. The amount of management responsibility the therapeutic recreation manager is willing to assume and

the careful use of information and data contribute to how the administration will react to the agency or organization budget as a whole.

Cutback Management

In a period of economic instability, increasing fund competition and resource scarcity, it is not unusual for program changes and downsizing to take place in health and human service organizations. Cutting back or downsizing on the part of the organization involves making hard decisions about who will be let go, what programs or services will be scaled down and/or terminated, and what consumers will be affected. At the same time, quality and access to services must be maintained. If therapeutic recreation managers are requested to present a plan for scaling down programs and practitioners, they must examine the department's mission, recognize programs of limited utility, use rational mechanisms for making choices, encourage the active participation of department practitioners, and retain department openness.

Because the "focus is on decreasing costs to maintain adequate profit margins in an area of diminishing compensation" (Sullivan & Decker, 2001, p. 115), managers are strongly motivated to be cost-effective. Managers rank programs by the cost of achieving objectives if cost-effectiveness is used as an economic evaluation method (Tomey, 2000). When cost-benefit analysis is used, the manager converts the costs of program operations and benefits into a dollar amount. If the benefit-to-cost ratio is one or greater, the investment is considered good (Tomey, 2000). In health care facilities another method used to evaluate cost-effectiveness is a critical clinical or care pathway (Marquis & Huston, 2003). These are predetermined courses of progress that define for a specific diagnosis or treatment an average length of stay and specific interventions to be completed at certain time intervals. If a client deviates from the plan, a variance analysis is undertaken to identify why the client is not in compliance. These techniques as well as others (e.g., inventory control) are used to monitor and to evaluate budget compliance. Staff participation on quality improvement teams may also serve to make staff aware of cost-effectiveness measures affecting their programs and status in the unit. Therapeutic recreation managers who have a thorough knowledge of the political, social, and economic forces that shape health and human services are positioned to be fiscally responsive to unit needs and overall fiscal health of the organization.

Summary

Initial consideration was given to a historical overview of the need for financial management in both community-based leisure service agencies and health care facilities. As a result of this need, therapeutic recreation managers must be more responsive in the fiscal management of their division or department.

Various revenue sources (i.e., appropriations, contributions, grants and contracts, fees and charges, and reimbursement) were discussed. These need to be considered when doing any kind of planning. The budget is a plan for the allocation of resources over a specific time period, and a control for ensuring that results comply with the plans. There are advantages and disadvantages to budgeting.

It was noted that prior to developing the budget several prerequisites need to be met, including participative approaches to budgeting. While there are many types of budgets, first-line managers are primarily associated with operating or revenue-and-expense budgets and capital expenditure budgets.

Most operating budgets are based on the previous year's budget and reflect day-to-day operations for the department. They include both revenues and expenses. Examples of items found in these respective budgets were provided. Unlike the operating budget, the capital budget is usually prepared for a longer period of time and incorporates major expenditure items. Another budgeting approach considered was program budgeting, which focuses on specific programs to meet goals. Revenues and expenses are budgeted for each program. Another budget tactic used frequently is zero-base budgeting, which is based on objectives for the coming year and demands that every expenditure, no matter how basic, be justified. The use of a decision package is the core of zero-base budgeting. Consideration was also given to a flexible budget, which is developed on the basis of a single estimate of expected volume.

This chapter concluded with a discussion of the importance of reviewing the budget periodically in association with financial accounting reports, downsizing, and cost-effectiveness measures that prevail in times of fiscal restraint.

Review Questions

1. Ask permission to photocopy an annual operating budget, regardless of setting, for a therapeutic recreation division, department, or unit. (The budget should not include individual salary figures to protect confidentiality.) Compare the budgeted distribution of available funds to the agency's or organization's goals, then try to work out a different distribution assuming 20% more available funds and 20% less available. What effect would the difference in funding have on the quality of and access to the therapeutic recreation service?

2. Develop a personal operating budget for a period of two weeks, including justifications. Compare it with what actually happened.

3. Regardless of setting, critique the value of a day-to-day operating budget with zero-base budgeting for a therapeutic recreation department, division, or unit.

4. If you were a manager of a therapeutic recreation department in a rehabilitation unit of a general medical hospital, what kind of information would you need concerning income and expenditure? Expand this question to any type of setting.

5. Consider the strategies the therapeutic recreation manager might take to secure reimbursement for services in a community-based leisure agency and a health care facility. How are they similar? How are they different?

6. Review a grant proposal and outline the contents.

7. Compare and contrast a grant proposal or process of a government agency with foundation requirements and procedures.

8. Study the Internet sites mentioned in the chapter to ascertain funding references and procedures.

9. Visit with a development or fundraising specialist and discuss strategies for securing external funds.

References

American Hospital Association. (1983). *Managing under Medicare prospective pricing.* Chicago, IL: Author.

Anthony, R. N. and Herzlinger, R. E. (1980). *Management control in nonprofit organizations.* Homewood, IL: Irwin.

Bart, C. K. (1988, November). Budgeting gamesmanship. *The Academy of Management Executive*, 285–294.

Berman, H. J., Weeks, L. E., and Kukla, S. F. (1990). *The financial management of hospitals* (7th ed.). Ann Arbor, MI: Health Administration Press.

Cincinnati Recreation Commission. (2004a). *Fund 323 status report.* Cincinnati, OH: Author.

Cincinnati Recreation Commission. (2004b). *050 summary report.* Cincinnati, OH: Author.

Connolly, P. and Garbarini, A. (1996). *Healthcare management and recreation therapy: Cost benefits*. Thiells, NY: National Council for Therapeutic Recreation Certification.

Cheek, L. M. (1977). *Zero-base budgeting comes of age*. New York, NY: AMACOM.

Crompton, J. L. (1999). *Financing and acquiring park and recreation resources*. Champaign, IL: Human Kinetics.

Esneault, C., Malkin, M. J., and Sellers, L. (1992). Third-party reimbursement for outpatient therapeutic recreation service. In B. Riley and J. Shank (Eds.), *Annual in therapeutic recreation* (Vol. 3, pp. 90–95). Hattiesburg, MS: American Therapeutic Recreation Association.

Malkin, M. J. and Skalko, T. (1992). Third-party reimbursement survey. *Expanding Horizons in Therapeutic Recreation, 14*, 23–51.

Marquis, B. L. and Huston, C. J. (2003). *Leadership roles and management functions in nursing: Theory & application* (4th ed.). Philadelphia, PA: Lippincott, Williams & Wilkins.

McCormick, B. P. (2002). Healthcare in America: An overview. In D. R. Austin, J. Dattilo, and B. P. McCormick (Eds.), *Conceptual foundations for therapeutic recreation* (pp. 185–206). State College, PA: Venture Publishing, Inc.

Melton, J. W. and Watason, D. J. A. (Eds.). (1977). *Interdisciplinary dimensions of accounting for social goals and social organizations: A Conference of the Department of Accountancy*. Columbus, OH: Grid.

Needleman, J. (1999). Nonprofit to for-profit conversions by hospitals, health insurers, and health plans. *Public Health Reports, 114*(2), 108–119.

Nowicki, M. (2001). *The financial management of hospitals and healthcare organizations* (2nd ed.). Chicago, IL: Health Administration Press.

O'Morrow, G. S. (2000). *Therapeutic recreation practitioner analysis*. Ashburn, VA: National Recreation and Park Association.

Pyhrr, P. A. (1973). *Zero-base budgeting: A practical management tool for evaluating expenses*. New York, NY: John Wiley & Sons.

Rosenberg, C. E. (1987). *The care of strangers*. New York, NY: Basic Books.

Skalko, T. K. (1998). Reimbursement. In F. Brasile, T. K. Skalko, and j. burlingame (Eds.), *Perspectives in recreational therapy issues of a dynamic profession* (pp. 447–462). Ravensdale, WA: Idyll Arbor.

Sullivan, E. J. and Decker, P. J. (2001). *Effective leadership and management in nursing* (5th ed.). Upper Saddle River, NJ: Prentice Hall.

Tappen, R. M. (2001). *Nursing leadership and management concepts and practice* (4th ed.). Philadelphia, PA: F. A. Davis Company.

Teaff, J. D. and Van Hyning, T. E. (1988). Third-party reimbursement of therapeutic recreation services within a national sample of United States hospitals. *Therapeutic Recreation Journal, 22*(2), 31–37.

Thompson, G. T. (2001). Reimbursement: Surviving prospective payment as a recreational therapy practitioner. In N. J. Stumbo (Ed.). *Professional issues in therapeutic recreation: On competence and outcomes* (pp. 249–264). Champaign, IL: Sagamore Publishing.

Tillock, T. C. (1981). Cost containment in the healthcare industry. *Aging and Leisure Living, 2*, 5–15.

Tomey, A. M. (2000). *Guide to nursing management and leadership* (6th ed.). St. Louis, MO: Mosby.

United Way of America. (1985). *Budgeting: A guide for United Ways and not-for-profit human service organizations*. Alexandria, VA: Author.

Chapter 9
Information Technology Systems: Enhancing Therapeutic Recreation Practice and Research

chapter revisions by M. Jean Keller

The development and application of information technology systems in therapeutic recreation has changed and will continue to evolve in ways that will impact therapeutic recreation. To take full advantage of this potential, therapeutic recreation professionals will need to understand the capabilities of information technology systems and to competently apply technology to management, practice, and research to improve the health and well-being of consumers of therapeutic recreation services.

Using information technology systems enhances therapeutic recreation services in a number of ways. For example, information technology systems support therapists' activities in providing direct consumer care, including presentation of data, documentation, and work flow (Eder, 2000). Advanced support tools may include pathways to services and efficacy research (Eder, 2000). Additionally, information technology systems help therapeutic recreation managers to make judgments about financial management, staffing, supplies and equipment, policies and procedures, program effectiveness, and communications.

The purpose of this chapter is to highlight the rationale for the development of information technology systems and show how these systems are effective tools in the provision, management, and research of therapeutic recreation. Information technology systems support the therapeutic recreation profession in terms of quality services, efficacy, best practices, research, evaluation, and cost effectiveness (Deluca & Enmark, 2002). A brief overview of terms is provided followed by a discussion of information technology systems and design, as well as computer applications for therapeutic recreation management, practice, and research.

Computer Hardware and Software

Computers are digital or electronic machines. Computers, along with other hardware and software, accept numerical or alphabetical characters, otherwise known as data, process these data in some way, and then record the processed data. Data that have been processed or manipulated are called *information*. Computer systems (made up of hardware and software) perform three functions: input (i.e.,

getting information into the computer), processing (i.e., manipulating information), and output (i.e., displaying results in some meaningful format; Deluca & Enmark, 2002). Computers need operating software (e.g., system utility) to tell the hardware what to do.

There are many general purpose application software programs available to meet therapeutic recreation needs, such as spreadsheet, word processing, database management, and graphic programs. As decisions are made regarding software programs, the criteria for use must be clearly defined. Considerations should be given to flexibility, validity, reliability, ease of use, conformity, performance, and compatibility. Word processing programs have options for enhancing the quality of the document, such as sizes of type, variety of type fonts, and printing. Word processing programs check for spelling and grammar errors and suggest alternative word choices if they contain a thesaurus. Most programs also have "Help" messages used for assistance if one has difficulty with a program function. Some programs even help one to write new programs. Printed documents may include memorandums, letters, policies, procedures, forms, and labels.

File or database management programs are the computer counterpart to the standard file cabinet and its contents. These electronic files are used to store data and are manipulated for information much like paper files. Once a database is created, one is able to add, update, display, or delete information as well as generate printed reports. For example, a therapeutic recreation manager could have last year's budget retrieved and last year's figures replaced with current year figures without typing a whole new document.

In association with budget development, therapeutic recreation professionals might want to incorporate a graphic that allows numerical data to be displayed visually, such as a pie charts or a bar graph. The old axiom about a picture being worth a thousand words is an understatement when it comes to computer-generated graphics, charts, and diagrams. Present-day spreadsheets produce a wide variety of charts and graphics. This is valuable because often the essence of quantitative analysis is captured more quickly and easily when depicted in the condensed form of a visual display (Purchase, 2000). Therapeutic recreation professionals also use graphics or charts to show progress toward achieving goals, number of participants in specific activities and programs, and demographic trends such as an increase in the number of elderly adults being served by a particular program.

Electronic Communication

Electronic communication systems enable the user to send text of any type electronically. The receiving location views the information on a video screen or in print. Electronic mail (e-mail) services transfer messages to sites around the world. Some electronic mail systems also include electronic calendars and ticklers (reminders) as substitutes for paper calendars, sequentially dated folders, or notes. Technology has advanced to allow communication through voice mail. Instead of using a keyboard for data entry, voice messages are digitized so they are transmitted and stored by the recipient's voice mail system. Last, there is facsimile (or fax) equipment for the electronic transmission of copies of documents from one location to another. Connectivity technologies are in growing demand among health and human service personnel and organizations (Deluca & Enmark, 2002).

Networks

Networking is tying together a group of computers via a common communications line and storing common applications and data on a single central computer (a server). Networks have other uses besides tying together data system devices. Modern network technology allows an organization to use common wiring and connectivity for voice, data, video, and telemetry applications.

Data Security

There are a number of tools designed to protect the security and confidentiality of data traveling over public and private networks. A *digital certificate* is one of several electronic means used to secure Internet-based transactions. Issued by a certificate authority, a digital certificate contains enough information to authenticate the identity of a person or organization sending or receiving data over the Internet. Digital certificates are increasingly being used in health and human service organizations as the amount of business and communication conducted over the Internet expands (Deluca & Enmark, 2002).

Encryption is another tool used to secure data being transmitted electronically. Encrypted data are converted from their original form into a form that cannot be understood except by the intended recipient of the data, who has possession of an algorithm that will unscramble the data.

Firewalls are electronic programs that provide an electronic barrier between an organization's internal, private data and operations and the outside world. Security and confidentiality of information in health and human

service organizations must be considered as information technology systems are developed, implemented, and evaluated.

Viruses are electronic programs that attach to computer files, changing their nature in some way. Some viruses are minor, causing little or no damage; others corrupt computer hard drives or networks, shutting them down, causing data loss, business stoppage, or other serious events. Viruses can infect executable program files, e-mail systems, or simple data (e.g., word processing, spreadsheet) files. Protecting systems from viruses requires a combination of organization policies, such as restrictions on what types and originators therapeutic recreation professionals may accept electronic files from and technical tools, such as antivirus software, which check new files against a list of known viruses.

Backing up data as well as storing data are additional factors that need to be considered when working with information technology systems. Some organizations will have data repositories or warehouses for storing large data sets, particularly clinical or financial data. As therapeutic recreation managers, specialists, and researchers use information technology systems, retrieval and storage of data needs to be considered.

Information Technology Systems

Information systems existed before computers. Today, an information technology system has become a necessity in health and human service organizations and is an integral part of the therapeutic recreation profession (Farley, 1987; Lorenzi & Riley, 1994).

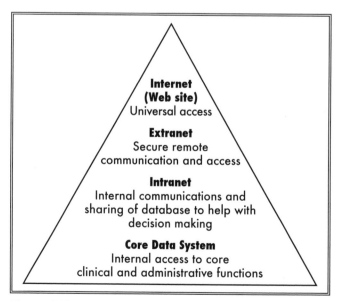

Figure 9.1
Layers of Information Technology Systems

A system is a set of related components (e.g., inputs, processes, and outputs) that collectively form a unified whole (Deluca & Enmark, 2002). Information technology systems are composed of people, hardware, software, data, and procedures. They support the provision of operational efficiency, functional effectiveness, quality service, and research in therapeutic recreation.

Understanding the multidimensional power of these systems requires knowledge of Intranet, Extranet, and Internet capabilities. These systems and technologies enable organizations to reach an increasingly diverse body of users and to establish and maintain communications both within and outside the organization. The Internet is likely to be a major force in the future delivery of therapeutic recreation services (Mitra, 2005). Figure 9.1 shows layers of information technology systems. Each layer broadens access to a new group of constituents or offers former ones value over and above what is already provided.

It is important to remember that the end goal of any information technology system is not technology. The goal is to incorporate the technology features and functions successfully into the daily operations of the organization to achieve specific goals and objectives (Deluca & Enmark, 2002).

Some therapeutic recreation professionals enthusiastically submerge themselves in the workings of information technology. Others avoid technical subjects as completely as possible. What is the "right" balance of information technology for therapeutic recreation professionals to enhance their work and best serve their constituents? There is no simple answer to this question. Designing and implementing effective information systems in a therapeutic recreation organization is a continuous process and managerial responsibility.

Systems Approach to Using Technology

A key to success of information technology systems in therapeutic recreation is improved outcomes and services. Effken (2002) created an approach to designing information technology systems. This approach may be useful in therapeutic recreation. Table 9.1 outlines an integrated model using cognitive work analysis (CWA) and Carper's (1978) four ways of knowing.

CWA was developed for exploring complex technology work domains where workers needed considerable flexibility in responding to external demands (Vicente, 1999). This approach focuses on work domains, control tasks, strategies, social/organizational functions, and staff competencies. This approach appears appropriate for the therapeutic recreation profession.

Table 9.1
Designing Computer-Based Information Systems

Cognitive Work Analysis Levels	Ways of Knowing			
	Empirical	*Ethical*	*Personal*	*Aesthetic*
Work domains	Data elements, values, and relationships	Accuracy and reliability of data and relationships	Organization, discipline, workgroup, novice-expert, and individual differences	Meaning derived from data and relationships
Control tasks	Diagnostic, therapeutic, and information management goals	Which control tasks are right and appropriate for each group of users	Organization, discipline, workgroup, novice-expert, and individual differences	Meaning derived from control tasks
Strategies	How data are processed and results used	Support effective strategies and discourage ineffective ones	Discipline, workgroups, novice-expert, and individual differences	Meaning derived from various strategies
Social/organizational functions	Roles, communication, collaboration, and coordination	Cultural, organizational, discipline, and workgroup values	Cultural, organizational, discipline, and workgroup differences	Meaning derived from cultural, organizational, workgroup, and discipline processes
Staff competencies	Skills needed, skills available, safety, security, and privacy	Individual, workgroup, cultural, discipline, and organizational values	Observed group competencies	Meaning derived from competencies

Adapted from Effken, 2002

Defining work domains helps the therapeutic recreation manager understand what information is needed to accomplish tasks and achieve goals. This in turn helps determine what underlying databases and relationships are needed.

Control tasks analysis examines control structures rather than data. This analysis creates procedures to help the therapeutic recreation manager achieve goals. This analysis also identifies which variables and relations of work domains are relevant for specific situations so the right information may be presented at the right time. For instance, under what conditions are prompts or alerts necessary to ensure the safety of a consumer of therapeutic recreation services? Strategies analysis looks at how work is to be done and provides input for designing appropriate human-computer dialogues as well as the flow of those dialogues.

The process of social-organizational functions analysis identifies the responsibilities of various players in the delivery of therapeutic recreation services. This helps identify the authority and communication patterns that are needed to support a viable organizational structure. Therapeutic recreation professionals' competencies and areas of needed professional development are also identified and addressed.

Work domains, control tasks, and strategies comprise areas of problem demands that an information technology system should support. Social-organizational functions and staff competencies relate to how to solve problems. To achieve an ideal system, a seamless fit between these two areas is created and implemented (Effken, 2002).

Effken (2002) proposed that Carper's ways of knowing complements cognitive work analyses by providing insights into the user's empirical, ethical, personal, and aesthetic values. Using this approach may be highly beneficial for therapeutic recreation professionals.

Empirical knowing deals with facts, theories, models, and relationships. It is the kind of knowing that addresses the following questions: What is the goal of the system? Who will use it? What data elements are needed? What reports must be prepared? Who will use them? How will they be used? How often will they be used? By asking and answering these types of questions, therapeutic recreation professionals enhance their capacity to create useful information technology systems.

In the area of ethical knowing the questions are different, and include the following: Is it good? Is it right? Is it just? How does an information technology system incorporate the organization's core values? How does the information technology system reflect the values, vision, mission, and goals of therapeutic recreation, its consumers, and its administrators within the organization? Given the differing constituents involved in therapeutic recreation,

there may be differing values important in the design of an information technology system (Berg, 1999).

Information technology systems must consider users and their personal knowing (Flach, Hancock, Caird & Vicente, 1995). For example, novices and experts have different information needs. Also, the styles of learning of therapeutic recreation professionals differ; thus, information presented in different ways may enhance learning. Technology may increase or decrease human interactions, as well as the sharing of information depending on how a system is designed.

How is data understood? This is what is meant by aesthetic knowing. Consider what role order plays in the design of data presentation and what role simplicity plays. Research has shown the aesthetics of a software display correlate with consumer usability and satisfaction (Tractinsky, Katz & Ikar, 2000).

This approach to creating an information technology system is time-consuming and ongoing because it approaches the analysis from individual, workgroups, and organizational perspectives. However, it offers flexibility, usability, and sustainability within complex and dynamic organizations where therapeutic recreation services are provided.

Successful information technology systems management requires competent and dedicated leadership and staff as well as a management structure that optimizes the use and maintenance of technology within an organization (Deluca & Enmark, 2002). As health and human service organizations evolve in response to financial, clinical, service, legal, and business issues and trends, so will information technology systems.

The role of information technology systems in therapeutic recreation will continue to unfold as professionals create new and more ingenious applications. Areas of interest, related to information technology systems and therapeutic recreation include maintaining consumer records, improving quality services and service delivery, supporting evidence-based and consumer-centered practice, and enhancing research.

Maintaining Consumer Records

Most consumer recordkeeping can be computerized in therapeutic recreation. Although the degree to which consumer charting in health and human service organizations is standardized varies from one facility to another, most have uniform procedures by which information is recorded and stored for later reference.

A computerized recordkeeping system may be very simple, merely listing categories under which information is classified, or it may be comprehensive. In a health care organization, an entire therapeutic recreation treatment protocol or plan—assessment, goals and objectives, interventions, progress notes, and discharge plans—may be included. Computerization also allows for the constant monitoring and evaluation of a treatment plan once it is designed and implemented. Moreover, computers allow for more uniformity in the monitoring of consumer progress across disciplines. This provides more reliable consumer observation records and in turn enhanced consumer improvement and satisfaction (Bates & Gawande, 2003).

One advantage of computers relative to consumer records is that the computer becomes an electronic reminder to therapeutic recreation professionals of what information should be recorded and where gaps exist. If properly formatted, the information is retrievable for measures of quality control (Berg & Goorman, 1999). Further, accrediting bodies such as the Joint Commission on Accreditation of Healthcare Organizations (JCAHO), the Commission on Accreditation of Rehabilitation Facilities (CARF), and other state and local regulations dictate types of consumer information that must be charted.

Another advantage of computer recordkeeping is that therapeutic professionals are quickly made aware of changes in a consumer's condition that may require a different intervention plan because information from another department is sent to all care providers. From still another perspective, the consumer record contains valuable information that permits periodic reevaluation of the effects of service or treatment with the consumer as well as providing data for therapeutic recreation research. The computer provides periodic reminder information to both consumer and professional on the need for follow-up review and service (Bates & Gawande, 2003).

Securing the confidentiality of consumer records is very important. The Health Insurance Portability and Accountability Act (HIPAA) of 1996 has two administrative standards dealing with privacy and security while promoting the greater use of electronic transactions (U.S. Department of Health and Human Services, n.d.; refer to Chapter 6 for discussion of HIPAA).

In some settings, therapeutic recreation professionals may be seen with hand-held wireless computers, answering preprogrammed prompts as they complete assessments or document consumer engagement. The documented information flows over a host computer in real time. This point-of-care recordkeeping has been shown to be a cost savings in terms of staff time, "back office" documentation, and paper reduction. Additionally, transcription errors are reduced and on-time documentation is improved (Bates & Gawande, 2003).

An individual in private practice shared that she was spending too much time and energy manually writing notes to referring physicians and insurance companies. Parry (personal communication, April 28, 2005) said she was attracted to voice recognition technology that com-

bined with consumer data imported from her practice management system. With these two information technology systems, Parry created electronic charts, complete with logo and letterhead, and reduced paperwork time by 27%.

Improving Quality Services and Service Delivery

Information technology systems allow basic descriptive statistics (e.g., mean, median, mode, standard deviation, variance, frequency) to be used to describe the distribution of data related to therapeutic recreation services and delivery as well as consumer outcomes and satisfaction. This type of descriptive information provides therapeutic recreation managers data to make decisions about therapeutic recreation services and service delivery. For example, all past consumer records containing reality orientation performed by therapeutic recreation professionals for a given period may be extracted. Information about the average length of a reality orientation session is discerned; variance analysis describes how an actual performance compared with others; and trend analysis assists in forecasting workload demand and resource usage related to offering reality orientation sessions. "What if" or scenario analyses are useful when exploring growth in a particular population or staff reductions. By altering variables in the equation, managers are able to determine impact (Lau, Kwok & Bay, 1993). Graphic output is an effective way to display this data for decision making and to enhance understanding of the data.

Information technology systems reduce the rate of errors in health and human service organizations by improving communications, making knowledge more readily accessible, requiring key information, assisting with calculations, performing checks in real time, assisting with monitoring, and providing decision-making supports (Bates & Gawande, 2003). Examples of how information technology systems are used in therapeutic recreation settings to improve services and safety are presented next.

Computerized coverage systems for signing in and signing out, hand-held personal digital assistants (PDA), and wireless access to electronic consumer records improve the exchange of information among therapeutic recreation professionals in a timelier manner. For instance, a consumer of therapeutic recreation services with Alzheimer's disease is in an adult day care center. The client wanders from an activity area and the therapeutic recreation professional is immediately alerted over the PDA. The same consumer is attending a birthday party and reaches for punch and cake. A newly hired therapeutic recreation professional checks the medical records on the PDA and is instantly aware the consumer has severe diabetes. In both illustrations, access to consumer data and information provided therapeutic recreation professionals opportunities to improve the quality and safety of services.

Another key to improving quality services and enhancing safety is access to reference information. A wide range of textbooks, references on drugs and tools to managing infectious diseases, as well as access to Medline database are available for desktop and even hand-held computers (e.g., htttp://www.epocrates.com, http://www.inbound-medicine.com). For instance, a ten-year-old boy, who is HIV positive, falls in the day camp cafeteria and knocks out a tooth. Body fluids are safely and effectively cleaned up by the cafeteria staff after the therapeutic recreation professional provides a checklist from a portable computer.

Another benefit of using computers for providing quality therapeutic recreation services is to implement a "forcing function" feature that may require a task to be completed in a certain way. If a therapeutic recreation professional is required to write a goal statement that is time bound and this is not done, the computer will not allow the professional to complete the documentation. Hence, documentation is more consistent and meets quality expectations. An additional example is when a consumer is referred to a program (e.g., pet therapy) a question immediately comes up on the computer (e.g., asking if the consumer is allergic to pets). Sound therapeutic recreation programming and service decisions are made based on these types of questions and information from well-designed information technology systems (Bates & Gawande, 2003).

Information technology systems help to design effective services for consumers of therapeutic recreation. For instance, an individual is receiving rehabilitation services and because all therapies are entered, it is noted that all the physical activities are clustered from 8:00 a.m. until 11:00 a.m. and the passive activities are from 2:00 p.m. to 5:00 p.m. By noticing this immediately, the consumer's schedule is adjusted to maximize endurance and promote rehabilitation by balancing active and passive activities.

Effective therapeutic recreation managers must have timely, accurate, and comprehensive information to perform their responsibilities. The application of information technology systems to therapeutic recreation management is broad and varied depending on the health and human services setting. Computers are well-suited to store and manipulate the range of data required for planning, budgeting, decision making, monitoring, and scheduling of staff and facilities, as well as purchasing and materials management (Deluca & Enmark, 2002). Some health and human services organizations have their own information management systems that support therapeutic recreation managers in planning, implementing, scheduling, accounting, and evaluating their services. Electronic spreadsheets and databases allow for the manipulation and monitoring of data and save first-line managers time with (a) preparing budgets and billing; (b) programming and

scheduling activities; (c) tracking consumer engagement in programs and activities; (d) identifying supply usage, purchasing supplies and equipment, and maintaining inventories; (e) scheduling and monitoring facilities; and (f) staff and volunteer scheduling, development, and training; and (g) recordkeeping (including attendance, turnover, skills, and credentials). Gathering data, both internal and external, making a decision with data, developing decision-making criteria or standards that will be used to compare data solutions, establishing goals and objectives, deciding how to allocate resources, and developing a variety of solutions to a problem are all possible with well-designed information technology systems (Deluca & Enmark, 2002).

More research is needed on how to improve the quality and delivery of therapeutic recreation services using information technology systems. However, the use of information technology systems in improving therapeutic recreation services demonstrates continued promise.

Supporting Evidence-Based and Consumer-Centered Practice

McCormick and Lee (2001), Stumbo (1996), and many others have shared the need for evidence-based therapeutic recreation service and practice. Therapeutic recreation managers must continue to ask and answer the following questions: How do we know that what we do is effective and how can our practice and service be improved? While appearing to be simple questions, they challenge the therapeutic recreation profession daily. Moving toward this type of evidence-based and consumer-centered practice and service is simplified with information technology systems.

Just as therapeutic recreation managers must partner with information technology personnel to design effective and useful systems, so too must therapeutic recreation managers partner with researchers to ascertain best practices and services. Information technology systems in therapeutic recreation have the potential to help researchers, students, and professionals formulate clear questions around consumers' problems, prognosis, activities' selection, outcomes, and evaluations. Part of the research process is to search relevant databases and literature; information technology systems make these processes more efficient and effective (McCormick & Lee, 2001). Additionally, information technology systems help researchers and managers discern and implement the best available consumer practices and then evaluate consumer outcomes to monitor or alter practice and service delivery.

Johnson and Ashton-Schaeffer (2003) indicated that communicating with technology, such as using the Internet, has the potential to improve leisure satisfaction, health, and quality of life for some individuals. Specific examples of how computer-mediated communication broke down social barriers and increased positive social support for single young mothers and reduced the number and length of hospitalizations for persons who were HIV-positive were shared in the article, "Virtual Buddies: Using Computer-Mediated Communication in Therapeutic Recreation." Johnson and Ashton-Schaeffer (2003) suggested that individuals with disabilities explore leisure interests, locate leisure resources, and learn leisure skills using computers. In the near future, therapeutic recreation professionals will communicate with consumers and provide treatment and leisure education over long distances. This will be a valuable, cost-effective method of service delivery and follow-up to therapeutic recreation consumers in remote areas and who are hard to reach.

Enhancing Research

Therapeutic recreation professionals have been challenged to create and to implement research (Compton, 1984; Howe, 1994/95; Witt, 1988). Information technology systems in therapeutic recreation settings may encourage the therapeutic recreation profession to aggressively address this challenge. There are many areas on which a profession may base its research, including where and how professionals work (i.e., scope of practice), skills needed to perform the work (i.e., education), and benefits/outcomes of the work (i.e., efficacy). Likewise, there are a number of different ways to explore these aspects of the profession. Several ideas are shared as to how information technology systems are a part of a research agenda for the therapeutic recreation profession.

In 2005, Mitra discussed how Web-based methods are used to collect data about recreation and leisure services. Using Internet technologies to collect information is convenient and efficient. Both quantitative and qualitative data may be collected. For instance, a Web-based public meeting may be hosted regarding accessibility issues. It could be interactive, where people have a discussion in real time. Potential benefits of this method of data collection include accessibility, convenience, affordability, monitoring, complete and accurate records, and possibly increased involvement. Posted surveys and questionnaires provide data and information for decision making that may not be available from other sources. While there are opportunities for data collection using technology, as in all research, consideration must be given to validity and reliability of the data.

The availability of large, comprehensive data bases, such as the Uniform Data System for Medical Rehabilitation (UDSMR) and Medline, allow therapeutic recreation managers access to data and research using technology information systems. Data is compared, contrasted, and analyzed using readily accessible information. Organizations may find comparing their own data with national,

regional, and state averages is useful for demonstrating effectiveness, efficiency, and identifying opportunities for improvement. Again, like in all research, precautions using electronic data bases are necessary to ensure uniformity in the use and interpretation of data.

Information technology systems enhance research using other designs as well. Case study, single-subject, daily experience, and mixed methods are research methods used to enhance practice and each benefits from information technology systems. Each method is highlighted and briefly discussed. The therapeutic recreation profession has expressed concerns with an overreliance on survey research; thus, exploring how various methods enhance knowing more about the profession is important. Information technology systems facilitate the use of these research methods.

A case study may be an individual, group, event, or community. When compiled for consumer recordkeeping and other purposes, data are used for research to understand actions in the context of a case (McCormick, 2000). While single-point studies are conducted, case studies also allow the collection of data over time to discern developmental patterns. Case studies allow managers and researchers to explore complex sets of decisions and to recount the effects of decisions over time. Data from technology information systems can be merged from various sources efficiently. The management of data over time may be expedited when computerized. Case study research, with support of information technology systems, may contribute valuable information to the theoretical, practical, and technical knowledge of therapeutic recreation (McCormick, 2000).

Single-subject research designs are used to examine the effects of therapeutic recreation. These research designs enhance program evaluation (Dattilo, Gast, Loy & Malley, 2000). Additionally, single-subject research designs complement the ability of therapeutic recreation professionals to meet the individual needs of consumers. Using information technology systems with well-documented intervention results to promote specific outcomes with consumers is a key part of single-subject research designs. Baseline data are important in these research designs and information technology systems facilitate the gathering and access to the data about consumers of therapeutic recreation. The documentation of repeated observations of consumers' behaviors over time is another aspect of single-subject research designs supported by information technology systems. Results of measurements are graphically displayed and inferences about relationships between interventions and changes in behaviors are enhanced with information technology systems. This type of formative evaluation and information about interventions applied in therapeutic recreation settings allows therapeutic recreation managers to make changes quickly to increase consumers' success. This information also allows researchers and managers to ascertain best practices.

Voelkl and Baldwin (2000) discussed the importance of understanding daily experiences among persons with disabilities and highlighted three methods for measuring daily experiences. Common to each approach (i.e., interval-contingent, signal-contingent, and event-contingent) is the collection of consumer responses to a set of questions during or immediately after the daily activity. Information technology systems support these research methods.

In the interval-contingent approach a consumer is given a checklist and asked at certain scheduled intervals to complete it. Interval-contingent methods examine variables one time, thus, this method is used to track consumers' responses to interventions or activities. This is completed online, tabulated using technology, and entered into an information system to be used for research, decision making, and best practice.

The signal-contingent approach asks consumers to describe their experience whenever they are signaled. This method has the potential to be used as a tool for examining the effects of an intervention in the daily lives of consumers of therapeutic research (Voelkl & Baldwin, 2000). Consumers are given a PDA and asked to share what they are doing and how they feel when they are doing it, when they are signaled. Consumers' entries are placed into an information technology system and then analyzed.

The event or activity-contingent method asks consumers to complete a self-report questionnaire each time an event occurs. This is a means to learn about specific consumer behaviors. Again, technology and information technology systems supports data collection, analyses, and interpretation.

There are issues and considerations when designing studies to measure daily experiences. Technology and information technology systems may be able to simplify the selection and training of consumers and simplify the complexity of data collection and analyses. Because the therapeutic recreation profession is designed to promote health and well-being during daily leisure experiences of individuals with disabilities, these methods, supported by information technology systems, enhance therapeutic recreation research and practice.

As shown here, various research methods are available to enhance the therapeutic recreation profession. Mactavish and Schleien (2000) discussed linking qualitative and quantitative data in mixed methods research design as a means to enhance the validity and reliability of studies. The strength of mixed methods research lies in the ability to facilitate the study of complex phenomena in ways that cannot be studied with a single approach; information technology systems support these research

designs (Bullock, 1993; Henderson & Bedini, 1993). Data analyses in mixed methods research include descriptive and comparative statistics along with the conversion of raw narrative data. Information technology systems in therapeutic recreation settings expedite these forms of data analyses from questionnaires and interviews. Bedini, Bullock, and Driscoll (1993) and Mactavish and Schleien (2000) provided examples of how mixed methods are used in therapeutic settings.

Information technology systems have the potential to enhance research in therapeutic recreation. The various research designs discussed here are well-suited for studying the intricacies that affect practice and knowledge in therapeutic recreation. Information technology systems promote these forms of knowing and best practice by making data accessible, easier to analyze, and more useful in decision making.

Barriers and Opportunities

Information technology systems and technology are advancing daily and continue to impact therapeutic recreation services and delivery. Like other professions, therapeutic recreation will continually need to understand information technology systems, how these systems enhance the profession, and how to employ these systems to improve practice, management, and research. Information technology systems support therapeutic recreation managers in identifying the services and supports that most effectively and efficiently meet the needs of consumers. Therapeutic recreation managers will need to collaborate with information technology professionals to advance the profession in the coming years. Information technology systems and technology are not end results, they are tools used by therapeutic recreation managers to promote their visions and missions.

Despite the substantial opportunities for improvement of therapeutic recreation practice, management, and research, the development, testing, and adoption of information technology systems in therapeutic recreation remains limited. Barriers to the use of information technology systems and technology in therapeutic recreation include financial limitations, lack of standards, privacy regulations, and cultural issues.

Therapeutic recreation managers will be challenged to find ways to overcome these barriers. The development of applications of information technology systems in health and human services has been for the most part, commercially motivated and funded. The focus has been on products to improve billing and reimbursements for services rather than on those that might improve services to consumers. For therapeutic recreation and organizations seeking to determine the investment costs of information technology systems, those costs can be high. Where systems are in place, the applications for therapeutic recreation remain highly variable (Bates & Gawande, 2003). The information technology systems approach described earlier in this chapter could enhance applications within a system.

There are few standards for representation of clinical or human service data. The result has been that most applications do not communicate well even within an organization, and the costs to interface are high. While a challenge, there are both short-term and long-term opportunities in these areas. The National Committee on Vital and Health Statistics (2002) released a report endorsing national standards for electronic data for key domains. This may be an area the therapeutic recreation profession considers in the future.

There is also a tendency for therapeutic recreation specialists, managers, and researchers to see information technology systems as relatively unimportant to their practice or knowledge development. This reluctance appears to have a number of causes. Technology in therapeutic recreation research remains relatively underused. A number of therapeutic recreation specialists are uncomfortable with computers due to legal and privacy issues along with technical competencies. A fundamental challenge in therapeutic recreation is execution of existing information technology systems. Providing reliable, efficient, individualized therapeutic recreation services requires a degree of mastery of data and coordination that will be achievable with increased use of information technology systems. Information technology systems in therapeutic recreation have the potential to help managers offer improved quality and safe services, promote evidence-based and consumer-centered practice, access data necessary to support sound decision making, and support various forms of research.

Summary

In many businesses and industries, information technology systems have made possible the efficient and reliable production of goods and services according to the highly personalized needs of individual customers (Bates & Gawande, 2003). The growing sophistication of technology

hardware and software allows information technology to play a key role in enhancing the health and well-being of individuals and those who support these goals. Creating information technology systems supports the therapeutic recreation profession in terms of quality services, best practices, research, evaluation, and cost effectiveness. An overview of a number of issues related to the design, implementation, and evaluation of information technology in therapeutic recreation settings was highlighted. Opportunities and challenges are plentiful as therapeutic recreation managers explore how to use information technology systems to enhance practice and research.

Will the therapeutic recreation profession take advantage of the best that modern technology can offer? This question needs to be addressed by therapeutic recreation professionals today and tomorrow. Information technology systems may be used to enhance therapeutic recreation practice, to support administrative decision making, to facilitate therapeutic recreation education, and to expand the body of therapeutic recreation knowledge through research.

Review Questions

1. Speculate how you might use a computer and information technology systems as a first-line manager in health and human service settings.

2. Visit a community-based leisure service setting and a health care facility. Compare and contrast how they use computers and information technology systems to manage and deliver services.

3. Explain how information technology systems assist the therapeutic recreation manager to achieve more efficient operations.

4. Conduct an Internet search to identify commercial hardware and software available to use to improve services and to promote consumer-centered practices.

5. Visit with a manager to observe how budget development and monitoring occur using data generated from information systems.

Glossary

Application software Computer program that carries out a specific business or personal task, such as registering a consumer, processing an order, or producing a bill.

Computer-telephone integration Technology that combines the functions and capabilities of telecommunications with computer application systems. Most commonly used to support call centers, continuing education, and consumer-oriented systems.

Consumer health systems Application directly targeted for use by health care consumers. Functions might include self-triage, self-service appointment scheduling, personal health record maintenance, and other patient-centered activities.

Data Representation of information in a form suitable for processing.

Database Electronic storage structure similar to a file.

Data integration Connectivity between and across application systems, allowing data input into one system to be accessed from others.

Data repository Data collection and storage tool that can incorporate consumer demographic, financial, and clinical information into one physical location, allowing data access and input throughout the enterprise or IDS. Often used synonymously with a data warehouse.

Data warehouse Data repository that incorporates strengthened data access and analysis tools.

Decision support systems Applications that allow service providers to collect and analyze data in sophisticated and complex ways. Activities supported include case mix, budgeting, cost accounting, clinical protocols and pathways, outcomes, and actuarial analysis.

Electronic data interchange (EDI) Automated exchange of data and documents in a standardized format. In health care, some common uses of this technology include claims submission and payment, eligibility, and referral authorization.

Electronic medical record (EMR) Application that aggregates consumer data from a variety of source systems; advanced EMRs allow access to text, graphics, clinical results, images, voice, and video.

Emerging technology Technology, unproven untested in the health care and human service industries, offering great potential benefits to organizations willing to accept the associated risks.

Enterprise system Application allowing a single point of access for consumer and resource management across a health system or set of connected organizations.

Extranet The part of an enterprise network or Intranet extended via secure means to specific outside users.

Foundation technology Technology that allows application systems to communicate more effectively; examples include networking technologies, data integration and interface tools, and computer-telephone integration.

General financial management systems Technologies that support the basic financial transactions required in the day-to-day operation of a health care enterprise (e.g., general ledger, payroll, materials management, human resources).

Hardware Equipment that runs application software or peripheral devices (e.g., printer, computer monitors) used in working with computers.

Health Insurance Portability and Accountability Act (HIPAA) U.S. law passed in 1996 requiring the adoption of standards for electronic health transactions and requiring specific patient data security and confidentiality measures.

Information systems Application software designed to automate a particular part of the health care or human service processes.

Information technology Technology designed to facilitate process or customer service automation in health care or human services. More than information systems, information technology encompasses application software, operating systems, database and data access systems, telecommunications equipment (e.g., networks, telephone), and computer hardware.

Information technology planning The formal process through which an organization assesses its information technology status and performance against industry standards, best practices, and current and future expected business requirements and then designs strategies and tactics to target future investment to meet key needs and objectives.

Interface Specialized software or hardware that permits the passing of information back and forth between two systems. Interfaces are of two types: batch and real-time.

Internet Worldwide network of networks, allowing public access to anyone with a computer and a service provider.

Intranet Private network for use within an enterprise (and therefore not available to the public).

Management information system System designed to manipulate information to assist in management decision making.

Remote processing Network configuration in which a data center is removed from the main user areas, as in another building or another country.

Research systems Application systems allowing the collection, consolidation, tracking, management, and analysis of data relating to clinical research efforts (including administrative, financial, and clinical data components).

Security Tools and techniques used to protect a computer system from unauthorized access.

Software Computer programs to control internal computer operations or to carry out the tasks for which an information system is designed.

Technical support unit Group operating within the information systems department that is typically responsible for general PC support and hardware or cabling plans and changes.

References

Bates, D. W. and Gawande, A. A. (2003). Improving safety with information technology. *New England Journal of Medicine, 348*, 2526–2534.

Bedini, L. A., Bullock, C. C., and Driscoll, L. B. (1993). The effects of leisure education on factors contributing to the successful transition of students with mental retardation from school to adult life. *Therapeutic Recreation Journal, 27*(2), 70–82.

Berg, M. (1999). Patient care information systems and health care work: A socio-technical approach. *International Journal of Medical Informatics, 55*, 51–60.

Berg, M. and Goorman, E. (1999). The contextual nature of medical information. *International Journal of Medical Informatics, 1*, 13–23.

Bullock, C. C. (1993). Ways of knowing: The naturalistic and positivistic perspectives on research. In M. J. Malkin and C. Z. Howe (Eds.), *Research in therapeutic recreation: Concepts and methods* (pp. 25–42). State College, PA: Venture Publishing.

Carper, B. (1978). Fundamental patterns of knowing in nursing. *Advanced Nursing Science, 1*, 13–23.

Compton, D. (1984). Research priorities in recreation for special populations. *Therapeutic Recreation Journal, 18*(1), 9–17.

Dattilo, J., Gast, D. C., Loy, D. P., and Malley, S. (2000). Using single-subject research designs in therapeutic recreation. *Therapeutic Recreation Journal, 34*(3), 253–270.

Deluca, J. M. and Enmark, R. (2002). *The CEO's guide to health care information systems with Web-enabled technologies.* Hershey, PA: Idea Group Publishing.

Eder, L. (2000). *Managing healthcare information systems with Web-enabled technologies.* Hershey, PA: Idea Group Publishing.

Effken, J. A. (2002). Different lenses, improved outcomes: A new approach to the analysis and design of healthcare information systems. *International Journal of Medical Informatics, 65*, 59–74.

Farley, J. M. (1987, Winter). Modelling the choice of automation. *Sloan Management Review*, 5–15.

Flach, J., Hancock, P., Caird, J., and Vicente, K. (Eds.). (1995). *Global perspectives in the ecology of human-machine systems* (Vol. 1). Mahwah, NJ: Lawrence Erlbaum Associates.

Henderson, K. A. and Bedini, L. A. (1993). Notes on linking qualitative and quantitative data. *Therapeutic Recreation Journal, 28*(2), 124–130.

Howe, C. (1994/95). Encouraging joint involvement in inquiry by therapeutic recreation specialists and educators: Potential outcomes for students from collaborative and cooperative models of research. In C. P. Carruthers (Ed.), *Annual in Therapeutic Recreation* (Vol, 5, pp. 48–56). Hattiesburg, MS: ATRA.

Johnson, D. and Ashton-Shaeffer, C. (2003). Virtual buddies: Using computer-mediated communication in therapeutic recreation. *Parks & Recreation, 38*(3), 71–79.

Lau, F., Kwok, H., and Bay, K. S. (1993). Some computer-based decisions support tools for the rehabilitation manager. *Physiotherapy Canada, 45*(1), 29–38.

Lorenzi, N. M. and Riley, R. T. (1994). *Organizational aspects of health information: Managing technological change.* New York, NY: Springer.

Mactavish, J. B. and Schleien, S. J. (2000). Beyond qualitative and quantitative data linking: An example from a mixed method study of family recreation. *Therapeutic Recreation Journal, 34*(3), 154–163.

McCormick, B. P. (2000). Case study research in therapeutic recreation. *Therapeutic Recreation Journal, 34*(3), 245–252.

McCormick, B. P. and Lee, Y. (2001). Research in practice: Building knowledge through empirical practice. In N. Stumbo (Ed.), *Professional issues in therapeutic recreation* (pp. 383–400). Champaign, IL: Sagamore Publishing.

Mitra, A. (2005). Weaving a Web. *Parks & Recreation, 40*(5), 49–51.

National Committee on Vital and Health Statistics. (2002). *Administrative simplification in health care, 2001: Annual report to Congress on the implementation of the administrative simplification provisions of the Health Insurance Portability and Accountability Act.* Retrieved March 27, 2004, from http://www.ncvhs.hhs.gov/reptrecs.htm

Purchase, H. C. (2000). Effective information visualization: A study of graph drawing aesthetics and algorithms. *Interactive Computing, 13*, 147–162.

Stumbo, N. J. (1996). A proposed accountability model for therapeutic recreation services. *Therapeutic Recreation Journal, 30*(4), 246–259.

Tractinsky, N., Katz, A. S., and Ikar, D. (2000). What is beautiful is useable. *Interactive Computing, 13*, 127–145.

U.S. Department of Health and Human Services. (n.d.). *OCR privacy brief summary of the HIPAA privacy rule. HIPAA compliance assistance.* Retrieved November 11, 2005, from http://www.hhs.gov/ocr/privacysummary.pdf

Vincente, K. J. (1999). *Cognitive work analogies: Toward safe, productive, and healthy computer-based work.* Mahwah, NJ: Lawrence Erlbaum Associates.

Voelkl, J. E. and Baldwin, C. K. (2000). Daily experience research: Methods and application in therapeutic recreation. *Therapeutic Recreation Journal, 34*(3), 227–243.

Witt, P. A. (1988). Therapeutic recreation research: Past, present, and future. *Therapeutic Recreation Journal, 22*(1), 14–23.

Chapter 10
Decision Making, Problem Solving, and Conflict Management

Much of the first-line manager's time is spent critically examining issues, making decisions, and solving problems (Marquis & Huston, 2003). Managers are expected to use knowledge from various disciplines along with their expertise to make decisions and to resolve problems and conflicts in dynamic situations (Sullivan & Decker, 2001). Decision making, problem solving, and conflict resolution are criteria on which management expertise is judged. The quality of decisions made and action taken weigh heavily on the degree of a manager's success. Yet, these tools are used with clients, staff, and administrators, and as we manage our day-to-day lives.

In this chapter the most basic of the decision making and problem solving processes, along with how to manage conflict, will be considered. Opening the chapter is a brief discussion of critical or reflective thinking. Critical thinking is an essential component of decision making and problem solving. Critical thinking is broader in scope and encompasses higher level reasoning and creative analysis (Marquis & Huston, 2003; Sullivan & Decker, 2001). Skills essential to critical thinking are found in rational decision making and problem solving.

A major portion of the chapter is devoted to decision making. This chapter section considers decision types and conditions under which decisions are made; policies, procedures, and rules; the decision-making process, including the role of creativity in the process; group decision-making; tools and techniques used in decision making; and personal and ethical elements of decision making. Therapeutic recreation managers develop skills that enable them to make effective decisions that are at the core of every management task.

Next the chapter considers problem solving. Decision making may or may not involve a problem yet requires the selection of one choice from among several, each of which may be appropriate; problem solving requires selecting the one correct solution. The problem solving process is reviewed, as are problem solving methods and group problem solving. Problem solving is analogous to the APIE (i.e, assessment, planning, implementation, evaluation) process. A gap exists between existing and desired conditions and this prevents realization of department goals. Using the APIE process, the manager resolves the issue, thus closing the gap and enabling achievement of department goals.

Finally, the chapter addresses conflict. Conflict is inevitable and can be constructive or destructive; it may be a prerequisite to change in people and organizations. Conflict is a warning to management that something is amiss and it should stimulate search for solutions through problem solving (Sullivan & Decker, 2001; Tomey, 2000). Causes and types of conflict are presented followed by approaches and strategies to conflict resolution. Complete elimination of conflict is unrealistic and not necessary. First-line managers minimize stress on staff and the organization and maximize effectiveness when they manage the sources and types of conflict.

Critical Thinking

A hallmark of an effective manager is the ability to make decisions and to resolve problems reflectively without being influenced by current opinions or perceptions (Tappen, 2001). Critical thinking is an attitude and process characterized by insight, intuition, empathy and a willingness to take action (Marquis & Huston, 2003; Tappen, 2001). Critical thinking involves "examining underlying assumptions, interpreting and evaluating arguments, imagining and exploring alternatives, and developing a reflective criticism" (Sullivan & Decker, 2001, p. 151) to justify a reasoned conclusion.

> It is a willingness to give fair consideration to any idea, but to accept an idea only after you have reflected carefully on it and evaluated it in terms of the evidence to support it and its congruence with your value system. (Tappen, 2001, p. 186)

Inherent in clinical practice and application of the self in helping relationships are reflection and critical analysis. When a manager or therapist examines a problem or makes a decision, a series of questions facilitates critical analysis (Sullivan & Decker, 2001; Tappen, 2001).

- What is the meaning and significance of the issue?

- What are the underlying assumptions?

- How does the evidence support the viewpoints?

- How are arguments evaluated and supported?

- What are the possible alternative viewpoints?

- How do the insights drawn from the conclusions impact practice?

Results of critical thinking may or may not be welcome, as they may lead to different views and creative solutions. Critical thinkers are using scientific problem solving to explore ambiguities found in clinical decision making and management practices.

Decision Making

Decision making is defined as choosing a particular course of action from among a set of alternatives (Marquis & Huston, 2003). The essence of decision making is choice. The person making a decision must recognize that a decision is necessary and identify a set of feasible alternatives before selecting one. Hence, decision-making processes rely on a scientific approach like the APIE process to

1. Identify the nature of the decision situation.

2. Explore the alternatives.

3. Consider the consequences.

4. Choose a desirable alternative.

5. Implement the decision.

6. Evaluate the outcomes (Tomey, 2000).

Decision making is a major component of each of the management functions discussed in Chapter 2. Decision making can be active; that is, a choice is made to do something different. Passive decision-making results in "deciding not to decide" or maintaining the status quo. Because organizational and department life is characterized by an environment of competing values, the decision-making requirements in the position of therapeutic recreation manager are complex. The choices that confront managers daily are rarely choices between something good and something bad. If this were the case, the job of managers would be relatively easy. Although rationality is the goal of managers, many decisions are affected by such nonrational factors as emotion, attitudes, and individual preferences and needs.

Types of Decisions

Therapeutic recreation managers must make many different types of decisions. In general, however, most decisions fall into one of two categories: programmed and unprogrammed (Robbins & Decenzo, 2001). Decisions are programmed to the extent they are repetitive and routine and to the extent a definite approach has been worked out for handling them so that they do not have to be treated as new or unusual each time they occur. Given a certain known situation, the manager need only evoke a learned and appropriate response. Consideration of an alternative step in the decision-making process is minimal or nonexistent. In many situations it becomes decision making by precedent; that is, the manager simply does what the manager or others have done in the same situation. Objectives, standards, procedures, rules, and policies all represent examples of programmed decisions (Sullivan & Decker, 2001). Routine decisions are more often made by first-line managers than executive-level managers (Sullivan & Decker, 2001).

Occasionally, decisions must be made concerning a relatively unstructured or different situation. No cut-and-dried solution exists because the matter has either never arisen before—its structure is vague, ambiguous, or complex—or it is so important that it deserves a custom-tailored approach (Robbins & Decenzo, 2001).

Unprogrammed decisions usually include the large and dramatic. Managers faced with these situations must treat them as unique by investing blocks of time, energy, and resources into exploring the situation from all perspectives. While top managers are usually involved in unprogrammed decisions, therapeutic recreation managers may very well be involved if the situation focuses on a new facility, legal issues, programs, or budgets.

Clearly, the greater the proportion of programmed knowledge and programmed application used, the simpler the job of the first-line therapeutic recreation manager. However, the manager has a particular responsibility when an unprogrammed situation arises. It is his or her responsibility to chart a course of action—to problem solve—in these circumstances. This does not mean that the manager will make all unprogrammed therapeutic recreation service or activity decisions. Indeed, the wise manager will use his or her best resource people for this purpose. Resource people can include experienced staff practitioners, personnel from other departments, or practitioners from other organizations who have special expertise. While it is not up to the first-line therapeutic recreation manager to make all decisions, it is clearly the responsibility of the manager to be creative and effective at finding the best resource people for each unprogrammed situation.

An aside to types of decisions as related to programmed knowledge is that it is also the responsibility of the manager to document new approaches and new theories of service as they are tested or used in the environment. Whenever satisfactory results are obtained from a new approach, it is important that the findings be preserved and shared with other therapeutic recreation practitioners. Results obtained in any given situation are shared so they may be tested again. In this way programmed therapeutic recreation knowledge grows and is verified.

Decision-Making Conditions

Just as there are different kinds of decisions, there are also different conditions in which decisions must be made. Managers sometimes have an almost perfect understanding of conditions surrounding a decision, but at other times they have few or no clues about these conditions. Decision theorists have identified three general circumstances that exist for the decision maker: certainty, risk, and uncertainty (Robbins & Decenzo, 2001; Sullivan & Decker, 2001).

Certainty

In theory, certainty means that a manager, when faced with a decision, knows the exact outcome of each alternative being considered. In reality, when managers have to make a decision, absolute certainty never exists.

Risk

A more common decision-making condition is a state of risk. Essentially a state of risk implies that the manager knows the probabilities associated with the possible outcomes of the alternative under consideration. Objective probability is based on statistical or recorded experience. Subjective probability estimates are the product of the manager's experience and judgment. In decision making under condition of risk, the level of risk is moderate. However, the ability to recognize and to take a calculated risk is a skill required of all managers.

Uncertainty

The final condition is uncertainty. In this situation, the manager does not know all of the alternatives, the risks associated with each, or the consequences each alternative is likely to have. This condition is the most ambiguous for managers. According to Ayert and De Groot (1984), the key to effective decision making under the condition of uncertainty is to acquire as much relevant information as possible and to approach the situation from a logical and rational perspective. Intuition, judgment, and experience play a major role in this condition as well.

Certainty, risk, and uncertainty may be viewed as a conceptual continuum that helps managers to visualize and to think about the decisions that face them. Although therapeutic recreation managers face decisions every day, they are more inclined to make decisions that fall between certainty and risk.

Policies, Procedures, and Rules

While there is a decision-making process, decision making is made easier by policies, procedures, and rules. In fact, these factors are essentially the guidelines of the organization (Bannon, 2002; Robbins & Decenzo, 2001). They are associated with planning, contributing to goals and objectives, budgeting, programming, purpose or mission, and thinking and action in decision making. In many organizations they are considered standing plans because they focus on programmed decision making (Marquis & Huston, 2003; Robbins & Decenzo, 2001).

First-line managers rarely make policies and procedures. Rather, they interpret and apply them. Department policies and procedures, when initiated, must be within the boundaries and guidelines established by organizational policies and procedures. All policies and procedures should be clearly written; that is, they should be precise and concise. Policies and procedures that are not intelligible are not likely to be followed. They should not only be documented but also be periodically updated and revised or abandoned if no longer usable or outdated. Policies and procedures are usually found within a policy and procedure manual. A copy of the manual should be in each department of the organization. In some organizations the department may have a separate manual with reference to the organizational manual. To a great degree, the type of manual will be influenced by the sheer number of policies and procedures, and that in turn is influenced by the size of the organization.

Even when policies and procedures exist, staff are not always as familiar with them as they should be. To ensure that policies and procedures are followed, orientation and training sessions for old and new employees should be an integral part of employee development. Further, all policies and procedures should be accessible; employees should know where to go to obtain specific information.

Policies and procedures usually develop over time, incrementally, as situations arise where decisions have to be made. These informal policies and procedures usually become a working part of the department. Longtime employees feel there is no need, or they do not have the time, to document what they are doing. However, as departments and organizations grow larger, and as employee turnover becomes more of a factor, documentation of policies and procedures becomes necessary to ensure the continued efficiency and effectiveness of the department.

Policies

Policies explain how goals will be achieved and serve as guides that define the general course and scope of activities permissible for goal accomplishments. They serve as a basis for decisions and actions, help coordinate plans, control performance, and increase consistency of actions by increasing the probability that different managers will make similar decisions when independently facing similar situations (Bannon, 2002; Tomey, 2000). Policies are comprehensive statements that "direct individual behavior toward the organization's mission and define broad limits and desired outcomes of commonly recurring situations" (Marquis & Huston, 2003, p. 68) while serving as guides to those who carry out the policies.

Policies establish the boundaries or limits within which a specified type of decision should be made. Within these boundaries, judgment must be exercised. The degree of discretion permitted varies from policy to policy. Some policies are broad in scope and permit much latitude and at the same time allow various departments to develop supplemental policies. Others are narrow and leave little room for interpretation.

Policies emerge in several ways: originated, appealed, or imposed. As noted previously, they may be originated by top management, but they can be generated at the department level. At times, policies may be formulated simultaneously from both directions. Policies are usually prepared through committee action and circulated for comments on potential effect before final approval. Thereafter they are embodied in the organization's policy manual.

The second way policies come about is through appeal. When a manager does not know how to solve a problem, disagrees with a previous decision, or otherwise wants a question reviewed, he or she appeals to a higher authority for a decision. As appeals are taken up the hierarchy and decisions are made, precedents are set, which guide future managerial actions (Tomey, 2000). Appealed policies are likely to be incomplete and unclear. Unintended precedents can be set when decisions are made for one situation without regard for effects across the department.

Finally, policies may be externally imposed. In many instances, health and human service organizations must conform to governmental laws, practice standards of professional associations (e.g., practice standards of the American Therapeutic Recreation Association [ATRA] and the National Therapeutic Recreation Society [NTRS]), accreditation standards in health care facilities (e.g., Joint Commission on Accreditation of Healthcare Organizations [JCAHO] and Commission on Accreditation of Rehabilitation Facilities [CARF]), and community-based agency accreditation program of NRPA and the Commission for the Accreditation of Park and Recreation Agencies (CAPRA).

Policies relative to therapeutic recreation are usually associated with delivery of services, personnel, external factors, and quite possibly with interdependent and intradependent relationships. Following are several simple guidelines for establishing a therapeutic recreation policy manual:

1. If possible the title of every policy should use the most common terminology (for easy location).

2. A brief description of the policy should be set out at the top of the document so that the reader can rapidly tell if it contains the desired information without having to read the entire procedure.

3. Objectives (i.e., purposes) for the policy should be stated. This facilitates periodic manual review. If the policy no longer meets the original objectives, it will be apparent.

4. A code system should be used to enable the reader to find related policy and procedural statements.

5. All policies should be authenticated by date and by either the therapeutic recreation manager or his or her supervisor.

Collaboration in the development of policies is encouraged by JCAHO (Paige, 2003). Collaboration across departments standardizes practice and creates opportunities to determine best practices. The use of consistent policy and procedures ensures compliance with standards and uniform client care. Further, staff are uniformly directed toward achieving department goals. With predictable interpretations, internal and external criticism is reduced (Edginton, Hudson & Lankford, 2001).

Figure 10.1 shows the table of contents of a therapeutic recreation policy and procedures manual for a day treatment program of the Rocky Mountain MS Center. The contents include protocols and regulations governing agency operation (MS Center) as well as the day program, the King Adult Day Enrichment Program (KADEP).

Procedures

Procedures are guides to action or execution. They detail an exact chronological sequence of steps to be taken in performing specific duties. They are used in communication, understanding, standardization, teaching, coordination, and evaluation. Procedures are intradepartmental or interdepartmental and consequently may not affect the entire agency or organization to the extent that policy statements do (Tomey, 2000). They usually become more exacting and numerous in the lower levels of the organization because of the necessity for more careful control while reducing the need for discretion in making a decision. In some instances, procedures provide a means for implementing certain organizational policies (Paige, 2003).

A procedure manual, like a policy manual, provides a basis for orientation and staff development and is a ready reference for all personnel. The manual should be well-organized, with a table of contents and an index. Each procedure should be easily replaceable with a revised one.

Rocky Mountain MS Center
KING ADULT DAY ENRICHMENT PROGRAM
POLICY AND PROCEDURE MANUAL
TABLE OF CONTENTS

continued…

Figure 10.1
Policy and Procedures Manual Content

Section 12
OPERATIONS/FACILITIES AND EQUIPMENT
Certificate of Occupancy
Colorado Department of Health Survey
Purchasing
Repairs and Maintenance
    Request for Maintenance
Building Security
    Alarms
Supply Inventory
Durable Medical Equipment
Therapy Garden
Safety Checks and Equipment Monitoring
Hazardous Materials
Health and Sanitation

Section 13 SAFETY
13.1 Emergency Preparedness
    Fires
    Weapons/Bombs
    Natural Disasters
    Power Failures
    Medical Emergencies
    - CPR and First Aid
    - First-Aid Kits
    - TRIP Books and Bags
    - Outing Checklist
    Safety during Violent Situations
    Internal/External Disasters
    Weather Emergencies
13.2 Infection/Exposure Control Plan
    Universal Precautions
    Sharps
    TB Testing
    Hepatitis B
    Cleaning/Housekeeping Standards
    Laundry
    Kitchen Sanitation/Food Handling
    Restroom Sanitation
    Handwashing
    Reporting Suspected Infection/Safety Issues
    Incident Reporting

Section 14
PUBLIC RELATIONS/MARKETING
Program Fact Sheet
Program Brochure
Informational Sheet for Professionals (GRID)
Video
KADEP Newsletter: Enriched News
RMMSC Newsletter: Inform
Media Coverage
Marketing Plan
Publications
Web Page

Section 15
QUALITY MANAGEMENT/ EVALUATION
Quality Management Plan
Program Evaluation
Participant Satisfaction Survey
Caregiver Satisfaction Survey
Case Manager Satisfaction Survey
Outcomes Monitors
Risk Management Plan
United Way Reporting
Foundation Reports
Board of Directors Reporting

Section 16
NUTRITION/MEAL SERVICE
Nutrition Policy
Meal Service
CACFP Program
Food Bank of the Rockies
Nutrition Assessment
Meal Records
Food Handling
Special Diets/Swallowing

Section 17
APPENDICES/ATTACHMENTS

Figure 10.1
Policy and Procedures Manual Content (continued)

It is important to review and to revise the procedure manual periodically.

Involving staff in establishing procedures increases the quality of departmental procedures and the likelihood that they will be implemented as desired. "Established procedures save time, facilitate delegation, reduce cost, increase productivity, and provide a means of control" (Marquis & Huston, 2003, p. 69). Standardized procedures provide a means of evaluating adherence to work protocols. Figure 10.2 illustrates the procedures associated with each policy of the animal-assisted activities program at the King Adult Day Enrichment Program (KADEP) of the Rocky Mountain MS Center Denver, Colorado. Procedures applicable to each aspect of the program are detailed. Additionally, reference to the Delta Society Policies and Procedures for Registered Pet Partners implies that volunteers also must adhere to protocols of this program as well as the volunteer requirements of KADEP.

Rules

Rules are specific statements of what must or must not be done in a given situation. Unlike policies, rules leave no room for discretion. Robbins and Decenzo (2001) noted that rules "are frequently used by managers who confront a well-structured problem because they are simple to follow and ensure consistency" (p. 125). Because rules describe only one choice of action, there should be as few rules as possible; yet they should be enforced to help morale from breaking down (Marquis & Huston, 2003).

The Decision-Making Process

Over the years a large number of decision-making models have been developed. Traditional theory holds that decision making requires a logical thought sequence, commonly called the *rational decision-making process.* Today recent advances in the field of cognitive science indicate that decisions made based on intuition (if verified on the basis of logic) by experienced managers can also be quite rational (Marquis & Huston, 2003). Researchers further suggested that intuition and the rational decision-making process do not have to be a completely independent process; rather, both can be integrated components in an effective decision system (Simon, 1987).

Although intuition can be an important aid to decision making, managers understand the importance of following a logical thought sequence in making decisions (Sullivan & Decker, 2001). However, it is well to review the research of Herbert A. Simon (1987) regarding how decisions are often made. According to his findings, managers often make decisions by using incomplete and imperfect information that is limited by their values, skills, or habits, and they tend to search only until an alternative

Animal Assisted Activities Program

PURPOSE: The Animal Assisted Activities (AAA/T) program will serve to enhance the quality of client's life by improving their health and via the positive psychological effect of human-animal interaction.

POLICY: Volunteer guidelines

Procedure:

1. AAA/T volunteers must be Delta-registered Pet Partners and, as such, agree to the Delta Society policies and Procedures for Registered Pet Partners (as described in the attached document)

2. Registered Pet Partners are covered by Delta Society's commercial general liability insurance.

3. As Delta-registered Pet Partners, volunteers will have specific training and pass rigorous screening from Delta-licensed instructors and evaluators and veterinarians. Re-testing every two years ensures program quality and consistency.

4. Current documentation of volunteer Pet Partners and animal credentials shall be maintained in the Volunteer Services Office.

5. Volunteers must fulfill all requirements for this facility's volunteer program as follows:

- Complete and submit volunteer application to the Volunteer Services Office.

- Complete and sign a volunteer "Confidentiality Agreement."

- Wear a picture ID badge issued by this facility while performing service.

- Have a mandatory TB test, follow-up test, and required annual tests in future.

- Wear approved volunteer garb.

- Wear closed-toe rubber-soled shoes (no sandals).

- Sign in and out as designated and record volunteer hours served.

- Abide by the policies outlined in the volunteer handbook.

- Supply program leader with results of yearly veterinary checkups, including vaccinations.

- Complete required visit documentation at completion of visits.

- Communicate changes in visit schedule in advance to program leader and reschedule missed visits.

- Maintain a professional and cooperative relationship with staff, clients, and other team members.

- Make required number of visits per month (minimum of 2).

- Remain current with Pet Partner registration.

6. Volunteers will read and become familiar with the AAA/T Protocol as outlined by this facility in cooperation with the Delta Society.

7. Volunteers and their animals are required to shadow a current Delta Pet partner for two visits before beginning their individual volunteer service.

8. Volunteers must be able to explain the program and answer any questions from clients of visitors.

POLICY: Volunteer Training and Orientation

Procedure: Volunteers must fulfill all requirements for the Volunteer Program as follows:

1. Complete/Submit application to the Volunteer Coordinator.

2. Attend initial Volunteer Orientation and complete annual refresher courses as required.

3. Complete and sign a volunteer "Confidentiality Agreement."

4. Wear Pet Partners picture ID badge.

5. Wear approved volunteer garb.

6. Wear closed-toe rubber-soled shoes (no sandals).

7. Sign in and out and record volunteer hours served.

8. Abide by the policies outlined in the volunteer handbook.

9. Be familiar with the AAA/T protocol as outlined by this facility in cooperation with the Delta Society.

POLICY: Staff Training

Procedure: An in-service training session will be given to staff who will be involved in AAA/T. It will be scheduled before Pet Partner visits are initiated. Staff will be instructed on:

Figure 10.2
Procedures: Animal Assisted Activities Program   >>

1. Goals of the program

2. How to identify clients who should not participate in an animal visit

3. Staff responsibilities before, during, and after an animal visit

4. What to expect from the volunteers

5. How to assist the volunteers

POLICY: Documentation

Procedure:

1. Volunteers shall check in at the staff desk and with the program leader before beginning their visit.

2. In case of an accident or unusual occurrence, volunteers shall follow Pet Partner policies and procedures for this instance, which includes completing a Pet Partners Incident Report Form.

3. Upon completion of each set of visits, volunteers shall complete a Visit report and leave it in the Pet Partners binder, which will be in its designated location. Staff suggestions or comments on the visit or for future visits are recommended.

4. In the event parental or physician consent is needed for an AAA/T visit, the appropriate forms must be completed in advance.

POLICY: Incident Reports

Procedure: In the event of an injury, the Delta Pet Partner is required to observe the following techniques as outlined in the current Delta Pet Partners team training course manual:

1. Secure the animal. Do not tie the animal to other people, equipment, or furniture, which have the possibilities of being unstable.

2. Get help for the injured person. Volunteers should never give medical aid to an injured client. Facility staff, and not volunteers, should be the ones to provide medical treatment to clients, even if the treatment is as simple as applying an adhesive bandage.

3. End the visit.

4. Notify the facility contact person in writing so the injury can be documented in the client's medical file.

5. Fill out all necessary documentation at the facility. Some facilities have accident or unusual incident report forms.

Upon notification of an incident, the program leader will contact the appropriate individuals and subsequently provide a copy of MS Society KADEP's "Incident Report" for follow-up.

POLICY: Animal Screening

Procedure:

1. Animals must be Delta-registered Pet Partners with current registration. This facility has chosen to limit visits to the following types of animals:

DOGS

2. Pet Partners will have completed specific training and passed rigorous screening from Delta-licensed evaluators.

3. Animals must pass a thorough examination by a veterinarian prior to registration.

4. Animals must be kept on a strict vaccination and parasite prevention schedule, administered and documented by a licensed veterinarian.

5. Animals must be clean and well-groomed. They shall be bathed and/or thoroughly brushed prior to a visit, nails clipped, ears clean and free of any odor, eyes clean, and have clean breath with teeth brushed.

6. Dogs shall wear a nylon, cloth, or leather buckle collar, or a head collar, such as the Gentle Leader.

7. Dogs shall be on a leash no longer than 6 feet in length, shall always remain with the handler, and shall be under control at all times.

8. Animals must wear their proper vest and ID badge (as appropriate).

Figure 10.2

Procedures: Animal Assisted Activities Program (continued)

that meets some minimum standard of efficiency is identified. Why the latter? The decision maker may be unable to weigh and evaluate a number of alternatives at the same time. Also, subjective and personal considerations often intervene in decision situations.

A manager who really wants to approach a decision rationally and logically should try to follow certain steps. It is important to recognize this step format as a thought process, as thinking in a specific directional pattern to arrive at a satisfactory solution. However, it is also important to recognize that at times several steps may be going on simultaneously. Nevertheless, this approach should clarify what is meant by the decision-making process.

Problem Identification

The decision-making process begins by determining that a problem exists; that is, there is an unsatisfactory condition. This is frequently expressed as a disparity between what is and what should be (Robbins & Decenzo, 2001). In other words, when a person perceives a discrepancy between what is and what should be, a problem exists, at least in the mind of that person.

Problems arise from many different sources. Internal reports may indicate areas of unsatisfactory performance on the part of the staff. Pressures may be exerted by consumers, regulator organizations, or pressure groups to initiate a new service or improve services. Then, too, managers may see the opportunity to emulate a successful program from another agency.

The key to good problem recognition is to define precisely what the problem is. This is easier said than done, however, because it is frequently difficult to distinguish the problem from its symptoms. The therapeutic recreation manager identifies the problem by analyzing the situation completely, including the specific objectives to be accomplished by the solution. "All too frequently decisions are made and implemented before all the facts have been gathered" (Tomey, 2000, p. 53).

To avoid this the manager should have a questioning attitude. What is the desirable situation? What are the presenting symptoms? What are the discrepancies? Who is involved? When? Where? How? With answers to these questions the therapeutic recreation manager can develop tentative hypotheses and test them against what he or she knows. Progressive elimination of hypotheses that fail to conform to the facts reduces the number of causes to be considered. Feasible hypotheses should be further tested for causal validity. Once the cause or causes of the problem have been identified and available information analyzed, the manager begins to explore possible solutions.

As a final note in problem diagnosis, managers may need to be aware of limits within which the solution may fall. Normally, problem analysis reveals the conditions that limit solutions. These limits may include budget constraints, agency or organization policy, organizational behavior, the individual characteristics of top managers, and just plain time (Simon, 1987).

Exploring Alternatives

Once the problem has been identified and the objectives and boundaries of an acceptable solution have been determined, the manager must explore and identify alternative or possible solutions (Tomey, 2000). If various alternatives are not explored completely, the course of action is limited. Griffin (1990) suggested that it is useful to develop both obvious, standard alternatives and creative, innovative alternatives. However, he cautioned that creative solutions run the risk of various kinds of constraints, such as legal restrictions, moral and ethical norms, and authority constraints.

Typical sources for initiating alternatives are experience, practices in other agencies and organizations, other managers, and other interested parties. There is no harm in obtaining input from others who are respected in decision making. Rarely can important decisions be made without input from others including those who may be affected by the decision. They may generate or identify other ways of looking at the problem. In addition, soliciting input from others shows respect for others' opinions and fosters open communication.

One may also generate alternatives from professional meetings, review of pertinent literature, continuing education, and correspondence with others (Tomey, 2000). Inductive and deductive reasoning are both appropriate. Last, doing nothing (i.e., maintaining the status quo) and postponing the decision to a later date, as noted earlier, are also alternatives (Griffin, 1990).

Creativity is essential to critical thinking processes. A mediocre decision-making team becomes an excellent team as a result of the quality and originality of thinking (Sullivan & Decker, 2001). "Creativity is the ability to develop and implement new and better solutions" (Sullivan & Decker, 2001, p. 168). Cultivating creativity is one way to keep a department viable. The right side of the brain is intuitive and conceptual and is used in creative thinking while the left side is analytical and sequential. Processes like brainstorming, think tanks, the Delphi technique, and modeling are avenues to promote the use of the right side of the brain. Creative thinking is paramount to exploring solution alternatives. The creative process has five steps that we can learn.

Felt Need. It is during felt need that creative solutions to problems may be developed. The creative process has steps similar to the problem-solving process, but the emphasis is different. Decision-making stresses the choice of a solution, while the creative process emphasizes the uniqueness of the solution (Tomey, 2000). Creativity is a latent quality activated when a person becomes motivated by the need for self-expression or by the stimulation of a problem situation. Thus the first phase of the creative process is a felt need. Similarly, when a decision maker is confronted with a problem, the maker starts seeking a solution (Tomey, 2000).

Preparation. The second phase of creative problem solving is a work stage known as preparation from which creative ideas emerge. Innovation is partially dependent on the number of options considered. By exploring relationships among potential solutions, one may identify additional solutions. Many decisions are made with little preparation and therefore result in commonplace solutions. "Superficial analysis of obvious information does not facilitate creative answers" (Tomey, 2000, p. 56). For example, extensive use of libraries for data collection is helpful. The creative person may take notes on readings, develop them into files with other clippings and ideas, review these materials, and combine the most appropriate aspects of old solutions into new answers (Tomey, 2000).

Incubation. Incubation, the third phase, is a period for pondering the solution. Repetition of some thoughts with no new ideas or interpretation is a sign of fatigue and indicates that it is a good time to start the incubation period. Switching one's attention provides a necessary respite, and yet the unconscious mind continues to deal with the problem. A time should be set to reexamine the situation and review the data collected during the preparation phase (Tomey, 2000).

Illumination. Illumination is the discovery of a solution. It may come to mind in the middle of the night or during the performance of another task. It is recommended that the idea be written down so the details can be preserved regardless of when the illumination occurs (Tomey, 2000).

Verification. It is rare for an illumination to be ready for adoption. Verification, the fifth and final phase of creative decision making, is the period of experimentation when the idea is improved through modification and refinement. The advantages and disadvantages of each alternative must be weighed, resources and constraints have to be evaluated, and potential technical and human problems must be considered. By comparing the advantages and disadvantages of options, the manager can choose the most desirable alternative (Tomey, 2000).

Evaluating Alternatives

This step is a continuation of the previous step, including the creative process. Consideration in this step needs to be given to the feasibility of the alternative, its satisfaction, and its consequences (Griffin, 1990).

The first question to ask is whether or not an alternative is feasible. Is it within the realm of probability and practicality? Limited human resources may preclude the initiation of a new program. A manager may want to write down the pros and cons for each alternative and analyze this information to make his or her decision.

When an alternative has passed the test of feasibility, it must next be examined to see how satisfactory it would be. Satisfaction refers to the extent to which the alternative will satisfy the conditions of the decision situation. For example, the therapeutic recreation manager wants to increase programming in the community sector by 50%. One alternative is to hire a new practitioner. If closer examination reveals that the employment of the practitioner would only expand programming by 35%, it may not be satisfactory. Depending on the circumstances, the manager may go ahead and employ a new practitioner and search for other ways to achieve the remaining 15% expansion, or the manager may simply drop the consideration until another day (Griffin, 1990).

Finally, if the alternative is both feasible and satisfactory, its probable consequences must be assessed. From a practical viewpoint however, one cannot project every possible consequence for every alternative. Still, questions need to be addressed. To what extent will a particular alternative influence or stress other parts of the agency or organization? What will the cost be to implement the alternative? Even when an alternative is both feasible and satisfactory, the consequences might be such that it must be eliminated from further consideration (Griffin, 1990).

Selecting an Alternative

The next step in the decision-making process is to select an alternative course of action to make a decision. In many situations the decision is obvious from the analysis, although managers should remember that it may be possible to have two or more acceptable alternatives.

Empirical studies indicate that managers' perceptions are colored by their personal values and that their decisions can be influenced by these values, either directly or through their perceptions (Marquis & Huston, 2003). Of course, the manager is influenced by many other things, such as staff acceptance, morals, cost, and risk of failure.

Before implementation, managers may want to test the soundness of the decision depending on the situation and solution. Several techniques may be employed. Herbert and Estes (1977) suggested that a person assume the role of "devil's advocate." Another possible method is to project the decision into detailed plans thereby revealing any serious flaws in the prospective course of action. Another answer is to ask others in similar managerial roles to give constructive feedback concerning the potential solution (Newman, 1964). Decisions may also be tested by trying them out on a limited basis, such as pilot testing. Last, the manager may want to review and take a second look, just as a second opinion can determine the ultimate success or failure of a solution. The manager should go back to the basics and ask: Will this decision accomplish the stated objectives or answer the needs? Is it workable and efficient? Will it prove effective as a long-term investment? When these questions and others have been answered to the manager's satisfaction, it is time to implement the solution (Griffin, 1990).

Once a decision has been made, the manager should be aware of the natural postdecision reaction called *cognitive dissonance* (Festinger, 1975). Very simply, cognitive dissonance means that once a person makes a decision, he or she is likely to develop second thoughts because of the favorable characteristics of some of the rejected alternatives. Moreover, the manager may talk to others about the positive aspects of the decision. In doing so the manager is attempting to convince himself or herself, as well as others, of the wisdom of the decision.

In general, the more desirable the characteristics of the rejected alternatives and the faster the decision had to be made, the greater the cognitive dissonance (Brehm & Cohen, 1962). Awareness of this natural human tendency should give therapeutic recreation managers greater objectivity in testing and evaluating their choices. Moreover, it should provide the manager with a helpful perspective in discussing with staff the merits of the decisions.

Implementing the Decision

After a decision has been reached, it needs to be implemented. In some decision situations implementation is easy; in others, it will be difficult. In the change process there are usually two types of resistance: that incurred by the nature of the change and that incurred by misperceptions of what the change might mean. Some individuals resist change, which is usually the result of insecurity, inconvenience, and fear of the unknown. Thus, the manager needs to communicate to appropriate staff in a manner that does not arouse antagonism (Tomey, 2000). The decision and procedures for implementation can be explained in an effort to win cooperation. A major decision requires a plan of action when "conveying the decision to those affected and getting their commitment" (Robbins & Decenzo, 2001, p. 119). Anticipating most questions helps the manager to explain the changes in ways that will alleviate groundless fears (Griffin, 1990).

The therapeutic recreation manager should not let himself or herself be tricked into making premature and ineffective responses to resistance as it develops. These ineffective responses include self-justification, advice giving (i.e., "What I would do if I were you…"), premature persuasion (i.e., "Later, you'll see it my way."), censoring (i.e., meeting opposition with disapproval), and punishing behavior.

Evaluating the Decision

Evaluation, the final step, is a matter of analyzing the positive and negative aspects of a solution derived by using a scientific thought process. Depending on the solution being evaluated, suggested methods to use alone or in combination include interviews, individual observations, surveys, quality assurance scales, audits, and various types of questionnaires. The bottom line is evaluating whether or not the alternative chosen has served its original purpose.

Evaluation examines both the objective and subjective result. Was the result the one expected, and was the result desired positive or negative? If the alternative appears not to be working, the manager can identify the second or third choice for adoption. The manager might decide to give it more time to work or begin the decision-making process all over again.

Evaluation can occur in relation to application for future problems, or it can occur in terms of the entire decision-making process incurred for this particular situation. Which steps were performed adequately or inadequately? What did the therapeutic recreation manager learn as a result of the process? Finally, evaluation allows for the identification of serendipitous findings.

Group Decision Making

The widespread use of participatory management, quality improvement teams, and shared governance in health care organizations requires therapeutic recreation managers weigh the desirability of using groups effectively (Sullivan & Decker, 2001). Group decision making places the manager in a facilitator and consultant role. "Compared to individual decision making, groups can provide more input, often produce better decisions, and generate more commitment" (Sullivan & Decker, 2001, p. 164).

The manager can promote effective group decision making by rewarding behavior that focuses on and values the uniqueness of each individual's ideas and feelings. Through communication of concern for, and trust in, others' ideas and feelings, positive norms are established. When the therapeutic recreation manager engages in promoting conformity to others' ideas and feelings, antagonism or mistrust results, and group development and decision-making ability are hampered. To avoid such problems when involved with a group making a decision in a staff meeting or committee meeting, the therapeutic recreation manager can request a member to record all the ideas as they are expressed. It is often useful to have laptops so that each member can record ideas. The usefulness of each person's ideas should be stressed rather than the weaknesses. The use of "yes, but" should be avoided as it may foster conformity to the manager's way of thinking at the expense of creative group decision making. Groups have a greater quantity and diversity of information, and as a result can identify more alternatives than can the manager (Robbins & Decenzo, 2001). Additionally, "decisions made by groups may be perceived as more legitimate than decisions made by a single person" (Robbins & Decenzo, 2001, p. 129). Lastly, group decisions tend to be more creative and accurate than do individual decisions.

One should also recognize the disadvantages to group participation in decision making. Group decisions may result from social pressures. The subordinate may be influenced by a desire to be accepted by the group or to appease the manager. Hierarchical pressures can lead the subordinate to acquiescence to the manager's desires. Formal status is likely to inhibit interaction when the manager has less expertise than the staff. A competent manager is more likely to possess self-confidence and to allow interaction.

Another disadvantage of group participation in decision making is the amount of work time a manager devotes to coordinating and facilitating group decisions. Also, the speed with which group decision making occurs is inferior to the time a manager might devote to the same decision situation. Other disadvantages to group participation in decision making may include the following:

- Every problem situation is not automatically a group issue.

- Some groups are not functioning at a level where they could produce a usable solution.

- Sometimes information about a problem cannot be shared with the staff, and the manager must make an independent decision.

- Some managers work best when they retain responsibility for all decisions because they are unable to share responsibility with a group.

- In a crisis situation, there may not be time for a group to convene and produce a solution, and the manager must do so.

Groups are best used in decision making when time and deadlines allow for group processes, the decision is multifaceted, members share the department goals, and there is a need for acceptance of the decision if it is to be properly implemented (Sullivan & Decker, 2001). When group members meet face-to-face they may pressure other group members into agreement witholding minority views. A number of techniques may be instituted by the manager to foster creative group decision making.

Interaction Group

One of the most common and popular forms of group decision making is an interaction group (Griffin, 1990). The format is simple: an existing or a newly designated group is asked to make a decision about something. Existing groups might be department staff or standing committees. Newly designated groups can be ad hoc committees, task forces, or teams. The group members talk among themselves, argue, agree, argue some more, form internal coalitions, and so forth. Finally, a decision is made. While there is value in this type of group, such as sparking new ideas and promoting understanding, the disadvantage is that it is open to political pressures.

Brainstorming

Another popular form of group decision making is brainstorming. Group members meet together, possibly away from the problem site, and generate lots of ideas without consideration of their relative value. Members do not

Alternative	Financial effect	Political effect	Departmental effect	Time	Decision
#1					
#2					
#3					
#4					

Figure 10.3
A Decision Grid

critique ideas as they are proposed but are encouraged to improve on each other's ideas. Merit of each solution follows after all ideas have been generated (Sullivan & Decker, 2001). Environment is the key to successful brainstorming and participants must be comfortable within the setting. These brainstorming sessions may be called *retreats* if they last for a number of days. Such a group form takes considerable planning. Time should be structured for the sessions as well as for relaxation and recreation. The major disadvantage with this form is cost and arranging a time that can accommodate everyone. Brainstorming is also a technique used in total quality management (TQM) and continuous quality improvement (CQI). However, time is not spent away from the setting.

Nominal Group Technique

In some settings and depending on the situation, the nominal group technique (NGT) might be appropriate. Nominal groups are used most often to generate creative and innovative alternatives or ideas. In the NGT process, the manager presents a problem to a group that usually consists of no more than ten people, and each member silently lists what he or she believes to be the best solution or alternative. After a brief period of time each participant is asked to give his or her idea, which is written down on a flip chart. This process continues without discussion, except for simple clarification, until all ideas have been recorded. Then an open forum takes place. After each idea is openly discussed, the participants privately rank the various alternatives from least acceptable to the one solution they believe to be the best. The decision idea that receives the highest overall rating is the first choice and is presented as the decision of the group. Unfortunately, the manager may retain the authority to accept or reject the group's decision.

Delphi Group Method

One group participative method is the Delphi group method. The basic format is very similar to the NGT process. The major difference is that the group membership is anonymous: Participants do not meet face-to-face. Ideas are collected through a sequence of questionnaires interspersed with manager-prepared summaries of participant ideas from each of the previously mailed questionnaires (Sullivan & Decker, 2001). Only the manager who has selected the participants knows the group mix. All information gathered about the problem and all of the suggested ideas and solutions proposed by the participants are given in writing to the manager only. Personal feedback is provided by the manager to each member with regard to all written suggestions. All members of the group are made aware of the other responses and reactions being generated. The selection process is handled in a similar fashion as the NGT, but communication remains confidential and identities anonymous. When a final decision is reached, it is presented as a group decision, but participants are not identified. The time factor associated with this form rules out routine, everyday decision use. However, its use with large numbers of participants is extensive.

Electronic Meetings

Computer technology enables managers to facilitate group generation of ideas by recording individual member ideas as they are presented during brainstorming and NGT sessions. Meeting rooms with individual terminals allow group members to enter responses onto computer screens. All comments as well as aggregate votes are displayed on a projection screen (Robbins & Decenzo, 2001). Technology increases the speed and anonymity of responses while allowing group members to be truthful. Expense and availability of the systems may be drawbacks.

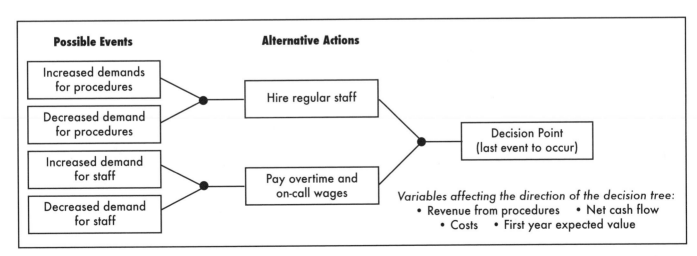

Figure 10.4
A Decision Tree

Tools and Techniques Used in Decision Making

A number of tools are available to the manager to "provide order and direction in obtaining and using information or… in selecting who should be involved in making the decision" (Marquis & Huston, 2003, p. 41). Some like NGT, Delphi technique, and electronic meetings have been noted in the discussion on group decision making. Some require the manager to use analytical skills while others are designed to increase intuitive reasoning.

Decision Grids

A spreadsheet is created to examine each alternative according to set criteria. These criteria are weighted so the final decision is based on a numerical value. When selecting a candidate for a position, this method might be helpful. A decision grid allows one to visually compare one alternative against each of the others (see Figure 10.3).

Decision Trees

A decision tree is a graphic representation that plots a decision over time as it is tied to the outcomes of other events. The tree plots the events with the alternative actions while introducing the variables affecting the direction of the decision tree. Hiring full-time versus using on-call staff illustrates managerial considerations when specific services like aquatic therapy are in demand. In Figure 10.4, variables affecting the direction of the decision tree include revenue from aquatic therapy, personnel expenses, net cash flow, and variability in demand.

Program Evaluation and Review Technique (PERT)/ Critical Path Method (CPM)

A PERT model is "a flow chart that predicts when events and activities must take place if a final event is to occur" (Marquis & Huston, 2003, p. 43). A critical path shows an activity that must occur in the sequence before management or staff may proceed. Often PERT/CPM are depicted in the same flow chart. A critical path is shown by lines that connect decision boxes according to time necessary to complete tasks. PERT charts are helpful during process evaluation as the decision-making process unfolds.

Personal and Ethical Elements of Decision Making

"Every decision maker brings a unique set of personal characteristics to his or her… efforts" (Robbins & Decenzo, 2001, p. 127). The assumption that each person who receives the same information and uses the same scientific process will come to the same decision does not hold true (Marquis & Huston, 2003). A manager who is creative and does not mind uncertainty develops decision alternatives differently than one who is less likely to take risks. Decision making involves both perception and eval-

uation. We perceive by sensation and intuition and evaluate our perceptions by thinking and feeling. Because each person has different values and life experiences, we perceive and think differently given the same set of circumstances (Marquis & Huston, 2003).

The therapeutic recreation manager's personality can and does affect how and why certain decisions are made and certain personal and professional problems are addressed or ignored. "Optimism, humor, and a positive approach are crucial to energizing staff and promoting creativity" (Sullivan & Decker, 2001, p. 167). One's culture, locus of control, self-esteem, age, developmental stage, values, personal preferences, and past experiences with illness, interventions, and decision making may influence the process (Noone, 2002). Value judgments affect the alternatives generated and the final choice selected; for some, certain choices are not possible because of their beliefs (Marquis & Huston, 2003). Although preferred, one alternative may not be selected because it is too risky with regard to time or costs a manager perceives must be devoted to the preference. Each decision maker brings past education and decision-making experience to the process. "The more mature the person and the broader his or her background, the more alternatives he or she can identify… Likewise, having made good or poor decisions in the past will influence a person's decision making" (Marquis & Huston, 2003, p. 37). Caring, credibility, a futuristic perspective, confidence, courage, flexibility, energy, creativity, and sensitivity tend to be qualities of successful decision makers (Marquis & Huston, 2003; Sullivan & Decker, 2001).

As decisions are made, the manager faces conflict among values. Ethical choices consider wants, needs, and rights and are predicated on one's values. At times, decisions among alternatives infringe on one's rights. Moral dilemmas result when decisions have equally unsatisfactory alternatives (Tomey, 2000). Value modification is a lifelong process as is moral development. One moral decision model outlines a decision-making process that parallels the APIE process (Marquis & Huston, 2003, p 551):

M Massage the situation and collect data on the ethical problem and who should be involved in the process.

O Outline the alternatives, causes and consequences.

R Review the alternatives against the values.

A Act or implement the decision.

L Look back and evaluate the decision making.

This framework does not solve the problem, but assists the manager in clarifying personal values and beliefs (Marquis & Huston, 2003). The manager working in concert with agency ethics committees makes choices that affect policy. Ethical issues associated with costs, privacy, efficacy, autonomy, and beneficence require the manager to invoke a moral decision-making process. Professional ethics codes guide managerial decisions that weigh wants and needs against personal rights.

As a final note, the therapeutic recreation manager needs to keep in mind that poor decisions will be made from time to time and will have to be lived with. Even when the best decision-making techniques are used, errors occur because of the complexity of situations. A competent manager realizes no one is perfect, or even nearly so, and that an accepting attitude is paramount in management.

In summary, decision making is defined as the selection of a preferred course of action from two or more alternatives. There are two types of decisions: standardized or programmed responses and unique responses to complex situations. These are called *unprogrammed decisions.* These two types of decisions are made under varying conditions referred to as certainty, risk, and uncertainty. The decision-making process is made up of six main steps. Group decision making takes on various forms, which include interaction groups, brainstorming, nominal group technique, Delphi group method, and electronic meetings. Decision grids, decision trees, and PERT/CPM models are used to obtain information and make decisions. The section closed with consideration of personal characteristics and the ethical nature of decision making.

Problem Solving

Problem solving is not the only skill needed by the first-line manager, but it is certainly a primary one. To oversimplify, management is the successful balance of two behaviors: solving problems and achieving goals. As noted at the beginning of this chapter, problem solving involves diagnosing a problem and solving it, which may or may not mean deciding on the one correct solution. Managers usually associate problem solving with the conflict that stems from antagonistic interaction among individuals. However, problems can develop from unfinished paperwork, delays and interruptions, complaints from staff and consumers, lost or damaged supplies and equipment, excessive time spent on an activity, and absenteeism or turnover of staff. Simply put, it's an obstruction, mental or physical, that presents itself to the individual—some undefined situation that keeps one from moving on. It is important, therefore, that the first-line manager be a resourceful problem solver. The manager must recognize when a problem exists and accept responsibility for its resolution.

Problem Solving Defined

Problem solving can be defined as a process used when a gap is perceived between an existing state and a desired state. Problem solving, like decision making, is a series of steps designed to organize available information to come up with the best possible solution. It is a deliberate, thoughtful way to deal with an immediate situation that is creating some kind of difficulty for which there is no ready-made solution. Instead of reacting to a problem without thinking it through, problem solvers try to sort out the complexities of the situation first and then bring some thought and organization to their actions to resolve the problem (Sullivan & Decker, 2001; Tappen, 2001).

Problem-Solving Purpose

Problem solving itself does not supply answers. It is only a process by which one arrives at an answer. Its major usefulness is in providing guidelines or structures when one is faced with a problem. As shown in Table 10.1, problem solving consists of steps quite similar to the therapeutic recreation process with which the reader is already familiar.

Therapeutic recreation process refers to the use of these steps in relation to the consumer or group, while problem solving refers to any kind of problem, whether it is related to the consumer, coworkers, or disorderliness in the department. In other words, it might be said that problem solving is a generic process that can be applied to any number of problems.

Table 10.1
Comparison of the Problem-Solving and Therapeutic Recreation Process

Steps	I	II	III	IV
Problem Solving	Collect data	Select strategies	Take action	Evaluate
Therapeutic Recreation Process	Assessment (including problem identification)	Planning (including goal setting, activity, plan, and evaluation criteria)	Implementation	Evaluation

Problem-Solving Process

Step 1A. Assessment: Collect Data

This first step is critical. The therapeutic recreation manager should insist on knowing all relevant facts. One should list as much information concerning the problem as possible. The experiences of the manager and everyone involved are sources of information. Some data may be inaccurate, yet some will be helpful in pursuing innovative ideas. If data are unreliable or too incomplete to define the problem, more will have to be gathered before proceeding. Sometimes a manager can include gathering more data as one of the selected strategies for resolving the problem. It should be remembered, however, that one is gathering data for a specific purpose and that when one has sufficient information to confirm or delete the hypotheses about the situation, one should proceed to the next step and not continue to gather unnecessary information.

Because information gathered is a combination of facts and feelings, it is important to state the data as objectively as possible, saving interpretation for the next step. One can do this by describing observed behavior instead of one's interpretation of that behavior. The following statements illustrate the difference between interpretative and objective data statements:

> *Interpretative:* The therapeutic recreation manager does not like the way I chart.

> *Objective:* The therapeutic recreation manager frowned when reading my chart notes, but said nothing.

It was noted in the previous section that soliciting input from others may be an appropriate approach in decision making. It is also appropriate in problem solving. A manager may involve everyone in every phase or engage different people in each, depending on the problem to be solved and input needed. Options for obtaining input may include one-to-one conversations, group discussions, memos requesting input, and electronic mail discussion.

When interviewing others to gain information for problem solving, open-ended questions and active listening should be used. The manager needs to take care not to judge others' suggestions or to convey, verbally or nonverbally, that he or she disapproves of their ideas. If the manager does not remain open to the information he or she solicits, others will sense that their input is not really important and will stop communicating with the manager.

Step 1B. Assessment: Define the Problem

Once a reasonably adequate amount of data has been collected, one can begin to analyze it. Is it a problem in its own right, or is it merely a symptom of a problem that

is broader in scope? It is important to look especially for patterns in the data as well as for clues to the underlying dynamics of the situation, remembering there are often multiple rather than single factors at work when a problem arises. Then a summary statement of the situation should be prepared in which the problem is defined as specifically and objectively as possible (Tappen, 2001). This summary should not include the solution to the problem. Jumping to the solution is tempting, especially when urgently needed, but it keeps one from exploring new avenues and selecting the best alternatives. It also prevents one from ensuring that the problem identification is correct before applying a solution.

Sometimes it is not possible to immediately define the problem, but only to come up with several alternative hypotheses. If this occurs, it is necessary to gather more information on each hypothesis before selecting one to follow through in the planning stage. Developing alternatives is also valuable when the manager is not able to implement the first-order solution (Sullivan & Decker, 2001).

Step 2. Plan: Select Strategies

Every alternative solution or appropriate action for any given problem that one can think of should be written down. None of these strategies should be discarded until all the possibilities have been considered. The identification of alternative solutions is needed to keep the problem solver flexible and open to the potentialities present in each situation. This action is a form of individual brainstorming.

Failure to generate enough alternatives is not the only possible defect at this stage of problem solving. Some situations simply offer an insufficient range of feasible solutions. Thus a lack of alternatives may reflect the environmental circumstances, or it may reflect a lack of creative thought on the part of the manager. The manager must consider the second of these explanations honestly before concluding that the first applies.

An even more complex situation is one in which there are unlimited potential alternatives. In this instance the problem solver must use categorization to select a representative but workable number of alternatives for consideration.

After having listed all of the possible actions, strategies should be selected that will be the most appropriate and effective strategies for the situation—select the strategies that are most feasible and satisfactory and have the fewest undesirable consequences. One's management skills and experience will help one to make the decision.

Step 3. Implementation: Take Action

Now one is ready to act. The manager has selected the strategies that in his or her judgment are most likely to be effective and appropriate for resolving the problem. As a plan is put into action, the verbal or nonverbal responses to it will indicate whether to proceed or to go back and think through the process again. If the solution involves change, the manager initiates change processes so the action is implemented (refer to Chapter 5 for discussion of organizational change factors). Staff respond to solutions when they fit in their acceptance zone; yet a manager does not abandon a course of action because a few object (Sullivan & Decker, 2001).

Step 4. Evaluation: Evaluate Results

At each step one needs to analyze critically the data being collected, to evaluate the responses gathered, and to evaluate the benefits of the solution. Thinking about what one is doing and what results one is gathering should be a continuous process so that one can revise one's plan where needed as one goes along. The evaluation can be subjective as well as objective, including not only the measurable results but also any feeling of accomplishment or satisfaction from having resolved the problem successfully. This evaluation should also provide clues for future action. For example, what changes have contributed to the success of the solution and will the solution continue to work? Evaluating an outcome to affirm that the solution solved the problem builds on the experience so problem solving becomes a skill used throughout the manager's career.

Approaches to Problem Solving

Individual or group approaches to problem solving vary little from what was discussed in the previous section. Research has indicated that people generally use one fundamental, perhaps even innate, approach that does not change easily even after they are taught a different method (Tappen, 2001). People generate hypotheses early in the problem-solving process and do not wait until all the facts are in before coming up with some solutions (Tappen, 2001). As noted earlier people also have a tendency to oversimplify or to choose a solution that has worked in the past. This desire for simplicity is strong enough that people will try to make new facts fit old facts to avoid having to redefine the problem (Tappen, 2001).

While the individual can approach each step of the problem-solving process, input from a group can promote the probability of more complete data collection, creative planning, successful implementation, and evaluation indicating problem resolution. As Brightman and Verhoeven (1986, p. 26) stated, "a team of problem solvers has greater potential resources than an individual, can have a higher motivation to complete the job, can force members to examine their own beliefs more carefully, and can develop creative solutions."

The various group techniques outlined and discussed in the previous section for decision making can be applied in group problem solving, such as Delphi and nominal group techniques, task forces, and various analytical tools. Quality circles are another form increasingly being used to solve problems.

In summary, the therapeutic recreation process and the problem-solving process are based on the same progression of events. Problem solving is particularly helpful in bringing a sense of order and manageability to a problem. However, some people have a tendency to try to define the problem quickly or to oversimplify it before they have all the facts.

Conflict Management

Conflict is inevitable and can be constructive or destructive. It may offer an individual personal gain, provide prestige to the winner, be an incentive for creativity, and serve as a powerful motivator. Conflict is an accepted consequence of people working together. "It is estimated that managers of organizations spend approximately 40% of their time refereeing conflict" (Herstine, 2001, p. 1). Actually, conflict is neither good nor bad but rather "it lies in the minds of the individuals who are parties to it" (Herstine, 2001, p. 1). Thus, the real meaning of conflict is defined by how it is managed. The ideal way of handling conflict is to lessen the perceptual differences so that the outcome is fair to everyone involved (Griffin, 1990). If conflict, on the other hand, goes beyond the invigorating stage, it becomes debilitating. Conflict is a warning to the manager that something is amiss (Tomey, 2000). When conflict is not recognized, it tends to go underground. It then becomes less direct but more destructive and eventually becomes more difficult to confront and resolve. Thus, the therapeutic recreation manager needs to learn the causes and types of conflict and how to manage them so "subordinates' motivation and organizational productivity are not adversely affected" (Marquis & Huston, 2003, p. 388).

Conflict Definition

Conflict is "internal and external discord that results from differences in ideas, values, or feelings between two or more people" (Marquis & Huston, 2003, p. 388). These real or perceived differences may be (a) within one individual, (b) between two or more individuals, (c) within one group, or (d) between two or more groups (Sullivan & Decker, 2001).

Causes of Conflict

When people work together in an agency, such as a community-based leisure service agency or a complex organization like a hospital, there are numerous causes of conflict. Further, conflict increases with both the number of organizational levels and the number of specialties (Tomey, 2000). Conflict is greater as the degree of association increases and when some parties are dependent on others (Tomey, 2000). In addition, conflict has an effect on both the psychological health of persons involved and the efficiency of organization performance. Unhealthy conflict relationships tend to involve feelings of low trust and low respect, which in turn are reflected in performance.

Competition for scarce resources coupled with ambiguous jurisdictions plus the need for consensus contribute to conflict. A manager depends on the allocation of money, personnel, supplies and equipment, and physical facilities or space to accomplish objectives. Inevitably, one department, division, or unit receives fewer resources than another does, and this can lead to perceptions of inequity and conflict (Marquis & Huston, 2003; Tomey, 2000).

Individuals may have different value systems and different perceptions of a situation, which may lead to conflict. For example, top management may perceive information provided by a report from first-line managers as valuable. But the first-line managers may view the time in preparing the report and the report itself as busy work and may in the future resist completing such reports.

Different managerial or personality styles can also result in conflict. For instance, one person's style may be to discuss problems thoroughly before taking action, whereas another prefers immediate action and becomes extremely impatient with lengthy discussions. In such a situation decision-making styles can cause conflict.

Associated with the previous example is conflict from interpersonal dynamics—in other words, the so-called personality clash when two persons distrust each other's motives, dislike one another, or for some other reason simply can't get along. Although standardized policies, rules, and procedures regulate behavior, make relationships more predictable, and decrease the number of arbitrary decisions, they impose added controls over the individual. Men and women who value autonomy are likely to resist such controls (Griffin, 1990).

Other conflicts arise from cultural differences, beliefs, language, education, experience, skills, professional values and norms, status, and pay differences. Work may be seen as a means to an end or as satisfying in itself. Change may be seen as progress or as an unfortunate disruption in the present order of things. Coupled with this is change as the result of a merger or "take over of an organization by another organization." Revealing personal feelings may seem natural to some people but inappropriate to others. Some people perceive teamwork as a threat to their professional identity and to the territorial rights of their profession.

Off-the-job problems can bring about on-the-job conflicts. These include marital discord, alcoholism, drug use, financial problems, and mental stress. Clearly, the sources of conflict are endless, and the number of conflicts increases as the number of unresolved differences accumulates (Tomey, 2000).

Richard Mayer, in his publication *Conflict Management* (1995, pp. 7–8), noted the following predictable factors associated with conflict:

1. When significant conflicts arise, each person involved typically believes he or she knows its cause (usually centered on other person or persons).

2. Actually, the protagonists in a conflict almost never know its cause; their diagnoses are almost always in error. More often than not, the cause they ascribe has little or no bearing on the conflict.

3. Conflicts perceived to be rooted in action and content are in reality often caused by communication failures, particularly in listening.

4. In spite of beliefs to the contrary, deliberate workplace attempts by one person to harm another in any way are extremely rare.

5. The need to be right—a strong drive in most men and women—is almost invariably a primary contributor to any conflict.

6. Many conflicts are fed by one's belief in the primacy of rational thinking and a one-to-one correspondence between words (especially written words) and their meanings. One tends not to recognize that everyone interprets reality subjectively and that the meanings of most words are rooted in individual experience. This leads to overreliance on words and insensitivity to nonverbal communication.

7. By the time a conflict has attained the proportions most people are willing to—or feel they have to—deal with, the apparent conflict is actually an accumulation of numerous half-forgotten, relatively minor incidents leading to a blowup over the last straw. Because of this underlying complexity, often coupled with faulty communication patterns, third-party assistance may be required for resolution.

8. Most interpersonal conflicts involve a dance—a series of moves and countermoves by each of the protagonists—with no one to blame.

In summary, research suggests conflicts can be separated into three categories: (a) communication differences that arise from semantic difficulties and misunderstandings; (b) organizational structural differences that relate to resource allocations, goals, decision alternatives, and performance criteria; and (c) personal differences that evolve from individual idiosyncrasies and personal value systems (Robbins & Decenzo, 2001).

Conflict Intervention and Resolution

Conflict resolution begins with preventive measures to reduce the number of conflicts within the division or department, between parties from different departments or units, or between internal and external parties (e.g., a therapeutic recreation university fieldwork supervisor has a conflict with the therapeutic recreation agency supervisor). Even before a conflict arises, a manager can take certain actions to prepare for conflict resolution.

It is especially helpful to create a climate in which individual differences are considered natural and acceptable. Although this does not sound difficult, there are strong pressures for conformity to counteract in establishing this climate. Encouraging open and honest communication, stressing to staff that department goals must take precedence over any individual or group goals, and having clearly defined tasks and areas of responsibility all help to reduce or avoid conflicts. A manager's effort to meet the needs of staff before a conflict arises can reduce the occurrence of conflicts.

The existence of a conflict within the department or with another department or unit within the same facility should not be interpreted as a symptom of serious malfunction but rather as a sign of a problem that needs to be resolved. It is helpful to maintain a realistically optimistic attitude that the conflict can be resolved. However, it is not unusual for those inexperienced in conflict negotiation to expect unrealistic outcomes. When there are two parties or more with mutually exclusive ideas, attitudes, feelings, or goals, it is extremely difficult, without the commitment and willingness of all concerned, to arrive at an agreeable solution and to meet the needs of both parties.

Before managers attempt to intervene in conflict, they must be able to assess its five progressive stages (Marquis & Huston, 2003; Sullivan & Decker, 2001; Tomey, 2000). In the first stage, latent conflict, antecedent conditions like short staffing or incompatible goals propel a situation toward conflict. If these preexisting conditions persist, a cognitive awareness of the stressful situation results; in this second stage of conflict, perceived conflict, one's personal perceptions can contribute to either an accurate or inaccurate assessment of the situation. Perceived conflicts may also result when individuals have limited knowledge of the situation or when they misunderstand each other's position. Felt conflict, stage three, occurs when the conflict is emotionalized. Felt emotions include anger, hostility, and mistrust. Some perceive the conflict but don't feel it (i.e., person views situation as only a problem to be solved), while others feel conflict but not the

problem (i.e., unable to identify cause of felt conflict). In the fourth stage, manifest conflict, overt behaviors like debate and covert behaviors like withdrawal are evident. These behaviors are learned early in life and tend to be unconsciously acquired; whereas, conflict resolution requires a conscious learning effort. In the fifth and final stage, conflict aftermath, positive or negative outcomes result. Resolution is found with mutually agreed-on outcomes; a win-lose situation finds only one party truly committed to the outcome. As a consequence, conflict issues remain and may resurface to cause more conflict. This model helps the manager to explain why conflict occurs and ultimately how to intervene with the least amount of negative aftermath.

Conflict resolution begins with a decision regarding if and when to intervene. The therapeutic recreation manager should make sure the parties know when he or she is likely to intervene. Failure to intervene can allow the conflict to escalate, while early intervention may be demotivating to the parties, causing them to lose confidence in themselves and to reduce risk-taking behavior in the future. On the other hand, some conflicts are so minor, particularly if they are between two people, that intervention is not necessary and may be better handled by the two people. However, where there is potential for considerable harm to result from the conflict, the therapeutic recreation manager must intervene.

If the manager decides to intervene, he or she must make decisions as to when, where, and how the intervention should take place. Routine problems can be handled in the manager's office, but serious conflicts should take place in a neutral location agreeable to both parties. The time and place should be one where distractions will not interfere and adequate time is available. Because conflict resolution takes time, the manager must be prepared to allow sufficient time for all parties to explain their points of view and to arrive at a mutually agreeable solution.

Other management techniques besides personal intervention can be used to resolve conflict. Some of these include changing or clarifying goals, developing subordinate goals, appealing to the hierarchy, providing cooling off periods, and establishing liaison persons. The latter approach is effective to reduce conflict between departments or units.

Approaches to Conflict Resolution

Despite everyone's best intentions, conflict is inevitable. There are several widely accepted approaches to the resolution of conflict.

Active Listening

A manager may very well be involved at some time in conflict with a member of his or her staff or with other personnel outside his or her department. According to Davis, Skube, Hellervik, Gebelein, and Sheard (1992), too often individuals involved in an argument spent most of their time talking instead of listening. When one person is speaking, the other is busy preparing a rebuttal or thinking of additional ways to support his or her viewpoint rather than listening to what is being said.

In addition, most people immediately judge the statements of others—either to agree or disagree. Frequently, the listener judges a statement from his or her point of view without consideration of the other person's perspective. True listening is not occurring—people hear what they expect or want to hear, rather than what the speaker intends to communicate.

Both of these behaviors can cause disagreements to escalate into arguments. When neither person stops to listen, there is a good chance that agreement will be delayed or prevented altogether. Moreover, when emotions run high, people may say or do things they later regret. Davis, Skube, Hellervik, Gebelein, and Sheard (1992) suggested the following techniques to improve the effectiveness of active listening:

- Listen carefully to what the speaker is saying, giving full attention without thinking about how one intends to respond and without judging the speaker's statements.

- Get the speaker to clarify his or her position by asking open-ended questions starting with phrases such as the following: Describe… Tell me about… Explain… How do you feel…

- Periodically paraphrase what the speaker has said to ensure that one understands.

- Determine whether one's interpretations are becoming more accurate as the discussion progresses.

- Avoid interrupting the speaker.

Further consideration of this topic is found in Chapter 13.

Collaborating/Problem Solving

The slogan of this form of conflict resolution is win-win. Time pressures are minimal and the issue is too important for compromise. Each party sets aside their original goal to establish a supra-ordinate common goal; the focus remains on problem-solving while expressing a high concern for others' and one's own needs (Herstine, 2002; Marquis & Huston, 2003).

Avoidance

One method of dealing with conflict is to avoid it. The conflict is simply not addressed: "If we don't talk about it, the problem will go away." Avoidance does not offer a permanent way out of resolving conflict, but it is an extremely popular short-run solution. However, if the problem is avoided for a period of time, the conflict situation may be taken to a higher authority. The technique is used in highly cohesive groups where participants do not want to do anything to interfere with good feelings each has for the other (Sullivan & Decker, 2001). It reflects a low concern for one's own needs and needs of others—a lose-lose scenario (Herstine, 2002).

Smoothing/Accommodating

Smoothing/accommodating can be described as the process of playing down differences that exist between individuals or groups while emphasizing common interests. It is a diplomatic way of dealing with conflict. Differences are suppressed in smoothing, and similarities are accentuated. Because most conflict situations have points of commonality between them, smoothing represents a way in which to minimize differences. This approach is used by managers to encourage someone to cooperate with another person. Although appropriate for minor disagreements, rarely are the conflicts actually resolved. This is a you win–I lose situation (Herstine, 2002; Marquis & Huston, 2003).

Compromise

This particular technique makes up a major position if resolution approaches. Compromise is a middle-of-the-road solution. Each party gives up something of value. While there is no clear winner, there is also no clear loser. Compromise has an advantage over restrictive and suppressive methods because conflicting persons or groups are less likely to feel hostility over the resolution of the problem. Compromise serves as a backup to resolve conflict when collaboration is ineffective. For compromise not to result in a lose-lose situation, both parties must give up something of equal value.

Authoritative Command

In an agency or organization context probably the most frequently used method for resolving opposing conflicts interacts with the use of formal authority. This kind of behavior uses intellectual and managerial power and strength to affect the actions of others. Organizational values, cooperation, and teamwork are emphasized. A weakness is that individuals may comply to the letter regarding responsibilities and fail to use their own initiative and judgment at times when independent action is desirable or necessary.

Competing/Forcing

The final technique considers changing the behavior of one or more of the conflicting parties. Competing occurs when one party seeks to win regardless of the cost to others. Managers may use this approach in situations involving unpopular, quick, or critical decisions (Marquis & Huston, 2003; Sullivan & Decker, 2001).

Strategies for Conflict Resolution

Filley (1975) identified three ways of dealing with conflict: win-lose, lose-lose, or win-win. Win-lose methods include the use of position power, mental or physical power, failure to respond, majority rule, and railroading a minority position. Win-lose outcomes often occur between groups. A potential negative consequence of this strategy is that frequent losing can lead to the loss of cohesiveness within groups and can diminish the authority of the manager. Lose-lose strategies include compromise, bribes for accomplishing disagreeable tasks, arbitration by a neutral third party, and resorting to the use of general rules instead of considering the merits of individual cases. If one uses this strategy, neither side wins. Moreover, using a third-party arbitrator can lead to a lose-lose outcome. Because an outsider may want to give something to each side, neither gets what is desired.

In win-lose and lose-lose strategies, the parties often personalize the issues by focusing on each other instead of on the problem. Intent on their personal differences, they avoid the more important matter of how to mutually solve their problem. Solutions are emphasized instead of goals and values. Rather than identifying mutual needs, planning activities for resolution, and solving the problem, each party looks at the issue from his or her own point of view and strives for total victory.

By contrast, win-win strategies focus on goals and attempt to meet the needs of both parties. They emphasize consensus and integrative approaches to decision making. The consensus process demands a focus on the problem (instead of on the other), on the collection of facts, on the acceptance of the useful aspects of conflict, and on the avoidance of averaging and self-oriented behavior. Integrative decision-making methods focus on the means of problem solution rather than the ends and are most often useful when the needs of the parties are polarized. Using integrative decision-making methods, the parties jointly identify the value needs of each, conduct an exhaustive search for alternatives that could meet the needs of each, and then select the best alternative. Both methods focus on defeating the problem, not each other.

In bringing this section and chapter to a close, it is well to note that managers need to be realistic in their conflict resolution expectations. When two or more individuals hold mutually exclusive ideas, attitudes, feelings, or goals, it is difficult to arrive at an agreeable solution that meets the needs of everyone without the commitment and willingness of all parties involved. If the reader is interested, he or she may want to read Sun-tzu's (1993) classic text *The Art of War*, which is a guide to conflict resolution without battle.

Summary

This chapter addressed three major issues of concern to therapeutic recreation managers: decision making, problem solving, and conflict management.

Decision making is the process through which choices are made. Managers make two distinct types of decisions: programmed and unprogrammed. Decisions may be made under states of certainty, risk, and uncertainty. Decision making is assisted by policies, procedures, and rules. The rational decision-making process follows a six-step sequence:

1. problem identification

2. exploring alternatives

3. evaluating alternatives

4. selecting an alternative

5. implementing the decision

6. evaluating the decision

There are also a variety of techniques available to the manager for testing the soundness of a decision. There are two basic criteria to consider in evaluating managerial decisions: the objective quality of the decision and the acceptance of the decision by those who must implement it.

The problem-solving process is similar in nature to the therapeutic recreation process: collect whatever data are needed and identify the problem, select appropriate strategies for dealing with the problem, take action, and evaluate results. It was noted that many individuals try to identify the problem without gathering all the facts or try to oversimplify the problem to make it more manageable. Various techniques were suggested for problem solving.

Conflict was defined as a disagreement between two or more individuals. Conflict management includes activities that attempt to resolve it. Possible causes of conflict include differences in perception and goals, scarce resources, nature of work activities, and other circumstances. Techniques and strategies for resolving conflicts were suggested. As a final point, it was noted that managers must be realistic in their conflict resolution expectations.

Review Questions

1. Which step in the decision-making process would be the most difficult for a therapeutic recreation manager in a health care facility? In a community-based leisure service agency? Why?

2. What are the pros and cons of decisions made by groups (e.g., committee or task force) as compared to decisions by one person or the manager?

3. Under what conditions, either in a health care facility or a community-based leisure service agency, would you expect group problem solving to be preferable to individual problem solving, and vice versa? Why?

4. Review department policy and procedure manuals from health care and community based agencies. Compare and contrast the content—What are similarities and differences? Explain how standards of accrediting bodies like JCAHO and professional standards of practice from ATRA and NTRS are reflected in the manuals.

5. How would conflict in a health care facility, therapeutic recreation department, or a community-based leisure service therapeutic recreation division agency be beneficial to the department?

6. Think of an important decision you have made, such as choosing a university or choosing a major or concentration. How did you make this decision? Write out your response, supplying as much detail as possible. Did you follow a rational decision-making process or use intuition? Was it some combination of the two?

References

Ayert, R. M. and De Groot, M. H. (1984). The maximization process under uncertainty. In P. D. Larkey and L. S. Sproull (Eds.), *Information processing in organizations* (pp. 47–61). Greenwich, CT: JAI Press.

Bannon, J. J. (2002, Fall). Developing personnel policies. *Management Strategy, 26*(3), 1, 4.

Brehm, J. W. and Cohen, A. R. (1962). *Exploration in cognitive dissonance.* New York, NY: John Wiley & Sons.

Brightman, H. J. and Verhoeven, P. (1986, January–March). Why managerial problem-solving groups fail. *Business,* 24–29.

Davis, B. L., Skube, C. J., Hellervik, L. W., Gebelein, S. H., and Sheard, J. L. (1992). *Successful manager's handbook.* Minneapolis, MN: Personnel Decisions.

Edginton, C. R., Hudson, S. D., and Lankford, S. V. (2001). *Managing recreation, parks, and leisure services: An introduction.* Champaign, IL: Sagamore Publishing.

Festinger, L. (1975). *A theory of cognitive dissonance.* Stanford, CA: Stanford University Press.

Filley, A. C. (1975). *Interpersonal conflict resolution.* Glenview, IL: Scott, Foresman and Company.

Griffin, R. W. (1990). *Management* (3rd ed.). Boston, MA: Houghton Mifflin.

Herbert, T. T. and Estes, R. W. (1977, October). Improving executive decisions by formalizing dissent: The corporate devil's advocate. *The Academy of Management Review, 2*(4), 662–667.

Herstine, J. (2001, Fall). Part I: Myths, causes and sources of conflict learn to recognize and appreciate them! *Management Strategy, 25*(4), 1, 7.

Herstine, J. (2002, Spring). Part II: Appropriately identifying and employing suitable conflict management and conflict resolution tools and techniques. *Management Strategy, 26*(1), 1, 4.

Marquis, B. L. and Huston, C. J. (2003). *Leadership roles and management functions in nursing: Theory & application* (4th ed.). Philadelphia, PA: Lippincott Williams & Wilkins.

Mayer, R. J. (1995). *Conflict management.* Columbus, OH: Battelle Press.

Newman, W. H. (1964). *Administrative action.* Englewood Cliffs, NJ: Prentice Hall.

Noone, J. (2002). Concept analysis of decision making. *Nursing Forum, 37*(3), 21–32.

Paige, J. B. (2003). Solve the policy and procedure puzzle. *Nursing Management, 34*(3), 45–48.

Robbins, S. P. and Decenzo, D. A. (2001). *Fundamentals of management essential concepts and applications* (3rd ed.). Upper Saddle River, NJ: Prentice Hall.

Simon, H. A. (1987, February). Making management decisions: The role of intuition and emotion. The *Academy of Management Executives,* 57–63.

Sullivan, E. J. and Decker, P. J. (2001). *Effective leadership and management in nursing.* Upper Saddle River, NJ: Prentice Hall.

Sun-tzu. (1993). *The art of war.* New York, NY: Quill.

Tappen, R. M. (2001). *Nursing leadership and management: Concepts and practice* (4th ed.). Philadelphia, PA: F. A. Davis Company.

Tomey, A. M. (2000). *Guide to nursing management and leadership* (6th ed.). St Louis, MO: Mosby.

Chapter 11
Marketing: New Approaches for Therapeutic Recreation

chapter revisions by Jane K. Broida

While it's not the first thing we think of in the field of therapeutic recreation, marketing is actually one of the first things that we do—or should be doing—after creating our programs. According to the American Marketing Association, "Marketing is the process of planning and executing the conception, pricing, promotion, and distribution of ideas, goods, and services to create exchanges that satisfy individual and organizational objectives" (Berkowitz, Kerin, Hartley & Rudelius, 2000, p. 9). It is a much broader concept than advertising or selling and must involve a two-prong process—you must not only find out what the prospective customer wants but also meet those "wants" by providing the appropriate products, goods, or services.

Marketing focuses on the wants and needs of the customer. What's the difference between those? A *need* is something essential. It can be either physical (e.g., food to survive) or psychological (e.g., contact with others). A *want* is a "felt need created by a person's knowledge, culture, and personality" (Berkowitz, Kerin, Hartley & Rudelius, 2000, p. 12). Effective marketing, then, helps to shape a person's "wants" by creating products that can help satisfy those "wants." Let's take an example of a nine-year-old child, Allie. Allie needs the basics to survive—food, clothing, and shelter. However, after watching the advertisements during her favorite television program, she wants all the latest toys and breakfast cereals. Through product marketing, the girl desires the unessential products she saw marketed.

How can we translate this concept to the field of therapeutic recreation? For many individuals, therapeutic recreation services are needed. Individuals in both clinical and community-based settings are referred for therapeutic recreation services, and we document client outcomes that support the value and benefits of those services. However, there are many other individuals that do not receive therapeutic recreation services who might also have beneficial outcomes from participation. How can we market therapeutic recreation services to create the "want" for therapeutic recreation services? While it would be unlikely that we would resort to mass marketing techniques (e.g., advertisements on television), we can utilize other approaches to inform potential consumers. Some of the more traditional approaches are noted in Table 11.1.

This chapter examines marketing basics and explores marketing approaches that first-line managers may choose to implement. The initial section considers fundamental marketing concepts the manager contemplates during service and relationship marketing. A marketing plan is designed to enable relationship building over an extended time. This process is similar to the therapeutic recreation process (i.e., assess, plan, implement, evaluate) and is presented in the next sections. The importance of branding is considered, as is the benefits approach to marketing

Table 11.1
Traditional Marketing Activities in Therapeutic Recreation

- Conduct an in-service about therapeutic recreation at your agency.

- Invite allied health professionals to therapeutic recreation association meetings.

- Conduct professional presentations at allied health meetings.

- Write an article about therapeutic recreation for your agency newsletter or an allied health journal.

- Celebrate National Therapeutic Recreation Week.

- Be part of a speaker's bureau where you can talk about therapeutic recreation services and benefits.

- Learn how to lobby and speak with Congressional leaders.

- Have your consumers write to their congressional representatives about the value of therapeutic recreation services they received.

- Speak to consumer groups about therapeutic recreation services.

- Teach volunteers how to be therapeutic recreation advocates.

- Develop promotional materials that can be used with various market segments, such as consumers, public, administrators, legislators.

- Conduct research that examines the outcomes of your services and disseminate the results.

- Speak at career fairs and health promotion workshops.

during the implementation of therapeutic recreation services. The closing sections of this chapter consider trends, strategies, evaluation, and the roles of first-line managers as they market therapeutic recreation services of their divisions or department. With creative strategies like the use of tag lines, logos, bundling, and focus groups, the first-line manager is able to establish community relationships and to advocate so services are maintained and extended to new and different consumers and settings.

Marketing Basics

In 1960, E. Jerome McCarthy first noted four critical elements necessary for a complete marketing program. The "four Ps" for a marketing mix include the following:

1. Product—a good, service or idea to satisfy the consumer's needs

2. Price—what is exchanged for the product

3. Promotion—means of communication between the buyer and the seller

4. Place—means of getting the product into the consumer's hands (pp. 45–47).

These four factors can be controlled by the organization/agency conducting the marketing. However, there are numerous other uncontrollable factors. For example, environmental factors cannot be controlled by the organization/agency, but they very much influence how we satisfy consumer needs. Environmental factors include the following:

- Social forces—demographic characteristics of the population (e.g., age, sex, ethnicity, income, occupation, culture)

- Technology forces—inventions and innovations, fast pace of development

- Economic forces—income, expenditures, and resources that affect the cost of running a business or household

- Competition forces—alternative firms that could provide a product to satisfy a specific market's needs

- Regulatory forces—restrictions placed by state and federal laws on the business with regard to the conduct of its activities

While the aforementioned environmental elements might be beyond our control, we still must be cognizant of their influence on therapeutic recreation marketing. For example, the Health Insurance Portability and Accountability Act (HIPAA) regulations ensure patient confidentiality and regulate release of patient information. This has a tremendous impact on how we must (or must not!) market in therapeutic recreation (e.g., maintaining patient anonymity).

Additional variables that impact marketing are noted by Cotte and Ratneshwar (2004). They indicated that "timestyle" or how a person customarily perceives and uses time, influences the choice of leisure goals and leisure services. Four dimensions to an individual's leisure choices will influence leisure behavior and include the following:

- Social orientation—categorization of discretionary time as either time for self or time with/for others

- Temporal orientation—preference of individuals to look back at events, live in the present, or look to the future

- Planning orientation—the continuum of "planners" to spontaneous engagements

- Polychromic orientation—preference for a multitasking style versus a monochromic, "one-thing-at-a-time" style

By understanding these influences, therapeutic recreation managers can better understand how to market therapeutic recreation services by having a clearer picture of how individuals make leisure choices.

What Do We Market?

Products/goods, services, or ideas can be marketed. Goods are defined as physical objects. In therapeutic recreation, one of our "goods" might include an innovative piece of adaptive equipment that we developed. Services, on the other hand, are intangible items. Therapeutic recreation services that might be marketed include leisure education activities, such as referral to community-based therapeutic recreation programs. Ideas are also intangibles but focus on thoughts about actions or causes. Creating an innovative, entrepreneurial therapeutic recreation consulting agency might be an "idea" that could be marketed. Historically, marketing has focused on a product-oriented approach. However, within the past 25 years, the marketing discipline changed, with services marketing becoming free from the product-oriented marketing approach.

Services Marketing

According to van der Zwan and Bhamra (2003), services have "distinctive characteristics which made them fundamentally different from products, such as an intangible nature" (p. 341). This service-oriented approach decreases the emphasis on the product and stresses the ability to deliver a constant quality found with total quality management practices. This approach focuses on identifying the need that the product fulfills and the way the product creates value. Is a service marketing approach viable in therapeutic recreation? Given that therapeutic recreation is a service-dominated field, this marketing approach might be especially significant for therapeutic recreation. The need of the consumers would be highlighted, along with demonstrating how therapeutic recreation services have fulfilled these needs. Similarly, relationship marketing—attracting and retaining business through a range of internal and external relationships—has become prominent and its principles can be applied to therapeutic recreation marketing.

Relationship Marketing: Application to Therapeutic Recreation

In recent years, companies are combining traditional marketing approaches with relationship marketing (Keep Asking the Customer, 2004). Relationship marketing has the principal concern for the establishment and maintenance of long-term customer relationships (Canning, 2004). Relationship marketing is characterized not only by the functional benefits received but also by the relational benefits of the good, product, or service (Coulter & Ligas, 2004). Coulter and Ligas (2004) noted that emotional attachment—an affinity and bond with the service provider—was important. In the area of health care services, customers must not only perceive their relationship as professional but also develop a lasting relationship with the provider. The authors noted service firms that

> implement programs and effectively train their personnel to make the customer feel at ease will go along way in terms of developing the strong emotional attachments evident in the long-term relationships. Trust building involves delivering quality service with a personal touch. (Coulter & Ligas, 2004, p. 489)

While therapeutic recreation personnel frequently create this personal-professional relationship, therapeutic recreation specialists seem to fail in capitalizing on this personal touch. Hence, we may be missing out on this long-term customer relationship. According to O'Brien

and Manross (2002), also important to building customer loyalty are identifying desired behavioral outcomes, reviewing the predictors of customer loyalty, keeping in touch with advocates and opponents, documenting facts, and acting on what is important to your constituents.

A Marketing Process for Therapeutic Recreation

To successfully market a therapeutic recreation product, good, or service, a coherent, organized plan is essential. A typical marketing plan is complex and includes information noted in Table 11.2.

Step One: Assessment

A simplified, four-step marketing process was presented by O'Morrow and Carter (1997). Step one of the marketing process involves assessment. Initially, it is important to assess your market. The market is comprised of individuals that have the desire and ability to buy a certain product

Table 11.2
Outline for a Marketing Plan

> I. Overall Objectives
> II. Market Analysis
>   a. Demographics and lifestyles
>   b. Economic conditions
>   c. Laws and government regulations
>   d. Technology
>   e. Competition
> III. Business Profile
> IV. Target Market Identification and Objectives
> V. Marketing Mixes
>   a. Product/service/location
>   b. Place/distribution
>   c. Price
>   d. Promotion
>   i. Selling
>   ii. Advertising
>   iii. Sales promotion
>   iv. Publicity
>   v. Word of mouth
>   e. Internal
>   i. Orientation to client
>   ii. Customer management
>   iii. Personnel training
>   iv. Personnel policies and incentives
>   v. Organizational communication
> VI. Budget
> VII. Implementation
> VIII. Evaluation

(Berkowitz, Kerin, Hartley & Rudelius, 2000). Critical to defining your market is identifying a key group or groups of potential consumers. This concept is called *target marketing*, whereby one or more specific groups of potential consumers are identified, and marketing strategies are applied to those potential customers. In therapeutic recreation, it is possible to have diverse target audiences. Figure 11.1 is a summary of possible target audiences that can be addressed by therapeutic recreation marketing.

Step Two: Planning

The second step in the marketing process is to develop a plan. Here, the therapeutic recreation professional should answer the 4 *P*s of the marketing mix presented earlier. O'Sullivan (1991) suggested including additional *P*s, such as physical evidence, people, policies and procedures, public image, and political impact.

According to O'Morrow and Carter (1997), therapeutic recreation physical evidence involves the area where the intervention occurs, tokens received from participation, and documented outcomes of the exchange. Therapeutic recreation managers should continually strive toward making the therapeutic recreation experience as attractive as possible. The second *P*, people, is critical to the provision of therapeutic recreation services. Of course, our consumers are our primary audience, but it is also essential that caregivers, family members, and other professionals be considered in the marketing process. Policies and procedures guide our marketing plans by regulating what can and cannot be done. The fourth *P*, public image, is also critical to consider when developing the marketing plan. While public image is an intangible, it can be greatly influenced by some concrete strategies, such as development of a tag line and logo. These strategies are discussed in detail during the last phase of the marketing process. Lastly, political impact is an ever increasingly important influence and must be considered when planning for therapeutic recreation marketing. According to O'Morrow

and Carter (1997), managers must learn about the political agendas of target audiences, including legislators, insurance companies, health care organizations, and potential philanthropic groups.

Step Three: Implementation

The third step of the marketing process involves implementation of the plan. The agency, prior to implementing marketing activities, should develop a marketing style guide. The marketing style guide ensures consistency of style throughout the organization. This is important, as the agency should create a similar look and feel to marketing materials. An example of one of the most comprehensive guides was developed by Ken-Caryl Ranch Metropolitan District. Their *Marketing Style Guide* (2004, March) includes, logo elements, logo colors, logo versions, logo don'ts, stationary, forms, envelopes, business cards, publications, staff uniforms, and nametags.

Branding Therapeutic Recreation Services: Can This Be Done?

"A brand name is a signifier, a shorthand explanation of what we are and do, how we do business, and what benefits will accrue to a consumer" (Peters, 1997, p. 320). What messages do we want to evoke in therapeutic recreation? What brand image do you think therapeutic recreation services have at your agency? Now, what would the therapeutic recreation department realistically like it to mean? How can we move the meaning from where it is to where we want it to be? This is the process of branding—branding can help you define yourself in the marketplace (Bashe & Hicks, 2000).

Health… quality of life… functional recreation skills—all might be concepts that could be used to help therapeutic recreation establish consistency of brand. Through joint efforts of the National Therapeutic Recreation Society and the American Therapeutic Recreation Association, the profession has the power to alter the

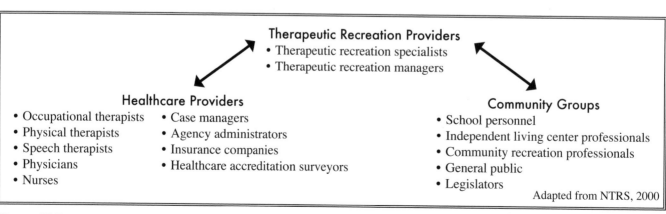

Figure 11.1
Target Audiences for Therapeutic Recreation Marketing

public's perception of therapeutic recreation services by solidifying behind a common brand concept.

Marketing Using a Benefits Approach

In 2000, the National Therapeutic Recreation Society (NTRS) began to promote the marketing of therapeutic recreation using a benefits approach. This might be an appropriate branding strategy for therapeutic recreation managers to consider.

The benefits movement in recreation and parks began in the 1990s and still has strong application to the field today. The benefits approach involves a focus on the outcomes to what we do instead of on the provision of activities, facilities, and programs (Bright, 2000; NTRS, 2000; O'Sullivan, 1999). In therapeutic recreation, utilizing a benefits approach is critical to enhancing the perceived value of our services and conveying the importance of this service as a viable treatment modality to improve functional abilities, knowledge of leisure resources, and integration into the community (NTRS, 2000).

According to NTRS (2000), "benefits-based therapeutic recreation is an approach that deliberately targets strategies that will ensure the identification and delivery of the benefits of therapeutic recreation to appropriate internal and external audiences" (p. 13). There are four steps necessary to the therapeutic recreation benefits movement:

1. Identifying benefits derived from therapeutic recreation services

2. Assigning resources to address and promote these benefits

3. Documenting the resultant outcomes

4. Promoting these outcomes

To market therapeutic recreation with a benefits approach, it is important to know the benefits of therapeutic recreation services.

Knowing the Benefits of Therapeutic Recreation

Both the literature and anecdotal evidence point to the importance of therapeutic recreation as a viable treatment modality. The *Therapeutic Recreation—The Benefits Are Endless…* (NTRS, 2000) training program and resource guide can be used to help you market the outcomes of therapeutic recreation services as physical, social, psychological/emotional, cognitive, and expressive benefits are noted and full citations in the literature provided. Additional resources provided in this manual are "success stories," which document the significance of therapeutic recreation services from a consumer, therapist, or caregiver perspective.

Two Examples: Benefits-Based Marketing Tools

Most agencies are required to develop an annual report, which reflects the activities of the agency throughout the entire year. These reports are factual accounts, providing quantitative data supporting the activities conducted. The City of San Jose, California, determined they were going to provide more information in their annual report. Interspersed throughout the pages of data were quotes from consumers and caregivers documenting the benefits accrued from participating in the therapeutic recreation programs. The annual report became more than just a "reporting" document, it became a living document reflecting the impact of the therapeutic recreation programs on the community residents.

Another creative therapeutic recreation specialist took the concept of "success stories" and developed an agency-specific version. The Certified Therapeutic Recreation Specialist asked residents of the assisted living facility to talk about the values derived from their therapeutic recreation participation. These true life stories, told from the client's perspective, were written down, bound into a book of "success stories," and made available in the agency waiting room. The book provides compelling documentation of the value of therapeutic recreation services to the consumers residing in the agency.

Step Four: Trends, Strategies, and Evaluation

The fourth and last step in the marketing plan is trends, strategies, and evaluation. Marketing trends should be employed in therapeutic recreation marketing approaches. The following discusses some important aspects of marketing that should be implemented by therapeutic recreation managers.

Tag Line

"Just Do It" (Nike)
"I'm Lovin' It" (McDonald's)

These are probably two of the best known product tag lines. Clearly, the public relations firms that created the campaigns for each company has been successful. We just need to hear the tag line, and we associate with the product.

What is a tag line? A tag line is a one- or two-line descriptor that comes after a product logo or agency name. A tag line used by the National Recreation and Park Association is "Healthy Lifestyles. Livable Communities." Perhaps a better known tag line in the recreation field is "The Benefits Are Endless." This has been adopted by many communities and seeks to have the public relate to countless tangible and intangible positive aspects of parks and recreation services provided to our communities.

Denoting excellent care, the Rehabilitation Institute of Chicago's tag line is "The best in healing and hope."

A tag line reinforces unique aspects or the position of your agency/organization. Table 11.3 shows the steps to follow in the development of a tag line for your agency/department.

Logo

We've all heard the expression, "A picture is worth a thousand words." That is what a logo is all about! Immediately when we see the "swoosh," we know that the product is Nike. The swish logo has helped to define the identity of the organization and that is exactly what a logo should do. Logos are pictorial representations that positively associate with the agency, product or good, and help to define the agency's identity. Research indicates that corporate logos can be extremely effective in creating positive associations with a company and that logos, with the company name behind the symbol, increase associations with the organization through the unique, compelling, and attractive symbol (van Riel & van den Ban, 2001). As the therapeutic recreation manager looks toward developing a logo for the agency/department, determine the image that should be conveyed and how this can best be symbolized through a picture.

Table 11.3
Steps to Developing a Tag Line

1. **Get data by answering the following questions:**
   - Who are your customers?
   - What benefits do you give your customers?
   - What feelings do you want to invoke in customers?
   - What action(s) are you trying to generate from customers?
   - Who is the competition and how are you different?
2. **Prepare to brainstorm**
   - Gather tag lines from other agencies, including your competition. Look in other categories besides your own
   - Write tag lines on index cards for mixing and matching
   - Pay attention to words used, how they are put together
   - Look for a unique angle for your tag line
3. **Brainstorm with a small group**
   - Generate a large number of ideas
4. **Consolidate your list**
   - Pull out the words with the best potential
5. **Choose the one best tag line**
   - Get opinions through a survey (possibly online) or through a focus group

Bundling Services: A Strategy for Therapeutic Recreation Marketing?

Why not have a cell phone for yourself… and each family member, along with high-speed Internet service? Why pay for your checking account when you can have a savings account with a free ATM card? Why only buy a Big Mac when for a nominal amount more you can get the drink and fries also?

These are but three examples of bundled services that are seen frequently in the business world. Bundling is defined as "the sale of two or more separate products in one package" (Legarreta & Miguel, 2004, p. 264). These packaged services assist in expanding to new target markets or to sell additional services.

If we examine the field of recreation and parks, we can find some examples of bundled services. Often when consumers buy memberships to recreation facilities, they get not only use of the facilities but also opportunities to participate in selected free programs.

In many clinical settings, therapeutic recreation services are already "bundled" by including them as part of the "per diem" or room rate in that hospital. By paying one room fee, patients not only get "the room" but also meals, nursing care, and therapeutic recreation services.

Let's think more creatively, though, in how we might further bundle therapeutic recreation services to expand to additional markets or increase our services. In clinical settings, perhaps we can offer more joint programs with related disciplines. For example

- a therapeutic cooking class supported by occupational therapy, dietary services, and therapeutic recreation

- an expressive arts drama program supported by speech-language and therapeutic recreation

While joint programming is not a new concept, marketing these programs to increase services to new markets (i.e., individuals who may not typically receive therapeutic recreation services) is unique.

Bundling services is also very appropriate for community-based therapeutic recreation programs (e.g., providing a recreation center membership when enrolling in three specialized therapeutic recreation programs). The therapeutic recreation program might see higher enrollments as individuals would register for more than one class while the recreation center would have an increase in center memberships, with the plan to retain that enrollee as a paying member in future years. This is a win-win situation for all—the client benefits as he or she increases participation and has access to center resources, the therapeutic recreation department increases its participation numbers, and the recreation department increases the number of members and the potential of future revenue. Mowen (2003) noted the importance of successful health partnerships, and perhaps these can be the basis for our bundling services—building relationships between health benefits and therapeutic recreation services.

Evaluation

Evaluation should be both formative and summative. Formative evaluation occurs on a continuous basis as the marketing plan is designed and implemented. This is critical to determining the ongoing effectiveness of the marketing efforts. Therapeutic recreation managers should assess what is and what is not working and seek to implement changes as needed. Quantitative data, such as increased number of participants, should be documented and qualitative, anecdotal comments should be noted. These records are useful to the manager in determining effectiveness of the marketing plan and approaches and can be used to justify marketing expenditures.

Similarly, summative evaluation is critical. Summative evaluation occurs at the end of the program and reflects how well the overall goals of the marketing plan have been achieved.

Focus Groups as an Evaluation Tool. Focus groups are a specialized form of evaluation and involve market research. Focus groups are used to assess user needs and feelings before a product, good, or service is implemented. Nominal groups, from six to nine users, are identified, and individuals participate in a discussion lasting from one to two hours. Groups are run by a moderator, typically an individual external to the agency with experience facilitating groups and synthesizing ideas. While focus groups appear free-flowing and relatively unstructured, the moderator goes in with a preplanned script of specific issues and goals that need to be addressed. The moderator must keep the discussion on track and at the conclusion of the meeting write a report that summarizes the mood of the group, using illustrations and examples (Neilsen, 1997). Table 11.5 provides tips for running a successful focus group.

A Final Thought: Thinking Creatively

Clearly, the time has come for therapeutic recreation professionals to understand the importance of marketing its services and programs. By using creative approaches, we will be able not only to maintain existing services but also to expand opportunities to new client groups and different settings. We, as therapeutic recreation specialists and managers, must learn to value the time spent marketing as an opportunity to exponentially expand opportunities and to secure the placement of therapeutic recreation in our clinical and community settings.

Managerial Roles

Therapeutic recreation managers are challenged to articulate the unique benefits and to create strategies that will ensure that therapeutic recreation services remain integral to the organization's markets. The first-line manager is the link between the department's mission, the organization, and the service quality that fosters relationships. A well-conceived and designed market plan supports value—added services that aim to give the consumer more than is anticipated. A first-line manager is the central figure in designing department tools like the marketing plan and cultivating the culture in which staff deliver quality services, engage in long-term relationships, and evaluate the outcomes of intangible elements like helping relationships and leisure resource awareness. Also, the manager is the link between the therapeutic recreation service, community groups and health care providers (refer to Table 11.4).

First-line managers advocate to build community relations that promote access, cost containment, resource sharing, social capital, and health and well-being among various constituent groups. Through educational programs, service learning, volunteering, sponsorships, and internship training, therapeutic recreation managers build networks and relationships that benefit their therapeutic recreation

Table 11.4
Tips for Running Focus Groups

Overplan
- Recruitment
- Content and flow of discussion topics

Manage the recruitment process
- Must have the right people in the group

Don't prejudge participants on physical appearance

Have a good moderator that is objective with expertise
- Must bring out the comments in people
- Listens well
- Ability to interpret results
- Communicates results accurately to client

Coordinate the objectives of the focus group between the client and the moderator
- Know the purpose of the group
- Conduct the "right" amount of focus groups
- Moderator should have a fast turn-around on the report
- Brief client observers prior to the start of the group
- Moderator needs to provide objective conclusions based on the interpretation of the data

Adapted from Greenbaum, T. L. September 14, 1998, *Ten tips for running successful focus groups.* http://www.groupsplus.com/pages/mn091498.htm

services while increasing their capacity to respond to consumer needs.

As professional advocates, managers articulate the merits of therapeutic recreation services with referral agents, third-party reimbursers, colleagues, and political agents. Managers use evidence-based practices and the results of efficacy studies to articulate the benefits of therapeutic recreation services. Additionally, they monitor legislation and communicate with decision makers the essence of their services. When professionals recruit students to be members of professional organizations or serve on professional committees, they are advocating for their professional future.

Summary

Managers assume key roles in the design of marketing approaches that create consumer friendly service environments and long-term relationships. The marketing process, like the therapeutic recreation process, involves assessment, planning, implementation, and evaluation. Therapeutic recreation services are used by diverse target audiences identified through assessment. Key to planning is studying the marketing mix or the 4 *P*s and several service *P*s for each audience or target market to present the right services to the right target group. During implementation each target audience's marketing plan is put into action. Strategies like branding and benefits-based marketing are used to highlight therapeutic recreation services. Creative approaches like tag lines, logos, bundling services, focus groups, and community relations strategies aim to retain consumers while extending to new audiences the benefits of therapeutic recreation.

As a first-line manager, the therapeutic recreation manager is the link between service quality and the accomplishment of the unit's and the organization's marketing goals. The manager garners the resources and creates the culture that enables relationship building. As the primary advocate, the manager articulates the benefits of evidence-based practices to community groups and health care providers.

Review Questions

1. Develop a marketing plan for a therapeutic recreation department.

2. Using a benefits approach, describe how a therapeutic recreation department can market its programs and services.

3. Lead a focus group to solicit feedback in the development of a logo or tag line for your therapeutic recreation department.

4. Visit three therapeutic recreation programs and compare and contrast their marketing activities.

5. Select a therapeutic recreation program in your area (either clinical or community-based) and brainstorm ways that services may be bundled.

References

Bashe, G. and Hicks, N. J. (Eds.). (2000). *Branding health services: Defining yourself in the marketplace.* Gaithersburg, MD: Aspen Publishers.

Berkowitz, E. N., Kerin, R. A., Hartley, S. W., and Rudelius, W. (2000). *Marketing* (6th ed.). Boston, MA: Irwin/McGraw-Hill.

Bright, A. D. (2000). The role of social marketing in leisure and recreation management. *Journal of Leisure Research, 32*(1), 12–17.

Canning, L. (2004). Book review: Relationship marketing: Dialogue and networks in the e-commerce era. *European Journal of Marketing, 38*(8), 1031–1032.

Cotte, J. and Ratneshwar, S. (2004). Choosing leisure services: The effects of consumer timestyle. *Journal of Services Marketing, 17*(6), 558–572.

Coulter, R. A. and Ligas, M. (2004). A typology of customer-service provider relationships: The role of relational factors in classifying customers. *Journal of Services Marketing, 18*(6), 482–493.

Greenbaum, T. L. (1998, September 14). *Ten tips for running successful focus groups.* Retrieved December 5, 2005, from http://www.groupsplus.com/pages/mn091498.htm

Keep asking the customer. (2004). *Strategic Direction, 20*(9), 24–26.

Legarreta, J. M. B. and Miguel, C. E. (2004). Collaborative relationship bundling: A new angle on services marketing. *International Journal of Service Industry Management, 15*(3), 264–283.

Marketing style guide. (2004, March). Littleton, CO: Ken-Caryl Ranch Metropolitan District.

McCarthy, E. J. (1960). *Basic marketing: A managerial approach.* Homewood, IL: Richard D. Irwin, Inc.

Mowen, A. (2003, May). Community efforts, community health: Seven tips for creating successful health partnerships. *Parks and Recreation, 38*(5), 36–39.

National Therapeutic Recreation Society. (2000). *The benefits of therapeutic recreation: A training and resource guide.* Arlington, VA: National Therapeutic Recreation Society.

Neilsen, J. (1997). The use and misuse of focus groups. *IEEE Software, 14*(1), 94–95.

O'Brien, P. and Manross, G.G. (2002, December). Building customer loyalty: Ten steps toward obtaining this valuable commodity. *Parks & Recreation, 37*(12), 50–53.

O'Morrow, G. S. and Carter, M. J. (1997). *Effective management in therapeutic recreation service*. State College, PA: Venture Publishing, Inc.

O'Sullivan, E. (1991). Marketing experiences: It's the how, not the what. *Parks & Recreation, 26*(12), 40–42.

O'Sullivan, E. (1999). *Setting a course for change: The benefits movement in parks and recreation*. Arlington, VA: National Recreation and Park Association.

Peters, J. (1997). Branded. *The TQM Magazine, 9*(3), 320–321.

van der Zwan, F. and Bhamra, T. (2003). Services marketing: Taking up the sustainable development challenge. *Journal of Services Marketing, 17*(4), 341–356.

van Riel, C. B. M. and van den Ban, A. (2001). The added value of corporate logos: An empirical study. *European Journal of Marketing, 35*(3/4), 428–440.

Chapter 12
Staffing

In labor-intensive organizations like health and human service agencies, the quality of personnel hired and retained determines whether the organization accomplishes its objectives (Robbins & Decenzo, 2001; Sullivan & Decker, 2001). Additionally, staff must be skilled and competent professionals to properly address client needs (Marquis & Huston, 2003). The quality of an organization is, in large part, determined by the quality of its staff (Robbins & Decenzo, 2001). Staffing decisions and methods are critical to ensuring that the right mix of personnel are hired and retained.

The human resource management (HRM) department or specialist and the first-line manager usually share staffing in health and human service organizations. First-line managers are most knowledgeable about therapeutic recreation job requirements and can best describe the position to candidates. HRM personnel may assist the manager with various staffing responsibilities. HRM personnel also monitor adherence to a number of legal and professional standards that affect hiring and personnel management practices. The intent of this chapter is to consider the essential elements of staffing.

Health and human services are undergoing major scrutiny as the demand to deliver quality services at contained costs escalates. First-line managers must consider the cost involved in all aspects of department functions. A major portion of the total budget is always personnel costs. Managers must also consider the cost of training and development, benefits, and retention. Therefore it is crucial to employ therapeutic recreation specialists who meet client needs while performing cost effectively.

First-line managers are impacted by a number of legal regulations and professional standards designed to protect the employee and employer and to promote fairness in the work environment. Professional standards also encourage employees to maintain and upgrade their professional competence. Managers who elect to incorporate these criteria into job specifications develop privileging protocols and policies and procedures to assure assessment of staff competence. Responsibility then rests with the manager to tie performance criteria to therapeutic recreation practices. The first portion of this chapter, therefore, covers legal and professional regulations and standards.

In the second section of this chapter, variables that affect human resource planning are reviewed. Managers may conduct human resource inventories as they develop a plan to ensure that the right mix and number of personnel are in place to address present client needs and prepare to meet future agency goals. Prior to recruitment—the process of locating, identifying, and attracting candidates—managers undertake job analyses. Information from analyses is used to update or develop job descriptions and specifications. Hiring is based on the information contained in these documents. Accurately predicting staffing needs and allocating staff resources result in efficient and effective services. Further, proactive staff planning fosters retention while preparing for fluctuating staffing needs.

The focus of the next segment of this chapter is on the selection process. The manager's task is to determine who is best qualified for the position. A number of screening and assessment processes are available. Managers may elect to use a combination of methods. A manager synthesizes gathered information, makes a decision, and presents a compensation package to the successful candidate. Compensation packages take into account employee benefits. These packages are quite varied and considered something each employee values (Robbins & Decenzo, 2001).

The last portion of this chapter addresses issues that arise throughout staffing. Human resource issues facing the therapeutic recreation manager range from job relatedness of recruiting and screening practices to workforce diversity, downsizing, fiscal accountability to the agency, and ethical accountability to staff. Selection of competent employees who represent the communities they serve is one of the most critical responsibilities of first-line managers and HRM departments. Staffing decisions are fundamental to ensuring an agency hires and keeps the right personnel.

Legal and Professional Regulations and Standards

Commencing in 1935, a number of federal laws and court decisions have been implemented that affect employment practices. Amendments to original legislation, court interpretations, and executive orders contribute to ambiguity and inconsistency in practice. Yet, the responsibility lies with the first-line manager to comply with the intent of laws and legislation. In an attempt to ensure quality consumer services, professional credentialing bodies and societies have recommended minimal and expected educational experiences and credentials. Further, in a number of practice settings, privileging practices to promote maintenance of staff competence are outlined. Noncompliance to laws exposes the manager to liability. Adherence to professional guidelines, however, facilitates the hiring of staff who are eligible to meet personnel criteria and who have been exposed to competencies believed essential to quality therapeutic recreation service delivery.

Legal Regulations

The National Labor Relations Act (Wagner Act) of 1935, the Labor Management Relations Act (Taft-Hartley Act) of 1947, Kennedy Executive Order 10988 of 1962, the 1974 amendments to the Wagner Act, and state right-to-work laws govern relationships among employees who are union or nonunion members and the first-line manager responsible for conducting fair labor practices. First-line managers interact directly or indirectly with unions as they employ and supervise staff. A public park and recreation department or a private hospital may be unionized and have union members within the agency. In either situation the manager needs to be familiar with union conditions and practices that govern collective bargaining. In some instances, first-line therapeutic recreation managers rely on union members to carry out supportive tasks critical to program delivery, such as room setup or equipment maintenance. Therefore, the manager must plan to accommodate stipulated work practices and include monies to cover the deployment of essential support services in the budget.

The Fair Labor Standards Act (FLSA) enacted by Congress in 1938 and amended numerous times since covers more than 85% of all nonsupervisory employees and tends to place a floor on wages and a ceiling on work hours (Marquis & Huston, 2003). The law set a minimum hourly wage and established overtime pay requirements in relation to hours worked for certain employee categories. Executive, administrative, and professional employees are exempt from minimum wages and overtime pay requirements. Overtime pay can be a significant budgetary consideration as first-line managers plan staffing schedules to cover weekend shifts or extended day programs.

The Equal Pay Act of 1963 (P.L. 88-38) prohibits pay discrimination on the basis of sex. This law requires the same pay for men and women "doing substantially equal work, requiring substantially equal skill, effort, and responsibility under similar working conditions" (Tomey, 2000, p. 297). This law and its amendments (e.g., 1972

Equal Employment Opportunity Act, P.L. 92-261) cover entry-level employees or nonsupervisory staff as well as first-line managers. Private as well as government institutions are required to comply. Thus, whether the department is part of a larger city or county government agency or a private hospital, first-line managers are required to have equitable pay scales.

The first-line manager is directly responsible for the enforcement of the fair employment provisions of the Civil Rights Act, Title VII of 1964. This law and its court interpretations ensure that discrimination in hiring, firing, wages, terms, conditions, and privileges of employment do not occur. The courts have decreed that an applicant is to be judged based on ability. Prerequisites for a position are to be job-related (BFOQ—bona fide occupational qualifications); therefore, if cardiopulmonary resuscitation (CPR) and first aid are employment requirements, they are to be tied to client safety during service provision. When employees are subjected to testing, it must be job-related (e.g., civil service tests administered by public agencies). Differential compensation rates and employment conditions may exist if part of a seniority system or merit program, yet they must not be discriminatory.

The Civil Rights Act was strengthened by Executive Order 11246 in 1965 as amended by Executive Order 11375 in 1967. All government contracting agencies are prohibited from discriminating against a job applicant or employee. Contractors are to take affirmative action to ensure those who historically were discriminated against are actively recruited to fill vacancies.

The Age Discrimination in Employment Act of 1967 (P.L. 90-202), amended in 1978 (P.L. 95-256), makes it illegal to discriminate against persons 40 years of age or older in employment selection, retention, promotion, and compensation. Employers affected are public and private agencies with 20 or more employees. The law prohibited mandatory retirement for persons under the age of 70. However in 1987, this upper age restriction was removed except for certain job categories (Marquis & Huston, 2003). As with Title VII, an employee may exercise BFOQ and the bona fide seniority system as exemptions (Sullivan & Decker, 2001).

The Equal Employment Opportunity Act of 1972 established the Equal Employment Opportunity Commission (EEOC) to enforce the 1964 and later the 1991 Civil Rights Act (P.L. 102-166). This law expanded Title VII to include employers with 15 or more employees and state and local government employers. Consequently, many first-line therapeutic recreation managers are affected. Although not specifically required by law, court orders have tended to support the preparation of affirmative action plans (Marquis & Huston, 2003). These plans identify guidelines affecting position advertising, application forms, and recruitment practices. Advertisement is to be nondiscriminatory in nature and must not indicate a hiring preference. Applications are to be job specific. During interviews, for example, the first-line manager cannot inquire about arrest records unless driving is a job requirement and the questions focus only on driving performance as it relates to job outcomes.

An affirmative action officer is identified within each organization. This person oversees the preparation of the affirmative action plan and reviews advertising, recruiting, and selection documents and processes to ensure compliance. An EEOC statement is developed and used on written communications (e.g., job position announcements, official documents). While affirmative action plans are aimed at seeking the members of underemployed groups, equal employment opportunities are aimed at preventing discrimination. For instance, when EEOC finds an employer has been discriminatory, a civil suit may be brought against the employer. When discrimination is found, an employer may be ordered to restore "rightful economic status" or back pay for up to two years. Within an agency the first-line therapeutic recreation manager may be appointed as the department officer or liaison to the affirmative action office.

Section 503 of the 1973 Rehabilitation Act (P.L. 93-112) required all employees with government contracts of more than $25,000 to take affirmative action to employ and to advance in employment qualified persons with disabilities (Marquis & Huston, 2003; Tomey, 2000). Similarly, Section 402 of the Vietnam Era Veterans' Readjustment Assistance Act of 1974 (P.L. 93-508) required contractors to take affirmative action to employ and advance disabled veterans and veterans of the Vietnam era. The act also provided employment rights with regard to positions held before the armed forces enlistment (Marquis & Huston, 2003; Tomey, 2000). In 1978 the Pregnancy Discrimination Act (P.L. 95-555) extended Title VII to include treatment of pregnant women; as a consequence, an employer who requires mandatory leave without regard to the employee's ability to work is in violation of the Civil Rights Act. Like the Vietnam Act, a job is protected during maternity leave.

Although job discrimination due to gender became illegal with Title VII in 1964, guidelines stating that sexual harassment in the workplace violates Title VII were not established until 1980 (Sullivan & Decker, 2001). "Under these guidelines, the employer can be held liable for acts… committed by employees whether or not the employer had any prior knowledge of the reported acts" (Sullivan & Decker, 2001, p. 84). Because of the public image and nature of therapeutic recreation jobs, professionals are exposed to situations in which sexual harassment might occur. Managers, therefore, must (a) recognize the serious consequences of sexual harassment, (b) take preventive strategies to deal with the issue, (c) impartially investigate any complaints, and (d) incorporate education about sexual harassment in new employee orientation and professional development (Marquis & Huston, 2003).

The Americans with Disabilities Act (ADA) of 1990 (P.L. 101-336), which became effective in July 1992, addresses discriminatory practices against persons with disabilities. Title I of this act addresses employment criteria in public or private settings with 15 or more employees. A first-line manager must make reasonable accommodations to provide access for a qualified person to a position. This may include technology, such as physical access at the site of employment and special hearing and/or reading equipment to do the job. Also, on-site and off-site locations for training and development programs must be accessible.

The Civil Rights Act of 1991 restored provisions (i.e., hiring, firing, or promotion) lost through Supreme Court decisions following the enactment of the 1964 law. Supervisors must be aware of hiring and promotion practices, known as the "glass ceiling effect" (e.g., artificial barriers) that adversely impact protected classes, seniority systems, and persons whose age might be considered an employment factor. In case of intentional discrimination, employees are permitted to sue for punitive damages (Robbins & Decenzo, 2001).

The Family and Medical Leave Act of 1993 (P.L. 103-3) affects all public employers and private employers with 50 or more employees. When an employee has worked for an employer at least 12 months, the employer must provide eligible employees with up to 12 weeks of unpaid leave per 12 month period for childcare, care of an immediate family member, and an employee's own serious health condition that precludes job performance. The law allows employees to maintain health insurance coverage while on leave and to return to the same or equivalent position following the leave period (Sullivan & Decker, 2001). With this particular law the first-line manager's concern becomes establishing policies to ensure that the law is implemented fairly and making sure that service quality is retained during staff absences.

Professional Standards

Laws and court decisions affect how first-line managers conduct staffing processes and what policies and procedures are developed to administer departments. Credentialing bodies and professional groups set standards that affect what managers include in job specifications. The minimal staff requirement delineated in professional standards of practice (ATRA, 2000; NTRS, 2004) for the therapeutic recreation specialists is state licensure, registration or certification, and certification with the National Council for Therapeutic Recreation Certification (NCTRC).

Additionally, the written plan of operation encourages professional development activities, periodic assessment of staff competencies, and the design of individual development plans so staff competencies are maintained and enhanced for safe and effective practice. NCTRC (2003a) defines the criteria for a bachelor's degree, with minimal credit hours in recreation, therapeutic recreation coursework, and supportive content courses. A culminating internship with a minimal number of clock hours and length of time under a CTRS is the eligibility criteria for the entry-level certification exam. Upon successful completion of the exam, certification extends for five years with annual renewal maintenance fees. Following the five-year period, accumulation of professional experience and continuing education in therapeutic recreation or successful reexamination ensures recertification (NCTRC, 2003b). The first-line manager may elect to include the requirement of state licensure, registration, or certification; CTRS certification; or eligibility to sit for the CTRS exam as job specifications. If this course of action is taken, the manager must relate job knowledge, skills, and abilities (KSAs) to the job tasks of the Therapeutic Recreation Specialist (refer to http://www.nctrc.org/certification/ctrsrecertificationandreentry.pdf).

Professional practice documents refer to therapeutic recreation specialists that maintain their competency and adhere to policies, procedures, and clinical privileges where appropriate (ATRA, 2000; NTRS, 2004). Specifically, standard of practice documents identify staff participation in competency opportunities that improve patient outcomes (ATRA, 2000). Regulatory bodies like JCAHO consider competency assessment programs or the assessment, maintenance, and continual professional development of staff as quality indicators. As a consequence, first-line managers document and maintain records of staff participation in programs that offer CEU (i.e., continuing education unit) opportunities. Where credentials specify minimal professional expectations, privileging identifies specific agency or department practice requirements. A privileging plan sets minimal employment criteria such as possession of the CTRS credential, CPR, first aid, and experience(s) in specific settings. These are considered provisional privileges. According to Hatfield (1991), when the probationary period is successfully completed, the new employee must display competence in specific department KSAs to gain full privileging rights and retain employment. Specific privileges are gained with higher or more specific levels of knowledge and training (e.g., assertiveness, stress management). Privileging is granted for a predetermined time period after which the employee must document the continuing competence essential to quality service delivery. A first-line manager in a setting may include privileging criteria in job specifications. In a public recreation setting, similar criteria may be listed without direct reference to privileging requirements. In both settings the use of professional credentials and specific privileging or performance criteria with the demonstration of ongoing competence requires that the manager continually ensure the relevance of job specifications to therapeutic recreation practice.

Human Resource Planning

Proactive human resource planning requires the first-line manager to continually assess and reassess staffing needs. As managers probe ways not only to streamline but also to diversify consumer services, staffing patterns remain in flux to accommodate new and changing department goals. The manager assesses current human resources, considers future needs, and develops a plan to ensure that the right mix and number of personnel are in place to meet future goals. Human resource planning takes into consideration staffing patterns, scheduling options, budget constraints, historical background of staffing needs and availability, diversity of client population served, personnel policies, educational and experiential levels of staff, mix of titles or classifications, and fluctuations in programs or seasonal offerings (Marquis & Huston, 2003; Tomey, 2000). Managers are alert to diversity in the communities served by the organization and attempt to recruit staff sensitive to that diversity. Managers are also aware of national and local economics and trends affecting health care delivery. Downsizing to achieve cost containment has resulted in decreasing length of stay in clinical settings and an increasing focus on inclusion. Therapeutic recreation specialists will become adept at wellness interventions, brief treatment, and training of recreation and support staff as legislation and health care reform focus on quality control and accountability. Advances in technology and treatment innovations are increasing demands for health care (Marquis & Huston, 2003). An educated consumer population with ready access to health care information is more knowledgeable about alternative interventions and service options. Services that are reimbursable and have revenue-generating potential will receive staffing priorities as budget tightening in the private and public sectors continue. In addition, as staffing needs fluctuate due to budget challenges or seasonal offerings, managers will introduce employee participation programs to maintain morale and productivity (Robbins & Decenzo, 2001). Proactive planning, therefore, involves assessing national issues and trends, analyzing historical patterns, keeping personnel statistics and client service records, and carefully monitoring agency priorities and goals.

Employment Assessments

An initial staffing function is an assessment of the department's current human resources. This involves developing an inventory of staff KSAs, including education, training prior to employment, credentials, and specialized skills and talents (Robbins & Decenzo, 2001). An inventory provides the manager with information on currently available KSAs. Another aspect of the current assessment is the completion of job analyses. The purpose of these is to assess or reassess the KSAs needed to successfully perform each job. A job analysis determines duties and responsibilities in a particular job, tasks inherent in these duties, and skills, abilities, and knowledge to perform successfully (Sullivan & Decker, 2001). The process is lengthy and may involve supervisory conferences between the first-line manager and staff to identify critical tasks. Observation of work performed, completion of checklists, interviewing, and maintaining self-report logs are techniques managers use to determine essential tasks and KSAs. Once identified, these job tasks may be compared to the NCTRC job tasks for the therapeutic recreation specialist to affirm competencies common to entry-level positions. Additionally, the manager develops or updates job descriptions and specifications used in the hiring process. With planning data on trends, financial forecasts, historical staffing patterns, current staff KSAs, and anticipated staff KSAs, a staffing plan to hire and retain competent professionals is developed.

Job Descriptions

A manager develops job descriptions by clustering job tasks so work that accomplishes the objectives of the department is done. A job description describes what, how, and why a job is done. Descriptions are fluid; managers redevelop them to address the changing human resource needs of the unit. Job descriptions portray job content, work environment and employment conditions. Managers use job descriptions to describe the job to potential candidates (see Figure 12.1, p. 172). Additionally, job descriptions help staff learn their duties by clarifying the outcomes management expects.

Job or position descriptions tend to be comprised of several parts: position title and classification, superior and subordinate relationships, objective or job statement, general and specific responsibilities, duties to be performed, qualifications, and skills. The first-line manager works with the human resource division or specialist to design job descriptions that reflect professional criteria (e.g., CTRS and department privileging criteria or performance standards). O'Morrow (2000) described the process organizations use to complete job evaluation studies to assign relative worth to job tasks so that each position is ranked or classified in relationship to every other organiza-tional position. Results of these studies are also used to set salaries and ensure pay equity. Usually the job description lists a job class or position as well as unique qualifications that are sought.

Job Specifications

Job specifications detail job descriptions. The specific minimum acceptable KSAs and the behavior required to effectively perform a given job are identified. "The job specification keeps the manager's attention on the list of qualifications necessary for an incumbent to perform a job and assists in determining whether candidates are qualified" (Robbins & Decenzo, 2001, p. 188). Because the description is used as a recruitment notice (see Figure 12.1, p. 172), information on application deadlines, procedures, and materials to submit may be listed. Job specifications may also include salary information, benefits, work conditions, employment date, and specific duties. In practice, subtle differences unique to each setting exist between job descriptions and job specifications (see Figure 12.2, p. 173).

The first-line manager in smaller organizations may prepare job specifications and receive applications when positions open. In larger agencies the first-line therapeutic recreation manager may assist the human resource department or specialist in the preparation of job specifications. When this occurs, materials are submitted to the human resource department or specialist who screens applications and forwards to the manager only those applications that satisfy the preferred specifications.

When positions do open, the position may be reevaluated to determine the necessity of the position in the achievement of department objectives and agency goals. The evaluation study may result in salary adjustments and/or job reclassification. Consequently, positions are eliminated or temporarily not filled and duties are reassigned with or without salary adjustments. If jobs are reclassified, the manager reexamines the effectiveness of the structure to achieve desired outcomes and determines the appropriate mix and number of needed staff.

Recruiting Process

With completion of the inventory, job analyses, job description, and job specification, the manager is ready to prepare a plan to recruit applicants who meet the department's human resource needs. The purpose of a recruiting plan is to locate and attract enough qualified applicants for a pool from which individuals can be selected. The manager determines where to look, how to look, when to look, and how to sell the department to potential recruits (Sullivan & Decker, 2001).

For most organizations the best place to look is within the geographic region. One approach is to recruit

City of Cincinnati
Job Opportunity

EXCEPTIONAL APPOINTMENT

PARKS/RECREATION PROGRAMMING COORDINATOR
(Certified Therapeutic Recreation Specialist)

Open to the Public and to City Employees

$31,382 - $42,365 ANNUALLY

APPLICATION DEADLINE: 4:30 p.m., Monday, July 19, 2004

The Cincinnati Recreation Commission is seeking to fill a Recreation Programming Coordinator (Therapeutics) position. Under the direction of the Service Area Coordinator, this employee has responsibility for planning, developing, coordinating, supervising and evaluating community-based recreation programs for individuals with disabilities. This position includes training and supervision of assigned staff as well as working as a team member in providing inclusive recreation programs. Candidates must possess strong organizational and communication skills with the ability to manage numerous programs as well as a large inclusion support caseload.

APPLICATIONS must be filed <u>in person</u> at Two Centennial Plaza, Suite 200, 805 Central Avenue, Cincinnati, Ohio 45202 or returned through the United States mail with a postmark no later than the deadline date for applications. Do **NOT** use the interdepartmental mail system.

Blank applications can be downloaded from the Internet at *http://www.cincinnati-oh.gov/cityhr/pages/-4278-/*

QUALIFICATIONS: Each applicant must be a Certified Therapeutic Recreation Specialist (CTRS) certified through the National Council for Therapeutic Recreation Certification (NCTRC), with a minimum of two years full time experience, which includes the supervision of part time and/or full time employees. Experience in community-based settings with multiple populations is desired. Each applicant must be willing to work evenings, weekends and irregular hours and be able to furnish own transportation to various program locations. Must have a valid Driver's license. You are required to show your valid Driver's license to the Department of Human Resources staff NO LATER THAN THE DEADLINE DATE FOR FILING APPLICATIONS. Must be a Hamilton County resident at the time of appointment.

CONTACT PERSON: Stephanie Knarr, 352-4055

City of Cincinnati, Human Resources Department
Two Centennial Plaza
805 Central Ave, Suite 200
Cincinnati, Ohio 45202

TDD: 352-2419
Announcement Number: 79
Date Issued: June 28, 2004

"Applications for City positions are considered public records under Ohio's Public Records Act. As a public record, applications maintained by the City shall be made available to any person requesting to view them".

AN EQUAL OPPORTUNITY EMPLOYER
REASONABLE ACCOMMODATION FOR QUALIFIED PEOPLE WITH DISABILITIES. TO HELP US ACHIEVE THE CITY'S GOAL TO RECRUIT QUALIFIED PERSONS WITH DISABILITIES, PLEASE SELF-IDENTIFY AT THE TIME OF APPLICATION AND AT EMPLOYMENT INTERVIEWS. HELP THE CITY HELP YOU!

Figure 12.1
Job Description

CITY OF CINCINNATI
CIVIL SERVICE COMMISSION
CLASSIFICATION SPECIFICATION
(draft 4/9/04)

EXCEPTIONAL APPOINTMENT
PARKS/RECREATION
SERVICE AREA COORDINATOR
(THERAPEUTIC RECREATION)

GENERAL STATEMENT OF DUTIES

Administrative responsibility for the operation and personnel management for Therapeutic Recreation Programs and Inclusion Support Services within a designated region (East, West, Central). Develops, organizes and implements specialized programs designed to meet the needs of individuals with disabilities. Develops, organizes and implements support services designed to facilitate the inclusion of individuals with disabilities in general recreation programs and services within designated region.

EXAMPLES OF WORK PERFORMED

(Illustrative only. Any one position within this classification may not include all of the duties listed nor do the listed examples include all of the tasks which may be performed.)

- Assesses recreational needs and interests of individuals with disabilities within region, develops TR programs and support services based on assessment.

- Prepares and monitors the budget for all TR programs and support services within the region; gathers information and data and organizes it to be interpreted and summarized by supervisor.

- Recruits, hires, trains and supervises staff to conduct regional TR programs and to provide support services.

- Develops and conducts training designed for community center staff in areas relating to inclusion.

- Develops and disseminates program/service promotional materials, oversees the program registration process and requests for accommodations.

- Collaborates and forms partnerships with various disability organizations and social service agencies to coordinate resources.

- Identifies risks associated with programs/services for individuals with disabilities and develops risk management plans; includes advising regional staff on responsibilities relating to Americans with Disabilities Act.

- Works with region Service Area Coordinators in planning for accessible programs and services.

- Works with other TR Service Area Coordinators in planning and implementing city-wide TR programs and events.

- Evaluates Service Area programs/services for quantity and quality as they relate to departmental standards.

- Applies and enforces all departmental policies and procedures.

SUPERVISION EXERCISED

- Supervises Community Center Directors, part-time staff and volunteers.

PARKS/RECREATION SERVICE AREA COORDINATOR (THERAPEUTICS) EXAMPLES OF REQUIRED KNOWLEDGE, SKILLS AND ABILITIES (KSAs)

(Illustrative only. Any one person may not require all of the listed KSAs nor do the listed examples include all the KSAs which may be required.)

Knowledge of:

- Operating policies and procedures of the department

- Emergency safety procedures

- Program goals and objectives of the department

- Principles of supervision

- Americans with Disabilities Act, accessibility guidelines (ADAAG), and laws governing recreation services for people with disabilities in city/government agencies (Title II)

- Various disabilities and their implication for recreation

- Therapeutic recreation competencies, including assessment activity, analysis, and activity adaptation

- Specific strategies for supporting inclusion, such as peer training, cooperative grouping and activity modification

- Behavior management principles and techniques

- Alternative communication methods and systems

- Community resources and existing support agencies related to TR and inclusion services

- Community resources and existing support agencies related to TR and inclusion services

- General safety practices, safety policies and procedures

Ability to:

- Establish work priorities

- Develop and monitor a budget

- Provide training to staff and volunteers

- Work as a team member with regional staff, outside agencies and others

- Assess needs and plan appropriate programs for targeted audiences

- Mobilize human resources

- Facilitate problem solving at the service area level

- Interview and access abilities of job applicants

- Develop behavior management plans

- Perform basic computer functions

- Write measurable performance objectives

- Evaluate staff, programs, and services

- Organize and facilitate meetings involving a variety of participants

REQUIRED EDUCATION AND EXPERIENCE

Each applicant must be a Certified Therapeutic Recreation Specialist (CTRS) certified through the National Council on Therapeutic Recreation Certification and must have a minimum of two years full-time supervisory experience in community-based therapeutic programs serving multiple populations or have five years full-time supervisory experience in community-based programs serving multiple populations.

Figure 12.2
Job Specifications

where past efforts have been successful. Also, an incremental strategy involves local recruiting first followed by expanding to larger markets until a sufficient pool is obtained. Geographic location makes a difference in earnings (O'Morrow, 2000). Professionals living in the southwest and northwest regions have higher average annual income ranges than practitioners living in other regions of the country do. Consequently, managers consider employment variables unique to their local communities and regions as they determine where they might look to attract recruits.

A second management decision is selecting recruiting sources. The Internet is emerging as a cost-effective way to recruit qualified job applicants worldwide. Managers desire to find a medium with the widest exposure; yet, this medium tends to be inefficient when compared to influential media like present employees (Sullivan & Decker, 2001). Consequently, word-of-mouth remains a popular recruiting tool as friends and associates have prior credibility and may communicate subtle information regarding the department or position. Most applicants are drawn to an organization by some form of advertisement (Sullivan & Decker, 2001). The type of position or level of responsibility for which applicants are being recruited also influences how positions are advertised. To illustrate, the ATRA Web site (http://www.atra-tr.org) and the therapeutic recreation directory (http://www.recreationtherapy.com) may be sources to use when recruiting for supervisory positions while local career fairs and newspapers are used to advertise entry-level positions. Employee referrals are considered to produce good candidates (Robbins & Decenzo, 2001). Other reliable sources are through university faculty and alumni, and colleagues from professional organizations. Active recruitment of employees who represent the diversity found in the organization's constituents is addressed in the recruiting plan and assures adherence to policy. HR specialists provide access to media appropriate to use with specific underrepresented individuals.

Careful planning ensures recruitment begins in advance of anticipated needs. The time frame is affected by organizational policies that, for example, require a position to be vacated two weeks prior to internal posting. Once posted, applications are accepted for a two-week period prior to external advertisement. Some positions remain open until filled while others are filled after the new fiscal year commences. Managers may retain an open file of unsolicited résumés received during annual conventions or from walk-ins who desire to relocate or are interested in making an employment change. Recruiting is on going. Events like college career fairs and annual conventions represent opportune times to sell the agency.

A marketing plan to sell the organization consists of the traditional *P*s: (a) product—aspects of each position like professionalism and standards of practice as well as job descriptions and specifications, (b) place—physical qualities like intervention resources and parking as well as the organization's reputation, (c) price—salary and compensation package, and (d) promotion—advertising media and messages to recruit staff. As the marketing plan is effected, managers focus on the fit between potential employees and organizational offerings. Employee retention is influenced by the manner in which managers use various recruiting strategies.

Selection Process

Recruitment results in a pool of potential applicants. The size of the pool, the nature of the position, and the size of the organization and department influence the manager's role in screening and selection decisions. The manager coordinates with human resource personnel to define screening criteria and to facilitate objective on-site selection procedures.

Preliminary Screening

In the absence of a perfect method to select candidates, first-line managers use a variety of screening methods to identify the most appropriate candidate. Traditional methods have included application forms, résumés and portfolios, written and performance-simulation tests, interviews, and background examinations. According to Robbins and Decenzo (2001), use of a number of selection devices intends to reduce accept and reject errors. An *accept error* is the selection of a candidate who subsequently performs poorly on the job, while a *reject error* is rejecting a candidate who would later have been successful on the job. In either situation, the outcome is costly because direct service time is ultimately lost and recruiting and screening are time-consuming and expensive. A correct decision is made when the applicant is predicted to be successful on the performance criteria used to evaluate therapeutic recreation specialists. Robbins and Decenzo (2001) noted that a correct decision also occurs when applicants are predicted to be unsuccessful and would not meet expectations if hired. Thus, the first-line manager chooses those screening methods that are most likely to predict which applicants will be successful if hired.

Screening methods must be valid, reliable, and in compliance with legal and legislative directives. Valid methods demonstrate a relationship between the screening tool and job performance. For example, experience with documentation and assessments is a valid screening method to use in the Rehabilitation Accreditation Commission (CARF) and Joint Commission on Accreditation of Healthcare Organizations (JCAHO) accredited settings where staff must complete these tasks. Likewise, skill proficiency in the use of wheelchairs and mobility aides is a valid screening method employed by community special recreation associations. Reliable screening tools yield consistent results. In other words, the characteristics being measured are considered to remain stable over time. To illustrate, if the NCTRC exam were chosen as a preliminary screening tool, each applicant's score would remain consistent over time because the test is a reliable measure of entry-level therapeutic recreation specialist job tasks.

The first screening step is to determine who is minimally qualified to perform the duties required in a particular position. It may be neither cost-effective nor time-effective to interview and test each applicant, so the manager uses application forms, résumés or portfolios, and/or background information to establish which candidates possess minimally desired qualifications. Weighing or rating systems are designed to assess information presented by applicants. Established criteria reflect job relatedness. For example, experience with aging adults with strokes would be weighted higher than would experience with well elderly when the manager is hiring for a rehabilitation unit, whereas the opposite would be true if the position were in a community senior center. An applicant who possesses the CTRS and CPRP credentials might be given higher ratings than the applicant who has yet to be declared eligible to sit for either exam if the manager chooses to tie the job responsibilities tested by each exam to the respective job tasks of the open position.

Application Forms

Application forms are one of the more traditional screening tools. The form should have sufficient questions to gain a picture of the applicant's potential but not be too lengthy as to discourage application completion. When the parent organization requires information irrelevant to the therapeutic recreation department, length may become an issue; conversely, the organization form may be so brief that the first-line therapeutic recreation manager must use a supplementary form. The form may be as brief as to require only name, address, phone, and emergency contacts or be as detailed as to require comprehensive profiles on education, experience, references, and KSAs related to particular therapeutic recreation positions. Demographic information is quickly acquired using application forms (Tomey, 2000). Applications help managers do a better job interviewing candidates (Woodward, 2000). Application forms assure information consistency among candidates. They also serve important legal functions like notifying candidates they must have proof of citizenship or give permission for their current employers to be contacted. Application forms provide a preliminary glimpse into applicants (Woodward, 2000). Like a first assignment,

they tell the manager how neat and detailed the candidate might be and how well they follow directions and spell. As applications are reviewed, the critical question to ask is whether applicants distorted their responses (Sullivan & Decker, 2001). Studies indicate "the application form may be one of the more valid predictors in a selection process" (Sullivan & Decker, 2001, p. 278).

Résumés and Portfolios

Résumés and portfolios provide detailed information on applicants' qualifications. Résumés may precede, accompany, or follow application submission. Managers may review unsolicited résumés then send an application to those who appear qualified. This practice serves as initial screening and cost savings as the processing of each application might involve review by a human resource specialist to ensure compliance with EEOC. Another scenario finds job descriptions written so that potential applicants request an application then submit the completed application form with a résumé, portfolio materials, reference sources, and actual reference letters. When this procedure is followed, the intent is twofold: (a) to determine if the applicant is truly interested in the position as demonstrated by actual follow-through and (b) to ascertain the applicant's ability to follow procedures. When résumés accompany applications, the human resource specialist and manager compare documents to determine if gaps need clarification or explanations require more detail and to assess how thoroughly the documents have been prepared and submitted. This also permits simultaneous review for EEOC and therapeutic recreation expectations by those most qualified to conduct the assessments. A third scenario finds submission of résumé and/or portfolio materials on managerial request following preliminary screening of application forms. This approach, as with the first, conserves time because the manager only reviews documents of applicants who have met minimal qualifications.

Background Data

Background data are a third category of preliminary screening information. Application forms, résumés, portfolios, references, and contacts managers make as potential applicants are referred serve as primary sources of background information. Verification of application information and employment history is a fact-finding process. The reliability of the applicant's information is ascertained at this stage. Outstanding references may not guarantee excellent job performance yet "poor references may help prevent a bad hiring decision" (Marquis & Huston, 2003, p. 246). "Emphasis should be placed on characteristics consistently cited and on the general tone of the letters" (Tomey, 2000, pp. 293–294). Some organizations do not permit supervisors to write recommendation letters. To avoid legal issues, letters may include only employment dates, salary, and whether the applicant is eligible for rehire (Sullivan & Decker, 2001). Reference checks, work experience, and credentials are verified prior to on-site interviewing.

Managers may have the opportunity to involve staff in preliminary and subsequent screening activities. In smaller agencies the therapeutic recreation manager and full-time and part-time employees are more likely to carry out the entire selection process. If materials are mailed directly to a human resource department or personnel specialist, preliminary screening is conducted at this level with or without input from the manager and therapeutic recreation staff. Those who meet minimal qualifications (e.g., possession of a bachelor's degree, CTRS or CPRP credential, specific population and setting experience) make up the applicant pool. The weighing or rating system prepared with human resource support is then used by the manager and/or staff to identify top candidates from the pool to participate in on-site screening. Phone interviews may be conducted prior to inviting finalists to participate in on-site screening. Finalists may be invited either individually or as a group to participate in on-site assessments.

On-Site Screening

On-site screening consists primarily of individual and/or group interviews and performance simulations. In public agencies, such as municipal leisure service departments, employees are required to take civil service tests. Test questions are developed from site-specific job specifications and existing professional standards, such as the NCTRC job tasks and knowledge areas. Tests are administered periodically through the human resource department. Therapeutic recreation managers serve as content experts for a personnel specialist who ensures compliance with legal mandates, test validity, and reliability standards. Applicants are ranked by score results. Agency-wide policies then determine who is selected for on-site interviews.

Performance Simulations

Performance simulations require candidates to demonstrate work-related skills, such as computer assessments, incident reporting, and writing client treatment or activity plans. Candidates also may be asked to participate in role-playing situations like those that occur as services are delivered (e.g., scenario requiring clinical judgment and problem solving). First-line managers may have their staff critique candidate performance according to the preset weighing or rating systems.

Interviews

Interviews, like application forms, are a universal screening criteria. The interview process is planned. Significance of the position, number of candidates, and the time devoted to interviewing procedures will affect the interview approach. One approach involves each candidate responding to the same set of questions; a second approach involves several candidates appearing before interviewers, sequentially or simultaneously, also responding to the same questions. Regardless of the approach used, the goals of a selection interview are threefold (Marquis & Huston, 2003):

1. The interviewer gathers enough information to determine the applicant's suitability for the position

2. The applicant with information from the interview is able to make an intelligent decision about the job, if it is offered

3. Regardless of the outcome, the applicant maintains a positive outlook toward the organization.

The interview brings the candidate into the work environment and culture. As a result of the interview, three fundamental questions are answered: "(a) Can the applicant perform the job? (b) Will the applicant perform the job? and (c) Will the candidate fit into the culture of the unit and the organization?" (Sullivan & Decker, 2001, p. 278).

The major challenge with interviews is subjectivity (Marquis & Huston, 2003). Interviewers use their judgments, biases, and values to make decisions after brief interactions with applicants, whereas applicants may be unduly influenced by the interviewer's personality (Marquis & Huston, 2003). Research has found that team interviewing utilizing a structured interview format will improve hiring decisions (Marquis & Huston, 2003; Shelton, 2000). Individual bias is reduced by using more than one staff member to interview job applicants. A structured interview allows the interviewer to be consistent and to compare all applicants' answers against a common base (Robbins & Decenzo, 2001). Comparability is maximized with the use of an interview guide (Sullivan & Decker, 2001). The interview guide is a written document listing questions, interviewer directions, and providing space for note taking. The guide provides a written record of the interview while using relevant (i.e., job-related) questions.

Planning an interview, therefore, involves arranging for the on-site visit, preparing staff, and developing an interview guide. A preparation step is to set up a schedule for the on-site visit. When managers interview one candidate at a time, the concern is to sequence the visit so that all staff and organization personnel who need to meet the candidate have an opportunity to do so. The manager must also make certain that the candidate has enough time to explore community concerns (e.g., housing, recreational opportunities). When all or most candidates are to be scheduled over several days or in one time frame, the manager ensures consistency with each candidate's schedule and plans staffing schedules to minimize service interruptions. Confidentiality becomes an issue when group interviews are scheduled. The manager plans for this through scheduling and discussion with candidates prior to the on-site visit.

The trend toward decentralization of decision-making encourages involvement of staff in the process. Managers coach staff on how to apply the rating criteria, when and what to document, and how to assess interviewee statements. The orientation also includes review of laws and regulations, tips for managing awkward situations (e.g., silence), and allows time to practice using the interview guide (Sullivan & Decker, 2001). The manager and staff may also develop a personal profile of what the person hired should be, including education, experience, and abilities. Standardization of interviews in this manner promotes nondiscriminatory hiring practices.

The first-line manager sets the tone of the interview through opening comments and introductions. The intent is to relax the applicant and to establish rapport. The manager uses the interview guide to structure the interview. The interviewee is informed that interviewers will take notes, the length of the interview, and the questioning procedure (e.g., each statement or question is made by the same interviewer and in the same sequence with each applicant). A brief orientation to the agency, therapeutic recreation service, and the position follows. Opening questions relate back to already presented background information so that the interviewee feels confident to respond to further questioning. Interviewers use probes, repetition, and paraphrasing to gain insight into how the applicant's KSAs relate to the job specifications. Silence also encourages response. Asking the interviewee if there are any details about the position, organization, or community that require clarification concludes the interview. Additionally, the manager identifies the next step in the hiring process (e.g., when a decision will be made, how the notification will occur, what follow-up steps might be required of the candidate). An interview guide outline with example questions (see Box 12.1) presents a standardized sequence.

A final question on the form may be recommendation to hire or not to hire (Marquis & Huston, 2003). The manager and staff independently complete the rating or weighing of responses as quickly as possible after each interview. Each interviewer weighs the applicant's qualities relative to degree of importance on the job, reliability of the data, and training potential. Dimensions likely to be learned in training are given less value than those less likely to be acquired through training, for example, using assessment tools vs. establishing helping relationships (Sullivan & Decker, 2001). Interviewers also examine any negative feelings (e.g., personal bias may not relate to criteria necessary for success on the job). Once independent ratings are completed, the team collectively studies results of analyzed ratings. During and following the interview, observation of gestures, mannerisms, and nonverbal cues may provide valuable clues about the applicant's "fit." Documentation of verbal and nonverbal responses and behaviors establishes if the candidate is qualified and likely to perform successfully in the position if hired.

Box 12.1: Interview Guide Outline

Heading

- Date, position, interviewer's names, candidate name, and application review comments
- Introductions and welcome: Names of personnel present, length of interview, outline of interview topics

Education

- How does your education prepare you for this position?
- Have you participated in continuing education opportunities?
- What specific intervention skills will you bring to client services?

Employment History

- What are your responsibilities in your current position?
- What tasks have you completed to demonstrate skills in teamwork, discharge planning, leisure education, and designing inclusion plans?
- May we contact your present employer?
- What skills have you gained in your previous positions that may help you be successful in this position?

Professional

- Do you currently hold the CTRS and/or CPRP credential(s)?
- In what professional organizations do you participate and how would this be of value to the position for which you are applying?
- What are your career goals and where do you see yourself in three years?

Personal Goals

- In what ways have you changed in the last five years?
- What are your greatest assets?

Questions From the Interviewee

- What questions do you have about the department, position, or community?
- What other questions do you have?

Closure

- Available start date, follow-up steps and dates, tour

Selecting

Selection and rejection are the final steps in the screening process. Data are compared across candidates. This lessens the impact of early impressions because each job element across the entire pool is considered (Sullivan & Decker, 2001). When qualifications of several candidates appear equal, the ability to fit into the department and meet future human resource needs are deciding factors. Does a match exist between the applicant's qualifications and the organization's expectations? Reference to the personal profile identifies a successful performer. Additionally, verifying the applicant's qualifications and work history is essential before an offer is made because an agency is liable for the character and actions of the employees hired. Although the first-line manager is responsible for the hiring decision, it is wise to work with the interview team and upper-level management to gain consensus and support. This is especially true if the new employee will be working with other organization employees and representing the department at agency events.

Notice to the selected candidate precedes rejection notification to unsuccessful candidates. In the case that a selected candidate rejects the offer, the door remains open to offer the position to the next most qualified candidate. A reasonable deadline is allowed for acceptance or rejection so that the manager is able to contact the next candidate without alerting him or her that he or she is not the first choice. Individuals who are seriously considered but not hired are possible candidates for future positions. If applicants are unlikely to be considered again, a personal letter explaining why their qualifications did not satisfy the job specifications is a professional courtesy. Offers are made in writing and managers request successful applicants to confirm their acceptance in writing. Pre-employment procedures like background checks are also clarified in writing. Documentation from all candidate screening is retained in the event questions about hiring and rejection decisions arise in the future.

A compensation package is negotiated and finalized with selection of a successful candidate. Job specifications usually identify a starting salary range commensurate with the applicant's qualifications. Additionally, a benefits package includes insurance, retirement, leave of absence, vacations, holidays, professional development incentives, unemployment benefits, and family-friendly benefits like summer day-camp for employee's children and extended school day programs for children of dual-career couples. A therapeutic recreation manager usually makes the decision about the exact amount of the starting salary while human resources presents the organization's alternative benefits packages. Whether or not the candidate elects to accept the offer may be determined by his or her perception of the total package and factors outside the actual offer (e.g., geographic location, community resources). Consequently, the manager is aware that extraneous factors may determine whether or not a candidate accepts or rejects a particular offer.

Probationary Periods

Organizations use probationary periods to confirm that a proper mix or match has been made. These periods vary from several weeks to a few months. This variation is due to the size of the organization and the position level. Usually the larger the organization and the more responsible the position the longer the period. During this period suitability of the new employee to the position and the position to the new employee is determined. Is the employee likely to perform successfully as a continuing member of the department? To predict the likelihood of success, managers incorporate personnel training, development, and evaluation processes into this orientation period. A new employee is introduced to position duties, trained in site-specific practices, and evaluated on service outcomes. Compatibility between the manager and employee is ascertained as the new employee is coached in the design of an individual development plan and becomes familiar with the department privileging and/or performance expectations. Managers use the new employee's development objectives and performance criteria from position specifications to evaluate progress toward performing the job tasks of the newly acquired position.

A candidate who does not perform successfully or appears unlikely to be able to develop the KSAs in the job specification is released. If the manager documents behaviors or performance that do not satisfy expectations, the candidate is released prior to or at the end of the probationary period. A candidate may voluntarily elect not to remain as an employee and terminate the probationary experience. The intent of the probationary period is to enhance the probability of making a correct decision rather than either an accept or reject error.

Staffing Issues

Several issues affect recruiting and selection processes. What the manager may say and do during candidate selection is governed by a number of laws, court decisions, and executive orders that affect the staffing process. Managers must ensure job relatedness of questions and statements. In therapeutic or caring relationships personal qualities and subjective characteristics, such as empathy and active listening skills, are perceived as essential yet may not be listed as specific job tasks. Consequently, asking a candidate a direct question about his or her abilities to be empathetic might be perceived by the candidate as inappropriate. Therefore, the manager develops simulation or role-playing scenarios to assess these types of communication skills to ensure the screening activities remain job related.

Another issue is the job relatedness of credentials such as the CTRS and CPRP. Is a person with these credentials likely to be more successful than the individual without the credentials? Although the competencies covered by the exams have been tied to job responsibilities, research has yet to link the competencies with indicators of quality in service outcomes. The same analogy holds true for experience. Do two years of experience with developmentally delayed persons prepare a candidate to complete the therapeutic recreation process in behavioral medicine? Further, persons who have experienced injuries or have experience with family members with disabilities may seek employment in therapeutic recreation. Interview questions on medical background and family history are illegal. Are these experiences relevant to the ability to perform as a therapeutic recreator?

Improving workforce diversity is a consideration in the selection process. Employee diversity is helpful in meeting the needs of an increasingly diverse client population. A diverse staff enriches morale and productivity in the organization (Marquis & Huston, 2003). Turning to listservs, newsprint, and training centers that target underrepresented individuals and persons with disabilities widens the recruiting net. The agency broadens its applicant pool by incorporating this type of outreach into its recruiting plan.

Outcomes of changing client care patterns and continuous quality improvements are "flatter" organizational structures and redesign of employee responsibilities to increase efficiency and maintain flexibility. Downsizing and rightsizing are used to balance staff with changing client needs or to link staffing levels with unit productivity goals like number of clients in programs or interventions provided. Fluctuations in staffing numbers and mix are necessitated by patient need, seasonal programming, reimbursement or revenue streams, personnel policies, workload budgets, regulations regarding staff-client ratios, and types of client classification systems used (e.g., inclusion programs define assistance levels whereas JCAHO defines care based on patient needs and severity level of disease or disability).

As the manager develops a human resource plan to meet actual and projected staffing needs, positions are defined by full-time equivalents (FTEs). One FTE equals 40 hours of work per week for 52 weeks, or 2,080 hours per year. Managers calculate the number of FTEs required to meet client needs for the number of days services are provided in a fiscal year. Positions in a budget are presented as FTEs. As staff schedules are developed, managers take into consideration the factors influencing fluctuations in staffing numbers and mix. With this information in hand, first-line managers estimate the number of full-time, part-time, and seasonals to recruit to meet FTE projections. This type of flexible scheduling allows managers to meet productivity levels while responding to organizational reductions in force.

Growing budget deficits at the federal and state levels have caused increased pressure for health care organizations to reduce costs (Marquis & Huston, 2003). Because personnel budgets are large in health and human service agencies, a small percentage cut in personnel may result in large agency savings. Managers are held accountable for providing safe, effective services while meeting client needs and remaining within the budget. Additionally staff "have the right to expect a reasonable workload" (Marquis & Huston, 2003, p. 305). Effective managers address their ethical accountability obligations by reviewing productivity components like job specifications, staff competencies, scheduling, and client needs. They also take into consideration numbers of staff and clients. Periodic evaluation is necessary to initiate change in the human resource plan.

When a manager works with human resource departments or specialists to screen applicants, the manager is the content or field expert whereas the specialist is the process or technical expert. The relationship a manager has with the department or specialist affects the degree of input managers have as each step is undertaken. When mutual respect and confidence exist, the therapeutic recreation manager is likely to be involved from the onset. Thus, when the applicant pool is complete, desired therapeutic recreation KSAs are evident in each candidate's materials. Although cumbersome and sometimes time-consuming, operating without assistance and clearance from specialists and EEOC personnel can place hiring decisions in jeopardy.

Assurance of the proper mix and number of competent staff rests with the first-line manager. The probationary period is a critical supervisory period, and experiences or patterns are valid predictors of future performance. Thus, behaviors and performance during this period are not to be overlooked or excused as "new employee" errors. Managers and employees take this probationary period more seriously when identifying that staff training needs in a personal development plan is a goal. In public agencies probationary employees can be dismissed without adhering to the traditional termination steps. Therefore, it is actually easier to let a probationary employee go than to terminate an employee after successful completion of the probationary period. The tendency of many is to presume the selection process is final when an offer is accepted. Yet, in reality, the selection is finalized with demonstration of the KSAs expected of a successful therapeutic recreation specialist during the probationary period.

Summary

Every first-line manager will be involved in staffing decisions. The nature of this involvement depends on whether the parent organization has a human resource department or specialist. In small organizations therapeutic recreation managers conduct recruiting and selection processes with consultation from a personnel specialist. In large organizations, however, the human resource department oversees and guides hiring practices. A manager is the content specialist whereas the personnel specialist gives technical and legal assistance. A therapeutic recreation manager, therefore, needs to be aware not only of the qualifications and performance expectations of therapeutic recreation specialists' positions but also of those standards and practices that impact how recruiting and selection are conducted. Ultimately, the first-line manager is responsible for selecting persons who are likely to perform successfully on the job. This chapter covered material on the standards that affect hiring and the strategies a manager uses to ensure an appropriate mix of human resources to deliver safe quality services.

A number of laws, court decisions, and executive orders have been enacted that influence recruiting and screening processes and decisions. These include the National Labor Relations Act, Labor Management Relations Act, Fair Labor Standards Act, Equal Pay Act, Civil Rights Act (Title VII), Age Discrimination in Employment Act, Equal Employment Opportunity Act, Section 503 of the 1973 Rehabilitation Act, Section 402 of the Vietnam Era Veterans' Readjustment Assistance Act, Pregnancy Discrimination Act, Americans with Disabilities Act, and the Family and Medical Leave Act. Professional standards of practice and credentialing bodies recommend qualifications that therapeutic recreation managers may choose to include in job specifications. The issue for the manager becomes establishing the job-relatedness of the credentials (e.g., CTRS, CPRP) and the recommended experience and educational standards (e.g., ATRA, 2000; NTRS, 2004). Privileging protocols use these criteria as entry-level expectations with site specific standards added to ensure competency assessment and maintenance.

The manager plans for present and future human resource needs, which change with the evolving directions of health and human services. As the manager develops job descriptions, an inventory of present staff KSAs is completed. This permits the manager to select candidates that have talents and capabilities to adapt to future transitions. Job analyses also help the manager to develop job specifications.

As a recruiting plan is developed, the manager considers those variables (e.g., salary, organization, community culture) that might influence one's decision to apply for a particular position. The recruiting plan details where to look, how to look, when to look, and how to sell the department to potential recruits. Recruiting materials are designed to target specific audiences. Job specification content is used to develop recruiting announcements.

Because no single screening method has been found to result in selection of the "right" candidate, a number of methods or tools tend to be used during the selection process: application forms, résumés and portfolios, background data, simulations, and interviews. The first three are used to form applicant pools. Simulations and interviews are costly and time-consuming. Usually the finalists are asked to complete performance simulations and interviews with staff and management. Team interviewing following a structured interview process that uses an interview guide tends to reduce interviewer subjectivity. Final selections occur after probationary periods of varying lengths are completed. Selection methods must be valid, reliable, job-related, and objective. Weighing and rating systems are developed to factor each screening tool into the final decision.

The probationary period is the final opportunity to assess compatibility and the proper staff mix. During this period the manager supervises training, development, and evaluation processes so that the final decision is correct and not an accept or reject error.

Issues arise throughout the staffing process. The manager's challenge is to ensure the best staff mix. Any decisions made must be tied to job relatedness. When CTRS or a bachelor's degree in therapeutic recreation are listed as job specifications, the manager documents the relationship between service quality and outcomes and the competencies represented by these criteria. Selected applicants must represent the diverse needs of constituents. Managers are financially and ethically accountable to ensure an adequate number of competent staff deliver safe quality services to meet client needs and accomplish organizational goals.

Review Questions

1. Identify and summarize the laws and professional standards of practice impacting staffing processes and decisions.

2. What are the primary steps in human resource planning?

3. Describe the contents of job descriptions and job specifications. What is the relationship between the two?

4. Conduct an Internet search to identify Web sites to recruit therapeutic recreation professionals. How do the competencies in the position announcements compare to the entry-level criteria of the CTRS?

5. What are the primary screening techniques and how is each used in relationship to each of the others?

6. What are predictors of a "proper" fit and how does a manager factor these into a final decision?

7. Summarize the issues a manager faces as staffing processes and decisions are carried out.

References

American Therapeutic Recreation Association (ATRA). (2000). *Standards for the practice of therapeutic recreation and self-assessment guide*. Alexandria, VA: Author.

Hatfield, R. (1991). Credentialing and privileging in therapeutic recreation: Practical professional necessities. In B. Riley (Ed.), *Quality management applications for therapeutic recreation* (pp. 163–172). Hattiesburg, MA: American Therapeutic Recreation Association.

Marquis, B. L. and Huston, C. J. (2003). *Leadership roles and management functions in nursing: Theory and application* (4th ed.). Philadelphia, PA: Lippincott Williams &Wilkins.

National Council for Therapeutic Recreation Certification. (2003a, August). *Part I: Information for new applicants. Candidate Handbook*. Retrieved February 23, 2004, from http://www.nctrc.org/certification/informationfornewapplicants.pdf

National Council for Therapeutic Recreation Certification. (2003b, August). *Part III: Recertification and reentry. Candidate Handbook*. Retrieved February 23, 2004, from http://www.nctrc.org/certification/ctrsrecertificationandreentry.pdf

National Therapeutic Recreation Society (NTRS). (2004). *Standards of practice for a continuum of care in therapeutic recreation*. Retrieved September 12, 2004, from http://www.nrpa.org/content/default.aspx?documentID=530

O'Morrow, G. S. (2000). *Therapeutic recreation practitioner analysis*. Ashburn, VA: National Therapeutic Recreation Society.

Robbins, S. P. and Decenzo, D. A. (2001). *Fundamentals of management* (3rd ed.). Upper Saddle River, NJ: Prentice Hall.

Shelton, M. (2000). Improve your interviewing technique team interviews help to reduce bad hiring decisions. *Camping Magazine, 73*(6), 26–29.

Sullivan, E. J. and Decker, P.J. (2001). *Effective leadership and management in nursing* (5th ed.). Upper Saddle River, NJ: Prentice Hall.

Tomey, A. M. (2000). *Guide to nursing management and leadership* (6th ed.). St. Louis, MO: Mosby.

Woodward, N. H. (2000). The function of forms. *HR Magazine, 45*(1), 66–73.

Part IV
Human Service Management

Chapter 13
Effective Communication

chapter revisions by Jean E. Folkerth and Marcia Jean Carter

People communicate even when they do not speak. The hallmark of an effective manager is effective communication, which is a complex process that requires skills on individual, group, and organizational levels. Managers participate in formal and informal communication, and the size of the organization influences the quality and formality of the communication. As a change agent, the manager's role is facilitative and integrative. Through communication the manager shares information and accesses resources so that others perform effectively to deliver quality services. The intent of this chapter is to explore both oral and written communication from an individual perspective as a supervisor or at the group level and within the organization.

What is successful communication? Is it overcoming resistance to change, gaining staff cooperation, negotiating higher salaries, and handling criticism? The first section of this chapter explores personal and interpersonal communication skills. As noted by Austin (2004), one must have basic interpersonal communication skills to perform as an effective helper. People communicate using a number of methods, yet even during personal interactions, barriers arise. The first portion of this chapter reviews strategies and techniques that foster effective interpersonal communication. The section closes with consideration of communication in a multicultural workplace.

The authors consider the relationship of effective communication as part of managerial roles and functions in the second portion of this chapter. Supervisory-subordinate relationships emanate from the "authority" position of the manager. Yet paradigm shifts in management to participatory styles affect communication between first-line managers and employees. Managers seldom see the end of a change event because they are busy and their work is fragmented. Information is transmitted orally and through a variety of media to accomplish goals of the department and organization. In addition to personal skills, an effective manager is able to run meetings skillfully and effectively along with using processes like delegation, negotiation, and collaboration to accomplish results.

In the concluding section of this chapter, communication within the organizational structure and as a professional representative of the organization and profession are explored. Within organizations formal and informal patterns of communication exist (Robbins & Decenzo,

2001). Protocols structure interactions. Barriers exist. Strategies that enhance organizational interactions also contribute to effective interpersonal and managerial communications that ensure employees have the information necessary to maintain and improve service quality. Therapeutic recreation managers represent their departments and organizations professionally. Oral and written interactions with associates, colleagues, clients, and caregivers leave an impression. Being able to effectively represent a department both verbally and in writing is a skill all managers need to utilize.

Communication Channels

Prior to sending a message, the manager must determine the message's purpose and how best to deliver the message. Additionally, Guffey (2004) suggested there are five factors a manager needs to consider prior to delivering a message: "the importance of the message, the amount and speed of feedback required, the necessity of a permanent record, the cost of the channel and, the degree of formality desired" (pp. 32–33). After determining the purpose of a message and reviewing these five factors, the manager selects the most appropriate channel. Table 13.1 (p. 186) outlines the different channels and their best use.

With the appropriate channel selected the manager then composes the message. Whether it is an oral or a written message the old adage of the five *P*s—prior planning prevents poor performance—is important to keep in mind. The next sections of this chapter consider oral and written communication skills.

Personal and Interpersonal Communication

The business of helping is a human enterprise that uses day-to-day communication skills. According to Austin (2004), the higher one's level of personal communication, the higher the potential to function effectively as a helping professional. The manager who does not communicate properly will have an ineffective department. Managers and therapists communicate formally and informally through a number of media. The intent of this communication is to share ideas, thoughts, or emotions with each other so the meaning of the content is understood by both. Liebler, Levine, and Rothman (1992) identified four pieces to the communication process: initiation, transmission, reception, and feedback. The sender begins interaction by transmitting the message formally or informally to a receiver. A receiver acts upon the message from a particular frame of reference through feedback. This feedback, according to Liebler, Levine, and Rothman (1992), acknowledges the information in the form of acceptance, nonacceptance, modification, or suppression. The effectiveness of communication is influenced overall by assumptions, perceptions, feelings, past experiences, present surroundings, and interpretations of the sender and receiver as well as the context in which the communication occurs. Understanding the ideas of others is essential to delivery of quality health and human services.

Communication Avenues and Influences

In formal communication each party is aware of the avenues used, whereas in informal communication one or the other party is unaware of the avenues being used or that a message even exists. This latter form of communication is referred to as the grapevine or the political context of communication. As listed by Robbins (1995), formal communication takes place through verbal and nonverbal communication, behavior, written documents, and technology (e.g., electronic mail).

Formal Communication

Verbal Communication

Verbal communication is perceived as a quick way to transmit information and as a way to build trust and support. In contrast to other avenues, the spoken word conveys a personal caring. Day-to-day managerial interactions rely heavily on the spoken word. A verbal exchange is comprised of voice, message, response content, and methods used to transmit and receive information. Emotions are expressed orally. Tone; word choice; use of silence, accents, and intonation; speed of delivery; clarity; and articulation are verbal exchange factors. Genetics and culture affect these qualities. Additionally, as noted by Liebler, Levine, and Rothman (1992), professional preparation trains managers and therapists to deliver information in a certain fashion.

Word meanings vary with the setting in which they are used. For example, boardroom and hallway conversations have different connotations. Content is also affected by the positions held by the receiver and sender. Famil-

Table 13.1
Choosing Communication Channels

Channel	Best Use
Face-to-face	When you want to be persuasive, deliver bad news, or share a personal message.
Telephone call	When you need to deliver or gather information quickly, when nonverbal cues are unimportant, and when you cannot meet in person.
Voice mail message	When you wish to leave important or routine information that the receiver can respond to when convenient.
Fax	When your message must cross time zones or international boundaries, when a written record is significant, or when speed is important
E-mail	When you need feedback but not immediately. Insecurity makes it problematic for personal, emotional, or private messages. Effective for communicating with a large, dispersed audience.
Face-to-face group meeting	When group decisions and consensus are important. Inefficient for merely distributing information.
Video or teleconference	When group consensus and interaction are important but members are geographically dispersed.
Memo	When you want a written record to explain policies clearly, discuss procedures, or collect information within an organization.
Letter	When you need a written record of correspondence with customers, the government, suppliers, or others outside an organization.
Report or proposal	When you are delivering considerable data internally or externally.

Source: Guffey, 2004

iarity with each other, the setting, and content information influence how well messages are understood. Methods used to transmit and receive information influence the meaning and understanding of messages. Talking on the phone or via teleconference is distant and not necessarily as revealing as face-to-face exchanges. Listening in a crowded hallway versus a private office introduces different distortions. Moreover, one's ability to listen and attend is influenced by communication methods. Listening as a message is transmitted by phone demands less attentiveness than listening during face-to-face interactions.

Nonverbal Communication

Nonverbal communication accompanies oral communication and is present in body language, posture, distance, eye contact, and body movements. Interaction is initiated through nonverbal avenues, such as eye contact or gestures, then continued through oral exchanges. Phone conversations are dependent on oral exchanges; however, silence and intonation convey unspoken thoughts. Talking at an intimate distance (18 inches or less) is less formal, usually, than discussion during public distances (12 or more feet). Folded arms and legs crossed away from the speaker suggest nonreceptivity, whereas open posture toward the speaker implies acceptance. Likewise, eye contact and hand gestures connote degrees of attending and active listening. A soft-spoken voice creates a different meaning from a loud voice. Robbins and Decenzo (2001) indicated that oral communication carries a nonverbal message, which is likely to have the greatest impact on the meaning and understanding of transactions. How something is said is as significant as what is said.

Dress is another nonverbal communication form. Unwritten and written rules govern professional attire. Written rules specify colors for specific therapies or days when staff shirts are to be worn, location and type of professional identification and appropriateness of accessories or apparel regarding safety issues or organizational protocols. For example, if practitioners were to wear sandals or jewelry, consumer interactions might be affected, and if the manager were to wear casual rather than formal attire on board meeting day, the impression left might be less than the desired professional image. Impressions are created by attire and personal identification—the impact of a briefcase, business card, and lapel name pin. These impressions reflect feelings or beliefs about the department and therapeutic recreation as a profession. Social norms and work culture determine dress protocols and standards. To illustrate, if Fridays are viewed as "casual attire" days, how are clients and staff distinguished during Friday night socials? Therapists promoted to managers consider the unwritten dress codes that influence how other professionals respond to the authority of the new position. As a result "meeting room" rather than "functional activity" attire is more frequently worn.

Conscious and Unconscious Behaviors

Conscious and unconscious behaviors affect oral communication. During conscious exchanges the speaker is aware of the content, direction, and intent of the interaction. Unconscious motives and behaviors, such as desires, fears, mind set, and beliefs are "hidden," yet they affect behavior. Word selection and use do the same. For example, to say "finish the report" as opposed to saying "please finish the report by the end of the workday" projects two very different attitudes.

Written Communication

Managers not only need good oral communication skills but also sound written communication skills. A manager is expected to write reports, to write and respond to letters, and, with technology becoming more ingrained in the workplace, to use e-mail effectively. It is important as a manager to be able to effectively express yourself using appropriate grammar and writing style.

Whether writing e-mail, a report, or a response to a letter, there is a process to be used. Guffey (2004) recommended a three-phase process.

Prewriting prepares the manager to write. During this phase a manager analyzes the audience and determines the purpose for writing. To analyze the audience the manager considers who the primary reader is, what the relationship is with this person, how much the person knows about this topic and, what kind of a response the manager might expect from this person. Also, keep in mind who else might see this message. The audiences vary with writing a report for use in the hospital's accreditation study to developing a department brochure to writing a performance review. After determining the audience, the purpose for writing is determined. Guffey (2004) suggested as the message is composed the writer asks (a) Why am I sending this message? and (b) What do I want to achieve? The response to these two questions determines how information is organized and presented.

Writing involves researching, organizing, and then writing the message. When writing a specific report, all the information is collected and synthesized. After collecting the information, focus on organizing the information. Consider how quickly to address the issue: Is the point immediately addressed or introduced slowly by describing the problem, presenting evidence and ending with a solution? The final step in writing is the actual composing of the message. When composing at the computer revisions are easily made.

Revising is the third phase and involves actual revising, proofreading, and evaluating the message. After writing the first draft, the time is taken to revise the message for clarity, conciseness, tone, and readability. Should the document be reorganized? Guffey (2004) noted this is the time to improve the organization and sound of the message. Proofreading is a very important part of this phase—check for correct spelling, grammar, punctuation, and format. After writing the document, take a break before beginning the final revision—this results in "fresh eyes" for proofreading. Depending on the importance of a document, someone else may review the material before it is sent. Another way to proof your work is to read it out loud. This is a slower process and encourages the reading of each word; thus, catching any errors that might have been missed.

As noted by Robbins (1995), written documents are official, have long-term implications, and present complex information. Written documentation is as simple as a memo and as sophisticated as an annual report. The message may be as personal or informal as "enjoy your birthday off" or as formal as the action plan following a performance review. Writing commits thoughts and feelings to record; a paper trail is created that later can become "permanent binding statements" to which a manager is legally committed. Although writing tends to reduce ambiguities, the reader may have a different understanding of the written material from the writer. Telephone messages or e-mail are examples of communication in which what is written may be as significant to the message as what is not written. Understanding written communication is affected by factors such as the type and quality of handwriting or printed word, word choice, composition level and complexity, volume, organization, and presentation of the material.

Technology

Technology has enhanced communication in therapeutic recreation management and personal interactions. Through computers, cellular phones, videoconferencing, and networking, personal communiqués are transmitted more quickly over longer distances, and access to others is easier. Because several people receive one message simultaneously, the volume and number of interpersonal exchanges are increased. These forms of communication rely on the manager's ability to use and access equipment. Consequently, they are not available to the same extent at all work sites. Another concern lies with the translation of the message to written word: Is the meaning lost? Or, are there thoughts that are not articulated?

E-mail

Michael Eisner (2000), former CEO of the Walt Disney Company, observed:

E-mail is changing our behavior, our way of interacting with people, our institutions. And, it is happening incredibly fast… Because its spread so fast, it has raced ahead of our abilities to fully adapt to this new form of communication. (p. 593)

E-mail appears to be here to stay. In the workplace its primary function is to exchange messages within an organization. This means that a manager must be able to write an effective e-mail using correct grammar and formality. Many people use e-mail to communicate with family and friends. This should not be the same style of e-mail that is used in the workplace. Cute forwarded messages, emoticons, and shorthand messages using letters, such as BCNU (be seeing you), should not be used in office e-mails.

Guffey (2004) stated that two important benefits can result from well-written e-mail. First, a well-written e-mail is likely to achieve its goal. Second, a well-written document enhances one's image within the agency. A manager who writes competently and professionally may be noticed and rewarded. E-mails maybe the most commonly used communication medium. Guffey (2004, pp. 100–108) presented the following guidelines:

- *Write on a single topic.* Whether it is to solve a specific problem or attend a specified meeting, limiting the topic helps the receiver respond appropriately. If there is more than one topic contained in the e-mail, not everything may be addressed by the receiver. The subject line should clearly identify what the e-mail topic is. This will help the receiver get to the "heart" of a message immediately.

- *It is OK to use a conversational tone.* Usually e-mail is sent to people we know. Thus, using a warm and friendly tone is acceptable. There should be nothing written in an e-mail that would not be said to a person's face. Sarcasm and emotion are not found in e-mails.

- *Be concise.* E-mail should only contain what is necessary to convey meaning and be courteous. Make every effort to contain e-mail to one screen. If more space is needed, consider writing a brief cover message and using the attachment function for the longer document.

- *Use graphic highlighting.* Consider using graphic highlights (e.g., bullets, numbers, headings) to help the receiver more easily identify the important points in a message. If there are important words, use bold type or italics. Use all capital letters with caution. Never write e-mail in all capital letters; this seems to SHOUT at the receiver.

- *Do not send out anything you would not want published.* E-mail does create a permanent record and can be retrieved even after being deleted. Thus avoid writing something that is too personal, confidential, inflammatory or potentially embarrassing. Rule of thumb: Do not write something that would embarrass you if your boss, colleague, or wife/husband read it. The news is full of reports of careless and casual e-mail that have become "smoking guns" in lawsuits.

- *Do not use e-mail to avoid contact.* E-mail is not appropriate for every message. It is inappropriate for breaking bad news or resolving arguments. If what is said could hurt someone's feelings than e-mail is inappropriate. Pick up the phone or find the person for a face-to-face conversation.

- *Avoid writing e-mail in anger.* Allow a cooling off period before responding to e-mail from someone who has upset you. First, after a "cool off" your responses are more clear, and time allows for the identification of some better alternatives. Second it is always better to deal with people face to face on an emotional topic, thus enabling problems to be worked through more quickly rather than firing back and forth emotionally charged e-mail(s).

- *Do not forward spam.* Make sure your e-mails are professional when sent to your work colleagues. Although friends and family may enjoy it, your colleagues do not need to see cute pet pictures.

- *Use spell check.* If an e-mail system has spell check as an option it is important to have it turned on. Very often the fingers seem to be slower than the mind and words and letters are missed when typing.

- *Change the subject line when responding if the e-mail content changes.* Nothing is more frustrating when opening e-mail and expecting the topic to be one thing only to find it has changed. Also if a person is looking for e-mail on "assessment protocol" and it is embedded in an e-mail entitled "community outing," the important information may be lost forever.

Informal Communication

Informal (i.e., unofficial) communication occurs through informal networks or the grapevine by word-of-mouth and through electronic means (Robbins & Decenzo, 2001). It is not uncommon for the person accountable for change to be the last one to become aware of desired actions or the impact of actions on others. Rumors begin for a number of reasons: words have different meanings or are interpreted differently, time lapses occur between senders and receivers, mediums are distorted, messages are incomplete, and anxiety creates ambiguity. Less time is available on a daily basis to communicate increasing amounts of information. Further, the personal context of a message is easily lost in an informal transmission.

One reacts differently to informal networks and grapevines, and these personal reactions affect how one responds personally and professionally to messages circulated in this manner. The grapevine does, however, act as a feedback loop to help judge accuracy and appropriateness of messages. To illustrate, if the message through the grapevine was that one appears to dominate conversations, one has the opportunity to assess interactions and to adjust verbal and nonverbal contributions accordingly.

Communication Barriers

A number of conscious and unconscious barriers contribute to the meaning of exchanges being confused or misinterpreted. These interferences can originate with the sender, receiver, methods of communication, and the message itself. Robbins and Decenzo (2001) suggested that barriers to effective communication result from word usage, poor listening or attending, limited feedback, perceptual differences, role or status differentials, use of inappropriate communication methods, variances between the sender and receiver with regard to honesty, emotions, and orientation and information overload.

Word Usage

There is a tendency to believe that the words and terms used to send messages have the same meaning for the receiver. Yet, the use of language is not uniform (Robbins, 1995). Age, education, culture, and role or status tends to influence language use. Witness the various meanings the words *play* and *leisure* have for a child, adult, and a professional therapeutic recreator. Likewise, qualitative words used to describe sizes, amounts, and ranges have unique meanings to each of these groups.

Listening or Attending

Listening and attending are distorted by one's mindset, perceptual defenses, sensory overloads, and thinking about the receiver or response one anticipates. Robbins (1995) suggested that a person tends to listen for agreement and disagreement rather than for meaning. Listening involves attending, interpreting, and remembering. Consequently, environmental distractions, inability to focus on the moment at hand, and/or the sender's behavior contribute to *inactive* listening. The friend who wears a color one dislikes, the loud radio on a colleague's desk, and the desire to be elsewhere at the moment are examples of situations that cause nonlistening.

Feedback

Feedback is essential information given by the receiver to the sender that helps the sender to judge the effectiveness of the transmitted message. Feedback reveals how behavior appears to others or affects others' feelings. Without reliable evaluative feedback, one does not know if the message has been received as intended (Robbins, 1995). There are several legitimate reasons for the absence of feedback: (a) receivers may choose not to respond, (b) responses may not be forthcoming as the respondent fears the consequence of giving feedback, and (c) the time to respond may not permit adequate responses.

Perceptual Differences

Perceptual differences between senders and receivers interfere with interpretation, transmission, and understanding of meanings. Assumptions, attitudes, past experiences, expectations, cultural perspectives, educational and philosophical orientations, and family and caregiver values influence how one interprets and responds. Thus, senders and receivers view a situation from their unique perspective. To illustrate, consider the differing viewpoints held by the public and those in health and human services toward disabilities that are visually apparent and those that are "hidden."

Role or Status Differentials

One engages in behaviors that typify the roles one plays (e.g., child, mother, father, employee, employer). Roles have certain expectations, for example, mothers nurture, children respect parents, employees and employers are loyal. These role expectations create differentials and a frame of reference from which communication is interpreted. Those in professional roles use technical terms or jargon not necessarily understood by other professionals. At any given time, one assumes multiple roles that may interfere with another. For instance, the desire to be home with the family after a program has ended contributes to the recording of brief notes on client outcomes.

Selection of Communication Methods

According to Robbins (1995), communication methods vary in the richness of information transmitted. Oral, one-to-one contact is more direct, complete, and personal than e-mail or phone contact. Complex, ambiguous messages are better committed to writing; however, time and resources may preclude accurate reporting. Out of frustration a request is committed to writing when a verbal reminder should bring about the desired change. One might say "thank you" when a letter in a personnel file

was justified. The nature of the message also influences selection of the communication method. However, these are not always matched, and issues arise as a consequence of the incongruity between content and process.

Sender and Receiver Variances

A number of factors contribute to the inability to be honest and open regarding communication. One may desire to avoid confrontation that causes someone to become upset or resistive. One may say what others want to hear to gain their support or a political advantage. One may temporarily withhold communication to allow for time to gather additional information or to calm tempers. Increased tension and creation of additional communication barriers is a consequence of not being open and timely with communication. Openness and honesty are compromised by extreme emotions, such as frustration and anger or excitement and happiness. As noted by Robbins (1995), one is likely to disregard rational thinking processes when these emotions are present. Time, place, situational set, and people in the environment influence emotional response and how messages are received and sent. The nature of the therapeutic recreation work environment is supportive to open communication, yet the practitioner may need to repeat the information in a formal meeting so that the consumer grasps the significance of the recommended intervention.

Information Overload

Individuals have a finite capacity for processing information. "When information exceeds our processing capacity," the result is information overload (Robbins & Decenzo, 2001, p. 381). When managers have more information than can be sorted or used, the tendency is to ignore, pass over, or forget. In some instances, managers quit processing until the overload dissipates. The demand of keeping up with e-mail, faxes, phone calls, and professional activities contributes to information overload and results in the loss of information and less effective communication (Robbins & Decenzo, 2001).

Senders and receivers are preoccupied with their respective orientations. Each is concerned with achieving his or her own objectives or sending and receiving messages that leave others with positive impressions. One becomes insensitive to the needs of others when one promotes the self. Communication is most effective when the sender anticipates how the receiver will respond and what the meaning of the message will be for the receiver.

Effective Communication Techniques

Effective communication results when the sender and receiver interpret the intended meaning of the message similarly and respond accordingly. Although some communication blocks, such as word usage and perceptual differences, are less pliable, techniques like feedback and active listening are improved with practice. Objective analysis also improves communication. As reported by Liebler, Levine, and Rothman (1992), objectivity involves observing, attending, responding to requests, and checking information. A skilled observer separates personal interpretations and perceptions from the reality of an event. Awareness of self permits one to understand a message as intended in its original meaning. A person who attends listens actively and focuses on what is said rather than what the response is likely to be. An active listener responds to the true—conscious and unconscious—meaning of a message. Further, communiqués are presented with differing agendas. Objective listeners sort through the layers to discover the real meanings of the exchanges. Finally, by requesting feedback, a listener checks for accuracy of the interpretation. Clarification, paraphrasing, and summarizing are techniques used to check information.

The personal characteristics of therapeutic helpers are believed to be effective in promoting communication (Liebler, Levine & Rothman, 1992). Qualities such as genuineness, empathy, caring, humor, congruence, respect, and trust enhance communication processes. Effective helpers and communicators display compatibility between what is known, how it is expressed, and the actions taken. They are true to their own feelings and accept the feelings of others; thus, information is shared openly. Respect and a mutual commitment are evident, and the significance, uniqueness, and contributions of each are affirmed.

Feedback

Misunderstandings occur without feedback. Feedback is a way of giving help. Without feedback, one is unaware of how one's communication, verbal or nonverbal, affects others or how one's behavior appears to others. Feedback is confirming or correcting. With either, one may choose or not choose to change or improve oneself and the quality of one's services. As suggested by Denton (1987) and Robbins and Decenzo (2001), several techniques improve the effectiveness of feedback:

- Specific rather than general statements are more accurate and lead to action (e.g., "Your reports will be read by colleagues when better organized" rather than "Your paperwork is sloppy").

- Action rather than inaction statements motivate change (e.g., "Is there a way that you could improve report writing?" rather than "There does not seem to be a way to improve the situation").

- Descriptive rather than evaluative statements help to clarify meaning (e.g., "When you do not document your observations, the team is unaware" rather than "Your documentation does not reflect client outcomes"). In other words, keep feedback impersonal.

- Feedback that presents options or is goal-directed is more likely to be received than input that does not permit choices (e.g., "Could you chart daily or work with a cotherapist?" rather than "Entries are required for each session").

- Feedback is given immediately or within a short interval between the behavior and receipt of feedback. During a time lapse, emotions build and more information is "stored up" than one is capable of accurately sending or receiving.

Active Listening

Active listeners receive and understand the whole message. Several factors cause people not to be active listeners. These include judging or speculating on the speaker's motive, planning responses while spoken too, interrupting the speaker with information that finishes the thought, and sensory overload. Additionally, as noted by Denton (1987), past experiences create a set of expectations that may either help one to understand the new ideas or cause one to mold the information to the present situation. Physical health or medical condition may discourage active listening as well. To improve active listening, one should become aware of these blocks and distortions.

The active listener understands the communication from the speaker's point of view. Robbins and Decenzo (2001) noted that this is accomplished by listening with intensity, empathy, acceptance, and a willingness to assume responsibility for completeness. Concentration permits the active listener to place each new piece of information into the context of preceding information. Empathetic listeners step into the "shoes" of the speaker suspending personal thoughts and feelings. Active listeners withhold judgment on the content until the speaker finishes. Further, Robbins and Decenzo (2001) suggested active listeners take actions necessary to receive the intended meaning of the communication (e.g., ask the speaker to restate the message).

Knippen and Green (1994) described four techniques used by effective active listeners: restatement, summarization, responding to nonverbal cues, and responding to feelings. Active listeners restate or repeat messages by paraphrasing in their own words what the speaker has said (e.g., "What I hear you saying is that you prefer briefer, more frequent meetings"). Summarizing occurs when the important points of the speaker are listed at the conclusion of the conversation as occurs during assessment interviews. The active listener often acknowledges and verbalizes nonverbal cues by stating the effect of nonverbal messages (e.g., "I hear you saying you don't mind adjusting your schedule yet your slow response time indicates otherwise"). Responding to feelings permits verbalization about perceptions and unexpressed feelings (e.g., An astute manager aware of staff concern about client progress might state "I see the lack of client progress and motivation are contributing to your frustrations").

A number of specific active listening strategies can be used to enhance communication effectiveness during conversations. They are summarized as follows:

1. Metzger (1982) suggested the judicious use of silence. When questions are asked at the beginning of conversations, allow silence to motivate response.

2. Open-ended questions allow the respondent to truly present the type of information perceived as important (Metzger, 1982).

3. Emotional filters cause misinterpretation when one feels strongly about a subject. Metzger (1982) suggested a third party or resource person be asked to join a conversation to facilitate objectivity.

4. Metzger (1982) noted most people listen for facts to the exclusion of feelings and the speaker's point of view. Paying attention to the way the speaker delivers the message clues the respondent into the speaker's true meaning. Impressions are checked by asking questions after the speaker concludes.

5. As noted by Robbins (1995), eye contact with a speaker focuses the respondent's attention, reduces the likelihood of being distracted, and encourages the speaker.

6. According to Denton (1987), a number of nonverbal techniques or backchannels indicate interest. An active listener uses affirmative head nods, facial gestures, and attending actions such as "uh-huh" to denote interest.

7. When time is limited, rather than interrupting the conversation, the stage is set to continue at another time (e.g., "Excuse me, I apologize for disrupting your thoughts. Could we plan to complete this conversation when time permits both of us to concentrate?"; Robbins, 1995).

8. A conversation is viewed as a "whole" rather than as separate pieces. Questions are asked that ensure understanding of the entire puzzle (e.g., "You have shared several ideas… Are we looking at the need to restructure program offerings?").

9. Confront biases that prohibit accurate evaluation of the message source. As illustrated by Robbins (1995), appearance, speaker credibility, and personal mannerisms cause one to draw premature conclusions about the speaker.

10. Statements that begin with "I" clarify, show ownership of conversations, receipt of messages, and reflect feelings, for example, "I understand the need for additional time to complete the project" (Denton, 1987).

11. Robbins (1995) recommended thinking before acting. What outcomes are expected? The message should be organized, and a method of delivery chosen that is congruent with desired outcomes and the receiver's needs and resources (e.g., e-mail is quick yet does not permit "rich" exchanges).

12. Language choice is critical. Jargon and professional terms facilitate meaning for those who understand but cause confusion for those unfamiliar with the terms (Robbins, 1995).

13. Actions give meanings to words. When words and actions are congruent, they act as motivators so credibility and trust can develop. Relationships are strained when actions do not back up words.

According to Robbins (1995) conversation may have at least six messages:

1. What the speaker means to say.

2. What the speaker actually says.

3. What the listener hears.

4. What the listener thinks he or she hears.

5. What the listener says.

6. What the speaker thinks the listener said.

Facilitation skills, especially the ability to communicate warmth and to be an active listener, are essential to helping and leading (Carter, Van Andel & Robb, 2003). Assertiveness training, values clarification exercises, and role-playing are methods to cultivate awareness of personal communication processes. A first-line manager's personal communication skills become evident during supervisory-subordinate relationships.

Communication in a Multicultural Workplace

As our world "becomes smaller" the health care facility is becoming a microcosm of multiculturalism. The manager works with consumers and other professionals who are from different cultures and backgrounds. Every country and, depending on the size of a country, region has its own common heritage, joint experience and shared learning. Combined, these shared experiences referred to as "culture" impact what we do and say. Consider the impact of cultural differences like eye contact, body language, and personal space on the therapeutic relationship (Austin, 2004). Miscommunication may result from cultural differences. Guffey (2004) identified the following strategies a manager may employ to reduce cultural miscommunication:

- *Use simple English.* Sentences should be short and to the point. Avoid using puns, slang, jargon, sarcasm or references to sports and the military. Especially watch the use of idioms such as "under the weather" or "talk a blue streak."

- *Speak slowly and enunciate clearly.* Speak slowly, using more pauses than normal. Talk slower, not louder.

- *Encourage accurate feedback.* Ask the listener to paraphrase what you said. A simple "head nod" may not reflect understanding. Paraphrase back to the speaker what you think he or she said when information is given to you.

- *Check frequently for comprehension.* Move to a second point only after you know the person understands what has been said or you understand what you have been told.

- *Observe eye messages.* If a person's eyes appear to be wandering or "glaze" over; the person probably does not understand what is being said.

- *Accept blame if a misunderstanding results.* If a misunderstanding does occur, graciously accept the blame for not clearly making a point.

- *Listen without interrupting.* Let others finish their sentences themselves. Try not to jump in and complete their thoughts or answer a question they have just begun to ask. According to Guffey (2004) it is believed that North Americans listen too little and talk too much.

- *Remember to smile.* A smile can ease all kinds of communication problems. It is thought to be the single most understood and most useful form of communication.

A manager will communicate with colleagues and consumers from a variety of cultures. It is important that a manager has the sensitivity and leadership skills to communicate with effectiveness and respect in the workplace.

Even when dealing with staff and stakeholders from the same cultural background, it requires administrative skill to decide whether to send an electronic or paper memo or to speak face-to-face or not to communicate on the matter (Marquis & Huston, 2003). In a multicultural healthcare setting, this complexity is greater. Additional suggestions that promote effective communication include (a) recognizing that culture is transmitted through communication, (b) using respect and ethical practices as the central core of working relationships, (c) avoiding slang or references to persons of particular ethnicity and using first or last names or titles differently infers comparison to "normative standards," and (d) accepting the uniqueness of each individual rather than expecting people of the same backgrounds to behave similarly creates respect and value for each communiqué.

Managerial Communication

The typical workday of a first-line therapeutic recreation manager consists of numerous meetings, informal interactions, one-on-one supervisory conversations, personal contacts with clients and caregivers, and colleague contact via phone, fax, and e-mail. Instead of following a detailed schedule, supervisors find they spend the day reacting to people and situations. Marquis and Huston (2003) and Robbins (1995) noted that the majority of time on a particular workday is spent communicating. Effective managers learn to separate important from insignificant messages and to manage their time so that disruptions do not prevent them from achieving department goals. Sometimes it seems that much of a manger's time is spent in meetings; running effective meetings demonstrates the abilities of a manager.

The power invested in a managerial position gives the first-line manager the authority to act through employees to achieve unit and organizational outcomes. Through processes such as delegation, negotiation, and collaboration, the work of practitioners, volunteers and seasonal employees is facilitated. Supervisory interactions do result in criticism, complaints, and confrontation, which can be managed to gain support for accomplishing work initiatives. The effectiveness of supervisor-employee exchanges determines the efficiency with which the unit operates to achieve its goals.

Social Context of Managerial Communication

A manager's communication is embedded in the social context or culture of the employing organization. Consequently, exchanges are judged within an organizational climate. Formal avenues of communication and the grapevine are channels of information exchange. For example, protocol may dictate how and when upper-level decisions on benefit packages or new services are to be communicated by the supervisor, while the grapevine simultaneously generates rumors speculating withholding and service adjustments. Managers are challenged to respond to organization protocols and to meet the information needs of department employees. As suggested by Marquis and Huston (2003, p. 338), the manager should assess the cultural context in which organizational communiqués take place:

- Who communicates with whom in the organization?

- Is the communication timely?

- Does communication within the formal organization concur with formal lines of authority?

- What modes of communication are used?

Managers consider a number of factors that affect organizational communication, such as

- The number of levels communication must filter through and how spatial distance affect communication.

- As the number of employees increases, the quantity of communication generally increases.

- Different subcultures have their own value systems that result in different translations of messages from management.

- Organizations are in a constant state of flux and it is difficult to communicate decisions to all people impacted due to constant change.

- Some men and women communicate and use language differently. Gender is a significant factor in organizational communication. (Marquis & Huston, 2003)

Effective Meetings

Meetings matter because that's where an organization's culture perpetuates itself. A person's ability to develop ideas, to motivate, and to move people and ideas to positive action is possibly the most critical asset in any career (Streibel, 2003). If a manager is able to effectively run a meeting, people will recognize that person's abilities. Thus, the ability to effectively run a meeting is a necessary skill for any manager to develop. There are specific strategies a manager may use to plan and run effective meetings. Many people are surprised to learn that any meeting must be planned, whether it is a treatment team meeting, a protocol development meeting or a strategic planning meeting; it does not just happen. Any meeting worth holding is worth planning. As Benjamin Franklin once said, "By failing to prepare, you are preparing to fail." The following are steps for planning a meeting:

1. Develop, finalize, and distribute an agenda.

When establishing an agenda, the manager needs to include date and time, place, purpose, and items to be discussed. If people have been invited to speak to specific agenda items, their names should be listed next to the agenda item. Some people like to follow *Robert's Rules of Order* when writing an agenda and include general topics such as committee reports, old business, and new business, with specific items listed under each. However, there are no specific rules for preparing an agenda as long as all topics are listed or added. It is important that as a manager you prepare your group prior to the meeting, so the agenda should be distributed no later than two weeks prior to the meeting and include any reports or materials that participants should read in advance. If it is an ongoing meeting, minutes from the last meeting should be included.

2. Determine the purpose for the meeting.

What do you want this meeting to do? If you are meeting because you always meet on Fridays or because you haven't met in a month, this is *not* a purpose. Perhaps a meeting is not the best way for communicating; if you simply need to relay information perhaps e-mail or a report would be more effective. Every meeting should be justified and if it is not justified, it should not be held.

3. Set goals for the meeting.

Based on the purpose, goals/outcomes for the meeting should be established. These goals don't need to be formally written; perhaps just listing topics would provide enough guidance for the meeting and next to the topics suggest methods for handling the topic. Make sure that if a decision needs to be made, enough information will be provided and also predetermine how that decision will be made. Streibel (2003, p. 19) suggested four ways to make decisions: *managerial* (i.e., the manager ends up making the decision), *majority or plurality vote* (i.e., the largest number for or against an issue determines what will happen), *consensus* (i.e., everyone agrees to an action), and *delegation* (i.e., certain members of the group make the decision).

4. Sequence and allocate time for the items.

When sequencing the items, look for the natural ebb and flow. Structure the agenda to keep the meeting from getting bogged down or burning out. Structure the meeting to vary the pace, maintain attention, and sustain involvement. Each item should have a designated amount of time thus an efficient manager should be able to determine the amount of time necessary for the meeting. Include five to ten minutes to open the meeting and 10–15 minutes to review the accomplishments of the meeting.

5. Determine who should meet.

There is nothing worse than sitting through a meeting that does not have any meaning to you. A manager should be stingy with invitations to meetings, invite only those people necessary to achieve the goals of the meeting. Streibel (2003) suggested a manager ask the question "How do you expect this person to contribute to the meeting?" If a person is unable to contribute because nothing within his or her role is being discussed, maybe that person doesn't need to be invited.

After deciding who should meet, determine if there are people outside the department or unit who need to be invited. Assign any specific responsibilities or give any requests to these people far enough ahead of the meeting for them to adequately prepare. Also, prior to the meeting the role of secretary or scribe should be assigned so that person is ready to take appropriate notes.

6. Determine when and where you should meet.

Time and place are very important to the running of an effective meeting. A manager may have few choices of when to meet depending on the schedule of the people needed at the meeting. However, a good manager will try to schedule a meeting either when everyone is free or, if that is impossible, when the people essential to the meeting are available. According to Arrendondo (2000) the majority of people who work days have two peak periods: 9:30 to 11:30 in the morning and 3:00 to 5:00 in the afternoon. During these times most people are at their creative and productive best.

When determining where to meet, a manager should consider the following when choosing a room: it should comfortably accommodate the number of people attending the meeting, it must allow for the proper atmosphere, and it must have adequate lighting. Prior to choosing a room

the manager checks with the people attending the meeting to determine if there are any audiovisual needs that might impact room selection.

7. Run the meeting.

As the manager it is up to you to start the meeting on time even if all invited persons have yet to arrive. At the stated time the manager gives a brief overview of the meeting, including the goal and length of the meeting, background or topics or problems, potential solutions/constraints, the proposed agenda, and any specific rules to be followed. If a person has not been identified to take the minutes, now is the time.

After the introduction the manager should say as little as possible. Remember the purpose of a meeting is to exchange views, so no one should dominate. When a topic comes up that takes the group off topic but is important, let the group know that it will be discussed at another time, possibly at the next meeting, and then go back to the original topic. As the group reaches consensus on a topic, the manager should summarize the position and make sure everyone agrees and then move on to the next topic.

End the meeting at the agreed-on time. The manager should summarize what has been decided, who is going to do what, and by what time. At this time it may be necessary to ask for volunteers to take responsibility for completing action items agreed to in the meeting. Some people use the technique of "once around the table" as a closure technique; everyone at the table gives his or her interpretation of what was accomplished at the meeting. The next meeting date and time should be set and everyone should be assured that they will be receiving minutes of the meeting.

8. Follow-up of the meeting.

The manager needs to ensure that the minutes are accurate and distributed within a couple days of the meeting. Also the manager should make sure that what was agreed on at the meeting is accomplished. Thus the manager may need to call or send out reminder e-mails to ensure that tasks are accomplished.

Running effective meetings is an important managerial task. Effective meeting management encourages professionals to attend and demonstrates effectiveness as a manager.

Delegation

To accomplish the work of the department the manager delegates responsibility to employees to make decisions and to take actions toward accomplishing unit goals. Delegation shifts "power" from the first-line manager to an employee. First-line managers may hesitate to relinquish a portion of their "authority" for a number of reasons (e.g.,

I can do the job better, time is of the essence, staff is inexperienced, work loads will become imbalanced). Consequently, they may *underdelegate*. *Overdelegation* occurs when the first-line manager relinquishes inordinate amounts of authority. A number of reasons such as dislike for certain paperwork tasks, feelings of being overworked, awareness that certain employees appear to be interested in specific tasks, and the manager's own inexperience in a management position contribute to overdelegation. Hansten and Washburn (1992) recommended consideration of the following four factors to determine when and what to delegate:

1. *The task*. Certain tasks remain the responsibility of first-line managers (e.g., personnel and fiscal matters, policy-related actions). Staff carries out direct service interactions such as initially responding to client and caregiver inquiries and soliciting programmatic input.

2. *The employee*. Employee job specifications, privileging protocols, and plans of operation identify who has specific knowledge, skills, and abilities (KSAs) and is to perform certain responsibilities. For instance, asking a volunteer rather than a department employee to dispense medications on an outing would be inappropriate and outside the purview of a volunteer's job duties.

3. *The message and the medium*. Written communication is used with significant messages, such as documentation of client outcomes, whereas e-mail or a hallway conversation is appropriate to gain an update on a coming special event.

4. *The feedback*. Evaluation during and after task completion ensures accountability and proper employee recognition. Feedback gives the manager a status report while acknowledging the employee's contribution to department goals. Thus, when tasks are assigned, time and resources are also planned to gain input.

Managers are increasingly leading by empowering their employees through participation in decisions that direct, coordinate, and control their work (Robbins & Decenzo, 2001). Delegation is the primary means a supervisor has to empower employees. Delegation is driven by the need to make quick decisions and to relieve the demands of increased load caused by the larger span of control managers' experience. A first-line manager accepts and expects mistakes within this process, but he or she institutes feedback controls so that the costs of errors do not exceed the learning that occurs (Robbins, 1995).

Redesigning job specifications is another process used to delegate. This occurs as positions are vacated, when mergers occur, and through restructuring. Job specifications are rewritten during retreats with employees and with design of employee professional development plans. As outlined by Robbins (1995), effective delegation is mutual: The task is clearly delineated, the employee has the authority and resources to accomplish the task, the employee has the competence and has agreed to accept the responsibility, other employees are informed of the delegation, the employee is expected to respond to problems that arise as the task is carried out, and feedback controls assure that the task will be completed on time and to the desired specification.

Negotiation

Managers communicate through negotiation. Effective negotiation sets up a win-win work environment. An effective negotiator recognizes the needs and objectives of others while expressing in a professional manner points of view that facilitate achievement of unit goals. Negotiation skills are used during performance reviews, employee coaching, conflict resolution, and planning quality and safety improvement programs. Official negotiations occur with collective bargaining and contract agreements. On a daily basis, the first-line manager negotiates for meeting times, program space or areas, employee benefits, and client contact time. Each of these encounters involves distribution of resources among work units to accomplish outcomes. The quality of manager-employee relationships and relationships with other organizational units is impacted by the manager's ability to look for solutions to promote positive outcomes among all parties.

Viewing an issue as one to be resolved jointly enhances the probability of a win-win situation. When a win-lose situation is created, those who lose become resentful while those who win may use power inappropriately; either condition is counterproductive to long-term working relations among people and organizational units. A problem-solving approach creates win-win situations (i.e., mutually define the problem, look for alternatives, select and implement the most feasible option, and evaluate and plan for follow-up). Robbins (1995) suggested the following guidelines as issues are negotiated:

• Consider the needs, interests, and strategies of all those affected by the situation.

• Consider the significance of the issue to the operation of the department and the needs of the unit's constituents (e.g., How critical is the pay raise or van access to employee morale or client programming?).

- Think small and positive. When initial overtures reflect reconciliation and agreement, others are also more likely to result in give-and-take.

- Depersonalize issues so that perceptions do not distort communication. Real issues are identified so feelings and misinformation don't become "fog" factors.

- Negotiating is a continuous process of informing and monitoring outcomes. Professionals agree to disagree professionally. Avenues to ensure continuous exchanges are established (e.g., weekly briefings).

- When third parties mediate, confidentiality of information is cautiously regarded.

Collaboration

Collaboration is the outcome of win-win situations. Robbins (1995) characterized collaboration as involving open discussions, active listening, understanding and identifying differences, and deliberating over all possible solutions. Team building and networking are collaborative. These efforts have become more critical in health and human services as a result of reduced resources, briefer intervention periods, increased accountability demands and attention to measuring outcomes, and the ongoing impact of change on service quality and improvements.

Managers empower staff by creating collaborative environments in which staff has the support and resources to react to and to change events. This occurs through communication that fosters feelings of trust, risk taking, openness, equity, and opportunity finding. According to Stevens and Campion (1994) several features define collaborative communication, including the following:

- Communication is behavior or event focused rather than "personal."

- Messages are specific rather than general, descriptive rather than evaluative, and make comparisons to objective standards rather than subjective standards.

- Congruence is evident among what collaborators do and say.

- A manager's messages validate staff feelings and decisions (e.g., they do not convey superiority or rigidity of position).

- Encounters are conjunctive, allowing everyone an opportunity to speak and be perceived as competent.

- Each party takes responsibility and is held accountable for its ideas and actions.

- Techniques that avoid conformity to majority opinions, such as brainstorming, nominal group techniques and simulations, facilitate change and empowerment.

- Discussions are scheduled when facts are fresh. Investigation and documentation prior to exchange save time and aggravation.

- Personal biases are confronted to dissipate strong feelings that could distort communication.

Successful collaboration depends on cohesion and dedication to a service mission that reflects common values. Managers create linkages among their staff that promote cooperation, respect, and integration of individual talents so that collective achievement of goals enables unit change.

Criticism, Complaints, and Confrontation

Although the desire is to create win-win situations (see Approaches to Conflict Resolution, Ch. 10, p.153), managerial exchanges and actions do result in criticism, complaints, and confrontation. These occur for a number of reasons, but primarily because no one is perfect all the time. Further, these outcomes need not always be perceived as negative because they are valuable self-assessment tools. The manager's challenge is to identify underlying issues or needs and to redirect energies toward effective encounters. Managers also separate the significant from the insignificant to identify those requiring responses.

This profession is naturally more vulnerable to criticism, complaints, and confrontation because one is on the "front lines" working with those who have health and well-being needs. Fear, frustration, and anxiety contribute to complaints, criticism, and confrontations. According to Deering (1993), practitioners make critical decisions in high-stress situations that do not always bring the desired success or help. A first-line therapeutic recreation manager is in the middle of the communication loop between upper-level managers who have the resources or authority and staff who use these resources to achieve organizational goals. This position requires interpreting communiqués from two viewpoints, which may or may not be congruent. A therapeutic recreation manager, therefore, is the potential recipient of criticism, complaints, and confrontation for a number of reasons and from a variety of sources.

A first-line manager must model ways to give and receive criticism, complaints, and confrontation to promote constructive outcomes. Complaints arise for a number of reasons. As Davidhizar (1991) noted, complaints may be an attempt to meet information needs, express discomfort, and gain control, or as the result of an effort to seek clarity in confusing situations. Criticism is caused by a negative evaluation of personal actions and is usually considered unpleasant (Davidhizar & Wysong, 1992). Confrontation results from discrepancies between performance and expectation. According to several authors (Davidhizar, 1991; Davidhizar & Wysong, 1992; Deering, 1993), the manager may elect to receive and respond in a number of ways to promote positive outcomes from criticism, complaints, and confrontational situations. The following list highlights some of these ways:

- Confidentiality promotes an atmosphere conducive to disclosing feelings (Davidhizar, 1991).

- Active listening enables the manager to listen to the verbal and nonverbal message and respond to the *whole*. A response like "I agree with you as do other staff" may be enough to enable the manager and staff member to cope with the situation.

- Credibility of the involved parties can be maintained by investigating, determining the real problem, and deliberating alternatives.

- To avoid escalation of the problem and embarrassment to those involved, consideration is given to the timing and location of intervention (Deering, 1993). When intervention does occur, the problem behavior and the desired behavior are identified so that the employee is able to regain control and to feel positive about self and work.

- When employees participate in actions that affect their responsibilities, job satisfaction tends to increase and negative input decreases. Employee confidence and cooperation is gained by explaining *why* and *what for*.

- Responses are presented in a manner of "kind firmness" and expectations are stated concretely with specific examples of acceptable and unacceptable responses.

- Even when formal grievances have been filed, the manager should respond with consistency and respect. Responses are nonthreatening and "save face" for the manager and employee. A request for feedback or an apology help the manager to gain additional evaluative information and to handle feelings of inadequacy that may have been projected onto staff.

- Therapeutic recreation managers work in stressful environments. Humor is a constructive mechanism that promotes communication. Davidhizar and Wysong (1992) suggested that an appropriately timed laugh creates avenues to exchange perceptions and interpretations with others while helping take the error more lightly.

- Practitioners tend to respond to fair challenges. The key to change is moving from small points of consensus toward overall agreement. The competent manager agrees with valid complaints, criticism, and confrontation and sets the expectations so that each change or accomplishment is acknowledged and rewarded. Sometimes public reward is all that is needed to gain positive momentum.

A prudent manager accepts complaints, criticism, and confrontation as an inevitable part of first-line supervisory duties. By modeling constructive ways to receive and respond to these situations, the first-line manager helps staff to gain insight into their own behaviors. Professional actions can correct the erring, consider personal communication styles, and initiate change so that problem behaviors are changed into constructive relations.

Through delegation, negotiation, and collaboration the manager empowers staff to carry out department goals. A positive response to criticism, complaints, and confrontations facilitates the risk taking necessary to change and improve. The first-line manager assumes a key role in organizational communication that usually implies a position somewhere between upward and downward channels.

Organizational and Professional Communication

To achieve organizational goals effective communication is essential. Formal communications are sanctioned and occur through meetings, memos, executive sessions, and individual management-staff supervisory sessions. Informal communication takes place through the grapevine and may or may not promote the goals of the organization. Organizational communication patterns have become more complex in health and human services. Factors like professional specialization, decentralization of service centers, use of cross-disciplinary teams, corporate mergers, and reductions in the number of mid-managers present challenges to the transmission of messages in a timely manner to appropriate personnel.

The first-line manager is a central figure who represents therapeutic recreation within the organization and to public and professional audiences external to the organization. Employees expect the manager to be informed and are quick to realize when their supervisor is "mouthing" organizational policy or has been bypassed in the communication chain. First-line managers direct and/or redirect formal communications from upper-level management. In their positions, first-line therapeutic recreation managers inform and educate department staff, organization employees, clients, caregivers, and colleagues about the mission of unit services and scope of professional practice. Through research, evaluation, presentations, and publication of written materials, the therapeutic recreation manager conveys the essence of the profession at the work site, within the community, and to the profession at large. This advocacy role is evident in management meetings, at community-wide special events, and during professional leadership functions.

Organizational Communication

Formal communication within an organization is directional and supportive of organizational goals. Usually, a hierarchy of roles guides the direction of communication (e.g., a first-line manager normally does not walk into the chief executive officer's office unannounced to request additional storage space). Formal verbal communication occurs at management meetings; board, committee, and team meetings; staff training and development sessions and meetings; and in strategic planning sessions, budget hearings, and public forums. Nonverbal formal communication is written or transmitted through goal statements, manuals, executive orders or directives, employee direct mailings, paycheck inserts, flyers, e-mail, bulletin boards, and training session handouts. As identified by Liebler, Levine, and Rothman (1992), informal communication is not necessarily directional and may circumvent formal channels. Gossip and rumors are not always accurate but they result from situations important to the employee (Robbins, 1995). Rumors persist until expectations causing the uncertainties are fulfilled and anxieties reduced. Managers use the grapevine as a barometer and feedback mechanism to judge success of formal communication and to identify relevant employee concerns. The informal network tends to be more accurate in an open rather than in an authoritative culture (Robbins & Decenzo, 2001).

Blocks to Organizational Communication

As with personal and interpersonal communication, a number of factors block or distort organizational communication. Liebler, Levine, and Rothman (1992) noted that the grapevine and a number of other factors associated with groups of people working together day-to-day in a structured environment influence communication, including the following:

- *Language.* Jargon or technical terms used by the practitioner may be unfamiliar to upper-level administrators or colleagues from other health and human service professions.

- *Unconscious motives.* Staff have thoughts or feelings based on real and/or perceived events that interfere with their ability to view the current events and communications from an objective perspective (e.g., previous budget cuts affect willingness to risk change and innovation).

- *Status and position.* Real and perceived differences in rank, title, and physical location of divisions or departments inhibit exchanges and interactions.

- *Organization size and structure.* The larger the organization the greater the number of contacts or channels through which messages are transmitted. Within self-governing teams and participatory management roles, the diversity of responsibilities assumed by managers and staff contribute to increasing numbers of employees becoming part of communication networks.

- *Logistical factors.* Support factors such as space, availability of technology and computers, skill and resources of available administrative assistants, work schedules, location of direct services in relation to management, and time permitted for clerical work affect the nature of face-to-face interactions, written communication, and feedback.

- *Work culture and environment.* Rapid client turn around or dramatic increases in the number of clients with diverse, multiple needs and severe deficits creates staff frustration that inhibits communication. When the intensity of the work varies with seasonal changes or client turnover, communication becomes labored and distorted as a result of staff stress and pressure.

- *Employee composition.* Each age group, gender, and culture brings unique features to the work environment. Values, beliefs, experiences, and expectations vary when there are employees from various age cohorts, cultures, and genders working together.

Improving Organizational Communication

Centrality of the manager's role to the flow of communication requires that conscious actions be taken to develop linkages throughout the organization. Strategies used to facilitate organizational networking include the following:

- The manager gains the confidence of others by remaining impartial and consistent, responding promptly to requests, and representing the interests of department employees to other management levels and throughout the organization.

- Accurate information is transmitted between levels. If communication bypasses levels or goes through informal channels, it is acknowledged.

- Individual efforts and the work of the department are recognized publicly and before upper management levels.

- The manager impresses on the staff that ineffective communication can mean wasted time and resources. Staff also is made aware that communication is subject to organizational controls as are other organizational functions (e.g., fundraising, marketing). This helps employees understand why compliance with protocols and proper use of communication tools enhance the image of the department.

- The manager uses multiple communication methods through which messages are transmitted so that the meanings benefit from the impact of repetition and everyone who needs to hear the message will.

Organizational communication is also enhanced by careful planning and analysis of formal and informal exchanges. Planning and evaluating the transmission of written documents and documentation improves the effectiveness of message sending and receiving. When forms are used properly and reports completed in a timely manner, others view the department positively. All persons associated with a situation are informed of the outcomes (e.g., minutes of staff meetings sent to upper-level management garner support and awareness). The appearance of official documents leaves an impression that influences responsiveness. Committing agendas and problem alternatives to writing, for example, allows others to prepare for exchanges. The first-line manager solicits input on the relevancy of communication methods to determine their appropriateness to various audiences. For example, paycheck inserts and e-mail may elicit more input than bulletin boards and flyers.

Verbal exchanges are also planned. Location of verbal exchanges is contemplated. Confidential material is discussed in private as is any topic that might arouse emotional responses. Discussion between staff and management regarding resource allocations occurs on *neutral territory*. Verbal exchanges are planned to occur after all facts are carefully analyzed for accuracy. Positions of communicators in the conversation are planned (e.g., space between speakers or height of speaker and respondents is arranged). Discussion is focused by controls such as time, *Robert's Rules of Order*, or third-party facilitation. The intent of conversations is stated at the outset, and summarization brings closure at the conclusion. Talking with constituents prior to structured meetings clarifies and gathers information and permits the manager to gain insight into the situation. Formally acknowledging hallway communications also helps informal communications to become barometers for needed formal communiqués. Conducting communication audits to request input on how information and ideas are shared and what the satisfaction level is with these patterns helps organizations to plan proper uses of formal verbal and nonverbal communication processes.

Professional Communication

The manner in which communication is shared within and outside the organization leaves an impression about therapeutic recreation. Through a number of media (e.g., in-services, presentations, reports, research, articles, voluntary contributions) the first-line manager is a role model for staff, a representative for the organization, and an advocate of the profession. As a role model, the first-line manager shares professional resources, publications, contacts, standards, and protocols with staff. Likewise, staff present information from off-site professional meetings to unit colleagues during in-services. Managers encourage their staff to present agency-wide in-services on therapeutic recreation. As noted by Austin (2004), first-line managers interact with staff during clinical supervision to ensure that their performance promotes department accountability which will be considered in more depth in Chapter 19.

First-line managers represent their departments and the organization as they network and collaborate in the agency, community, and profession. Their poise, appearance, mannerisms, promptness, and timeliness are qualities reflective of personal professional standards of excellence. The manager's written and oral accuracy, follow-through, receptivity, and quality of delivered materials, project an *image*. Real and perceived impressions of the manager affect others' thoughts and feelings about the manager, organization, and profession.

Managers are also judged by the "company they keep." Power associated with positions and roles is communicated through associations. Responsiveness to a manager occurs in a political context. Judgments affect what and how others share information. Before a manager communicates externally, organizational protocol requires that proper internal personnel have been informed and that information to be disseminated has received clearance. Professionals ensure that the positions and roles of others are respected, and in return they expect the same of colleagues.

When a therapeutic recreation manager disseminates publications, research findings, and results of service evaluations, information representative of the profession is being conveyed to clients, caregivers, and colleagues. Through professional writings, presentations, and community service projects, therapeutic recreation is promoted as a viable health and human service. The advocacy role is evident in one-on-one interactions and during professional conferences. This advocacy role is carried out in a number of ways, such as program tours, advisory board meetings, support group facilitation, resource sharing, volunteerism, cosponsorships, and student intern training.

Professional communication is unique because of the distance communication travels and the impact it makes on audiences wider than those within the organization. E-mail, telephones, formal letters, committee reports, and conference calls are impersonal and do not permit the message to project feelings or subjective interpretations. Each professional reads and hears the message from his or her own perspective. Because this frame of reference is unique, the sender and receiver ascribe different meanings to the message. Therefore, to ensure congruence the first-line manager carefully constructs the message, seeks review prior to transmission, and solicits feedback from the receiver(s) to gauge accuracy of understandings. A correspondence file permits revisiting previous communications to verify information transmitted. Additionally, the manager devotes certain daily time periods to prioritized communications. Brief notes are made summarizing appointments, calls, and contacts. Busy work times (e.g., Monday mornings or budget hearings) are avoided. A resource file is maintained to ensure ongoing communication and networking.

Organizational and professional communication is multidirectional and multifaceted. The first-line manager is often the person through whom organizational messages are transmitted. Communicating the right message at the right time to the right person is a major responsibility of management. Internal and external professional exchanges leave long-lasting impressions and are primary tools through which the professional and profession mature. How, what, and when messages are conveyed influence perceptions others have of therapeutic recreation.

Summary

This chapter began by identifying the components of interpersonal communication and the nature of formal and informal communication processes. The interchange between formal written and verbal exchanges is influenced by the nonverbal manner in which messages are conveyed. Successful communicators exhibit congruency in the manner messages are shared and received. Also, effective communicators consider the barriers that occur and result in real or perceived differences in message content and inter-

pretation. Personal characteristics of "effective helpers" promote effective communication. Feedback and active listening are two tools that enhance communication when used properly. In a multicultural work environment, the manager is sensitive to communication strategies that promote open and accurate interpretations.

Interpersonal communication skills are employed during managerial exchanges. A first-line manager's day-to-day transactions are brief yet focused so that employees have the support and resources to perform department tasks. As a clinical supervisor, the first-line manager ensures that those within the unit and those that support unit activities have timely, factual, accurate information. Through meetings, delegation, negotiation, and collaborative processes, the manager communicates so that win-win situations accomplish unit and organizational goals. When criticism, complaints, and confrontation do arise, the manager separates the significant from the not so critical to discern real needs and action steps. With humor the stress created in problem situations can be dissipated.

Organizational and professional communications extend the first-line manager's network beyond the division or department. These exchanges inform and educate others about therapeutic recreation while advocating for the contributions made by professionals. Although barriers exist within the organization and public domain, the professional is able to analyze situations so that the appropriate image is projected and clients, caregivers, and colleagues have accurate impressions of the nature of the profession.

Review Questions

1. Identify the avenues of formal and informal communication and describe how each affects message transmission.

2. Using the guidelines presented in this chapter, critique e-mails you have received. Identify features that enhance and detract from the information sent by e-mail.

3. Explain the critical roles of active listening and feedback in overcoming communication barriers.

4. What steps can be taken to improve message sending, transmission, receiving, and feedback?

5. Attend a formal meeting in an agency. Critique the effectiveness of the meeting using the steps presented in this chapter.

6. What steps can a manager take to improve the processes of delegation, negotiation, and collaboration?

7. How are criticism, complaints, and confrontation managed so win-win situations result?

8. Identify organizational blocks to communication.

9. How does a manager enhance organizational communication? Explain how culture is transmitted through communication in the workplace.

10. What practices contribute to effective professional communication?

References

Arrendondo, L. (2000). *Communicating effectively.* New York, NY: McGraw-Hill.

Austin, D. R. (2004). *Therapeutic recreation processes and techniques* (5th ed.). Champaign, IL: Sagamore Publishing.

Carter, M. J., Van Andel, G. E., and Robb, G. M. (2003). *Therapeutic recreation: A practical approach* (3rd ed.). Prospect Heights, IL: Waveland Press.

Davidhizar, R. (1991). The employee who complains: Understanding and responding to staff complaints. *Hospital Topics, 69*(4), 16–19.

Davidhizar, R. and Wysong, P. R. (1992). Positive and negative criticism: Strategies for professional growth. *Critical Care Nurse, 12*(6), 94–99.

Deering, C. G. (1993). Giving and taking criticism. *American Journal of Nursing, 93*(12), 56–62.

Denton, P. L. (1987). *Psychiatric occupational therapy: A workbook of practical skills.* Boston, MA: Little, Brown and Company.

Eisner, M. (2000, July 15). Enlightened communication, *Vital Speeches,* 593.

Guffey, M. E. (2004). *Essentials of business communication* (6th ed., p. 32). Mason, OH: Thomson Publishers.

Hansten, R. and Washburn, M. (1992). How to plan what to delegate. *American Journal of Nursing, 92*(4), 71–72.

Knippen, J. T. and Green, T. B. (1994). How the manager can use active listening. *Public Personnel Management, 23*(2), 357–359.

Liebler, J. G., Levine, R. E., and Rothman, J. (1992). *Management principles for health professionals* (2nd ed.). Gaithersburg, MD: Aspen Publishers.

Marquis, B. L. and Huston, C. J. (2003). *Leadership roles and management functions in nursing: Theory & application* (4th ed.). Philadelphia, PA: Lippincott Williams & Wilkins.

Metzger, N. (1982). *The healthcare supervisor's handbook* (2nd ed.). Rockville, MD: Aspen Systems Corporation.

Robbins, S. P. (1995). *Supervision today.* Englewood Cliffs, NJ: Prentice Hall.

Robbins, S. P. and Decenzo, D. A. (2001). *Fundamentals of management* (3rd ed.). Upper Saddle River, NJ: Prentice Hall.

Stevens, M. J. and Campion, M. A. (1994). The knowledge, skill, and ability requirements for teamwork: Implications for human resource management. *Journal of Management, 20*(2), 503–530.

Streibel, B. J. (2003). *The manager's guide to effective meetings.* New York, NY: McGraw-Hill.

Chapter 14
Motivation

The amount and quality of work accomplished through a first-line manager is a direct reflection of their motivation and that of their subordinates (Marquis & Huston, 2003). Since motivation comes from within the person, managers cannot directly motivate subordinates, yet they can create an environment that maximizes the development of each staff member's potential. Motivation is the result of the interaction between the employee and the work situation (Robbins & Decenzo, 2001). A therapeutic recreation manager's challenge is to create a work environment that encourages or empowers staff to carry out mutually developed division or department goals. Productivity and accountability result when practitioners are "turned on" to their job tasks. To motivate effectively, a manager must be in tune to each practitioner's personal needs and the interchange between the work environment and employee needs and abilities. The intent of this chapter is to explore the relationships among employee motivation, department outcomes, and the manager's responsibility to create a productive work environment.

What is motivation? Motivation is a degree of readiness or the desire or willingness within an individual to pursue a goal. As suggested by Robbins and Decenzo (2001), motivation is "the willingness to exert high levels of effort to reach organizational goals" (p. 313). First-line managers choose how to motivate their employees. The challenge is to create work opportunities whereby "individual employees can meet their individual needs while meeting the goals of the organization" (Edginton, Hudson & Lankford, 2001, p. 151). The manager seeks to create an environment in the department that enhances each practitioner's willingness to work.

Each staff member is unique. What is significant to one person is not necessarily important to another. Likewise, what motivates a practitioner at one particular time may not be something that fulfills a personal need in the future. The first section of this chapter considers the significance of motivation in a knowledge-based work environment. Factors that motivate a diverse workforce are outlined, along with factors that influence people's capabilities to cope with work demands.

A number of theories explain motivation. The principles derived from these theories are universal. The effective first-line manager is the one who creates an environment in which employees are highly motivated and therefore highly productive (Tappen, 2001). Successful managers focus on factors that stimulate worker satisfaction and productivity. The second section of this chapter reviews the theories that explain a manager's choice of motivational strategies.

A positive supportive environment is created by effective application of motivational concepts. While remaining aware of personal needs, the first-line manager seeks to expand the zone of acceptance within staff for department goals. This chapter's third section presents strategies a manager uses to create a supportive environment that promotes managerial and staff performance. A supportive work environment deters factors like burnout that negatively impact morale, job satisfaction, and productivity.

In a knowledge-based work environment, employees are significant organizational assets. The diversity and dynamics of the department influence their needs and how they go about meeting them. Therapeutic recreation practitioners of the future are likely to be more demanding, mobile, and to have a different value perspective about work than current staff. A first-line manager will experience challenges unique to a diverse work force. The closing section of this chapter highlights a few of the issues likely to influence choices managers make as they balance practitioner needs with the changing work environment.

Motivation and Individual Need Fulfillment

Why is motivation significant to the first-line therapeutic recreation manager? The most important resource in any organization is human capabilities and competencies. A manager assumes responsibility to maintain productivity, accountability and quality while encouraging employee job satisfaction. Because intrinsic motivation comes from within, to be intrinsically motivated, an employee must value job performance. Intrinsic motivation is related to each person's level of aspiration (Marquis & Huston, 2003). Upbringing, cultural background, and expectations influence achievement drives.

The job environment enhances extrinsic motivation. Motivation is the effort put forth to achieve a goal that satisfies an unmet need. Motivated employees try hard, yet managers cannot assume that employee efforts will be channeled in the direction that benefits the department nor that they have adequate levels of intrinsic motivation to achieve organizational goals (Robbins & Decenzo, 2001). As a consequence, the manager must create a climate that stimulates employees' intrinsic and extrinsic drives to use their skills and competencies to achieve worthwhile endeavors.

In a knowledge environment, employees have access to more information and opportunities for growth. When the manager provides recognition and support in these work environments, efforts result in increased productivity, employee retention, and worksite harmony (Edginton, Hudson & Lankford, 2001). Motivated employees channel their efforts toward improved service quality and efficiency. Motivated employees are willing to do more with less.

As suggested in Chapter 5, personality is one of the factors that affects work performance. Robbins and Decenzo (2001) identified five specific personality traits that affect employee responses to work demands. These traits explain factors that motivate employee behavior. The first, locus of control, describes a person's belief about being the master of his or her fate. Persons with an internal locus of control perceive they are responsible for their own actions and, as a consequence, are less likely to blame the outcomes of their actions on luck or chance. Need fulfillment is their assumed responsibility. Staff members who attribute actions and their outcomes to someone other than themselves display an external locus of control. Persons with this focus are likely not to assume responsibility for their actions and attribute consequences to factors over which they have little control. Persons with an internal locus of control are inclined to satisfy their needs through inherent work values, while those with an external locus of control are more apt to gain work satisfaction through rewards such as paychecks.

A second factor that tends to affect individual perceptions about work is employee perceptions on how to gain and maintain power. Some employees perceive power to be inherent in their positions. Others perceive that power results from achievement of outcomes. In the former situation, a staff member is more prepared to be accepting of department protocol. An employee motivated by the end product is more apt to "bend the rules" to achieve department outcomes.

Self-esteem, a third factor, is a personality trait that influences one's degree of self-acceptance. According to Robbins and Decenzo (2001), persons with high self-esteem believe they have the ability to perform while those with low self-esteem are more susceptible to external influences and are motivated by the expectations and external reinforcement of others.

A successful employee adapts to the work environment and is capable of adjusting to changes in the workplace. Robbins and Decenzo (2001) referred to this fourth characteristic as the ability to "go with the flow" or to be self-monitoring. Self-monitoring personalities are more likely to discern situations that require change and flexibility. Persons who are low self-monitors tend to be rigid and to show their "true colors" when their course of action is disrupted. Someone who self-monitors is more capable of performing in diverse work roles and with team members having various expectations.

A final characteristic that influences behavior is the ability to assume risk or to take chances (Robbins & Decenzo, 2001). Some people are more willing to act with less information than are others. Those with high levels of confidence tend to make more rapid decisions because they believe in their ability to operate with the resources available. Thus, a risktaker is more willing to try a new technique or to initiate a new service than is an employee who dislikes risk taking. Risk taking facilitates change. The manager's challenge is to decide the degree of risk necessary to support staff as they adapt to the changing work environment.

Individual Needs and Work

Accepting and understanding individual uniquenesses helps the manager plan alternative motivational strategies for staff. Efforts to hire, train, and develop the "right" staff are likely to have negligible impacts on performance and "organizational fit" if managers are unsuccessful in matching motivational strategies with staff needs. Staff and volunteers are motivated to work in therapeutic recreation for a variety of reasons. The desire to help others, to contribute to health and well-being, to improve the system, and to give back time and support to others and the community are needs met through volunteerism and paid positions. In-depth interviews with childcare workers in a residential treatment center found that employees viewed their jobs "as a sort of personal fulfillment, a way of giving and receiving intangible rewards" (Moses, 2000, p. 120). Reasons given for working with behaviorally disturbed youth were a sense of pride and an opportunity to repay a debt of gratitude for help received in a time of need.

According to Edginton, Hudson, and Lankford (2001), affiliation, power, achievement, financial rewards, status, recognition, worthwhile work, growth and learning, and opportunities to be innovative and creative are factors a manager may influence to alter employee effort. The unique demands of the human service work environment have lead researchers to consider "a motivating work environment as one in which staff members are effectively supported to work diligently as well as to enjoy their day-to-day employment" (Parsons, Reid & Crow, 2003, p. 96). Examples of supervisory techniques used to motivate staff to work hard and enjoy their work include the following:

- reward items, like an extra day off following good work performance

- positive feedback, like sending congratulatory notes to reflect favorable performances

- participatory management, like active listening and making staff feel their opinions count

- assisting staff to carry out their responsibilities, like covering their duties in an emergency situation

- attending to staff job structure and functions, like providing adequate training and resources to perform assigned duties

Positive supervisory feedback was noted as the most effective way to motivate staff working with individuals with developmental disabilities in the community (Parsons, Reid & Crow, 2003). Tangible rewards may be motivational at times yet should not be relied on to help employees meet the demands of their day-to-day work responsibilities.

Personal needs and group interactions motivate employees. Relationships formed with colleagues on treatment teams or staff in the department motivate effort. Likewise, interactions between staff and support groups, advisory committees, and/or parents stimulate staff initiatives. Summer staff and volunteers return, in part, because their relations with staff have been enjoyable.

Edginton, Hudson, and Lankford (2001) reported that staff are likely to strive for excellence in the work environment when they experience opportunities for growth. Growth experiences are unique to each individual. For some, the opportunity to apply new interventions constitutes growth, whereas for other practitioners a change of clientele or setting is enough to stimulate the interest in learning and acquiring skills.

The first-line manager who is aware of individual differences also accepts the significance of personal needs as motivators in the work environment. No single work incentive addresses the complexity of human behavior. Motivation comes from within the staff member and department. Employees perform because they desire to do so. Employee behavior impacts others and, as a consequence, contributes to other's harmony with department protocols and directions.

Motivational Approaches

The goal of a first-line manager is to accomplish department goals while giving practitioners the opportunity to meet their needs. A number of theories have attempted to interpret alternative approaches for motivating employees. These theories change with time and tend to reflect the psychosocial views prevalent during particular time periods. A brief review of these views reveals shifting explanations for employee motivation.

Maslow's Hierarchy of Needs

Maslow's hierarchy of needs is associated with the humanistic perspective of management. As a result of Maslow's work, managers realized employees have many needs motivating them at any one time (Marquis & Huston, 2003). His efforts provided insight into factors that stimulate satisfaction and productivity while eliminating worker dissatisfaction (Tappen, 2001). From the humanistic perspective, the most effective manager is one who creates an environment in which people are highly motivated and, as a consequence, highly productive. Because motivation is internalized, if productivity is to increase, managers must help employees to first meet lower-level needs, then employees will have the motivation to work toward higher level needs like self-actualization. Maslow's hierarchy of needs theory suggests the key to motivation is to determine where along the developmental continuum (i.e., physiological, safety, social, esteem, self-actualization) an employee is functioning and focus motivational efforts at this level. For example, money is essential to satisfy physiological needs—an adequate paycheck becomes a desirable goal when securing a position. Employees pursue goals to satisfy their needs. The need to fulfill one's potential is at the highest level of the continuum. Consequently, employees strive for growth through professional training, job advancement or sharing, and employment with different agencies. Needs from each of the five levels are important at different times. No need is ever fully met, yet a substantially satisfied need (e.g., comfortable income) no longer motivates one's actions.

Clayton Alderfer's Modified Need Hierarchy

Clayton Alderfer proposed a three-level need hierarchy that collapsed Maslow's five levels and suggested that frustrated higher-level needs cause regression to next lower-level needs in the hierarchy (Sullivan & Decker, 2001; Tomey, 2000). Alderfer also suggested that more than one of the three needs—existence (i.e., physiological and safety), relatedness (i.e., belongingness or social), and growth (i.e., self-esteem and self-actualization)—may be operative at any one point in time. Satisfaction of lower level needs like affiliation activates a need at the highest level. Participation in staff development activities and continuous quality improvement projects are built on recognition and growth needs of employees in a knowledge-based work environment.

Herzberg's Two-Factor Theory

Frederick Herzberg's concept of motivators parallels concepts of need levels and satisfaction seen in Maslow's and Alderfer's hierarchies. Herzberg investigated what people wanted from their jobs (Robbins & Decenzo, 2001). He believed, on one hand, that motivators or job satisfiers are present in work itself and that they give people the desire to work and work well, and on the other hand, there is a need to meet organizational goals yet these hygiene or maintenance factors do not act as real motivators (Marquis & Huston, 2003). So factors that lead to job satisfaction are separate and distinct from those that lead to dissatisfaction (Robbins & Decenzo, 2001). As a consequence, when managers eliminate factors that create job dissatisfaction, they may not be necessarily motivating employees.

Intrinsic factors like achievement, recognition, responsibility, and the potential for growth and work itself lead to job satisfaction. Extrinsic factors like relationships with supervisors and peers, salary, job security, and working conditions when lacking or inadequate can lead to employee dissatisfaction. However, if paired with motivators like advancement, an extrinsic factor like salary can be a powerful motivator. Herzberg's work suggested that managers motivate by building on maintenance factors and empowering employees to move toward higher-level needs. For instance, an effective reward system is created when the manager gives employees greater responsibilities, recognition, and commensurate forms of compensation when work is well done.

Argyris' Maturity-Immaturity Continuum

First postulated in the late 1950s, the Argyris maturity-immaturity continuum is also based on a behaviorist perspective and is grounded on a continuum approach. Individuals vary in their level of maturity along a relative continuum from total immaturity to total maturity. The manager's challenge is to view each employee from his or her respective maturity level and to create a work environment that recognizes each employee's uniqueness. Thus, employees require a management style commensurate with their level of maturity and one that will create harmony between their needs and the goals of the organization (Edginton, Hudson & Lankford, 2001; Tomey, 2000). Consequently a manager creates satisfaction by taking advantage of employee interests and helping personnel meet their needs for self-actualization because employees tend to exert more energy to meet their needs than those of the organization.

McClelland's Three Needs Theory

David McClelland identified three basic needs that guide people to action: achievement, affiliation, and power (Marquis & Huston, 2003; Robbins & Decenzo, 2001; Tomey, 2000). Some practitioners strive for personal achievement through seeing their work through to successful completion. Robbins and Decenzo (2001) suggested the drive to succeed, rather than rewards of success, compels these individuals. McClelland described this drive for personal achievement as a higher level need similar to Maslow's esteem and self-actualization higher order needs. An employee operating with this motif is intrinsically motivated, displays a high degree of self-control, and desires to perform more efficiently. High achievers avoid risky tasks or those that might succeed or fail if outcomes were left to chance. The manager's task becomes assigning responsibilities of moderate risk while delegating enough authority so the employee is self-regulating and receives appropriate recognition. Staff with high affiliation needs seek out human service settings and meaningful relationships; they are more interested in high morale than overt productivity. Managers who support cooperative team interactions are creating satisfying work environments among affiliation-oriented employees. Finally, people who are power-oriented need to be in control and influence others. They are motivated by the power gained from specific outcomes. Thus, a manager might assign a power-oriented person to a task like retrenchment that involves an unpleasant consequence because they strive for control and are unaffected by decisions that might alienate staff.

McGregor's Theory X and Theory Y

Coincidental with Herzberg's and Argyris' theories, McGregor presented Theory X and Theory Y to explain two types of management. McGregor observed from studying traditional organizational structures that some workers dislike their work, avoid responsibility, lack initiative, and prefer strong direction (i.e., Theory X). Motivation is derived from satisfaction of lower level needs (e.g., salaries, fringe benefits). This approach has been labeled the "carrot-and-stick" management style. A manager who operates according to Theory X leads with an authoritative hand or bribes employees to perform using extrinsic motivators such as financial reward. This theory assumes the lowest levels of need satisfaction like Maslow's and Argyris' motivate behaviors.

McGregor proposed an alternative theory, Theory Y, based on higher levels of need satisfaction. Motivators create opportunities for self-control, self-direction, and self-esteem building. The assumptions undergirding this theory view human behavior positively and hold that work is as natural as play. McGregor believes people seek self-control under the right conditions, learn to accept responsibility, commit themselves to meaningful tasks or department goals, and seek quality in personal and professional tasks. The manager is challenged to create an environment in which Maslow's higher order social and self-esteem needs are achieved (Robbins & Decenzo, 2001). A manager uses incentives like recognition, opportunities for individual growth, and participation on self-regulating teams to realize staff needs and to achieve department goals. Staff can be trusted to put forth adequate effort when committed to department goals (Tappen, 2001).

Vroom's Expectancy Theory

In the mid-1960s a number of theories purported that behavior is not merely motivated by need satisfaction alone—employees' perceptions and expectations of the work environment influence outcomes of work behaviors. Expectancy theory suggests that an employee must expect that his or her behavior will lead to satisfaction or a desired outcome. Robbins and Decenzo (2001) outlined the relationship among three primary tenets of the theory: effort-performance, performance-rewards, and attractiveness. An employee is motivated when effort leads to positive performance appraisal and proper recognition that attain desired outcomes valued by the employee. Expectancy theory emphasizes rewards so a manager must align rewards with employee desires.

Vroom's theory suggests the manager should be aware of the unique needs and values of his or her staff. Each staff member places different value on work motivators such as security, financial reward, and recognition. Likewise, the needs fulfilled by work vary. Some therapeutic recreation specialists need praise from a supervisor while others need collegial recognition; some need "to give or help" while others need to be a part of a "medical team." Also evident from this theory is the significance of a manager's explanation of the reward structure and performance expectations. Consequently, to motivate, first-line managers must clearly articulate the relationship between performance and departmental goals and the significance of the department's award structure to each member's individual goals (Tomey, 2000). Managers applying the principles of expectancy theory promote leadership among employees while they attempt to better understand employee values, strengths, and willingness to take risks (Isaac, Zerbe & Pitt, 2001; Marquis & Huston, 2003).

Equity Theory

Similar to the expectancy theory, equity theory describes the relationship between individual effort and reward and employees' perceptions of the effort and reward received by others. Equity exists when an employee subjectively determines that the ratio of his or her input to reward or outcomes is comparable to that of other employees. When an imbalance exists, the tension that is created causes the employee to be motivated to reduce the inequity and to achieve fairness (Tomey, 2000). When staff "feel overworked and underpaid, they are likely to decrease their productivity" (Tomey, 2000, p. 81).

Employee input includes a number of factors, such as effort, experience, education, and competence. Reward is also broadly defined to include salary level, fringe benefits, recognition, working conditions, and department rewards. Tension is created when, for example, two employees of the same age and years of accumulated work experience are rewarded differently. Robbins and Decenzo (2001) indicated this theory helps to explain why employees reduce their work efforts when they perceive they are not rewarded fairly. Inequitable rewards lead to lower job satisfaction and poor job performance. In an economically unstable environment when organizations are being redesigned and positions reduced, problems with employee's perceptions of equity can be anticipated (Sullivan & Decker, 2001).

Ouchi's Theory Z

William Ouchi described a contemporary motivational approach that focuses on increasing productivity through participatory management. As noted in Chapter 2, Theory Z supports both Theory X and Theory Y, because employees and managers alike participate in making decisions that effect department outcomes. Theory Z evolved from the Japanese culture and assumes that increased satisfaction and productivity result from using collective decision making with long-term employment, slower promotions, indirect supervision, and a holistic concern for employees (Tappen, 2001).

A holistic perspective permeates management. Each staff member's efforts are significant to the department and work of the team. Quality circles work on solving job-related quality problems, such as client scheduling and/or transportation. As a result of feeling a sense of commitment from the department, employees tend to plan a lifelong career with the unit. Close working relationships develop within the team and each member's contributions are thoroughly evaluated. Supervision is subtle as workers become a part of the culture and peer approval supports group behavior. Relationships forged by group efforts support each employee's individual needs and job satisfaction.

To summarize this section, each theory offers alternatives to creating motivating environments that contribute to employee satisfaction and productivity. Traditional theories tend to limit motivation to behaviors that satisfy needs. Fundamental differences in these theories relate to descriptors of lower and higher level needs that create satisfied employees. More recent theories attribute motivation to broader concepts of need satisfaction. These theories suggest employee behaviors tend to be affected by perceptions and judgments of relationships among a number of factors, including how employees compare and relate to one another. Systematic management practices derived from the most recent theories acknowledge the influence of the total work environment on the achievement of personal needs and on the inherent relationship between satisfaction of personal needs and department goals.

Creating a Motivating Work Environment

A manager's challenge is twofold: (a) to hone personal professional qualities and practices to engage staff in experiences that result in need fulfillment and (b) to create a work environment supportive of personal satisfaction, development, and achievement of department goals. Thus, the manager is aware of personal qualities and work environment factors that promote productivity and job satisfaction. As a result, actions are taken to orchestrate a mutually supportive work experience.

Because the organization impacts extrinsic motivation, it is important to examine the organizational climate and culture that affect morale and motivation (Marquis & Huston, 2003). Factors within the environment like extensive paperwork requirements, a sense of powerlessness, long hours, and client losses lead to negative interaction between expectations and behaviors of health care professionals and the work environment (Tappen, 2001; Tomey, 2000). Low morale and job dissatisfaction result. Prevention is the best strategy to manage burnout.

In this section, motivation is considered from the manager's and department's perspective. Managerial guidelines drawn from the theories and study of the organizational climate and culture are presented. First-line managers have a tremendous impact on motivation at the department level. Their role in creating positive reinforcers or rewards and designing jobs is key to a supportive work setting.

As a role model, the manager consistently uses strategies that are supportive and encouraging. The commitment and energy level displayed as the manager interacts with various constituents directly affects employee morale and productivity. Motivational strategies used vary with the employee and the situation. Some strategies are extrinsic like those associated with organizational reward systems while others are intrinsic like those evident when the manager's behavior reflects the qualities and actions that influence other's behaviors.

Organizational Climate and Work Culture

A number of variables within the work climate directly influence motivational levels of managers and staff. First-line managers have the opportunity to affect change in some of these variables, whereas other variables remain outside their realm of influence. With an awareness of these variables, managers are open to opportunities that promote achievement of staff and department goals.

One variable over which a first-line manager has minimal influence is the complexity of the department and/or relationship of the unit to the organization. Communication flows through more channels in larger organizations. Structure of the department and its relationship to other units and/or the organization also is a function of size. Formal policies and procedures codify behavior in larger complex work environments. Where size and complexity are factors, managers hope to structure unit tasks so that practitioners perceive trust, openness, and support within the department for their needs.

A variable over which the manager does have some influence is the climate within the department. Within the department a manager structures the physical environment to support interpersonal relationships and a collective commitment to the mission. Amenities like flextime work, educational opportunities, childcare, and comfortable office space boost morale. The degree of control a first-line manager has within the unit is relational to organizational variables. Consequently, the climate set at the macrolevel permeates managerial actions within the service unit. Individual work units are only as healthy as the overall work environment.

A number of administrative processes, such as personnel selection, reward structures, financial management, the interpersonal relationship between the supervisor and employee, and job design, affect department environments. Competent personnel can be expected to perform if given necessary support, resources, and appropriate recognition. Conversely, marginally qualified persons are not as likely to perceive their jobs in a positive manner regardless of the quality of work environment and reward system. Achievement is promoted by properly rewarding performance. Motivation results when staff value the reward and the reward is commensurate with their efforts. The degree of financial solvency within the division, department, and organization contributes to worker security and morale. For example, uncertainties about pay raises or fringe adjustments create discomfort and lead to job dissatisfaction.

"The interpersonal relationship between an employee and his or her supervisor is critical to the employee's motivation level" (Marquis & Huston, 2003, p. 323). The manner in which the first-line manager communicates with staff affects employee attitude toward the organization.

The manager assesses individual employee values and needs and the organization mission then uses his or her authority to bring these values together. Managers create a climate that demonstrates positive regard for their employees, recognizes achievement, and encourages open communication, growth, and productivity.

One of the more specific functions of a first-line manager is the job design process. To release employee work capacity, a manager has to design a job that will be conducive to employee motivation (Edginton, Hudson & Lankford, 2001). Through the job design process, managers enrich employees' jobs and increase their motivation. One approach suggests every job has the following five key dimensions, and when each is present to a high degree the job is potentially motivating (Robbins & Decenzo, 2001):

1. degree of skill variety (i.e., routine or multifaceted)

2. degree of task identity (i.e., whole or partial completion)

3. degree of significance (i.e., minimal to substantial impact on others)

4. degree of autonomy (i.e., discretion to carry out treatment protocol)

5. degree of feedback (i.e., degree to which carrying out job duties results in the employee obtaining direct and clear information about effectiveness of therapeutic recreation services)

In a knowledge-based society, working is no longer a matter of salary or increasing incentives with anticipation that the employee's behavior and motivation should increase proportionately. Managers must structure work so it is meaningful, satisfying, and productive and employees have opportunities to achieve and grow. Designing motivating jobs requires the manager to contemplate the inherent motivational features of each position. The manager considers how each employee's needs will be fulfilled and how each employee's achievements relate to department goals. One approach suggested by Flannery (2002) is to match each employee's psychological contract or those things like professional advancement and flexible work hours that make a job worth doing for the employee with organizational tasks that need to be addressed and are consistent with the manager's vision for future directions.

Work culture broadly describes the atmosphere and nature of a job setting. A number of factors over which the first-line manager has varying degrees of control and influence contribute to the work climate. For instance, the size, complexity, and structure of a department and organization directly affect job comfort and performance. Satisfaction is enhanced with the presence of amenities and open interactions. The manner in which a manager

transacts duties also sets a certain tone and sends specific messages. A positive work environment finds manager and staff equally committed to the achievement of personal goals and the department mission.

Burnout

Persons who enter helping professions usually do so with enthusiasm; they want to help people and desire to impact their well-being (Tappen, 2001). A supportive work environment and success nourish their efforts, while situational factors like long hours, sense of powerlessness, lack of appreciation, unresponsiveness to client needs, and arduous amounts of paperwork lead to negative interactions. "Burnout is a syndrome of physical and emotional exhaustion that leads to negative attitudes and behaviors" (Tomey, 2000, p. 85). Burnout leads to excessive absenteeism, turnover, job dissatisfaction and decreased productivity. As suggested by Bedini and Anderson (2003) with increased professional stressors like corporate reengineering, increased caseloads, managed care issues, and subsequent burnout, therapeutic recreation professionals are likely to feel less secure in the workplace. Prevention is the best strategy; a supportive workplace can protect against burnout (Marquis & Huston, 2003; Tomey, 2000).

The manager can create a pleasant work environment. A manager helps staff to set realistic goals, to prioritize work, to balance undesirable with preferred tasks, to recognize achievement of personal and departmental goals, and to create supportive networks. As role models, managers project enthusiasm, high levels of self-care, and morale. Managers balance and replenish their energy with proper diet, exercise, relaxation, spiritual renewal, emotional support and guidance. They mirror physical and emotional health desired of their employees. By virtue of their positions, managers use formal authority to reduce dissatisfiers. Informally, they project behaviors and attitudes to encourage job satisfaction that result in increased organizational productivity.

Guidelines To Build a Positive Motivational Atmosphere

A successful manager blends individual needs with department goals. Edginton, Hudson, and Lankford (2001) suggested a motivating environment be characterized by mutually agreed on goals, managerial assistance meeting employee goals, and managerial recognition of employee efforts that accomplish goals. A manager creates the tension necessary to maintain quality while encouraging subordinates' achievement of personal goals so organizational goals are also realized (Marquis & Huston, 2003). If the work environment creates a spirit of camaraderie, staff and volunteers feel empowered to communicate with candor and openness. There are many actions a manager can take to promote worker desire to achieve personal and departmental goals. A number of authors (Edginton, Hudson & Lankford, 2001; Marquis & Huston, 2003; Tager, 2002) presented guidelines managers should consider as they organize the work setting to promote worker satisfaction and quality. The following list highlights these guidelines:

- Integrate staff needs with department goals and organization vision.

- Communicate candidly so that each staff member and volunteer feels informed and significant to department outcomes.

- Increase practitioner ability to achieve personal and professional goals through training and opportunities for growth.

- Introduce challenges so that expectancy is increased, performance is improved, and workers experience a higher level of job satisfaction.

- Be a firm decision maker and encourage commitment to the course of action by involving staff and volunteers in decision-making processes so that commitment to the course of action results.

- Promote the concept of teamwork, because unity results in productive units.

- Structure the work environment so that practitioners have the freedom to accomplish clearly delineated tasks, then reinforce productivity with positive feedback.

- Encourage cooperation and respect for each person's unique contributions by individualized reinforcement, praise, and recognition.

- Epitomize ethical behaviors, such as being consistent, objective, equitable, and reliable.

- Maintain a positive, enthusiastic image as a role model.

- Maintain a healthy lifestyle on and off the job.

- Assign work duties commensurate with employee abilities.

- Mentor and coach practitioner actions and review progress by setting up observable, measurable goals and planned formal and informal sessions.

- Use legitimate authority to provide formal feedback and positive feedback to reward individual employees.

- Identify achievement and affiliation needs of staff and develop strategies to meet these needs.

- Communicate expectations to employees clearly.

- Change the routine, constantly innovate, and stretch staff to promote self-growth and self-actualization.

Managerial actions that promote motivational environments are interrelated. Also, when one element (e.g., individualized recognition) is in place, another is likely to be positively impacted (e.g., performance reviews). The autonomy of the therapeutic recreation department may determine the manager's relative control over motivational strategies. A number of these guidelines appear to have evolved from previous theories (e.g., expectancy, equity, Theory Z). Management views tend to promote work environments that facilitate satisfaction of higher level needs (e.g., self-esteem, self-fulfillment) through staff and volunteer involvement in day-to-day decisions and planning. This stimulates cohesiveness and unity between personal and unit goals.

Motivating a Diverse Work Force

A number of management trends, health care initiatives, and social demographics create challenges in the work environment. Health and human service work settings will experience increasing rates of change, accountability, and quality concerns with a reduced work force and resource base. Cultivating a work environment supportive of staff needs will become increasingly challenging. Traditional motivators, such as promotional opportunities, blanket health care coverage, and wage increases, will become less significant in the employee recognition process. Human resource management will focus on productivity and quality through conscious efforts to match personal and professional growth needs to achieve measurable outcomes.

Participatory management, accountability, and quality monitoring are trends impacting employee motivational strategies. Self-regulating teams, supervisor-employee design of development plans, and management-staff operational planning exemplify participatory functions likely to influence practitioner motivation. Managers empower staff to become intimately involved in these activities to encourage self-efficacy and department advocacy and growth. Decision-making opportunities promote perceptions of value, worth, and control—qualities necessary for one's self-fulfillment.

A focus on accountability requires each practitioner to assume responsibility. Accountability is known through feedback. Positive feedback affirms responsible actions and fosters motivation. First-line managers transfer to practitioners an increased degree of authority to ensure responsible use of limited departmental resources and client contact time. Managers help staff through the time-consuming "paper trails" so that practitioners are made acutely aware of the results of their interventions. Formal and informal acknowledgments reward contributions.

Continuous quality improvement processes focus on individual staff efforts, garnering necessary support, and maintaining competent professionals. Managers guide staff in their self-assessments and team building. Increasingly, first-line managers advocate for necessary resources and devote their time to staff enhancement, change, and growth. Managers possess training and financial management skills and create a work environment of expectancy and self-direction.

Health and human service professionals are experiencing decreased direct client contact, blending of professional roles, and relocation of services. These trends either motivate or demotivate. Managers will facilitate personnel transformations, assist during periods of role ambiguity, and train staff as referral and transition specialists. Without adequate managerial support, employees are likely to perceive job insecurities, feelings of incompetence, and professional abandonment. Mentoring programs that facilitate job satisfaction and advancement are especially important to women and minorities in therapeutic recreation (Bedini & Anderson, 2003).

Managers face the challenge of helping staff to realize their contributions to the whole intervention or program process regardless of service setting. Therapeutic recreators will apply the therapeutic recreation process across disciplines and settings. Managers will also help their staff and volunteers to advocate for the significant role therapeutic recreation assumes in quality of life and well-being. Additionally, a work culture will cultivate flexibility and adaptability so that helping skills are applied not only at one work site but also in several delivery settings. Feedback from delivery networks will help staff realize that the therapeutic recreation process is carried out even when settings change and jobs are not titled "therapeutic recreation specialist."

Just as the work setting and way work is managed are changing, so is the nature of the work force. The work force will be more diverse and individually value laden. As noted in Chapter 5, the workforce is becoming more diverse in a number of ways. A diverse workforce brings to the work setting an array of needs. Men place more importance on autonomy in their jobs than women do. Convenient work hours and good interpersonal relations are more important to women than men (Bedini & Anderson, 2003; Robbins & Decenzo, 2001). "Younger people tend to be more interested in income, whereas older people are interested in security" (Tomey, 2000, p. 86). Many of the motivational theories were developed and validated on American workers (Robbins & Decenzo, 2001). Priorities like self-interest and achievement are less evident in cultures that value team-based efforts and loyalty to the organization. Employees, therefore, have different personal needs they are hoping to satisfy on the job. Many of the motivation theories recognize that employees are not homogeneous. As a consequence, managers must vary their motivational techniques with the situation and employee involved.

A shifting value system will orient inward toward individualized commitments and inherent worth of personal services rather than commitment to company outcomes and department recognition. As Robbins and Decenzo (2001) noted, loyalty of employees is to their profession rather than a particular work site. Future employees will tend to be as sensitive to job design as to money. They value support with work itself being their chief reward (Robbins & Decenzo, 2001). To remain current, employees regularly update their knowledge. Therefore, educational opportunities become meaningful rewards as do recognition of individual differences and participation in goal setting and decision-making. As with volunteers, "what's in it for me" will become the double-edged sword of management.

To motivate, managers will focus on intangibles as well as tangibles in the work setting. Factors like autonomy, variety, group cohesiveness, peer recognition, personal development options like mentoring, and self-determined work schedules will become commonplace in the work environment. Amenities like onsite childcare and access to alternative program resources through telecommunications will accompany the coffee pot and company mentoring and wellness programs as standard employment benefits. Staff and volunteers will more readily achieve productivity in a work culture supportive of flexibility, professional growth, and self-management. The manager's challenge becomes communicating options through strategies like delegation, negotiation, and job sharing. Traditional management preparation tends to focus on day-to-day tasks like budgeting, marketing, and supervision. Future processes will emphasize concepts found in clinical supervision, self-efficacy, and human resource development.

Summary

Motivation is an inherent feature of management. The future will see an increased focus on the first-line manager's ability to motivate staff and volunteers. This is due in large part to the changing nature of the work environment, work force, and health and human services dynamics.

As traditional motivators like money and advancements become less available, the manager's ability to manipulate areas that influence the work environment become more critical to effective department operations. The intent of this chapter was to present options managers introduce into the work environment to empower staff so that work outcomes are mutually beneficial to staff and department goals.

The initial section of this chapter dealt with a motivation prerequisite—the fulfillment of individual needs. A number of factors (e.g., locus of control, perceptions about power, self-esteem, employee fit, risk taking) contribute to individual differences. When a manager recognizes these uniquenesses, it is easier to match individual need satisfiers with performance outcomes. The manager shapes the work environment or work culture. The support and resources of the environment add or detract from relationships formed in the work environment. Thus, the manager blends the work culture with uniquenesses of employees to accomplish personal goals and department outcomes.

A number of theories have explained motivation. Each purports concepts applicable to manager-practitioner motivational variables. One of the more elementary but significant theories is Maslow's hierarchy of needs. Several behaviorists—such as Alderfer, Herzberg, Argyris, and McClelland—employed the concept of need satisfaction along a continuum from lower to higher order needs to describe the significance of need satisfaction to personal development and achievement in the work setting. McGregor's now infamous Theory X and Theory Y also applied similar concepts to explain the difference between workers who require a carrot-and-stick approach and those who are motivated by self-growth opportunities. Theories proposed since the 1960s (e.g., expectancy, equity) suggest that behavior alone does not motivate action. Workers are also motivated by perceptions of others and comparisons between their efforts and rewards and that of other employees. The more recent Theory Z contends that participatory management strategies enhance workplace motivation.

From these theories and management writings, a number of motivational guidelines are drawn. In the third section of the chapter, factors that contribute to a supportive work environment are summarized. Complexity, structure, administrative processes, and interpersonal relationships impact the work culture. First-line managers have varying degrees of control over these factors, some of which create stress and may result in burnout. As the manager designs each job, consideration is given to the inherent motivational features of the position. Yet, the manager is cognizant of extrinsic factors like lack of appreciation, managed care issues, and arduous amounts of paperwork that can contribute to burnout. As a role model, the manager assures that the use of self and that consistent application of specific motivational techniques create a positive open work environment.

A closing section addressed challenges created by a dynamic work setting and diverse workforce. Management trends, health care initiatives, and social demographics are causing dynamic work settings, diverse work forces, and adjustments to the way therapeutic recreation is practiced. In the future, managers will focus on tangibles and intangibles to create motivating workplaces. Further, traditionally assumed motivators like financial reward will be supplemented by creative job design, access to educational opportunities, mentor relations, and management of the social fabric of one's work cultures. Managers will need to craft flexible, supportive networks where interpersonal and professional development focus on achievement of personal needs and productivity to achieve departmental goals.

Review Questions

1. What are the five primary factors that explain individual differences in the workplace? Explain how each influences motivation.

2. What are the key theoretical concepts that have influenced management of employee motivation? Summarize points of each that will influence futuristic management styles.

3. What individual factors may a manager influence to alter employee effort in a knowledge-based human service work environment?

4. What work culture variables influence employee motivation?

5. In therapeutic recreation work environments, what elements might contribute to burnout? How might the manager create an environment to minimize these factors?

6. What is the manager's role as it relates to job design in a dynamic diverse work environment?

7. How will managers motivate in the 21st century?

References

Bedini, L. A. and Anderson, D. M. (2003). The benefits of formal mentoring for practitioners in therapeutic recreation. *Therapeutic Recreation Journal, 37*(3), 240–255.

Edginton, C. R., Hudson, S. D., and Lankford, S. V. (2001). *Managing recreation, parks, and leisure services: An introduction.* Champaign, IL: Sagamore Publishing.

Flannery, R. B. (2002). The psychological contract: Enhancing productivity and its implications for long-term care. *American Journal of Alzheimer's Disease & Other Dementias, 17*(3), 165–168.

Isaac, R. G., Zerbe, W. J., and Pitt, D. C. (2001). Leadership and motivation: The effective application of expectancy theory. *Journal of Managerial Issues, 13*(2), 212–226.

Marquis, B. L. and Huston, C. J. (2003). *Leadership roles and management functions in nursing: Theory & application* (4th ed.). Philadelphia, PA: Lippincott Williams & Wilkins.

Moses, T. (2000). Why people choose to be residential child-care workers. *Child & Youth Care Forum, 29*(2), 113–126.

Parsons, M. B., Reid, D. H., and Crow, R. E. (2003). Best and worst ways to motivate staff in community agencies: A brief survey of supervisors. *Mental Retardation, 41*(2), 96–102.

Robbins, S. P. and Decenzo, D. A. (2001). *Fundamentals of management* (3rd ed.). Upper Saddle River, NJ: Prentice Hall.

Sullivan, E. J. and Decker, P. J. (2001). *Effective leadership and management in nursing* (5th ed.). Upper Saddle River, NJ: Prentice Hall.

Tager, S. (2002). Motivating staff. *Camping Magazine, 75*(6), 50–53.

Tappen, R. M. (2001). *Nursing leadership and management: Concepts and practice* (4th ed.). Philadelphia, PA: F. A. Davis Company.

Tomey, A. M. (2000). *Guide to nursing management and leadership* (6th ed.). St. Louis, MO: Mosby.

Chapter 15
Performance Appraisal

Appraising staff performance is one of the most important and complex employee relations duties of the first-line manager (Arnold & Pulich, 2003). Performance appraisals let employees know their level of job performance and organizational expectations while generating information used in administrative decisions like salary adjustments, disciplinary actions, and terminations (Marquis & Huston, 2003). No other task is as personal as appraising the work of others, because work is an important part of our identity and we are sensitive to how others feel about our performance. For this reason, the performance appraisal is a significant tool an organization has to motivate and to develop employees (Marquis & Huston, 2003).

Performance appraisals are formal periodic evaluations of how well staff have actually performed their job duties during a specified time period (Herringer, 2002). Appraisals create a system for achieving organizational goals through employee performance. Performance appraisals are completed for a number of reasons, including the following:

- to provide managers with the opportunity to give constructive feedback to their employees

- to serve as the basis for administrative decisions like pay adjustments, promotions, and corrective actions

- to comply with Fair Labor Employment practices and regulatory bodies like JCAHO (Herringer, 2002)

- to provide an opportunity for managers to plan training and development programs with their employees

- to create the opportunity for the manager to discuss the organization's goals with employees

- to recognize staff accomplishments and to motivate staff toward higher achievement.

The design of performance appraisal and management systems involves structuring informal and formal reviews and communicating on a continuous basis. In performance management systems "the manager places his or her efforts into ongoing coaching, mutual goal setting, and leadership training of subordinates" (Marquis & Huston, 2003, p. 485). The manager spends more regularly scheduled time with subordinates. In the first section of this chapter, the authors introduce a number of factors considered as the manager engages in ongoing performance evaluations. The second section considers the design and implementation of performance measures, including the appraisal interview or review. A third section outlines the steps and alternatives that result from formal reviews. Performance problems result from an employee mismatch, rule violations, inadequate training, and unsatisfactory performance, practices, or behaviors. These issues are also considered in the third section. Evaluation of others is inevitable. If done on a continuous basis, outcomes are motivational, encouraging stronger worker relationships among the management team members and commitment to accomplish organizational goals.

Planning Personnel Evaluation Systems

Personnel evaluation is a vital component of human resource management. Persons who possess the desired knowledge, skills, and abilities (KSAs) are hired. They are then oriented and trained to perform their jobs so that department goals are achieved and, finally, they are evaluated to ensure that the mix of personnel and resources remain optimal. Performance appraisal is an ongoing activity that translates organizational goals into clear expectations for each employee. Evaluation demonstrates both the employee's and the health care organization's responsibility to the public to provide quality care (Tappen, 2001). By judging caregiver's actions against an accepted standard, accountability is achieved. Therefore, a personnel evaluation system must be congruent with the protocols of the organization and uphold the tenets of the profession. Like other human resource functions, evaluation systems must be free of bias and job related.

If performance appraisals are to have positive outcomes, an important consideration is how the employee views the process (Marquis & Huston, 2003). Appraisals guide employees' behaviors and influence productivity and organizational commitment (Miller, 2001). Factors that influence employee satisfaction with appraisal processes include the following (Marquis & Huston, 2003; Miller, 2001):

- Employees must believe appraisals are based on standards to which other employees are held, such as job descriptions or objectives developed at the time of hire.

- Employees should have a voice in developing the standards on which their performance is judged.

- Prior to implementation, employees must know the consequences of not meeting performance standards.

- Employees need to know the sources of information and the weighting procedures used with collected information.

- First-line managers who observe employees' work should conduct the process in concert with team members who observe the day-to-day interactions of team members.

- To be effective, performance appraisals are conducted in an environment of mutual trust and professional respect.

Legal Considerations

Evaluation is a serious activity with consequences for the manager, employee, and organization. Federal and state laws cover decisions based on appraisals, such as layoffs. The Equal Pay Act of 1963, Title VII of the Civil Rights Act of 1964, and the Age Discrimination in Employment Act of 1967 require that employees document quality of employee performance prior to decisions on selection, training, transfer, retention, and promotion (Sullivan & Decker, 2001; Tomey, 2000). Although a manager can never be sure a system is legally defensible, several steps help ensure nondiscrimination:

- Contents of appraisals should be in writing, occur regularly, at least once per year, and be based on job analysis.

- Standards, results, an appeal process, and anti-discrimination laws should be communicated to personnel.

- Employees should have an opportunity to respond in writing to appraisals.

- Managers should observe and document performance throughout the evaluation period. Documentation from more than one source is desirable and each should be accompanied by written instructions.

- Anecdotal notes from critical incidents should be shared with the employee throughout the evaluation period.

- Evaluators should be trained to carry out the process.

- Counseling on performance deficits and corrective actions prior to termination are steps included in a performance review process.

Organizational Considerations

The organization in which the therapeutic recreation program is housed greatly influences the manager's role in performance reviews. It is not uncommon for an organization to use or to recommend the use of standardized forms and/or review processes during formal evaluations. In some instances an abbreviated or generic form is provided, and the manager assumes the responsibility to identify individual employee job factors and quality indicators to be included during actual evaluation sessions. Managers develop job descriptions and specifications and select staff according to organizational policies and protocols. Within any organization, personnel carry out their duties according to operational codes. Managers cognizant of these organizational factors incorporate assessment of organizational expectations into the evaluation.

Politics and the culture within the organization also impinge on worker performance and are considered as systems are designed. Results of evaluations have implications for relationships among employees, employees and managers, and managers and upper-level administration and they are important in salary, promotion, and retention actions. A manager's budget requests to upper-level administration include personnel justifications. Employees' perceptions of their manager rest upon how well the manager has fostered their potential and has supported their resource needs. While working together to improve client well-being, each employee anticipates a return for his or her contribution to the client's satisfaction. Therefore, there is an ever-present reality that employees, the manager, and upper level administrators are influenced by the political consequences of actions directly or indirectly tied to performance evaluations.

A number of precipitating factors have contributed to the manager's role as a department facilitator. Decreases in funding and staffing levels, increases in accountability measures, shorter length of stays, and reduced length of program sessions have fostered collaboration and teamwork. Clients gain from collective expertise and resource access. Collaboration, networking and teamwork rely on each employee to contribute to the team and to be a good team player. Peers rather than first-line managers often observe these qualities. As a consequence, appraisal systems that integrate supervisory, peer, and self-review provide the best results for the employee, manager, and organization alike (Template Topics, 2001).

Professional Considerations

The manager's responsibility to ensure compliance with professional practice standards in the workplace has contributed to closer scrutiny of the tie between organizational and departmental personnel evaluations and professional training and credentials. A manager is aware that qualified therapeutic recreation specialists with similar credentials (e.g., CTRS), have varying practice styles based on training and experience (Sullivan, 1994). Also, part-time and seasonal employees with credentials in other health and human service professions may be qualified to practice in specific positions, such as day camp leaders, aquatic supervisors, and adventure-challenge specialists, where their expertise is applicable and contributes to improved client functioning. Managers design evaluation systems to recognize differences while noting acceptable practice modalities. Where staff hold credentials outside the professional purview of therapeutic recreation managers, appraisal systems incorporate performance indicators that assess contribution to departmental outcomes but do not require the manager to judge the competence of the staff member as, for example, a special education teacher or nurse. The manager's challenge is to create performance systems that determine if competent professionals are able to apply their KSAs clinically or functionally in practice. Standards of practice (ATRA, 2000; NTRS, 2004) define service scope and depth and describe the types of services to be delivered by competent professionals. In essence, these are worker-oriented jobs because they present what content experts see as essential to successful therapeutic recreation practice. Inclusion of evaluative criteria that recognize these practices enhances the validity of appraisals.

Quality Management Considerations

Because performance appraisals are intended to motivate individual staff, to aid employees to realize their potential, and to measure their contributions to the department's productivity, each performance appraisal is unique. As the manager assesses the situation, reviewing and collecting available documents and using recommended evaluation techniques can add to the credibility of the implemented processes. A number of strategies are recommended for planning and conducting performance reviews so that they are congruent with quality management principles and the unique features of a particular work environment:

1. A successful process considers past, present, and future employee performance and achievements (Scotto, 2000). Review of the past year is accomplished by reviewing the actual written review of the previous year. The present is considered by discussing the employee's role in the department and organization. Future planning entails conveying to employees where the department will be within the next year and where the employee fits into the scheme.

2. Performance appraisal is a year-long process for managers. The process consists of general information and recordkeeping throughout the year, a midyear evaluation, preparation for the appraisal meeting, the appraisal meeting, and appropriate follow-up (Scotto, 2000).

3. Specific tasks recommended to create a performance evaluation system include the following: (a) develop evaluation form, (b) identify performance measures, (c) set guidelines for feedback, (d) create disciplinary and termination procedures, and (e) set an evaluation schedule (Capko, 2003).

4. Training leads to more accurate rating and evaluation of employee and system factors. Employee evaluations are tempered by the knowledge that the behaviors and/or outcomes the rating is based on are influenced by factors within the organization and department over which the employee has no control or responsibility.

5. Evaluation considers employee potential and barriers to potential improvement and growth. Feedback is less confrontational when the emphasis is placed on improvement rather than blame for specific problems. Assessment of potential allows the employee to project future career options and growth targets.

6. Raters observe behavioral indicators defined by the acronym "SMART" (i.e., specific, measurable, achievable, results-oriented, time-bound).

7. Absolute, or noncomparative, and relative, or comparative, standards are combined in the design of performance criteria. Absolute standards direct employees toward quality output without concern about a competitive position with their peers. Relative standards inhibit teamwork and minimize actual variability among employees, yet facilitate individual awareness of behaviors perceived significant within the team or department. Using both absolute and relative standards enables the manager to present information relative to other personnel in the organization as each unit manager may use different rating forms and assign values to rankings differently.

8. Questions a manager should consider as staff performance reviews are planned include the following:

- Has the employee been efficient and effective in his or her work?

- Does the employee add value to the team?

- What support and training is required to assist the employee to reach his or her goals?

- Does the employee's performance match or exceed expectations in the job description?

- What is the employee's potential for promotion?

- Does the employee have an action plan to follow to achieve his or her goals? (Ashurst, 2000)

Designing and Implementing Personnel Evaluations

By assessing the environment in which personnel evaluations are to occur, the manager becomes aware of resources, guidelines, and constraints that will affect the design and implementation of evaluations. The next step is to determine the performance measures, to communicate these expectations, and to gather information or data to use in making judgments on performance. During orientation and probationary periods, the manager and employee review job descriptions and specifications and discuss the evaluation process. In these discussions the distinction among setting performance objectives for development plans, reviewing development plans, and completing formal performance appraisals is clarified. The relationship of each activity to the reward system is also explained. The time frame for setting objectives varies with the time necessary to measure accomplishment of the behaviors described in each objective. Development sessions follow measurement of individual development plan objectives and serve the purpose of revising development plans based on the assessment of objective outcomes. The usual pattern of activity involves holding a yearly session dedicated to performance appraisal that incorporates information from ongoing objective and development sessions.

A number of reward systems exist in organizations; the most predominant is financial. Usually salary adjustments occur after the probationary period and at regular intervals thereafter—none of which are necessarily congruent with or contingent on the time frame of objective setting or development plan discussions. Shortly after being hired, therefore, the manager and employee define performance expectations and the context in which personnel evaluations and reviews occur and are linked to the organization's reward system.

Determine Performance Measures

The initial task in the performance review process is to translate job descriptions and specifications into performance measures and relate these to employee objectives. Job performance areas included on most performance evaluations are job knowledge and skills, quality of work, quantity of work, habits, and attitudes (Capko, 2000). Also considered are employee's people skills, ability to motivate and to provide direction, overall communication skills, and the ability to build teams and solve problems. The manager works with employees to select key components of the position that can be objectively measured. Quantitative and qualitative data that reflect the practice of therapeutic recreation are identified as indicators of employee job knowledge and skills.

As the job roles and responsibilities are clearly identified, consideration is given to how performance criteria integrate into quality controls and improvement plans of the department and organization. Individual development plans reflect each employee's contribution to the unit outcomes. To illustrate, one criterion might read, "Participates in department operations demonstrating professional behavior, supporting unit goals, and maintaining an accounting of resource use." Rewritten as a quality control measure, the statement would be broken into several components:

- The employee contributes to writing unit goals that improve operations.

- The employee exhibits ethical, safe behaviors that comply with standards of practice and protocol.

- The employee recommends cost-effective ways to deliver therapeutic recreation services with available resources.

Organization personnel policies and performance appraisal handbooks may outline generic areas to be appraised. For example, all employees are to meet standards in the areas of resource management and organization, quality of service and role accountability, interpersonal skills and teamwork, and knowledge and skills of their profession. A second example might list the following areas: professional development, ability to supervise, program development, budgetary and communication skills, and work performance as a practitioner. Generally, generic forms also allow for the projection of improvement areas and reporting of recognized contributions (refer to Figure 15.1).

The challenge for the manager is to integrate into the generic form and/or process each position's performance

City of Cincinnati
EMPLOYEE PERFORMANCE EVALUATION

NAME: **CLASSIFICATION:**

Employee ID#:   **DEPT/DIV:**

Due Date of Rating:

☐ **ANNUAL REVIEW**   ☐ **PROBATIONARY**   ☐ **SPECIAL REVIEW**

---

1. **QUALITY OF WORK:** Includes accuracy; achievement of work assignments, completion of work on schedule; initiative and resourcefulness; neatness of work product; soundness of decisions.

RATING: ☐ Does Not Meet Expectations   ☐ Meets Expectations   ☐ Exceeds Expectations
                    (Needs improvement)   (Valued employee)

Explain why:

---

2. **QUANTITY OF WORK:** Includes amount of work performed.

RATING: ☐ Does Not Meet Expectations   ☐ Meets Expectations   ☐ Exceeds Expectations
                    (Needs improvement)   (Valued employee)

Explain why:

---

3. **RULES AND REGULATIONS:** Includes compliance with rules, policies, and directives; practices safety and proper use of tools and equipment; ethical conduct.

RATING: ☐ Does Not Meet Expectations   ☐ Meets Expectations   ☐ Exceeds Expectations
                    (Needs improvement)   (Valued employee)

Explain why:

---

4. **INTERPERSONAL SKILLS:** Includes participation and teamwork; contribution to unit morale; working cooperatively with the public, peers, and subordinates; accepting advice and counseling from supervision.

RATING: ☐ Does Not Meet Expectations   ☐ Meets Expectations   ☐ Exceeds Expectations
                    (Needs improvement)   (Valued employee)

Explain why:

---

5. **CUSTOMER SERVICE DELIVERY:** Practices and exhibits effective customer service skills both internal and external to users of City services.

RATING: ☐ Does Not Meet Expectations   ☐ Meets Expectations   ☐ Exceeds Expectations
                    (Needs improvement)   (Valued employee)

Explain why:

Figure 15.1
Employee Performance Evaluation   >>

NAME: **CLASSIFICATION:**

Employee ID#:   **DEPT/DIV:**

Due Date of Rating:

6.   ATTENDENCE: Meets normal standards, including tardiness and observance of work hours; number of chargeable incidents of absence during rating period _____ to _____.

RATING: ☐ Does Not Meet Expectations   ☐ Meets Expectations   ☐ Exceeds Expectations
               (Needs improvement)   (Valued employee)

Explain why:

7. SUPERVISORY SKILL (Supervisors Only): Includes planning and assigning work; making decisions; training, instructing, and evaluating employees; leadership; employee safety and welfare.

RATING: ☐ Does Not Meet Expectations   ☐ Meets Expectations   ☐ Exceeds Expectations
               (Needs improvement)   (Valued employee)

Explain why:

RATER'S OVERALL EVALUATION— Check only one rating factor.

____   Exceeds Expectations   Consistently remarkable, distinguished performance. Employee displays initiative and creativity. Employee has substantially enhanced department efficiency and/or effectiveness. Supervisor must provide specific reasons for rating.

____   Meets Expectations   Employee is performing as required and expected in a satisfactory manner.

____   Does Not Meet Expectations   Performance does not fully meet job requirements as described below. Supervisor must provide employee with specific improvement guidelines. "Needs Improvement."

Rater's Name (Please Print) _____

Rater's Signature_____ Title _____

- -

Reviewer's Overall Rating:

RATING: ☐ Does Not Meet Expectations   ☐ Meets Expectations   ☐ Exceeds Expectations
               (Needs improvement)   (Valued employee)

Reviewer's Comments: (If Reviewer disagreed with Rater's overall rating, Reviewer must explain in detail.)

Reviewer's Signature _____ Title _____

To the employee: Your signature is requested here only as an indication that you have seen this report. Your signature is not intended to imply that you agree with the ratings.

I saw this appraisal on_____ Signature: _____

Employee Comments (Optional):

Figure 15.1 (continued)
Employee Performance Evaluation

expectations and to interpret the relationships of each position's expectations within departmental or organizational criteria. This would apply also to seasonal and part-time employees who might not have formal objective setting or development plan sessions but would be expected to meet operational standards and carry out protocols. For these employees, the link between performance expectations and financial reward is viewed from a different perspective than that of a full-time practitioner; the opportunity to retain part-time hours or to return the following summer might be as significant as salary adjustment.

Determine Format for Performance Review

After the manager and employee have determined the criteria that either stand alone or become integrated into existing forms and processes, the format for collection of data is either designed or reviewed (if in place with generic forms and processes). Information is gathered using absolute or relative standards, objectives, and eclectic measurements that involve self-appraisal, peer review, and 360-degree feedback.

Absolute methods do not compare employee performances to one another. Formats include essays, anecdotal notes from critical incidents, checklists, rating scales, and behaviorally anchored rating scales (BARS; Marquis & Huston, 2003; Sullivan & Decker, 2001; Tomey, 2000). The essay or free-form narrative is a descriptive response format that enables the manager to elaborate on the quality of the employee's performances in each performance category or for each criterion. Commonly, this subjective format is used with more objective rating scales. Essay results may reflect the manager's writing ability rather than the employee's performance. The use of anecdotal notes or the critical-incident approach permits the manager to observe employee performances in specific situations over time. The longer the manager is familiar with the employee and the more incidents that are documented, the more accurate the evaluations tend to be. This documentation type permits the manager to explain why performance is effective or ineffective, although the approach does not guarantee that observations of relevant behavior will occur. Checklists allow the manager to note whether performance has or has not occurred using yes-no criteria (e.g., "Does the employee maintain progress notes on each client?" "Is the weekly petty cash report accurate?"). The same yes-no criteria can be used when the list consists of only the behaviors essential to successful performance, yet this does not guarantee the observed behavior is persistent. Checklists tend to reduce critical criteria to absolutes; however, adding narrative comments to each question offsets this disadvantage.

Rating traits and behaviors is among the oldest and most popular appraisal formats according to Marquis and

Huston (2003). Each performance criterion is rated on a Likert scale along a continuum that best describes the employee's behavior. Numeric rating scales use numbers against which a list of behaviors are rated while graphic rating scales list characteristics rated from 5 (*high*) to 1 (*low*). The format is appropriate with objective criteria such as quality of service, job skills, and knowledge. The scales are popular because items are standardized, data are easily compiled, and they are less time-consuming than, for example, essay and critical-incident formats. Table 15.1 (p. 222) presents an illustration of generic criteria presented in a graphic rating scale format.

A frequently used format, BARS or BES (i.e., behavioral expectation scales) combines major elements of the critical incident and rating scale methods. Managers rate employees along a scored continuum according to actual behaviors performed on the job. Each job responsibility or dimension is defined as having varying performance levels using observable, measurable behaviors. Each scale is used with only one job or cluster of similar jobs so these scales are time-consuming and expensive to develop. Yet, the process of developing the instrument is valuable because it clarifies to both manager and employee the quality of performance expected. To illustrate, one of the National Council for Therapeutic Recreation Certification (NCTRC) knowledge areas, selection of programs and interventions, is presented in the BARS format in Table 15.2 (p. 222; NCTRC, n.d.).

The second category of formats uses relative standards. Relative standards compare one employee's performance with other employee evaluations. Ranking systems use a standard distribution curve or a comparison of individual employees to obtain a ranked list (Houston, 1995). The effectiveness of this method varies with department size and would be inappropriate with smaller units. The manager using a group ranking places employees in classification categories described by the normal distribution curve (e.g., top one third or two thirds). For individual ranking, the manager lists employees in order from highest to lowest performance. As Robbins (1995) pointed out, the major disadvantage of ranking systems is that a mediocre employee may score high because he or she is "the best of the worst" while an outstanding employee is rated poorly because he or she is evaluated against others who are also performing as expected.

Management by objectives (MBO) uses the individual development plan objectives or performance objectives prepared with each employee as the focus of results or outcome evaluations. The manager and employee meet and agree on principal duties and responsibilities from the employee's job description. Objectives used to evaluate accomplishments of goals are specified. The manager and employee agree on a time frame to complete the objectives. Time frames vary from one month to one year (Marquis & Huston, 2003). The first-line manager and employee meet regularly to discuss progress; thus, continuous performance review is accomplished. In Figure 15.2, a generic agency review form illustrates the categories for which the employee and manager develop goals and maintain progress notes during on going review periods.

MBO directs work activities toward organizational goals, makes the manager a coach rather than a judge, provides objective appraisal criteria, and creates a motivational environment in which employees are vested in the accomplishment of their self-defined goals (Tomey, 2000). MBO assumes employees will define suitable standards and managers understand their limitations and will focus on results rather than activities that seem to indicate results.

Eclectic measurements draw information from a variety of sources and may involve self-appraisal, peer review and 360-degree feedback. Self-appraisal is found in participatory management settings that use employee improvement plans and view the manager as a coach rather than a judge (Tomey, 2000). Increasingly employees submit portfolios of their work-related accomplishments and productivity (Marquis & Huston, 2003). The portfolio also contains an employee's goals and action plan for accomplishing these goals. Self-appraisal ensures employees are ready for the performance review and it increases the perception of fairness. However, some employees may under value their accomplishments or feel uncomfortable giving themselves high marks. Thus, used alone self-appraisal might be inaccurate. Development of a personal

Table 15.1
Graphic Rating Scale Format

Criterion	Performance Ratings				
	5	4	3	2	1
Resource Management	Uses time productively; maintains supplies and equipment at highest level	Uses time wisely; reports problems with equipment and supplies	Usually uses time wisely; does acceptable job in maintaining equipment; only rarely wastes supplies	Occasionally misuses time and equipment in unproductive effort	Often misuses time, equipment, and supplies; does not report problems
Quality of Service, Role Accountability	Produces well-organized work; maintains all documentation	Produces high-quality work; usually keeps updated documentation	Work is acceptable with some corrections and documentation sometimes falls behind	Fair quality of work with errors and corrections needed in documentation	Work and documentation have errors and require correction routinely
Interpersonal Skills, Teamwork	Always cooperates and contributes to group effort	Willing to help and support work of others	Helps others and usually contributes to group effort	Frequently has difficulty working with others and contributing to group initiative	Cannot comfortably contribute as a group member
Therapeutic Recreation Specialist Skills, Knowledge	Exhibits KSAs required of position; executes job exceptionally	Exhibits KSAs; seldom requests manager assistance	Completes routine tasks; seeks help with some tasks	Seeks assistance with client-related duties and supportive roles	Usually seeks help from others with client and supportive duties

Table 15.2
Behaviorally Anchored Rating Scale

CTRS Criterion: Selection of programs and interventions	Rating
Could be expected to select services that enable each client to achieve program/treatment plan objectives	5
Could be expected to recommend services that enable client achievement of program/treatment plan objectives with ocassional supervisory guidance	4
Could be expected to identify alternative services appropriate to client objectives for staff review and program determination	3
Could be expected to seek approval for recommended services to achieve objectives from staff and manager	2
Could be expected to seek assistance from staff and manager for identifying appropriate alternatives to achieve client objectives	1

City of Cincinnati
Initial and Interim Performance Review

Name: _____ Classification _____

Dept/Div. _____ Work Section _____

(Annual P.R. Date) Start Date _____ Mid Date _____ Special Date_____

ALL CATEGORIES REQUIRE COMMENTS (Use additional sheets as necessary)

1. Quality of Work:

- Goals:

- Progress:

2. Quantity of Work:

- Goals:

- Progress:

3. Rules and Regulations:

- Goals:

- Progress:

4. Interpersonal Skills:

- Goals:

- Progress:

5. Customer Service Delivery:

- Goals:

- Progress:

Figure 15.2
Initial and Interim Performance Review

6. Attendance:

- Goals:

- Progress:

7. Supervisory Skill (Supervisor Only):

- Goals:

- Progress:

Training (includes training identified by supervisor, employee, others):

- Goals:

- Progress:

Additional Employee Activities (includes special assignments, projects, committees, recognition/awards):

- Goals:

- Progress:

Employee Comments:

<u>Initial Review</u>

Employee Initials/Date: _____ Supervisor Initials/Date:_____

Next Review Month: _____

<u>Interim Review</u>

Supervisor Signature: _____ Date: _____

Employee Signature: _____ I saw this report on: _____

Copies to: Department/Division, Supervisor, Employee

Figure 15.2
Initial and Interim Performance Review (continued)

portfolio ensures collection of documents from a variety of sources. Having this information enables the manager to examine congruencies among available data.

Peer review occurs when peers assess work performance. The manager's review of an employee is not complete unless some type of peer review data are gathered (Marquis & Huston, 2003). Peer review provides valuable feedback for employee growth while providing peer reviewers learning opportunities. Job satisfaction results from peer recognition. If peer review is used, tools are developed, the process is determined, staff are oriented, who will evaluate whom is decided, and an interview to provide feedback is planned (Tomey, 2000). Typically peer evaluation includes review of self-appraisals, projects, care plans, and essential intervention elements (e.g., assessments, past performance, performance evaluation by the first-line manager). A committee may be elected, appointed, or randomly selected to review the employee's portfolio. Feedback is shared during an interview with the employee or the employee and his or her supervisor. Even though the process is time-consuming, peer review has the potential to increase performance appraisal accuracy while promoting increased professionalism and learning among all employees (Marquis & Huston, 2003).

As a multisource assessment system, 360-degree feedback involves anyone who interacts directly with an employee on a regular basis. Appraisal includes input from the first-line manager, peers, clients, agency administrators, and caregivers. Each individual completes an appropriate form (Arnold & Pulich, 2003). An advantage of this system is that others interact with the employee being appraised when the manager is not present, bridging a gap in the appraisal process. All evaluators are instructed about the process. This approach reduces supervisor bias and supports a team environment and performance management system (Tomey, 2000).

Performance Review Errors

A combination of formats is commonly used to gather information. Results-centered (e.g., management by objectives) behaviorally anchored rating scales (BARS) and eclectic approaches that combine outcomes with behavioral appraisals tend to be the most job related and fair. In preparation for gathering information, the manager reviews existing forms and formats and attends supportive training sessions. Training allows practice with the tools and opportunities to give feedback and to coach employees on their performances. These sessions also alert managers to the types of errors likely to occur as information is gathered. Introduction of personal bias or imposition of subjective judgment into personnel evaluations reduces the legitimacy of the results. Through training, a manager becomes aware of these errors and how to avoid them.

The tendency of a manager to overrate staff performance is a *leniency error* (Sullivan & Decker, 2001). A positive leniency error underestimates performance, which reduces the ability to discriminate among employees' performances. By using multiple raters and combining relative with absolute standards, this tendency is minimized.

An inherent difficulty with most appraisal systems is the length of time over which employees are formally evaluated, usually every 12 months (Sullivan & Decker, 2001). Typically there is a tendency to give more weight to what happened last week than to the performance of two months ago. This is referred to as the *recency error*. As a consequence of remembering the most recent events, the performance rating reflects what the employee has contributed lately rather than over the entire period (Sullivan & Decker, 2001). Also, the manager more clearly recalls recent performance, including poor behaviors the employee has not yet had time to correct (Arnold & Pulich, 2003). Anecdotal notes kept with critical incidences lessen the impact of recency errors.

There also is a tendency, known as the *halo effect*, to rate all factors high or low as a result of remembering the most notable performances during the whole evaluation period. A halo error is made when the manager allows one trait to influence the evaluation of other traits or rates all traits on the basis of a general impression (Tomey, 2000). Halo errors are minimized when the manager ensures that appraisals are based on all the important criteria for performance of every staff member (Arnold & Pulich, 2003). Accuracy of ratings is further increased by continually gathering information and involving peers, clients, and colleagues in the evaluation process.

A manager may evaluate based on qualities like organization and timeliness that the manager possesses so that an employee with similar behaviors is assessed differently from the employee who does not display these characteristics. This is a *similarity error*.

When a manager does not like the exhibited behavior, the horns effect is present. The *horns error* is opposite the halo effect. The manager perceives one negative aspect about performance and generalizes it into an overall poor appraisal rating (Arnold & Pulich, 2003). Use of BARS tends to compensate when this form of personal bias is introduced. The use of objectives and participatory evaluations also balances these rating errors.

It is possible regardless of who is being evaluated or what format and criteria are being used that the pattern remains the same: The manager tends to rate everyone in the middle rather than discriminate "outstanding" from "unacceptable." Consequently, performances appear more homogeneous than they really are, the *error of central tendency* (Marquis & Huston, 2003). Using multiple raters and combining formats (e.g., essay with critical incident) helps to improve accuracy and to reduce uniform ratings.

The first-line manager who is aware of his or her own biases and values guards against subjective attitudes influencing appraisals. Appropriate and accurate data collection and recordkeeping ensure fairness in performance reviews. Review effectiveness is enhanced by ongoing communication between the manager and employee and documentation of growth and achievement as well as areas where development is desired.

The Appraisal Interview

As managers supervise, they may choose to note performances informally, to record anecdotal notes, and to document observations and discussions with employees using department and organization personnel forms or guidelines. Additionally, most organizations require formal reviews and appraisals at least once or perhaps twice each year. During new employee orientation or probationary periods, the manager and employee review informal and formal processes and forms, and plan the time for the formal biannual or annual appraisal to coincide with the unit and organization time requirements (e.g., anniversary date of employment, fiscal year dates). Common practice has the manager gathering data year-round from multiple sources, completing a performance appraisal form, and then conducting an interview with the employee to discuss and consider or reconsider collected information, self and peer appraisals, and all the assigned ratings. At the conclusion of the appraisal discussion, a document is signed by the employee and manager and placed in an official personnel file.

Formal reviews serve important functions that benefit the manager and employee. Communication is enhanced when time is set aside for face-to-face conversations that build positive rapport and allow the manager to reassure employees of how appreciative the manager is for all the work done by staff members (Feuer, 2003). Additionally, time together builds more effective teamwork while reinforcing organizational values and emphasizing employee roles related to organizational performance and personal and professional development (Feuer, 2003; Template Topics, 2001). "The appraisal interview is the first step in employee development" (Sullivan & Decker, 2001, p. 318). The review offers a time to consider what would improve performance and the ways a manager can work to ensure staff accomplish what is expected of them. Linkage between performance and rewards that motivate employee performance is accomplished with the interview. The manager establishes that performance has been

clearly assessed, and when appropriate, rewards will be forthcoming (Sullivan & Decker, 2001). Developmental activities are identified to incorporate into individual plans and agency training programs.

Preparation for the formal appraisal is critical. It is better to meet earlier in the workweek than later because it allows time for follow-up before the weekend. An agenda with objectives is mutually prepared. The review is scheduled at least two or three days in advance with the time convenient for both parties (Feuer, 2003; Marquis & Huston, 2003; Sullivan & Decker, 2001). Also, both identify an uninterrupted time period sufficient in length to discuss input from all parties. Holding the meeting in a private conference room, rather than the manager's office, neutralizes positional power, assures privacy, and promotes a seating arrangement that supports a collegial problem-solving process. Reiterating the significance of positive outcomes establishes an improvement-oriented climate and assures two-way communication. It is also important for the manager to reaffirm the primary objective of the review is to identify how the manager and staff member can work together to improve performance and relate individual goals to organizational performance.

Before beginning the session it is important for each participant to be at ease. "The review will probably always have an element of anxiety" for both the manager and employee (Scotto, 2000, p. 8). One of the manager's responsibilities is to create a relaxed yet professional atmosphere. If the manager has given continuous feedback, some nervousness should be reduced. Another approach is to commence with small talk and to ignore employee tension (Sullivan & Decker, 2001). The use of coaching techniques with a nondirective participatory manner fosters responses from the interviewee and encourages two-way communication throughout the review (Marquis & Huston, 2003). Specific strategies to encourage a positive professional approach throughout the interview include the following:

- Let the employee know that the organization and manager are aware of his or her valuable contributions and accomplishments.

- Clearly state the objectives and agree on confidential content.

- Encourage discussion of present and past performance as well as what has been gained or learned.

- Initiate conversation with positive feedback and specific examples rather than vague generalities (e.g., "You were late in completing three client assessments last month" rather than "You are always late").

- Move into areas of improvement with feedback consistent with previous informal and formal communications.

- Mutually set specific goals and time tables so that each participant knows what has been done well, what requires improvement, what the plans are to improve, and what performances are expected in the future.

- Realize most employees believe they are meeting expectations and are surprised to hear otherwise (Feuer, 2003).

- Focus on two or three specific areas needing improvement while systematically reviewing each rating; this technique may prevent both from becoming defensive.

- Be available for employees to return to elaborate and clarify unexpected information (Marquis & Huston, 2003).

- Specify a follow-up plan to examine progress with identified review dates four to six months after the interview.

- Close with an expression of confidence in the employee's ability to improve and perform.

If generic organization forms are used, the manager and employee review performance within each category interpreting how the employee's performance did or did not meet the standards and why specific ratings were assigned. Each job task on the position specification is also reviewed. Through the exchange it may be discovered that position descriptions require rewriting. Time is also devoted to assessing each employee objective. This helps the manager and employee acknowledge achievement and validate performance. Designating a finish time is useful because the tendency is to continue discussions beyond comfortable active listening limits. Before closure, the manager's feedback is checked via paraphrasing or rephrasing as with routine therapeutic intervention sessions. Action steps to be taken by the manager and employee are committed to writing to ensure follow-up and to affirm session outcomes. Both the manager and employee sign the form to affirm that the review was held and the employee received the information.

Actual documents considered and comments recorded during the appraisal session are placed in the employee's personnel file and, if appropriate or required, shared with the human resources department or personnel specialist.

Managing Action Plans and Performance Issues

The purpose of appraisal is to effect change in the performance of others. Yet, the outcomes of personnel evaluations are factored into a number of management functions and decisions that affect the employee and manager. Immediate tasks resulting from completed appraisals are to design an employee action plan and to process information to use with quality controls and improvements. In addition, evaluation outcomes are used to take personnel actions like promotions or terminations, to plan training and development programs, to adjust system operations or department management, and to reward performances.

Designing an Action Plan

According to Marquis and Huston (2003), a follow-up plan identifies time or dates by which goals will be achieved, roles of employee and manager, and resources necessary to realize the employee's potential and to enhance service quality. This also encourages the identification of long-term coaching needs. With day-to-day feedback regarding performance, coaching methods are one of the best ways to improve work performance and build a team approach (Marquis & Huston, 2003). This plan is prepared as a stand-alone document; however, statements from the document are integrated into quality improvement plans, development plans, training inventories, and staff performance objectives. Thus, both the employee and manager are planning for the measurement and reward of future performance. The format of the plan might resemble a client's discharge plan or transition plan with a listing of objectives, target dates to review accomplishments, required resources, and progress notations. With this form of ongoing communication incorporated into routine supervisory sessions, fear created by once-a-year reviews is minimized and energies are refocused toward personal success and department or organization improvements.

The action plan is a tool used to improve quality. The plan identifies steps an employee might take to gain the KSAs necessary to deliver services in compliance with job specifications and professional standards of practice. Team effectiveness might be improved by changes in staffing assignments or other work processes that encourage interdepartmental communication and coordination. To illustrate, an objective on an employee's action plan might be to improve documentation or to incorporate assessment results into referral plans so that the team is more accurate in projecting length of stay. With seasonal or part-time staff, action plans help managers to judge appropriateness of staff assignments. For example, teachers who have experience with special needs students are often hired in summer day camps. A job responsibility is to lead a variety of therapeutic recreation activities. A first-line manager may discover after a month of the program that day campers are repeating the same activities weekly. Together the manager and summer employee plan to add diversity to the offerings and base these offerings on client objectives for the summer. If a second review a month later were to also note no new or additional services, the manager might recommend additional training prior to authorization for hiring the employee the following summer. Time is an essential quality control factor. An employee's action plan may require improvements in completion time of work tasks, such as individual assessments or preplanning for large group activities like outings or family events. The completion of these tasks in a timely manner is essential if subsequent services dependent on these initial actions are to be expedited efficiently. The action plan commits the manager and employee to ongoing communication and problem solving. The focus becomes what can be done better rather than what is being done incorrectly. An action plan used to assess team effort is presented in Figure 15.3. The supervisor and staff develop mutually agreed upon goals in each "key ingredient" area. Each goal is given a priority and together the supervisor and staff evaluate quarterly the status of each goal.

Performance Issues

Evaluation outcomes are used in personnel decisions. If outcomes of formal reviews are positive, the manager reinforces the behavior with incentives through the reward system and the development plan. If the manager determines that performance does not satisfy expectations, corrective action is incorporated in the follow-up document. Generally issues result from variances in expectations related to attendance, safety, performance, and conduct (Edginton, Hudson & Lankford, 2001). Attendance issues result from excessive absences and tardiness. Safety concerns occur when emergency procedures are not adhered to or equipment and medical protocols are improperly used or not followed. Performance problems relate to work quality, productivity or incompetence. Conduct that results in performance issues includes sexual harassment, substance abuse, policy or rule violation, and illegal acts like possession of a weapon or crime conviction. The first-line manager may engage coaching strategies to help employees improve their performance. Self-discipline and constructive discipline are used to help employees grow. When staff fail to meet expected standards of achievement progressive discipline may be in order. These processes may also involve grievances and termination.

Coaching

The day-to-day process of coaching or helping employees to improve their performance is an important yet difficult management task (Sullivan & Decker, 2001). Coaching is used when standards are met yet improvement remains possible. Coaching is less threatening than an enforcer role and over time helps employees to "improve their performance to the highest level of which they are capable" (Marquis & Huston, 2003, p. 505). Coaching eliminates small problems before they become big ones. Coaching sessions focus on variances in safety and performance practices, like misuse of equipment and supplies or procedures for conducting assessments and completing client documentation. A coaching session may be as brief as a few minutes. Issues are approached using the problem-solving approach:

1. The targeted performance is identified in behavioral terms.

2. Consequences of the problem are tied to clients, the organization, and or the employee's job description.

3. Reasons for the problem and suggestions on how to solve the problem are mutually explored.

4. A follow-up time is set to share performance feedback. (Sullivan & Decker, 2001)

Positive Discipline

Variances in adherence to rules, policies, and codes of conduct result in attendance and conduct problems. Positive discipline intends to transform negative work behaviors into positive outcomes. The emphasis in constructive discipline is to assist the employee "to behave in a manner that allows them to be self-directive in meeting organizational goals" (Marquis & Huston, 2003, p. 495). Ideally all employees would internalize rules and would have adequate self-control to meet agency expectations; yet, this does not happen. The following practices are required if discipline is to be growth producing (Marquis & Huston, 2003; Tomey, 2000):

1. Staff must know and understand the purpose of the rules and consequences for nonadherence prior to the incident.

2. Discipline is administered promptly, privately, carefully, and with a positive attitude.

3. Each time the transgression occurs, the rule is enforced consistently with an explanation of the required behavior to prevent further disciplinary action.

Recreation Center/Area

20__ Action Plan

Key Ingredient: Facility Maintenance & Improvement	PRIORITY*	QUARTERS**				Comments
		1	2	3	4	

Key Ingredient: Leisure Programs	PRIORITY*	QUARTERS**				Comments
		1	2	3	4	

Key Ingredient: Community Involvement	PRIORITY*	QUARTERS**				Comments
		1	2	3	4	

* Priorities: VH=Very High, H=High, M=Medium
** B=Begin, E=End

Figure 15.3
Action Plan

Key Ingredient: Department Image	PRIORITY*	QUARTERS**				Comments
		1	2	3	4	

Key Ingredient: Professional Growth	PRIORITY*	QUARTERS**				Comments
		1	2	3	4	

Key Ingredient: Management Operations	PRIORITY*	QUARTERS**				Comments
		1	2	3	4	

* Priorities: VH=Very High, H=High, M=Medium
** B=Begin, E=End

Figure 15.3
Action Plan (continued)

4. The discipline is impartial and flexible taking into account the entire performance record of the employee.

This approach keeps morale from breaking down while helping staff gain new skills and behave appropriately in the future. Coaching and positive discipline encourage employees to operate independently and to make decisions that control their performance.

Progressive Discipline

If employees continue undesirable conduct like breaking rules or not performing their job duties adequately, progressively stronger discipline forms are employed. The model of progressive discipline was developed in response to the National Labor Relations Act of 1935. The act required discipline and discharge to be based on "just cause" (Marquis & Huston, 2003). Specific steps in a progression are followed with repeated infractions of the same rule. The first step is an informal reprimand or verbal admonishment. During a meeting the manager and employee discuss the broken rule or performance deficiency and ways to alter the employee's behavior to meet the standard (Marquis & Huston, 2003). The manager may place an anecdotal note in the employee's personnel file documenting the infraction, consequences, and follow-up action (Tomey, 2000).

A formal reprimand or written admonishment is the second step. If the same rule is broken or a behavior like insubordination occurs again, a meeting is held; the rule/policy and consequence of future repetition are presented in written form (with reference to the previous verbal warning) along with the plan of action to meet agency expectations (Marquis & Huston, 2003; Tomey, 2000). Both the manager and employee sign the form to verify the meeting and discussion; witnesses also may sign the document to affirm discussion of the document and that a copy was given to the employee. The employee may choose to respond in writing to the document, after which both documents are filed in the employee's personnel folder. The employee retains a copy as well, and after a definitive time period, outlined in the reprimand, the manager and employee meet again to review behavioral changes and the status of compliance with expectations.

A third step is usually suspension from work without pay. As with the second step, a meeting is held, previous documentation of the incident along with the current infraction is reviewed, and comments are recorded and verified by witnesses. The suspension is immediate yet may vary in length according to the nature of the incident (e.g., excessive unexcused tardiness would result in a suspension of lesser length than threatening language toward a client).

Involuntary separation or dismissal is the last step in progressive discipline. An employee may choose to resign rather than experience termination. A termination meeting is similar to the disciplinary meetings except future improvement is not considered. The human resource department may provide procedures and documentation forms. The sequence of events during the meeting involves the following:

1. The manager stating the facts, providing concrete examples of the variance(s), and explicitly stating termination is the outcome.

2. The termination process and agency procedures are explained by the manager with each party signing agency forms.

3. The employee is given the opportunity to explain behaviors at issue and respond to termination procedures.

4. The manager closes with clarification of the agency's position regarding future references and assists the employee in departing immediately without undue embarrassment (Marquis & Huston, 2003; Sullivan & Decker, 2001).

Careful documentation throughout may allow the manager to encourage an employee to leave prior to dismissal. Also, documentation helps managers to adhere to agency disciplinary and grievance procedures.

A *grievance procedure* is a statement of wrongdoing or a procedure followed when staff believe a wrong has been committed (Marquis & Huston, 2003). It may be used at any time as well as during disciplinary proceedings when employees believe they have not been fairly treated. As a due process procedure, complaints are put in writing and include (a) situation causing dissatisfaction (i.e., who, where and when), (b) why the situation is a grievance (i.e., what needs to be rectified), and (c) what specific actions should be taken (Edginton, Hudson & Lankford, 2001). Once in writing, a sequence similar to progressive discipline is followed. An oral presentation to the first-line manager is followed by written submission to middle then top-level management. Both parties must show good will in attempting to resolve a grievance. Negotiation, compromise, and collaboration as quickly as possible result in win-win resolution and clear, fair, two-way communication that promotes morale and productivity.

Performance Outcomes and Rewards

Performance outcomes considered in employee rewards are more likely to be repeated. Also, motivation to continue to perform as desired is encouraged if the reward is contingent on performance. The desirable scenario is to reward employees for the attainment of specific development plan or performance goal accomplishments. Yet the timing of a formal annual or biannual reward may not coincide with individual employee goal achievement. To compensate for this difference managers have instituted recognition systems like "employee of the week" (or month), newsletter features, and yearly service awards. These formal signs of recognition are accompanied by informal "thank yous" and letters placed in personnel files.

Employee promotion also recognizes performance and fosters growth and motivation just as do other forms of compensation, such as salary increases, bonuses, payment of educational fees, and on-the-job childcare facilities. Formal annual rewards, like pay grade increases or promotional opportunities, may coincide with the agency fiscal year rather than individual performance reviews. The manager recognizes that favorable performance reviews are intrinsically motivational, while benefits like paid holidays, flextime, and employee assistance programs, although extrinsic in nature, are also motivational. Consequently, action plans incorporate agency compensation and benefit options. Additionally, first-line managers work with human resources to assure their staff are fairly and adequately compensated throughout the year for the positions they hold.

Summary

This chapter began by establishing that appraisal is concerned with gathering information to determine if employees have achieved work expectations and performance goals and have contributed to organizational goals. Appraising staff performance is one of the most important public relations and motivational tasks a first-line manager completes. Rarely does the first-line therapeutic recreation manager have sole responsibility for designing, implementing, and conducting performance follow-up. Through a human resource department or personnel specialist, the manager acquires and perhaps gives input into forms and processes used agency-wide. The manager's primary role of gathering information, giving feedback, and determining the support needed by each employee to perform as expected and to maximize his or her potential is critical to maintaining unit productivity and morale.

The authors cited sources that suggest a number of strategies a manager can take to ensure instruments and processes satisfy legal, organizational, and professional standards. Outcomes, behaviors, and traits identified by the manager and incorporated into the agency form or used to design individual review forms were discussed. Format for information collection may include essay, anecdotal notes from critical incidents, behaviorally anchored rating scales (BARS), rating scales, rankings, management by objectives (MBOs), and eclectic approaches. More recent performance management systems use quality control methods that incorporate self, peer, and 360-degree feedback approaches because they are more job related, fair, and promote employee growth and increased professionalism.

The manager may use several techniques to compensate for potential rater errors (i.e., leniency, recency, similarity, central tendency, and the halo and horns effects). Informal collection of information is ongoing. Formal reviews usually occur once or twice a year, which allow the manager to share informal observations and encourage the employee to continue to improve, achieve, and remain productive. A manager's feedback is tailored to the employee, department, and organization needs and processes.

A follow-up action plan jointly prepared and routinely discussed emphasizes continued improvement, quality control, and employee potential. Objectives and target dates encourage ongoing employee-manager communication. The plan is also a correction control tool, as it helps the employee perform as expected so that problems do not escalate. The plan also aids the manager in correcting inappropriate operational standards and performance criteria. In essence, the follow-up plan prescribes what the employee and manager must do together to avoid disciplinary action.

Performance issues generally result from variances in expectations related to attendance, safety, conduct and performance. Coaching through day-to-day exchanges promotes employee improvement and continued growth. Positive or constructive discipline is used to promote employee self-direction while progressive discipline is implemented with continued undesirable conduct and inadequate performance. Grievance procedures are used at anytime or during disciplinary proceedings when employees believe they have been unfairly treated.

Performance outcomes are weighed in a number of management decisions, including planning and evaluation of training and development sessions, reward and recognition processes, department management changes, and adjustments within the organization. The manager's challenge is to create a supportive environment that focuses energy and resources on those areas of employee performance, which contribute to quality, productivity, and ongoing service improvements.

Review Questions

1. Describe the legal, organizational, and professional factors a manager considers as personnel appraisal systems are designed.

2. Describe several strategies a manager takes to design performance reviews that are congruent with individual staff needs as well as unique organizational features.

3. Identify and explain the two types of performance criteria.

4. Explain and give the advantages and disadvantages of each method used to rate information gathered during performance reviews.

5. What are the appraisal errors commonly made by managers and what control features are introduced to reduce these tendencies?

6. What techniques are used during formal reviews to create a problem-solving approach to performance issues?

7. What is a follow-up action plan and how does it relate to performance issues and disciplinary actions?

8. Summarize the manager's role as a "coach" in performance appraisals. Discuss how the outcomes of performance reviews impact other management functions.

References

American Therapeutic Recreation Association (ATRA). (2000). *Standards for the practice of therapeutic recreation and self-assessment guide*. Alexandria, VA: Author.

Arnold, E. and Pulich, M. (2003). Personality conflicts and objectivity in appraising performance. *Health Care Manager, 22*(3), 227–232.

Ashurst, A. (2000). How to develop a staff appraisal system. *Nursing & Residential Care, 2*(12), 596–597.

Capko, J. (2003). Five steps to a performance evaluation system. *Family Practice Management, 10*(3), 43–47, 69-70. Retrieved March 8, 2004, from Infotrac One File database.

Edington, C. R., Hudson, S. D., and Lankford, S. V. (2001). *Managing recreation, parks, and leisure services: An introduction*. Champaign, IL: Sagamore Publishing.

Feuer, L. (2003). The management challenge: Making the most of your next performance appraisal. *Case Manager, 14*(5), 22–24.

Herringer, J. M., (2002). Once isn't enough when measuring staff competence. *Nursing Management, 33*(2), 22.

Houston, R. (1995). Integrating CQI into performance appraisals. *Nursing Management, 26*(3), 48A–48C.

Marquis, B. L. and Huston, C. J. (2003). *Leadership roles and management functions in nursing: Theory and application* (4th ed.). Philadelphia, PA: Lippincott Williams & Wilkins.

Miller, J. S. (2001). Self-monitoring and performance appraisal satisfaction: An exploratory field study. *Human Resource Management, 40*(4), 321–332.

National Council for Therapeutic Recreation Certification (1997). *1997 JA report: NCTRC report on the national job analysis project for certified therapeutic recreation specialists*. New City, NY: Author.

National Therapeutic Recreation Society (NTRS). (2004). *Standards of practice for a continuum of care in therapeutic recreation*. Retrieved September 12, 2004, from http://www.nrpa.org/content/default.aspx?documentID=530

Robbins, S. P. (1995). *Supervision today*. Englewood Cliffs, NJ: Prentice Hall.

Scotto, D. (2000). Performance appraisals: More than just going through the motions. *Medical Laboratory Observer, 32*(8), 14–17. Retrieved March 8, 2004, from Infotrac One File database.

Sullivan, C. A. (1994). Competency assessment and performance improvement for healthcare providers. *Journal of Healthcare Quality, 16*(4), 14–19, 38.

Sullivan, E. J. and Decker, P. J. (2001). *Effective leadership and management in nursing* (5th ed.). Upper Saddle River, NJ: Prentice Hall.

Tappen, R. M. (2001). *Nursing leadership and management: Concepts and practice* (4th ed.). Philadelphia, PA: F. A. Davis Company.

Template Topics. (2001). Conducting effective performance appraisals. *Clinical Leadership & Management Review, 15*(5), 348–352.

Tomey, A. M. (2000). *Guide to nursing management and leadership* (6th ed.). St. Louis, MO: Mosby.

Chapter 16
Staff Training and Development

First-line managers are expected "to sustain a viable, productive workforce to provide quality, cost-effective patient care" (Parsons & Stonestreet, 2003, p. 121). This translates into a need to maintain and to upgrade therapeutic recreation specialists' knowledge and skills. Managers must provide responsive training programs that address staff needs quickly, cost-effectively, and accurately.

Effective 21st century organizations are characterized as learning organizations. A culture of continuous learning empowers staff to implement new ideas and to adapt to new technologies (Pesavento, Bator & Ross, 2001). McConnell (2002) suggested "given the pace of technological change in health care and elsewhere and social change in the world at large" managers and employees must continue to acquire new knowledge and learn new skills (p. 4). Another trend contributing to the growing interest in employee training and education programs is the use of systems management approaches like total quality management (TQM). TQM philosophy values the role that employees play in the success of health and human service agencies. Each system component, such as the employees, contributes to organizational outcomes. "The knowledge base of a facility's staff and management is the foundation of that facility's quality of care" (Klusch, 2002, p. 2). The goals of continuous improvement, high-quality service, cost-effectiveness, worker efficiency, and adaptation to change require that managers and staff be in a constant state of learning and development.

Training refers to learning experiences that result in a relatively permanent change in an individual that improves his or her ability to perform on the job (Robbins & Decenzo, 2001). As described by Grayson (2001), this change occurs in the practitioner's knowledge, skills, attitudes, and/or behavior. It is expected that as a result of training employees that acquire new skills will create a better product or be more productive (Marquis & Huston, 2003). Staff development is the broader concept that includes training and intends to prepare practitioners for continuous growth (Marquis & Huston, 2003). Developmental training is a long-range training program directed toward improving work performance by providing employees an opportunity to expand personal knowledge, skills, and abilities (KSAs; Edginton, Hudson & Lankford, 2001).

The first section of this chapter considers regulations, legislation, and professional standards that support training and development. Various types of training and development are also presented. Personnel needs assessments are described in the second section. Meeting the educational needs of a culturally diverse staff is considered in this section. Also assessed are internal and external resources available for training and development programs. With this information a comprehensive training and development program is designed. The third section of this chapter addresses the learning theories and principles of adult learning that influence the delivery methods and teaching strategies used with adult learners to present material. Implementation of training and development programs—section four—involves the manager in a number of tasks, the result of which is delivery of relevant and useful options. The manager's role in short- and long-term coaching is considered, as are the roles of mentoring and technology in the implementation of training and development programs. The next section considers evaluation of training and development programs. Evaluation helps to justify training expenditures. The manager conducts evaluations to ascertain if staff enhancement has occurred and if outcomes are relevant to organizational and client needs. Specific evaluation strategies are introduced in the fifth section of this chapter. This chapter concludes with an overview of trends and issues in therapeutic recreation training and development.

Throughout this chapter, the role of a first-line manager in training and development is considered because responsibility for knowledge of department personnel competencies lies with the first-line manager. The manager is also aware of the problems to be resolved and decisions to be made as personnel adapt to change within the organization and profession. Further, managers oversee the budget. Changes in productivity and outcomes are reflected in the budget, and a manager's task is to relate the cost of training and development to changes in worker productivity and outcomes. Formalized training and development programs address the needs of all personnel (i.e., seasonal, part-time, interns, volunteers, on-call as-needed staff [PRN], and full-time employees) as each contributes to the department's accomplishment of service goals and outcomes. Thus, managers monitor comprehensive programs that meet their needs and the needs of those who carry out the unit's mission.

Composition of Training and Development Programs

Societal changes affecting employment have occurred so rapidly and dramatically that the ways in which a manager manages have changed completely (McConnell, 2002). Changes have come about as a result of regulations and legislation that focus on individual rights, client care, and confidentiality (Aylward, Stolee, Keat & Johncox, 2003; Blair, 2003; McConnell, 2002). "Continual development of staff knowledge and understanding will result in greater competency, broader awareness and increased… safety" (Schirick, 2001, p. 15). Professional standards documents (ATRA, 2000; NTRS, 1990, 2004) also present criteria that encourage professionals to remain competent through continuing education and design of individual development plans.

Commencing in the mid to late 1980s the need for training in long-term care was realized (Aylward, Stolee, Keat & Johncox, 2003). A report in 1986 by the Institute of Medicine encouraged training interventions to improve skill, boost self-esteem, and improve resident care (Wood, Cummings, Schnelle & Stephens, 2002). The U.S. Omnibus Budget Reconciliation Act (OBRA) of 1987 (P.L. 100-203) focused on resident care mandating individual care plans to ensure optimal functioning. To support this focus, mandatory training hours for nursing assistants were increased and regular performance assessments were required to show skill competency (Aylward, Stolee, Keat & Johncox, 2003). The 1996 Health Insurance Portability Accountability Act (HIPAA) addressed client confidentiality and required employees throughout health care and social service agencies to be trained in a relatively brief time frame (Blair, 2003). Training needs of staff were highlighted in a national survey that found more than one in four assisted living facilities had at least one training deficiency between 2000 and 2002 (McCoy & Hanson, 2004).

A second focus of legislation, individual rights, calls on managers to remain informed about employment rights. Since the 1964 Civil Rights Act, a number of laws have been passed that have an effect on how managers can or must deal with employees. These include legislation like the Americans with Disabilities Act (ADA), Family and Medical Leave Act (FMLA), and the Employee Retirement Income Security Act (ERISA, P.L. 93-406; McConnell, 2002). Continuing education is as important for first-line managers as it is for employees in any rapidly changing technical or human service field.

A third impetus to address staff and manager training needs comes from professional standards of practice documents. Criteria are cited as either stand-alone or plan of operation standards. A department written plan of operation includes policies that promote training and development and procedures for periodic assessment of therapeutic recreation staff educational needs (ATRA, 2000). Also, as an element of continuous quality improvement (CQI), staff are to participate in periodic evaluation of the department's professional development plan and make recommendations for improvement (ATRA, 2000). A professional development plan supports a wide range of opportunities for continuing education and training. This plan identifies policies that establish minimum staff participation and guidelines for practitioners' individual development plans (ATRA, 2000; NTRS, 1990).

Literature sources (Edginton, Hudson & Lankford, 2001) and professional standards (NTRS, 1990) suggest that a number of types of formal training are incorporated in a comprehensive staff training and development program. The first type, an orientation program, is a systematic training aimed at introducing new employees to the department. This orientation generally introduces staff to several different components of the organization's culture, including the following:

1. vision, mission, goals, objectives, and services

2. policies, procedures, structure, and plan of operation

3. areas, facilities, resources, and workstations

4. protocols and standards of practice

5. clientele and coworkers

6. performance expectations and privileges associated with each position (Klusch, 2002; Pesavento, Bator & Ross, 2001)

Practical or "survival" training helps the new employee become comfortable in the environment. Communication skills, core clinical requirements, competency testing, and mentoring of new employees by selected staff are orientation topics that help staff feel as though they are part of a team (Klusch, 2002). Managers also present the expectation that learning will be an ongoing part of the job.

The goal of in-service training, the second type of staff training and development, is to enable practitioners to fulfill the expectations of their positions with the highest degree of competence possible and to maintain performance at that level as long as the position is held. According to Edginton and associates (2001), keeping staff at peak performance and up-to-date requires that opportunities be provided to review previous knowledge and skills (e.g., documentation) and to acquire new information and technological advancements (e.g., computerized assessments). Organized in-service training programs occur through regularly scheduled staff meetings; agency-sponsored workshops and seminars; and the use of outside consultants, media, and technology (NTRS, 1990).

Professional development programs, a third type of staff training and development, are becoming increasingly more important. As managers and staff must meet the changing health and human service needs of clients within a dynamic environment, development training addresses both department needs and practitioner needs. Development education considers recertification requirements of the CTRS and CPRP as well as employee career development (Marquis & Huston, 2003). Self-improvement and expansion of personal KSAs occur through classes on time management and conflict resolution. The intent is to improve work performance while allowing staff and managers to realize their growth potential.

Retraining, a fourth type of training and development, has emerged to accommodate practitioner needs to remain abreast of changing work environments and demands. Evidence of the rapid rate of change in the clinical setting is the more frequent publishing of the Joint Commission on Accreditation of Healthcare Organization's (JCAHO) standards and the decreasing length of client stays. In the community, practitioners respond to legal directives like the Americans with Disabilities Act (ADA) and the fairly recent acute health needs of persons returning to their homes from clinical settings. As a result of impacts such as these, managers are faced with new and changing roles that must be affected immediately if standards are to be met and costs recovered. The intent of these experiences is to ensure staff gain the KSAs necessary to stay productive and marketable while delivering quality services efficiently. "Retraining also provides employees with an opportunity to survive downsizing" (Marquis & Huston, 2003, p. 603). Retraining promotes employee and manager retention while creating a motivational environment necessary for career advancement (Parsons & Stonestreet, 2003). Retraining occurs through position exchanges, long-distance learning, computerized self-paced programs, acquisition of credentials in other professional areas, cross-training, return to school, and conventional in-service programs.

Training and Development Assessments

The first step in an effective training and development program is a needs assessment to determine educational needs of staff and management (Sullivan & Decker, 2001). A comprehensive needs assessment gathers relevant data from the department, identifies alternative training resources and performance expectations, and ultimately creates a department-wide atmosphere supportive of training and development programs. Assessments consider the needs of each staff member while taking into consideration organizational goals. The first-line manager is the link between upper-level management strategic goals and the tasks that must be completed to achieve these goals. Consequently systematic determination of staff operational needs based on organizational and departmental goals is the basis for determining specific content.

Marquis and Huston (2003) outlined the following processes in planning and evaluating staff development programs:

- Identify the desired staff and manager knowledge and skills.

- Identify present level of competence.

- Determine deficit between competence and desired performance levels.

- Identify resources to meet needs.

- Implement alternative programs.

- Evaluate outcome of programs.

Powell (2002) suggested the process commence with examining existing documents, like job descriptions, performance reviews or action plans, and safety-related reports, and also with considering the recommendations and future projections of experts. Certification requirements (NCTRC, n.d.) and federal, state, and local regulations (e.g., infection control, emergency safety, quality improvement, handling hazardous materials) are also considered (Sullivan & Decker, 2001). Staff development specialists and managers use audits, peer evaluations, case conferences, accreditation and practice standards, coaching, mentoring, and clinical observations to determine specific positional needs.

To determine the needs of a particular position a traditional form of needs assessment is a job or task analysis. This analysis determines what is to be performed, how often or frequently the task is performed, how important or significant the task is to services provided, and how difficult it is to develop the KSAs to perform the task. Job descriptions, performance appraisal criteria, professional certification plans (NCTRC), and licensure requirements are resources of expected therapeutic recreation specialist job responsibilities. Task analyses prepared from review of such documents are used to compare staff performance with competencies expected of professionals in similar positions. Discrepancies become the focus of individual development plans. Each plan identifies specific performance outcomes to alleviate deficits found in actual job behaviors. The manager uses data from staff development plans and department assessments to prepare training and development goals. These goals identify information to be acquired by practitioners and the challenges they will face as newly acquired knowledge and skills are put into practice.

First-line managers can expect to work with a more diverse workforce, including professionals from different age cohort groups as well as staff and consumers with various cultural backgrounds. Learners with diverse backgrounds and learning styles perceive the content and delivery methods differently than persons who have been prepared in the mainstream. Older professionals learn differently than new graduates (Marquis & Huston 2003). Mentoring programs have been used as career development tools and as a means to reduce stereotypes (Bedini & Anderson, 2003). Education to support diversity, like case studies and experiential learning, along with mentoring, facilitates team development and effectiveness. Consequently, as the manager assesses departmental needs, consideration is given to the strengths and challenges presented by heterogeneity of staff backgrounds and preparation.

Because managers are responsible for the performance of their staff, it becomes their responsibility to ensure that employees are properly trained and the resources are available for training. The role assumed by the first-line manager depends on a number of the following factors identified during the assessment process: the size of the department, funds available for training, the manager's and employees' training skills, and access to resources internally and externally. Robbins (1995) indicated that the larger the department or agency, the more likely there will be a separate training department or human resource specialist with support resources to conduct specialized training. Whether or not internal rather than external resources are used may depend on the extent of the human resource department's or specialists' expertise and available technology and financial support. Supervisors' training and clinical supervision skills vary. Some have developed particular expertise through training and experience and are comfortable planning and conducting educational sessions. Likewise, staff with special experience are also able to develop and present programs. Additionally, the availability of technology, such as teleconferencing and CD-ROM, may influence whether training occurs both internally and externally. Although internal education is usually a lower cost per person, external options like conferences provide more instructors and a greater variety of instructional approaches.

Affiliation with state and national professional organizations is a conduit to training and development expertise and materials. Other therapeutic recreation, health, and human service personnel in the community bring expertise to bear on issues of common concern. Community and professional contacts, in essence, validate the findings of assessments. Additionally, they provide resources to help managers and staff remain abreast of global professional issues. Attendance and participation in community and professional activities is, therefore, one avenue to access training and development resources while also remaining aware of management trends.

Design of Training and Development Programs

After staff and management needs are determined, the next step is to plan the types of formal training and development programs. This involves identifying objectives and matching them with educational or delivery methods (Sullivan & Decker, 2001). These objectives are measurable statements that delineate employee behavioral changes to occur within a specific time frame. Objectives in each employee's development plan guide the manager as programs are planned. Also considered in the selection of education or delivery methods are the learning needs and styles of adult learners and the teaching strategies that promote transfer of acquired knowledge and skills to performance. Adult learners are self-directed people who have learned from life experiences and are focused on solving problems that exist in their immediate work environments (Marquis & Huston, 2003).

Adult learning theory suggests that children and adults have different learning styles. Androgogy, or adult learning, suggests strategies appropriate to adult learning. Specific implications for training and development include the following (Marquis & Huston, 2003; Sullivan & Decker, 2001):

- Adults enjoy participating in the planning of learning experiences.

- Experiential techniques work best.

- Mistakes are opportunities for learning.

- Readiness is greatest when there is a need to know.

- Adults need quick application of learned material.

- Adults need to be involved in evaluation of their progress.

- Adults think of learning as a way to be more effective in solving today's problems.

- Adults see themselves as capable of self-direction and desire others to also view them from this perspective.

Social learning theory, outlined by Bandura, suggests people learn most from direct experience and observation with behaviors retained through positive rewards (and vice versa). The following four processes are fundamental to social learning theory (Marquis & Huston, 2003; Sullivan & Decker, 2001):

1. People learn as a result of the effects of their actions from direct experience.

2. Knowledge is obtained through vicarious experiences like observation.

3. People learn as a result of judgments voiced by others.

4. People evaluate the soundness of new information using inductive and deductive logic.

The anticipation of reinforcement influences what people observe. Consequently, observational learning is more effective when the learner is informed in advance about the benefits of adopting certain behaviors because behavior is learned through cognitive processes before it is performed (Sullivan & Decker, 2001).

Another theory, relapse prevention, teaches learners to anticipate potential problems and to remain confident as coping strategies are applied (Sullivan & Decker, 2001). By learning self-control and coping strategies, trainees retain newly learned behaviors. In the neutral environment of training and development, learners identify potential problems and alternative ways to cope with situations. Trainees then practice such situations using the newly acquired skills.

Marquis and Huston (2003) indicated several additional concepts have planning implications with adult learners:

- Readiness to learn refers to maturational and experiential prerequisite skills, knowledge or behavior necessary for the next stage of learning. Without prerequisites, training may meet with limited success.

- When informed in advance of the training benefits and adopting new behaviors, adults are more motivated to attend and learn.

- Once acquired, behavior needs reinforcement until internalized. On-the-job rewards and benefits from managers and mentors influence leaning maintenance.

- Task analysis, whole/part/whole learning, and overlearning facilitate retention of complex tasks.

The goal of training is to transfer new skills to the work setting and "the biggest problem in training is the loss of transfer that results from lack of use" (Tyler, 2000, p. 102). This situation is managed by creating similarity between the training and work experience, practicing and overlearning in a variety of situations, and presenting underlying principles so the learner is capable of adapting the task to accommodate situational demands. Transfer is also facilitated by scheduling training as close as possible to the time employees need to use the skill and having trainees teach others within 24 hours of their training (Tyler, 2000).

Ability to retain information varies between experienced and inexperienced professionals. Organizing material into groups—three or four ideas in oral presentations and four to six when using visual aids—enhances retention.

Measurable objectives inform employees of work expectations and are a means to assess their progress. Learning is also enhanced when knowledge of results is immediate and meaningful to the work assignment.

Learning styles vary among practitioners. Ismeurt, Ismeurt, and Miller (1992) described two types of learning styles in their research. Field-dependent learners tend to prefer discussion, guided discovery, and demonstration methods whereas field-independent adults tend to prefer observation, experimentation, and interaction with others to acquire new information and skills (Ismeurt, Ismeurt & Miller, 1992). Field-dependent trainees tend to be influenced by feedback while field-independent trainees tend to be self-motivated and to respond better to situations that permit active participation and leadership. Therefore, as the manager designs the content and plans for the practice of newly acquired staff knowledge and skills, adult learning styles are considered.

People learn differently (Hanover, 2001). Therefore, as education or delivery methods are selected, teaching strategies that recognize adult learner needs and theories are considered. One training format appropriate to adults is grounded on the premise "tell them, show them, and ask them to tell you." This approach supports transfer of information and encourages an interactive format conducive to learner retention (Hanover, 2001). Strategies that promote retention, transfer, and learner motivation to change incorporate a number of considerations:

- Scheduling 15- to 30-minute sequenced sessions two to three times per day or over two days before programs or shift changes when learners are rested results in information transfer as will scheduling training immediately prior to when the information is needed (Klusch 2002; Schirick, 2001).

- Applying new information to real-life problems through role-playing, simulations and case studies is motivational and encourages retention.

- Organizing trainees into small groups, followed by teaching each other, motivates participation (Grayson, 2001).

- The military model of repeated trainings in real situations is effective as people, under pressure, tend to resort to experience as opposed to knowledge (Grayson, 2001).

- A format that uses skill demonstration, discussion, and problem solving to augment brief lectures is more effective than lecture-only training formats (Klusch, 2002).

- Learners are responsive when they are aware that their competency will be evaluated or is an issue. Consequently, posttests on class content are used immediately following training to assess learner outcomes (Klusch, 2002).

- Scheduling several staff from the same program may pose coverage issues, yet in the long run may result in joint problem solving, which boosts retention (Tyler, 2000).

- Retaining learning is enhanced when staff have visuals, checklists, and CDs they take from the training for later use (Tyler, 2000).

- Stimulation of as many senses repeatedly and minimizing distractions like access to e-mail during training breaks also fosters use of new materials (Tyler, 2000).

- Teaching the essentials in a concise manner and teaching how to access additional information at a later date encourages interest.

Evidence suggests people learn 10% of what they read, 30% of what they see and 50% of what is heard and seen while they remember 90% of what is both said and done (Dickerson, 2003; Hanover, 2001). Thus using different delivery strategies keeps presentations alive and promotes learner retention.

Overcoming reluctance is critical to helping trainees apply classroom learning to change in practice. A question like, "What will help you implement what you have learned today?" stimulates learner application prior to leaving the session and generates a plan for dealing with jobsite challenges (Dickerson, 2003).

Using reflection during training promotes its use during practice. A question like,"What factors will help you implement this intervention?" stimulates critical thinking and creative learning. "Spending the time on creative learning and reflection increases employee's job satisfaction… which in turn leads to higher… retention of quality staff" (Dickerson, 2003, p. 249).

As outlined by Marquis and Huston (2003), managers first complete needs assessments to identify desired staff and managerial knowledge and skills and available resources; this is followed by preparing objectives, then educational or delivery methods are selected that promote transfer of information to practice. These methods are compatible with adult learner behaviors as well as the types of training and development (i.e., orientation, in-services, professional development, and retraining). Finally, prior to implementation of a comprehensive training and development program, therapeutic recreation managers plan how to evaluate the outcomes of the program (i.e., summative evaluation) and each training and development opportunity presented (i.e., formative evaluation). Training objectives tied to CQI plans and staff development plans become indicators of outcome achievement. Habel (1994) noted that an outcome-based service focus requires evaluation to demonstrate the difference training and development makes in job performance and ability to adapt to future professional challenges.

Training and development effectiveness is judged by how well staff performance addresses agency, department, and personal and professional goals. Thus, evaluation assumes a three-dimensional perspective. Upper-level managers are generally concerned with whether employees work efficiently to meet agency goals. First-line managers, however, focus on the quality of client services. Arnold and McClure (1989) suggested employees measure training and development by how much they can apply to their immediate responsibilities and future obligations. Similar to needs assessments, a number of methods are available to validate learning and its impact on service outcomes. According to Habel (1994), primary evaluation approaches are verbal and written feedback, demonstration, and observation of job performance following introduction of new knowledge and skills. The manager's task is to identify an approach and to design tools appropriate to each evaluation audience. Ultimately, the manager must prepare an evaluation plan that projects how achievement of objectives will be measured and reported to document the effects of training and development on job performance and service outcomes (Habel, 1994).

Implementation of Training and Development Programs

When preparing to conduct or facilitate participation in training and development programs, the first-line manager undertakes the following tasks to ensure the delivery is relevant and useful:

- Inform staff about the opportunities.

- Arrange for staff attendance or access.

- Prepare the delivery methods and setting.

- Ensure that offerings are related to staff development plan goals.

- Plan for applicability of programs to the job or professional growth of each trainee.

- Project follow-up and continued training and development needs.

While training and development programs are in progress, the manager monitors change through formative evaluations with upper-level management, trainees, ser-

vice recipients, and anyone affected by therapeutic recreation services. Formative or process evaluations involve the manager in coaching, work site observations, portfolio reviews, performance appraisal documentation, financial reporting, mentoring, and CQI or service quality monitoring.

Informing Staff

Informing staff about training and development opportunities is essential for several reasons. If behavioral change is expected, staff must know about and be motivated to attend programs to gain access to knowledge and skills. When participation occurs during work time, impact on programming and direct client services is considered. Additionally, the manager plans for the equitable distribution of time and financial resources among personnel. One information method is a training and development calendar (see Figure 16.1). This calendar identifies on-site programs for a period of time (e.g., a month, fiscal or calendar year). This helps managers plan for service continuity, and staff select opportunities that best relate to their particular needs. Also, the calendar becomes an educational tool that apprises colleagues of common issues

TRAINING AND DEVELOPMENT CALENDAR – June 20__

Educational Services
Iowa Health System
Woodland Center
1313 High, Ground Floor
Des Moines, Iowa

Preregistration is required for all classes. To register, call #6398.
For detailed information on these classes, consult your online Educational Services Catalog.

MONDAY	TUESDAY	WEDNESDAY	THURSDAY	FRIDAY
			1	2
5 New Employee Orientation 8–4:30; IMMC–Hill Auditorium	6	7	8	9 Q2/Care 8:30–4; Woodland Center #3
12	13 Q2/Care 4–9 p.m.; ILH–Conf. Room A/B	14	15	16
19 New Employee Orientation 8–4:30; IMMC–Hill Auditorium	20	21	22 Q2/Care 8:30–4; Woodland Center #3	23
26	27 Supervisors' Forum 1:30–2:30 p.m.; IHL–Conf. Room	28 Supervisors' Forum 8:30–9:30 a.m.; IMMV–Hill Aud	29	30

Used with permission of Iowa Health Des Moines, Methodist, Lutheran, Blank Hospitals

Figure 16.1
Training and Development Calendar

and networking opportunities. During short-term or day-to-day coaching sessions when managers are engaged in 5- to 10-minute "teachable moments" or "two-way talks" with staff, they may suggest participation in structured training and development sessions as appropriate follow-up to, for example, assist with socialization into the department culture or identify alternative interventions to accomplish client objectives (Marquis & Huston, 2003; Sullivan & Decker, 2001). Other methods used to announce training and development opportunities include flyers, e-mail, table tents, listserv bulletins, and department circulars. Techniques used to inform personnel of off-site professional workshops and conferences are association mailings and Internet announcements.

Facilitating Access

Managers facilitate access to training and development when they circulate information, arrange program coverage, plan coaching sessions, and prepare for mentoring relationships. Lead-time is required to submit financial requests and to plan adequate service supervision when external programs are attended. With brief lunch or before-program in-services, circulating a sign-up sheet permits employees to rearrange personal schedules and managers to have the proper amount of training materials. Department membership in professional organizations and the opportunity to attend a national conference are staff motivators. Managers conscious of these employment perks budget accordingly.

A key facilitative role assumed by the manager is support of long-term coaching sessions and mentor relationships. These processes build reflective teams and promote succession and retention while increasing productivity, job satisfaction, and professional growth (Bedini & Anderson, 2003; Greene & Puetzer, 2002; Marquis & Huston, 2003). A manager plans annual coaching sessions with employees that occur at a time other than during the performance appraisal review. The focus of the session is on advancing the employee's knowledge and skills and exploring future career options.

Managerial support of mentoring is demonstrated through financial incentives, staffing and scheduling flexibility, and title and leadership recognition (Greene & Puetzer, 2002). The manager facilitates mentoring relationships through ongoing orientation and development opportunities between the seasoned professional (i.e., mentor) and the new hire (i.e., mentee). The manager sets aside time for mentor-mentee formal and informal evaluations and recommends mentor-mentee meeting guidelines. Job descriptions include titles and incentives to recognize mentoring. Performance reviews and reward systems acknowledge mentor-mentee relationships.

Preparing Delivery Methods

Training and development programs are conducted in ways that help trainees remember and use information and skills. The environment in which programs take place and the resources used during programs are arranged or planned to support trainee goals. As previously noted, presentation methods recognize the nature of the content and learning needs of practitioners. When the training environment resembles the work setting, trainees transfer the newly acquired information and skills more quickly. Further, when training and development experiences closely align with work tasks, transfer is facilitated. Presentation methods, such as case studies, simulations, gaming and role-playing, enable practice of therapeutic recreation situations. Nontraditional devices, such as equipment used in therapy sessions and during recreation experiences, motivate participation by appealing to the primary senses and the desire to "learn by doing."

Training health care professionals is a challenge due to burnout that causes poor motivation, time constraints caused by heavy workloads, frequent deadlines, numerous training requirements, and the shift-nature of work. The use of technology like online modules, self-paced instructional videos, CD-ROM, and internal e-mail systems offers a number of training advantages to health care staff and managers (Blair, 2003; Brenner, 2003; Harrington & Walker, 2002; Pastuszak & Rodowicz, 2002; Wood, Cummings, Schnelle & Stephens, 2002):

- Staff may schedule training at their convenience.

- Managers do not have to coordinate staff coverage schedules nor plan for trainer availability.

- Modules are designed for take-home or application and transfer of information.

- New employee training is readily available.

- Training is self-paced and individualized.

- Retention is enhanced by material that encourages trainee interaction and sensory stimulation.

- Technology approaches are more economical than conventional instructor-led sessions.

One disadvantage of technology-based training might be the availability of equipment and tech support. Also, the practice of a physical skill, like debriefing a group session, is necessary to supplement computer-based training. Overall, the advantage of technology as a delivery method with adult learners is the ability to provide education on demand at a time and place that meets their educational needs.

Relating Training and Development to Staff Needs

A manager helps to ensure the relatedness of training and development programs to staff needs by including staff in program design and implementation. Staff participate in needs assessment processes and the preparation of the department's annual training and development plan. Also, along with the manager, staff develop goals for each program. This fosters interest and enthusiasm, which motivates staff to learn, remember, and use acquired information and skills (Arnold & McClure, 1989). Managers also encourage staff to link their individual development plan goals to those for each training and development program. Each learning opportunity is then linked to the goals of the department's annual plan. When staff conduct programs, they are more likely to relate training content and outcomes to their particular situational needs.

Applicability of Training and Development

Another technique to motivate change, retention, and growth is to relate learning outcomes to practice and professional development. This is accomplished in programs that include situational sets found in therapeutic recreation practice. When staff conduct programs or attend programs presented by other therapeutic recreators, they benefit from "ownership" of the experience and relating to "common" professional issues. Attendance at professional meetings also exposes staff to analogous situations. Evaluations that require respondents to identify how session knowledge and skills will be applied to practice also helps trainees to realize how they are expected to improve or change performance as a result of attendance.

Projecting Follow-Up

A final management task prior to implementing training and development programs is to project what follow-up is necessary after staff participation. Dramatic change in the work environment requires additional practice, managerial feedback and support, and recognition of achieved training and development goals. Follow-up occurs when staff return to the work site to present materials and resources acquired at professional meetings to those in the department who did not attend. Follow-up also involves planned observations and reviews of tapes to critique practices and compare "before" with "after" performances. The use of written checklists to confirm completed job tasks is a follow-up strategy and self-correcting tool to incorporate into personnel appraisal processes. Follow-up needs are projected to prepare the resources and continued training and development opportunities that ensure use of newly acquired abilities and to overcome challenges to the introduction of new behaviors in the work setting.

Implementing Training and Development Programs

While training and development is in progress, the manager oversees program delivery, facilitates application of knowledge and skills, and conducts formative evaluations. Specific tasks include managing site logistics, collecting and analyzing evaluation information, monitoring application of learned skills, documenting and verifying continuing education credits, tracking financial and travel reimbursements, long-term coaching, supporting mentor relationships, and ensuring continuity of department programs and services. Through postevent follow-up, managers observe how newly acquired knowledge and skills relate to department services and professional practice. A primary concern for the manager is the match between individual development goals, department annual development goals, and the outcomes of each particular training and development experience. When incongruencies are observed, the task becomes reconciling available opportunities with annual staff and department development plans. Locating and offering different opportunities and/or revising staff and department plans are options. Change has a domino effect. As change resulting from training and development is monitored, performance expectations and development plans are updated to ensure that indicators of quality improvement are continually achieved.

Implemented training and development programs vary with the needs of the staff, situation, department, and agency. The needs of volunteer, intern, seasonal, and part-time employees are more diverse than full-time staff. As a consequence, orientations and in-services cover broader topics, but they are less in-depth. With full-time staff, development and retraining are focused and in-depth while emphasizing the knowledge and skills necessary to update, enhance, and/or revitalize performance.

Situational needs also influence program implementation. Resources and interventions are unique to each setting. Professionals who relocate may find it necessary to attend orientations or in-services to become familiar with protocols peculiar to new positions. Implementation is also affected by relationships and timing of department and agency programs. The therapeutic recreation manager monitors the timing and content of department and agency programs to encourage maximum staff involvement and support and to avoid duplicating efforts.

First-line managers are leading increasingly complex and rapidly changing work environments. As a consequence of reengineering, downsizing and organizational flattening, managers are spread more thinly than ever (McConnell, 2002). Spans of control have increased and responsibilities expanded. It is difficult to learn how to manage better in this environment. Yet, the need for continuing education is ever present. Managerial development and retraining programs are critical components of comprehensive staff development programs.

Implementing Orientation Programs

Managers involve staff in conducting orientations (e.g., with summer or seasonal employees, new full-time employees). Content acquaints personnel to the mission and direction of the department and agency operational policies. Topics presented by managers and staff include but are not limited to the following:

- agency vision, mission, culture, and structure
- department clientele, services, and operating protocols (see Figure 16.2)
- areas, facilities, resources, and use procedures
- risk management, infection control, client rights, and quality and safety plans
- employee benefits, forms, policies, performance expectations, and competency evaluation
- work rules and standards
- privileging procedures and professional opportunities
- mentoring and coaching processes
- team building
- personnel introductions
- credentialing requirements and opportunities

Implementing In-Service Programs

In-services are generally implemented on site in brief time periods (e.g., over the lunch hour, during "nonprogram" time). Employees, human resource specialists, and managers present information helpful to current job performance. Some general, yet not all-inclusive, in-service topics include the following:

- marketing and promotion
- referral and transition planning
- managing safety and risk
- regulatory standards, reviews, and documentation
- interdisciplinary and teamwork strategies
- managing assistive devices
- volunteer management
- caregiver training and support

- application of specific interventions (e.g., brief treatment)
- inclusion training and adapting resources (see Figure 16.3, p. 246)
- workplace diversity
- technology tools and resources

Implementing Development Programs

Development opportunities like attendance at local workshops or professional conferences address systematic issues such as the following:

- legislation and legal directives
- mentoring skills
- technological and scientific discoveries
- ethics and professionalism
- innovative interventions
- philosophical paradigms
- research and efficacy
- health and human service reforms
- changing demographics and clientele needs

Managerial development programs encompass how to manage taking into consideration employee and client rights as well as leadership, financial, and technical skills necessary to function successfully as a manager: Specific topics cover the following (McConnell, 2002; Sullivan, Bretschneider & McCausland, 2003):

- organizational alignment and alliance
- developing subordinates
- facilitating team functioning
- managing time
- recruitment and retention
- conflict resolution
- strategic planning and networking
- regulatory and compliance responsibilities
- human resource issues (see Figure 16.4, p. 247)
- life-work balance management
- mentoring, developing and motivating staff
- research in practice

Therapeutic Division

Pre-Season Training

❖ **First Aid / CPR** (Full Certificate Course)

Day One
New Employee Orientation (New Employee Only)

Day Two
Adapted Aquatics / Epilepsy information (New Employees Only)

First Aid / CPR Review Course (Returning Staff with Current Certification)

Day Three
Positive Behavioral Support and CPI
Mandatory for Camp Directors, select returning staff, and new employees

Day Four
Team Building and Leadership Skills

Prior To Monday Planning – at the Dunham Recreation Center

Week One
Activity Leadership and Special Populations (Individuals and Group Leadership Techniques)

Week Two
Sensory Activities, Activities for Severe / Profound Disabilities

Week Three
Director's Meeting (Issues in Supervision, etc.)

After Monday Planning – at the Dunham Recreation Center

Week Two
CPI — Part II, Team Holds
Mandatory for Program Directors and selected staff

Week Five
Adaptive Aquatics Refresher

Source: Cincinnati Recreation Commission, 2004b

Figure 16.2
Orientation Program

CincinnatiRecreationCommission

Inclusion Training

Day One: 8:30 a.m. – 5:30 p.m.

❖ **Overview of Inclusion**   8:30 a.m. – 9:30 a.m.
  ▪ What is Inclusion? Definition
  ▪ CRC Policy
  ▪ Confidentiality
  ▪ Legislature / ADA
  ▪ Eliminating Barriers / Types of Accomodations
  ▪ Benefits
  ▪ Terminology / People First Language
❖ **The Job of the ISA?**   9:30 a.m. – 10:15 a.m.
  ▪ Team Roles / Relations
❖ **Break**   10:15 a.m. – 10:30 a.m.
❖ **Disability Awareness**   10:30 a.m. – 11:15 a.m.
  ▪ Autism / Asperger's, MRDD, ADD, ADHD
❖ **Lunch**   11:15 a.m. – 12:00 p.m.
❖ **Fostering Socialization**   12:00 p.m. – 2:00 p.m.
  ▪ Guest Speaker
  ▪ Expand on Fostering Socialization
  ▪ Tips for Success
❖ **CPI**   2:30 p.m. – 5:30 p.m.

Day Two: 8:30 a.m. – 5:00 p.m.

❖ **Presentation from CITE**   8:30 a.m. – 12:30 p.m.
  ▪ Behavior Management
  ▪ Communication Strategies / Visual Strategies
  ▪ Sensory Needs
  ▪ Strategies for Social Inclusion
❖ **Lunch**   12:30 p.m. – 1:15 p.m.
❖ **CPI**   1:15 p.m. – 5:00 p.m.

Source: Cincinnati Recreation Commission, 2004a

Figure 16.3
In-Service Program

Implementing Retraining Programs

First-line managers and staff may be unaware of the impact of change. The need to retrain, therefore, becomes a viable retraining program to implement. Attitudinal and behavioral change occurs over time and through novel approaches, like job sharing and mentoring. Self-monitoring of continuing education units (CEUs) through readings, tapes, and videos permits access to newly developed resources. Clinical supervision of interns is a form of retraining because students tend to bring recently acquired resources to placement locations. When orientation, in-service, and development sessions expose trainees to updated therapeutic recreation practices, retraining occurs. Implementation of retraining is critical during transitions like mergers and restructuring or reorganizing. Training is provided by persons already in similar positions from within the agency or agencies with similar cultures. Retraining sessions are implemented over extended time periods or through intermittent briefings.

Managers monitor the selection of content and the implementation of training and development programs to assure immediate staff performance and long-term growth and professional development. Monitoring also ensures compatibility between agency and department efforts and the appropriate balance among orientation, in-service, development, and retraining programs. Collection of formative data enables immediate adjustments to staff, department, and agency development plans. As systems analysts, managers measure immediate outcomes and monitor quality indicators to project future plans and directions.

Evaluation of Training and Development Programs

How are the results of training and development programs measured? What indicators verify adaptation to the domino effect of change? Reorganizing staffing patterns, implementing cost-effective delivery systems, and improving quality within a framework of declining resources mandate that management and staff respond to change. Training and development are the tools that enable change to take place; evaluation determines the effectiveness of training and development. The complexity of change and each person's responsiveness to change result in a variety of content and methods being used to accomplish training and development goals. Systematic evaluation strategies are, therefore, needed to validate achievement of planned outcomes.

Managing Diversity

Date:	March 30, 20__
Time:	8:30 a.m. – 12:00 p.m.
Place:	Educational Services, Classroom #3
Intended Audience:	Managers and Supervisors of Central Iowa Health Systems
Purpose:	To discuss the multicultural work force of the future, to explore the differences of managing the work force, and how to use coaching techniques.
Objectives:	At the completion of this program, the participant should be able to:

    1. Identify six (6) basic diverse work groups at CIHS.
    2. Examine three (3) steps in understanding and managing these diverse work group.
    3. Discuss the changing attitudes and values in today's work environment and the impact on patient care.

Faculty:	Educational Services
Register:	Call 241-6898 or online at cihs.org

MCE-3.5

This program has been approved for four (4) contact hours/0.4 CEUs by Iowa Approved Provider #31, Educational Services, Iowa Health System.

Figure 16.4
Development Program

Evaluation has several benefits. For instance, evaluative measures determine if programs are producing the results for which they were intended, thereby justifying the time and money budgeted. The feedback provided enables the manager to improve offerings. A comprehensive evaluation plan is prepared during the design phase to assess each training and development program. Jeska (1994) reported that managers determine the focus of evaluation plans by considering cost, volume, and significance of each program. The higher or more crucial each of these variables is to the trainees and service quality indicators, the more intense the evaluation effort. Orientation and retraining sessions typically focus on new staff or new procedures and are more costly, time-consuming, and significant to service outcomes than are in-service or development programs. As a result, data collection is more carefully planned and carried out with the former than with the latter types of programs.

Training and development evaluations have tended to focus on trainee opinions of programs and perceptions of what trainees have learned. Robbins (1995) noted these forms of evaluation are unduly influenced by the difficulty of the learning experience, its entertainment value, and the personality of the instructor. According to Jeska (1994), Marquis and Huston (2003), and Sullivan and Decker (2001), a comprehensive objective evaluation plan measures five facets: employee reactions, learning, transfer of new knowledge and skills to job performance, results or impact on service outcomes, and cost effectiveness. Additionally, Sims (1993) suggested that evaluation of each training and development session has five goals that influence the manager's selection of evaluation audiences and determination of the evaluation schedule:

1. to determine how well or what the trainee does during each session

2. to determine if objectives of individual, department, and agency development plans are achieved

3. to determine whether trainee effectiveness is improved (e.g., Is there an impact on consumer services?)

4. to ascertain if the session was efficient and cost effective or if alternative types of training and development might achieve the same objectives

5. to ascertain relevance of content and methods to training and development objectives (e.g., Were topics related to job and career goals? Were appropriate methods used to deliver content?)

To obtain maximum benefit from a program, trainees must like the opportunity. Employee reactions are usually evaluated by conducting interviews or administering questionnaires immediately following the program. The intent, according to Sims (1993), is to determine if trainees liked the program, if they felt the instruction was helpful, and if they learned from the presented materials. Typical questions may include the following:

- How well were trainees' personal objectives met?

- How well were the identified program objectives met?

- How effective was the instructor in delivering the content?

- Were the environment and instructional aids conducive to learning?

Learning evaluations, the second form of evaluation, determine if the trainee is able to demonstrate understanding of presented content. Skill demonstrations, cognitive tests, role playing, interactive video, and case study analyses determine trainees' grasp of the information. Test performance may neither reflect what is actually learned nor the ability to apply the KSAs to work or career goals; however, when used at the conclusion of a program, tests are reliable, easy to administer, and objective in their assessment of the trainees' grasp of presented content.

Transfer of new information toward improving job performance and/or agency effectiveness is one of the most critical outcomes of training and development (Sims, 1993). Information is of little value unless behavior or performance changes. The main question becomes, "Does the trainee assimilate learning within the practice setting?" This form of evaluation occurs at defined intervals after participation in training and development. The amount of time to incorporate new information into behavioral patterns varies with the difficulty level of the competencies. For example, soon after an in-service on new petty cash (e.g., administrative competency) or equipment use (e.g., technical competency) procedures, the therapeutic recreation manager observes and/or interviews staff to confirm use of the new procedures. Self-assessments and peer reviews evaluating outcomes of work delegation (e.g., interpersonal competency), time management (e.g., leadership competency), or strategic planning (e.g., conceptual competency) sessions occur on several occasions over extended periods of time because of the complexity of behavioral change. The following are some questions to assess the transfer of information to job improvement:

- Compared to two months ago, has the supervisor delegated work assignments more effectively?

- Do recorded work activities of this month reflect improved time management as compared to the calendar kept prior to the in-service last month?

- Have practitioners revised their individual development plans since the implementation last month of the department's new mission and plan of operation?

The fourth component of comprehensive evaluation is the result or impact of training and development on service outcomes. The purpose of training and development is to increase or to improve effectiveness through achievement of department goals. In health and human service agencies the primary evaluative question is, "Did training and development result in enhanced client well-being?" In therapeutic recreation the manager might ask, "Was service maintained or improved through cost reductions, enhanced use of personnel or physical resources, and the application of specific interventions?" Impact measurements consider quality of care, productivity, cost-benefit analyses, and follow-up information from client and caregiver surveys. Results of this form of evaluation are directly correlated to department goals. A manager reconciles impact outcomes with staff and agency development goals, and adjustments occur when goals are not reached or incongruencies are evident among development plans.

The final or fifth element measured is cost-effectiveness. Whether training is carried out by mentors, external sources, through coaching or online, activities should be quantified (Marquis & Huston, 2003). One example of cost-effectiveness, noted as an advantage with computer-based training, is the cost savings found with online customized modules available to employees at their convenience. On-line training "tracks the investment of employee time for the organization" (Blair, 2003, p. 10). Cost-related data "provide evidence to higher administration that educational efforts do affect organizational effectiveness" (Sullivan & Decker, 2001, p. 334).

The evaluation plan is based on the department's training and development needs and goals and the objectives of each particular program. A manager prepares instruments and identifies techniques to collect data in each of the five areas—reaction, learning, performance, impact, and cost-effectiveness—for each training and development opportunity provided. The task is to match each form of evaluation with the type of training used to reach identified outcomes. As shown in Table 16.1, performance and impact evaluations are appropriate to development and retraining sessions, while reaction and learning evaluations are administered with orientation and in-service sessions—cost-effectiveness is determined with each type of training. With each training and development program one or more evaluation audiences (e.g., staff, managers, clients, caregivers, administrators) respond to or are the subject of assessing outcomes. After an in-service, managers interview staff to ascertain if they learned how to conduct client assessments differently. However, after a retraining session, both managers and staff participate in peer reviews on adapting to agency-wide changes. A comprehensive evaluation plan depicts the department's assessed needs, the programs designed and implemented to meet these needs, and the forms of evaluation used to collect the data to determine the benefits of training and development (see Table 16.1). An evaluation plan, therefore, interrelates the assessment, design, implementation, and evaluation steps of comprehensive planning.

Managers revise, replace, or retain programs based on evaluation outcomes. These decisions relate training and development outcomes to performance and service delivery effectiveness. Compatibility among the department, agency, and staff development goals and evaluation results is assessed. The manager determines which behaviors and performances have changed, the longevity of the

Table 16.1
Training and Development Evaluation Plan

Domain	Goal/Need	Program	Evaluation Type	Audience
Conceptual	Adapt to change	Retraining	Impact/ Cost-effectiveness	Manager and staff
Leadership	Build teams	Development	Performance/ Cost-effectiveness	Staff and clients
Interpersonal	Manage conflict	Development	Performance/ Cost-effectiveness	Staff and colleagues
Administrative	Design development goals	Orientation	Reaction/ Cost-effectiveness	Staff and administrators
Technical	Conduct computer-based assessments	In-service	Learning/ Cost-effectiveness	Staff

changes, and the relationship of the changes to service outcomes. Goals in each of the plans are rewritten and training and development opportunities are reconsidered if incongruencies exist. For example, the orientation content or schedule might be revised and in-service sessions replaced by more relevant or current topics on medication side effects and accessible transportation alternatives. The therapeutic recreation manager uses evaluation results to make immediate adjustments in development goals and to plan for long-term development that will impact future department services.

Training and Development Trends and Issues

Society is undergoing very rapid change in a number of ways, including the manner in which the practice of therapeutic recreation is conducted. Dynamic work and social environments require that professionals continually update knowledge and skills to adjust to the needs of clients and the profession. Health and human service organizations are a portion of the growing service industry where "people skills" are fundamental to quality of services delivered. It is evident that therapeutic recreators rely on communication skills to maintain and to improve client well-being. Further, information is acquired and communicated more rapidly with the computer and other electronic and technological resources. The increasing significance of information as a commodity is evidenced in network information systems and through emerging forms of electronic leisure. The pace of change intensifies with information exchange.

Each manager and therapist will continue to need knowledge and skills about how to process and access information via technology. Increasing amounts of information will be communicated in the practice setting to consumers, caregivers, and colleagues. As demands for accountability, quality, cost reductions, and service redistributions magnify, the time to communicate becomes less while the necessity to communicate the value of therapeutic recreation becomes greater. Consumer well-being is the central focus of intervention. The challenge is to synthesize vast amounts of information so that the intent of professional practice is properly communicated and consumer well-being is maintained and enhanced.

Therapeutic recreation specialists will continue to need to develop communication skills, and management will have to evolve to meet changing social philosophies. Competency in communication skills, such as conflict resolution, negotiation, individual and group facilitation, public speaking, problem solving and empathetic listening, are fundamental to service delivery approaches that emphasize participatory management and interactive leadership. As the information age brings people closer together, communication with others whose culture, age, experience, and education are more unique and varied increases. Consequently, communication is an avenue to cultural awareness and sensitivity skill building. Advocacy depends on effective communication. The intent of therapeutic recreation is communicated through research, evaluation, and efficacy studies. Thus, competence in all forms of communication is necessary and continues to be a training and development need.

Training and development provide opportunities to study ethical dilemmas. To illustrate, "doing the right thing" receives mixed signals in the workplace, profession, and society. Therapists increasingly experience dilemmas in situations that involve service marketing and competition, financial reimbursement, consumer confidentiality and self-determination, and collegial interactions (e.g., teamwork and networking). Training and development teach the facilitation skills necessary to resolve situational and professional practice dilemmas and to communicate the beliefs and ethical standards of therapeutic recreation.

How does one cope with change? The interpersonal aspect of therapeutic recreation contributes to the need to adjust to the changing perspectives of clients, caregivers, and management. Therapeutic recreators, like other members of health and human service teams and networks, require support as the work environment becomes more people and information intensive. Support can be found in time and stress management sessions and self-help books that represent an attempt to adapt personally to changing professional interactions and pressures. Training and development offer avenues to adapt to changes that would otherwise contribute to "professional burnout."

Summary

The intent of this chapter was twofold: to introduce the tasks in preparation and delivery of staff training and development programs and to explore the roles and responsibilities of first-line managers in staff training and development. The need for such training and development has evolved out of the rapid rate of change in society and the workplace. Impetus for first-line managers and staff to participate in training and development has come from a number of federal regulations, legislation, and professional standards. Regulations and legislation on client care and confidentiality and individual rights necessitate continuing education so quality of care is maintained and managers remain informed about employee rights. Professional practice standards include guidelines pertaining to annual department development plans and personnel training and development goals. A therapeutic recreation manager is the intermediary between the development goals of the agency, department, and staff and is expected to know the competence of employees and outcomes of each position. Consequently, the manager is held responsible for achieving agency and department goals through staff activities. A comprehensive training and development program is integral to continuous quality improvement and cost-effective productivity.

Four types of staff training and development include orientation, in-service, professional development, and retraining. Training needs and goals are established through assessments, and a plan is developed to address specific objectives. These objectives guide the selection of training content and delivery methods. A number of learning theories and adult learner characteristics are taken into consideration as the first-line manager selects content and teaching strategies. Also considered is the compatibility of methods to the type of training program (i.e., orientation, in-service, professional development, and retraining). Managers facilitate access to training and development opportunities, conduct sessions and monitor services to assure newly acquired information results in improved practices and growth of staff.

The manager also designs an evaluation plan that collects formative and summative data to ascertain if newly acquired practices result in client-related benefits. A comprehensive evaluation plan assesses five types of trainee outcomes: reaction, learning, performance, impact, and cost-effectiveness. The type of evaluation chosen is compatible with the training offered. Where higher levels of resources are invested, evaluation efforts are more intense.

Viable training and development topics continue to be adaptation to change and the use of technology to access information and apply newfound knowledge and skills to practice. A number of training and development topics emanate from the aspect of therapeutic recreation that deals with different people day in and day out. The manager's challenge is to validate the linkage between training and development, professional practices, and client services.

Review Questions

1. Describe the content and delivery methods of orientation, in-service, development, and retraining programs.

2. Outline the criteria on training and development presented in professional standards documents.

3. How does the manager facilitate participation in training and development programs?

4. Conduct an Internet search on managerial coaching and mentoring. What roles are assumed by the manager, and how does the manager benefit from these experiences?

5. Explain how adult learner theories and behavior characteristics impact implementation of training and development programs.

6. Explain how the manager selects and uses each type of evaluation. What are the goals of training and development evaluations?

7. Generate responses to the following statement: In the future training and development in therapeutic recreation will likely focus on _____ and will be delivered through _____ media.

References

American Therapeutic Recreation Association (ATRA). (2000). *Standards for the practice of therapeutic recreation and self-assessment guide*. Alexandria, VA: Author.

Arnold, W. E. and McClure, L. (1989). *Communication training and development*. New York, NY: HarperCollins.

Aylward, S., Stolee, P., Keat, N., and Johncox, V. (2003). Effectiveness of continuing education in long-term care: A literature review. *The Gerontologist, 43*(2), 259–271.

Bedini, L. A. and Anderson, D. M. (2003). The benefits of formal mentoring for practitioners in therapeutic recreation. *Therapeutic Recreation Journal, 37*(3), 240–255.

Blair, R. (2003). HIPAA training comes of age: Oregon IDN trades its classroom approach to HIPAA training for online education and experiences overwhelming acceptance by employees. *Health Management Technology, 24*(7), 30. Retrieved April 28, 2004, from InfoTrac One File database.

Brenner, P. (2003). Advanced practice. High-tech training offers flexibility for staff, facilities. *Nursing Spectrum, 12*(8). Retrieved May 20, 2004, from http://www.nursingspectrum.com

Cincinnati Recreation Commission. (2004a). *Inclusion training* [flier]. Cincinnati, OH: Author.

Cincinnati Recreation Commission. (2004b). *Preseason training* [flier]. Cincinnati, OH: Author.

Dickerson, P. S. (2003). Ten tips to help learning. *Journal for Nurses in Staff Development, 19*(5), 244–252.

Edington, C. R., Hudson, S. D., and Lankford, S. V. (2001). *Managing recreation, parks, and leisure services. An introduction*. Champaign, IL: Sagamore Publishing.

Grayson, R. (2001). Staff training best practices: Targeting attitude. *Camping Magazine, 74*(6), 40–43.

Greene, M. T. and Puetzer, M. (2002). The value of mentoring: A strategic approach to retention and recruitment. *Journal of Nursing Care Quality, 17*(1), 63–70. Retrieved May 1, 2004, from InfoTrac One File database.

Habel, M. (1994). Planning an agency-wide in-service. *Journal of Nursing Staff Development, 10*(3), 133–136.

Hanover, C. (2001). Making the most of year-round training creating a learning environment at your camp. *Camping Magazine, 74*(4), 26–29.

Harrington, S. S. and Walker, B. L. (2002). A comparison of computer-based and instructor-led training for long-term care staff. *The Journal of Continuing Education in Nursing, 33*(1), 39–45.

Ismeurt, J., Ismeurt, R., and Miller, B. K. (1992). Field-dependence/independence: Considerations in staff development. *The Journal of Continuing Education in Nursing, 23*(1), 38–41.

Jeska, S. B. (1994). Evaluation: An important aspect of staff development service. *Journal of Nursing Care Quality, 8*(4), 55–65.

Klusch, L. (2002). The basics of staff education: It involves much more than mandatory in-services, and pays off in many ways. *Nursing Homes, 51*(4), 18–22, 68–69. Retrieved April 28, 2004, from InfoTrac One File database.

Marquis, B. L. and Huston, C. J. (2003). *Leadership roles and management functions in nursing: Theory & application* (4th ed.). Philadelphia, PA: Lippincott Williams & Wilkins.

McConnell, C. R. (2002). The manager and continuing education. *Health Care Manager, 21*(2), 72–83. Retrieved May 1, 2004, from InfoTrac One File database.

McCoy, K. and Hansen, B. (2004, May 25). Havens for elderly may expose them to deadly risks, analysis of data on 5,300 facilities finds medication errors and lapses in training. *USA Today*, 1A, 10A.

National Council for Therapeutic Recreation Certification. (n.d.). *1997 JA report, NCTRC report on the national job analysis project for certified therapeutic recreation specialists.* New City, NY: Author.

National Therapeutic Recreation Society (NTRS). (2004). *Standards of practice for a continuum of care in therapeutic recreation.* Retrieved September 12, 2004, from http://www.nrpa.org/content/default.aspx?documentID=530

National Therapeutic Recreation Society (NTRS). (1990). *Guidelines for the administration of therapeutic recreation services.* Alexandria, VA: Author.

Parsons, M. L. and Stonestreet, J. (2003). Factors that contribute to nurse manager retention. *Nursing Economics, 21*(3), 120–126, 119.

Pastuszak, J. and Rodowicz, M. O. (2002). Internal e-mail: An avenue of educational opportunity. *Journal of Continuing Education in Nursing, 33*(4), 164–167.

Pesavento, L. C., Bator, M. G., and Ross, J. E. (2001). Research update, staff development practices: Is your organization "learning" in the 21st century? *Parks & Recreation, 36*(6), 24–32.

Powell, G. M. (2002). Staff training planning for next summer can start with recruitment and retention now. *Camping Magazine, 75*(6), 46–49.

Robbins, S. P. (1995). *Supervision today.* Englewood Cliffs, NJ: Prentice Hall.

Robbins, S. P. and Decenzo, D. A. (2001). *Fundamentals of management essential concepts and applications* (3rd ed.). Upper Saddle River, NJ: Prentice Hall.

Schirick, E. (2001). Risk management continuing training all summer. *Camping Magazine, 74*(4), 14–15.

Sims, R. R. (1993). Evaluating public sector training programs. *Public Personnel Management, 22*(4), 591–615.

Sullivan, E. J. and Decker, P. J. (2001). *Effective leadership and management in nursing* (5th ed.). Upper Saddle River, NJ: Prentice Hall.

Sullivan, J., Bretschneider, J., and McCausland, M. P. (2003). Designing a leadership development program for nurse managers and evidence-driven approach. *Journal of Nursing Administration, 33*(10), 544–549.

Tyler, K. (2000). Focus on training. *HR Magazine, 45*(5), 94–102.

Wood, S., Cummings, J. L., Schnelle, B., and Stephens, M. (2002). A videotape-based training method for improving the detection of depression in residents of long-term care facilities. *The Gerontologist, 42*(1), 114–121.

Chapter 17
Volunteer Management

chapter revisions by Glenda Taylor and Marcia Jean Carter

Volunteering is in the process of transition… as it adapts to a changing environment (Pidgeon, 1998). Social, economic, political and technological change has altered the volunteer's response and responsibilities. With societal change, there is a potential for disenfranchisement and disadvantage among individuals that has placed many agencies at risk for being overwhelmed with the needs of their communities. In an environment of fiscal constraint, service demand requires human capital to organize, manage, and provide quality services. Within this context the core business of health care is to provide for the well-being of the consumers.

In the 21st century environment, volunteering is crucial to the well-being of the agency as a means to shore-up a fragile workforce while providing multiple satisfactions to service constituents. The spirit of volunteerism has become a basic tenet of the social fabric and concerned people, such as the old and the young. For many people the consequences of volunteering may be in expressing their identity or their values (Wilson & Musick, 1999). The literature reveals a wide range of economic values when estimating the worth of volunteer services, and these appear to be increasing. Sources estimated an annual worth in 1990 of 150 million dollars and in 1999 of 225 billion dollars (Henderson & Silverberg, 2002; Phoenix, Miller & Schleien, 2002). Although nonprofit organizations predominate in the use of volunteers, national surveys report that government-based programs account for an estimated 25% to 30% of all volunteer efforts (Brudney, 1999). In terms of human and social capital, volunteerism is big business.

Management of volunteers is an integral component of personnel management, as agencies embrace the human resource management model. The significance of volunteers to practice is noted by the inclusion of governing standards in professional practice documents (NTRS, 2004). The intent of this chapter is to present an overview of volunteering as a crucial element of service delivery and to address each phase of volunteer management in therapeutic recreation. Material is organized according to those areas a manager needs to cover when designing a volunteer program. The design, planning, and implementation of a volunteer program may be the sole responsibility of the therapeutic recreation manager or shared with those responsible for the agency-wide recruitment, placement, supervision, and evaluation of volunteers. Issues and dilemmas that arise as staff, consumers, and volunteers interface are introduced. Illustrations are drawn from actual agency and department materials.

Volunteer Planning

Volunteer preparation begins with the organization of program staff and resources to ensure recruitment and selection of mutually compatible volunteers. After this has been completed, a cadre of volunteers is chosen to extend, enhance, and expand programs, services, and resources. Organization involves the following:

1. assessment of the department strategic plan

2. identification of standards and practices impacting volunteer management

3. delineation of relevant management policies and protocols

4. determination of staff, consumer, and volunteer roles and responsibilities

5. design of job descriptions and management documents

With completion of organization tasks a department is ready to recruit volunteers. Recruitment alerts potential volunteers to the needs and benefits of giving of their time and resources. Recruitment entails developing a marketing plan to

1. Identify target volunteer audiences.

2. Coordinate internal (i.e, agency, division, or department) and external (i.e., community) promotions.

3. Disseminate information about the department, clientele, and services.

4. Evaluate the effectiveness of the marketing plan to ensure the retention of a volunteer pool.

Volunteer recruitment is an ongoing process. Selection is ongoing and/or periodic (i.e., coincides with program start-up or staff development cycles). Volunteer selection involves the following:

1. application and credential review and verification

2. candidate screening and interviewing

3. candidate disposition and documentation

Results of planning for volunteer management include a structure, policies, and job descriptions to organize volunteer operations and relationships of volunteers, staff, and consumers; a marketing plan and promotional materials to use in recruitment and retention; and strategies and processes to use in initial screening and review of potential volunteers. The nature of this planning is influenced by the agency's mission, and the therapeutic recreation department's role in achieving that mission. To illustrate, when the department is in a primary care hospital where length of stay averages less than two weeks, volunteers provide hospital-wide support with assistance during special events and pet therapy sessions. When the department is an autonomous entity as in a transitional living center or special recreation district, volunteers support staff in all phases of service delivery and are trained specifically to meet client needs during therapeutic intervention.

Volunteer Organization

Assessment of the department's mission and strategic plan are undertaken to determine the attitude toward volunteers and the roles and relationships of volunteers within the agency to the department. The vision, mission, and goals guide the manager's planning (Carter, VanAndel & Robb, 2003). Study of organizational charts also shows the relationship of volunteers within the agency to each department (refer to Figure 17.1). Instilling the mission and values of the agency to the new volunteer occurs during training. To illustrate, the Virginia Beach City Volunteer Council is responsible for training that incorporates orientations into each city department that uses volunteers. When volunteers are identified in these documents, their functions are essential to service outcomes, and resources are devoted to volunteer management.

Review of these documents also reveals whether volunteer management is centralized or decentralized. In centralized management settings, such as veterans affairs hospitals, one unit is responsible for hospital-wide volunteer coordination. This centrality is noted by identification of an autonomous unit that has parity with other hospital-wide units (e.g., marketing, finance, research). In decentralized management, each department, such as therapeutic recreation or Region I (i.e., geographic unit), is responsible for volunteer coordination in its particular unit. To illustrate, when volunteer management is centralized, one or more persons manage volunteer operations of the entire hospital. In decentralized settings, staff in each program, such as aquatics, inclusion, and pet therapy, oversee direct service responsibilities and manage the volunteers assigned to their areas.

A number of publications include volunteer management guidelines. Professional organizations (NTRS, 2004) incorporate statements in standards of practice on management of therapeutic recreation services. Literary sources (Tedrick & Henderson, 1989) report practices in health and human services, nonprofit organizations (Pidgeon, 1998), and the public sector (Brudney, 1990). Accreditation statements (NRPA, 2004) reference volunteers in personnel management standards. All recommend that procedures similar to management of permanent staff be instituted with volunteers. These sources also present samples of tools (e.g., job descriptions, evaluation forms).

Volunteer management practices are governed by general and specific policies emanating from the agency and department. General practices are found in placement procedures, contracts, orientation and training materials, job descriptions, supervisory and evaluation plans, productivity measures, risk management plans, safety policies, infection control plans, and personnel codes on workman's compensation.

Specific policies cover legal and risk concerns and client and staff functions and interactions. Legal and risk documents identify specific volunteer roles on outings, when transporting, in emergencies, and when documenting or reporting client information. Treatment protocols specify client-volunteer interactions. To illustrate, volunteers may not be permitted to transfer patients without a qualified therapist present, or while in the community a volunteer may not be permitted to refer to an agency by name if the reference would violate client confidentiality. The Health Insurance Portability and Accountability Act of 1996 (HIPAA) regulations have further tightened the rules surrounding privacy, and confidentiality; these are referred to as protected health information (PHI; Thacker, 2003).

Generally allowable roles are defined by agency and department policy documents. The manager assesses unit needs to determine desired volunteer skills, expertise, and roles. Roles and responsibilities usually fall within three categories: direct service, supportive services, or administrative services. Direct service roles involve provision of services, programs, and resources to clients. When a volunteer assists a client during Special Olympics or on a challenge course, it is direct service. Volunteers who complement and supplement staff during group sessions provide supportive service. Administrative roles enable service delivery but do not directly involve clients, such as when volunteers repair equipment, secure alternative funds, or write computer programs.

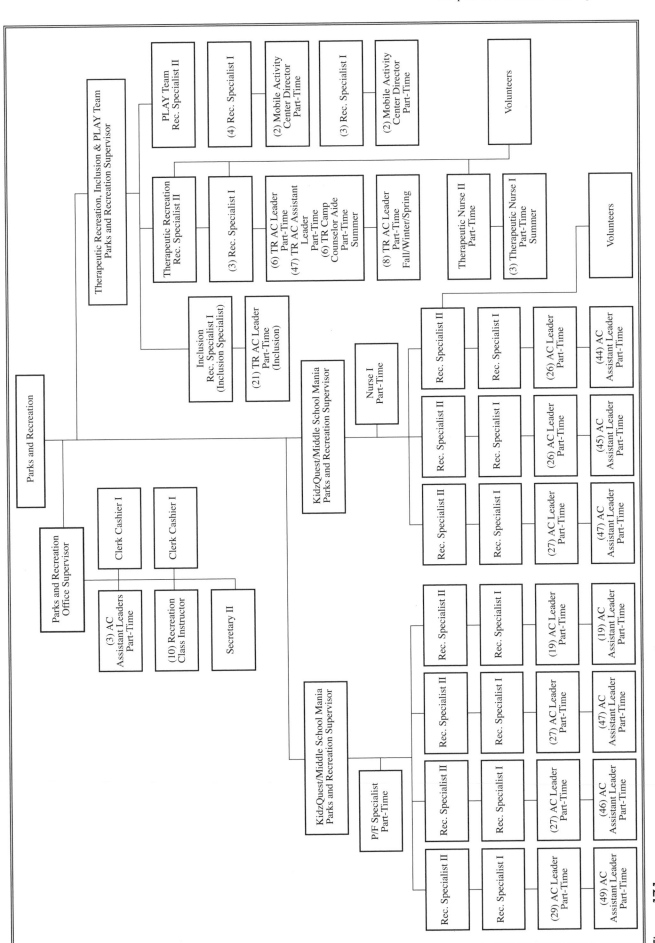

Figure 17.1
Virginia Beach Parks and Recreation Organizational Chart

Volunteer roles are intended to extend, enhance, and expand current staff capabilities and consumer services. A number of factors influence volunteer roles, including the following:

- number of staff available, their competence and interests
- staff-to-consumer ratio
- consumer abilities and preferences
- length and nature of interventions
- safety, risk, and emergency practices
- available work stations, space, and resources
- policies governing consumer interactions

The manager develops an inventory listing volunteer needs. From this list, job descriptions are generated. These are developed for each direct, supportive, and administrative role. Each description presents information in the following categories:

- agency and department information, position title, work sites
- purpose or objective of job
- performance expectations
- job requirements (e.g., duration, hours, days, orientation, training)
- qualifications (e.g., job-related education, training, competence, credentials, experience, membership dues, insurance, equipment, dress, medical tests and treatments, legal screening, transportation)
- authority and supervision (e.g., limits to authority, relationships with staff, consumers, other volunteers, job supervisor, and evaluation, separation, and recognition procedures)
- comments (e.g., in-kind benefits, unusual job site demands, medical coverage, emergency protocols, disclaimers)
- date of job description preparation, revision, and approval

As with descriptions for permanent positions, these descriptions are updated periodically and used as recruiting tools. Because they define expectations, they are foundational to supervisory and evaluation plans. Contracts are written after the review of job descriptions and unit policies.

Contracts detail the relationship between each volunteer and the placement site. Therefore they usually consist of two parts: one portion outlines the volunteer's commitment while the second describes the placement's responsibilities. Volunteer contracts outline minimal practice standards and performance expectations. Consequently, along with job descriptions they are used to formulate volunteer supervisory plans and evaluations. Signed contracts are placed in volunteer personnel files. A direct service contract might include the following:

The volunteer agrees to

1. become familiar with department policies and procedures
2. work a certain number of hours at a particular site in a particular position
3. report to work according to the schedule and maintain a record of hours worked by clocking in and out
4. provide 24-hour notice of nonattendance and notification of one week in advance of a leave of absence
5. attend orientation and training sessions and undertake continuous educational development
6. accept right of the manager to dismiss a volunteer for poor performance and attendance
7. exercise caution when acting on behalf of the department to protect the confidentiality of the unit and its clientele
8. abide by department rules specifically related to health, risk, safety, and emergencies
9. accept supervisory actions and functions as a team member contributing to professional working relationships among staff, clientele, and volunteers

The unit agrees to

1. train volunteers to a level permitting them to commence and continue work confidently and competently
2. provide work conditions equal to paid staff
3. conduct routine evaluations and provide references on request
4. offer promotions, new assignments and/or more responsible jobs upon mutual agreement and with commensurate training
5. keep volunteers informed of activities and policies
6. recognize volunteer service

7. include volunteers in program planning where possible

8. provide benefits as appropriate (e.g., parking, proper identification tags, meals, access to medical library, fee waivers for CPR and first-aid classes)

Sometimes more than one person from a service organization donates time in supportive or administrative volunteer roles to a department. In this situation a manager prepares a standard form letter that describes group responsibilities and serves as a contract between the department and service organization. For example, the letter details volunteer roles of the group for a one-time project, such as a birthday party on the pediatric unit or spring cleanup of the challenge course area.

Volunteer Recruitment

Securing volunteers is critical to agency goals, and is a core part of business for the not-for-profit agency (Pidgeon, 1998). Designing a marketing plan to systematically recruit volunteers begins by determining the roles to be played by volunteers in reaching the department mission. What are potential roles of volunteers as services are provided in achieving unit goals? And as volunteers provide these services, what benefits do they receive? Volunteering is an exchange; the department provides growth, challenge, and experiences while volunteers give time, expertise, and resources. The design of a marketing plan begins with generating responses to questions such as the following:

- What does the unit offer volunteers in exchange for what is desired from them?

- What motivates volunteerism?

- What rewards are volunteers seeking?

- What type of service commitment is desired?

Not all volunteers desire the same benefits or have the same motives, and each experience uniquely impacts each volunteer. The first-line manager must have identified the nature of the program/service, to target appropriately whether the service will require an individual, individuals, or groups of people. As a consequence, the manager identifies target volunteer audiences to maximize each volunteer's "life cycle." Promotional effectiveness is more likely when the manager is aware of the type of service commitment and benefits anticipated by each target audience (refer to Figure 17.2).

Several target volunteer audiences are likely to have an interest. Among these are older adults, students of medicine and health-related professions, caregivers, youth, court-assigned volunteers, former consumers, and present consumers. Each of these audiences brings a particular perspective and expectation to the volunteer experience. To recruit these groups a first-line manager determines how to use their skills while offering an experience that both suits their personal needs and achieves the unit's goals. The key is to use the right people rather than the convenient person in the right position (Pidgeon, 1998).

Between the ages of 55 and 74 individuals traditionally relinquish paid work and some family responsibilities. Choices about how to use their expanding discretionary time may include volunteerism (Mutchler, Burr & Caro, 2003). These older persons were often at the cutting edge

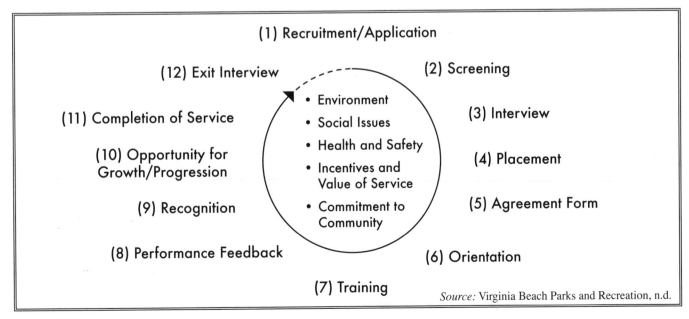

Figure 17.2
Volunteer Life Cycle

of service delivery during their professional careers. Their knowledge, skills and abilities are of benefit to the agency's consumers. Older adults gain a sense of belonging, recognition, companionship, and opportunities to remain a part of the social mainstream as they share their personal expertise plus encounters they may have had with health care settings. Volunteering is also a valued leisure pursuit for this group.

Students in medicine and health-related professions desire to receive evaluated work experience, to explore career possibilities, and to receive professional training. When a caregiver volunteers, focus may be on a member of his or her family or other persons with illnesses or disabilities served by the same agency (e.g., extended care facility). Caregiver needs encompass an opportunity to advocate, to make system changes, to alleviate boredom, to compensate for losses, and to process grief. For a caregiver, volunteering is a form of leisure and self-help within a safe and supportive environment.

Youth volunteers bring novelty, energy, unconditional positive regard, acceptance, and a desire to help and to have fun to their experiences. Some desire to explore career options while others gain a sense of social responsibility desired by their parents or legal authorities. If volunteers are assigned by the courts their primary objective may be to avoid institutional detainment, but authorities recognize the rehabilitative potential of volunteerism. Court-assigned volunteers also have a need to contribute to change, use their skills, and be a part of a group with socially acceptable leisure outlets. Former consumers have a vested interest and are influential recruiters (e.g., adult wheelchair athletes promote youth leagues). Former consumers take part in family evenings and special events in hospitals and agencies, thus providing inspiration, motivation and hope to the newly injured family member. For this group, their needs stem from a desire to give back to those who have enhanced their well-being and to advocate for constituent group needs (e.g., accessibility). Studies (Miller, Schleien, Rider, Hall, Roche & Worsley, 2002) document the benefits of inclusive volunteering for individuals with and without disabilities.

Person-to-person contacts and support from satisfied volunteers are the most effective recruiting tools. Managers select and coordinate the use of internal and external promotional resources suited to each target audience. Several details are considered as the medium is selected. Each message presents an "opportunity" through particular roles and unique experiences. Volunteers respond to familiar situations and those with known credibility. To illustrate, potential volunteers are more responsive to a call from the "hospital" coordinator of volunteer services than the less familiar department manager. Because people usually do not respond immediately to a call for volunteers, managers select media outlets that will keep their story continuously in full view. Some of the very best recruiters are current volunteers.

To facilitate coordination of recruiting efforts a matrix is designed that identifies the media and contacts used with each target audience (see Table 17.1). This matrix is intended to ensure that each audience receives the proper amount of information in a timely manner. The matrix presents several target organizations as potential volunteer sources. Social service clubs and corporations periodically contribute both money and group efforts. These communal efforts create individual awareness and collective advocacy. Likewise, when educational institutions and professional organizations donate expertise, they also advocate for persons with disabilities.

Information dissemination results as the manager and therapeutic recreation specialists communicate with clients, caregivers, colleagues (e.g., doctors, nurses, social workers, other therapists), residents, and organizations. This communication is usually ongoing but can intensify at times coinciding with seasonal program cycles. When contacts are made, documentation on the matrix helps to determine if and when the audience should again be contacted. Although few volunteers drop in, a method should be in place to record both the nature of each inquiry and the source of information about the opportunity. Initial information to share with all audience types includes the following:

- benefits of the opportunity

- length, frequency, clientele, location, educational, and experiential requirements (e.g., certifications)

- training expectations

- application and placement dates and deadlines

- screening tests or procedures (e.g., references, police)

- incentives

Marketing outcomes are evaluated by identifying the number of new and retained volunteers. Marketing also educates others to client referral needs, such as access to other hospital or community resources. Consequently, evaluation encompasses situations such as phone inquires, mail requests, newspaper clippings, observed television and radio releases, invitations to make presentations, number of visits to agency Web site, and expanded client reentry opportunities. One approach is to allow space on the initial volunteer application for identification of where or how the volunteer became familiar with the opportunity.

Documentation of marketing costs is part of evaluating the benefits of a volunteer program. Figures on media and dissemination expenses are included in administrative budgets or individual program budgets. The manager compares the cost of gaining and retaining volunteers to worker-year equivalents (e.g., 2,080 hours equal one worker year) or service extensions. Ultimately, evaluation determines if the form of marketing used was suitable to each target audience. Managers consider whether the right story has been told to a sufficient number of the right people. Marketing continues as volunteers are trained, supervised, and recognized. When satisfied volunteers are retained, the recruiting of new qualified volunteers is made easier.

Volunteer Selection

With constrained personnel budgets, the roles and responsibilities of volunteers are changing. Volunteers are taking on tasks once performed by full-time employees. Consequently, much more effort must go into the selection of qualified volunteers. Grossman and Furano (2002) suggest the following is important to the success of any volunteer program:

1. a screening process to select adults most likely to be successful volunteers

2. orientation and training to ensure that volunteers have the specific skills needed to be effective and realistic expectations of what they can accomplish

3. management and ongoing support of volunteers employed by staff to ensure that volunteers' hours are not squandered

Selection of qualified volunteers commences with application and credential review and verification. This review affirms the match between a volunteer's skills, priorities, and expectations and the department's goals and needs. During the recruitment process potential volunteers are given job descriptions and materials that delineate respective roles, needs, and expectations. They then complete applications (e.g., in-person, online, mailed) that require presentation of personal information plus any credentials related to their job competence and qualifications.

When volunteer services are managed agency-wide, the application form may or may not present specific options (e.g., therapeutic recreation, hospice, special events). When decentralized, each unit solicits and processes applications. Generally, applicants present information in several areas:

- personal and business address, phone, e-mail, emergency contacts, and procedures

- employment and volunteer experiences with addresses and references

- credentials and certifications, specialized training and skills, and educational preparation

Table 17.1
Volunteer Recruitment Matrix

Target Audience	Benefit	Media/Contacts	Record*
Older Adults	Recognition, companionship	RSVP, church group, radio, newspaper, displays, talks	
Students	Work experience, career choice	TV, classroom, career fairs, listservs, e-mail	
Caregivers	Compensation, support	Open house, cable TV, support groups	
Youth	Social responsibility, careers	Television, service club, internet, high school counselor	
Court Assignment	Rehabilitation	Social workers, voluntary action center, flyers	
Former Client	Advocacy	Personal contact, incentives	
Social Service Agencies	Community welfare	Referral agencies, PSAs, human interest stories, listservs	
Corporations	Public relations	Gift brochures, chamber of commerce, posters	
Educational Institutions	Education	PTA(O), displays, bumper stickers	
Professional Organizations	Advocacy	Annual conventions, letter writing, internet, publications	

* Name of contact person, address, response, type of media used, and dates of use

- commitment, time, duration, reason for seeking the opportunity, and source of information about the opportunity

- previous experiences related to therapeutic recreation (e.g., setting, clientele, intervention)

- job-related insurance, medical checkups, police record verification

A preliminary review validates accuracy of presented information, ascertains appropriateness of a volunteer to available positions, recommends further screening to specific agency and department interviews, and determines whether or not to refer the volunteer to other placements. A volunteer may appear to have compatible needs and goals yet lack proper training or experience, or the desired opportunity may not be available at the time of application. Managers inform volunteers of such assessments and request that they return after training or at a later date.

During the selection process, managers involve staff associated with placements. This contact facilitates volunteer supervision and evaluation as staff carry out these tasks. Staff also have information about volunteers from previous contacts and are responsible for recruiting volunteers to their programs. This enables staff and managers to consider the merits of volunteer placements from both the management and programmatic perspective. Volunteer needs may emanate from altruism—a sincere desire to be therapeutic helpers and to promote inclusive practices, to give back to the community, or to be agents of change. Managers and staff balance these values during the selection process.

Preliminary reviews result in one of the following actions:

1. information confirmation and referral of a volunteer to appropriate manager or staff member for interview and screening placement

2. referral to another volunteer opportunity within the agency or community

3. recommendation that further training or credentials be acquired with application at a more compatible time

4. nonselection because the applicant's skills and the department's needs and expectations are incompatible

After successful reviews, candidates are screened and interviewed. These processes are used to match the volunteer with placement options, to identify training needs, and to orient the volunteer to the organization. The nature of each volunteer job influences the screening and interviewing processes. When applicants are being assessed for supportive roles (e.g., computer processing) rather than direct consumer services (e.g., community buddies), the process is briefer because fewer consumer-related skills are evaluated. If the intent is to create a registry or list of potential volunteers, screening is also less detailed and time-consuming.

Screening is done with individuals or groups by phone or in person. A manager informs applicants of the agency's and department's intent, operating parameters, and needs. Specifically, the volunteer is apprised of time commitments, work schedules, health care and childcare options, employee processing procedures, incidentals (e.g., parking, out-of-pocket expenses, insurance coverage), and client protocols. In turn, the volunteer clarifies and explains how his or her qualifications relate to the position. Screening may result in referral or application withdrawal because time commitments may be incompatible or education and training may not be appropriately balanced. If there does appear to be a match, formal on-site interviews are planned.

The interview continues the orientation process while confirming if a match between the volunteer and department is likely. Individual or group interviews are conducted by the manager and therapeutic recreation staff. Interviews for administrative or support positions are conducted by the manager while staff are likely to be included when applicants interview for direct service positions. Initial interviews help management and staff to determine if volunteers and staff are compatible and if volunteers are likely to contribute to consumer health, well-being, and leisure functioning. During initial interviews consideration is given to the following:

- program goals and client descriptors

- agency and department structure

- volunteer positions, roles, and responsibilities

- relationships and communication among management, staff, and volunteers

- commitment requirements (e.g., resources, time)

- ethics and practice protocols

- training and supervisory requirements

- volunteer selection, placement, evaluation, recognition, and separation procedures

An interview begins with the verification and clarification of information in application forms and credentials. Noting the way with which these documents were presented as well as the professional manner displayed during the interview are an indication of the volunteer's perception of the significance of the position. After clarifying application information, an interviewee responds to specific questions about each opportunity. Through the interview, management and staff become aware of how the applicant's personal and professional competencies and character will or will not enhance program and client outcomes. Therefore attributes of effective helpers like empathy, unconditional positive regard, interviewing skills and any previous exposure to persons with disabilities are areas of investigation. Questions that might lead to interpreting personal-professional philosophies and practices include the following:

- What do you anticipate will be the outcomes of this experience?

- How have you become aware of this opportunity?

- What do you perceive to be the benefit of therapeutic recreation with our clients?

- What do you believe to be essential qualities of effective helpers?

- Describe your previous roles and interactions with health care systems and clients.

- What kind of challenges do you expect from this volunteer position?

- What do you need from us to help you do your job?

- What three characteristics do you value most in people with whom you work?

- Why do you recreate?

- What are your personal career goals?

- Interpret your assets and liabilities as related to the particular job.

Presentation of situations helps to determine how a volunteer might respond to emergencies and to routine behaviors exhibited by various consumers. Also the volunteer becomes aware of the types of behaviors, needs, and situations that he or she is likely to encounter. Types of questions that illustrate possible scenarios include the following:

- What would you do if you and members of our staff were intervening when a consumer becomes resistive or combative?

- How would you respond if a consumer becomes disoriented and confused?

- How would you react to a consumer who uses inappropriate language to describe your character?

Direct questioning about the interviewee's health is inappropriate unless it is related to performance expectations (e.g., assisting with patient transfers). If the interviewee indicates need for job accommodations, the manager is obligated to discern what can be done to effect necessary changes (e.g., assign the volunteer to a unit where consumers do not require physical assistance). Volunteer placements can be made contingent on outcomes of job-related physical examinations.

During the interview process, time is permitted for the interviewee to ask questions and to observe activities at various work stations. Managers seek permission to check references, to conduct a police record check, and to contact former supervisors and employers. At the conclusion of the interview, the manager summarizes factors that either confirm or negate a match, referral, training needs, and/or trial placement.

With acceptance, rejection, or referral written notification is sent to the volunteer and placed in permanent volunteer records. Acceptance letters are accompanied by contracts that inform volunteers of their assignments, workdays and hours, length of commitment, client and program protocols, training, supervision, and recognition processes. Rejection letters to volunteers present other options, suggest needed training, encourage application at a later date, recommend trial placements, and/or cite reasons for incompatibility.

Volunteer Training and Supervision

Successful completion of volunteer planning results in a cadre of volunteers who appear to be compatible with the agency and department. The next phase of volunteer management involves placing volunteers, providing education and training on their roles, and supervising their performance. Specifically, placement involves

1. orientation to the agency and department

2. introduction to specific jobs

3. trial and final placement

After probationary periods volunteers begin their jobs. Preparation to perform day-to-day tasks is acquired during in-service training and professional updating occurs through continuing education. Training and education of volunteers involve

1. designing training and education materials

2. providing job-related training and education

3. facilitating access to continuing professional development

4. monitoring and facilitating staff and volunteer infusion

Managers supervise staff and volunteers as they work together to provide consumer services. Managers communicate and interact while documenting volunteer performance and maintaining records. Supervision involves

1. communication with volunteers and staff

2. documentation in personnel and department records

3. retention and promotion or termination and separation

Adequate training and supervision enables effective volunteer performance and efficient volunteer management. Training and supervision, like planning, are influenced by the agency mission and relationship of the therapeutic recreation department to agency goals. Consequently, managers either assist the agency-wide volunteer manager or assume total responsibility for these functions in their unit.

Volunteer Placement

Appropriate placement is essential to quality services for both the volunteer and the consumer. Inappropriate placement may create tension and lead to anxiety, stress, and burnout for the volunteer. Orientation introduces volunteers to the working environment and to expectations. The goal of orientation is to ensure basic awareness and compliance with policies and codes while acquainting volunteers with department mission, resources, and personnel. Orientation periods extend over a period of time to avoid information overload. Orientation may be implemented hospital-wide, at set periods of time, and include a mix of full-time and part-time employees, as well as the volunteers. Others may insist on unit orientation and training for their volunteers because of the specificity of tasks and responsibilities. Consumers and caregivers remain involved as volunteers are made aware of the unique focus of the department. Orientation topics and activities include the following (refer to Figure 17.3):

- history and mission of department

- volunteer roles in the department

- organizational structure, management team, and staffing protocols

- financial and promotional protocols

- personnel policies relating to insurance, liability, consumers' rights, parking, personal identification, reimbursement, emergency, safety and infection controls, disaster plan, health codes, ethical conduct, and personal recordkeeping (e.g., time cards)

- management, staff, volunteer introductions, responsibilities, and interrelationships

- volunteer "boundaries" and performance criteria

- identification and location of agency-wide service units and resources

- medical, health, and legal clearances and reporting of test results

Introduction to specific work assignments and job responsibilities occurs either as the volunteer is oriented to the agency or as a department orientation is conducted. This orientation takes place at the conclusion of the agency orientation or at a subsequent time period. Orientation activities attempt to instill confidence in the volunteer through a thorough understanding of assigned roles and tasks. Orientations are conducted by staff and managers and as a consequence staff-volunteer relationships are developed and staff learn to manage volunteers. Orientation to specific job responsibilities includes the following:

- introductions to staff, volunteers, and associated personnel in the unit, including their roles, the chain of command, and the process for communicating among professionals, consumers, and caregivers (e.g., specifically things that can and cannot be said)

- identification of supervisory procedures, evaluation documents, and promotion and separation processes

- location of space for personal items, what to do when reporting to work, specific identification tags, and parking assignments

- review of job description, recordkeeping procedures, how to perform tasks, and location of people and resources

- specific consumer and caregiver information, staffing and volunteer protocols, intervention protocols, and client management

- managing consumer emergencies and unexpected work absences

- review of operation plan, internal and external accreditations, and professional standards of practice

When orientations are completed, staff and volunteers have had opportunities to develop "teamwork" behaviors, and each accurately interprets the other's roles and

Virginia Beach Department of Parks and Recreation
"On the Job Training Orientation"
A Checklist for New Volunteers

✓	Items To Be Reviewed	
	Mission/Values	
	City Mission	
	Organizational Values	City Volunteer Council
	Department Mission Goals	Volunteer Council
	Organizational Chart/Responsibilities	
	Department	
	Unit Protocol	
	Job Description/Expectations	
	Overview of Department	
	Parks and Recreation Services	Video
	Brochure (seasonal)	
	Overview of the Unit/Site Policies & Procedures and Responsibilities	
	Site orientation	Unit Policies & Procedures
	Work schedule	
	Staff phone numbers	
	Time distribution sheets	
	Leave	
	Emergency/Inclement weather	
	Documentation (e.g., accident, incident, statistical, communication log)	
	Training requirements/opportunities/mentoring	
	Dress code	
	Program/Services	
	Volunteers	
	Facility usage and maintenance	Safety
	Partnerships with other organizations (e.g., community, city agencies)	
	Equipment and supplies	
	Volunteer Performance Feedback	

I, _____, have completed the orientation for those items checked off. These topics were explained to me and I understand them.

Date: _____ Signature:_____
                                                                                                     Volunteer

Date: _____ Signature:_____
                                                                                         Staff conducting orientation

Figure 17.3
Virginia Beach Parks and Recreation Checklist for New Volunteers

responsibilities. Volunteers have experienced a sampling of tasks, and trial placements can occur as volunteers circulate through each work opportunity.

Trial placements encourage volunteers to explore where their skills and interests are best utilized while staff judge their suitability to program operation. For instance, trial rotations at each work site might determine that the best fit is with group experiences rather than during one-on-one sessions. Trial placements are also important because they help the manager identify types of in-service training and continuing education needed by volunteers. The scope of the program and a volunteer's skills influence the number and length of trial placements. Written documentation records placement activities including decisions made about final assignments, referrals, and recommendations.

Final assignments are made during—or following—trial placements by the manager and staff taking into consideration volunteer preferences. Assignments are made in writing and include workdays and hours, length and location of commitment, in-service training requirements, supervisory procedures, and client-related protocols (e.g., confidentiality, public disclosure, record access; refer to Table 17.2). If a contract is required, both the manager and volunteer sign the document a copy of which is placed in the volunteer's permanent file.

Volunteer Training and Education

As the new volunteer feels embraced by the agency, and is valued as a contributor to the mission, the volunteer is assimilated into the agency culture through education and training. Volunteer motivation and commitment is linked through learning about the organization, the job, and oneself (Serafino, 2001). Education material, written or oral, is presented to the volunteer in accordance with their developmental level, learning styles, and application to the task, responsibility or job. Therefore training begins with orientation and continues as long as necessary to ensure the volunteer remains updated. Education refers to those opportunities, which enhance the volunteer's comprehension of practice (e.g., professional development experiences). Training and education experiences are intended to develop job-related skills, to expand practice knowledge, to facilitate volunteer-staff partnerships, and to provide opportunities that might lead to promotion. Managers prepare and organize in-service and educational materials. Volunteer job descriptions and department goals guide the manager in this task. Volunteer manuals are developed which serve as training and education resources. A content outline for a manual reflects the volunteer management process and the unique features of a particular department (see Figure 17.4).

In addition to the manual, a manager organizes staff and resource people, including caregivers, to present in-services on topics such as communicating with a recently traumatized patient or lifestyle monitoring in cardiac rehabilitation or providing knowledge about inclusive practices

Table 17.2
Volunteer Assignment

Job Title	Therapeutic Recreation Program Assistant—Aquatic, Adult, Youth and Wheelchair Sport
Goals	To assist Therapeutic Recreation Staff in a variety of youth, adult and aquatic programs for persons with disabilities
Duties	Assist Staff in planning and implementing activities, demonstrating specific skills, and supervision of program participants
Qualifications	Must be age 14 or older and have a desire to work with individuals with disabilities
Training Required	Specific training mandatory prior to aquatic program: • One hour of orientation to TR Programs. • Onsite orientation by part-time unit Staff. • Forty (40) hours of training offered for summer programs.
Time Commitment	• Afternoon and evening hours primarily M–F and occasional weekends. • Forty (40) hours of training offered for summer programs. • Duration of 8–12 weeks during fall and winter/spring
Benefit/Value	• Sense of accomplishment • Job training • Experience working with individuals with disabilities • Recognition

Source: Virginia Beach Parks and Recreation, n.d.

in the community. Managers also develop resource files, Internet links, PDF files, and libraries to support volunteer training and education.

Job-related training and education sessions are scheduled with orientation sessions and during probationary or trial periods. Also, managers plan intermittent sessions to coincide with natural program breaks and client routines. To illustrate, shortly after volunteers begin their trial placements, managers can conduct volunteer-staff training to review compliance with protocol, to monitor staff-volunteer working relationships, and to require monthly in-services to update staff and volunteers on new equipment or resources.

Managers facilitate access to continuing professional development opportunities through other resources, such as service organizations (e.g., Red Cross) and professional associations (e.g., ATRA, NTRS). Volunteer contracts require acquisition and retention of credentials (e.g., first aid). Managers also elect to send volunteers to educational sessions as incentives or for promotional opportunities (e.g., state or regional ATRA or NTRS training). Consultants and educational sessions are brought into a facility via satellite or telecommunications. Each training and education session is evaluated to ensure that volunteers perceive experiences to be applicable to their respective assignments and to the goals of the department.

Department Background
- Vision, mission, goals
- Service description
- Consumer needs
- Volunteer opportunities

Department Information
- Policies, standards of practice
- Ethical practices
- Therapeutic recreation process and interventions
- CQI and risk management practices
- Records and documentation
- Safety and security protocols

Volunteer Program
- Organization and structure
- Volunteer jobs and contracts
- Staff-volunteer communication and protocols
- Volunteer screening, selection, placement processes
- Orientation content and procedures
- In-service content and procedures
- Professional development opportunities
- Evaluation tools and procedures
- Retention, promotion, recognition standards

Figure 17.4
Content Outline of a Volunteer Manual

Managers oversee volunteer/staff/client interactions. Staff varies in their degree of exposure to volunteer supervision. As a consequence, managers facilitate communication links and encourage the proper balance between authority and delegation of responsibility. Appropriate volunteer-client interactions are monitored. With staff, managers instill respect for volunteer roles so that volunteers are not taken for granted while they guide volunteers to ensure they do not overstep boundaries by assuming professional roles for which they are not qualified. As a manager, one may have to address paid staff attitudes and reservations about volunteers (Bannon, 1999). To overcome attitudinal barriers, managers guide staff and volunteers as they focus on consumer goals and outcomes.

Volunteer Supervision

Literature has addressed the ongoing support of the volunteer as being a crucial element of management, whether the experience is a short-term or long-term commitment (Serafino, 2001). Important to this support is the ongoing supervision and communication of performance to each volunteer. Documenting volunteer performance for the purpose of retention, promotion, or termination is integral to the management process. When successful, supervision enables volunteers to perform skillfully with enthusiasm and motivation. Volunteer retention diminishes with inadequate supervision and limited personal contact. Managers guide volunteers, create good working climates, encourage interest, and maximize volunteer effectiveness through communication.

Feedback is ongoing, positive, corrective, and supportive. Routine one-on-one conferences are supplemented with e-mail, phone contact, observation, informal discussion, and brief written "thank yous." Communication clarifies expectations, recognizes quality performance, monitors performance, and ensures safety. Constructive criticism promotes understanding (e.g., identifying a subtle client cue such as a change in body temperature that signals a need for professional staff attention). To have the most impact, feedback focuses on *how* rather than *why* and is given just prior to the time when the skill is to be used again. Giving feedback in the time closest to the event occurring creates an emotionally safe environment for the volunteer, rather than waiting for a more formal time to process observations.

Motivation is a key element in volunteer supervision. Maintaining high levels of motivation is just as important in settings where volunteer work is performed as in paid work settings. Actually, volunteer motivation may be more difficult because of the lack of monetary incentive; thus, when the "carrot is not the paycheck" effective management is imperative (Peach & Murrell, 1995; Ross, 1992). A manager balances volunteer needs with department goals so that the volunteer achieves his or her needs through assigned roles. "What's in it for me?" aptly describes this task. Volunteers are empowered through job enhancement, relationships with staff and clients, and confirmation that their roles contribute to department goals. Volunteers are motivated by their perception of contributing to the well-being of others or "helping" someone to improve his or her health. This volunteer role can also be significant because the volunteer may be adjusting to the unexpected presence of an illness in his or her own family. The reciprocity or exchange between volunteer peers may also provide newfound support systems for one's own life changes. Motivations for volunteering are multidimensional and require supervisors' respect and support.

Documentation is essential to volunteer management. Formative and summative supervisory evaluations are recorded in volunteer files or data banks. Information is used in planning, budgeting, quality control and improvement, risk management, job promotion, termination, and recognition. Quantitative data are collected using computer programs to generate statistics on number of volunteer hours, equivalent dollar value of volunteer hours, "prototype volunteers," and ratio of volunteers to clients. Managers document volunteer roles and responses in incident and accident reports necessary for liability and risk management. Routine supervisory sessions permit documentation of volunteer compliance with job assignments while casual observations permit documentation of skill development needs or quality of performance. Routine documentation occurs periodically during volunteer service (e.g., formative evaluation) and when volunteers complete their assignments (e.g., summative evaluation).

Volunteers outgrow their assignments, develop new interests, feel unneeded, burnout, experience change in their time commitments, develop improper attitudes, and/or become dissatisfied. Managers are challenged to maintain volunteer satisfaction. Consequently, naturalistic observation techniques are used to note behaviors to determine if volunteers have reached plateaus and would benefit from promotion or reassignment (Sarfit & Merrill, 2002; see Figure 17.5). A promotion results when a volunteer assists with another consumer or in another program area, and/or leads while staff provide support. Such an experience might lead to retention as the volunteer perceives his or her talents are better utilized. Administrative or supportive assignments may seem to be monotonous due to the repetitive nature of a particular task. In this situation a manager promotes retention by reassigning the volunteer to direct service tasks or places the volunteer on call until his or her talents can be better utilized.

Performance reviews conducted during supervisory meetings compare volunteer performance with job descriptions and contract specifications. Termination or

---

Volunteer Observation

Volunteer Name _____   Site _____   Date _____

✓ = appropriate   ✗ = needs improvement

____ Dressed appropriately   Comments: _____

____ Relation/Rapport with youth   Comments: _____

____ Relation/Rapport with staff   Comments: _____

____ Initiative/Works with minimal direction   Comments: _____

Activities Observed:

_____

_____

_____

Staff Comments:

_____

_____

Source: Virginia Beach Parks and Recreation, n.d.

Figure 17.5
Volunteer Observation Form

separation results when expectations are not met. Volunteers experience changes in their personal commitments that prevent them from fulfilling their intended obligations. In this situation the volunteer may choose to separate from the department by submitting a brief written request to relinquish the position. During sessions, managers may observe a sympathetic rather than empathetic relationship that compromises the consumer's goals. Managers might overhear conversations that compromise the consumer's integrity or confidentiality. In the latter situations, after due process, volunteers are assigned to positions without consumer contact or they are terminated. Following formative and summative supervisory meetings, managers document their actions (i.e., retention, promotion, or termination) in permanent files or data banks. These data are used to evaluate the operation of the volunteer program, recognize volunteer contributions, and prepare future references, verifications or recommendations.

Volunteer Evaluation and Recognition

A quality recognition plan assists the agency in the retention of volunteers (Pidgeon, 1998). Formal recognition during the initial volunteer experiences further facilitates motivation and commitment—put simply, if they do not feel appreciated they will not stay (Ross, 1992). Recognition is a critical element of volunteer management.

As managers formally and informally guide volunteers during supervisory interactions, the evaluation process commences. Volunteer program evaluation is one aspect of a comprehensive evaluation process. Comprehensive evaluation plans address personnel, programs, resources, clients, and management. Several tasks are involved in design and implementation of a comprehensive evaluation program, including the following:

1. Design the evaluation plan.

2. Collect data, analyze results, and implement outcomes.

3. Maintain records and financial data.

Data from supervisory sessions and evaluation reviews guide the manager's decisions concerning recognition. Informal and formal recognition enhances volunteer retention and staff support of volunteer efforts. Additionally, public recognition promotes therapeutic recreation. Thus, managers oversee informal volunteer and staff recognition and formal and public volunteer and staff recognition.

Evaluation Plan

A comprehensive evaluation plan is an element of professional practice standards (ATRA, 2000) and is a recommended programming practice (Rossman & Schlatter, 2003). Use of volunteers is impacted by or influences each element of comprehensive evaluations—consumers, programs, resources, personnel, and management. Evaluation plans are developed by responding to the following questions:

- What will be evaluated?

- When will evaluation occur?

- How will data be collected and analyzed?

- Who will administer and who will respond to the measurements?

- How will the results be used and disseminated?

What to evaluate is determined by department goals and professional and regulatory criteria. Fundamental questions to raise about the volunteer program include the following:

- What should the volunteer have done? Was it done? Why or why not?

- Did the volunteer's support improve client services or embellish service offerings?

- Were the volunteer's efforts successfully meshed with staff competence to create supportive relationships and an effective team?

- Was each phase of the volunteer process (e.g., planning, training, supervision, evaluation, recognition) successful? Why or why not?

Quantitative data are helpful during continuous quality improvement (CQI) planning. Examples of outcome measures that might be useful to quality improvement include length of service, turnover rate, total amounts of individual and group volunteer time, number of volunteers with demographic variables, dollar value equivalents of hours contributed, costs per consumer or per program, expenditure per volunteer, and staff time per volunteer. Each of these factors provides information helpful to extension or enhancement of services.

Qualitative data collection techniques, such as focus groups or individual in-depth interviews, enhance an understanding of the meaning of the experience to the volunteers and provide insights into motivation and retention strategies for the future. Volunteers often "see things with new eyes." They give refreshing perspectives to old problems and assist the agency in considering new service delivery methods. Henderson and Silverberg

(2002) suggested, "much more needs to be learned about volunteering" (p. 34).

The nature and length of a volunteer job, influences the frequency and formality of evaluation. When volunteer assignments are in direct service rather than administration or supportive areas, more frequent formal evaluations are likely. Direct service volunteers are governed by practice standards that mandate research and evaluation. Also, the consequence of error in direct service provision is more critical to client well-being than in nonconsumer contact functions. When volunteer commitments are short term, evaluations also are less detailed. The evaluation plan identifies approximate times of formal and informal reviews so that both formative and summative information are made available to the manager as needed for day-to-day decisions and future improvements.

A number of data collection tools and methods are available. Selection is influenced by the following qualities:

- validity (i.e., Does the instrument measure what it should?)

- reliability or dependability (i.e., Does the instrument have the same results with repeated use?)

- usability (i.e., Are resources available to administer evaluations, do staff have support for analysis, and is the evaluation method economical?)

- meaningfulness (i.e., Are significant features of the volunteer program assessed in an objective manner?)

- timeliness (i.e., Is the instrument used in a reasonable length of time and are the results readily available?)

- operational (i.e., Is the information unique, does it contribute to action, and is the maximum amount of information gained through minimum effort?)

- understandability (i.e., Are directions clear and are results readily interpretable?)

The intent of evaluation influences the type of tool or method selected. Managers may use questionnaires, interviews, observations, checklists, case studies, audits, self-appraisals, consumer ratings, cost-effectiveness studies, critical incidents, and a variety of participatory techniques (e.g., focus groups, quality circles, advisory groups, staff-volunteer councils). Managers may also use standardized forms prepared by the human resource department for use throughout the agency (refer to Figure 17.6). Decisions made using data from a number of methods add objectivity to actions taken following evaluations. To illustrate, a triangulated evaluation approach

might be used if the purpose is to determine appropriateness of a volunteer's placement and his or her ability to perform assigned tasks. Data are collected from three sources: the manager uses a checklist formulated from the job description and supervisory observations, the volunteer completes a self-appraisal, and the consumer gives input on a satisfaction scale.

The *who* are those impacted by the volunteer program. Thus, evaluation audiences include volunteers, staff, consumers, caregivers, managers, committee or board members, colleagues, and peers. Each audience evaluates its respective roles with respect to each of the other audiences. For example,

- Staff respond to questionnaires noting volunteer compliance with job descriptions.

- Volunteers complete surveys on training and supervisory effectiveness of staff and managers.

- Consumers report their satisfaction with programs and personnel during exit interviews.

- Managers gain reactions of volunteers and staff to operational efficiencies during quality circles.

Managers determine who is most directly affected by the evaluation concern or purpose and then design the evaluation plan so all audiences are involved appropriately. Additionally, managers either administer or oversee information collection or delegate the responsibility to appropriate personnel.

The last step in designing an evaluation plan is to determine how the results will be used and disseminated to improve program quality. Managers determine how each aspect (e.g., consumers, program, resources, personnel, management) may be improved. Also, the manager decides how each evaluation audience is to be informed and incorporated into follow-up as the evaluation results are used. The three options managers have are to maintain the status quo, to reassign or revise, and to terminate or discontinue. When results support achievement of performance indicators in the plan of operation, no change is necessary. When managers determine, for instance, that volunteer-staff relationships have not contributed to improved consumer functioning, reassignments or termination are plausible considerations. When the latter occurs and termination is necessary, it should involve the volunteer administrator, supervisor, and an ombudsperson; counseling and confidentiality are stressed (Lundin, 1996). Evaluation information is considered confidential and disseminated with discretion. Results are placed in appropriate files and are included in reports to administrators and governing boards.

VOLUNTEER PERFORMANCE EVALUATION
THERAPEUTIC RECREATION UNIT
DEPARTMENT OF PARKS AND RECREATION
CITY OF VIRGINIA BEACH

VOLUNTEER: _____   PROGRAM: _____

RATING SCALE: 3 = ABOVE AVERAGE   2 = AVERAGE   1 = BELOW AVERAGE

CATEGORY	RATING	COMMENTS	CATEGORY	RATING	COMMENTS
Appearance			Punctuality		
Creativity			Integrity		
Dependability			Follows Directions		
Willingness to Learn			Leadership		
Communications Skills – with participants – with parents – with staff			Planning Skills		

1. Was the volunteer qualified to work in the program? _____
_____

2. What has been the volunteer's contribution to your program? _____
_____

3. Do you have any comments/suggestions that may assist this volunteer to improve their performance? ___
_____

4. Additional comments: _____
_____

5. Would you recommend this volunteer for employment with this department/unit? ____ Yes ____ No   Explain: _____
_____

_____   _____
Volunteer/Date   Program Coordinator/Date

_____
Program Supervisor/Date

Source: Virginia Beach Parks and Recreation, n.d.

Figure 17.6
Volunteer Performance Evaluation

Collect Data, Analyze Results, and Implement Outcomes

Data are collected using the tools or methods selected or prepared by the department manager or agency-wide volunteer coordinator. Formative evaluation is done as volunteers complete their assigned tasks; summative evaluation occurs at the conclusion of particular duties. Forms incorporate more than one evaluation aspect (e.g., program evaluations include volunteer functions), or each major component may have individualized evaluations (e.g., personnel, programs, resources, clientele, management).

Analysis of formative data leads to immediate adjustments, such as the following:

- additional in-services on ethics in the workplace or a recreation therapist's contributions to consumer health and well-being

- reassignment of volunteers to another unit or a different consumer

- referral of a volunteer to supportive or administrative services

- recommendation of a promotion to another job

Analysis of summative data allows the manager to make judgments about future actions to improve services. Minimal change may be required or revisions and discontinuation may require major adjustments. Revisions that might result include additions to the orientation and training schedule (e.g., more hands-on experiences with clients), modifications in the supervisory process (e.g., additional self-assessments), alterations in contracts to better clarify job parameters, and/or redesign of evaluation tools to incorporate caregivers' comments.

Termination or discontinuation is the third summative evaluation outcome. Volunteers can be fired. Documentation corroborates contract violations and unmet job expectations. Termination results from noncompliance with consumer protocol, staff directives, ethical and professional standards, and operational policies. This action is appropriate regardless of the length of the intended commitment (e.g., after an outing or one event a volunteer is released if his or her actions placed the consumer in an at-risk position). When supervisory communiqués are ineffective over an extended time, volunteers are relieved of their duties. To illustrate, volunteers may tend to talk among themselves rather than focus on the consumer's needs, and although this is not detrimental to the consumer's health, over time such actions detract from consumer skill acquisition and program quality.

Maintain Records and Financial Data

Managers maintain records on each program aspect. A number of computer programs are available which permit data manipulation so that productivity measures and impact figures are generated to use in both annual and monthly trend reports. Records facilitate preparation of cost-effectiveness data and strategic plans. Volunteers use records for income tax statements and educational and employment applications. Managers use records to support supervisory feedback and recognition programs.

Volunteer records document work outcomes and performance-related activities. Permanent reports and records include job descriptions, contracts, supervisory plans, training results, performance appraisals, recommendations, referrals, promotions, terminations, recognitions, service data, staff evaluations, risk management, and continuous quality improvement (CQI) information.

Henderson (1988) suggested that relative worth of a volunteer to the agency is determined by cost-effectiveness analysis. Figures kept show output per dollar spent on each volunteer and are similar to productivity measures. Managers use statistics to show costs per volunteer, per consumer, per program, and per volunteer service hour. The intent of presenting this information in annual and monthly reports is to show the value of added service that contributes to reduced health care costs and increased consumer and staff effectiveness. Managers use 2,080 hours, or one worker year, and the salary ranges of equivalent professional positions to generate dollar value amounts contributed through volunteer service hours. Financial reports are shared with current supporters and prospective external funding sources to promote the department and to solicit future resources.

Informal Volunteer and Staff Recognition

Recognition energizes the work environment by supporting and motivating staff and volunteers. Because it promotes the worth of volunteers and therapeutic recreation to the agency and community, recognition is also a form of public relations. Recognition and praise counter feelings of insecurity and inadequacy. When consumers are unable to express appreciation, acknowledgment from staff is imperative.

Intrinsic recognition tied to performance motivates behavior. Therefore, informal recognition associated with task completion tends to enhance retention and recruitment. Because volunteers value peer recognition and acknowledgment of their competence, a thank you, handshake, e-mail, or sticky note can heighten motivation. Informal meetings among volunteers, staff, and management facilitate recognition and feedback. During supervisory sessions the suggestion of an additional assignment or promotion to another work area rewards quality and encourages service continuation.

Formal and Public Volunteer and Staff Recognition

Formal awards are based on performance criteria. Specific goals or service levels, each with commensurate forms of recognition, identify volunteer service hours, financial contributions, innovative programming, and resource acquisition. A comprehensive recognition program acknowledges quality as well as quantity so traits such as dependability and promptness as well as extraordinary hours of service are rewarded. To foster support for the program and to design meaningful equitable criteria, managers solicit volunteer and staff assistance to select tangible rewards and plan public ceremonies. Family members and caregivers are frequently willing to participate in recognition events.

Recognition considerations include the following (Virginia Beach Department of Parks and Recreation, n.d.):

- granting recognition in a public forum preferably among the peer group of volunteers

- timing recognition to capture all constituent groups

- tailoring recognition to the individual

- assuring that recognition is given sincerely

- assuring that recognition is fair

Managers use documented work hours, projects completed, funds raised, number of newly recruited volunteers, innovative programming ideas, and suggestions resulting in time-saving service improvements as achievement indicators. The recipient must perceive the chosen form of recognition as valuable. For example, a senior citizen who works on the pediatric unit would enjoy a luncheon, while a news clipping in the local newspaper would be more relevant in recognizing a service club. The nature of the contribution being recognized influences the nature of the tangible reward. Thus, if documented service hours is the chosen criterion, the value of the reward increases as the hours escalate (e.g., pins are given for 500 hours, plaques are presented for 1,000 hours). When ideas result in service improvement (e.g., adapting equipment, developing innovative programs, securing state or federal grants), the contributions warrant a write-up in the agency newsletter.

Managers recognize staff for their support of the volunteer program. Staff train, supervise, and recognize volunteers. Such tasks consume additional time and effort worthy of recognition. Team efforts are the result of staff facilitating cohesiveness among consumers, volunteers, and colleagues. Managers incorporate recognition of such contributions into job performance standards on volunteer supervision, documentation of supervisory experiences, released time for special training in volunteer management, letters of commendation in personnel files, and public acknowledgment before agency administrators, volunteers, consumers, and caregivers. Informal staff recognition (e.g., interoffice phone call, e-mail) creates a cooperative work environment and garners support of management.

Related Considerations

A number of trends and issues affect volunteerism. With workplace changes, people move in and out of volunteer experiences, making shorter rather than long-term commitments. Volunteerism is a component of service learning in high schools and colleges. As social inclusion continues, volunteer buddies become more integral to accessing relevant experiences. Also, with health care focusing on community and caregiver intervention, volunteerism becomes an essential element of the support network in home health care, outpatient, and transitional services.

A number of issues arise from these economic, social, and health care trends. Youth under age 18 seek out volunteer opportunities as alternatives to inaccessible paying positions and as service learning projects. Identification of placements appropriate to the youth and clients may be a challenge. For example, youth unaware of secondary outcomes of a disability like head injuries or strokes become uncomfortable with inappropriate client behaviors or statements, yet are bored if assigned supportive tasks. However, using a young person with a disability as a volunteer facilitates peer education that enhances community service delivery (Phoenix, Miller & Schleien, 2002).

Quality control and cost containment evident in the health care industry, along with social inclusion necessitate intensive volunteer training and higher levels of competence to assist during consumer transitions. Staff train volunteers as advocates, companions, and aides. This is time-consuming, because the process is ongoing and individualized to each consumer's needs. Managers, therefore, institute staff development programs to train entry-level staff as trainers so they "coach" volunteers to monitor individual client progress. The importance of devoting time to volunteer training is further complicated by reduced amount of consumer contact time with professional health care providers and implementation of quality control standards.

The use of consumers as volunteers presents several issues. Consumers perceive that through volunteering they may secure a permanent position yet may not have the physical or emotional tolerance to work full time. Problems arise when former consumers perceive that they are capable of helping recently traumatized patients while still adapting to their own changed lifestyles. Adult athletes who sponsor and train youth wheelchair athletes are effective role models as are formalized support groups where consumers and caregivers in various stages of recovery mentor one another.

Volunteer supervision has become more complicated due to the increasing number of standards, regulations, laws, and work demands. Managers monitor records pertaining to safety and risk issues as well as financial and personnel outcomes. Firing a volunteer and holding staff accountable for volunteer-consumer interactions require time and attention to protocols and standards of practice. Staff may perceive that volunteers are available to be used in tasks they would prefer not to undertake and/or that volunteers are available to carry staff overloads. Managers articulate expectations while carefully discriminating between professional and volunteer roles and the importance of each task to operation of the department. Volunteer management is becoming increasingly professional (Kerka, 1998), therefore managers need to ensure that the supervisors of volunteers are also kept abreast of new models of supervision, regulations, and the needs of the 21st century volunteer.

of the department within the agency. In-services prepare volunteers to complete daily assignments properly while educational sessions expose them to professional practices and issues. Supervision ensures compliance and performance of job expectations and a partnership among staff, volunteers, and management that benefits consumers.

Through informal and formal supervisory contacts, managers make decisions about volunteer retention, promotion, reassignment, and termination. Evaluative data affirm compliance with contractual expectations and contributions to service quality. Collected information is used to recognize volunteers and staff and to inform agency publics of the value of their efforts to program enrichment and improvement. Statistics used in cost-effectiveness ratios quantify the value of volunteers. Productivity measures incorporate cost of volunteer operation per client, per program, and per hour, as performance is assessed. Trend reports document value of volunteer hours per worker year (e.g., 2,080 hours times the hourly rate of a comparable position time's number of volunteers equals dollar value of volunteers to the department). Issues arise with volunteer management. Age and maturity of volunteers, amount of time devoted to training, appropriateness of training materials, presence of client volunteers, relationships among staff, volunteers, and consumers, and accountability measures are management considerations.

Summary

Volunteering is a crucial element of service delivery. The intent of this chapter was to present information on each phase of volunteer programs within the context of social, economic, political, and technological change. Major tasks in this process were briefly presented. Planning encompasses the paperwork steps prior to actual operation of a volunteer program: Is a volunteer program an element of the strategic plan and department mission? Are resources available to support the program? Professional standards, agency needs, and regulatory criteria guide design of volunteer policies, job descriptions, and contracts. Recruitment and selection of the right volunteer for the right job are fundamental. Target audiences, such as older adults, students, caregivers, youth, court-assigned volunteers, and consumers, each bring to the volunteer experience certain needs and anticipated outcomes matched with department goals.

Training and education begin with volunteer placements. Usually an orientation period introduces volunteers to the overall agency and department operation and its significance to services and outcomes. Orientation in therapeutic recreation includes responsibilities of volunteers within the unit and information about the focus and intent

Review Questions

1. Identify and explain the outcomes of each phase of department preparation of a volunteer program: organization, recruitment, and selection.

2. Explain the essential orientation topics to be covered as volunteer placements are made.

3. Conduct an Internet search to locate available volunteer training and education resources. Resources may be found on the following sites:
   - Corporation for National and Community Service http://www.cns.gov
   - National Retiree Volunteer Coalition http://www.nrvc.org
   - Association for Research on Nonprofit Organizations and Voluntary Action http://www.arnova.org
   - National Civic League http://www.ncl.org
   - Independent Sector http://www.independentsector.org
   - Service Leader http://www.serviceleader.org

4. Feedback and motivation are integral to volunteer supervision. Explain the manager's role with each.

5. What types or forms of documentation and evaluation should managers retain with volunteer programs?

6. What is the significance of recognition in volunteer management?

7. Explore how health care trends impact use of volunteers in therapeutic recreation.

8. Examine the pros and cons of client placement in volunteer roles.

9. Discuss the relationship of volunteer contributions to cost analysis and accountability (e.g., How should volunteer management costs and benefits be reflected in the budget)?

References

American Therapeutic Recreation Association (ATRA). (2000). *Standards for the practice of therapeutic recreation and self-assessment guide.* Alexandria, VA: Author.

Bannon, J. (1999). *911 management: A comprehensive guide for leisure service managers.* Champaign, IL: Sagamore Publishing.

Brudney, J. L., (1990). *Fostering volunteer programs in the public sector.* San Francisco, CA: Jossey-Bass Publishers.

Brudney, J. L. (1999). The effective use of volunteers: Best practices for the public sector. *Law and Contemporary Problems, 64*(4), 219.

Carter, M. J., VanAndel, G. E., and Robb, G. M. (2003). *Therapeutic recreation: A practical approach* (3rd ed.). Prospect Heights, IL: Waveland Press.

Henderson, K. (1988). Are volunteers worth their weight in gold? *Parks & Recreation, 23*(11), 40–43.

Henderson, K. and Silverberg, K. (2002). Good work, if you can get it. *Parks & Recreation, 37*(11), 26–36.

Grossman, J. B. and Furano, K. (2002). *Making the most of volunteers.* Philadelphia, PA: Public/Private Ventures. Retrieved September 26, 2003, from http://www.ppv.org

Kerka, S. (1998). *Volunteer management trends and issues alert.* Columbus, OH: ERIC clearinghouse on adult, career, and vocational education. (ERIC Document Reproduction Service No. ED414430).

Lundin, S. (1996). When all else fails: Releasing a volunteer. *Journal of Volunteer Administration, 15*(11), 15–18.

Miller, K., Schleien, S., Rider, C., Hall, C., Roche, M., and Worsley, J. (2002). Inclusive volunteering: Benefits to participants and community. *Therapeutic Recreation Journal, 36*(3), 247–259.

Mutchler, J. E., Burr, J. A., and Caro, F. (2003). From paid worker to volunteer: Leaving the paid workforce and volunteering in later life. *Social Forces, 81*(4), 1267–1293. Retrieved November 14, 2005, from Academic Search Premiere (EBCO) database.

National Recreation and Park Association (NRPA). (2004). *Standards and evaluative criteria for baccalaureate programs in recreation, park resources and leisure services.* Asburn, VA: Author.

National Therapeutic Recreation Society (NTRS). (2004). *Standards of practice for a continuum of care in therapeutic recreation.* Retrieved September 12, 2004, from http://www.nrpa.org/content/default.aspx?documentID=530

Peach, E. B. and Murrell, K. B. (1995). Reward, recognition system for volunteers. In T.D. Conners. (Ed.), *The volunteer management book* (pp. 222–243). New York, NY: John Wiley & Sons.

Phoenix, T, Miller, K., and Schleien, S. (2002). Better to give than to receive. *Parks & Recreation, 37*(10), 26–33.

Pidgeon, W., Jr. (1998). *The universal benefits of volunteering.* New York, NY: John Wiley & Sons.

Ross, D. (1992). Managing volunteers—When the carrot is not a pay cheque. *CMA Magazine, 66*(9), 30. Retrieved November 14, 2005, from Academic Search Premiere (EBCO) database.

Rossman, J. R. and Schlatter, B. E. (2003). *Recreation programming: Designing leisure experiences* (4th ed.). Champaign, IL: Sagamore Publishing.

Sarfit, R. D. and Merrill, M. (2002). Management implications of contemporary trends in volunteerism in the U.S. and Canada. *Journal of Volunteer Administration, 20*(2), 12–23.

Serafino, A. (2001). Linking motivation and commitment through learning activities in the volunteer sector. *Journal of Volunteer Administration, 19*(4), 15–20.

Tedrick, T. and Henderson, K. (1989). *Volunteers in leisure.* Reston, VA: American Alliance for Health, Physical Education, Recreation and Dance.

Thacker, S. B. (2003). *HIPAA privacy rule and public health guidance from CDC and the U.S. Department of Health and Human Services.* Retrieved June 3, 2004, from http://www.cdc.gov/mmwr/preview/mmwrhtml/m2e411a1.htm

Virginia Beach Department of Parks and Recreation. (n.d.). *Staff and volunteer manual.* Virginia Beach, VA: Author.

Wilson, J. and Musick, M. (1999). The effects of volunteering on the volunteer. *Law & Contemporary Problems, 62*(4), 141. Retrieved November 14, 2005, from Academic Search Premiere (EBCO) database.

Chapter 18
Intern Management

chapter revisions by Claire M. Foret, Kathy Jack, and Marcia Jean Carter

The internship plays a vital role in therapeutic recreation education and is generally considered the culminating experience in the undergraduate educational experience (Zabriskie & Ferguson, 2004). The internship is the bridge for assisting students to hone application skills from class work and to make the transition from a student identity to that of an emerging professional (Smith, O'Dell & Schaumleffel, 2002). Following a study to assess the various features of the intern experience, Zabriskie and Ferguson (2004) noted, "Therapeutic recreation educators consider the internship experience to be an essential component of their curricula" (p. 33). Yet one challenge faced by educators is how to manage the experience to minimize the potential of placement sites to be chance academic environments (Smith, O'Dell & Schaumleffel, 2002).

For purposes of this publication, the authors have chosen to define the internship and fieldwork experiences as follows: An *internship* is a structured career-related full-time work experience (e.g., 32 hours or more per week) of one or more quarters or semesters in duration (e.g., 12–16 weeks) for which the student receives academic credit and which occurs following the completion of the majority of major coursework during the junior and senior years in an upper division institution. A *fieldwork* and/or *practicum* experience precedes the internship experience and/or is the title assigned to experiential learning in the two-year or lower division institution. This experience or series of experiences is usually less than full time (e.g., 32 hours per week), may be completed as major coursework is taken, may or may not be graded independently of coursework, and serves as a prerequisite to the culminating internship.

Internships and fieldwork require agency preparation and devotion of staff time, resources, and expertise. Watson (1992) noted that cost-benefit analyses suggest that costs are rarely fully recovered. Why then would a manager consider having interns? According to Feldman and Weitz (1990); Steffes (2004); and Cunningham, Sagas, Dixon, Kent, and Turner (2005) college students benefit by the practicum and intern experiences in several ways: professional interests and values are affirmed, the transition from the academic setting to the work environment is made easier, classroom knowledge is solidified, and the opportunity to secure employment is enhanced. Further,

managers also benefit by having the opportunity to cultivate and observe potential employees, to link to academic settings creating avenues of information and resource exchange, and to look at things from a new or different perspective as a result of intern inquiries. A cooperative internship also provides a feedback loop with site supervisors helping validate and refine curricula and specific academic course work (Zabriskie & Ferguson, 2004).

Tasks undertaken, documents developed, management policies and responsibilities, and issues faced prior to, during, and following student placements are similar to volunteer management activities. The manager undertakes four major types of activities: preplacement preparation, orientation, supervision and training, and evaluation and termination. Preplacement planning encompasses tasks necessary to establish a relationship with university programs including the delineation of department, student, and academic responsibilities; the incorporation of internship policies and procedures into department documents; the dedication of personnel and resources to support student experiences; and the preparation of documents and agreements used in student selection and training. Orientation commences with initial student contact and recruitment and continues as the student becomes familiar with the agency, department, staff, and potential learning experiences.

While students assume increasing degrees of responsibility and autonomy, managers both provide supervision and conduct training to enhance the intern's ability to respond to the new demands. Formal written evaluations take place at midterm and termination periods with intermittent weekly or biweekly reports submitted through the manager to the academic supervisor. Throughout the placement, the manager mentors, advises, models, and challenges the student to acquire and demonstrate ethical behaviors. Performance is guided by personnel standards, professional practice standards, on-site protocols, and the student's personal-professional philosophy. During the placement, and as the experience terminates, issues may arise that require resolution. To illustrate, the intern may observe differing management styles between the academic and site supervisors. As the student internship ends, both the college and site supervisor address transitions to be made by staff, students, clients, and caregivers.

This chapter is organized according to the primary steps completed in preparation, orientation, supervision and training, and evaluation and termination of interns (refer to Table 18.1). The intent is to present strategies a manager might use to ensure the agency environment is not a "chance" setting but rather one that facilitates deliberate academic applications and transitions among the student, agency and university partners. The focus is on the for-credit undergraduate experience. Graduate students may, however, enroll in such a course to gain additional experience or satisfy credentialing criteria. Watson (1992) noted that those students who are closely supervised and receive academic credit tend to be more reliable and motivated, and the agency is legally protected from accusations of unfair labor practices. Campbell and Kovar (1994) suggested that successful internships provide the proper balance of academic and agency guidance and independence so students mature professionally.

Preplacement Planning

Preplacement planning tasks organize the department to support internships, to formalize relationships with academic institutions, and to secure a pool of internship applicants. Internship preparation, therefore, involves a number of the following management tasks:

1. Delineate specific internship goals and objectives.

2. Establish policies and procedures, including termination policies.

3. Prepare staff and resources to support interns.

4. Develop training materials.

5. Delineate department, academic, and intern responsibilities.

6. Negotiate affiliation agreement.

7. Develop selection procedures.

8. Design application and screening process.

9. Disseminate information and recruit potential interns.

10. Select and interview intern candidates.

With the completion of these steps, interns are under contract, academic institutions have committed to fulfill specific contractual obligations and the manager and staff are prepared to involve interns in daily department operations (see Table 18.1).

Department Preparation

An initial management task is to delineate within the department mission/vision the nature of an internship program. The scope and outcomes of structured internships are articulated in goals and objectives that appear in agency operating documents, marketing materials, and internship manuals. Collectively, these statements present the internship focus and substantiate contributions of the department to internship training. These documents establish the parameters for the management of the internship program. These directives guide subsequent management tasks. Table 18.2 (p. 278) notes the therapeutic recreation internship goals of a community-based special interest agency.

Existing department policies and procedures are studied to determine whether the manager will work with existing statements or develop new statements to define pertinent intern protocols. Intern policies and procedures are prepared and placed in internship manuals, affiliation agreements, recruiting materials, department policy manuals, and informative brochures presented to interested students and faculty. Statements are developed to describe personal and professional expectations and the resources that will be made available to students during the internship. Table 18.3 (p. 279) illustrates information for the student from an internship policy and procedures manual.

The manager involves department staff in internship preparation to encourage their commitment to internship training. Student policies and procedures are incorporated into staff training in anticipation of student arrival. Sessions devoted to intern management prepare practitioners for transitions they will undergo as student interns assume increasing degrees of autonomy and responsibility. Simulations and role-playing during staff training help staff to visualize the significance of their roles, to anticipate areas in which students might require assistance, and to gain familiarity with procedures and forms used during the internship. The manager prepares the staff guidelines and includes the guidelines with internship documents.

The value placed on internship training by the manager is reflected in the access to resources provided to the student during the internship. For the student intern to complete assignments and communicate with the department and academic supervisors, access to office space, computers, fax, e-mail, telephone, duplication services, and supplies are necessary. Access to professional and medical libraries on site or through practitioners also helps the student to make connections between theory and practice. Visits and observations with area practitioners and settings permit the student to become aware of relationships, issues, and practice similarities and differences. Opportunities to network through professional meetings and seminars heighten student awareness of the significance

Table 18.1
Internship Triad: Student, University, and Agency

	STUDENT	UNIVERSITY	AGENCY
Preplacement Preparation	• Complete academic coursework • Complete application to do internship • Review internship manual • Complete site visits to agencies • Complete interviews with prospective supervisors • Select site with agency and academic approval • Complete contract for placement	**With Agency** • Update manuals (e.g., overall goals, objectives) • Visit and recruit agency CTRS personnel at various sites • Meet with agency CTRS, review university procedures and policies, discuss resources • Sign affiliation agreements with agencies **With Student** • Ensure coursework is complete • Meet with student to review internship manual, procedures and policies • Discuss resources available • Discuss role of university supervisor: visits, report due dates, documentation to university	• Develop and prepare internship manual: agency's policies and procedures, including termination procedures • Prepare staff to supervise interns • Preinterview: site visit by potential interns • Interview and select interns • Update contracts with each intern and university • Sign contract with students, agency and university
Orientation	• Set goals and objectives for internship • Meet supervisor to set goals and objectives • Participate in agency orientation process • Review agency's internship requirements, policies, manual, and procedures • Review evaluation procedures with site and university supervisors	• Formalize goals and objectives with intern • Outline due dates and documentation for assignments • Delineate NCTRC job tasks • Review evaluation and supervisory processes and procedures: number of visits, placement dates, tasks	• Formalize goals and objectives with intern • Discuss weekly assignments and tasks as outlined by NCTRC job analysis • Discuss assignment due dates • Review policy manual • Discuss specific agency and CTRS program guidelines and procedures (e.g., parking, dress codes) • Orient to facility resources, personnel, and protocols
Supervision and Training	• Follow weekly schedule of job tasks • Document experiences through forms provided by agency and university • Meet with university supervisor on predetermined dates • Meet with agency supervisor weekly/daily and as needed • Display initiative, openly communicate with supervisors, maintain university contacts, comply with agency and professional protocols during client interactions and services	• Set due dates for assignments, observation visits, other communications • Discuss intern progress with supervisor biweekly and/or routinely • Set up procedures to maintain additional communication and contacts	• Set due dates, methods and procedures to write program plans, interventions, service delivery, evaluations and documentation • Review plans prior to service delivery • Follow weekly schedule of training and clinical tasks • Meet weekly to review and discuss performance • Maintain open communication among intern, supervisor, staff and university
Evaluation and Termination	**Formative** • Turn in reports on time • Discuss with supervisor performance on specific tasks • Follow recommendations of supervisor • Document daily **Summative** • Write up summative evaluation of experience • Evaluate performance of university and agency supervisor **Termination** • Evaluate preservice and internship program	**Formative** • Document observations of visits, use evaluation tools designed for observation • Discuss observations with intern and agency supervisor • Discuss intern performance with agency supervisor **Summative** • Review agency supervisor evaluation with intern • Discuss intern's overall performance • Assign grade for internship **Termination** • Assist intern in career options • Review agency and intern exit questionnaire • Follow-up with letter of appreciation for supervising interns	**Formative** • Discuss intern performance on weekly/biweekly basis • Provide feedback in a timely manner on specific task interventions and weekly performance • Document recommendations and procedures to follow **Summative** • Evaluate performance on NCTRC job tasks, agency and university forms • Discuss summative evaluation and recommendations with intern **Termination** • Answer university exit questionnaire on qualifications of intern and university program

of professional membership and continuing professional development. The time at the intern site is dedicated to internship-specific activities. If "downtime" on site occurs, time is used to research, prepare future programs, or observe other clinical disciplines.

Training materials, including an internship manual and recruiting packages, are prepared to guide the student as the internship is completed. Contents and materials are similar to volunteer materials and are guided by professional standards (Grote & Hasl, 1998; NTRS, 1997). A manual contains materials used in planning, orienting, training, supervising, and evaluating students, including disciplinary action and termination procedures. Items from the manual are used to recruit students. Managers organize packets to send to academic institutions or place on the Internet that invite applicants and specify how to develop relationships between the department and academic program. Documents sent or posted might include application forms, job descriptions, agency background information, and agreement forms. The contents likely to be found in an internship manual are listed in Figure 18.1.

Department and Academic Relationships

The internship experience is a triad relationship among students, agencies, and academic programs. Introductory materials help define the expectations of each entity in

Table 18.2
Goals of Student Internship Program

The following are the therapeutic recreation staff goals for students involved in the internship program:

1. Provide students with the opportunity to practice skills learned in the classroom.

2. Promote the expansion of knowledge gained in the academic setting.

3. Facilitate the student's refinement of interpersonal skills and development of work attitudes.

4. Provide feedback for on-the-job performance with the purpose of guiding the student toward improved effectiveness.

5. Encourage the development of self-evaluation and problem-solving skills.

6. Provide role models for clinical therapeutic recreation treatment.

7. Serve as a transition from the role of student to the role of therapeutic recreation specialist.

8. Meet the fieldwork requirements of the NCTRC.

9. Prepare the student for an entry-level position in the field of therapeutic recreation.

Used with permission of the Rocky Mountain Multiple Sclerosis Center, Denver, Colorado

detail. These expectations are further defined in a memorandum of agreement (MOA) between agency and academic programs and in contracts between the student and the department. Professional practice standards (ATRA, 2000; NTRS, 2004), professional guidelines (Grote & Hasl, 1998; Kinney & Witman, 1997; NTRS, 1997), and credentialing criteria (National Council for Therapeutic Recreation Certification [NCTRC], 2005a) provide directives helpful in developing relational documents. The supervisor of the internship should be qualified as a certified therapeutic recreation specialist (CTRS) with some experience in the position in addition to professional experience and should ensure a highly structured experience that encompasses the practice as defined by the NCTRC job analysis (NCTRC, 2005b), professional standards of practice (ATRA, 2000; NTRS, 2004) and other external agents like the accreditation criteria of the Council on Accreditation (COA) of the National Recreation and Park Association and the Association of Physical Activity and Recreation (APAR). The length of the internship experience and the number of required hours ranges from 20 hours per week for 24 weeks to 40 hours for a 12- to 16-week quarter or semester. A minimum of 480 clock hours to a maximum of 600 clock hours is recommended.

Students, agencies, and academic partners enter into agreements after confirming each is able to satisfy the other's expectations. To illustrate, managers may wish to only accept students who have majors in therapeutic recreation, attend Council on Accreditation (COA) therapeutic recreation accredited programs, and/or are supervised by an educator who holds the CTRS credential. Academic institutions may desire placements with agencies where at least two CTRSs are employed, where exposure to a variety of client populations rather than one particular clientele is guaranteed, and where the supervising CTRS has a certain amount of experience before taking student interns (Zabriskie & Ferguson, 2004). Agreements specify who is responsible for purchase of liability insurance and who completes specific supervisory tasks. MOAs are usually in effect for a definitive time period or until one party dissolves the relationship. As agreements require legal development and review, it is not unusual that three or more months of lead time are required to consummate a relationship.

Intern Selection Procedures

Intern selection processes are similar to the procedures used to hire employees. Selection processes require resumé submission, on-site or phone interviews, verification of academic coursework, proof of liability and health insurance, background checks, and in some instances, training in universal precautions, health screenings, and

Table 18.3
Student Intern Information and Guidelines

1. Meals are available in the dining room. Students receive the same discount rate on meals as employees.

2. Dress code is casual and appropriate according to activities. Athletic shoes are permitted but must be white leather and clean. Exercise attire can only be worn for exercise or sport activities. No blue jeans are allowed. Keep in mind the hospital is a professional setting and you want to present yourself in a professional manner.

3. Phone calls. When answering the department phone identify the department and yourself. Department phones should mainly be used for business matters. Personal calls should be kept to a minimum and should not interfere with work responsibilities.

4. Working hours. Minimum 40 hours per week, minimum 15 weeks. Schedule is determined by unit. Evenings and weekends may be involved.

5. Breaks. You are entitled to a 30-minute lunch or dinner. You are expected to be in the building during working hours. If you leave the building, let your supervisor know (and have approval). Your supervisor should be aware of your schedule.

6. Documenting hours. You must document hours (time of arrival and departure) on your weekly schedule.

7. Illness. If you are ill and cannot report to work, notify your supervisor by 8:30 a.m. Any hours missed due to illness or other personal matters will have to be made up if they interfere with the number of hours needed for completion of internship.

8. Holidays are observed as follows: New Year's Day, Memorial Day, Independence Day, Labor Day, Thanksgiving Day (and the day after), and Christmas Day. You may be scheduled to work during a holiday weekend but usually not on the day the holiday is actually observed.

9. Educational materials. Books, videos, and other materials belonging to the Recreation Therapy Department or Medical Library are available to students but must be signed out and returned.

10. Housing. Students are responsible for living arrangements. The Student Coordinator can be contacted for possible resources.

11. Parking. Do not park in the visitor parking areas. Please refer to the parking memo.

12. Smoking. This hospital is a smoke-free hospital. No smoking is allowed within the hospital or on the hospital campus. An outdoor smoking area for patients is located on the West End.

13. Nametags. You will be provided with a nametag. You will be expected to wear this during working hours.

Used by permission of Recreation Therapy Department, Chelsea Community Hospital, Chelsea, Michigan

updating immunizations. More detailed procedures require the following:

- transcript and copies of certification documents

- recommendation and/or verification letters

- prerequisite experience in similar setting and/or with similar clientele

- specific coursework (e.g., clinical psychology)

- maintenance of a specific grade point average in therapeutic recreation classes

- completion of all therapeutic recreation classes

- application form and self-assessment profile

- philosophical statement and career goals

- selection after department interview and university approval

Managers base selection decisions on a first-come, first-served basis; preference may be given to students from academic programs with presigned agreements. Selection may also be based on the quality of each applicant. Submission of materials by specified deadlines also determines who is given further consideration. Agency-wide preset starting dates (e.g., June 1, September 1, January 15) can also be used by the manager to select

Agency Overview
- Vision, mission, goals, objectives
- Organization, operational information
- Clientele and service scope

Department Service
- Vision, mission, goals, objectives
- Organization and staffing
- Services, scope of care, standards

Internship Program
- Affiliation policy and agreement
- Responsibilities of department, student, academic program
- Procedures for selection and placement
- Goals, objectives, prerequisite competencies
- Department policies, personal guidelines
- Job description
- Application procedures
- Schedule and weekly expectations
- Learning outcomes and assignments
- Supervisor profile
- Personnel and evaluation forms
- References and resource material

Figure 18.1
Content Outline of an Internship Manual

students available at these rotation intervals. Some highly competitive internship sites set earlier application deadlines and post announcements with criteria on the Internet.

After the selection criteria are determined, a process is developed to receive and evaluate application forms and supportive student documents. This process is affected by a number of variables: size of the department, presence of an agency-wide clinical coordinator, supervisory assignments from semester to semester, existence or nonexistence of an agency-wide intern program, and the number of on-site student rotations available per semester (e.g., aquatic, outpatient, substance abuse). These variables also influence who is involved in actual intern selection and how and when selection takes place. A formal rating system that collapses a large amount of subjective information into quantitative terms may be used to assess the quality of the prospective intern's application, and/or the decision may be made by the manager with input from staff assigned to supervise interns. Selection criteria consider the "goodness of fit" between student and department.

A pool of applicants can be recruited by personal contacts, participation on academic advisory committees, class presentations, mailing of materials to campus career centers, Internet postings, and through professional contacts. During professional meetings, department information is displayed and distributed. Managers who serve on boards or make presentations have captive audiences with whom to share internship opportunities. Mailings to persons on professional membership lists access students. Academic programs host job and internship fairs, and alumni and agency placement days. Agency CD or media presentations are used in introductory and seminar classes to inform students of intern options.

An important step in the selection of interns is the interview. Managers may elect to screen prospective applicants with interviews granted to a select number of students. Managers may require on-site interviews or use alternatives like teleconferences, videotaped or written responses/e-mail to questions, and/or phone interviews. These experiences are similar to hiring staff and placing volunteers. Interview questions emphasize the student's career goals and specific needs that might be served by a particular internship.

Interviews determine the "goodness of fit." Students may discover during an interview that they are not interested in a particular type of setting, or managers may ascertain that the student's goals would be suited to placement with clientele other than those served by the department. Interview outcomes are reported to the student as well as to the academic advisor in writing so that appropriate corrective action and/or follow-up can be taken. When a student is accepted, managers request return of an acceptance letter within a definitive time period. This

is then followed by mailing of orientation materials including an internship manual. This begins to prepare the student for the department orientation.

Department Orientation

Volunteer and intern orientations are similar. The structure of the internship experience is planned during the orientation. Student supervision, work schedules, assignments, evaluations, and communication protocols are arranged, and responsibilities and department-academic expectations are clarified. At this time, a student-department contract is formalized with clearly stated objectives, due dates, and tasks. Primary orientation activities include the following (refer to Table 18.1, Internship Triad):

1. introduction to agency, department, and other allied health disciplines

2. identification of training needs and expectations

3. review of supervisory and evaluation processes and procedures

4. student-department contract negotiation

Introduction to Agency and Department

Topics like those under volunteer training and supervision are incorporated into an intern orientation. When a site is a clinical training site for a number of disciplines, a general agency orientation may occur independently of the department orientation. Regardless, the orientation period ranges from a few days to a few weeks. Informal orientation continues as the manager meets routinely with the intern. Documentation of these interactions is ongoing. An orientation checklist (see Figure 18.2) helps the student to organize tasks and responsibilities during the experience (Fox Valley Special Recreation Association, 2003; Grote & Hasl, 1998).

Contents of the internship manual are reviewed and used to familiarize the student with the agency and department and to help the student become comfortable with the supervisor's management style. When objectives are outlined in the manual, students and supervisors review the evaluative criteria so that students can anticipate internship outcomes. Visits to other sites and discussions with peer professionals during the orientation help the student become familiar with health care and human services and the role of therapeutic recreation across disciplines. When several services comprise a department, students rotate among the areas prior to actual placement with particular services. Academic expectations, assignments, and forms are considered. Decisions are made as to which forms and assignments will be required. Recommendations from these discussions help the student focus on particular NCTRC job tasks, professional practice standards, and personal goals and needs.

Identification of Training Needs and Expectations

Managers expose students to the full range of division or department services and alternative placement assignments to acquaint the student with the day-to-day expectations and potential internship outcomes. This may entail brief time periods devoted to each service, clientele group, and staff role, or more extended rotations after which the student is either assigned to rotate among particular staff and service areas or the student selects a specific area where the majority of the experience will occur. During introductory rotations the manager identifies potential roles and contributions that are likely to be made by the intern. Simultaneously, the academic supervisor and student review assignments (e.g., assessment, documentation, program, treatment planning) to discern which are most compatible with the intern's anticipated goals. Together the manager, student, and academic supervisor determine specific training needs and outcomes beneficial to the department and intern.

A schedule of rotations, job tasks, and learning assignments is prepared. Goals and objectives that specify a sequence of tasks to be completed as the intern assumes

---

480–600 hour (15–16 week) Internship

Week 1: General Orientation to Agency
1. Orient to facility, department, and Therapeutic Recreation Program
2. Review Department Policy and Procedure Manual
3. Observe sessions with patients/clients
4. Attend agency orientation
5. Attend department staff meeting

Orientation to Work Environment
1. Observe the role and function of the multidisciplinary team
2. Review Therapeutic Recreation Department manual, including Standards of Practice and Code of Ethics
3. Review daily schedule
4. Complete assignment on specific disability
5. Demonstrate and train on adaptive equipment

Week 2: Orientation to Therapeutic Recreation Department
1. Review assessment, documentation and progress note procedures
2. Review payment systems used at agency
3. Develop transfer and transport techniques
4. Discuss professional boundaries while working with patients/clients
5. Schedule regular weekly meetings with supervisor

Week 3: Presentation Skills/Disability Awareness
1. Complete assignments on specific disabilities
2. Select a program or activity with appropriate adaptive equipment and/or techniques
3. Learn appropriate abbreviations for agency
4. Write progress notes on clients observed

Weeks 4–6: Program Planning
1. Carry a case load of one patient/client
2. Complete one assessment on patient/client
3. Colead one group session
4. Attend the Functional Community Outing
5. Meet with supervisor weekly for feedback, questions, answers

Weeks 7–9: Assessment/Program Leadership
1. Colead two to three group sessions per day
2. Carry a case load of five patients/clients
3. Plan one group session with appropriate goals and interventions
4. Complete assignment on specific disability
5. Complete mid-term evaluation with supervisor

Weeks 10–12: Program Planning
1. Complete five assessments with appropriate interventions
2. Lead all group sessions
3. Report reevaluation findings on five patients/clients at Team Conference
4. Maintain caseload of five patients/clients
5. Meet with supervisor weekly for feedback, questions, answers

Weeks 13–14: Program Planning
1. Develop and implement one new program for group sessions
2. Review and assess internship using NCTRC National Job Analysis
3. Demonstrate functional knowledge of the process for documentation/evaluation
4. Complete assignments on specific disabilities
5. Present final project via in-service to multidisciplinary staff

Weeks 15–16: Completion/Evaluation/Termination
1. Complete closure process with patient/client/staff
2. Review professional guidelines and standards and demonstrate an understanding of entry-level competencies in therapeutic recreation
3. Complete all assignments
4. Turn in all badges, keys, agency equipment and supplies
5. Complete final evaluation

Figure 18.2
Sample Internship Timeline

increasing levels of responsibility and autonomy define student expectations. Specific due dates, assignments, and projects compatible with job tasks are defined. These are often organized in weekly increments (see Figure 18.3; Fox Valley Special Recreation Association, 2003; Grote & Hasl, 1998). Interns are required to organize increasingly more hours daily as they perform higher order job tasks with equally high levels of effectiveness and less direct supervision.

Review of Supervisory and Evaluation Process and Procedures

Managers, interns, and academic partners review criteria and forms to be used during supervisory contacts and performance reviews as the sequence of intern events is planned. Project, midterm and final evaluation forms are found in department and academic internship manuals. Additionally, student-generated documents like journals, logs, portfolio projects, and weekly reports are tools used

Weeks 1–2: Orientation/Observation/Policies and Procedures	Date Completed	
☐ Attend new employee orientation	_____	_____
☐ Complete all necessary paperwork	_____	_____
☐ Review employee handbook	_____	_____
☐ Tour facility	_____	_____
☐ Review Agency's Mission/Vision Statement, Policies and Procedures and Plan of Operation	_____	_____

Weeks 3–6: Presentation Skills/Disability Awareness/ Program Planning			
☐ Review screening and assessment procedures	_____	_____	_____
☐ Review procedures for documentation of treatment plan, evaluation, re-evaluation and discharge planning	_____	_____	_____
☐ Shadow agency's therapeutic recreation staff and observe treatment/programs, assessments, evaluations	_____	_____	_____
☐ Study agency's approved list of abbreviations and documentation protocols	_____	_____	_____
☐ Demonstrate and practice procedures for escorting, transporting and transferring patient/client	_____	_____	_____

Weeks 7–10: Assessment/Program Leadership			
☐ Maintain caseload of five patients/clients	_____	_____	_____
☐ Colead two to three group sessions per day	_____	_____	_____
☐ Complete midterm evaluation	_____	_____	_____
☐ Report reevaluation information at staffing	_____	_____	_____
☐ Submit all assignments on time	_____	_____	_____

Weeks 11–14: Program Planning			
☐ Lead all group sessions	_____	_____	_____
☐ Develop and implement one new program	_____	_____	_____
☐ Observe multidisciplinary staff treatments	_____	_____	_____
☐ Complete Special Project	_____	_____	_____
☐ Complete five assessments with appropriate interventions	_____	_____	_____

Weeks 15–16: Completion/Evaluation/Termination		
☐ Complete and present Special Project	_____	_____
☐ Accomplish closure with patients/clients and staff	_____	_____
☐ Complete final evaluation with site supervisor	_____	_____
☐ Turn in all required projects, papers, evaluations	_____	_____
☐ Turn in all agency issued supplies, equipment	_____	_____

Figure 18.3
Weekly Assignment Checklist

to assess intern progress and growth toward anticipated personal and professional goals. The nature and procedures for using these indicators help the manager plan feedback and debriefing processes.

Department supervision is influenced by a number of variables. Distance between the academic program and placement site affects the frequency and nature of contact between supervisors. To illustrate, internships completed more than a few hundred miles from the academic program necessitate phone, fax, and/or e-mail contacts rather than in person exchanges. Staff-intern assignments determine whether or not the manager devotes time to student supervision or the manager supports staff in their supervision of students. When the manager is the only department staff person, time permits two or three formal reviews at designated times with casual observations during routine service provision. If interns rotate among staff or services, several supervisors provide input to the manager. Size and location of the service influences how frequently managers are able to complete casual observations and make informal contacts with the intern (e.g., with outreach services or community-based services that cover extended geographic areas fewer contacts are likely as compared to services in one facility).

As the manager and student review performance criteria, they establish a mutually beneficial communication process. Success of intern management, like volunteer management, is somewhat dependent on how effective the manager is in motivating, interpreting, and clarifying. Managers help the student to apply knowledge to practice and to realize the impact of personal behaviors on therapeutic relationships. They have the arduous task of helping the student assimilate the impact of the "self" on therapeutic outcomes. Each must feel comfortable in approaching the other, giving and receiving constructive criticism, resolving interpersonal and professional conflicts, and respecting the other's competence and professional integrity. Awareness of alternative management styles is a benefit of the internship experience.

Negotiate Student-Department Contract

Throughout the orientation period, managers, students, and academic supervisors work together to clarify and delineate internship assignments and learning experiences. Once finalized, they are organized on a document signed by the manager and intern and submitted to the academic supervisor with initial weekly reports. This document contains the intern's goals and objectives, due dates, projects, learning activities, and special notations. The contract also specifies the dates on which interns are to submit reports to the manager and academic supervisors. It is desirable for the student first to submit materials to the manager and respond to feedback before sending reports to the academic supervisor. This allows the academic supervisor to benefit from the manager's input and perspectives. Contract items are renegotiated when the manager detects that an intern's progress and task completion justify alterations. Adjustments are reported to the academic supervisor in revised weekly reports.

Supervision and Training

Throughout an internship, managers monitor and model professional competencies, personal skills, and performance desired of interns. Training is planned to enhance the intern's skills and to permit the intern to share expertise brought to the placement. Volunteer and intern supervision and training are similar and entail three major tasks:

1. communication with and observation of the intern

2. documentation of intern activities and experiences

3. provision of training and education opportunities

With supervision and training, the professional growth of the intern is promoted, and entry-level practice competencies are reinforced. Managers also ensure that the intern is operating within department policies while contributing to its outcomes (refer to Table 18.1, Internship Triad).

Communication and Observation

Formal communication processes are identified when the student and manager negotiate the contract. Projects and reports guide the nature and timing of a manager's observations. Thus, prior to the due date, managers plan conferences and observations to ensure interns have completed tasks and are reporting factual, accurate information according to protocol. A weekly time period dedicated to discussion and review of the preceding week's events helps track progress and alerts the manager to impending issues and challenges.

Informal observations and contact occur throughout an internship. Managers focus on the quality with which the intern performs duties delineated in the job description and the internship objectives. Midterm and/or final evaluation forms are useful as guides for debriefing sessions and recommending corrective actions. When the intern keeps a log or diary, the manager is able to gain additional insight into his or her personal needs and perceptions. The manager draws student attention to qualities and performances that enhance or detract from the department's mission and the student's ability to perform interventions through helping relationships. Emotional, behavioral, and attitudinal qualities and characteristics are also addressed.

Communication between the manager and academic supervisor occurs as the student is supervised. Preset phone calls permit three-way conversations and correspondence by fax and e-mail expedite contacts. Managers who choose to send written comments with intern reports are creating avenues for three-way communication. Intern progress is reported and suggestions on curriculum needs and resources are shared. Academic supervisors, in turn, confirm student preparation experiences and prior clinical training. Each supervisor is made more aware of what facets of professional practice and personal development are perceived as significant.

Documentation of Activities and Experiences

The managers guide the interns as documentation skills are acquired and practiced. They also assist the students in setting aside time to complete department and academic projects. Managers help the interns process issues and concerns resulting from their daily experiences. The type and amount of previous clinical experience may influence the interns' ability to document internship occurrences. Managers direct students to subtle cues and clinical manifestations that corroborate clinical decisions. When managers review intern reports that are to be submitted to the academic program, they make recommendations that help the interns clarify their actions. Managers also help interns organize their time to accomplish required written experiences. Last, managers encourage interns to complete self-assessments and to analyze their personal diaries to gain insight into real and perceived problems or successes. In each situation, the desire is to enhance the interns' ability to document the effectiveness of therapeutic recreation interventions and helping relationships.

Managers document intern activities in several ways. First, they review academic assignments and agency projects to provide informal feedback. Second, they use periodic formal evaluations like the midterm and final reviews to present written critiques. Third, managers review interns' actual documentation on services as they cosign reports. And, finally, they retain personnel files on each intern in which they document performances similar to those kept with personnel performance plans. The information accumulated from these sources helps the manager to judge intern progress and take corrective actions. For instance, managers may require additional training, recommend alternative placements, or encourage adjustment in time spent in the department or on assigned tasks.

Provision of Training and Education Opportunities

As managers prepare for the arrival of interns, they organize department resources useful to the advancement of the intern's education. Through the orientation experience and follow-up supervision, the manager ascertains the nature of the intern's training needs as well as the resources brought to the department by the intern. Interns have a need to acquire knowledge and apply skills in day-to-day operations as well as to gain insight into current professional issues and agendas.

In-services conducted by staff make interns aware of policies and operating protocols. Attendance at area professional meetings helps students build networks and become aware of the professional scope of service. Intern led in-services bring new theories and resources to department staff. Intern completion of a project incorporated into ongoing services also is mutually beneficial because interns and staff gain resources and contacts as the project is developed, implemented, and evaluated. Visits to other departments and interviews with colleagues in the agency and community facilitate intern application of academic knowledge and awareness of professional expectations and issues.

Evaluation and Termination

Formative and summative evaluations occur routinely during and at the termination of the internship experience. They involve each of the three partners' (e.g., student, manager, academic supervisor) assessments of each other's contributions and needs. As the internship nears completion, a number of factors are considered. The manager makes decisions on how transitions will occur so minimal service disruption results. The intern brings closure to a significant life phase and anticipates transition into the career world. Major challenges and issues arise. Evaluation and termination of an internship involves the following (refer to Table 18.1, Internship Triad):

1. formative evaluations

2. summative evaluations

3. termination tasks and issues

Formative Evaluations

Throughout the internship, students, managers, and academic partners evaluate interrelationships and processes to ensure growth and development of the intern (see Table 18.6). According to Lamb, Cochran, and Jackson (1991), focus of student evaluation is on knowledge and application of professional standards, competency, and personal functioning. Department evaluation considers the manager's effectiveness to supervise and to communicate with the academic supervisor and intern, the adequacy of department resources to support the internship, and the managerial compatibility with the intern's needs and goals.

The academic program is assessed by considering the adequacy of student preparation, management of the internship, intern supervision, and department relations. During the orientation, the procedures and criteria to assess each of these areas are mutually agreed on.

As noted by Lamb, Cochran, and Jackson (1991), timely and early feedback enables the manager and intern to address anxiety issues, to identify areas of concern, and to articulate specific training recommendations. Formative evaluation commences with initial supervisory sessions and continues as the manager reviews reports, monitors performance, and submits comments to the academic supervisor. Assessments consider how well the student integrates into the department and is able to apply knowledge to practice. The intern's ability to work with other staff and to follow operating codes is closely monitored. Skill deficits are noted so remediation strategies are incorporated into the internship.

Formative evaluation tools are intern reports, midterm written evaluations, and contacts between the manager and academic supervisor. If the internship is planned around a sequence of increasingly more difficult or autonomous responsibilities, evaluation focuses on the student's competence and willingness to assume these tasks and obligations and perform effectively. Managers document performance adequacy and recommend training needs. If there is impairment in the intern's performance other than what can be corrected by training, the manager, intern, and academic supervisor agree on appropriate alternatives, which could include reassignment or immediate withdrawal from the placement.

Summative Evaluations

Summative evaluation occurs near the completion of the internship period. Managers complete forms that critique the student's personal and professional competence, the academic preparation and supervision of the student, and interactions with the academic supervisor. Students assess the adequacy of their preparation and the department to support the internship as well as their interactions and compatibility with both supervisors. Academic supervisors consider appropriateness of the manager's supervision and the department's support, compatibility of practice with standards purported in academic experiences, and the student's ability to synthesize theory and practice.

At the completion of an internship, the student has been given the opportunity to demonstrate entry-level practice standards as defined by ATRA and NTRS and the credentialing body NCTRC. Managers use the standards documents of these organizations as measurements of the intern's potential to perform successfully as an entry-level practitioner. One approach to evaluate student progress is to use the National Job Analysis Skills of NCTRC (2005b)

to verify the experience has incorporated all of the entry-level areas described by the CTRS credential. A second approach is to use standardized professionally developed tools like the Therapeutic Recreation Intern Evaluation (Cincinnati-Dayton Area Recreation Therapy Association, 1997). The tool is useful for both midterm and final evaluations and contains categories compatible with existing credentialing and professional standards. Further, as noted by Zabriskie and Ferguson (2004), the respondents in their national study desire a standardized tool that evaluates all aspects of the academic/personal/professional experiences and transitions.

The manager also considers how well the intern integrates professional standards into his or her repertoire of professional behaviors. Additionally, the manager assesses the degree to which the intern has been able to respond positively to feedback. Comparison of midterm with final ratings reveals whether corrective action and training have resulted in progress and behavior change.

Summative evaluation considers changes and growth in the intern's personal functioning. How well did the student respond to supervision, manage stress and time, and work with and for other staff? What was the intern's comfort level with clients of diverse lifestyles? What was the intern's responsiveness to unexpected client behaviors? Did performance anxiety interfere with helping relationships? Are there mannerisms or behaviors that discourage active team participation? A number of personal qualities are essential to effective practice. The internship is the first opportunity to ascertain how well personal attributes, values, and attitudes intertwine with professional roles. The internship connects the theoretical with the practical. Transition between the two is enhanced by discussion of the exchanges between personal and professional roles and qualities. If the student has a portfolio, this is an ideal time to review its contents and incorporate documentation of experiential components of the internship with CDs of programs delivered or interventions practiced. This documentation "assists the student in projecting to employers the value of" the internship (Anderson, Schroeder & Anderson, 2001, p. 110).

Termination Tasks and Issues

The internship brings closure to academic preparation while serving as the transition step into a professional role. Managers and staff transition back into responsibilities partially or completely assumed by the intern. As the student separates from consumer, staff and department contacts, managers provide emotional support. Procedures are instituted to integrate the intern's project into department services.

Before the completion date nears, planning the next professional step has begun. Managers expose interns to future opportunities through various professional contacts and meetings. Managers coach the intern on job search strategies and interview techniques.

A number of issues surface as transitions are made. The intern reflects on interactions with consumers and supervisors and their readiness to assume professional challenges. As the intern terminates helping relationships, issues of confidentiality and client autonomy arise. Consumer dependency behaviors may trigger the student's desire to share personal information and maintain contact after the internship. Although absolute confidentiality may not be attainable, relative consumer and department confidentiality are necessary and supported as the manager communicates to the intern permissible forms of follow-up.

The internship experience may be the first opportunity to compare personal management styles. Did intern experiences reflect academic underpinnings? Were communiqués from the supervisors to the intern relevant? Was feedback useful and focused on the intern's needs? An internship devoid of conflict would be unusual. The manager's task is to help the intern learn to disagree without resentment. The manager and academic supervisor each have expectations. Issues arise when they are not compatible or vary in their level of expectancy. Managers and academic supervisors help the intern gauge the degree of autonomy achieved during an internship and their readiness to undertake future professional challenges.

Evaluations help the academic and department supervisor prepare for future interns. Managers cognizant of intern's perceptions about department acceptance, degree of assistance, quality of learning opportunities, and accomplishment of internship goals are able to make adjustments before the next interns arrive. More important, if the intern reports feelings of token acceptance or difficulty in approaching personnel or accessing resources, managers take immediate action as the intern's judgments are likely to be apparent with other department staff. The manager and academic supervisor guide the intern to experiences that resolve present issues while fostering future life and career successes. Interns are directed to alternative employment settings or clientele groups or asked to reconsider their chosen career field. Re-administration of self-assessments facilitates rethinking of life and career goals and directions.

Summary

Contents of this chapter have been divided into four sections descriptive of the steps undertaken as managers design, implement, and evaluate internship programs. A major portion of the time devoted to intern management actually occurs during the initial step or preplacement planning. Division or department preparation involves determining the intent and nature of the intern program within the unit and preparing the staff and resources necessary to support student placements. This step is followed by, or occurs as, cooperative partnerships between the department and academic setting are affected, which may involve negotiating MOAs. With legal documents in place, intern selection commences. These procedures are similar to employment processes and serve as a first step in the student's transition from academics to the work world.

The second step, department orientation, introduces the intern to agency operations and/or department services. Supervision and training are actually begun during orientation periods. Managers detail their expectations and clarify student assignments and academic requirements. The feedback loop begins as the manager and intern negotiate a student contract that structures the intern's weekly activities.

During supervision and training, step three of intern management, managers guide student acquisition of job-related knowledge and skills and professional competence and functioning. Through ongoing communication and observations, managers discern progress so that increasing degrees of autonomy are given to the intern. Through documentation and personal contacts, managers share constructive criticism and corrective actions with interns and academic supervisors. Training facilitates increased exposure to application of academic knowledge and helps the intern become aware of current practices.

Finally, evaluation and transition prepare the intern to bring closure to the academic experience while moving into a new life stage. Evaluation processes begin during orientation and continue throughout the experience. Formative evaluation occurs as the manager reviews intern reports and projects routinely submitted to the academic supervisor. Summative evaluations generate information on the intern's knowledge and application of professional standards, entry-level competence, and personal functioning.

Issues arise during the internship. Managers encourage conflict resolution and development of problem-solving skills. Yet, interns experience real-world dilemmas, such as client confidentiality, supervisor approachability, and relevancy of academic preparation to practice. Clinical experiences initiated early in the academic program permit the student to apply knowledge and skills to practice while acquiring professional skills supportive of transition into a career.

Review Questions

1. Conduct an Internet search of possible intern sites to discover requirements, forms used, and agency expectations.

2. Review the standards of practice of ATRA and NTRS and the NCTRC Job Analysis to identify entry-level competencies to incorporate into an internship experience.

3. What are the major tasks completed by a manager as the site is prepared to serve as a training site?

4. What activities occur during the orientation that are critical to the outcomes of the intern's entire experience?

5. Discuss the significance of supervisory feedback as it relates to the intern's training needs and the academic and department expectations.

6. Discuss techniques that the manager and academic supervisor use to support increasing degrees of intern work autonomy and progress toward the application of knowledge to practice.

7. What types of formative and summative evaluation tools are used to assess intern performance? How do these tools measure the critical outcomes of an internship experience?

8. Consider the issues that might arise as an intern prepares to bring closure to the internship experience. Discuss how they might impact the intern's professional and personal goals.

References

American Therapeutic Recreation Association (ATRA). (2000). *Standards for the practice of therapeutic recreation and self-assessment guide.* Alexandria, VA: Author.

Anderson, L. S., Schroeder, T., and Anderson, D. A. (2001). The use of portfolio advising with recreation and leisure services majors. In J. A. Busser (Ed.), *Schole: A Journal of Leisure Studies and Recreation Education* (Vol. 16, pp. 107–123). Ashburn, VA: National Recreation and Park Association.

Campbell, K. and Kovar, S. K. (1994). Fitness/exercise science internships: How to ensure success. *Journal of Physical Education, Recreation and Dance, 65*(2), 69–72.

Cincinnati-Dayton Area Recreation Therapy Association (1997). *Therapeutic recreation intern evaluation (TRIE).* Available from ATRA, 1414 Prince St., Suite 204, Alexandria, VA 22314, http://www.atra-tr.org

Cunningham, G. B., Sagas, M., Dixon, M., Kent, A., and Turner, B. A. (2005). Anticipated career satisfaction, affective occupational commitment, and intentions to enter the sport management profession. *Journal of Sport Management 19*, 43–57.

Feldman, D. C. and Weitz, B. A. (1990). Summer interns: Factors contributing to positive developmental experiences. *Journal of Vocational Behavior, 37*(3), 267–284.

Fox Valley Special Recreation Association. (2003). *Internship manual.* North Aurora, IL: Author.

Grote, K. A. and Hasl, M. A. (1998). *Guidelines for internships in therapeutic recreation.* Hattiesburg, MS: American Therapeutic Recreation Association.

Kinney, T. and Witman, J. (1997). *Guidelines for competency assessment and curriculum planning in therapeutic recreation: A tool for self-evaluation.* Hattiesburg, MS: American Therapeutic Recreation Association.

Lamb, D. H., Cochran, D. J., and Jackson, V. R. (1991). Training and organizational issues associated with identifying and responding to intern impairment. *Professional Psychology: Research and Practice, 22*(4), 291–296.

National Council for Therapeutic Recreation Certification (NCTRC). (2005a). *Certification standards part I: Introduction for new applicants.* Retrieved June 15, 2005, from http://www.nctrc.org/pdf/1_New_Ap_0605_CB.pdf

National Council for Therapeutic Recreation Certification (NCTRC). (2005b). *Certification standards part V: NCTRC national job analysis.* Retrieved June 15, 2005 from http://www.nctrc.org/pdf/5_Job_Analysis_0605_CB.pdf

National Therapeutic Recreation Society (NTRS). (1997). *NTRS internship standards and guidelines for therapeutic recreation.* Alexandria, VA: National Recreation and Park Association.

National Therapeutic Recreation Society (NTRS). (2004). *Standards of practice for a continuum of care in therapeutic recreation.* Retrieved September 12, 2004, from http://www.nrpa.org/content/default.aspx?documentID530

Smith, D. A., O'Dell, I., and Schaumleffel, N. A. (2002). Building a learning community for fieldwork students: A case study example. In J. A. Busser (Ed.), *Schole: A Journal of Leisure Studies and Recreation Education* (Vol. 17, pp. 21–36). Asburn, VA: National Recreation and Park Association.

Steffes, J. (2004). Creative powerful learning experiences beyond the classroom. *Change, 36,* 46–50.

Watson, K. W. (1992). An integration of values: Teaching the internship course in a liberal arts environment. *Communication Education, 41*(4), 429–439.

Zabriskie, R. B. and Ferguson, D. D. (2004). A national study of therapeutic recreation field work and internships. In Y. Lee and B. P. McCormick (Eds.), *Annual in therapeutic recreation* (Vol. 13, pp. 24–37). Alexandria, VA: American Therapeutic Recreation Association.

Part 5
Consumer Management

Chapter 19
Service Delivery Management

The therapeutic recreation manager is responsible for delivering quality service to the consumer. This service is based on one's knowledge and professional standards and, in some settings, regulatory standards. However, there are also other perceptions of quality that must be managed and achieved.

There are a variety of customers in varied settings and organizations (e.g., clinical and community-based leisure agencies, Joint Commission on Accreditation of Healthcare Organizations [JCAHO], Commission on Accreditation of Rehabilitation Facilities [CARF], Medicare) who define quality differently from the therapeutic recreation manager. If their definition of quality is not met, and their perception of quality is not achieved, they will think that quality service does not exist. Health and human service organizations cannot tolerate much variability in quality service. The room for error in quality has become narrow, and it affects in many instances financial outcomes and public outcry.

This chapter considers specific factors associated with improving the quality of service delivery provided by the practitioner within health care facilities and community-based leisure service agencies. Quality work gets done when practitioners are encouraged to develop their strengths and abilities. This approach addresses both the need to accomplish the task at hand and the need to make an investment in the practitioner so that future work activities can be accomplished more efficiently and effectively.

Initially considered is scheduling. Assigning, staffing, and scheduling are the ways in which goals of the therapeutic recreation department are converted into concrete acts.

The next consideration is the therapeutic recreation process, a systematic approach to meeting consumer and group needs through therapeutic intervention. There exists a number of therapeutic recreation service models (Mobily, 1999) that provide the conceptual foundation and guide the delivery of therapeutic programs. The common thread among the models is a four-step process—assessment, planning, implementation and evaluation (APIE)—referred to as the therapeutic recreation process. Although these steps are discussed in detail in other texts, the concern here is to summarize briefly the salient characteristics of the steps because all managers need to be acutely aware of the steps to meet consumer and group needs and the knowledge and abilities needed by the practitioner to carry out the process and assure quality. Accountability pressures from regulators, third-party payers, consumers, and the public to assure quality care have resulted in a professional focus on outcome measurement and evidenced-based practices. A discussion on outcomes research and evidenced-based practices considers the responsibilities of professionals to adhere to standardized practices that assure accountable results. In addition, brief consideration is given to protocols. Protocols standardize the therapeutic recreation process. They are procedures or courses of action to be taken in specific situations.

Another responsibility of the manager in association with the therapeutic recreation process is documentation. The manager has a responsibility to ensure proper documentation, its appropriateness and correctness. Documentation is also linked to risk management programs (see Chapter 20).

Last, consideration is given to monitoring and reviewing practitioner performance relative to program effectiveness to meet organizational goals including those of the division or department. Discussion of this responsibility is focused on the day-to-day performance of the practitioner and the interaction that takes place between the practitioner and manager or supervisor to improve job performance, thereby enhancing service quality. The manager's responsibilities as an administrative supervisor are distinguished from clinical supervisory tasks. Also reiterated are features of long-term and short-term coaching (refer to Chapters 15 and 16).

Scheduling

Scheduling is developing a plan for where and when personnel are to work within the parameters dictated by the organization. The therapeutic recreation manager is usually responsible for developing the schedule because he or she is aware of consumer needs as well as the expertise, limitations, and personal needs of the staff. The chief goal is balance. "Staffing requires a balance between the quantity of staff available and the numbers needed to provide quality" service while staying within the budget (Sullivan

& Decker, 2001, p. 285). Therapeutic recreation managers, when possible, involve staff in decisions regarding the staffing plan and thereby obtain their commitment to the results. In this way, plans become more individualized, promoting staff satisfaction and productivity. However, assigning program activities and consumer cases by matching work to be done with the experience of the practitioner can lead to more effective and efficient service delivery. Heavy workloads may necessitate the setting of priorities among various program activities and cases. Regardless of the assignments given to a practitioner, assignments must be allotted reasonable time to produce results. In health care facilities this may be difficult given the length of stay as dictated by insurance.

A number of variables are considered in making scheduling decisions in health care and community settings. Primary factors include client census and acuity, staff skill mix (allowing for nonproductive time like vacation, holiday, and sick time), and adequacy of the budget (Tappen, 2001). Additional factors a first-line manager considers include legislation concerning work time, regulatory criteria from bodies like JCAHO that require care based on specific client needs and severity level, agency personnel policies and scope of service, resources available, job descriptions, and mix of work titles or personnel classifications.

Factors that complicate scheduling within varied health care facilities might be types of consumers, consumer expectations, fluctuations in admissions, length of hospitalization, referrals, physicians' orders, nursing procedures, and services provided by other departments. In schedule planning, consideration must also be given to demands of staff that are not related directly to consumer service. In-service programs, staff meetings, charting, attending conferences, and getting supplies and equipment together are all necessary, but they take time away from the consumer.

Unfortunately there is no therapeutic recreation scheduling model to follow regardless of setting, although one might want to consider various nursing models if the staff is large (e.g., self-scheduling, flex-time, alternating or rotating work shifts, permanent shifts, cyclical scheduling, computerized scheduling). With self-scheduling, staff assume responsibility to develop their schedules following guidelines agreed on for the department. Flex-time allows staff to select time schedules that best meet their personal needs while still meeting their work responsibilities. With alternating work shifts, staff rotate among shifts while with permanent shifts staff select a preferred shift. In cyclical scheduling, the same schedule is used repeatedly. Computerized schedules may be generated with centralized management of scheduling through human resources to ensure agency-wide adherence to vari-

ous standards. Each scheduling approach has advantages and drawbacks. Scheduling significantly influences job satisfaction and retention. Periodically, managers assess staff to gauge satisfaction and assure ongoing input while making adjustments to meet client needs (Marquis & Huston, 2003).

Goals of Scheduling

Regardless of the setting or scheduling approach selected, goals of scheduling can be summarized as follows:

1. achievement of department objectives, especially those related to consumer service

2. accurate match of department needs with staff and volunteer abilities and numbers

3. maximum use of personnel resources

4. equity of treatment to all employees (or equal treatment for all employees within a similar job classification) and volunteers

5. optimization on use of professional expertise

6. satisfaction of practitioners (both as to hours worked and as to perceived sense of scheduling equity) and volunteers

7. consideration of unique needs of staff and volunteers as well as consumers

Staffing Variables

As mentioned, a number of factors are considered when first-line managers develop schedules. Client census and acuity are primary considerations. Managers schedule a certain number of staff with specific educational and experiential backgrounds to programs so clients achieve their treatment or program outcomes. Managers consider staff skill mix when they assign, for example, intervention specialists or inclusion coaches to support CTRSs. Staff skill mix influences the number of staff scheduled to cover specific programs.

When schedules are developed managers also consider direct service versus nonproductive time. In-service programs, staff meetings, charting, attending conferences, and gathering supplies and equipment are all necessary, yet take time away from the consumer. Nonproductive time includes paid time-off for funerals, vacation, holidays, education, and sick leave. "Some types of nonproductive time can be predicted and planned for, whereas others cannot" (Tappen, 2001, p. 257). Managers have to assign temporary staff to cover programs if full-time staff are not present to assure delivery of services that meet standards and address client needs.

Therapeutic recreation managers have the dual responsibility of planning for sufficient staff numbers to meet client needs while being mindful of remaining within the unit staffing budget (Tappen, 2001). Staffing budgets may be based on prior year productivity and budget figures. Managers involved in the budget process account for staff overtime, part-time staff, changes in salary scales, unexpected consumer fluctuations or referrals, accrued vacation time, and resignations. Discussion in Chapter 8 (Financial Management and Budgets) considered full-time equivalents (FTEs), which are used in staffing formulas to calculate the number of staff needed to cover anticipated and unplanned personnel leaves.

In devising schedules the therapeutic recreation manager needs to be aware of laws concerning work time. As noted in Chapter 12 (Staffing), there are federal, state, and even local laws and regulations which deal with wages and hours that must be followed. In most health and human service organizations the organization's personnel policies or human resources (HR) can inform the manager of the work hours for his or her department. If employees are unionized, it is important that the manager review any labor contracts for their impact on his or her staffing and scheduling.

Agency personnel policies influence the manager's staffing assignments and may result from legislative and regulatory criteria. Policies "represent the standard of action that is communicated in advance so that employees are not caught unaware regarding personnel matters" (Marquis & Huston, 2003, p. 298). When developed in collaboration with human resource departments, the first-line manager is assured of expertise, for example, pertaining to union contracts, state labor laws, and organizational-level protocols. With periodic staff input, managers bring flexibility to policy design and implementation. Policies related to staffing that might be cooperatively designed and implemented include rotation or shift policies; time and location of schedule posting; weekend and holiday policy; tardiness policy; low census procedures; procedures for requesting time and days off; absenteeism policies; procedures for funerals, vacations, and holiday time requests; emergency request policies; procedures for resolving conflicts regarding days off; education and training request procedures; and procedures for monitoring computerized time reports. Environmental resources, like available agency resources, affect scheduling. With assistance from HR personnel and staff input, the manager remains abreast of directives and staffing variables that impact the scheduling process.

Scheduling Challenges

Because of rapid turnover and retrenchment to accommodate the cost of services today, many health and human service organizations combine full-time and part-time practitioners in a therapeutic recreation department. While part-time practitioners may be qualified, there are usually problems or disadvantages in hiring them. These problems may consist of inequity in salary and benefits wherein the part-timer may feel inequitably treated. Use of part-time practitioners may pose a threat to continuity of service. It is also thought that part-time employees lack the commitment to the organization and consumer that is found with permanent employees. In addition, part-time employees are usually involved in in-service training or ongoing education programs. Last, full-time practitioners may be shown some form of favoritism, for example, work time scheduling.

While there is no universal solution to these problems, the manager, in cooperation with higher management, may be able to develop a benefit package that would be equitable for both full-time and part-time practitioners. Equity may involve pay or benefits in compensation for preferential hours. Full-timers may be more understanding of some favoritism in hours extended to a part-timer if they know that they have some recompensing factor, such as vacation prorated at a higher level, a higher pay scale, or some other benefit that compensates and equalizes the situation.

Abuse of sick time is another factor that can ruin a well-planned schedule. Some practitioners perceive sick time as time that is owed to them. They use sick days whether or not they are ill. Such practices can be curtailed by good personnel policies concerning chronic absences. Some organizations give back a proportion of unused sick days as extra days off. Other organizations allow the accrual of unlimited sick leave.

These scheduling matters are not the only concerns of the therapeutic recreation manager. Other matters associated with the manager's role in scheduling may or may not include: verifying to the fiscal office services provided to consumers for billing purposes or collecting fees, monitoring supplies and equipment used, approving department staff payroll, monitoring personnel schedules (e.g., sick time, volunteers), and monitoring productivity (e.g., cost of Program A relative to Program B, effectiveness relative to efficiency in the economic sense). Monitoring productivity is especially difficult for all health professionals who tend to work from a model of service in which all persons are entitled to the best professional service possible.

Regardless of the challenges inherent in scheduling, a management function is accountability for a prenegotiated budget. Because personnel budgets are a major portion of health and human service organizations, "a small percentage cut in personnel may result in large savings" (Marquis & Huston, 2003, p. 305). It is just as important for the manager to use staff to provide safe and effective care economically as it is to be ethical to clients and staff. Staff have the right to expect reasonable work loads. So as managers address the challenges and take into consideration a number of variables that affect scheduling, they "must ensure that adequate staffing exists to meet the needs of staff and patients" (Marquis & Huston, 2003, p. 305).

Therapeutic Recreation Process

A process is a series of planned actions or operations directed toward a particular result. The therapeutic recreation process is a systematic, rational method of planning and providing therapeutic recreation to the consumer (O'Morrow & Reynolds, 1989). To carry out the process at least two people must participate: the consumer and the therapeutic recreation practitioner. However, in some instances, a group or even a family may participate. A group is more likely to be seen in a community-based leisure service organization, whereas a specific group would be involved in a leisure experience (e.g., wheelchair basketball).

The consumer or group participates as actively as possible in all phases of the therapeutic recreation process. The therapeutic recreation practitioner, by contrast, requires interpersonal, technical, and intellectual skills to put the process into action. Interpersonal skills include communicating; listening; conveying interest, compassion, knowledge, and information; developing trust; and obtaining data in a manner that enhances the individuality of the consumer. Within the group, interpersonal skills promote integrity both personally and collectively and contribute to the viability of the community. Technical skills are manifested in the use of specialized equipment and the performance of procedures. Intellectual skills required by a therapeutic recreation practitioner include problem solving, critical thinking, and making therapeutic recreation judgments. Decision making is involved in every component of the therapeutic recreation process (O'Morrow, 1986).

The therapeutic recreation process consists of a series of four components, including assessing, planning, implementing, and evaluating. In some settings the process is assisted by protocols. An overview of the four-step process is as follows:

1. *Assessing* is collecting, verifying, and organizing data about the consumer or group. Data is obtained from a variety of sources (e.g., formal or informal interviews, assessment instruments) and is the basis for decisions made in subsequent phases. Skills of observation, communication, and interviewing are essential to perform this phase of the therapeutic recreation process. Once data are collected, problems or potential problems can be identified, and goals for the consumer can be developed.

2. *Planning* involves a series of steps in which the practitioner writes goals or expected outcomes, establishes therapeutic recreation interventions designed to solve or minimize the identified problems of the consumer, prepares a written plan, and informs others of the plan through announcements and meetings.

3. *Implementing* is putting the written plan into action. During this phase the practitioner continues to gather data and validates the therapeutic recreation plan. Continued data collection is essential not only to keep track of changes in the consumer's condition or group's reaction but also to obtain evidence for the evaluation of goal achievement in the next phase.

4. *Evaluating* is assessing the consumer's and group's response to therapeutic recreation interventions and then comparing the response to predetermined standards. The practitioner determines the extent to which goals or predetermined outcomes have been achieved, partially achieved, or not met. If the goals have not been met, reassessment of the plan is needed.

One must keep in mind that the various steps in the process are not discrete entities but an overlapping, continuing subprocess. As an example, assessing, the first step of the therapeutic recreation process, may also be carried out during implementing (i.e., intervention) and evaluating. Each step must be continually updated as the situation changes. Likewise, each step of the process affects the others; they are closely interrelated. For instance, if an inadequate database is used during assessment, the incompleteness will certainly be reflected in the next three steps. Incomplete assessment means unequivocal evaluations because the practitioner will have incomplete criteria against which to evaluate changes in the consumer and the effectiveness of the intervention. Table 19.1 provides a summary of the selected knowledge and abilities needed for the therapeutic recreation process.

Accountability and Therapeutic Recreation Process

Accountability is the condition of being associable and responsible to someone for specific behaviors that are part of the therapeutic recreation manager's and practitioner's professional role. The therapeutic recreation process provides a framework for accountability and responsibility in therapeutic recreation and maximizes accountability and responsibility for standards of service (e.g., JCAHO, CARF, continuous quality improvement [CQI], NTRS, ATRA). A brief review of accountability and the therapeutic recreation process follows.

Assessing

The therapeutic recreation practitioner is accountable for collecting information, encouraging consumer participation, and judging the validity of the collected data. When assessing, the practitioner is accountable for gaps in data and conflicting data, inaccurate data, and biased data. In addition, the practitioner is accountable for the judgments made about the consumer problem. For example, is the problem recognized by the consumer? Did the practitioner consider the consumer's values, beliefs, and cultural practices when determining the problem?

Planning

Accountability at the planning stage involves determining priorities, establishing consumer goals, predicting outcomes, and planning evidence-based practices. They are all incorporated into a written plan and shared with a team.

Table 19.1
Selected Knowledge and Abilities Needed for the Therapeutic Recreation Process

Component	Knowledge	Abilities
Assessing	• Biopsychosocial systems of humans • Developmental needs of humans • Health • Disability/illness • Etiologic factors of health problems • Pathophysiology • Family system • Culture and values of self and client • Normal measurement standards	• Observe systematically • Communicate verbally and nonverbally • Listen attentively • Establish a helping relationship • Think critically • Develop trust • Conduct an interview • Understand consumers' attitudes toward society • Identify patterns and relationships • Organize and group data • Make inferences • Reason inductively and deductively • Make decisions or judgments
Planning	• Consumers' strengths and weaknesses • Values and beliefs of the consumer • Resources available to implement therapeutic recreation strategies • Roles of other health care personnel • Measurable outcome criteria that relate to the goals • Design of evidence-based therapeutic recreation practices • Organizational goals • Varied activities • Use of supplies and equipment	• Problem solve • Make decisions • Write consumer goals that relate to the therapeutic recreation process • Write measurable outcome criteria that relate to goals • Select and create therapeutic recreation stratgies or interventions that are safe, appropriate, and link outcomes to meet consumer goals • Sharing and eliciting the cooperation and participation of the consumer and other health care personnel • Adapting activities
Implementing	• Leadership roles • Physical hazards and safety • Procedures • Use of supplies and equipment • Organization • Management • Change theory • Advocacy • Consumer rights • Consumers' developmental levels	• Observe systematically • Communicate effectively • Use self therapeutically • Perform psychomotor techniques • Act as a consumer advocate • Counsel consumers • Maintain confidence
Evaluating	• Consumers' goals and outcome criteria • Consumers' responses to therapeutic recreation intervention • Validate evidence-based practices	• Obtain relevant data to compare with outcome criteria • Draw conclusions about goal attainment • Relate therapeutic recreation actions to outcome criteria (i.e., link interventions to outcomes) • Reassess the therapeutic recreation plan

Implementing

Therapeutic recreation practitioners are responsible for all their actions in delivering services. Although the manager has delegated or assigned practitioners to consumer activities, the practitioner is still accountable for the assigned action. Whatever action takes place, it should be noted after being carried out. In health care facilities it will be the chart that provides a written record. In other settings it may be in the consumer's file or if a group activity, it may be a daily or weekly activity report that is kept by the practitioner or manager.

Evaluating

By establishing the degree to which the objectives have been attained, the practitioner is accountable for the success or failure of therapeutic recreation actions. The practitioner must be able to explain why a consumer goal was not met and what phase or phases of the process may require change and why.

Although the therapeutic recreation manager is ultimately responsible for practitioner activity relating to accountability and the therapeutic recreation process, the role of the manager relative to this process also incorporates the following:

- Update assessment tools.

- Review treatment and program plans to ensure interventions match individual and group needs and objectives.

- Collect data and audit evaluations to ensure achievement of individual, group, division, and department outcomes that validate evidence-based practices.

- Facilitate documentation process via monitoring routine maintenance records.

- Communicate to practitioner organization changes that impact division or department services and programming process.

- Ensure training on new interventions.

Protocols

In recent years therapeutic recreation practitioners and educators have given attention to the design, development, and implementation of protocols that provide for consistency and quality in therapeutic recreation practice (Grote, Hasl, Krider & Mortensen, 1995; Kelland, 1995; Stumbo & Peterson, 2004). Knight and Johnson (1991, p. 137) noted that "protocols distinguish therapeutic recreation's role in treatment and the uniqueness of our service."

A *protocol* is a series of actions required to manage a specific problem or issue. These problems are associated with the physical, psychological, social, and cognitive functioning of the individual. In addition, according to Smith-Marker (as cited by Ferguson, 1992), a protocol may be *collaborative* (in association with other disciplines), *independent* (wherein the problem is addressed specifically by the therapeutic recreation specialist), or *interdependent* (from the perspective that the problem requires the skills of two disciplines and is so noted by the physician). While protocols have been developed for use in health care facilities, they are also found in community-based leisure service organizations.

The protocol or clinical practice guideline provides instructions on what to do for a particular problem (Stumbo & Peterson, 2004). A protocol may address a specific therapeutic recreation department program or service or a consumer's therapeutic recreation comprehensive treatment plan from admission to discharge including assessment, intervention, and outcome. Therefore, there are two kinds of protocols. *Treatment* or *program protocols* provide the framework to assess, plan, implement, and evaluate programs based on one area of care. *Diagnostic* or *problem-based protocols* provide the framework for how a specific group of clients with a common "diagnosis" or "problem" is served in a program (Stumbo & Peterson, 2004). Because practice procedures are standardized, protocols facilitate the use of the best practices available to be effective with certain diagnoses.

While there is no specific standardized protocol found in use today, Table 19.2 and Table 19.3 suggest outlines for the development of each type of protocol. Table 19.2 shows the outline for a diagnostic protocol as developed by Lanny Knight and Dan Johnson as part of the 1989 Protocol Committee of ATRA and modified by Ferguson (1992). A program protocol outline is illustrated in Table 19.3. This protocol outline was initially developed by Roy Olsson (1990) with modification by Ferguson (1992).

Table 19.2
Outline for Developing Diagnostic Protocols

> I. Diagnostic Grouping
> II. Specific Diagnosis
> III. Identified Problem
> IV. Defining Characteristics
>   A. Subjective Data
>   B. Objective Data
> V. Related Factors or Etiologies
> VI. Process Criteria (Therapist will…)
> VII. Outcome Criteria (Client/Patient will…)

Used with permission of the Curators of University of Missouri, Columbia, Missouri

The development and application of protocols, according to NTRS can

1. Promote a better understanding of the therapeutic recreation service as it relates to the performance of others on the treatment team,

2. Provide a process of systematic program and treatment planning, and

3. Allow for program coverage by a replacement/secondary therapist without impacting the treatment plan. (1989, p. III)

In addition, according to Knight and Johnson, "protocols can be the basis for both the process and the evaluation of outcomes in quality assurance programs" (1991, p. 138).

Table 19.4 is a sample protocol. The outline is similar to the program protocol format. As noted, there is neither consistency in title nor format yet the use of diagnostic and program protocols brings standardization to program delivery and evaluation. As practice guidelines, they improve the quality of care delivered, reduce variability of services, and increase skills of service providers (Hood, 2003).

With the growing interest in protocols, the therapeutic recreation manager has three responsibilities associated with protocols: (a) overseeing the development and revision of protocols, (b) advocating the role of therapeutic recreation throughout the organization with protocols as an illustration of the contribution of therapeutic recreation to outcomes, and (c) supporting and conducting research

Table 19.3
Outline for Developing Program Protocols

I. Program Title

II. General Purpose

III. Description of the Program (very brief)

IV. Appropriate Presenting Problems Which May Be Addressed

V. Referral Criteria

VI. Contraindicated Criteria

VII. Therapeutic Recreation Intervention Activities or Techniques to be Employed

VIII. Staff Training/Certification Requirements (e.g., CTRS, Water Safety Instructor)

IX. Risk Management Consideration

X. Outcome Expected

XI. Program Evaluation (i.e., frequency and method)

XII. Approval Signature and Data

Used with permission of the Curators of University of Missouri, Columbia, Missouri

Table 19.4
Sample Program Protocol: Fitness

GENERAL PROGRAM PURPOSE
To increase the ability of clients to manage independently their individual fitness needs, while improving and/or maintaining their current physical fitness level.

PROGRAM DESCRIPTION
Clients are consulted regarding their current fitness needs and are assessed on their knowledge of fitness and weight equipment. An individual fitness program is developed using on-site facilities and equipment, while taking into account facilities and equipment available in the community. Once established on a program, clients are introduced to the basics of physical fitness and weight equipment and are encouraged to increase both their knowledge of fitness and their fitness level. Clients are assisted with their program to the level necessary.

DEFICITS THE PROGRAM MIGHT ADDRESS
- Poor fitness level
- Social inappropriateness
- Overweight or underweight
- Low self-esteem
- Poor knowledge of community fitness facilities
- Lack of leisure activity skills

FACILITATION TECHNIQUES
- Individual and small group skill instruction and demonstration
- Behavior modification techniques (e.g., role modeling, shaping, chaining, positive reinforcement)
- Motivational techniques
- Audiovisual aids and handouts
- Exposure to community facilities

STAFF RESPONSIBILITIES/REQUIREMENTS
(1) Recreation Therapist
- Program Protocol
- Program Plan
- Risk Management Considerations
- Program Evaluation
- Program Observations
- Program Delivery
(2) Recreation Therapy Assistant
- Program Profile
- Program Observations
- Program Delivery

EXPECTED PROGRAM OUTCOMES
- Increase knowledge and ability to use equipment
- Increase ability to follow and understand a fitness program
- Maintain or increase present fitness level through an established fitness program
- Increase ability to transfer skills to community facilities

Source: Kelland, J. (1995). *Protocols for recreation therapy treatment plans.* State College, PA: Venture Publishing, Inc. Reprinted with permission.

and evaluation with protocol implementation and collection of data to verify outcomes of intervention application.

Documentation

Professional responsibility and accountability in therapeutic recreation are among the most important reasons for documentation. Documentation is part of the practitioner's total responsibility in providing service, and it is the manager's responsibility to note its appropriateness and correctness through coaching, training, and auditing. With the development and initiation of the therapeutic recreation process as a framework for practice, documentation has evolved as an essential link between the provision of service and evaluation of service. The purpose of documentation is to facilitate service, to enhance continuity of service, to describe the service, to identify researchable problems, and to evaluate not only the effectiveness of the service in achieving individual and/or group goals but also the consumer's response to the service (Austin, 2004). Basically, evaluation of documentation ensures quality management.

While documentation is important regardless of setting, it is a requirement within health care facilities in response to meeting various regulatory standards. Probably the most notable regulatory agencies for health care and as related to therapeutic recreation are JCAHO, CARF, and Centers for Medicare and Medicaid Services (CMS). As was mentioned earlier, without accreditation from JCAHO, hospitals are not eligible for any government funds, such as Medicare or other health care insurance programs. Along with JCAHO's standards, health care facilities must comply with the documentation regulations issued by the state department of health in its state. For reimbursement both Medicare and Medicaid require documentation. CMS regulations and U.S. Omnibus Budget Reconciliation Act (OBRA; P. L. 100-203) stipulate completion of the Minimum Data Set for Resident Assessment and Care Screening (MDS; Austin, 2004). In addition, ATRA (2000) and NTRS (2004) have established standards of therapeutic recreation practice which associate themselves with JCAHO and CARF regulatory standards. These standards of practice are based on the framework for providing service and the therapeutic recreation process.

Documentation today has assumed new importance, with the current emphasis placed on monitoring the quality of health care as evidenced by consumer outcomes. Prospective payment systems and limited health care resources have made quality of health care a major issue. Consumers, insurers, and government agencies are seeking more information on clinical performance and related dimensions of good care. In response to these concerns,

JCAHO adopted an *Agenda for Change* with the primary focus of evaluating organizational and clinical performance outcomes (JCAHO, 1987).

Documentation Evaluation

While the therapeutic recreation practitioner will document the assessment, planning, and implementation phase of the therapeutic recreation process, documentation of the evaluation phase is an important and ongoing part of the process. Evaluation of the consumer's status, progress, or achievement of outcomes is provided through a progress note. Progress notes are not only vital for evaluation purposes but also used for protection from liability and for reimbursement in health care facilities.

Progress notes document the consumer's status in relation to the desired outcomes (Shank & Coyle, 2002). The consumer's responses are compared with the outcomes defined in the treatment or program plan. The frequency with which to document progress depends on organization policy. Within a community-based leisure service organization it may be on a weekly, monthly, or seasonal basis. In health care facilities the type of charting system used in the organization may define how often one should document an evaluation. Therapeutic recreation protocols may specify frequency. Last, the therapeutic recreation department, or its intervention procedures, may specify frequency.

In writing a progress note, the practitioner and manager need to be aware that such notes are used to document pertinent observations and responses to interventions. In addition, using specific, definitive words when describing a consumer's or group's status is very important. Such expressions as "appears" and "apparently" are not always appropriate. Objective observations should be included without qualifying phrases. Also, only specific pertinent comments should be included, and the use of stock phrases or basket terms which convey little or no meaning is to be avoided. Another common error is to project the future or potential outcome of participating in a specific activity.

Leisure education is an important activity in many settings. Unfortunately it is not always noted in progress notes, and the consumer's response to education is seldom noted. Merely providing information does not guarantee learning. That is why it is necessary to evaluate responses to any teaching or education effort. To determine whether learning is taking place the following methods may assist in deciding results of leisure education programs: demonstrations, written tests, diaries, discussion, observation, questionnaires, problem solving, and simulation.

One last point on documentation evaluation specifically related to health care facilities is the transfer and discharge information. Transfer forms are used to communicate important information about the consumer's status when the consumer is moved within the health care facility, between two facilities, or between home and an agency. The consumer's most significant therapeutic recreation information should be discussed to provide a clear picture of the consumer's participation in therapeutic recreation service and the needs of the consumer for follow-up.

In some settings therapeutic recreation is incorporated in discharge summaries. Depending on the setting, therapeutic recreation discharge information would describe the consumer's involvement in the program (without going into extensive detail), how well the consumer achieved the planned outcomes, condition of the client at discharge and any specific instructions/information/referrals given to the client and/or caregiver (Shank & Coyle, 2002). In some agencies, the opportunity is provided for referral to a community-based leisure service agency if the consumer has been involved in a leisure education program.

Legal Aspects of Documentation

Regardless of setting, legible, accurate documentation is imperative. Records communicate important information about the consumer to a variety of professionals. In the event of a lawsuit, the record may form the basis for the plaintiff's case or the therapeutic recreation practitioner's or manager's defense. The following briefly lists charting techniques and strategies to improve documentation (Austin, 2004; Shank & Coyle, 2002):

1. *Write neatly and legibly.* Sloppy illegible handwriting creates confusion and wastes time. If the information is unclear, misunderstandings can occur. In some settings computerized records have reduced difficulties associated with handwriting (Austin, 2004).

2. *Use proper spelling and grammar.* Progress notes filed with misspelled words and incorrect grammar create negative impressions. They imply that the practitioner has limited education or intellect, or he or she is careless and distracted when charting.

3. *Document in blue or black ink.* The use of either color has become a trend in health care settings.

4. *Use authorized abbreviations.* Most agencies have a list of approved abbreviations. This list needs to be available to all personnel who document.

5. Depending on the charting system, *the consumer's name should be on every page.*

6. *Chart promptly* (if possible). Chart as close as possible to the time of making an observation. When charting is left to the end of the morning or afternoon, details that are important are often forgotten.

7. *Chart after the delivery of service, not before.* Some practitioners get in the habit of charting before an activity because they believe they know how participants are going to behave. It is a dangerous practice if something happens to the consumer during the activity.

8. *Identify late entries correctly.* There are times when one cannot chart. Most health care facilities have a procedure for adding late entries.

9. *Correct mistaken entries properly.* Each health care agency has an approach for correcting mistakes. One of the more common ones is to draw a single line through the entry so that it is still readable and then to initial and date it.

10. *Do not tamper with the record.* This involves changing the date of entry, placing inaccurate information into the record, omitting significant facts, rewriting the record, and destroying the record.

11. *Chart only service provided.* Therapeutic recreation practitioners should sign only those notes describing service they provided or supervised. Cosigning others' notes is occasionally necessary. Student interns' notes are frequently cosigned by the practitioner, manager, or student intern coordinator.

12. *Avoid using charts to criticize others.* Finger pointing and accusations of incompetence do not belong in a chart.

13. *Document comments any consumer makes about a potential lawsuit against the agency or other drastic measures,* such as the consumer talking about suicide or harming others. This type of information should be described in the progress notes and reported to the appropriate person in the facility. Other factors would include violent behavior and antisocial characteristics.

14. *Eliminate bias from written descriptions* of the consumer. Avoid using words that reveal negative attitudes toward the consumer, such as abusive, drunk, lazy, spoiled, demanding, or disagreeable.

15. *Document potentially contributing consumer acts.* There are situations when the practitioner needs to chart acts on the part of the consumer which may contribute to injury or failure to respond to a treatment or program procedure. These would include noncompliance with interventions, leaving an activity without permission while on an off-grounds

trip, or having unauthorized items (e.g., alcoholic beverages, razors) on his or her person.

16. *Sign the progress note* including one's position title, credential, and date of entry.

Charting Systems

Various methods of charting consumer health care plans in health care facilities have evolved over the years. Some of the more popular ones include source-oriented or narrative charting (describing the consumer's status, any interventions, treatment, and consumer response to the interventions), *SOAP* (i.e., subjective data, objective data, assessment, and plan), *SOAPIER* (i.e., same as SOAP but *I* for interventions, *E* for evaluation, and *R* for revision), PIE (i.e., problems, interventions, and evaluation), *focus for current concern* (a method of identifying consumer concerns and organizing the narrative documentation to include data (D), action (A), and response (R) for each identified concern), and *CBE* (i.e., charting by exception) of only significant or abnormal occurrences (Austin, 2004; Shank & Coyle, 2002; Stumbo & Peterson, 2004).

Today most health care facilities, especially hospitals, have shifted to computerized information systems. Hospital Information Systems (HIS) form a framework for electronically linking departments throughout the facility. In addition, personal computers can be found at the bedside. The 1996 Health Insurance Portability and Accountability Act (HIPAA; P.L. 104-191) requires the maintenance of client confidentiality as information is created or received through computerized documentation systems. Computerization provides the opportunity to integrate the best aspects of various documentation systems.

Data can be entered into the computer in a number of different ways. Depending on the type of terminal or computer used, the therapeutic recreation practitioner may use a light pen to touch the screen, a touch-sensitive screen that responds to a finger, a keyboard or keypad, a hand-held terminal, a barcode reader, or a mouse. Speech-input interfaces are gaining more acceptance (Sullivan & Decker, 2001).

Depending on the type of computer in use, the practitioner may enter data into the system by filling in blanks, entering words or phrases to construct sentences, using blank text or free-form data entry, or selecting from a menu to highlight critical pieces of data such as changes in consumer responses (Lansky, 1989).

Regardless of which documentation system is used, all incorporate assessment, planning, care plans, progress notes, and a discharge summary. Effective documentation assures clients receive quality services. It facilitates coordination among service providers and is the primary means of accountability among professionals. First-line managers are responsible for assuring their unit's documentation identifies and evaluates client outcomes and measures evidence of clinical intervention using the therapeutic recreation process.

Monitoring and Consulting Practitioner Performance

Monitoring and assessing new and experienced practitioner performance represents one of the more challenging responsibilities of a human service manager. The responsibility is a difficult one because of the complexity of making judgments about the very people managers rely on and the colleagues with whom they have developed close working relationships. Nevertheless, the manager is a supervisor whose task is to create and sustain within the department a work environment that supports and facilitates quality service delivery efforts of staff and encourages them to actualize their knowledge and skills in relation with consumers. As Schermerhorn (1987, p. 52) pointed out, "Even the most competent employee will not achieve high performance unless proper support for the required work activities is available." He goes on to say, "The effective manager, working in concert with upper management, helps to provide the requisite resources to achieve high performance from his or her employees" (p. 54). As research has noted, performance is one of the strongest predictors of an individual's general satisfaction with a job (Feldman, 1980).

It is important to recognize that policies and practices within the organization over which the manager has little control also constitute an important part of the work environment. Inadequate salaries, funding cutbacks, and unclear organizational directives are some of the many other factors that influence the attitudes and behavior of staff. While the manager can sometimes mediate the worst effects of these environmental influences, in the final analysis they will be part of the reality that impinges on staff.

While these factors are important aspects of the work environment, the concern here initially is to consider the monitoring and informal assessment by the manager that takes place on a daily or weekly basis. In other words, the focus is on the work of practitioners, including interns, as related to the therapeutic recreation process and tasks that affect the recipients of service. Thereafter, the manager becomes a consultant who imparts knowledge and cultivates professional skills of the direct service practitioner. In some respects, the manager may serve as a kind of senior practitioner and role model; demonstrating valued behavior, attitudes, and/or skills that aid the practitioner in achieving competence, confidence, and a clear professional identity. To accomplish these specific functions, the manager must have

1. knowledge of the delivery service deemed appropriate and used by therapeutic recreation professionals

2. therapeutic recreation knowledge, techniques, and skills

3. conceptualization of the social, cultural, and behavioral patterns of consumers (including individuals, groups, and organizations)

4. adequate interpersonal skills such as self-disclosure, conflict management, and giving and receiving feedback

5. knowledge and understanding of one's own interpersonal behavior including motives plus affective sensitivity to one's own feelings as they are experienced in interpersonal situations

Much of what is discussed in this section is associated with the term *coaching*. Coaching, according to Robbins (1995, p. 274), is a day-to-day, hands-on process of helping employees recognize opportunities to improve their work performance. There are three general coaching skills that managers should exhibit if they are to assist employees in their performance, including the ability to

1. analyze ways to improve an employee's performance and capabilities

2. create a supportive climate

3. influence employees to change their behavior (Robbins, 1995, pp. 281–82)

As noted in Chapter 15 (Performance Appraisal), coaching is integral to actions taken by managers following performance reviews: In Chapter 16 (Staff Training and Development), coaching and mentorship roles are considered as the manager facilitates access to training and education with new and experienced staff. Day-to-day or *short-term coaching* helps employees improve their performance and involves spontaneous teaching that assists with socialization and short-term problems (Marquis & Huston, 2003). *Long-term coaching* occurs over the duration of employment and is broader in scope than a mentoring relationship. Long-term coaching helps employees to expand their career opportunities and is effective in building teams and increasing productivity and retention (Marquis & Huston, 2003).

Effective coaching will develop strengths and potentials of practitioners and help them to overcome their weaknesses. It is a positive motivator when it is specific and behavioral. While coaching takes time, it will save time, money, and errors by practitioners, which in the long run will benefit all—the manager, the practitioners, the organization, and the consumers. Thus short-term and long-term coaching represent managerial or administrative supervision. This form of supervision monitors and evaluates staff performance and growth while ensuring adherence to unit and agency policies (Austin, 2004).

A second form of supervision, *clinical supervision*, focuses on the therapeutic recreation process as experienced by clients and staff (Shank & Coyle, 2002). Clinical supervision intends to assure effective clinical practice and growth of a reflective practitioner. The manager and staff member engage in a nonjudgmental supportive relationship focusing on the client. A manager assumes the role of a clinical coach who consults and mentors to develop competent professionals (see Chapter 7, "Professional Clinical Supervision," p. 93).

Supervisory needs of practitioners vary. A developmental approach to clinical supervision reflects how supervisory needs and abilities of staff change over time (Shank & Coyle, 2002). Entry-level practitioners with limited direct experience are preoccupied with their lack of technical skills and depend heavily on their supervisors for information, technical direction, and support. When staff have resolved their anxiety over their clinical work, they become aware that there are no "cookbook" answers that work with all clients. At this intermediate level, staff vacillate between self-confidence and feeling dependent. Supervisors offer choices yet realize supervision may be uncomfortable for both parties. At this level, a major supervision task is to learn how the helping relationship is influenced by one's personal characteristics and how this interaction impacts clinical practice (Shank & Coyle, 2002). When the supervisee is open to challenges regarding feelings of competence and autonomy "and accepts responsibility for addressing underdeveloped areas of clinical competence, he or she is ready to transition to" the next level of development (Shank & Coyle, 2002, p. 258). At the last level, staff integrate their understanding of clinical practice with self-awareness and are capable of understanding the client's context—they have *practice wisdom*. At this level, formal supervision is replaced by periodic consultation (Shank & Coyle, 2002).

This developmental approach to clinical supervision finds the manager assuming three distinct roles. At level one, the manager is a teacher focusing on clinical practice skill instruction (Austin, 2004). During the intermediate stage, the manager assumes a counselor role to facilitate the supervisee's self-growth as a clinician. Lastly, as a consultant the manager encourages the supervisee to assume responsibility as a therapist (Austin, 2004). The outcome of effective clinical supervision is a competent professional who is aware of the therapeutic use of self during the therapeutic recreation process and who assumes responsibility for his or her decision making and judgment during clinical practice.

Monitoring Practitioner Performance

Monitoring may be broadly defined as that managerial task concerned with checking and reviewing the day-to-day work activity of the practitioner. Monitoring is a means employed by managers to generate immediate ongoing feedback about work activities and accomplishments so as to determine whether corrective action is necessary. It may be an on-the-spot forum to collect and to analyze information from the practitioner about work activity and outcomes while ascertaining whether steps should be taken to alter the activity of the practitioner or mode of operation. It may also be an individual conference as a result of reading or hearing case records/presentations or treatment plans. Previewing case records allows the manager to identify problem areas as practitioners pursue their responsibilities. Monitoring may or may not be associated with the annual performance review or the formal appraisal interview.

Close monitoring is most critical for inexperienced, new practitioners. At the same time, professional development continues throughout one's practice, and practitioners who have had experience also need assistance at times. However, the manager must be sensitive to possible defensiveness on the part of the experienced practitioner. Practitioners who have been monitored previously in their place of work may have positive or negative expectations about upcoming supervision. If the previous experience was negative, the present manager must overcome this mindset.

What might be some reasons for daily or weekly monitoring? Reasons for monitoring include to

1. Assess practitioner's attitudes about the job, responsibilities, organization, and the supervision.

2. Further the manager's understanding of the practitioner.

3. Help the manager observe the practitioner more closely to improve the consulting or teacher relationship. The manager must keep in mind the timing and location of the coaching experience. Excellent coaching at the wrong time or wrong place may prove to be of more harm than help.

4. Obtain feedback on practitioner's work activity (e.g., complying with regulations, protocols, standards of practice and procedures, achieving desired results).

5. Assist the manager in becoming more aware of differences among practitioners for better practitioner deployment.

6. Assist in clarifying activities associated with annual performance reviews.

7. Assist the manager in analyzing practitioner strengths and weaknesses to enhance strengths and reduce weaknesses. Monitoring charting activities, for example, may demonstrate compliance with documentation as well as the staff's knowledge, strengths, and deficits.

8. Assist the manager in making decisions about in-service training needs.

9. Assist the manager in verifying inadequate work performance demonstrated by a practitioner.

10. Assist the practitioner in his or her self-evaluation.

11. Enable the manager to represent the accomplishments of the program to the organization and to the larger community—a process crucial for building support, correcting misinformation, and defending against unwarranted criticism.

The manager must always keep in mind that the responsibility for monitoring is clearly shared by the manager and practitioner through the joint process of building a relationship which encourages free discussion of job-related responsibilities. It is assumed that practitioners will become more involved in their work when they utilize the freedom to discuss their work responsibilities. This form of supervision is a productive, rather than reactive, management tool.

Consultant and Practitioner Performance

Many managers view the term *consultant* as something reserved only for the expert or the outsider. While this view may be correct in some instances, its use here is viewed as a process whereby the manager, as a supervisor, provides assistance to others on the basis of a request for assistance or on the basis of developing an atmosphere for requesting assistance. From another perspective, consulting may be considered a method which gives service indirectly by assisting the practitioner in handling problems associated with the consumer. Regardless of the method, the ultimate goal of consulting is to increase the competence of the practitioner.

While the manager may be involved in consulting relative to giving colleagues insight into what is going on around them, within them, among them and other people, or in program consulting wherein the manager is invited by top management to assist in organizational planning and program development, the focus here is on therapeutic recreation process consulting. The consulting process begins with the recognition by the practitioner that his or her program responsibility could be enhanced by consulting with the manager. The manager assists practitioners in resolving particular problems related to a consumer or group for which the practitioner is responsible. The manager may engage in consulting related to helping the practitioner develop a more comprehensive diagnosis of the consumer's problems, expanding the practitioner's options regarding alternative methods of intervention and activities that might be used to bring about change, or assisting the practitioner in recognizing the relationship of the practitioner's personal feelings and anxieties to the consumer's problems.

The manager's method of intervention will vary according to his or her personality and professional background as an experienced practitioner, facilitator, and educator. These roles may be conceptualized along a continuum from most directive to least directive, most authoritative to least authoritative. As an experienced practitioner, the manager may be viewed as an expert and therefore authoritative and directive, one who imparts special knowledge or skill, and may be expected to have magical cures. A common occurrence is the desire of the practitioner to be as competent as his or her manager. While such aspirations of this type are a positive motivation for the practitioner to learn the knowledge and skills of the therapeutic recreation profession, it is wise for the manager to disclose his or her own errors, doubts, and disappointments. Good consulting requires that the manager not see himself or herself as an oracle but admits fallibility and devotes energy to furthering growth and building strength in the practitioner.

On the other hand, the manager as a consultant may assume a facilitator role. This involves the manager in a communication process which utilizes the collective resources of both the manager and the practitioner in problem solving. By skillfully using questions to help define and explore problems, the manager tries to generate alternative solutions from the worker and then discusses the pros and cons of each alternative. The manager might add alternatives not mentioned by the practitioner. Next, the manager helps the practitioner choose the approach that seems most likely to be successful and, equally important, one consistent with practice service delivery. By helping the practitioner to evaluate and choose an approach, the manager is not only assisting the practitioner with the development of professional competency but also is communicating confidence in the practitioner's practice ability, thus encouraging the practitioner to take a major role in the learning process.

The role of the manager as consultant-educator to the practitioner is one of the most widely recognized roles. The educator role may involve anything from on-the-spot teaching (e.g., giving evaluative reactions to a specific service delivery approach to the consumer, offering suggestions of what to do differently to be more effective) to citing specific articles or books relevant to the problem faced by the practitioner. The manager might also demonstrate a particular technique or approach by role playing with the practitioner. Then, too, the manager may offer strategies or techniques for the practitioner to implement.

The practitioner is an active participant in the learning process. The consultant's job is to present ideas and to monitor the way in which the practitioner relates to the ideas. This may range from simply watching the practitioner's eyes to make sure he or she is understanding the directions for charting to having regard for the practitioner's feelings while trying to help him or her tackle a difficult treatment plan. It can also mean being sensitive to the subtle interplay taking place between the consultant and the practitioner that has been described as the authority item. The effect resulting from this relationship can enhance the learning or can generate major obstacles to the integration of new ideas. Of course, some anxiety will be created by any supervisory technique or discussion, but most managers would agree that some techniques produce more anxiety than others. Also, some practitioners become anxious more quickly and to a greater extent than others. It is suggested that one should begin with a low-anxiety approach rather than a high-anxiety approach. However, the entire issue of supervisory intervention rests, to some extent, on the manager's belief about conflict. As noted in Chapter 10, conflict can have positive value as well as negative value. The authors view supervision here as the management of changes in the practitioner toward ideal professional behavior.

The eventual goal of the consulting role is the engagement of the manager and practitioner in a mutually responsible collegial relationship that values the participation of the practitioner equally with that of the manager. The result of this engagement should assist the practitioner in being able to integrate and apply basic practice skills in the delivery of therapeutic recreation service with consistency. Competency gives a practitioner credibility so that others will tend to seek out and respond to his or her suggestions. As long as both the new and old practitioner and the manager communicate openly and recognize and respond to each other's needs and expectations mutual development will continue, and the satisfaction of all will be enhanced.

Summary

Consideration was initially given to scheduling, including the goals and problems associated with scheduling. Consideration must be given to many variables and challenges in developing a schedule such as consumer needs and staff skills. Thereafter the therapeutic recreation process and accountability for the process were reviewed. Associated with this review and accountability was protocols, actions that address specific programs or treatment plans. Outlines of a diagnostic and program protocol were provided. Documentation and its importance in evaluation was considered next. It was pointed out that while there are various charting systems in use in health care facilities, many hospitals have shifted to computerized information systems.

Last, attention was given to the monitoring process of practitioner performance and the role of the manager as a consultant to both the new and older experienced practitioner. The monitoring process is one element of coaching closely aligned with managerial or administrative supervision. Clinical supervision, a second type of supervision, involves the manager in teaching, counselor, and consultative roles.

Review Questions

1. How is scheduling related to other managerial functions and activities?

2. Ask yourself, "What do people have to do to get positive feedback from me?" Evaluate your expectations.

3. Develop program and personnel schedules using various computer packages.

4. Compare different progress note formats and charting systems in clinical and community-based leisure service organizations.

5. Visit a therapeutic recreation manager and "walk through" the program development process reviewing the relationship between various types of schedules (e.g., individual/group, session/seasonal/annual).

6. Prepare either a program or diagnostic protocol based on the outlines found in this chapter (Tables 19.2 and 19.3).

References

American Therapeutic Recreation Society (ATRA). (2000). *Standards for the practice of therapeutic recreation, and self-assessment guide.* Alexandria, VA: Author.

Austin, D. R. (2004). *Therapeutic recreation processes and techniques* (5th ed.). Champaign, IL: Sagamore Publishing.

Feldman, D. A. (1980). A socialization process that helps new recruits succeed. *Personnel, 57,* 163–174.

Ferguson, D. D. (1992). Problem identification and protocol usage in therapeutic recreation. In G. L. Hitzhusen, L. T. Jackson, and M. A. Birdsong (Eds.), *Global therapeutic recreation II* (pp. 1–11). Columbia, MO: Curators of University of Missouri.

Grote, K., Hasl, M., Krider, R., and Mortensen, D. M. (1995). *Behavioral health protocols for recreational therapy.* Ravensdale, WA: Idyll Arbor.

Hood, C. D. (2003). Standardizing practice and outcomes through clinical practice guidelines: Recommendations for therapeutic recreation. In N. J. Stumbo (Ed.), *Client outcomes in therapeutic recreation services* (pp. 149–164). State College, PA: Venture Publishing, Inc.

Joint Commission on Accreditation of Healthcare Organizations (JCAHO). (1987). *Agenda for change.* Chicago, IL: Author.

Kelland, J. (Ed.). (1995). *Protocols for recreation therapy programs.* State College, PA: Venture Publishing, Inc.

Knight, L. and Johnson, D. (1991). Therapeutic recreation protocols: Client problems centered approach. In B. Riley (Ed.), *Quality management: Applications for therapeutic recreation* (pp. 137–147). State College, PA: Venture Publishing, Inc.

Lansky, D. (1989). Hospital-based outcomes management: Enhancing quality of care with coordinated data systems. In L. M. Kingland (Ed.), *Proceedings of the thirteenth annual symposium on computer applications in medical care: Enhancing quality of care with coordinated data systems* (pp. 732–736). Washington, DC: IEEE Computer Society Press.

Marquis, B. L. and Huston, C. J. (2003). *Leadership roles and management functions in nursing: Theory & application* (4th ed.). Philadelphia, PA: Lippincott Williams & Wilkins.

Mobily, K. E. (1999). New horizons in models of practice in therapeutic recreation. *Therapeutic Recreation Journal, 33*(3), 174–192.

National Therapeutic Recreation Society (NTRS). (1989). *Protocols in therapeutic recreation.* Arlington, VA: National Recreation and Park Association.

National Therapeutic Recreation Society (NTRS). (2004). *Standards of practice for a continuum of care in therapeutic recreation.* Retrieved September 12, 2004, from http://www.nrpa.org/content/default.aspx?documentID=530

Olsson, R. H., Jr. (1990). *Recreational therapy protocol design: A systems approach to treatment evaluation.* Toledo, OH: International Leisure Press.

O'Morrow, G. S. (1986). *Therapeutic recreation: A helping profession* (2nd ed.). Englewood Cliffs, NJ: Prentice Hall.

O'Morrow, G. S. and Reynolds, R. (1989). *Therapeutic recreation: A helping profession* (3rd ed.). Englewood Cliffs, NJ: Prentice Hall.

Robbins, S. P. (1995). *Supervision today.* Englewood Cliffs, NJ: Prentice Hall.

Schermerhorn, J. R., Jr. (1987). Improving healthcare productivity through high-performance managerial development. *Health Care Management Review, 12,* 49–55.

Shank, J. and Coyle C. (2002). *Therapeutic recreation in health promotion and rehabilitation.* State College, PA: Venture Publishing, Inc.

Stumbo, N. J. and Peterson, C. A. (2004). *Therapeutic recreation program design: Principles and procedures* (4th ed.). San Francisco, CA: Pearson Benjamin Cummings.

Sullivan E. J. and Decker, P. J. (2001). *Effective leadership and management in nursing* (5th ed.). Upper Saddle River, NJ: Prentice Hall.

Tappen, R. M. (2001). *Nursing leadership and management: Concepts and practice* (4th ed.). Philadelphia, PA: F. A. Davis Company.

Chapter 20
Risk Management

The first decade of the 21st century experienced the convergence of several forces that triggered changes across health care systems to improve patient safety. "Legislation, financial pressures, organizational restructuring, overwhelming administrative requirements, declining resources, and an explosion of technology" (Hemman, 2002, p. 419) served as springboards to create cultures of safety within health care organizations. This increasing focus on patient safety, plus the continuing insurance crisis, has changed the nature of risk management ("Risk Managers at the Crossroads," 2002).

In 1999 the Institute of Medicine (IOM) of the National Academy of Sciences released a report, *To Err Is Human: Building a Safer Health System*. This report became the catalyst for a national patient safety agenda and the instigator to shift the role of risk management from a reactive case-by-case identification of error to a proactive focus on providing quality experiences in a safe surrounding (Hemman, 2002; Peterson & Hronek, 2003). This report summarized the human cost of medical errors and found that most medical errors result from flaws in the system rather than individual recklessness. The report concluded that with adequate leadership, awareness, and resources, errors may be reduced by half within five years (Hemman, 2002). A subsequent IOM report, *Crossing the Quality Chasm: A New Health System for the 21st Century*, suggested the risk management focus must become more strategic and systems based in order to create safer health care environments (Kuhn & Youngberg, 2002). In the park and recreation arena it was not until after the mid-1970s that risk management programs became operational as a result of increased judgments against public entities and judgments for the plaintiffs who were injured in leisure activities (van der Smissen, 1990). Likewise, as a result of an increase in medical malpractice cases during the 1970s and 1980s, attention was given to loss prevention and risk management in health care facilities (Kuhn & Youngberg, 2002).

Risk management has been evolving since its inception. Initially, the focus was on managing monetary losses from plaintiff's judgments. More recently, concern for patient and consumer safety has been the impetus to align risk management and quality initiatives. The evolution of risk management as summarized by one source, outlines four distinct periods coinciding with the closing decades of the 20th century ("Risk Managers at the Crossroads," 2002):

- 1970s—The Birth of Risk Management. Risk management was closely tied to insurance companies with a focus on professional liability and general liability losses. Quality management consisted of counting incident reports.

- 1980s—The Good Old Days. Risk management evolved as an independent function and a move to integrate risk management and quality improvement commenced. Measurement included trending of incident reports.

- 1990s—Risk Management Under Fire. Distinctions between risk and quality initiatives blur with risk focusing on regulatory compliance and a soft insurance market encouraging complacency.

- 2000—Risk Management Eclipsed by Patient Safety. The IOM report focuses attention on medical errors.

A concern for patient safety shifts the focus to systemic organization changes that support quality. A number of entities, including the Veterans Health Administration and the Joint Commission on Accreditation of Healthcare Organizations (JCAHO) use root-cause analysis, a total quality management (TQM) approach to improve care (Vincent, 2003). The JCAHO published national patient safety goals requiring collaborative efforts among organizations and professionals to identify barriers to and strategies for improving patient safety. Further, the National Patient Safety Foundation (NPSF) of AMA was developed to serve as the catalyst through research and education for transitioning from a culture of blame to one of safety (Hemman, 2002).

Voelkl (1988) suggested that risk management is a component of quality assurance in therapeutic recreation. She stated, "Quality assurance and risk management appear to be natural partners in ensuring the highest level care for recipients" (Voelkl, 1988, p. 3). Because of similarities in the goals of these management activities, the trend is understandable. Both risk management and quality management must have ongoing monitoring and evaluating to improve financial and quality service continuously. In addition, risk management and quality management are concerned with patterns of noncompliance, either with safety practices or with goals, objectives, policies, procedures, and standards. The point of both management programs is to develop procedures that will provide feedback to the service providers so that services can be improved. As noted by Peters, "When quality goes up, costs go down. Quality improvement is the primary source of cost reduction" (1987, p. 79).

The therapeutic recreation manager needs to understand the basic concepts of risk management, namely the risk management program and its elements, as well as the problems and concerns associated with risk management. This chapter does not attempt to provide answers to all risk management administrative matters; rather, it gives therapeutic recreation managers a better understanding of the importance of risk management in providing quality service. Risk managers will experience new tasks as the paradigm shifts from reactive reporting of incidents that cause financial losses to a culture of safety. Within a TQM environment, loss control encompasses not only consumers but also safety and security of employees, volunteers, and guests. This chapter considers responsibilities of managers as they introduce workplace safety measures to assure employee, consumer, and caregiver security. Managers' duties now address threats to security and personal safety triggered by natural causes (e.g., weather, plants, animals) and actions attributed to crime and terrorism. JCAHO's standards require the design of emergency management plans. These plans require timely community-wide responses to local and national disasters. Thus, first-line managers develop plans to handle sensitive information with leisure service and health care providers in their home communities as well as globally.

Risk Management Program

A risk management program consists of policies and tasks that must be in place and performed on a daily basis. A risk management program is a concern of top management as well as of every employee and should be an integral part of planning. It is an organization-wide program since it calls for a team approach involving all departments within the organization. Further, it incorporates input from staff and feedback to management to accomplish its objective. Ultimately, the governing authority legitimizes the agencies' responsibility to promote quality and safety through a policy or philosophical statement on service quality and security relative to its constituents community-wide (Peterson & Hronek, 2003). In large organizations

and governmental units the program is formal; a risk management department and a full-time risk manager are in place. In smaller organizations the direction of the program is usually the responsibility of a manager who has other assigned duties. In some health care facilities the risk management manager and quality improvement manager may be the same.

Risk has been described as the probability or predictability that something will happen. A negative connotation is associated with risk. A consumer incident or a family's expression of dissatisfaction regarding service not only indicates some slippage in quality of service but it also indicates potential liability. In this regard, Stein (1993, p. 37) noted, "Too many recreation leaders—whether in regular or special programs—do not take all steps necessary and mandated to acquaint program participants with potential dangers in activities." A distraught, dissatisfied, complaining consumer is a high risk; a satisfied consumer is a low risk.

Risk management, on the other hand, usually refers to positive results achieved through some form of activity. Thus, a risk management program is a planned approach to deliver safe, quality services (Carter, VanAndel & Robb, 2003). Its purpose is to identify, analyze, and evaluate risks, followed by a plan for reducing the frequency and severity of accidents and injuries. Often, a risk management program focuses on general liability, general health and wellness within the environment, worker's compensation, and property or equipment loss due to vandalism, theft, fire, and fraud (Kaiser, 1986; Rios, 1992). According to Kaiser and Robinson (1999, p. 713) risk management "provides a framework for balancing and understanding the risks inherent within the programs and services of the organization and for empowering staff to make good choices in dealing with those risks." Rios (1992, p. 163) commented, "Risk management is simply a decision-making process to identify and control risk."

The concern for patient safety requires providers to focus on prevention and health promotion and a return to evidence-based practices (Hansen, Durbin, Cochran, Vaughn, Longowski & Gleason, 2003). The risk manager's focus is on an organization that functions consistently and reliably over a period of time without error ("Risk Managers at the Crossroads," 2002). In this culture, the risk manager takes into account both human and system factors that result in error (Hughes, 2004). Also, the risk manager is involved in strategic planning that promotes standardization of procedures and practices that improve performance (Kuhn & Youngberg, 2002). As a consequence, the risk manager considers system characteristics that influence patient safety, such as regulatory quality standards (e.g., JCAHO), staffing, the work environment, and the training and education of consumers and service providers (Hansen et al., 2003).

In brief, the development of risk management programs is the result of, but not limited to, the following:

- injury or death from environmental hazards found in parks, forests, and recreation areas

- poorly maintained or dangerous equipment in parks and playgrounds

- inadequately supervised recreation activities

- user behaviors

- changes in reimbursement and cuts in government health programs

- consumer requirement for accountability in the health areas

- increased cost of premiums for liability coverage

- increased litigation

- huge judgments or awards granted by courts

- a demand for service when previously there was less demand

- expectations regarding patient safety and quality services

As a result of these factors and many others, management of risks and concern for safety and security has gained significance in terms of priorities within community-based leisure service agencies and in health care organizations. In the final analysis, a risk management program serves as evidence of intent to act responsibly and protect the safety of agency constituents.

The degree of involvement of therapeutic recreation managers in the development of risk management and safety programs will vary from setting to setting. Some will be directly involved as a result of being a manager of a therapeutic recreation department within an organization. Managers of special recreation associations and community-based freestanding independent recreation centers for persons with disabilities will certainly be responsible for the development of risk and safety programs in their specific settings. Others need both to be involved and aware of what composes exposure to loss, threats to constituent well-being, and risk and safety problems.

Elements of a Risk Management Program

Elements of risk and safety programs include writing and disseminating policy statements; identifying, analyzing, and evaluating risks and threats; and selecting, implementing, and monitoring the plan.

The key to an effective risk management program is the development of a philosophy regarding risk for the entire organization. Merely knowing about the program and what is involved will not do the job. There must be an emotional acceptance and positive attitude about a risk management program. The statements of policy

> should set forth or delineate what risk management encompasses and its importance to the organization; the scope of authority and responsibilities of personnel and where risk management fits into the organization structure; and the extent and nature of the approaches to be used in managing risk. (van der Smissen, 1990, p. 4)

The organization board or policy-making body of the organization becomes involved and stays involved by approving these statements. A portion of the employee safety and health policy incorporated in a city risk management plan is presented in Figure 20.1 (p. 310). The policy of risk management is to be reviewed annually and updated with approval by the agency policy entity.

The initial activity of the therapeutic recreation manager, like other managers, is to identify risk and safety concerns that may result in loss to the organization. Kaiser and Robinson (1999) suggested by considering the legal-based classes of loss, hazards, and the constituents at risk, the nature of organizational risks is identified. Most providers experience a combination of the following five legal classes of loss:

- property loss: natural and human causes like terrorism

- financial business losses: theft and employee injuries

- contractual losses: breach of service contract being provided by another organization

- tort liability: negligence and malpractice

- human rights: equal opportunity and ADA (Kaiser & Robinson, 1999)

A second way to consider risks is by identification of hazards an organization may experience. Hazards may be associated with the following:

- environmental conditions

- infrastructure design, maintenance or inspection

- programming (e.g. supervision, activity selection)

- emergency care

- transportation of clients (Kaiser & Robinson, 1999)

NO. 100 CITY OF CINNCINNATI EMPLOYEE
SAFETY AND HEALTH COMMITMENT

Safety and Health Protection is a quality of worklife issue which has a high priority in all our activities. Our goal is to minimize human injury or illness, and property loss or operation interruption caused by accidents, fire or other hazards.

The City believes that safe working conditions for every one of its employees can be attained through the use of safety equipment, by proper job instruction, frequent review of safe practices, and proper supervision.

To support these vital actions toward our goal, the City is committed to:

Develop processes; design, build and maintain plants and equipment; and establish operating methods with full consideration of safety and health effects.

Seek out the best available information on hazards and risks, and communicate it to all concerned for decision-making application.

Provide leadership, organization, funds and other appropriate resources for comprehensive safety and health programs.

Foster safe behavior and initiative, both on and off the job, through education, training and publicity.

Minimize the undesirable effects of accidents by providing rescue equipment and training, first aid, and medical systems.

Recognize and reward achievements in health and safety planning, management and performance.

Require all supervisors to consider it an essential part of their job to administer the safety program and terminate unsafe activities.

Inform all employees that they are required, as a condition of their employment, to follow all established safety practices.

Have each Department/Division prepare a definite safety plan by means of which safe working practices will be brought to the attention of every employee.

Michael B. Gunn
Michael B. Gunn, Ph.D.
Assistant to the City Manager
Employee Safety/Environmental Compliance Division

Figure 20.1
City of Cincinnati Employee Safety and Health Commitment

Lastly, agency constituents like volunteers, board members, caregivers, interns, and employees are exposed to varying degrees of risk as they carry out their obligations. Initially, the focus on consumer safety and security broadens the identification of risks to consideration of "near misses" and continual monitoring of any threat or root causes that may result in error. Secondly, this broader framework reduces the focus on individual error and recognizes contributory factors are a reflection of organizational and system failures (Hughes, 2004; Vincent, 2003). Thus, risk identification commences with a system-wide analysis of casual factors that may result in "harm" to the organization's constituents.

According to Carter, Van Andel, and Robb (2003), risk is associated with therapeutic recreation service in three ways: (a) staffing, (b) programming, and (c) participant management. In staffing, for example, consideration needs to be given to the practitioner's knowledge and experience to successfully fulfill the responsibilities associated with the position. Managers, as noted by Stein (1993), are asking for legal problems if they assign a practitioner to conduct and supervise programs and activities without adequate training and education.

Program management uses American Therapeutic Recreation Association (ATRA, 2000) and National Therapeutic Recreation Society (NTRS, 2004) standards of practice as well as Joint Commission on Accreditation of Healthcare Organizations (JCAHO, http://www.jcaho.org), Rehabilitation Accreditation Commission (CARF, http://www.carf.org), National Committee for Quality Assurance (NCQA, http://www.ncqa.org), and Centers for Medicare and Medicaid Services (CMS, http://www.cms.hhs.gov) standards to ensure continuous performance improvement and focus on delivery of safe quality programs. Other standards that need to be considered are those which have been legislated by law (e.g., statutes, ordinances, regulations) and those set forth by organizations concerned with specific activities (e.g., American Camping Association, National Playground Safety Institute). "Ignorance of such standards is no excuse for failing to comply" (van der Smissen, 1990, p. 45). A policy and procedure manual is another source which will provide insight into program practices necessary to decrease losses and injuries (e.g., facility and equipment use and inspection, clinical privileges). It is extremely important in community-based leisure service agencies that sites, facilities, and programs conform with American with Disabilities Act (ADA) regulations. Consideration needs to be given to the procedures associated with handling emergencies, releases and waivers, injury precaution sheets, and agreements to participate. For example, contents of agreement to participate forms may need to be presented in large print or Braille. In other situations, sign language or visual supplements (e.g., videotape) will be necessary.

Participant management focuses on such things as assessment guidelines and information, including consumer chart updating, electronic documentation, and documentation of participation and degree of involvement. The broader the therapeutic recreation manager's knowledge of the department's operation, the more exhaustive and accurate will be the identification of loss exposures and unsafe practices. Risks must be identified before they can be managed. Thus, the manager reviews policies, procedures, and activities to make recommendations regarding changes that will prevent errors or threats and reduce potential loss.

Other matters and concerns, not exhaustive, that need to be addressed by therapeutic recreation departments' are shown in Figure 20.2.

After the identification of risks, the manager will probably be asked to analyze and evaluate the frequency, severity, and causes of specific types of incidents that might impact constituents and the organization. Because no two risks, errors, or threats are alike, each is analyzed and evaluated. This assessment relies on organizational data, staff assessment, and data from other agencies or similar programs (Kaiser & Robinson, 1999). The risk management team collects and aggregates "data that represent the total cost of risk presented by a specific behavior, the cost of managing or eliminating that risk, and the identification of benchmarks so that… the organization can more precisely develop a strategic plan" (Kuhn & Youngberg, 2002). Data are categorized with rating scales applied to represent the probability, high, medium, or low of the risk occurring. Severity of injury and organizational impact is also placed on scales (e.g., fatal to low and catastrophic to minimal financial losses). The team then can prioritize the identified risks and design a strategy to manage future incidents. Some managers will find that sufficient historical data are not available for reliable objective analysis. In such cases, intuitive analysis can be used, or the manager can compare data to that of a similar department within the same organization (e.g., occupational therapy) or to a like therapeutic recreation department in another organization.

As the manager and employees consider selection of risk management strategies, the mission of the organization and its financial status is matched with the nature of the identified risks and the frequency and severity of the losses (Kaiser & Robinson, 1999). Managers may select one or a combination of four options to control risk factors: avoidance, reduction, retention, and transference. Avoidance is simply doing away with the service or activity because its risk is too great. Reduction considers minimizing the contingencies through planning, staff training,

information management, and better procedures. The keeping of risk is retention (e.g., fee adjustments, self-insurance). There will always be risk, and the organization

1. Use of toxic materials.

2. Storage of flammable materials.

3. Kiln is periodically inspected and used by only experienced staff members.

4. Storage of equipment (to prevent people from using without proper supervision).

5. Proper space is available for program to be run safely.

6. Equipment is in good condition and regularly inspected.

7. Proper clothing is required for participation in certain activities (i.e., gym shoes for volleyball).

8. Staff-client ratio is an established policy.

9. Clients are informed of possible risks and means of preventing risks.

10. A first-aid kit is kept in the vehicle used for out trips. The kit is regularly checked to ensure it contains adequate supplies.

11. Out trip sites are inspected for accessibility, direct and safe entry ways, and services provided prior to taking clients.

12. Proper approval is obtained for clients to be involved in any activities.

13. Specific standards exist for the running of each program.

14. Assumptions are not made regarding clients' past experiences or skills.

15. Vehicles for out trips are regularly inspected.

16. Staff are involved in planning programs, policies, procedures, and standards.

17. Area is checked prior to activity.

18. Proper level and sequence of instruction is provided for each activity.

19. Proper supervision is provided for each activity.

20. All areas utilized in supervised or unsupervised activities are regularly inspected for safety.

21. Staff are always prepared to act in case of an emergency.

22. Clients are not allowed to participate in any general recreation or therapeutic recreation programs until staff have completed an assessment.

Source: Voelkl, J. E. (1988). *Risk management in therapeutic recreation*. State College, PA: Venture Publishing, Inc. Reproduced with permission

Figure 20.2
Therapeutic Recreation Department's Risk Management Concerns

accepts a certain level of loss. Transference is having the responsibility of risk carried by an individual, contract, lease, bond, or harmless clauses.

The next step in the risk management process is implementation. This step incorporates implementation and inclusion of all aspects of the program and its administrative procedures within the organization's and department's policy and procedures manual, including the various forms used to document incidents. Rios (1992, p. 172) suggests the following basics for inclusion:

1. a plan for supervision of all therapeutic recreation staff

2. standards of practice referencing accreditation and professional standards

3. ethical standards of conduct

4. credentialing standards and clinical privileging

5. process for reporting and investigating accidents and incidents

6. process for safety inspections

7. procedures for preventative maintenance

8. procedures for routine maintenance

9. emergency plans (e.g., search and rescue, fire evacuation, power outage)

10. procedures for managing untoward behavior (e.g., unauthorized leave)

11. procedures for managing aggressive behavior

12. safety guidelines for swimming

13. specific program guidelines for any individual program of moderate frequency or severity of risk (*moderate risk* includes any injury, such as minor fractures, strains, sprains, or infected lacerations vs. *inconsequential injuries*, such as minor lacerations, contusions, or abrasions)

14. job descriptions that include duties and responsibilities; reportability; minimum knowledge, skills and abilities to provide service; and level of supervision

15. internal peer review system

Figure 20.3 illustrates the risk management process as developed by Kaiser (1986), Kaiser and Robinson (1999) and Hronek and Spengler (2002). Its modification to therapeutic recreation by Rios (1992) is illustrated in

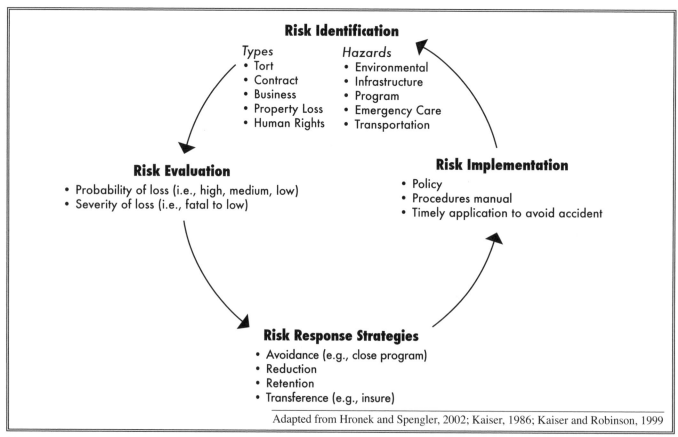

Figure 20.3
Risk Management Process

Figure 20.4. The scope of the decision-making process in therapeutic recreation has broadened to encompass activities that enhance safety, security, and promote quality improvements. Thus, the manager and risk management team consider guidelines like the JCAHO National Patient Safety Goals and their requirements to plan cooperatively with the community as emergency or disaster management plans are written: Also considered are laws like the Health Insurance Portability and Accountability Act of 1996 (HIPAA) that cover medical records and other individually identifiable health information, ADA, and OSHA (Occupational Safety and Health Administration) guidelines of 1998 that include policy recommendations to help prevent work place violence (Buppert, 2002; Henry & Ginn, 2002; Threats Create a Need to Coordinate With Providers, 2003; Unsafe for Every Need, 2002). Collectively, these resources guide the manager and team as they design goals and objectives for risk and constituent safety

and security. These goals and objectives identify benchmarks to meet and they become the criteria against which the effectiveness of program implementation is judged (Peterson & Hronek, 2003).

Once a risk management program has been developed, the therapeutic recreation manager will be involved in monitoring the program as it relates to the department recommending, if need be, preventive or corrective action. Certainly he or she will evaluate, on an ongoing basis, the effectiveness of the program and will provide reports to the administration or risk management manager for the agency or organization. The therapeutic recreation manager will gather information from staff and regularly inspect and observe current practices. The manager involves the staff in determining desirable practices and establishing safety rules, regulations and procedures. This involvement fosters a safety awareness attitude and makes routine safety inspections more palatable. Additionally, the upkeep

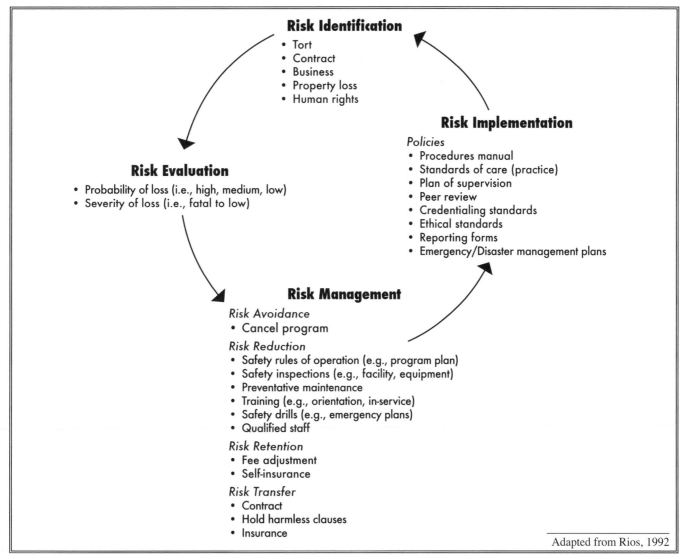

Adapted from Rios, 1992

Figure 20.4
Risk Management Decision-Making Process in Therapeutic Recreation

and maintenance of information documentation systems becomes a shared and significant responsibility of everyone. The manager may find useful a checklist to adequately cover all aspects of risk exposure and safety. Information gathered needs to be integrated into the department's computer risk management analysis program.

In the review process of developing a risk management plan, volunteers and student interns need to be involved. Volunteers and interns are subject to legal actions against them in a manner similar to regular paid employees, although they are generally liable for their own acts of negligence. It is probably wise to include participants as a review resource especially in community-based agencies. It also may be wise to require students to have personal liability insurance prior to starting their internship; however, the organization may have a policy on this matter that should be checked.

Education about risk is another major element. For a risk management program to be effective, every employee must be involved, including staff, volunteers, and interns. Staff and volunteers must understand the significance of hazards and associated liabilities. This means all those liabilities associated with negligence and/or malpractice. Merely knowing what to do and the liabilities associated with the risk is not acceptable. There must be an emotional acceptance, as has been noted, of risk management by the manager and practitioners of the department.

Highly reliable organizations rely on the standardization of practices, leadership dedicated to safety, data-driven outcomes, and an open, nonpunitive reporting culture (Kuhn & Youngberg, 2002). A wealth of information is generated as programs are delivered. It is a matter of educating professionals to look for quality and safety indicators and the importance of taking a role in safety initiatives. Health and human service "professionals are generally highly trained, skilled, dedicated people working together in complex systems" (Hughes, 2004, p. 84). Yet knowledge and technology are constantly changing as are their responsibilities; thus, the manager fosters a work environment conducive to ongoing learning as the costs associated with errors that "result in legal charges of negligence or malpractice outweigh the costs of conducting simulations and training programs" (p. 84).

Incident Report

Regardless of safety rules and procedures pertaining to consumer participation in program services and practitioners who deliver the services, incidents do occur. Incident reports are made for every accident, error, or anything unusual that occurs in the course of client's involvement in treatment or programs (Marquis & Huston, 2003). They are used to collect and to analyze future data for the purpose of determining risk control strategies. The report needs to be completed with extreme care because it can be used as evidence if a lawsuit is brought against the organization or any person involved. Because incident reports are used to defend an agency, they are considered confidential; yet, if reports are disclosed to the plaintiff they are no longer considered confidential and can be subpoenaed in court (Marquis & Huston, 2003). Consequently, no entry is placed in clients' records indicating incident reports have been written, only enough information about the occurrence is reported so proper care is given. Depending on the state, lawsuits can be filed until the statute of limitations runs out; thus, reports are maintained in agency files for a number of years.

At times there is a reluctance on the part of practitioners to report incidents due to fear of the consequences. This can be alleviated by two techniques: (a) staff education programs that emphasize objective reporting and (b) a clear understanding that the purpose of the incident reporting process is for documentation and follow-up and the report will not be used for disciplinary action. All incidents must be reported—even cases in which an unfavorable result follows the performance of a standard procedure. No segment of the department's staff is excluded from this responsibility.

According to Sullivan (2003), the principal purposes and functions of prompt reporting anytime an incident occurs in which a client, caregiver, staff, or volunteer could be injured or a deviation from established policy and procedures occurs are as follows:

- to identify and correct problems

- to track trends and ensure policies are revised or new systems implemented to prevent recurrence

- to identify potential lawsuits before a claim is made, triggering an immediate investigation of the event or deviation from standard protocols

- to determine whether restitution is necessary and how to explain the incident to minimize bad feelings or a perception of cover-up

- to protect staff and ensure they have the paperwork needed for workers' compensation

- to provide a permanent record of the occurrence

Although all organizations will develop their own incident report form and provide instruction for completion, van der Smissen (1990, pp. 54–56) and Sullivan (2003) suggested the following should be included in the report information:

1. identification information

2. date, time and exact location of occurrence, or if unknown, date and time of discovery

3. action of injured

4. sequence of activity

5. preventive measures by injured (e.g., What could or should have been done to have prevented the accident?)

6. procedures followed in rendering aid, including notification of caregivers

7. disposition, including securing report in a locked file

Figure 20.5 (p. 316) illustrates a report used when any risk or safety incident occurs, Figure 20.6 (p. 317) shows an example of an incident report used when any person associated with a program is involved in a potentially harmful situation, and Figure 20.7 (p. 318) is an accident report form used with participants. Incident reports are mandated by such agencies as JCAHO and by some state laws. Error notification is as critical as maintaining client documentation: This preventative measure helps to create a harm-free environment and protect the agency and professional from potential liability as well (Sullivan, 2003).

Risk Management Problems

Although there are many types of risk management problems, two categories will be considered here: negligence and malpractice. These two categories are associated with the term *liability*, which is used to describe a circumstance wherein an individual or organization has failed to carry out a responsibility required by law or through a contractual agreement. This responsibility may relate to the organization's judgment, professional practice, and/or negligence in conduct of activities and operations (van der Smissen, 1990).

Negligence is defined as "the omission to do something that a reasonable person, guided by the considerations that ordinarily regulate human affairs, would do or as doing something that a reasonable and prudent person would not do" (Marquis & Huston, 2003, p. 578). According to Kaluzny, Warner, Warren, and Zelman (1982), negligence is not a fixed standard, but must be determined in each case by reference to the situation and knowledge of the parties and the attendant circumstances.

Common acts of negligence associated with therapeutic recreation, regardless of setting, would include high-risk activities, falls, property loss, poor safety directions or measures, failure to communicate inappropriate activities, defects in equipment, and a variety of other activities or circumstances wherein the participant feels the

agency or organization failed in its responsibility to prevent the incident or injury. In most of these examples, a number of principles must apply or be proven before a claim based on negligence can be won. In other words, there is an approved standard of behavior that protects the individual against risk. In a court of law, the standard of behavior is defined by four criteria (Hronek & Spengler, 2002; Peterson & Hronek, 2003):

1. The defendant has a legal duty of care (i.e., is legally responsible) to the plaintiff.

2. The plaintiff must prove either failure to conform to standards or a breach of duty.

3. The plaintiff must prove the breach of duty was proximate cause of the injury.

4. The plaintiff must prove actual physical injury, mental anguish, or financial loss (i.e., damages).

For a claim to be considered there must be a breach of duty. While there are any number of breaches, the following are common (Hronek & Spengler, 2002; Peterson & Hronek, 2003):

- *contributory negligence:* conduct on the part of the injured party that helped to cause the accident

- *comparative negligence:* the amount of contribution to the accident assessed each party, with damages assessed accordingly

- *assumption of risk:* the injured party assumes part of the responsibility or participates in the activity knowing that harm may happen based on the activity and actions of others

- *governmental immunity:* the government is usually immune from suits related to personnel actions, budget distribution, and decisions involving planning and policy

- *failure of proof:* the injured party is unable to prove all four elements of negligence

- *act of God:* the direct cause of the accident was the result of an unusual situation or circumstance (e.g., flood, tornado)

- *notice of claim:* federal, state, and local governments require an injured or damaged person to file a claim in 30 to 120 days. This allows time for proper investigation and payment of legitimate claims. Failure to provide notice negates proceedings

- *statute of limitations:* states have varying time periods between the accident and when the suit

CINCINNATI RECREATION COMMISSION
"AS OCCURS REPORT"

LOCATION:

DATE OF HAPPENING:

REASON FOR REPORT: Crisis/Emergency   _____
(CHECK)   Accident to Employee   _____
                      Accident to Participant   _____
                      Police Action   _____
                      Potential Poor Publicity   _____
                      Vandalism/Damages   _____
                      Health/Building Violation   _____
                      City Hall Request   _____
                      Significant Staff Change   _____
                      Other: _____   _____

STATUS:

WHAT HAPPENED:

WHERE:

WHEN:

WHO INVOLVED:

WHY:

ACTION TAKEN:

SUPERVISOR MAKING REPORT:

DATE REPORT MADE:

Figure 20.5
Risk or Safety Occurrence Form

Rocky Mountain MS Center
KING ADULT DAY ENRICHMENT PROGRAM
INCIDENT REPORTING FORM

Name of Individual(s) involved: _____

_____	Client	_____	Staff
_____	Volunteer	_____	Family
_____	Other (specify) _____		

Date/Time of event _____

Description of event (Please describe in detail) _____

_____

_____

_____

Location of event _____

_____	In house	_____	On grounds
_____	Community	_____	Other (specify) _____

Nature of injury or illness (Identify body parts affected, sites of injury, etc.) _____

_____

Damage to property or equipment _____

_____

_____

Action(s) taken _____

_____

_____

_____	Emergency medical response
_____	First aid onsite
_____	Behavioral intervention/education
_____	Repairs initiated
_____	Other (specify) _____

Factor(s) contributing to incident _____

_____

_____	Equipment failure	_____	Lack of supervision
_____	Environment	_____	Inadequate instruction
_____	Act of nature	_____	Medical/Physical
_____	Other (specify) _____		

Recommendation(s) for minimizing risk in the future _____

_____

_____

Form completed by _____   Date _____

Witness to event _____   Date _____

Incident documented in chart? _____YES _____ NO   by _____

Figure 20.6
Rocky Mountain MS Center Incident Reporting Form

CRC 11 Rev. 7/03

Cincinnati Recreation Commission
Report of Accidents to Participants

Center Name _____   Date and Time of Accident _____

Location of Accident _____

Name _____   Telephone (day) _____ (evening) _____

Address _____   City/State _____ Zip _____

Date of Birth _____   Age _____ Sex _____ Race _____

Witnesses

Name _____ Address _____ Phone _____

Name _____ Address _____ Phone _____

Nature of Injury   **Part of Body Injured**

_____ Abrasion   _____ Laceration   _____ Head   _____ Arm   (R or L)

_____ Bruise/Bump   _____ Other   _____ Neck   _____ Hand   (R or L)

_____ Burn   _____   _____ Trunk   _____ Leg   (R or L)

_____ Fracture/Sprain/Strain   _____ Multiple   _____ Foot   (R or L)

                                                _____ Other _____

Description of Accident: (How did it happen? What was participant doing? Where was participant? Specify any apparatus or equipment involved and location of accident.) _____

_____

_____

Staff Person Present When Accident Occurred: _____

Action taken: _____

_____

First Aid Treatment Rendered By: _____

Describe First Aid Treatment: _____

_____

Was EMS Called?   Yes _____   No _____   Time Called _____ Arrival Time _____

Was Parent/Guardian or Emergency Contact Notified   Yes _____ No _____

Name _____ Telephone _____ Contacted By _____

Additional Comments: _____

_____

_____

Name and Title of Person Making Report _____ Date _____

Copies: (White) Director (Canary) Facility

Figure 20.7
Cincinnati Recreation Commission Report of Accidents to Participants

can be filed, one to three years for injury or property loss and up to five for wrongful death

- *waivers, releases, agreements to participate:* these documents are effective when (a) they involve adults and target specific dangers in an experience, (b) minors and their parents have read the specific dangers and rules of conduct required for safety, and (c) the parents have allowed their minor children to participate and agree to inform them of the rules and safety aspects of the program

Malpractice refers to an unreasonable lack of skill in professional duties, illegal or immoral conduct, or professional misconduct. There are many forms of malpractice, including educational and managerial. From a health care perspective, Marquis and Huston (2003, p. 78) defined it in these terms: "The failure of a person with professional training to act in a reasonable and prudent manner." Malpractice incorporates disregard of rules or principles, carelessness, and acts occurring as a result of a lack of knowledge that a professional should have (Richards & Rathburn, 1983). Similar to negligence, there must be a standard of care (i.e., degree of quality considered adequate by professional), a breach of duty, a foreseeability of harm (i.e., professional has knowledge or available information that not meeting standard of care could result in harm), failure to meet standard (i.e., provable correlation between improper care and client injury), and actual injury (Marquis & Huston, 2003). The major difference between malpractice and negligence appears to be the involvement of the professional. Any individual may be negligent, but the professional has a specific duty to perform in a way that requires some skill, knowledge, and behavior which meets a standard. Failure to meet the standard in performance of the duty by the professional constitutes malpractice (Richards & Rathburn, 1983).

Therapeutic recreation managers or practitioners have a responsibility to ensure that certain service expectations are met. Therapeutic recreation licensure laws, and to a lesser extent certification requirements, are designed to protect the public and to ensure a safe environment. When consumer expectations are not met, liability and the potential for litigation are possible.

While it is not the intent to consider the legal process if litigation arises, because it would be extensive, it is important to define terms which are used in the process. Table 20.1 provides a brief list of legal terms, which will aid in better understanding the process.

Any professional person may be called on to testify in court regarding standards of quality in his or her own agency or in some other agency or organization if there is a lawsuit. The expertise of a witness in a trial or hearing largely depends on education, experience, and recognition

by colleagues in the field. Such testimony may have a profound influence on litigation involving therapeutic recreation services or the quality of service provided by an agency or organization.

Therapeutic recreation managers need to have a basic understanding of law or familiarity with types of law. There

Table 20.1
Legal Terms

Litigation	Refers to a lawsuit.
Complaint	A document noting the complaint and asking for certain relief from the party against whom the plaintiff is complaining.
Plaintiff	The party who files the complaint.
Defendant	The party complained against, although the party may also be known as the *respondent*.
Jurisdiction	Refers to the rules governing where a case will be tried (i.e., federal, state, or local systems). May also include level of trial courts.
Summons	The complaint is filed together with a summons, and a U.S. Marshal or the Sheriff serves the summons and a copy of the complaint to all defendants.
Answer	A response to the various allegations in the complaint by the defendant.
Deposition	The giving of testimony (by plaintiff or defendant) under oath, normally in an attorney's office based upon oral questioning that is reduced to writing for later use in court or for discovery purposes.
Interrogatories	Questions in writing which must be answered by either the plaintiff or defendant in writing.
Motion	An application made to a court or judge for purpose of obtaining a rule or order directing some act to be done in favor of the applicant.
Damages	Parties to the litigation may be seeking either money or something other than money (i.e., equitable relief) as compensation for loss or injury.
Appeal	Once a judge makes a decision, either party may appeal to the appellate court. The appellate court does not retry the case but reviews the case and renders a decision. The decision may be to uphold the decision or reverse the decision and remand the case for further proceedings.

Source: Garner, B. A. (1999). *Black's law dictionary* (7th ed.). St. Paul, MN: West Group.

are a number of publications in the traditional parks, recreation, and leisure resource management field including several which focus specifically on legal aspects of parks and recreation (e.g., Hronek & Spengler, 2002; Kaiser, 1986; Peterson & Hronek, 2003; van der Smissen, 1990). *Parks & Recreation* also devotes a monthly column to this very issue. In addition, there are many health and human service publications, which address all aspects of the law and legal process that affect health service organizations. An appreciation of the law and legal process and its applications is necessary for the successful manager.

Many health care facilities cover employees in the event of a lawsuit. On the other hand, some agencies require their employees to purchase professional liability insurance. Some agencies require students to show proof of personal liability before beginning an internship or fieldwork experience.

Other Risk Management Concerns

This risk management section highlights a number of additional concerns associated with risk management programs and the therapeutic recreation manager, including patient rights, consumer charts, invasion of privacy, confidential communication, research, informed consent, and employee security and safety.

Some of the *rights of consumers* (i.e., patients) are spelled out in legal statutes or have been tested in court; others are not found in law books and might simply be considered the patient's human rights. Legal rights may vary from state to state, and therapeutic recreation managers should be aware of what their state laws require of them. Conversely, human rights are felt to exist by the very nature of the relationship between consumer and health care provider. As noted in the earlier chapter on ethics (Chapter 6), individuals have the human right to existence and, therefore, have the right to choose or make decisions concerning themselves as long as they are willing to accept any consequences. As also noted in Chapter 6, specifically defined sets of rights have developed in society by various agencies, organizations, and professional associations. A bill of rights that has become a state regulation has the most legal recourse; those developed by organizations and associations although not legally binding may influence "funding and certainly should be considered professionally binding" (Marquis & Huston, 2003, p. 591). Today's consumers are more involved and informed about their health. Their participation has led to conflicts in the areas of consumer charts and informed consent. Depending on the setting, therapeutic recreation managers need to be aware of consumer rights and adhere to them.

Malpractice claims are won or lost in many instances on the basis of *consumer charts* (i.e., patient charts); they are a legal document. A medical record and documentation are pivotal to avoiding medical malpractice (Miller & Glusko, 2003). Consumer's goals, objectives, and prognoses relative to their involvement in the program are key items to be charted. The court assumes that if one did not write something down, it did not happen. One should never wait, for instance, until the end of the day to chart if it can be helped. The quality of service given will be compromised by charting the little that can be remembered.

As noted in Chapter 19, charting is to be as thorough as possible. It is important for the therapeutic recreation manager to instill in therapeutic recreation staff the habit of accurate and concise documentation. Sloppy, illegible handwriting creates confusion and wastes time. Likewise, misspelled words and incorrect grammar creates negative impressions. Improper or too many abbreviations creates unnecessary confusion when others try to decipher the charting. In addition, one should chart as close as possible to the time an observation is made or service is provided. Last, one should never backdate or tamper with records. If this is detected, the organization and anyone involved face ethical dilemmas and possible legal action.

Therapeutic recreation managers and their staff may become liable for *invasion of privacy* if they divulge information from a consumer's medical record to improper sources or if they commit unwarranted intrusions into the consumer's personal affairs. However, there are occasions when one has a legal obligation or duty to disclose information as required by law. While therapeutic recreation practitioners enjoy taking pictures of their programs with consumer involvement, pictures should not be taken without the consumer's consent. To be completely on the safe side, the consent of the agency's or organization's administrator should also be sought.

Confidential communication is also a concern as related to treatment, observation, or conversation. It is associated with invasion of privacy. One has a professional obligation to keep secret information relating to a consumer's illness or treatment which is learned during the course of professional duties. It is a tenet of the therapeutic recreation code of ethics. There are federal and state statutes that address this matter and health care organizations have their own regulations.

With the final regulations published August 14, 2002, for HIPAA, managers are required to review their policies and procedures in view of a national health privacy framework (Buppert, 2002). Clients may set boundaries on the use and release of their health records, request and obtain audits on how providers disclosed their personal medical information during the previous six years, file complaints about privacy violation, and trigger an investigation. Under the HIPAA guidelines, providers must do the following (Buppert, 2002):

- Give patients notice that states (a) how their health information may be used, (b) their right to access their information, (c) their right to have their information amended, and (d) their right to limit disclosure of information.

- Make a good faith effort to have patients acknowledge in writing they've reviewed the notice.

- Obtain written authorization to use patient information for purposes other than treatment, payment, or operations.

- Draft policies and procedures to protect patient information (e.g., not leaving files in public places).

- Designate a professional to oversee adherence to these policies and procedures.

- Offer reasonable safeguards to administrative, technical, and physical protection of patient privacy.

- Provide employee training regarding these policies and procedures.

- Secure patient records so the minimum number of professionals who need them have access (e.g., password protected).

Research on humans requires consent to be obtained in writing from consumers or their representatives. In all health care organizations there is a committee responsible for reviewing human research proposals. As therapeutic recreation research becomes more prevalent outside university centers, therapeutic recreation managers will find more requests for access to consumers to investigate evidence-based practices. While research provides the opportunity to validate the theoretical or conceptual basis for practice, it must be proposed and conducted in a professional manner.

Informed consent is obtained when a person is undergoing a procedure, surgery, or treatment. The following three conditions define informed consent:

1. Individual capacity is determined by age and competence. Legal age status varies from state to state. Generally adults are considered competent when they can make choices and understand the consequences of those choices (Sullivan & Decker, 2001). A legal guardian or parent may give consent for a child or incompetent adult (Marquis & Huston, 2003).

2. Persons giving consent act voluntarily without force or deceit.

3. Information that is understandable must be given to clients, including an explanation of the inter-

vention and expected results, risks, benefits, alternatives. Additionally, the professional is to answer any questions or allow the client to withdraw consent at any time (Sullivan & Decker, 2001).

Each therapist delivering a service is responsible to provide informed consent information. In intervention plans, department protocols specify informed consent statements. Policies also clarify procedures to obtain informed consent from minors and persons whose competence is in question.

Safety and security of employees, interns, volunteers, contracted personnel, and temporary staff is a managerial responsibility. The health care work environment is unique. Professionals are exposed to infections, hazards, products that trigger allergic reactions and hypersensitivity, such as latex, violence-prone individuals, substance misuse, job-related stress triggered by low staffing levels or organizational changes, and vulnerable distraught clients and caregivers (Henry & Ginn, 2002; Tappen, 2001). Additional threats that may result in staff harm come from inadequate supervision, employee error, unsafe equipment, unsafe or unsecured facilities (e.g., slippery floors, unsecured continuous access health care facilities), and those caused by weather or the actions of others (e.g., crime, terrorism; Peterson & Hronek, 2003; Tappen, 2001).

The Occupational Safety and Health Act of 1970 (OSHA; P.L. 91-596) covers any workplace with at least one employee excluding government workers and domestic employees and was designed to minimize specific on-the-job risks to employees (Sullivan & Decker, 2001; Tappen, 2001). In 1980 OSHA introduced new guidelines to identify risk factors and recommend policies to mitigate workplace violence in health care and social service agencies (Henry & Ginn, 2002). Accreditation agencies (e.g., CARF, JCAHO) incorporate OSHA, Environmental Protection Agency (EPA), Food and Drug Administration (FDA), and Centers for Disease Control and Prevention (CDC) standards in their criteria.

The manager initially assesses the degree of risk and reasonable preventative actions. Then a plan to provide optimal staff protection is designed. Like client safety, the plan is monitored and evaluated by the management team. The manager oversees policy development and staff training on safe practices. A supportive work culture created by team building, staff empowerment, and effective communication is conducive to incident reporting and documentation. A manger's decisions and actions greatly influence the social climate, which in turn affects employee health and safety.

Summary

In the 21st century, the focus of risk management is primarily on client and constituent health and safety. A number of factors from technology to terrorism has created a paradigm shift and triggered adjustments in organizational cultures from cautious reporting of incidents to comprehensive safety planning and continuous quality improvements geared toward prevention.

Initial consideration was given to the importance of a risk management program and constituent safety to improving quality service. Thereafter it was noted that the elements of a risk management program included a policy statement; identification, analysis, and evaluation of risks; and selecting, implementing, and monitoring the plan. Examples of what should be included in a policy and procedures manual relative to risk management and safety were provided. The importance of an incident report was discussed followed by identifying two major risk management problems: negligence and malpractice. The section concluded with a discussion of other concerns associated with risk management including consumer rights, consumer charts, invasion of privacy, confidential communication, research, informed consent, and employee safety and security. Although the degree of involvement varies, the first-line manager is likely to be directly involved in the design and monitoring of risk management and safety programs because a major portion of a manager's responsibility is overseeing day-to-day service delivery.

Review Questions

1. Collect and compare contents of incident forms.

2. Review policy and procedures manuals to identify risk management statements.

3. Visit with risk management and quality assurance personnel to consider their roles and responsibilities.

4. Ask a therapeutic recreation manager, regardless of setting, what advice would you give to your practitioners concerning avoidance of liability suits?

5. How have federal and state legislative enactments as well as professional standards of practice and organizational standards affected therapeutic recreation service?

6. Search the Web sites listed in this chapter to identify standards affecting risk and patient safety in a variety of settings.

7. Visit a therapeutic recreation division or department, regardless of setting, and identify loss exposures.

References

American Therapeutic Recreation Association (ATRA). (2000). *Standards for the practice of therapeutic recreation, and self-assessment guide*. Alexandria, VA: Author.

Buppert, C. (2002). Safeguarding patient privacy. *Nursing Management, 33*(12), 31–36. Retrieved June 27, 2004, from Academic Search Premier (EBSCO host) database.

Carter, M. J., Van Andel, G. E., and Robb, G. M. (2003). *Therapeutic recreation: A practical approach* (3rd ed.). Prospect Heights, IL: Waveland Press.

Garner, B. A. (Ed.). (1999). *Black's law dictionary* (7th ed.). St. Paul, MN: West Group.

Hansen, M. M., Durbin, J., Cochran, R. S., Vaughn, A., Longowski, M., and Gleason, S. (2003). Do no harm provider perceptions of patient safety. *Journal of Nursing Administration, 33*(10), 507–508.

Hemman, E. A. (2002). Creating healthcare cultures of patient safety. *Journal of Nursing Administration, 32*(7/8), 419–427.

Henry, J. and Ginn, G. O. (2002). Violence prevention in healthcare organizations within a total quality management framework. *Journal of Nursing Administration, 32*(9), 479–486.

Hronek, B. B. and Spengler, J. O. (2003). *Legal liability in recreation and sports* (2nd ed.). Champaign, IL: Sagamore Publishing.

Hughes, R. G. (2004). First do no harm—Avoiding near misses. *American Journal of Nursing, 104*(5), 81–84.

Institute of Medicine (IOM). (1999). *To err is human: Building a safer health system*. Washington, DC: Author.

Institute of Medicine (IOM). (2001). *Crossing the quality care chasm: A new health system for hte 21st century*. Washington, DC: Author.

Kaiser, R. A. (1986). *Liability and law in recreation, parks, and sports*. Englewood Cliffs, NJ: Prentice Hall.

Kaiser, R. and Robinson, K. (1999). Risk management. In B. van der Smissen, M. Moiseichik, V. J. Hartenburg, and L. F. Twardzik (Eds.), *Management of park and recreation agencies* (pp. 713–742). Ashburn, VA: National Recreation and Park Association.

Kaluzny, A. D., Warner, M. D., Warren, D. C., and Zelman, W. N. (1982). *Management of health services*. Englewood Cliffs, NJ: Prentice Hall.

Kuhn, A. M. and Youngberg, B. J. (2002). The need for risk management to evolve to assure a culture of safety. *Quality and Safety in Health Care, 11*(2), 158–163. Retrieved June 27, 2004, from Infotrac One File database.

Marquis, B. L. and Huston, C. J. (2003). *Leadership roles and management functions in nursing: Theory & application* (4th ed.). Philadelphia, PA: Lippincott Williams & Wilkins.

Miller, J. and Glusko, J. (2003). Standing up to the security of medical malpractice. *Nursing Management, 34*(10), 20–21. Retrieved June 27, 2004, from Academic Search Premier (EBSCO host) database.

National Therapeutic Recreation Society (NTRS). (2004). *Standards of practice for a continuum of care in therapeutic recreation*. Retrieved September 12, 2004, from http://www.nrpa.org/content/default.aspx?documentID=530

Peters, T. (1987). *Thriving on chaos*. New York, NY: Alfred A. Knopf.

Peterson, J. A. and Hronek, B. B. (2003). *Risk management* (4th ed.). Champaign, IL: Sagamore Publishing.

Richards, E. P. and Rathburn, K. C. (1983). *Medical risk management: Preventive legal strategies for healthcare providers*. Rockville, MD: Aspen Systems Corporation.

Rios, D. (1992). Risk management. In R. M. Winslow and K. J. Halberg (Eds.), *Management of therapeutic recreation services* (pp. 163–176). Arlington, VA: National Recreation and Park Association.

Risk managers at the crossroads: Take advantage of opportunities: Be careful: The job description changes rapidly. (September, 2002). *Healthcare Risk Management, 24*(9), 97–101. Retrieved June 27, 2004, from Infotrac One File database.

Stein, J. U. (1993). Critical issues: Risk management, informed consent, and participant safety. In S. C. Grosse and D. Thompson (Eds.), *Leisure opportunities for individuals with disabilities: Legal issues* (pp. 37–52). Reston, VA: American Alliance for Health, Physical Education, Recreation and Dance.

Sullivan, G. H. (2003). Incident reports are a must. Legally speaking. *RN, 66*(11), 71–74. Retrieved June 27, 2004, from Infotrac One File database.

Sullivan, E. J. and Decker, P. J. (2001). *Effective leadership and management in nursing* (5th ed.). Upper Saddle River, NJ: Prentice Hall.

Tappen, R. M. (2001). *Nursing leadership and management: Concepts and practice* (4th ed.). Philadelphia, PA: F. A. Davis Company.

Threats create a need to coordinate with providers. (January, 2002). *Healthcare Risk Management, 24*(1), 5–6. Retrieved June 27, 2004, from Infotrac One File database.

Unsafe for every need: Too many details for patient safety goals can be trouble: Some efforts to comply with goals can backfire. (2003, August). *Healthcare Risk Management, 25*(8), 85–88. Retrieved June 27, 2004, from Infotrac One File database.

van der Smissen, B. (1990). *Legal liability and risk management for public and private entities* (Vol. 2). Cincinnati, OH: Anderson Publishing.

Vincent, C. (2003). Understanding and responding to adverse events. *New England Journal of Medicine, 348*(11), 1051–1056.

Voelkl, J. E. (1988). *Risk management in therapeutic recreation: A component of quality assurance*. State College, PA: Venture Publishing, Inc.

Chapter 21
Quality Service Management

Quality and consumer safety are major concerns of health and human service organizations and health and human service providers. The task of the therapeutic recreation manager focuses on ensuring high-quality, safe services to consumers.

In the early 1960s health and human service organizations were viewed by society as providing low-quality and ineffective services. Over time these organizations were forced to raise the cost of providing services as a result of real budget problems or deficits coupled with the determination on the part of society to hold professionals, agencies, and organizations accountable for providing safe, high-quality care.

One approach society used to assure higher quality was to take individuals, agencies, and organizations to court when services were inadequate, or outcomes in a health care facility were less than satisfying. Another was to lobby for stricter legal regulations. A third approach was simply to go elsewhere to participate in leisure experiences or, if it was health related, to seek a better service of care. In fact, all three of these approaches are very much alive today.

Each successive decade since the 1960s has seen the appearance of at least one concept or managerial method that was supposed to be the solution to improving health and human services. Many of these concepts and methods of management were borrowed from business and industry.

The 1960s saw the advent of program planning and budgeting system (PPBS). Management by objectives (MBO) appeared on the scene in the early 1970s, followed in the latter part of the decade by zero-base budgeting (ZBB) and quality circles (QC). The 1980s has been called a period of consciousness raising regarding quality (Albrecht, 1992). It was during the early 1980s that quality assurance (QA) came into being. This concept gave way in the late 1980s to the application of total quality management (TQM) and continuous quality management (CQM). In the mid-1990s the Joint Commission on Accreditation of Healthcare Organizations (JCAHO) initiated a process in the health care field called Improving Organizational Performance (IOP), also referred to as performance improvement (PI). This process incorporated core concepts of TQM and CQI (Cunninghis & Best-Martini, 1996).

The 21st century saw the paradigm shift to a culture of client safety with quality-related activities viewed as important safety checks (Caramanica, Cousino & Petersen, 2003). Improved care and safety depend on disciplines using scientific information to perform their roles (Caramanica, Cousino & Petersen, 2003). Evidence-based practices are motivated by not only minimizing risk but also maximizing the quality of care (Lee & McCormick, 2002). JCAHO's implementation of Shared Visions—New Pathways (January 1, 2004) reinforced the paradigm shift from structure and process focused accountability to comprehensive evaluation of outcomes: The provision of safe, high-quality care results from continuous systematic and operational improvements (Joint Commission Resources, 2004).

Historically, quality referred to the achievement of some preestablished standard of service. Today, quality has taken on a broader meaning. Health and human service organizations' focus and direction are provided by the quality needs and preferences of the consumer (in health care TQM the consumer is referred to as a customer) and ongoing attempts to assure their safety as well as satisfy the concerns of other stakeholders who interact with the system.

This chapter initially focuses on TQM and CQI and its unique characteristics. Attention is given to TQM and CQI and therapeutic recreation service, including its implementation into CQI. The topics are considered primarily from a health care facility perspective. A well-developed and stable quality movement in community-based therapeutic recreation divisions within public parks and recreation departments has been noted through a concept of QA since the 1980s. The benefits-based programming approach presents a framework for measuring the quality of the performance of a service (Zimmermann, Cooper & Allen, 2001). This approach gained popularity in the 1990s as professionals shifted from the identification of outputs—participants served to measurement of performance or outcomes (e.g., behavioral changes) in participants. A concluding section of the chapter addresses outcome measurement and evidence-based therapeutic recreation practices. As noted by McCormick (2003), "The future is likely to only intensify the emphasis on data-driven decision-making. Health and human service professions that are able to employ basic quantitative methodologies will be well-equipped to participate in their own destinies" (p. 224).

TQM as a Philosophy of Management

TQM as a philosophy of management differs from previous managerial waves. Past managerial waves, like PPBS, MBO, and ZBB, were essentially tool-based systems. These tools could be adopted by a health and human service organization without any significant changes being made in its basic approach to management. TQM is different. TQM is a proactive, innovative management philosophy applied to all individuals, departments, and units within an organization. TQM or a variation of it is found in nearly all general medical hospitals as well as in other types of health care facilities. When continuous quality improvement (CQI) becomes a management philosophy that permeates all aspects of an organization, CQI becomes TQM (Tappen, Weiss & Whitehead, 2004). Its goal is to involve everyone who provides care and the organization itself in the provision of the highest quality of care. TQM is based on the premises that the client is the focal point on which services depend and that the quest for quality is an ongoing process (Marquis & Huston, 2003). Thus, TQM is both process driven and consumer oriented. TQM recognizes that consumer requirements are the key to consumer quality and that these requirements change over a period of time for various reasons (e.g., age, education, economics). As a result these changes require continuous improvements in all organizational activities or processes, including agency-wide procedures, client admissions, or program registration; management functions, risk, and safety; and clinical interventions, protocols, and programs (Sullivan & Decker, 2005).

The success of TQM requires top management support and implementation over a period of time. The goal of quality management is to empower employees to make a difference in the service they provide (Sullivan & Decker, 2005). Based on the premise that employees understand and value their jobs and feel encouraged to improve through risk taking and creativity, TQM trusts employees to be knowledgeable and accountable and provides training for employees at all levels (Marquis & Huston, 2003).

A review of the literature notes the identification of six key elements of TQM as a philosophy of management (Carr & Littman, 1990; Milakovich, 1990). These six key elements are noted in Figure 21.1.

CQI and Its Characteristics

"TQM is the overall philosophy, whereas continuous quality improvement (CQI) is the process used to improve quality and performance" (Sullivan & Decker, 2005, p. 184). It blends or overlaps with earlier efforts initiated in the mid-1980s to improve quality through programs called quality assurance and risk management. CQI involves a systematic monitoring, evaluation, and improvement of the effectiveness and efficiency of work procedures through teamwork. A key characteristic of CQI is that it empowers staff to bring about improvements. As noted in Chapter 5, self-managed teams are integral to assuring quality in today's health care environment. One of these teams provides advice (e.g., improves quality). Problem-solving teams are the most frequently formed teams within TQM and CQI. They are empowered to discuss quality problems, investigate the causes of problems, recommend solutions, and, in some instances, take corrective action. According to Tappen and associates (2004), teamwork is at the core of CQI.

Historically, hospital organizations have promoted the idea of discrete and separate departments with each department's functions and processes viewed as independent from each other. This type of organizational culture promoted departmental conflicts in a "turf-oriented" environment. The CQI process crosses both departmental and discipline lines so all employees relate their jobs to the department's and organization's mission.

A basic assumption of CQI is that problems or quality deficiencies are neither the result of a single person, nor are they limited to a single department. Therefore, the development of multidisciplinary teams is used to realize improvements. A team approach requires cooperation and reduces or replaces competition as the interpersonal value to be maximized. At the same time it provides for a greater understanding of the function of each discipline in the process as well as a greater understanding of the roles and responsibilities of management (Triolo, Hansen, Kazzaz, Chung & Dobbs, 2002).

CQI recognizes two groups of consumers as customers: internal and external (Sullivan & Decker, 2005). *Inter-*

---

1. Quality is a primary organizational goal.

2. Customers determine what quality is.

3. Customer satisfaction drives the organization.

4. Variation in processes must be understood and reduced.

5. Change is continuous and is accomplished by teams and teamwork.

6. Top management commitment promotes a culture of quality, employee improvement, and a long-term perspective.

Source: Martin, L. L. (1993). *Total quality management in human services organization* (p. 24). Newbury Park, CA: Sage Publications, Inc. Reproduced with permission.

Figure 21.1
Elements of TQM as a Philosophy of Management

nal customers are the professionals and employees of the organization as well as departments or units that provide services of various kinds to each other and to the consumer. *External customers* comprise the patients or clients (i.e., consumers), friends and family members of the consumer, regulatory agents, and third-party payers. The community is also considered an external consumer because some of its needs are met by the health care facility (e.g., suppliers of equipment; Macintyre & Kleman, 1994).

Deming Cycle and CQI

A key aspect of improving quality is measurement. One tool developed to identify areas for process and quality improvement applies the scientific method found in the APIE process and active problem-solving. CQI incorporates what has come to be known as the Deming cycle—the Plan-Do-Check-Act (PDCA) cycle. It was adapted by W. Edwards Deming from Walter Shewhart (Deming, 1986). In short, this approach is similar in nature to active problem solving. Figure 21.2 illustrates the Deming cycle.

In brief, the Deming cycle begins with the plan stage. At the plan stage, a proposal is made to implement a change that hopefully will result in correcting a quality problem. The proposed improvement has not been arrived at by "seat of the pants" guesswork, but rather by the analysis of data to determine the most probable cause of the quality problem and the most likely solution. One of the CQI tools used to generate as many ideas as possible about the causes of a quality problem is brainstorming. The do stage is the actual implementation of the proposed change while holding constant all other aspects of the system or process. At the check stage, the results of the change are evaluated. Did quality improve? At the act stage, the change, if successful in improving quality is made a standard operating procedure. If the change does not improve quality, then it is abandoned, and other probable causes of the quality problem are studied. In either case, the Deming cycle is never completed; there is no end state to the pursuit of quality improvement. It focuses on continuous improvement to increase consumer satisfaction, to enhance productivity, and to lower cost (Deming, 1986; Tindill & Stewart, 1993).

What Is Quality?

In beginning this section, it is interesting to note that the first recorded instance of quality of care in hospitals was instituted in France in 1793 by the National Convention of the French Revolution. The measure decreed that there should be only one patient in a bed, as opposed to the usual two to eight, and that beds should be at least three feet apart (Rosenberg, 1987). In the United States, the oldest recognized quality control is that of hospital accreditation which began in 1918 when the American College of Surgeons (1946) drew up a one-page list of basic criteria and standards for hospital facilities. In 1951 the Joint Commission on Accreditation of Hospitals (JCAH; now JCAHO), which included the Canadian Medical Association, was formed. Standards developed by the American College of Surgeons over a period of some 35 years were adopted by JCAH. JCAH officially began to survey hospitals in 1952 using 11 standards (Scalenghe, 1994). In 1966, the Commission

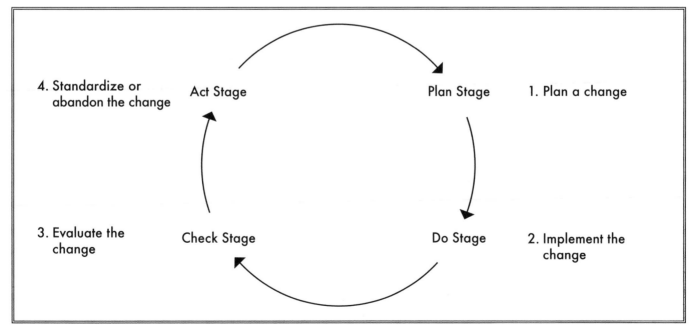

Figure 21.2
The Deming Cycle

on Accreditation of Rehabilitation Facilities (CARF) was established and entered into an administration relationship with JCAH (changed from JCAH to JCAHO in 1987) for accreditation purposes. It became an independent organization in 1971 (Toppel, Beach & Hutchinson-Troyer, 1991).

The interpretation of "quality" is embedded in the evolution of practices related to comprehensive program evaluation in health and human services (McCormick, 2003; Stumbo & Peterson, 2004). JCAHO's initial efforts to provide standards to accredit hospitals brought to the attention of the public and other professional bodies the importance of adequate care. Public Health Law 92-603 in 1972 created the establishment of Professional Standards Review Organizations (PSRO) to review quality and cost of care in federally supported programs like Medicaid and Medicare. Quality assurance programs became a focus of review processes. This concept gave way to total quality management. The focus on improvement and customer satisfaction was described as "the right thing to do the first time, on time, all the time" (Tomey, 2000, p. 383). Legislation like the Health Care Quality Improvement Act (P.L. 99-660) in 1986 created a federal data bank to identify incompetent practitioners: The Health Insurance Portability and Accountability Act (HIPAA) of 1996 created the Healthcare Integrity and Protection Data Bank (HIPDB) "to combat fraud and abuse in both health care insurance and health care delivery" (Sullivan & Decker, 2001, p. 135).

JCAHO standards in the early 1990s emphasized monitoring and evaluating important aspects of care (McCormick, 2003). The objective was to provide quality health care in the appropriate setting at the most economical cost (Tomey, 2000). Continuous quality improvement became the evaluative tool to assure quality and service delivery success. In the late 1990s JCAHO instituted its agenda for change that shifted the focus of accreditation from organizational structure and process to performance or outcomes (Marquis & Huston, 2003; McCormick, 2003). Performance improvement (PI) is concerned with identifying the needs of constituents and systematically improving organizational ability to meet these needs (McCormick, 2003). With JCAHOs Shared Visions—New Pathways in January 2004, the dimension of safety was included in the concept of quality. A number of factors contributed to concern for workplace safety and security early in the 21st century (see Chapter 20, Risk Management). As a consequence, federal agencies, regulatory bodies, and professional organizations incorporated health and safety at all times for all constituents in practice standards.

What began with accreditation efforts to evaluate adequate client care in the 1950s has evolved in the 21st century to a focus on evidence-based practices (Lee & McCormick, 2002). These practices result from systematic and operational improvements designed to provide safe, high-quality care. Evidence-based practice relies on scientific information to improve client care and safety. Although terminology changes have occurred, the intent of professional and regulatory agencies is to document quality through accountability processes that measure ongoing improvements in consumer safety and care.

No universally accepted definition of the term *quality* exists, although one is aware of it when it is lacking. Quality, like beauty, lies in the eye of the beholder. What the professional considers to be a substantial achievement, the consumer may consider to be less so. In a society where a major automobile company proclaims that "quality is job one" and a small-town doughnut shop advertises that "quality isn't our only goal, it's our standard," the precise meaning of quality is obscured. The problem is that quality actually possesses several distinct dimensions. When people disagree about what quality is, they are often simply demonstrating preferences for differing quality dimensions. As O'Leary (1993, p. 219) observed: "Quality of care is a judgment shaped by the interests of the individual or group making the judgment." In the conduct of health care utilization review, "quality" refers to the treatment process being reviewed or managed. Both provider and reviewer maintain their own perspective—the provider wants to correct the quality of his or her work, and the reviewer wants to assess the quality of that work. However, the provider is also interested in the quality of the review being conducted by the reviewer. According to Peterson (cited in Rhodes, 1991, p. 84) "between 54 and 78 percent of consumers feel that they can tell which hospitals provide quality care."

In TQM and CQI the consumer as a customer determines the relative importance of quality (Crosby, 1986; Juran, 1989). As Kaluzny and McLaughlin (1994, p. 202) noted, "[It]… is a shift from a technical definition of quality to a recognition that effective care requires a subjective as well as technical evaluation. Specifically, a definition of health care quality is inadequate if it does not include the customer." In general, this is the way it should be since consumers in health care facilities tend to judge quality of care by the interpersonal aspects of the clinical process because these aspects are the most obvious to them. Consumer-defined quality, regardless of setting, represents a way of achieving the health and human service goal of putting the needs of consumers first.

The consumer is not the only one concerned with quality. Each department within a health care facility is concerned with quality as determined by various organizational standards. Organizations such as JCAHO, CARF, National Committee for Quality Assurance (NCQA), Centers for Medicare and Medicaid Services (CMS), and community-based leisure services agencies have set expectations about quality that must be met. Quality is inherent in the American Therapeutic Recreation Association

(ATRA) and National Therapeutic Recreation Society (NTRS) standards of practice. Third-party payers have specific perceptions of quality—ones that can be described by cost per case, length of stay, and other measurable criteria. Quality is also found in statutes which have been enacted over the years at all levels of government to protect the public. Other quality dimensions associated with health and human services would include accessibility, consistency, humanness, effectiveness, efficiency, legitimacy (i.e., conformance to social and ethical principles), and equity (Tappen, Weiss & Whitehead, 2004).

Quality is a moving target. Because expectations constantly change, what is considered exceptional quality today will be routinely expected tomorrow. Unfortunately, quality is the most difficult, expensive (at times), and time-consuming factor to evaluate. Regardless of the quality views of professions and professionals, and the quality dimensions and standards specified in regulations and laws, the end result is quite clear: Quality is determined, or defined, by consumers (Martin, 1993).

QA and CQI Comparison and Therapeutic Recreation

Quality Assurance

Around the mid-1980s therapeutic recreation managers and practitioners became involved with the concept of quality assurance (QA), a process directed toward ongoing monitoring and evaluation of the quality of therapeutic recreation services provided in health care facilities through standards, and implementing mechanisms for ensuring that these standards were met to evaluate therapeutic recreation services. Others added to this the giving of feedback to individual and group providers of the services so that services could be improved. Over the intervening years, therapeutic recreation managers and practitioners working in community-based leisure service agencies and organizations integrated concepts of QA into their programs and services.

While several conceptual frameworks exist regarding quality service within health and human service organizations, Avedis Donabedian's (1969) approach to improving the efficiency and effectiveness of the services rendered had the widest application and is associated with QA. Donabedian's framework has the advantage of being simple yet comprehensive.

Comprehensive QA includes the structure in which service is given, the process of service, and the outcome of that service (Donabedian, 1969). The ATRA *Standards for the Practice of Therapeutic Recreation and Self-Assessment Guide* (2000) are presented in the format of structure,

process and outcome. Moreover, the standards are relative in two areas: (a) direct practice in therapeutic recreation and (b) management of the practice in therapeutic recreation. The latter area is concerned with monitoring and evaluating practice to improve services. These standards, according to ATRA, apply in a variety of settings. The NTRS *Standards of Practice for a Continuum of Care in Therapeutic Recreation* (2004) note standards relative to application of the therapeutic recreation process in a variety of settings. Criteria are outlined within each standard but not in the structure, process, and outcome format. Consideration of the different measures of quality as applied to a therapeutic recreation department follows.

Structure

Structure not only refers to the setting or location where services are provided but also includes the resources. While the setting is perhaps the easiest of the three aspects to measure, it is many times overlooked in some evaluation procedures. The following offers examples of some of the structural aspects:

- *facilities:* accessibility, adequate space to conduct programs, convenience of areas, safety

- *equipment:* adequate supplies and equipment, staff ability to use it

- *staff:* credentials (e.g., state licensure, certification), continuing education and professional development, performance evaluation, absenteeism

- *finances:* adequate budget, adequate salaries

- *management:* written statements of purpose, philosophy, and objectives; ethical statement of practice; scope of practice

- *organizational arrangement:* management structure, organization of practice, styles of supervision

- *legal authority:* accreditation, licensure

- *program or treatment plan:* procedures associated with assessment, planning, implementation, evaluation, and documentation of treatment plan appropriateness

None of these structural factors alone can guarantee that good service will be given, but they are factors that make good service more likely to occur (Tappen, Weiss & Whitehead, 2004). These factors "ensure a safe and effective environment but do not address the actual care provided" (Marquis & Huston, 2003, p. 451). As Riley (1991, p. 57) noted, "…structure variables measure the probability or propensity for quality care." Without adequate policies and facilities, for example, the process of delivering service is impeded, and outcomes are adversely affected.

Process

Process refers to the nature and sequence of activities carried out by therapeutic recreation management and practitioners. It usually involves two aspects: the technical and the interpersonal. Process standards assess the performance of specified and, at times, prescribed therapeutic recreation activities. Protocols and best-practice guidelines standardize practices and serve as process standards. It includes psychosocial interventions (such as teaching a skill or leisure education), program leadership, formulating an individual treatment plan, assisting in discharge planning and referral, evaluating (i.e., formative and summative) and documenting intervention results as well as contributing to the advancement of therapeutic recreation as a profession through participating in research projects. It also encompasses what is and what is not done, and what should or should not be done. A critical difference between structural and process standards is that process standards require a professional judgment to determine whether a criterion has been met.

There are several ways to collect process data. The most direct is by observation of practitioner activities. Another is self-reporting done by the practitioner. A third source is a review of the chart or records that are kept, and last, various kinds of assessment tools can be used.

Whatever source of data collection is used, some set of objectives (i.e., protocols or best practices) is needed as a standard against which to compare the activities. This set of objectives should be specific and measurable such as listing the steps in the development of a treatment plan. The objective is not only to collect valid, appropriate, and comprehensive data but also to collect these data in an efficient, standardized, and error-free manner.

Outcome

An *outcome* is the end result of a process and is the product of actions. It refers to the results of the activities in which the practitioners have been involved. The result of a process must be consumer oriented; adequate quality leaves the consumer in a state or condition that is considered desirable. Outcome measures evaluate the efficiency and effectiveness of these activities by answering questions such as the following:

- Did the service to the consumer improve?

- Is the consumer more independent?

- Were there unexpected or unanticipated consequences to activity participation?

Other consumer outcomes might include rehabilitation potential, health status, satisfaction, costs, resource consumption, and quality of life, including leisure-related knowledge, skills, and awareness (Stumbo, 2003a). The focus on safe, high-quality services through continuous systematic performance improvement broadens the realm of relevant outcomes from the client to a number of internal and external audiences; outcomes valued by multiple stakeholders are considered as are the system-wide influences impacting safety and quality in the environment (McCormick, 2003).

Whether the questions are general or specific, a major problem in using outcome measures in evaluation is that they are influenced by many factors, not by just one factor or by just one person (e.g., medication, diagnosis, assessments by various staff disciplines, treatment plans, documentation, age of the consumer). Outcomes are particularly sensitive to subjective value judgments. Thus, it is extremely important to determine criteria that indicate if standards are being met and to what degree they are met. Three forms of outcome measures are goals and objectives, standards and criteria, and instruments.

Goals and objectives are an important measurement device in any organization. Therapeutic recreation departments use goal and objective statements to provide direction and to identify the degree to which a program achieves its intended goals and objectives. Therapeutic recreation practitioners incorporate goals and objectives into the design of comprehensive and specific therapeutic recreation programs (Stumbo & Peterson, 2004). Measurable improvements evaluate change in clients as a result of their program participation (Carruthers, 2003). "Effectiveness evaluation determines the extent to which a program meets its intended goals and objectives" (Carruthers, 2003, p. 187).

The basic principles of outcome measurement rely on well-defined standards. Standards are a criterion for judging the work of a practitioner, team, or organization and they vary in their specificity. They supply a basis for comparison. Within an organization they form a consensus of professional thinking. In addition, standards are established and derived from a variety of sources. Managers must determine what standards will be used to measure the quality of therapeutic recreation service, then develop and implement a quality improvement program that can measure end results against the developed standards. Thereafter, managers have the responsibility to monitor the quality of the care or service to the consumer.

The major reason for setting standards is to increase objectivity by defining as clearly as possible what is acceptable and what is not acceptable. In addition, they must be achievable, measurable, and objective (Marquis & Huston, 2003). Realistic standards that are achievable lessen the likelihood of frustration, increase the motivation to perform well, and are more acceptable to staff. Without this approach, the judgments that take place in the evaluation process can be variable, subjective, and susceptible to the biases of the evaluator. The ATRA *Standards for the Practice of Therapeutic Recreation and Self-Assessment Guide* (2000) and the NTRS *Standards of Practice for a Continuum of Care in Therapeutic Recreation* (2004) are the standards for quality in therapeutic recreation service. They also define the scope and dimensions of professional therapeutic recreation. ATRA (2000) has published a self-assessment guide with its standards. The guide incorporates a rating scale for use by the manager or practitioner in evaluating the various standards. The final score provides information about how well there is compliance with the standards. In addition to the guide, ATRA has developed a "documentation audit" form which focuses on whether or not standards of therapeutic recreation practice are being met. The audit provides the manager or practitioner with a means to determine the quality of services rendered.

A second function of standards is to communicate clearly to everyone involved (i.e., staff, administrators, consumers, accreditors, and regulators) what level of service is expected in the department. This can be done only if the standards are available to everyone. The implementation of standards and their measurements for evaluating performance may vary from organization to organization, the purpose of the evaluation, and the evaluator.

There are a variety of instruments that can be used to measure outcomes in therapeutic recreation practice. Some of these include Comprehensive Evaluation in Recreational Therapy (CERT), Psych/Behavioral, Community Integration Program (CIP), and Leisure Competence Measure (burlingame & Blaschko, 2002). The therapeutic recreation practitioner in a medical rehabilitation setting will undoubtedly use the Uniform Data System for Medical Rehabilitation's Functional Independence Measure (FIM; 1993), which measures functional competence of the consumer in several areas that are important in rehabilitation and return to the community (see Table 21.1). The findings can be applied to a treatment plan in association with leisure skills, leisure education and resources, and community reintegration. There are also program-oriented instruments that involve a number of disciplines providing services as opposed to a single discipline-oriented instrument.

Further consideration of QA from a therapeutic recreation perspective is found in *Quality Management* edited by Bob Riley (1991) and in *Quality Assurance* by Richelle N. Cunninghis and Elizabeth Best-Martini (1996) as related to activity programs in long-term care facilities.

Continuous Quality Improvement

With the advent of CQI in health care facilities in the early 1990s, QA became integrated into CQI. The major problem with QA was that it looked at the past or what had been delivered, identified areas for improvement, and made changes. In summary, it was retrospective in its approach, identified problems impacting care outcomes, and lacked information on indicators of quality (McCormick, 2003).

According to Mayfield (1992), CQI complements and broadens the scope of QA. In many respects, QA can

Table 21.1
Functional Independence Measure

Description of the Levels of Function and Their Scores
Independent
Another person is not required for the activity (NO HELPER).
7 **Complete Independence**—All of the tasks described as making up the activity are typically performed safely, without modification, assistive devices, or aids, and within a reasonable amount of time.
6 **Modified Independence**—One or more of the following may be true: the activity requires an assistive device, the activity takes more than reasonable time, or there are safety (i.e., risk) considerations.
Dependent
Subject requires another person for either supervision or physical assistance in order for the activity to be performed, or it is not performed (REQUIRES HELPER).
Modified Dependence: The subject expends half (50%) or more of the effort. The levels of assistance required are:
5 **Supervision or Setup**—Subject requires no more help than standby, cueing or coaxing, without physical contact, or, helper sets up needed items or applies orthoses or assistive/ adaptive devices.
4 **Minimal Contact Assistance**—Subject requires no more help than touching, and expends 75% or more of the effort.
3 **Moderate Assistance**—Subject requires more help than touching, or expends half (50%) or more (but less than 75%) of the effort.
Complete Dependence: The subject expends less than half (less than 50%) of the effort. Maximal or total assistance is required, or the activity is not performed. The levels of assistance required are:
2 **Maximal Assistance**—Subject expends less than 50% of the effort, but at least 25%.
1 **Total Assistance**—Subject expends less than 25% of the effort.

be considered the baseline of service delivery while CQI considers and implements improved service delivery. The integration of QA and CQI provides an opportunity to build on the better of these two approaches to reach the goal of continual improvement in quality (Tindill & Stewart, 1993). There is a fine line that differentiates QA from CQI. The focus for CQI is not on assuring quality but rather on continuously improving the quality of consumer services. The concept is that there is always room for improvement (Peters, 1993). In reality, CQI is concerned with excellence.

CQI, as has been noted, is a movement from the standard definition of quality, which looked back at the work already done, to a method of improvement. CQI involves defining and meeting consumer needs that eventually lead to exemplary services (Berwick, 1990). It requires the health care facility or any health and human service organization that adopts CQI to demonstrate a consistent endeavor to deliver consumer care and service that is optimal within available resources and consistent with achievable goals. Peters (1993) noted that CQI is concerned with improving QA. She further commented that quality monitoring and evaluation is an ongoing process, "…not retroactive and is based on reality, what is actually being done, not what was supposed to be done" (p. 82). In addition, according to Berwick (1990), QA is a specialized staff function while CQI is the primary job of every manager because it involves an organization-wide commitment to excellence. CQI is concerned not only with doing what is good now but also improving or making it better than what it is. To modify an old adage, "If it ain't broke, it can be improved."

Application of CQI to therapeutic recreation requires a different way of thinking about how to provide services to the consumer. The focus of attention is on the consumer, but the structure, process, and outcome are similar in nature to QA.

Consumer

The term *consumer* (or *customer*) is used to signify the role that a person or unit plays when receiving the service. Consumers, as noted earlier, can be external—meaning the consumer, family, and the general community. Consumers can also be internal—internal consumers are all departments or units that exchange input or output to ensure CQI. The therapeutic recreation department is a consumer in the hospital, but it is not the only one. Physicians are consumers for whom the therapeutic recreation department provides input. The therapeutic recreation department is a consumer of the medical records department if the department is requesting information about a patient.

Structure

Structure incorporates all of those resources under which it is likely that good therapeutic recreation service will take place and that good consumer outcomes will occur. However, it does not ensure that consumer goals will be achieved; process and outcome are involved.

Process

Process is the combination of activities, actions, or steps that repeatedly come together to transform input into output or have impact on the consumer. Typically applied to therapeutic recreation service, process tells what the practitioner will do and how—actual interaction between practitioner and consumer or consumer group. While outcomes are the ultimate measure, how one achieves the results or outcomes is extremely important. Process is analogous to a football game. One doesn't score any points looking at the scoreboard. The game is won and lost on the field. The scoreboard only records the outcome. Process focuses on setting standards, determining criteria to meet those standards, data collection, evaluating how well the criteria have been met, making changes based on the evaluation, and following up on change implementation.

Outcome

Outcomes represent the ultimate goal of therapeutic recreation service measurement, for if the consumer outcome is unsatisfactory, it matters little what therapeutic recreation processes were used or what resources (i.e., structure) supported the treatment plan. Outcome focuses on the benefit to the consumer. Benefit refers to a judgment that is made in relation to the values and expectations of the customer relative to the service. Managers have a responsibility to assess and promote consumer satisfaction whenever possible. One must keep in mind that outcome is in the eyes of the beholder. Thus, any study of benefits requires an understanding of and knowledge about the needs and expectations of the consumer. Only when the consumer is involved in the process can therapeutic recreation managers or practitioners truly understand the consumer's point of view. While there are obvious direct care outcomes, there are also behavioral, physiological, and psychosocial outcomes (Batalden, 1993).

To assist in determining better outcomes in association with CQI as well as fiscal responsibility, a tool called *critical paths* was implemented in many health care facilities in the late 1980s. Critical paths are a compilation of multidisciplinary input driven by a specific time oriented outcome. Petryshen and Petryshen (1993/1994, pp. 111–112) described the implications of critical paths as follows:

> Identification of critical steps in the management
> of patient care facilitates consistent treatment

leading to discharge within the recommended length of stay. A consistent method of performing care activities is established, and caregivers are provided with advance knowledge of the outcomes toward which they are working, how these outcomes will be attained, and the time frame within which they should be achieved. Furthermore, because an entire course of care is outlined on a single care map, caregivers from all disciplines follow the same plan. A true interdisciplinary approach to care is created and, from an economic perspective, inappropriate, redundant, and excessive use of resources is minimized. As well, standard care plans for case types promote increased productivity through more efficient use of staff since the time required for caregivers to develop individualized plans for patients with similar needs is significantly reduced.

Petryshen and Petryshen (1993/1994) also noted that critical paths have therapeutic recreation implications in providing opportunities for program evaluation and research. Specifically, managers and practitioners "will be in a position to make credible decisions, discontinue ineffective routines, and refine practice patterns to the benefit of the patient and the health care system" (p. 112).

Indicators

Associated with QA and CQI are indicators. An indicator is a predetermined (i.e., written), measurable, well-defined component of an aspect of care or service. Indicators may evaluate the structure, process, or outcome of service although they are more associated with outcome. Structural indicators may include staffing, correct use of equipment, and adherence to policies. Processes consist of appropriate assessment of the consumer on admission and documentation of therapeutic recreation service given. The actual results of consumer service are the outcomes that show or reflect achievement or nonachievement of goals. In developing indicators the following guidelines need to be kept in mind:

1. Decide whether the indicators should evaluate compliance, appropriateness, or outcome. *Compliance* refers to procedures found within policies while *appropriateness* is concerned with the adequacy of service, and *outcome* is the result of the performance (or nonperformance) of a process.

2. Indicators should be limited to a few important or critical indicators based on standards.

3. Indicators should be stated in positive terms.

4. Indicators should ask for one piece of information. Each point to be addressed should be the subject of a separate indicator.

5. Indicators should be reliable, valid, and tested. Indicators are usually selected from practice standards, policies, protocols, and guidelines. After they are developed, others should review them for clarity. The reliability and validity of the indicators should be evaluated.

6. Determine if exceptions to the indicators will be allowed. While there should be no exceptions, there may be situations that do develop.

7. Establish the threshold for evaluation. The threshold for evaluation of an indicator is established before the monitoring process begins. When the results are less than hoped for, some type of problem solving is indicated. The projected threshold is the number or percentage established when the monitoring activity is developed or planned. Thresholds are usually expressed by number or percentage. It is unrealistic to set thresholds for evaluation at 100% although the percentage may change after testing.

Figure 21.3 (p. 334) illustrates an example of therapeutic recreation indicators which may form a therapeutic recreation section within a hospital or rehabilitation patient survey or be a separate form distributed to patients by the therapeutic recreation department at the time of discharge. The survey form can be either an open or closed questionnaire. The department would determine the threshold of acceptance. For example, 95% of the time consumers would rate each item as good or better. Examples of other types of indicators might include the following:

- *Assessment*—Complete a leisure assessment of patient leisure abilities within 72 hours after admission to the unit 95% of the time.

- *Program*—Patient is seen by the therapeutic recreation specialist a minimum of three times during hospitalization 95% of the time.

- *Discharge plan*—Complete a discharge plan with patient involvement no later than 24 hours prior to discharge 90% of the time.

Outcome Measures and Evidence-Based Therapeutic Recreation Practices

Once an organization shifts the focus from systematic and continuous performance improvement to measurement of outcomes and indicators of safe, high-quality services, the therapeutic recreation department must determine what values are important in providing services. Covey (1990) stated that these values serve as maps and enable one to know where one is going. Every person and every organization has values that mark their way in life. People see the world through their values. Moreover, values are the motivation of their beliefs and actions and are the energy source of accomplishments. Managing by values is rendering services with personal and organizational values clearly defined. Decisions about future directions to take or about what to do in a given situation can then be based on those values. Thus the therapeutic recreation manager manages by facts (i.e., values) and not by intuition.

The values important to the therapeutic recreation department are set forth in the mission statement. Quality is determined by the degree to which the department adheres to its mission and those values, or how well the department is doing what it set out to do as defined in its mission or purpose.

The next step is quality planning. In quality planning one looks to professional standards, which are internal or external quality mechanisms set in place for the purpose of maintaining and/or improving certain aspects of quality. Services provided must be safe and effective, and result in the essential outcomes within a reasonable amount of time and cost. Professionals plan to measure the final results of interventions in which consumers are involved (Neuman,

2003). Thus a critical planning task is identification of targeted consumer goals expected to result from standardized interventions (Stumbo, 2000, 2003a; Stumbo & Peterson, 2004). Therapists use three criteria to judge the appropriateness of outcome measures, relevance, importance, and attainment: "What outcomes are relevant? What outcomes carry the greatest importance to clients? What outcomes are attainable during (especially brief) interventions?" (Stumbo, 2000, p. 37). Targeted outcomes are based on evidence of empirically based, integrative, standardized services resulting in predictable, measurable changes in clients (Stumbo, 2000). Because APIE is a systems approach, it assists in the planning and evaluation of quality indicators. The process describes casual relationships between selected interventions and client changes outlined in targeted outcomes.

After the completion of quality planning, organizing quality becomes the next major task. During this step, the manager decides how to measure the targeted outcomes. This involves

1. translating the requirements of customers and/or professional standards into operational specifications

2. selecting performance measures or key indicators

3. weighing performance measures or key indicators

4. planning and monitoring key indicators

This approach provides a scientific basis for making decisions. A systematic approach is used to identify documentable information that demonstrates therapeutic recreation intervention effectiveness (Stumbo, 2003a). Outcome measurement quantifies data and compares relative costs of achieving outcomes (Neuman, 2003). Performance measures quantify efficiency and effectiveness of service-

	Circle the number that best represents your feelings				
	very poor	poor	fair	good	very good
The courtesy of your therapeutic recreation therapist	1	2	3	4	5
The degree to which you were able to participate in setting your therapeutic recreation goals	1	2	3	4	5
How well did the therapeutic recreation specialist explain your treatment and progress?	1	2	3	4	5
The adequacy of your therapeutic recreation program	1	2	3	4	5
The availability of recreational activities (e.g., crafts, games, entertainment)	1	2	3	4	5
The helpfulness of the instruction/information given about your postdischarge recreational activities	1	2	3	4	5

Figure 21.3
Therapeutic Recreation Survey Form

delivery methods (Zimmermann, Cooper & Allen, 2001). Professionals choose performance measures that reflect cost, quality, and time concerns (Leandri, 2001). Cost measures cover economical aspects of performance like cost-benefit analysis. Quality or effectiveness measures address how well services meet client needs, preferences and satisfaction; and, contribute to behavioral changes and quality of life issues like leisure options. Time measures reflect efficiency of using resources to deliver services (e.g., unit cost per participant, performance relative to regulatory or professional practice standards; Zimmermann, Cooper & Allen, 2001). Once the manager decides how to measure outcomes, training is planned to assure staff preparedness to continuously monitor and document relationships among interventions and consumer outcomes.

The last step is evaluating quality using a systems approach with a feedback loop. The quality improvement process itself deals with structure and process while the ultimate improvement is reflected in the outcome. Evaluating quality requires evaluating outcome of the implemented therapeutic recreation plan. It is essential to monitor both process and outcome indicators to determine if modifications in service delivery (processes) are necessary to improve (performance). The application of systems like APIE is cyclical: The manager has evidence to make decisions relative to structure and process factors that impact outcomes or benefits. With outcomes measurement, therapeutic recreation practices are based on evidence of practice effectiveness (e.g., Does *A* program produce *B* outcomes with *C* consumers?; Stumbo & Peterson 2004). Using evidence-based practices, professionals rely on the best available information gained through scientific processes to improve performance and remain accountable.

"Evidence-based practice improves the predictability and causality of service outcomes and provides regulators, payers, and consumers increased assurance of quality care" (Stumbo, 2003b, pp. 25–26). In an evidence-based setting, a therapist is providing the best possible program that is known to have the most desirable, intended, and meaningful outcomes (Stumbo, 2003b). Evidence-based practice or empirically based evidence is an accountability tool. "It is motivated not only by the minimization of clinical risk but also by maximizing the quality of care" (Lee & McCormick, 2002, p. 166). Accountability is a key managerial and ethical responsibility. Consequently, the manager operationalizes evidence-based practice by supporting systematic research and effectiveness evaluations: This is accomplished by using findings in practice and continuously evaluating the impact of change in practice (Stumbo, 2003b). "Evidence-based practice is a reflective process" (Lee & McCormick, 2002, p. 167). Reflective practitioners gather and assess evidence as they plan interventions. Staff that are encouraged to use the APIE process or the

Plan-Do-Check-Act model as decisions are made concerning program offerings are developing the ability to "think on their feet" and reflect, as services are offered, roots of evidence-based practice.

To summarize, CQI consists of four basic elements. The first of these elements is teamwork. A team approach is essential to effective CQI, especially the ability to function as part of an interdisciplinary team in which each discipline is accorded recognition for its contribution to consumer care and service. Consumer participation is the next element. In the past, the consumer's point of view was often omitted. Today, both consumer outcomes and consumer satisfaction are considered. The third and perhaps most essential element of measurement is that of work processes. This includes both baseline measures and measures after changes have been instituted. The data collection and evaluation are as objective as possible. The final element is the adequacy of the resources available to support improvement. This ranges from administrative support for any changes indicated to adequate staff, adequate equipment, and technology.

Although each term—quality assurance, continuous quality improvement, and performance improvement—may have a unique meaning created by its sponsoring agency (e.g., JCAHO, CARF, NCQA, CMS), the goal is similar—"to document accountability for improvement of health care services for all individuals" (Stumbo & Peterson, 2004, p. 388). Accountability is concerned with the extent to which program's goals are achieved and whether resources are used efficiently. Improvement refers to changes made to increase service effectiveness and efficiency to ensure consumers receive the safest, highest quality of care with available resources (Widmer, Zabriskie & Wells, 2003). Decision making is an end result of evaluating; evaluation provides information to the manager to make informed decisions for future action (Stumbo & Peterson, 2004). When a therapeutic recreation manager uses the APIE process, performance measures identify expected outcomes reached through standardized interventions. Decisions concerning future services are based on knowledge and clinical judgment that guide evidence-based practices.

Summary

This chapter focused initially on understanding TQM and CQI and its characteristics, including the Deming cycle in health and human service organizations. Since the early 1990s, TQM has been used to identify an innovative management philosophy which focuses on quality service and is applied throughout many health and human service organizations today. TQM is process-driven and consumer outcome oriented. With the advent of TQM came CQI which replaced QA. CQI is concerned with continuous service improvement to increase customer satisfaction while QA is retrospective in its approach to service improvement. However, QA can serve as a baseline for CQI. Consideration was also given to defining quality from various perspectives—consumer, standards, and organization. Thereafter, the concepts of QA and CQI were compared in relation to structure, process, and outcomes in association with therapeutic recreation service. The function of critical paths and indicators to improve quality service was noted. This chapter concluded with the application of outcome measurement and evidence-based practices in therapeutic recreation. A shift to client safety with quality-related activities viewed as safety checks requires therapeutic recreation managers to use evidence-based practices like the APIE process to improve care and safety while documenting measurable outcomes. An overview of how to implement outcome measurement in therapeutic recreation practices was briefly considered.

Review Questions

1. Complete an internet search for the ATRA (http://www.atra-tr.org) and NTRS (http://www.nrpa.org) standards of practice. Identify how performance improvement and outcome measurement are incorporated into the standards.

2. How can a therapeutic recreation manager determine the effectiveness of a program or services? Its efficiency?

3. Interview therapeutic recreation managers in various settings regarding how they measure the quality of their services. Compare results and discuss.

4. Conduct an Internet search of selected national organizations that look at outcomes (e.g., CMS, http://www.cms.hhs.gov; NCQA, http://www.ncqa.org; CARF, http://www.carf.org; JCAHO, http://www.jcaho.org). Identify criteria effecting therapeutic recreation services.

5. Generate examples of structure, process, and outcome indicators.

6. Discuss the differences and interrelations among risk management, TQM, and CQI initiatives.

7. Describe the therapeutic recreation manager's role in total quality management within a health care facility or a community-based leisure service agency.

References

Albrecht, K. (1992). *The only thing that matters*. New York, NY: Harper Business.

American College of Surgeons. (1946). 29th annual hospital standardization report. *Bulletin of the American College of Surgeons, 31*(4), 301–308.

American Therapeutic Recreation Association (ATRA). (2003). *Standards for the practice of therapeutic recreation and self-assessment guide*. Alexandria, VA: Author.

Batalden, P. B. (1993). Organization-wide quality improvement in health. In A. F. Al-Assaf and J. A. Schmele (Eds.), *The textbook of total quality in healthcare* (pp. 60–74). Delray Beach, FL: Saint Lucie Press.

Berwick, D. M. (1990). Quality: How do QI and QA differ? Expert illustrates the answer. *Hospital Management Review, 9,* 2–13.

burlingame, j. and Blaschko, T. M. (2002). *Assessment tools for recreational therapy and related fields* (3rd ed.). Ravensdale, WA: Idyll Arbor.

Caramanica, L., Cousino, J. A., and Petersen, S. (2003). Four elements of a successful quality program, alignment, collaboration, evidence-based practice, and excellence. *Nursing Administration Quarterly, 27*(4), 336–343. Retrieved July 16, 2004, from Academic Search Premier (EBSCO host) database.

Carr, D. and Littman, I. (1990). *Excellence in government—Total quality management in the 1990s*. Arlington, VA: Coopers and Lybrand.

Carruthers, C. (2003). Objectives-based approach to evaluating the effectiveness of therapeutic recreation services. In N. J. Stumbo (Ed.), *Client outcomes in therapeutic recreation services* (pp. 185–200). State College, PA: Venture Publishing, Inc.

Covey, S. R. (1990). *The seven habits of highly effective people*. New York, NY: Simon & Schuster.

Crosby, P. B. (1986). *Quality is free: The art of making quality certain*. New York, NY: McGraw-Hill.

Cunninghis, R. N. and Best-Martini, E. (1996). *Quality assurance* (2nd ed.) Ravensdale, WA: Idyll Arbor.

Deming, W. D. (1986). *Out of the crisis*. Cambridge, MA: MIT Center for Advanced Engineering Study.

Donabedian, A. A. (1969). *A guide to medical care administration, II: Medical care appraisal—Quality & utilization*. New York, NY: American Public Health Association.

Joint Commission Resources. (2004). The launch of Shared Visions—New Pathways. *Joint Commission Perspectives, 24*(1), 1–2. Retrieved July 24, 2004, from http://www.jcaho.org/accredited+organizations/svnp/jcp-2004-january.pdf

Juran, J. (1989). *Juran on leadership for quality: An executive handbook*. New York, NY: Free Press.

Kaluzny, A. D. and McLaughlin, C. P. (1994). Managing transitions: Assuring the adoption and impact of TQM. In C.

P. McLaughlin and A. D. Kaluzny (Eds.), *Continuous quality improvement in healthcare* (pp. 198–206). Gaithersburg, MD: Aspen Publishers.

Leandri, S. J. (2001). Measures that matter: How to fine-tune your performance measures. *The Journal for Quality and Participation Profound Change at Work 24*(1), 39–41.

Lee, Y. and McCormick, B. P. (2002). Toward evidence-based therapeutic recreation practice. In D. R. Austin, J. Dattilo, and B. P. McCormick (Eds.), *Conceptual foundations for therapeutic recreation* (pp. 165–184). State College, PA: Venture Publishing, Inc.

Macintyre, K. and Kleman, C. C. (1994). Measuring customer satisfaction. In C. P. McLaughlin and A. D. Kaluzny (Eds.), *Continuous quality improvement in healthcare* (pp. 102–126). Gaithersburg, MD: Aspen Publishers.

Marquis, B. L. and Huston, C. J. (2003). *Leadership roles and management functions in nursing: Theory & application* (4th ed.). Philadelphia, PA: Lippincott Williams & Wilkins.

Martin, L. L. (1993). *Total quality management in human services organization.* Newbury Park, CA: Sage Publications.

Mayfield, S. (1992). Quality assurance and continuous quality improvement. In R. M. Winslow and K. J. Halberg (Eds.), *The management of therapeutic recreation service* (pp. 137–162). Arlington, VA: National Recreation and Park Association.

McCormick, B. P. (2003). Outcomes measurement as a tool for performance improvement. In N. J. Stumbo (Ed.), *Client outcomes in therapeutic recreation services* (pp. 221–232). State College, PA: Venture Publishing, Inc.

Milakovich, M. (1990). Total quality management for public sector productivity improvement. *Public Productivity and Management Review, 14,* 19–32.

National Therapeutic Recreation Society (NTRS). (2004). *Standards of practice for a continuum of care in therapeutic recreation.* Retrieved September 12, 2004, from http://www.nrpa.org/content/default.aspx?documentID=530

Neuman, K. M. (2003). Developing a comprehensive outcomes management program: A ten-step process. *Administration in Social Work, 27*(1), 5–21.

O'Leary, T. (1993). Defining performance of organizations. *Journal of Quality Improvement, 19*(7), 218–223.

Peters, D. A. (1993). A new look for quality in home care. In D. F. Al-Assaf and J. A. Schmele (Eds.), *The textbook of total quality in healthcare* (pp. 80–90). Delray Beach, FL: Saint Lucie Press.

Petryshen, P. M. and Petryshen, P. R. (1993/1994). Managed care: Shaping the delivery of healthcare and creating an expanded role for the caregiver. In R. Kunstler (Ed.), *Annual in Therapeutic Recreation* (Vol. 4, pp. 108–114). Hattiesburg, MS: American Theraeutic Recreation Association.

Rhodes, M. (1991). The use of patient satisfaction data as an outcome monitor in therapeutic recreation quality assurance. In B. Riley (Ed.), *Quality management: Applications for therapeutic recreation* (pp. 83–106). State College, PA: Venture Publishing, Inc.

Riley, B. (Ed.). (1991). *Quality management: Applications for therapeutic recreation.* State College, PA: Venture Publishing, Inc.

Rosenberg, C. E. (1987). *The care of strangers.* New York, NY: Basic Books.

Scalenghe, R. (1994, October 13). *In introduction to the JCAHO.* Presentation at the National Therapeutic Recreation Institute, Minneapolis, MN.

Stumbo, N. J. (2000). Outcome measurement in health care: Implications for therapeutic recreation. In B. Riley (Ed.), *Annual in Therapeutic Recreation, Special Edition: Outcome Measurement in Therapeutic Recreation* (Vol. 9; pp. 1–8). Hattiesburg, MS: American Therapeutic Recreation Association.

Stumbo, N. J. (2003a). Outcomes, accountability, and therapeutic recreation. In N. J. Stumbo (Ed.), *Client outcomes in therapeutic recreation services* (pp. 1–24). State College, PA: Venture Publishing, Inc.

Stumbo, N. J. (2003b). The importance of evidence-based practice. In N. J. Stumbo (Ed.), *Client outcomes in therapeutic recreation services* (pp. 25–48). State College, PA: Venture Publishing, Inc.

Stumbo, N. J. and Peterson, C. A. (2004). *Therapeutic recreation program design: Principles & procedures* (4th ed.). San Francisco, CA: Pearson Benjamin Cummings.

Sullivan, E. J. and Decker, P. J. (2001). *Effective leadership and management in nursing* (5th ed.). Upper Saddle River, NJ: Prentice Hall.

Sullivan, E. J. and Decker, P. J. (2005). *Effective leadership and management in nursing* (6th ed.). Upper Saddle River, NJ: Prentice Hall.

Tappen, R. M., Weiss, S. A., and Whitehead, D. K. (2004). *Essentials of nursing leadership and management* (3rd ed.). Philadelphia, PA: F. A. Davis.

Tindill, B. S. and Stewart, D. W. (1993). Integration of total quality and quality assurance. In A. F. Al-Assaf and J. A. Schmele (Eds.), *The textbook of total quality in healthcare* (pp. 209–220). Delray Beach, FL: Saint Lucie Press.

Tomey, A. M. (2000). *Guide to nursing management and leadership* (6th ed.). St. Louis, MO: Mosby.

Toppel, A. H., Beach, B. A., and Hutchinson-Troyer, L. (1991). Standards: A tool for accountability the CARF process. In M. E. Crawford and J. A. Card, *Annual in Therapeutic Recreation* (Vol. 2, pp. 96–98). Hattiesburg, MS: American Theraputic Recreation Association.

Triolo, P. K., Hansen, P., Kazzaz, Y., Chung, H., and Dobbs, S. (2002). Improving patient satisfaction through multidisciplinary performance improvement teams. *Journal of Nursing Administration, 32*(9), 448–454.

Uniform Data System for Medical Rehabilitation. (1993). *Guide for the uniform data set for medical rehabilitation*

(Adult FIM^{SM}) version 4.0. Buffalo, NY: State University of New York at Buffalo.

Widmer, M. A., Zabriskie, R. B., and Wells, M. S. (2003). Program evaluation: Collecting data to measure outcomes. In N. J. Stumbo (Ed.), *Client outcomes in therapeutic recreation services* (pp. 201–219). State College, PA: Venture Publishing, Inc.

Zimmermann, J. A., Cooper, N., and Allen, L. R. (2001). Performance measurement: It's a benefit. *Parks & Recreation, 36*(6), 70–78.

Legislative Acts and Executive Orders Cited

1947 Amendments to the National Labor Relations Act of 1935 (Wagner Act), 49 Stat. 449, as amended, (29 U.S.C. §151 et seq.)

Age Discrimination in Employment Act of 1967, Pub. L. 90-202, Dec. 15, 1967, 81 Stat. 602 (29 U.S.C. §621 et seq.)

Age Discrimination in Employment Act Amendments of 1978, Pub. L. 95-256, Apr. 6, 1978, 92 Stat. 189 (29 U.S.C. §621 et seq.)

Americans with Disabilities Act of 1990, Pub. L. 101-336, Jul. 26, 1990, 104 Stat. 328 (42 U.S.C. §12101 et seq.)

Balanced Budget Act of 1997, Pub. L. 105-33, Aug. 5, 1997, 111 Stat. 251

Budget Improvement and Protection Act of 2000, Short title, see 42 U.S.C. §1305 note

Civil Rights Act of 1964, Pub. L. 88-352, Jul 2, 1964, 78 Stat 241. (42 U.S.C. §1981 et seq.)

Civil Rights Act of 1991, Pub. L. 102-167, Nov 21, 1991, 105 Stat. 1071. (42 U.S.C. §1981 et seq.)

Consolidated Omnibus Budget Reconciliation Act (COBRA) of 1985, Pub. L. 99-272, Apr. 7, 1986, 100 Stat. 82

Employee Retirement Income Security Act of 1974, Pub. L. 93-406, Sept. 2, 1974, 88 Stat. 829 (29 U.S.C. §1001 et seq.)

Equal Employment Opportunity Act of 1972 Pub. L. 92-261, Mar. 24, 1972, 86 Stat. 103, (42 U.S.C. §1001 et seq.)

Equal Pay Act of 1963, Pub. L. 88-38, June 10, 1963, 77 Stat. 56. (29 U.S.C. §201 note)

Executive Order 10988 of 1962, 27 FR 511, Jan. 17, 1962 (see 5 U.S.C. §7101)

Executive Order 11246 of Sept. 24, 1965, 30 CFR 12319, 12935, 3 CFR (1964-1965 Comp.), p. 339. (42 U.S.C. 2000e nt)

Executive Order 11375 of 1967, 3 FR 14303, 3 CFR (1966–1970), p. 684. (see 42 U.S.C. §2000e note)

Fair Labor Standards Act of 1938 (FLSA), Jun 25, 1938, ch. 676, 52 Stat. 1060 (29 U.S.C. §201 et seq.)

Family and Medical Leave Act of 1993, Pub. L. 103-3, Feb. 5, 1993, 107 Stat. 6 (5 U.S.C. §6381 et seq.; 29 U.S.C. §2601 et seq.)

Health Care Quality Improvement Act of 1986, Pub. L. 99-660, title IV, Nov. 14, 1986, 100 Stat. 3784 (42 U.S.C. 11101 et seq.)

Health Insurance Portability and Accountability Act of 1996, Pub. L. 104-191, Aug. 21, 1996, 110 Stat. 1936.

Health Maintenance Organization Act of 1973 (PL 93-222), Pub. L. 93-222, Dec. 29, 1973, 87 Stat. 914 (42 U.S.C. §300e et seq.)

Hill-Burton Act (Hospital Survey and Construction Act of 1946), Aug. 13, 1946, ch. 958, 60 Stat. 1040, amended 1949, Oct. 25, 1949, ch. 722, 63 Stat. 898

Hill-Harris Hospital and Medical Facilities Amendments of 1964, Pub. L. 88-443, Aug. 18, 1964, 78 Stat 447 (42 U.S.C. §291 et seq.)

Individuals with Disabilities Education Act Amendments of 1990, Pub. L. 101-476, Oct. 30, 1990, 104 Stat. 1103 (20 U.S.C. §1400 et seq.)

Labor-Management Relations Act of 1947 (Taft-Hartley Act), Jun 23, 1947, ch. 120, 61 Stat. 136 (29 U.S.C. §141 et seq.)

National Health Planning and Resource Development Act of 1974, Pub. L. 93-641, Jan. 4, 1975, 88 Stat. 2225 (42 U. S.C. §201 note)

National Labor Relations Act of 1935 (Wagner Act), Jul 5, 1935, ch. 372, 49 Stat. 449 (29 U.S.C. §151 et seq.)

Occupational Safety and Health Act of 1970, Pub. L. 91-596, Dec. 29, 1970, 84 Stat. 1590 (29 U.S.C. §651 et seq.)

Pregnancy Discrimination Act of 1978, Pub. L. 95-555, Oct. 31, 1978, 92 Stat. 2076 (42 U.S.C. 2000e(k))

Rehabilitation Act of 1973, section 503, Pub. L. 93-112, Sept. 26, 1973, 87 Stat. 355 (29 U.S.C. §701 et seq.)

Social Security Amendments of 1965, Pub. L. 89-97, July 30, 1965, 79 Stat. 286 (see 42 U.S.C. §1305 note)

Social Security Amendments of 1972 (PL 92-603) Pub. L. 92-603, Oct. 30, 1972, 86 Stat. 1329 (see 42 U.S.C. §1305 note)

Social Security Amendments of 1983, Pub. L. 98-21, Apr. 20, 1983, 97 Stat. 65 (see 42 U.S.C. §1305 note)

Tax Equity and Fiscal Responsibility Act (TEFRA) of 1982, Pub. L. 97-248, Sept. 3, 1982, 96 Stat. 324 (see 26 U.S.C. §1 note)

U.S. Omnibus Budget Reconciliation Act (OBRA) of 1987, Pub. L. 100-203, Dec. 22, 1987, 101 Stat. 1330

Vietnam Era Veterans' Readjustment Assistance Act of 1974, section 402, Pub. L. 93-508, Dec. 3, 1974, 88 Stat. 1578 (see 38 U.S.C. §101 note)

Index

21st Century Leisure: Current Issues, Second Edition
  by Valeria J. Freysinger and John R. Kelly

The A•B•Cs of Behavior Change: Skills for Working with Behavior Problems in Nursing Homes
  by Margaret D. Cohn, Michael A. Smyer, and Ann L. Horgas

Activity Experiences and Programming within Long-Term Care
  by Ted Tedrick and Elaine R. Green

The Activity Gourmet
  by Peggy Powers

Advanced Concepts for Geriatric Nursing Assistants
  by Carolyn A. McDonald

Adventure Programming
  edited by John C. Miles and Simon Priest

Assessment: The Cornerstone of Activity Programs
  by Ruth Perschbacher

Behavior Modification in Therapeutic Recreation: An Introductory Manual
  by John Datillo and William D. Murphy

Benefits of Leisure
  edited by B.L. Driver, Perry J. Brown, and George L. Peterson

Benefits of Recreation Research Update
  by Judy M. Sefton and W. Kerry Mummery

Beyond Baskets and Beads: Activities for Older Adults with Functional Impairments
  by Mary Hart, Karen Primm, and Kathy Cranisky

Beyond Bingo: Innovative Programs for the New Senior
  by Sal Arrigo, Jr., Ann Lewis, and Hank Mattimore

Beyond Bingo 2: More Innovative Programs for the New Senior
  by Sal Arrigo, Jr.

Boredom Busters: Themed Special Events to Dazzle and Delight Your Group
  by Annette C. Moore

Both Gains and Gaps: Feminist Perspectives on Women's Leisure
  by Karla Henderson, M. Deborah Bialeschki, Susan M. Shaw, and Valeria J. Freysinger

Client Assessment in Therapeutic Recreation Services
  by Norma J. Stumbo

Client Outcomes in Therapeutic Recreation Services
  by Norma J. Stumbo

Conceptual Foundations for Therapeutic Recreation
  edited by David R. Austin, John Datillo, and Bryan P. McCormick

Constraints to Leisure
  edited by Edgar L. Jackson

Dementia Care Programming: An Identity-Focused Approach
  by Rosemary Dunne

Dimensions of Choice: A Qualitative Approach to Recreation, Parks, and Leisure Research
  by Karla A. Henderson

Diversity and the Recreation Profession: Organizational Perspectives
  edited by Maria T. Allison and Ingrid E. Schneider

Evaluating Leisure Services: Making Enlightened Decisions, Second Edition
  by Karla A. Henderson and M. Deborah Bialeschki

Everything from A to Y: The Zest Is up to You! Older Adult Activities for Every Day of the Year
  by Nancy R. Cheshire and Martha L. Kenney

The Evolution of Leisure: Historical and Philosophical Perspectives
  by Thomas Goodale and Geoffrey Godbey

Experience Marketing: Strategies for the New Millennium
  by Ellen L. O'Sullivan and Kathy J. Spangler

Facilitation Techniques in Therapeutic Recreation
  by John Datillo

File o' Fun: A Recreation Planner for Games & Activities, Third Edition
  by Jane Harris Ericson and Diane Ruth Albright

Functional Interdisciplinary-Transdisciplinary Therapy (FITT) Manual
  by Deborah M. Schott, Judy D. Burdett, Beverly J. Cook, Karren S. Ford, and Kathleen M. Orban

The Game and Play Leader's Handbook: Facilitating Fun and Positive Interaction, Revised Edition
  by Bill Michaelis and John M. O'Connell

The Game Finder—A Leader's Guide to Great Activities
  by Annette C. Moore

Getting People Involved in Life and Activities: Effective Motivating Techniques
  by Jeanne Adams

Glossary of Recreation Therapy and Occupational Therapy
  by David R. Austin

Great Special Events and Activities
  by Annie Morton, Angie Prosser, and Sue Spangler

Group Games & Activity Leadership
  by Kenneth J. Bulik

Growing With Care: Using Greenery, Gardens, and Nature with Aging and Special Populations
  by Betsy Kreidler

Hands On! Children's Activities for Fairs, Festivals, and Special Events
  by Karen L. Ramey

Health Promotion for Mind, Body and Spirit
  by Suzanne Fitzsimmons and Linda L. Buettner

In Search of the Starfish: Creating a Caring Environment
  by Mary Hart, Karen Primm, and Kathy Cranisky

Inclusion: Including People With Disabilities in Parks and Recreation Opportunities
  by Lynn Anderson and Carla Brown Kress

Inclusive Leisure Services: Responding to the Rights of People with Disabilities, Second Edition
  by John Datillo

Innovations: A Recreation Therapy Approach to Restorative Programs
  by Dawn R. De Vries and Julie M. Lake

Internships in Recreation and Leisure Services: A Practical Guide for Students, Third Edition
  by Edward E. Seagle, Jr. and Ralph W. Smith

Interpretation of Cultural and Natural Resources, Second Edition
  by Douglas M. Knudson, Ted T. Cable, and Larry Beck

Intervention Activities for At-Risk Youth
  by Norma J. Stumbo

Introduction to Outdoor Recreation: Providing and Managing Resource Based Opportunities
  by Roger L. Moore and B.L. Driver

Introduction to Recreation and Leisure Services, Eighth Edition
  by Karla A. Henderson, M. Deborah Bialeschki, John L. Hemingway, Jan S. Hodges, Beth D. Kivel, and H. Douglas Sessoms

Introduction to Therapeutic Recreation: U.S. and Canadian Perspectives
  by Kenneth Mobily and Lisa Ostiguy

Introduction to Writing Goals and Objectives: A Manual for Recreation Therapy Students and Entry-Level Professionals
  by Suzanne Melcher

Leadership and Administration of Outdoor Pursuits, Second Edition
  by Phyllis Ford and James Blanchard

Leadership in Leisure Services: Making a Difference, Second Edition
  by Debra J. Jordan

Leisure Services in Canada: An Introduction, Second Edition
  by Mark S. Searle and Russell E. Brayley

Leisure and Leisure Services in the 21st Century: Toward Mid Century
  by Geoffrey Godbey

The Leisure Diagnostic Battery: Users Manual and Sample Forms
  by Peter A. Witt and Gary Ellis

Other Books by Venture Publishing, Inc.

Leisure Education I: A Manual of Activities and Resources, Second Edition
by Norma J. Stumbo

Leisure Education II: More Activities and Resources, Second Edition
by Norma J. Stumbo

Leisure Education III: More Goal-Oriented Activities
by Norma J. Stumbo

Leisure Education IV: Activities for Individuals with Substance Addictions
by Norma J. Stumbo

Leisure Education Program Planning: A Systematic Approach, Second Edition
by John Dattilo

Leisure Education Specific Programs
by John Dattilo

Leisure in Your Life: An Exploration, Sixth Edition
by Geoffrey Godbey

Leisure Services in Canada: An Introduction, Second Edition
by Mark S. Searle and Russell E. Brayley

Leisure Studies: Prospects for the Twenty-First Century
edited by Edgar L. Jackson and Thomas L. Burton

The Lifestory Re-Play Circle: A Manual of Activities and Techniques
by Rosilyn Wilder

The Melody Lingers On: A Complete Music Activities Program for Older Adults
by Bill Messenger

Models of Change in Municipal Parks and Recreation: A Book of Innovative Case Studies
edited by Mark E. Havitz

More Than a Game: A New Focus on Senior Activity Services
by Brenda Corbett

The Multiple Values of Wilderness
by H. Ken Cordell, John C. Bergstrom, and J.M. Bowker

Nature and the Human Spirit: Toward an Expanded Land Management Ethic
edited by B.L. Driver, Daniel Dustin, Tony Baltic, Gary Elsner, and George Peterson

The Organizational Basis of Leisure Participation: A Motivational Exploration
by Robert A. Stebbins

Outdoor Recreation for 21st Century America
by H. Ken Cordell

Outdoor Recreation Management: Theory and Application, Third Edition
by Alan Jubenville and Ben Twight

Planning and Organizing Group Activities in Social Recreation
by John V. Valentine

Planning Parks for People, Second Edition
by John Hultsman, Richard L. Cottrell, and Wendy Z. Hultsman

The Process of Recreation Programming Theory and Technique, Third Edition
by Patricia Farrell and Herberta M. Lundegren

Programming for Parks, Recreation, and Leisure Services: A Servant Leadership Approach, Second Edition
by Debra J. Jordan, Donald G. DeGraaf, and Kathy H. DeGraaf

Protocols for Recreation Therapy Programs
edited by Jill Kelland, along with the Recreation Therapy Staff at Alberta Hospital Edmonton

Quality Management: Applications for Therapeutic Recreation
edited by Bob Riley

A Recovery Workbook: The Road Back from Substance Abuse
by April K. Neal and Michael J. Taleff

Recreation and Leisure: Issues in an Era of Change, Third Edition
edited by Thomas Goodale and Peter A. Witt

Recreation and Youth Development
by Peter A. Witt and Linda L. Caldwell

Recreation Economic Decisions: Comparing Benefits and Costs, Second Edition
by John B. Loomis and Richard G. Walsh

Recreation for Older Adults: Individual and Group Activities
by Judith A. Elliott and Jerold E. Elliott

Recreation Programming and Activities for Older Adults
by Jerold E. Elliott and Judith A. Sorg-Elliott

Reference Manual for Writing Rehabilitation Therapy Treatment Plans
by Penny Hogberg and Mary Johnson

Research in Therapeutic Recreation: Concepts and Methods
edited by Marjorie J. Malkin and Christine Z. Howe

Simple Expressions: Creative and Therapeutic Arts for the Elderly in Long-Term Care Facilities
by Vicki Parsons

A Social History of Leisure Since 1600
by Gary Cross

A Social Psychology of Leisure
by Roger C. Mannell and Douglas A. Kleiber

Special Events and Festivals: How to Organize, Plan, and Implement
by Angie Prosser and Ashli Rutledge

Stretch Your Mind and Body: Tai Chi as an Adaptive Activity
by Duane A. Crider and William R. Klinger

Therapeutic Activity Intervention with the Elderly: Foundations and Practices
by Barbara A. Hawkins, Marti E. May, and Nancy Brattain Rogers

Therapeutic Recreation and the Nature of Disabilities
by Kenneth E. Mobily and Richard D. MacNeil

Therapeutic Recreation: Cases and Exercises, Second Edition
by Barbara C. Wilhite and M. Jean Keller

Therapeutic Recreation in Health Promotion and Rehabilitation
by John Shank and Catherine Coyle

Therapeutic Recreation in the Nursing Home
by Linda Buettner and Shelley L. Martin

Therapeutic Recreation Programming: Theory and Practice
by Charles Sylvester, Judith E. Voelkl, and Gary D. Ellis

Therapeutic Recreation Protocol for Treatment of Substance Addictions
by Rozanne W. Faulkner

The Therapeutic Recreation Stress Management Primer
by Cynthia Mascott

The Therapeutic Value of Creative Writing
by Paul M. Spicer

Tourism and Society: A Guide to Problems and Issues
by Robert W. Wyllie

Traditions: Improving Quality of Life in Caregiving
by Janelle Sellick

Venture Publishing, Inc.
1999 Cato Avenue
State College, PA 16801
Phone: 814-234-4561
Fax: 814-234-1651